dition

# the best campsites
# in Britain & Ireland

alan rogers  publishing
experts in camping for over 40 years

Compiled by: Alan Rogers Guides Ltd

Designed by: Vine Design Ltd

Additional photography: T Lambelin, www.lambelin.com
Maps created by Customised Mapping (01769 540044)
contain background data provided by GisDATA Ltd

Maps are © Alan Rogers Guides and GisDATA Ltd 2010


© Alan Rogers Guides Ltd 2010

Published by: Alan Rogers Guides Ltd,
Spelmonden Old Oast, Goudhurst, Kent TN17 1HE
www.alanrogers.com  Tel: 01580 214000

British Library Cataloguing-in-Publication Data:
A catalogue record for this book is available
from the British Library.

ISBN 978-1-906215-46-0


Printed in Great Britain by Stephens & George Print Group

# Contents

# Alan Rogers - in search of 'the best'

Alan Rogers Guides were first published over 40 years ago. Since Alan Rogers published the first campsite guide that bore his name, the range has expanded and now covers 27 countries in five separate guides. No fewer than 20 of the campsites selected by Alan for the first guide are still featured in our 2011 editions.

There are well over 5,000 camping and caravanning parks in Britain and Ireland of varying quality: this guide contains impartially written reports on almost 600, including many of the very finest, each being individually inspected and selected. We aim to provide you with a selection of the best, rather than information on all – in short, a more selective, qualitative approach. New, improved maps and indexes are also included, designed to help you find the choice of campsite that's right for you.

We hope you enjoy some happy and safe travels – and some pleasurable 'armchair touring' in the meantime!

" ...the campsites included in this book have been chosen entirely on merit, and no payment of any sort is made by them for their inclusion."

**Alan Rogers, 1968**

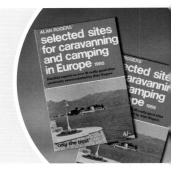

### How do we find the best?

The criteria we use when inspecting and selecting campsites are numerous, but the most important by far is the question of good quality. People want different things from their choice of site so we try to include a range of campsite 'styles' to cater for a wide variety of preferences: from those seeking a small peaceful park in the heart of the countryside, to visitors looking for an 'all singing, all dancing' park in a popular seaside resort. Those with more specific interests, such as sporting facilities, cultural events or historical attractions, are also catered for.

The size of the park, whether it's part of a chain or privately owned, makes no difference in terms of it being required to meet our exacting standards in respect of its quality and it being 'fit for purpose'. In other words, irrespective of the size of the park, or the number of facilities it offers, we consider and evaluate the welcome, the pitches, the sanitary facilities, the cleanliness, the general maintenance and even the location.

## Expert opinions

We rely on our dedicated team of Site Assessors, all of whom are experienced campers, caravanners or motorcaravanners, to visit and recommend campsites. Each year they travel some 100,000 miles around Europe inspecting new campsites for the guide and re-inspecting the existing ones. Our thanks are due to them for their enthusiastic efforts, their diligence and integrity.

We also appreciate the feedback we receive from many of our readers and we always make a point of following up complaints, suggestions or recommendations for possible new campsites. Of course we get a few grumbles too – but it really is a few, and those we do receive usually relate to overcrowding or to poor maintenance during the peak school holiday period. Please bear in mind that, although we are interested to hear about any complaints, we have no contractual relationship with the campsites featured in our guides and are therefore not in a position to intervene in any dispute between a reader and a campsite.

## Independent and honest

Whilst the content and scope of the Alan Rogers guides have expanded considerably since the early editions, our selection of campsites still employs exactly the same philosophy and criteria as defined by Alan Rogers in 1968.

### 'telling it how it is'

Firstly, and most importantly, our selection is based entirely on our own rigorous and independent inspection and selection process. Campsites cannot buy their way into our guides – indeed the extensive Site Report which is written by us, not by the site owner, is provided free of charge so we are free to say what we think and to provide an honest, 'warts and all' description. This is written in plain English and without the use of confusing icons or symbols.

## Looking for the best

Highly respected by site owners and readers alike, there is no better guide when it comes to forming an independent view of a campsite's quality. When you need to be confident in your choice of campsite, you need the Alan Rogers Guide.

- Parks only included on merit
- Parks cannot pay to be included
- Independently inspected, rigorously assessed
- Impartial reviews
- Over 40 years of expertise

Written in plain English, our guides are exceptionally easy to use, but a few words of explanation regarding the layout and content may be helpful. For England we have used official tourist board regions and the counties within them. For Wales, Scotland and Ireland (North and South) we use the counties.

## Index town
### Park name
Postal address (including county) T: telephone number. E: email address
alanrogers.com web address (including Alan Rogers reference number)

A description of the park in which we try to give an idea of its general features – its size, its situation, its strengths and its weaknesses. This section should provide a picture of the park itself with reference to the facilities that are provided and if they impact on its appearance or character. We include details on pitch numbers, electricity (with amperage), hardstandings etc. in this section as pitch design, planning and terracing affects the park's overall appearance. Similarly we include reference to pitches used for caravan holiday homes, chalets, and the like. Importantly at the end of this column we indicate if there are any restrictions, e.g. no tents, no children, naturist sites.

### Facilities
Lists more specific information on the park's facilities and amenities and, where available, the dates when these facilities are open (if not for the whole season). Off site: here we give distances to various local amenities, for example, local shops, the nearest beach, plus our featured activities (bicycle hire, fishing, horse riding, boat launching). Where we have space we list suggestions for activities and local tourist attractions.

Open: Park opening dates.

### Directions
Separated from the main text in order that they may be read and assimilated more easily by a navigator en-route. Bear in mind that road improvement schemes can result in road numbers being altered.
O.S.GR: Ordnance Survey grid references are included for those using OS maps.
GPS: references are provided in decimal format. All latitudes are North. Longitudes are East unless preceeded by a minus sign e.g. 48.71695 is North, 0.31254 is East and -0.31254 is West.

### Charges 2011 (or a general guide)

## Maps, campsite listings and indexes

For this 2011 guide we have changed the way in which we list our featured campsites and also the way in which we help you to locate the parks within each region.

We now include a map immediately after our Introduction to that region. These maps show the towns near which one or more of our featured parks are located.

Within each regional section of the guide, we list these towns and the park(s) in that vicinity in alphabetical order.

You will certainly need more detailed maps for navigation, for example the Ordnance Survey road atlas. We provide O.S. references and G.P.S. coordinates for each park to assist you. Our three indexes will also help you to find a park by its reference number and name, by region and park name, or by the town where the park is situated.

# Understanding the entries

## Facilities

### Toilet blocks

We assume that toilet blocks will be equipped with WCs, washbasins with hot and cold water and hot showers with dividers or curtains, and will have all necessary shelves, hooks, plugs and mirrors. We also assume that there will be an identified chemical toilet disposal point, and that the campsite will provide water and waste water drainage points and bin areas. If not the case, we comment. We do mention certain features that some readers find important: washbasins in cubicles, facilities for babies, facilities for those with disabilities and motorcaravan service points. Readers with disabilities are advised to contact the site of their choice to ensure that facilities are appropriate to their needs.

### Shop

Basic or fully supplied, and opening dates.

### Bars, restaurants, takeaway facilities and entertainment

We try hard to supply opening and closing dates (if other than the campsite opening dates) and to identify if there are discos or other entertainment.

### Children's play areas

Fenced and with safety surface (e.g. sand, bark or pea-gravel).

### Swimming pools

If particularly special, we cover in detail in our main campsite description but reference is always included under our Facilities listings. We will also indicate the existence of water slides, sunbathing areas and other features. Opening dates, charges and levels of supervision are provided where we have been notified.

### Leisure facilities

For example, playing fields, bicycle hire, organised activities and entertainment.

### Dogs

If dogs are not accepted or restrictions apply, we state it here. Check the quick reference list at the back of the guide.

### Off site

This briefly covers leisure facilities, tourist attractions, restaurants etc. nearby.

## Charges

These are the latest provided to us by the parks. In those cases where 2011 prices have not been provided to us by the parks, we try to give a general guide.

## Opening dates

These are advised to us during the early autumn of the previous year – parks can, and sometimes do, alter these dates before the start of the following season, often for good reasons. If you intend to visit shortly after a published opening date, or shortly before the closing date, it is wise to check that it will actually be open at the time required. Similarly some parks operate a restricted service during the low season, only opening some of their facilities (e.g. swimming pools) during the main season; where we know about this, and have the relevant dates, we indicate it – again if you are at all doubtful it is wise to check.

Sometimes, campsite amenities may be dependant on there being enough customers on site to justify their opening and, for this reason, actual opening dates may vary from those indicated.

## Special pitches

We note an ever increasing number of 'special' pitches under a variety of fancy names (for example, Executive, Panorama, Super). These provide a range of extra facilities such as waste water disposal, TV and phone connections, hardstanding, patios, etc. and they are often booked up well in advance. Readers interested in such pitches should contact the park concerned to check exactly what is provided. People with disabilities are also advised to telephone before turning up to ensure that facilities are appropriate to their particular needs.

# You're on your way!

Whether you're an 'old hand' in terms of camping and caravanning or are contemplating your first trip, a regular reader of our Guides or a new 'convert', we wish you well in your travels and hope we have been able to help in some way.

We are, of course, also out and about ourselves, visiting parks, talking to owners and readers, and generally checking on standards and new developments.

## Our Holiday Home section

**324**

Over recent years, more and more parks in Britain and Ireland have added high quality holiday home accommodation in the form of caravan holiday homes, chalets and lodges. In response to feedback from many of our readers, and to reflect this evolution in campsites, we have decided to introduce a separate section on caravan holiday homes and chalets (see page 324). If a park has decided to contribute to this section, it is indicated above our site report in the main body of the guide with a page reference where the full details are given. We feature parks offering some of the best accommodation available and have included full details of one or two accommodation types at these parks.

Please note however that many other campsites listed in this guide may also have a selection of accommodation for rent.

**We wish all our readers thoroughly enjoyable Camping and Caravanning in 2011 – favoured by good weather of course!**

The Alan Rogers Team

Scotland
page 258

Northern
Ireland
page 289

Northumbria
page 223

Cumbria
page 212

North West
England
page 204

Yorkshire
page 186

Republic of Ireland
page 297

Heart of England
page 161

Wales
page 230

East of England
page 144

Southern
England
page 102

South West England
page 12

South East
England
page 127

London
page 140

Channel Islands
page 320

# The Alan Rogers Awards

**Campsites Award**
**2010**
**Camping du Domaine de la Rive**
**Winner**
The Alan Rogers Progress Award

**Campsites Award**
**2010**
**Kawan Village le Coin Tranquille**
**Winner**
The Alan Rogers Welcome Award

The Alan Rogers Campsite Awards were launched in 2004 and have proved a great success. Our awards have a broad scope and before committing to our winners, we carefully consider more than 2,000 campsites featured in our guides, taking into account comments from our site assessors, our head office team and, of course, our readers.

Our award winners come from the four corners of Europe, from southern Portugal to Slovenia, and this year we are making awards to campsites in 13 different countries.

Needless to say, it's an extremely difficult task to choose our eventual winners, but we believe that we have identified a number of campsites with truly outstanding characteristics.

In each case, we have selected an outright winner, along with two highly commended runners-up. Listed below are full details of each of our award categories and our winners for 2010.

## Alan Rogers Progress Award 2010

This award reflects the hard work and commitment undertaken by particular site owners to improve and upgrade their site.

| Winner | |
|---|---|
| FR40100 | Camping du Domaine de la Rive *France* |

| Runners-up | |
|---|---|
| AU0060 | Ferienparadies Natterer See *Austria* |
| IT60360 | Camping Ca'Pasquali *Italy* |

## Alan Rogers Welcome Award 2010

This award takes account of sites offering a particularly friendly welcome and maintaining a friendly ambience throughout reader's holidays.

| Winner | |
|---|---|
| FR38010 | Kawan Village le Coin Tranquille *France* |

| Runners-up | |
|---|---|
| NL6630 | Camping Ter Spegelt *Netherlands* |
| IT62485 | Camping Conca d'Oro *Italy* |

**Our warmest congratulations to all our award winners and our commiserations to all those not having won an award on this occasion.**

The Alan Rogers Team

## Alan Rogers Active Holiday Award 2010

This award reflects sites in outstanding locations which are ideally suited for active holidays, notably walking or cycling, but which could extend to include such activities as winter sports or water sports.

**Winner**

| DE3820 | Camping Havelberge *Germany* |

**Runners-up**

| SV4415 | Camping Terme Catez *Slovenia* |
| FR65090 | Camping du Soleil de Pibeste *France* |

## Alan Rogers Motorhome Award 2010

Motorhome sales are increasing and this award acknowledges sites which, in our opinion, have made outstanding efforts to welcome motorhome clients.

**Winner**

| NL6200 | Camping Erkemederstrand *Netherlands* |

**Runners-up**

| UK1340 | Cornish Farm Touring Park *England* |
| FR30120 | Campéole Ile des Papes *France* |

## Alan Rogers 4 Seasons Award 2010

This award is made to outstanding sites with extended opening dates and which welcome clients to a uniformly high standard throughout the year.

**Winner**

| ES81300 | Camping Int. de Calonge *Spain* |

**Runners-up**

| UK0970 | Cofton Country Holidays *England* |
| DE3455 | Gugel's Dreiländer Camping *Germany* |

## Alan Rogers Seaside Award 2010

This award is made for sites which we feel are outstandingly suitable for a really excellent seaside holiday.

**Winner**

| FR83120 | Camp du Domaine *France* |

**Runners-up**

| CR6716 | Camping Lanterna *Croatia* |
| ES82000 | Camping Cala Llevadó *Spain* |

## Alan Rogers Country Award 2010

This award contrasts with our former award and acknowledges sites which are attractively located in delightful, rural locations.

**Winner**

| NL6425 | Camping De Twee Bruggen *Netherlands* |

**Runners-up**

| FR24010 | Kawan Château le Verdoyer *France* |
| UK7830 | Glen Nevis Caravan Park *Scotland* |

## Alan Rogers Rented Accommodation Award 2010

Given the increasing importance of rented accommodation on many campsites, we feel that it is important to acknowledge sites which have made a particular effort in creating a high quality 'rented accommodation' park.

**Winner**

| SV4270 | Kamp Koren Kobarid *Slovenia* |

**Runners-up**

| FR66070 | Yelloh! Village le Brasilia *France* |
| ES84830 | Camping Tamarit Park Resort *Spain* |

## Alan Rogers Unique Site Award 2010

This award acknowledges sites with unique, outstanding features – something which simply cannot be found elsewhere and which is an important attraction of the site.

**Winner**

| PO8175 | Zmar-Eco Camping Resort *Portugal* |

**Runners-up**

| DK2170 | Klim Strand Camping *Denmark* |
| ES80330 | Camping Las Palmeras *Spain* |

## Alan Rogers Family Site Award 2010

Many sites claim to be child friendly but this award acknowledges the sites we feel to be the very best in this respect.

**Winner**

| ES80400 | Camping Las Dunas *Spain* |

**Runners-up**

| IT60030 | Centro Vacanze Pra' Delle Torri *Italy* |
| LU7620 | Europacamping Nommerlayen *Luxembourg* |

## Alan Rogers Readers' Award 2010

We believe our Readers' Award to be the most important. We simply invite our readers (by means of an on-line poll at www.alanrogers.com) to nominate the site they enjoyed most.

The outright winner for 2010 is:

**Winner**

| IT60200 | Camping Union Lido Vacanze *Italy* |

## Alan Rogers Special Award 2010

A special award is made to acknowledge sites which we feel have overcome a very significant setback, and have not only returned to their former condition, but can fairly be considered to be even better than before. In 2010 we acknowledge one campsite which suffered storm damage and we feel qualifies for this award, but also wish to acknowledge the campsites of the Argens valley, Var, France, which suffered serious flood damage in June 2010 and have made highly impressive recoveries.

| FR17340 | Camping Au Port-Punay *France* |

The campsites of the Argens valley *Var, France*

The West Country is a diverse region of beautiful sandy beaches, steep craggy cliffs, desolate moors and rolling green hills. Home of clotted cream teas, it also boasts a range of historical and modern attractions, including the celebrated Eden Project.

**THE SOUTH WEST COMPRISES: CORNWALL, DEVON, SOMERSET, BATH, BRISTOL, SOUTH GLOUCESTERSHIRE, WILTSHIRE AND WEST DORSET.**

With its dramatic cliffs pounded by the Atlantic ocean, and beautiful coastline boasting warm waters, soft sandy beaches and small seaside towns, Cornwall is one of England's most popular holiday destinations. The coast is also a surfers' paradise, while inland the wild and rugged Bodmin Moors dominate the landscape. In Devon, the Dartmoor National Park has sweeping moorland and granite tors, where wild ponies roam freely. Much of the countryside is gentle rolling green fields, dotted with pretty thatched cottages. The coastline around Torbay is known as the English Riviera which, due to its temperate climate, allows palm trees to grow. Stretching across East Devon and West Dorset is the fossil-ridden Jurassic Coast, a World Heritage Site. West Dorset is also home to Lyme Regis and Weymouth, which comes alive in summer when regular entertainment, including a carnival and fireworks, is held along the seafront. Famous for its cider and cheese, Somerset is good walking country, with the Exmoor National Park, which also straddles Devon. Wiltshire's natural attractions include the Marlborough Downs, Savernake Forest and the River Avon. It also boasts one of the most famous prehistoric sites in the world, the ancient stone circles of Stonehenge.

### Places of interest

*Bath:* World Heritage Site full of Roman and Georgian architecture, elegant streets such as the Circle and Royal Crescent, Roman baths.

*Bristol:* steeped in maritime history with the world's first great Ocean Liner; Brunel's Clifton Suspension bridge; a range of museums and art galleries.

*Cornwall:* seaside town of St Ives; Land's End; Eden Project; Penzance and St Michael's Mount.

*Devon:* popular seaside resorts of Torquay, Paignton and Brixham; cities of Exeter and Plymouth.

*Somerset:* Weston-Super-Mare; Wells Cathedral; Glastonbury; Cheddar Gorge and Wookey Hole caves.

*West Dorset:* Dorchester, home of Thomas Hardy; Isle of Portland; Abbotsbury village, with swannery.

*Wiltshire:* Salisbury; Longleat stately home and safari park.

### Did you know?

Chesil Beach is an 18-mile stretch of fortress-like walls of pebbles, formed 12,000 years ago.

There are numerous white horses carved into the landscape across the South West.

The Jurassic Coast is a Natural World Heritage Site stretching for 95 miles.

The black death entered England through the port of Weymouth in 1348.

Britain's oldest complete skeleton, Cheddar Man, was buried in Gough's Cave 9,000 years ago.

At 404 feet, Salisbury Cathedral has the tallest medieval spire in the world.

# Bodmin

## Ruthern Valley Holidays

Ruthernbridge, Bodmin PL30 5LU (Cornwall) T: 01208 831395. E: camping@ruthernvalley.com
**alanrogers.com/UK0306**

This is a little gem of a site set in eight acres of woodland, tucked away in a peaceful little valley not far from Bodmin. Run by Andrew and Nicola Johnson, the park was landscaped over 30 years ago with an amazing range of trees and shrubs and plenty of animal wildlife. There are 16 touring pitches, informally spaced but numbered, in the main, tree-lined field, six with 10A electricity, and a further 13 in smaller fields and alcove areas amongst the woods with a small stream meandering through and alive with bluebells when we visited. There are also 12 wooden chalet/bungalows and a number of wooden 'camping pods' which blend naturally into the environment. Four caravan holiday homes will be replaced with 'pods' in due course. The larger pods have basic equipment; the smaller have none – you bring everything but your tent! The bubbling stream is an attraction for children and now there are some chickens and small animals to watch in an additional field, not to mention some adventure-type play equipment in an area set away from the pitches.

### Facilities

Small, fully equipped toilet block with solar heated water. Washing machines and dryer. Shop with basic provisions shares with reception (reduced hours in low season). Barbecue hire. Play area including five-a-side goal posts. Field with small animals. Bicycle hire (delivered to site). Free WiFi. Dogs are not accepted in July/Aug.
Off site: Nearest pub 3-4 miles. Fishing 2 miles. Riding, pony trekking and golf 4 miles. 10 miles to the coast.

Open: All year.

### Directions

Approaching Bodmin from A30 or A38 turn right at first mini roundabout and proceed anti-clockwise on the inner ring road. Go straight over double mini-roundabout, leaving Bodmin on A389/A391 towards St Austell. Ignore first Nanstallon - Ruthernbridge sign, after 1.5 miles, at top of hill, turn right. At Nanstallon village sign (0.75 miles), turn left then filter left. Continue into Ruthernbridge. Turn left before bridge. Site is on left in 300 yards.
O.S.GR: SX012668. GPS: 50.46455, -4.8019

### Charges guide

| | |
|---|---|
| Per unit incl. 2 persons | £ 12.00 - £ 16.00 |
| incl. electricity | £ 15.00 - £ 19.00 |
| extra person (over 3 yrs) | £ 3.00 - £ 4.00 |
| pet (max. 1, low season only) | £ 1.00 |

## Bodmin

### South Penquite Farm

South Penquite, Blisland, Bodmin PL30 4LH (Cornwall) T: 01208 850491. E: thefarm@bodminmoor.co.uk

alanrogers.com/UK0302

South Penquite offers real camping with no frills, set on a 200-hectare hill farm high on Bodmin Moor between the villages of Blisland and St Breward. The farm achieved organic status in 2001 and runs a flock of 300 ewes and a herd of 40 cattle and horses. The camping is small scale and intended to have a low impact on the surrounding environment. Tents or simple motorcaravans (no caravans) can pitch around the edge of three walled fields, roughly cut in the midst of the moor. You can find shelter or a view. Four yurts – round Mongolian tents – are available to rent in one field, complete with wood burning stoves. Camp fires are permitted with wood available from the farmhouse. You will also find horses, ponies, chickens, geese, ducks and turkeys which show their approval or not by the skin around their necks changing colour! A farm walk of some two miles takes you over most of the farm and some of the moor taking in a Bronze Age hut settlement, the river and a standing stone. It is also possible to fish for brown trout on the farm's stretch of the De Lank river, a tributary of the Camel. The farm's website offers a fascinating insight into life and work at South Penquite.

#### Facilities

A smart new pine clad toilet block, with a separate provision of four family-sized showers, with solar heated rainwater. Two covered dishwashing sinks (H&C) and two outside Belfast sinks. Washing machine and dryer. Small fridge and freezer. Home produced lamb, burgers and sausages available. LPG gas. Facilities for field studies and opportunities for educational groups and schools to learn about the local environment. Bushcraft days. Fishing (requires an EA rod licence and tokens available from the West Country Rivers Trust). Dogs are not accepted. Off site: Walking. Riding and cycling 1 mile. Sustrans Route 3 passes close by. North and south coasts within easy reach. Inns 1.5 and 2.5 miles.

Open: 1 May - 1 November.

#### Directions

On the A30 over Bodmin Moor pass Jamaica Inn and sign for Colliford Lake and watch for St Breward sign (to right) immediately at end of dual-carriageway. Follow this narrow road over open moor for 2 miles ignoring any turns to left or right. Also ignore right turn to St Breward just before the South Penquite sign. Follow track over stone bridge beside ford through farm gate and then bear to left to camping fields. Walk back to book in at Farm House. O.S.GR: SX104752. GPS: 50.5445, -4.671833

#### Charges guide

| | |
|---|---|
| Per person | £ 6.00 |
| child (5-16 yrs) | £ 3.00 |

Less 10% for stays of 5 nights or more.
No credit cards.

## Bodmin

### Eden Valley Holiday Park

Lanlivery, Bodmin PL30 5BU (Cornwall) T: 01208 872277. E: enquiries@edenvalleyholidaypark.co.uk

alanrogers.com/UK0280

A pleasant, peaceful touring park, Eden Valley Holiday Park has plenty of sheltered green space and a natural, uncommercialised atmosphere. This has been enhanced by careful planting of trees and shrubs to form a series of linked paddocks with an unfenced stream running through. With 56 numbered touring pitches in total, each paddock contains 10-15 pitches spread around the perimeter. There are 20 hardstandings and 40 pitches have electricity connections (5/10A). Awning groundsheets must be lifted on alternate days. A separate field contains 35 private caravan holiday homes. A large, well equipped activity play area with adventure type equipment on grass is in one of the hedged paddocks. The park is now owned by Darren and Ginny Hopkins and their young family and they welcome families and couples to enjoy their park with its colourful trees and grassy paddocks. They plan to add some log cabins for rent. The village pub is within walking distance and there are several good local restaurants. Indoor tennis courts (Bodmin) and a swimming pool are nearby. The Eden Project is very close. The nearest beach at Par is some 4 miles.

#### Facilities

Two well-equipped toilet blocks, one with individual cubicles. En-suite family washroom and unit for disabled visitors. Fully equipped laundry room. Motorcaravan service point. Gas supplies. Play area. TV room. Games room. Putting green. Torch useful. Off site: Fresh water fishing 1.5 miles or sea fishing 3 miles. Beach 4 miles. Bicycle hire 4 miles. Riding 2 miles. Golf 1.5 miles.

Open: Easter/1 April - 31 October.

#### Directions

Park approach road leads off A390 road 1.5 miles southwest of Lostwithiel. Follow white or brown camping signs. No other approach is advised. O.S.GR: SX083592. GPS: 50.40191, -4.69805

#### Charges guide

| | |
|---|---|
| Per unit incl. 2 persons and electricity | £ 11.00 - £ 15.00 |
| extra person | £ 1.50 - £ 2.00 |
| child (4-15 yrs) | £ 1.00 - £ 1.50 |
| dog | £ 1.00 - £ 2.00 |

No single sex groups
(excl. bona fide organisations).

For latest campsite news visit
**alanrogers.com**

## Bodmin

### Mena Caravan & Camping Park

Lanivet, Bodmin PL30 5HW (Cornwall) T: 01208 831845. E: mena@campsitesincornwall.co.uk
alanrogers.com/UK0270

A peaceful, simple park, Mena is tucked away in the Cornish countryside, yet close to the main routes, and a warm welcome awaits visitors. A few years ago it was a field for cows and with hard work and care it has been developed into a comfortable, yet natural site. Set in 15 acres of secluded countryside, it is spacious and never crowded offering only 25 level grass pitches on well drained, slightly sloping grass. There are 21 electricity connections (10A). The land includes a small fishing lake and a wooded area. Now open all year, developments include a new reception and shop.

**Facilities**

Four toilet and washbasin cabins are in an older wooden building. Two new showers and two toilets are behind the veranda building. On the opposite side of the site is a new en-suite facility for disabled visitors, part of a building housing a large games room with a snooker table, TV and darts. Shop (with gas). Swings, etc. for children in the central grass area. Fishing lake (licence required). Two mobile homes for hire. Off site: Lanivet village with shop and pub 2 miles. Riding 1 mile. Golf 2 miles. Bicycle hire 3 or 5 miles. Nearest beach 8 miles. Eden Project 4 miles.

Open: All year.

**Directions**

From A30 Bodmin bypass, exit at A30/A391 Innis Downs roundabout. Take the A389 north signed Lanivet and Bodmin. After 0.5 miles take first right (filter lane) and pass under the A30. Turn first left (Lostwithiel, Fowey) and in 0.25 miles turn right at top of hill. Continue for 0.5 miles and take first right into lane and site in 100 yds.
O.S.GR: SX041625. GPS: 50.430267, -4.757167

**Charges guide**

| | |
|---|---|
| Per unit incl. 2 persons and electricity | £ 15.50 - £ 23.00 |

## Bude

### Wooda Farm Holiday Park

Poughill, Bude EX23 9HJ (Cornwall) T: 01288 352069. E: enquiries@wooda.co.uk
alanrogers.com/UK0380

326

Wooda Farm is spacious and well organised, with some nice touches. A quality, family run park, it is part of a working farm set within 40 acres, under two miles from the sandy, surfing beaches of Bude. In peaceful farmland with plenty of open spaces (and some up and down walking), there are marvellous views of sea and countryside. The 220 large touring pitches are spread over four meadows on level or gently sloping grass. There are 142 with electricity connections (16A), 83 hardstanding hedged 'premier' pitches (electricity, water, waste water) and five premier pitches with Sky TV, linked by tarmac roads. A late arrivals area has electricity. Beside the shop and reception at the entrance are 55 caravan holiday homes for let. Tractor and trailer rides, archery and clay pigeon shooting with tuition are provided according to season and demand, plus woodland (find the pixies) and orchard walks and excellent coarse fishing.

**Facilities**

Three well maintained toilet blocks, one heated, include a unit suitable for disabled visitors, two baby rooms and five en-suite family bathrooms for hire (small charge). Two laundry rooms. Motorcaravan service point. Self-service shop with off-licence. Courtyard bar/restaurant and takeaway. Play area in separate field. 9-hole 'fun' golf course (clubs provided). Games room with TV and pool. Badminton. Tennis. Fitness suite. Coarse fishing in 1.5 acre lake (permits from reception, £1.50 per half day, £2.50 per day). Certain breeds of dog not accepted. Caravan storage. Internet access. WiFi. Off site: Local village inn is five minutes walk. Leisure Centre and Splash Pool in Bude.

Open: End March - end October.

**Directions**

Park is north of Bude at Poughill; turn off A39 on north side of Stratton on minor road for Coombe Valley, following camp signs at junctions.
O.S.GR: SS225080. GPS: 50.84331, -4.51857

**Charges guide**

| | |
|---|---|
| Per unit incl. 2 persons and electricity | £ 14.00 - £ 24.00 |
| incl. water and drainage | £ 17.00 - £ 27.00 |
| extra person | £ 3.50 - £ 5.00 |
| child (3-15 yrs) | £ 2.00 - £ 4.00 |

For latest campsite news visit
**alanrogers.com**

## Bude
### Widemouth Bay Caravan Park

Widemouth Bay, Bude EX23 0DF (Cornwall) T: 01288 361208.
alanrogers.com/UK0373

Widemouth has a wonderful situation on the edge of Widemouth Bay amidst rural farmland. Covering 50 acres in total, a number of areas have mobile homes carefully fitted into the hillside. There are some 180 touring pitches on undulating meadowland at the top of the hill, with 16A electricity available and some level hardstandings. The views are magnificent. The sandy beach, just a 15 minute walk away, is very popular with bathers and surfers and the indoor heated swimming pool is a bonus. This is a big and lively park in season, very well catered for with a well stocked shop, a bar serving food and nightly entertainment for children and parents. Bude is some ten minutes away by car and Tintagel is close enough to visit if the tales of King Arthur, Merlin and the round table interest you; otherwise Port Isaac is the 'Port Wenn' of the Doc Martin TV series. A regular local bus service operates from outside the Manor Hotel, hourly in the low season and half hourly in the main season. In the main season you go to the touring field to book in with the wardens.

### Facilities

Two traditional, fully equipped toilet blocks. Facilites for babies and an en-suite unit for visitors with disabilities. Launderette. Microwave. Shop, bar with food, and takeaway (limited hours). Indoor heated pool with lifeguard. Entertainment, quizzes, disco. Kids' club. Amusement arcade. Play area. Internet café/WiFi. Mini Golf. Bus service. Mobile homes to rent. Off site: Tennis and riding nearby. Fishing and boat trips from Bude.

Open: 5 March - 31 October.

### Directions

Using the A39 bypass Bude and after approx. 3 miles watch for righthand turning for Widemouth Bay. Follow to beach and continue south alongside beach until road bends inland by the Manor Hotel. Lane to site on right. GPS: 50.78033, -4.5613

### Charges guide

| | |
|---|---|
| Per unit incl. 2 persons and electricity | £ 14.00 - £ 38.00 |
| dog | £ 3.00 |

## Bude

### Sandymouth Holiday Park

Bude EX23 9HW (Cornwall) T: 01288 352563

alanrogers.com/UK0375

Sandymouth is a popular family park with a good range of amenities. The beautifully maintained site is situated on the side of a valley with wonderfull views but also a lot of up and down walking. Serviced pitches, 22 in all, with hardstanding are arranged either side of a tarmac roadway. A number of electric tenting pitches are to one side of the large, sloping open tenting field. where there are ten acres for camping. Pitches here are grassy and enjoy excellent views of Bude and Sandymouth. There is also a good range of fully equipped mobile homes, chalets and lodges available for rent. On-site amenities include an indoor pool (with water slide), sauna and free membership of the Ocean Bar and Club. There is a great deal here for children – notably the Black Pearl Adventure Play area which comprises a five-deck galleon with slides, walkways and a 24 m. cableway. There is a nightly programme of entertainment in peak season. Sandymouth beach is a 15 minute walk from the site with firm hard sand and rockpools, a National Trust car park and small café. From May 2010 the site is under new ownership so there may be some changes.

**Facilities**

Fully equipped toilet block. En-suite facilities for visitors with disabilities. Shop. Bar. Restaurant/snack bar. Takeaway. Ocean Bar and Club. Indoor swimming pool with small slide. Sauna. Adventure playground. Soft ball area. Minigolf. Sports field. Activity and entertainment programme. Children's club. Amusement arcade. Fishing. Internet access in reception. Mobile homes, chalets and bungalows for rent. Off site: Summerleaze and Sandymouth beaches. Clovelly 13 miles. Fishing. Surfing.

Open: 13 March - 31 October.

**Directions**

Approaching on the M5 motorway, leave at exit 27 and take the A361 and A39 towards Bideford and Bude. After passing through Kilkhampton turn right towards Stibb. Follow this road to Stibb and after the village turn left and the park is on the left.
O.S.GR: SS215105. GPS: 50.866973, -4.53752

**Charges guide**

| | |
|---|---|
| Per unit incl. 2 persons and electricity | £ 20.00 - £ 30.00 |
| extra person | £ 3.00 - £ 4.00 |

## Camelford

### Lakefield Caravan Park

Lower Pendavey Fm, Camelford PL32 9TX (Cornwall) T: 01840 213279. E: lakefieldcaravanpark@btconnect.com

alanrogers.com/UK0360

Lakefield is a small, simple touring park on what was a working farm. Now the main focus is on the BHS approved equestrian centre. With only 40 pitches, it is no surprise that the owners, Maureen and Dennis Perring, know all the campers. The well-spaced pitches backing onto hedges and with 24 electric hook-ups (16A) are in view of the small, fenced lake watched over by one of Cornwall's first wind farms. The white-washed café/reception, converted from one of the old barns is open all day offering traditional Cornish fare. A dozen colourful picnic tables are dotted about the site. Children will love the animals and 'Wabbit World'. With over 30 horses, the riding school is very much part of the site, offering lessons and hacks with qualified supervision and instruction.

**Facilities**

Simple but adequate toilet block. Washing machine and dryer in the ladies' and a dishwashing sink and a laundry sink outside but under cover. Toilet for disabled visitors at Riding Centre. Shop and tea room. Gas supplies. Torches may be useful. Off site: Fishing (sea 4 miles, coarse 5 miles). Golf 2 miles.

Open: 1 April - 30 September.

**Directions**

Follow B3266 north from Camelford. Park access is directly from this road on the left just before the turning for Tintagel, clearly signed.
O.S.GR: SX097852. GPS: 50.635058, -4.687648

**Charges guide**

| | |
|---|---|
| Per unit incl. 2 persons | £ 11.50 - £ 14.50 |
| extra person (5 yrs and over) | £ 1.00 |

For latest campsite news visit
**alanrogers.com**

## Falmouth

### Pennance Mill Farm Chalet & Camping Park

Maenporth, Falmouth TR11 5HJ (Cornwall) T: 01326 317431. E: pennancemill@amserve.com

**alanrogers.com/UK0450**

Pennance Mill Farm has been in the hands of the Jewell family for three generations and is listed as a typical Cornish farmstead in an Area of Outstanding Natural Beauty and you can enjoy the woodland walk with 200-year-old beech trees. In the high season skittles, country games and barbecue evenings are organised, all in keeping with the relaxed and friendly atmosphere generated by the owners. The camping area is in four sheltered south-facing and fairly level fields with views over the countryside and providing 75 pitches, all with 16A electricity and eight with hardstandings. Caravans are accepted but this is not a site for those who like neat manicured lawns and flower beds. An old mill wheel reminds one of the site's origins and you book in at the farmhouse. A private foot and cycle path takes you to the sandy beach at Maenporth safe for bathing, windsurfing and diving. An hourly bus service now runs to the beach and the town centre. The owners recommend visiting in May and June when the hedgerows are ablaze with colour from buttercups, campion and foxgloves.

#### Facilities

The two toilet blocks are fully equipped. Original block near the entrance is well kept with hot water, washing machine, dryer, laundry and dishwashing sinks. The newer block is heated and includes dishwashing sinks. Small farm shop including some basic provisions (open 09.00-10.30 and 17.30-18.30). Gas supplies. Small play meadow with new play equipment. Off site: Beach and watersports 2 miles. Indoor heated pool 2 miles. Riding 4 miles. Bar/restaurant/takeaway 5 miles. New Maritime Museum. Tennis courts, golf course and pitch and putt within walking distance. Coastal footpath to Helford River.

Open: Easter - November.

#### Directions

From Truro, follow signs for Falmouth on A39. At the first roundabout pass Asda then turn right at next roundabout signed industrial estates (on Bickland Water Road), next roundabout signed Maenporth. Follow the brown international camping signs for 1.5 miles and continue down the hill to site on your left as the road bends to the right.
O.S.GR: SW789307. GPS: 50.134983, -5.092667

#### Charges guide

| | |
|---|---|
| Per person | £ 6.00 - £ 7.00 |
| child (over 3 yrs) | £ 2.50 - £ 3.00 |
| pitch | £ 5.00 - £ 6.00 |
| electricity | £ 2.50 |

No credit cards.

## Fowey

### Penhale Caravan & Camping Park

Fowey PL23 1JU (Cornwall) T: 01726 833425. E: info@penhale-fowey.co.uk

**alanrogers.com/UK0285**

Penhale is a traditional campsite on four and half acres of rolling farmland with magnificent views across the countryside to St Austell Bay. The Berryman family run an arable and beef farm alongside the campsite. The atmosphere here is relaxed and there is plenty of room in the touring fields. The fields do slope but a number of pitches have been levelled. In total, there are 56 pitches for all types of units, 34 with 16A electricity hook-ups. Ten holiday caravans occupy a separate field. It is possible to walk to Polkerris beach a mile away and Fowey is just a mile and a half. The attractive, busy town of Fowey with its narrow streets is on the river of the same name and is a sailor's paradise (Regatta week is late August). Daphne du Maurier's association with the town is celebrated at the Literary Centre and with an annual Arts Festival in May. This is the landscape of wooded valleys, hidden coves and sandy beaches that inspired her books. There are many lovely walks and the site has produced directions. There are no public footpaths direct from the site but permission has been given to access the footpaths across private property.

#### Facilities

One fully equipped toilet block at the bottom of the touring fields. Laundry room. Reception at the farmhouse stocks basic necessities. Off site: Sandy beach, pub and watersports centre at Polkerris beach 1 mile (windsurfing, sailing, paddle surf, kayak). Fishing and boat launching 1.5 miles. Three golf courses within 7 miles. Shops and restaurants Fowey 1.5 miles. Garage with shop 600 yds. Bicycle hire 5 miles.

Open: Easter/1 April - 8 October.

#### Directions

From the A390 take B3269 for Fowey and 1 mile before town turn right at roundabout by petrol station on the A3082 St Austell road. Site is about 600 yds on the left. O.S.GR: SK105526.
GPS: 50.34309, -4.66848

#### Charges guide

| | |
|---|---|
| Per unit incl. 2 persons and electricity | £ 11.00 - £ 17.00 |
| extra person | £ 4.00 - £ 5.00 |
| child (4-15 yrs) | £ 2.00 |
| dog | £ 1.00 - £ 2.00 |

# Fowey

## Penmarlam Caravan & Camping Park

Bodinnick-by-Fowey, Fowey PL23 1LZ (Cornwall) T: 01726 870088. E: info@penmarlampark.co.uk

alanrogers.com/UK0195

Penmarlam is situated high above the estuary opposite Fowey, close to the village of Bodinnick, famous for being the home of Daphne du Maurier. The original field is level and sheltered with 30 pitches which are semi-divided by bushes. The newer field with 35 pitches has a slight slope, is divided with wild banks and enjoys good countryside views. Both fields have circular concrete access roads. All pitches have 16A electricity and six also have water and drainage. The modern reception, shop and the toilet facilities are well situated between the two fields. Reception is fitted with a loop system for deaf visitors and the owner can 'sign' as well as speaking French, Spanish and some German!

### Facilities

The modern, heated toilet block is fully equipped including a baby and toddler room in the ladies' and a separate unit for disabled visitors which can double as a family room. Laundry facilities. Well stocked, licensed shop with fresh fruit and vegetables. Coffee machine (available for reduced hours in low season). Video, DVD and book library. Off site: Fishing and boat launching 500 m. Beach 1 mile. Riding 3 miles. Golf 6 miles. Car or passenger ferry for Fowey. Annual Daphne du Maurier Festival of Arts and Literature held in Fowey (May). Fowey Regatta (mid Aug).

Open: 1 April - 31 October.

### Directions

From the main A390 road at East Taphouse take B3359 towards Looe. After 5 miles fork right, signed Bodinnick and ferry. Site is signed on the right 1 mile past village of Lanteglos Highway, just before Bodinnick village. O.S.GR: SK130527. GPS: 50.34434, -4.62289

### Charges guide

| Per unit incl. 2 persons | |
|---|---|
| and electricity | £ 13.00 - £ 22.50 |
| extra person | £ 3.50 - £ 7.00 |
| child (3-15 yrs) | £ 1.50 - £ 3.00 |

# Gorran Haven

## Sea View International

Boswinger, Saint Austell PL26 6LL (Cornwall) T: 01726 843425. E: holidays@seaviewinternational.com

alanrogers.com/UK0150

Sea View is an impressive, well cared for park. The enthusiastic owners, Mr. and Mrs. Royden, and their team are continually improving the park with the aim of providing quality camping. The new area at the top of the park with uninterrupted views is very smart, with 31 large, hedged, fully serviced grass pitches and a new toilet block providing excellent, en-suite family shower rooms. The remaining, established pitches (163, also with views) all have 16A electricity and 43 are fully serviced, including 12 hardstandings suitable for large motorhomes. There are 38 caravan holiday homes for hire in a separate area. Although somewhat exposed, the park is colourful with flower beds and flowering shrubs and has well manicured grass of exceptional quality. The area around the swimming pool is particularly attractive with sunbathing areas with free sunbeds on tiled terraces surrounded by flowers creating private little areas, all with magnificent views of the sea and the distant headland. Adjacent is a barbecue area with tables set out to take advantage of the view. A large recreation field provides play equipment as well as tennis, football and crazy golf. There is plenty to do and see in this area, from the gardens of Heligan and Trelissick, to Lanhydroc House and the seal sanctuary, not forgetting the safe beaches, one of which is only a half mile walk from the park. A member of the Best of British group.

### Facilities

Excellent toilet facilities are well maintained and heated providing for all needs, including en-suite facilities, bathrooms (on payment), baby baths and facilities for disabled visitors. Campers' kitchen. Well equipped laundry. Motorcaravan service point. Shop and off-licence with gas (June-end Sept). Takeaway (Whitsun-mid Oct). Swimming pool (heated end May-mid Sept). Large recreation field. Fenced play area for under 7s. Adventure playground. Games room. WiFi. Breeds of dog are not accepted. Off site: Fishing and boat launching 2 miles. Riding 2 mile. Bicycle hire 5 miles. Golf 9 miles. Community bus picks up at the park.

Open: 1 April - 31 October.

### Directions

From St Austell take B3273 towards Mevagissey; 1 mile before Mevagissey village turn right at Gorran and campsite sign and continue towards Gorran for 5 miles. Fork right at sign and follow signs to park. O.S.GR: SW991412. GPS: 50.2369, -4.820033

### Charges guide

| Per unit incl. 2 persons | |
|---|---|
| and electricity | £ 6.00 - £ 32.50 |
| serviced pitch | £ 8.00 - £ 35.00 |
| super pitch (fully incl.) | £ 10.00 - £ 56.00 |
| extra person (over 5 yrs) | £ 3.00 - £ 5.00 |
| dog (limited breeds and numbers) | £ 3.00 |

For latest campsite news visit

## alanrogers.com

## Helston

### Boscrege Caravan Park

Ashton, Helston TR13 9TG (Cornwall) T: 01736 762231. E: enquiries@caravanparkcornwall.com

alanrogers.com/UK0480

A pretty site covering 12 acres and hidden deep in the countryside in an Area of Outstanding Natural Beauty, Boscrege will suit those who want a quiet peaceful base for their Cornish holiday. The main large touring field nestles at the foot of Tregonning Hill with its striking hilltop cross, and has neatly cut grass with a gentle slope from the top. The pitches are generously spaced around the edge, backing on to hedging and leaving plenty of room in the centre for ball games. There are two small, attractive paddock areas with 26 caravan holiday homes and a field for touring units, providing a total of 51 pitches, 40 with 10A electricity. A nature trail has been developed which will help you identify the birds which can be seen around the park. This park is a welcome retreat for couples and families with young children.

**Facilities**

Traditional, fully equipped toilet block is showing its age but has been newly painted and includes a smaller basin for children (M/F). Washing machine, dryer and microwave. Two play areas for smaller children and central ball area. Amusement machines, pool table and TV room. Nature trail and dog-walking area. Plans to include WiFi. Off site: Godolphin House and garden. Whole of the tip of Cornwall easily accessible – the Lizard, Lands End. Nearest beach (Praa Sands) 2 miles. Fishing 1 mile. Golf and riding 2 miles. Bicycle hire and boat launching 5 miles.

Open: Easter/1 April - 31 October.

**Directions**

From Helston take A394 for Penzance. At top of Sithney Common Hill turn right just before Jet garage onto B3302 (Hayle) road. Pass Sithney General Stores on left and take next left for Carleen and Godolphin Cross. Continue to Godolphin Cross village and turn left at side of Godolphin Arms signed Ashton. Proceed up hill bearing left at top until you see camp signs where road turns sharply left and go straight over into lane leading to Boscrege. O.S.GR: SW593305. GPS: 50.12501, -5.36751

**Charges guide**

| | |
|---|---|
| Per unit incl. 4 persons and electricity | £ 13.00 - £ 22.45 |
| extra person | £ 2.00 |
| No charge for dogs (max. 3) | |

## Helston

### Silver Sands Holiday Park

Gwendreath, Ruan Minor, Helston TR12 7LZ (Cornwall) T: 01326 290631. E: info@silversandsholidaypark.co.uk

alanrogers.com/UK0070

Silver Sands is a small, peaceful, 'away-from-it-all' park, under new ownership, in a remote part of the Lizard peninsula, the most southerly part of mainland Britain and an Area of Outstanding Natural Beauty. It is tucked away behind two other holiday home parks (possible noise in season). The park itself has 16 caravan holiday homes, along with 36 touring pitches of which 20 have 10A electrical hook-ups. The pitches are large, attractively situated and divided into individual bays by flowering shrubs and bushes. The adjoining tent field has similar pitches (seven with electricity) where the shrubs are growing (some pitches are slightly sloping). The park is only reached after passing Culdrose Naval Base and the Goonhilly Earth Station down a single track road. A half mile footpath leads down through a small valley to the twin beaches of Kennack Sands (one is dog-free) divided by a small headland. This is generally an unspoilt walking area with the coastal path passing through and under the care of English Nature. A member of the Countryside Discovery group.

**Facilities**

The fully equipped toilet block includes an en-suite room for disabled visitors, doubling as a family room. Some play equipment. An undeveloped three-acre field can be used for walking, kite flying, etc. Off site: Restaurant nearby, pub within walking distance. Fishing 1 mile. Bicycle hire 5 miles. Boat launching 2 or 7 miles. Riding 5 miles. Golf 6 miles.

Open: Easter - mid October.

**Directions**

From Helston take A3038 Lizard road. After Culdrose turn left on B3293 passing Goonhilly after 4 miles. At next crossroads turn right (Kennack Sands), continue for 1.5 miles then left to Gwendreath on single track road - site is 1 mile. O.S.GR: SW732170. GPS: 50.00900, -5.16900

**Charges guide**

| | |
|---|---|
| Per unit incl. 2 persons, 2 children and electricity | £ 14.00 - £ 19.50 |
| extra person | £ 3.20 - £ 4.10 |
| child (under 16 yrs) | £ 1.80 - £ 2.50 |

## Helston

### Lower Polladras Touring Park

Carleen, Helston TR13 9NX (Cornwall) T: 01736 762220. E: lowerpolladras@btinternet.com

alanrogers.com/UK0475

Lower Polladras is a small, friendly park located north of Helston in beautiful rolling Cornish countryside. There are 44 touring pitches here as well as a number of mobile homes (for rent) and seasonal pitches. The site has a strong conservation interest and is actively working towards carbon neutral status. A two-acre area adjoining the park accommodates play equipment for children and a sports area. The upper level here is reserved for 28-day camping in the peak season. A nature and dog walk has been developed around the perimeter. There are some excellent walks and cycle tracks in the surrounding countryside and the park's owners will be pleased to recommend possible routes. This part of Cornwall has a great deal of interest. The Eden Project is within easy reach and Helston is a delightful town, best known perhaps for its annual Furry Dance. Beyond Helston, the Lizard Peninsula, is a stunning stretch of coastline leading to Lizard Point, the most southerly point of mainland Britain.

**Facilities**

Two traditional toilet blocks, both clean and light, with preset showers and hairdryer (20p). Baby changing area. Visitors with disabilities should check with site. Shop for basics. Playground. Sports area. Nature and dog walk. Tourist information. Mobile homes for rent. Off site: Helston (shops and restaurants). Golf, boat launching 3 miles. Fishing 4 miles. Riding 6 miles. Walking and cycling. Eden Project. Lizard Peninsula.

Open: 1 April - 2 January.

**Directions**

Take the A394 from Helston towards Penzance. On the edge of Helston, turn right on to the B3302, signed Camborne and Hayle. Take the second left to Carleen. Once in the village take the second right and follow signs to the park. O.S.GR: SW616308. GPS: 50.130156, -5.337199

**Charges guide**

| Per unit incl. 2 persons | |
|---|---|
| and electricity | £ 14.00 - £ 20.00 |
| extra person | £ 2.00 - £ 3.00 |
| child (3-16 yrs) | £ 1.50 - £ 2.00 |

## Liskeard

### The Colliford Tavern Campsite

Colliford Lake, Saint Neot, Liskeard PL14 6PZ (Cornwall) T: 01208 821335. E: info@colliford.com

alanrogers.com/UK0300

Colliford Tavern is quietly situated high on Bodmin Moor near Colliford Lake but hidden and protected by tall pines with a camping area and a tavern. The camping area is quiet and simple and has been kept very natural with short grass (helped by the rabbits) and sheltered from the moor by tall pines. The main field provides 40 fairly level pitches with 19 electric hook-ups (16A) and six hardstandings. Reception is in the tavern building. The tavern is run as a free house with a bar, dining room, a family room with outside terrace, garden, water wheel and a good, fenced play area. It is open to campers and caravanners and the public. Ideally situated for Colliford Lake and the Moor, be it for walking, fly fishing (permits available) or birdwatching, the park is also suitable for excursions to both the north and south coasts.

**Facilities**

The pine-fitted, heated toilet block is fully equipped and includes a baby room and unit for disabled visitors (no shower). Service wash and tumble dry (Monday to Friday). Restaurant and bar. Play area. Some occasional family entertainment. Eden Project tickets (20-30 minutes by car). Barbecues permitted with prior permission.

Open: All year.

**Directions**

Approaching on the A30 travelling south, pass the Jamaica Inn and site is signed a further 1-1.5 miles on the left. Follow for 0.5 miles and site is signed beside Colliford Lake Park. O.S.GR: SX168730. GPS: 50.536933, -4.582267

**Charges guide**

| Per unit incl. 2 persons and electricity | £ 18.00 |
|---|---|
| extra person (over 12 yrs) | £ 4.00 |
| child (5-12 yrs) | £ 2.00 |

For latest campsite news visit

**alanrogers.com**

## Mevagissey

### Tregarton Park

Gorran, Mevagissey, Saint Austell PL26 6NF (Cornwall) T: 01726 843666. E: reception@tregarton.co.uk

alanrogers.com/UK0155

Run by the welcoming Hicks family, Tregarton Park itself dates back to the 16th century. It is little wonder that the listed buildings have created some problems in providing modern facilities, although the Hicks have done well with their conversions to create a pleasing environment. The 12-acre caravan park is made up of four meadows with wonderful rural views. The 125 pitches, all with 10A electric hook ups, some with hardstanding, are of a generous size with most separated by either hedges or fencing. All have been terraced as the park itself is quite hilly. Reception provides a well stocked shop and a takeaway service offering freshly cooked food including a daily delivery of Cornish pasties. The large, heated, outdoor pool is surrounded by decked terraces, with tables and chairs where one can relax and watch the children, and is the focal point of the park. An adventure playground is in one meadow, where there is also an impressive all-weather tennis court.

**Facilities**

The fully equipped toilet block has been completely revamped and includes some excellent features. Facilities for disabled visitors. Laundry room. Well stocked shop with groceries and camping supplies, takeaway (all 28/5-24/9). Gas supplies. Heated swimming pool (28/5-2/9). Tourist information. Dog exercise meadow. Adventure playground. All weather tennis. WiFi. Max. 2 dogs. Off site: Bus stop at entrance. Bicycle hire 3 miles. Golf 5 miles. Heligan Gardens 2 miles. Mevagissey 2 miles. Beaches 2 miles. Eden Project 9 miles. Fishing trips available from Mevagissey and Gorran Haven.

Open: 1 April - 30 October.

**Directions**

Leave St Austell travelling south on the B3273 and pass through London Apprentice and Pentewen. Follow Tregarton Park's brown tourist signs by turning right at the crossroads at the top of the hill towards Heligan and Gorran Haven. Do not go into Mevagissey. O.S.GR: SW989435.
GPS: 50.2588, -4.829417

**Charges 2011**

| Per unit incl. 2 persons, | |
|---|---|
| electricity and awning | £ 9.00 - £ 25.00 |
| extra person (4-17 yrs) | £ 3.00 - £ 18.00 |
| dog (max. 2) | £ 1.00 - £ 3.00 |

## Mullion

### Franchis Holidays

Cury Cross Lanes, Mullion TR12 7AZ (Cornwall) T: 01326 240301. E: enquiries@franchis.co.uk

alanrogers.com/UK0485

A small rural site, Franchis is ideally situated for exploring the Lizard peninsula in an Area of Outstanding Natural Beauty. Mature trees edge the site's two fields (a total of four acres) that slope slightly, with 70 pitches arranged around the perimeters. There are 33 with 10A electricity. Natural woodland areas and a stream will keep children occupied. Continuing past the fields into a wooded area are six small bungalows and six mobile homes, some privately owned and some to rent. There is a small toilet block for each field and a small shop that opens morning and evening. Phil and Kate, the young couple who have owned the site for the last three years, will be pleased to welcome you and advise you in exploring the area. The Lizard is a unique area and well worth exploring with unspoilt coves and the Helford river. Goonhilly Earth station is just up the road and you pass by the extensive Culdrose Naval base on your way to the site. Helston is known for its famous 'floral dance', the origin of which is not certain, but for one day in May each year the inhabitants dress up and dance through the streets to celebrate.

**Facilities**

Two traditional small toilet blocks. Two washing machines and two driers. Freezer for ice blocks. Small shop (18/7-30/9). Tourist Information. Small library. Play area. Dog exercise field. Tourist information. Mobile homes and chalets for rent. Off site: Helston 5 miles. Beach 2 miles. Fishing and boat launching 2 miles. Sailing 4 miles. Riding and golf 2 miles.

Open: Easter - 31 October.

**Directions**

From Helston take the A3038 road for the Lizard. After passing Culdrose take the A3083 signed Mullion and after about 2 miles watch for site directly on the right. O.S.GR: SW696204.
GPS: 50.039, -5.21843

**Charges guide**

| Per unit incl. 2 persons | |
|---|---|
| and electricity | £ 12.00 - £ 16.00 |
| extra person | £ 1.00 - £ 1.50 |
| dog | £ 1.00 - £ 1.50 |

## Newquay
### Sun Haven Valley Holiday Park
Mawgan Porth, Newquay TR8 4BQ (Cornwall) T: 01637 860373. E: sunhaven@sunhavenvalley.com
alanrogers.com/UK0215

An attractive, well maintained holiday park, Sun Haven Valley is on the edge of a small valley with views of the opposite hills. Owned and thoughtfully run by the Tavener family, it caters mainly for couples and families with children. On a gently sloping hillside, around 30 caravan holiday homes for rent border the top field with a central area of neatly cut grass left free for play. The lower field is edged by a small trout stream (unfenced) and provides over 100 level, grass touring pitches (in standard and large sizes), marked by tram lines and accessed by a circular road. In peak season, extra pitches are provided in a field on the other side of the road. The facilities and play area are situated between the two fields and some up and down walking is required. A footpath involves a 15-20 minutes' walk to reach the beach and the small village of Mawgan Porth which was buzzing with surfers and families out to enjoy the beach when we visited. There are eating places within walking distance and an organic farm with a shop next door – apparently Tesco and Asda will deliver to the site! An unusual recycling activity whereby any left behind body boards, chairs, tables and toys can be borrowed by other campers seems to be much appreciated. Local bus services pass through the village.

#### Facilities
A large, central toilet block is fully equipped, a smaller one is in the far corner. Two en-suite family rooms have facilities for disabled visitors. Laundry. Fridge and freezer. Microwave. Toaster. Basic foodstuffs in reception. Play area. TV room. Games room with computers and games machines. WiFi (around reception). Mobile homes and chalets for rent. Off site: Two pubs, restaurant, bistro, takeaway and supermarket in village. Beach 0.75 miles. Fishing 100 yds. Golf 1 mile. Riding 5 miles.
Open: Easter - 31 October.

#### Directions
From B3276 at Mawgan Porth take narrow unclassed road up the Vale of Lanhorne for 1 mile. Site is on the left. O.S.GR: SW861667. GPS: 50.46203, -5.01385

#### Charges guide
| | |
|---|---|
| Per unit incl. 2 adults and electricity | £ 15.00 - £ 27.00 |
| child (5-13 yrs, first one free) | £ 2.00 - £ 3.50 |
| dog (max. 1 in high season) | £ 1.00 - £ 4.00 |

## Newquay
### Trekenning Tourist Park
Saint Columb Major, Newquay TR8 4JF (Cornwall) T: 01637 880462. E: holidays@trekenning.co.uk
alanrogers.com/UK0310

Trekenning is a very useful park with easy access just off the A39 roundabout at St Columb Major. It comprises a large sloping field with neatly cut grass and all the facilities tucked into the top corner. There are 75 pitches, 68 with 10A electricity and semi-terraced. The A39 runs parallel to one side of the site, so there may be road noise. The star of the show is the kidney shaped pool and paddling pool which are in a garden-like setting with gazebos and sun loungers surrounded by lawn and overlooked by a patio bar at the top – lovely for summer evenings. The bar complex, with a conservatory and decked area, serves local real ales and food. Entertainment is provided most nights in the main season.

#### Facilities
Two toilet blocks, one with showers and washbasins, the other with two en-suite bathrooms (50p) and six large family showers, well refurbished. Laundry room. Freezer service. Shop for basics (July/Aug). Bar (all season) with food on demand. Takeaway including breakfasts (B.Hs and July/Aug). Play area. Outdoor pool with poolside bar (Whitsun-end Aug). Games room. Off site: Fishing 1 mile. Riding and golf 2 miles. Bicycle hire 6 miles.
Open: All year.

#### Directions
Take A3059 turning to Newquay from St Columb Major then turn immediately left; park is signed (this was the old road). O.S.GR: SW907625. GPS: 50.42182, -4.94265

#### Charges guide
| | |
|---|---|
| Per unit incl. 2 persons | £ 15.00 - £ 20.00 |
| extra person | £ 4.75 - £ 7.00 |
| child (3-15 yrs) | £ 2.00 - £ 4.50 |

For latest campsite news visit
**alanrogers.com**

# Newquay

## Trethiggey Touring Park

Quintrell Downs, Newquay TR8 4QR (Cornwall) T: 01637 877672. E: enquiries@trethiggey.co.uk

alanrogers.com/UK0530

Trethiggey is a garden-like park with a ten month season, set some three miles back from the busy Newquay beaches and night life, with an enjoyable, informal style. With natural areas including a small wildlife pond and fishing lakes to enjoy, conservation is high on the agenda. There are 157 pitches, 110 with 16A electricity, some with hardstanding and four with water and sewage connection. Some level pitches are formally arranged, with others more informal on gently sloping grass amidst 12 caravan holiday homes. A tent field is opened for the main season. A bistro and barbecue bar are very popular. Facilities maintain the informal touch with reception alongside the Trethiggey Trading Post which provides basic supplies, an off-licence and a small library. The attractive bistro-style café and terrace operate in school holidays for breakfasts and simple evening meals, with children catered for. At weekends in peak season the barbecue bar is an added attraction.

### Facilities

Two fully equipped, heated shower blocks, one in traditional style. En-suite facilities for families and disabled visitors. Baby bathroom. Motorcaravan service point. Laundry facilities and wetsuit wash. Games room at each toilet block with TV and amusement machines. Shop, (all season). Café, bar and takeaway (June-Sept). Adventure play area and recreation field. Coarse fishing. WiFi (on payment). Off site: Riding 2 miles. Golf and bicycle hire 3 miles. All the delights of Newquay within 3 miles with nightly minibus service (book in shop). Pub within walking distance.

Open: 2 March - 2 January.

### Directions

Site is a few hundred yards south of roundabout where A393 crosses the A3058 at Quintrell Downs (beside the A3058). O.S. GR:SW846596. GPS: 50.396833, -5.0283

### Charges guide

| Per unit incl. 2 persons | |
|---|---|
| and electricity | £ 15.45 - £ 22.05 |
| extra person | £ 4.65 - £ 7.95 |
| child (3-15 yrs) | £ 1.70 - £ 5.30 |
| dog | £ 2.70 - £ 2.85 |

*See advertisement opposite.*

# Newquay

## Newperran Holiday Park

Rejerrah, Newquay TR8 5QJ (Cornwall) T: 01872 572407. E: holidays@newperran.co.uk

alanrogers.com/UK0160

Newperran is a large, level park in rural Cornish countryside. Being on high ground, it is quite open but this also gives excellent views of the coast and surrounding countryside. The owners, Keith and Christine Brewer, have rebuilt the reception, shop and pub to a very high standard. The traditional layout of the park provides a number of flat, well drained meadows divided into over 370 individual pitches with 10/16A electricity. Some fields have larger and reservable spaces with more free space in the centre. There are now 77 fully serviced pitches, some with hardstanding and a TV point. Newperran is only 2.5 miles from Perranporth beach, but there is a free heated swimming pool with sunbathing area and paddling pool on the park. A state of the art entrance barrier is now in place operating on recognition of your number plate. The pub, or 'cottage inn' as it is called, is a very comfortable area with a log burner for low season warmth and family entertainment such as quiz nights in high season. A separate café operates on a franchise basis. This is a well run park with plenty of space and activities for families with a few caravan holiday homes to rent. There are plans to provide a specialist naturist area but advanced booking will be required.

### Facilities

Toilet facilities comprise four clean blocks, two heated and all refurbished to a very high standard. Facilities include washbasins in cabins, family rooms, baby room, hairdressing room and a unit for disabled visitors. Laundry room. Well stocked self-service licensed shop. Licensed bar (mid May-Oct). Café (all season). New outdoor heated swimming pool with paddling pool (Whitsun-Sept). Adventure playground and separate toddlers' play area. Games room with TV. TV room. Off site: Riding or golf 2 miles. Fishing 1 mile. Goonhavern village within walking distance with pubs and post office. Beach 2.5 miles.

Open: Easter - October.

### Directions

Turn off A3075 to west at camping sign 7 miles south of Newquay and just north of Goonhavern village. O.S.GR: SW794546. GPS: 50.350433, -5.101817

### Charges guide

| Per pitch incl. 2 persons | |
|---|---|
| and electricity | £ 13.90 - £ 20.60 |
| extra person | £ 4.50 - £ 7.85 |
| child (3-15 yrs) | £ 2.35 - £ 6.10 |

*See advertisement opposite.*

For latest campsite news visit
**alanrogers.com**

# orth Beach
### ist Park • Newquay

y 100m
n the beach...

h, Newquay, Cornwall, TR7 3NH
37 876531   e:info@porthbeach.co.uk
.porthbeach.co.uk

## NEWPERRAN
### Holiday Park

Peaceful family holiday park, renowed for its spacious, at perimeter pitching, with breathtaking open countryside and sea views.

**Call for a Brochure**
**Tel: 0845 1668407**
Fax: 01872 571254

- new luxury toilet blocks
- free showers
- family rooms
- disabled facilities
- launderette
- cafe/takeaway
- premium all-service pitches
- shop/off licence
- entertainments
- TV/games room
- Cottage Inn
- adventure playground
- toddlers play area
- new swimming pool and paddling pool with sunbathing terraces
- internet access
- caravan storage

Rejerrah, Newquay, Cornwall TR8 5QJ    **www.newperran.co.uk**

---

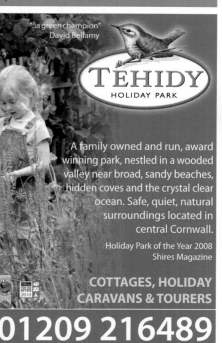

"...a green champion"
David Bellamy

## TEHIDY
### HOLIDAY PARK

A family owned and run, award winning park, nestled in a wooded valley near broad, sandy beaches, hidden coves and the crystal clear ocean. Safe, quiet, natural surroundings located in central Cornwall.

Holiday Park of the Year 2008
Shires Magazine

**COTTAGES, HOLIDAY CARAVANS & TOURERS**

# 01209 216489
## ww.tehidy.co.uk
oliday@tehidy.co.uk
oliday Park, Harris Mill, Illogan, Redruth, Cornwall. TR16 4JQ

---

*A park for all seasons*
## Trethiggey Holiday Park
Quintrell Downs, Newquay, Cornwall TR8 4QR

Set in beautiful countryside, Trethiggey is an award-winning touring park just minutes from Cornwall's "Coast of Dreams" and some of the finest beaches in Europe.

Centrally positioned for top attractions including the Eden Project, we're only seven miles from Newquay International Airport.

Tel: 01637 877672
E-mail: enquiries@trethiggey.co.uk
Online booking: www.trethiggey.co.uk

camping ★ touring ★ holiday homes

# Hendra
## HOLIDAY PARK

01637 875778
**www.hendra-holidays.com**
Hendra Holidays, Newquay, Cornwall, TR8 4NY

Family run park for families & couples with top rated facilities & the fantastic Oasis indoor & outdoor Fun Pools co

★ five star park ★ five star facilities ★ five star holiday ★ five star fu

---

**Open All Year**

Dolbeare
Park caravan & camping

An award winning park
located in the beautiful Cornish countryside close to
Plymouth and the unspoilt beaches of the Rame
Peninsula - a park for all seasons
~1 mile easy access from A38
~60 large gravel & grass pitches with electric
~Children's Adventure Play Area ~ WiFi
~Shop, Off Licence & Takeaway ~ Calor Gas
~Visit our website for reviews and **Special Offers**

www.dolbeare.co.uk   01752 851332

Heated
swimming pool

Licensed
family bar

Free
entertainment

Café/takeaway

On site shop

TV and
games room

Adventure
playground

Electric hook-up

Treloy golf
course nearby

Treloy
Touring Park

Telephone:
**01637 87206**
Or visit us at:
**www.treloy.co.**
Newquay, Cornwall TR8 4.

## Newquay
### Trevornick Holiday Park
Holywell Bay, Newquay TR8 5PW (Cornwall) T: 01637 830531. E: bookings@trevornick.co.uk
alanrogers.com/UK0220

Trevornick, once a working farm, is a modern, busy and well run family touring park providing a very wide range of amenities close to one of Cornwall's finest beaches. A modern reception with welcoming staff sets the tone for your holiday. The park is well managed with facilities and standards constantly monitored. It has grown to provide caravanners and campers (no holiday caravans but 68 very well equipped Eurotents) with 440 large grass pitches (350 with 10A electricity and 55 fully serviced with electricity, water, drainage and TV connection with DVD channel) on five level fields and two terraced areas. There are few trees but some good views. Providing 'all singing, all dancing' facilities for fun packed family holidays, the farm buildings now provide the setting for the Farm Club. Recently refurbished, it provides much entertainment from bingo and quizzes to shows, discos and cabaret. The Stables Grill also opens for breakfast and the Hungry Horse provides takeaway food. The rest of the development provides a pool complex, an 18-hole golf course with a small, quiet club house offering bar meals and lovely views out to sea and three fishing lakes. Next door is the Holywell Bay 'fun' park (reduced rates) and the sandy beach is five minutes by car or a downhill walk from the park. An innovative idea is the Hire Shop where it is possible rent anything you might have forgotten, from sheets, a fridge, travel cot, etc. to a camera or a wet suit to catch the famous Cornish surf!

### Facilities
Five modern toilet blocks provide showers (20p), two family bathrooms, baby bath, laundry facilities and provision for disabled visitors. Well stocked supermarket with bread made on site (from late May). Hire Shop. Bars (with TV), restaurant, cafe and takeaway. Entertainment (every night in season). Pool complex with heated outdoor pool, paddling pool, sunbathing decks, solarium, sauna and massage chair. Health and beauty salon. Super Fort Knox style adventure playground, crazy golf, Kids' Club and indoor play area (supervised for 2-8 yr olds at a small charge). Amusement arcade and bowling alley. 18-hole pitch and putt with golf pro shop. Bicycle hire. Coarse fishing with three lakes. Dogs are accepted in one field only. Only limited facilities open at Easter and from 8 Sept. Off site: Riding within 1 mile. Bicycle hire 4 miles.

Open: Easter - mid September.

### Directions
From A3075 approach to Newquay - Perranporth road, turn towards Cubert and Holywell Bay. Continue through Cubert to park on the right. O.S.GR: SW776586. GPS: 50.384983, -5.128933

### Charges guide
| | |
|---|---|
| Per person | £ 4.95 - £ 9.30 |
| child (4-14 yrs) | £ 1.30 - £ 6.55 |
| electricity | £ 4.75 |
| 'super premium' or 'jumbo' pitch incl. electricity | £ 8.95 |
| dog | £ 3.45 - £ 3.75 |

Families and couples only.
Many special discounts.
*See advertisement on page 27.*

## Newquay
### Hendra Holiday Park
Newquay TR8 4NY (Cornwall) T: 01637 875778. E: jn@hendra.co.uk
alanrogers.com/UK0210

Hendra is a long-established holiday park for all the family with a wide range of facilities and a comprehensive entertainment programme. There are comedians, show bands, cabaret, dancing, bingo, discos, plus a super pool complex. The 548 touring pitches are on well mown, mostly terraced grass fields with country views and mature trees, some more sheltered than others. There are 280 caravan holiday homes to rent in separate fields. With tarmac roads and lighting, 311 pitches have electricity (16A) and 28 pitches are fully serviced including water, electricity, light, sewerage, satellite TV connections and some innovative awning pads (dogs are not accepted on these pitches). The entrance and reception are very attractive with a mass of well tended flower beds which, along with the other facilities, form an attractive, village-like centre to the park. The 'star of the show' at Hendra is the Oasis complex consisting of an indoor fun pool with flumes, river rapids and beach; it is open to the public. The outdoor heated pool with grass sunbathing area is free to campers and activities are well catered for with a range of amenities. The park is 1.5 miles from Newquay and its fabulous surfing beaches and a bus passes the gate. Hendra welcomes families and couples. A member of the Best of British group.

### Facilities
Three modern fully equipped toilet blocks including facilities for babies and disabled visitors. Large launderette. Motorcaravan services. Gas supplies. Well stocked shop. Various bars and restaurants, open all season (limited hours in early season). Pizzeria (main season only). Takeaway. Outdoor swimming pool. Indoor pool complex (cost £2.70 per person or, if pre-booked, £13.90 for 7 tickets). Various play areas including one for soft play. Minigolf. Bowling. Off site: Fishing or riding 1 mile. Bicycle hire or golf 2 miles. Beach 1.5 miles.

Open: 23 March - 31 October.

### Directions
Park is on left side of A392 Indian Queens - Newquay road at Newquay side of Quintrell Downs. O.S.GR: SW833601. GPS: 50.402433, -5.04915

### Charges guide
| | |
|---|---|
| Per unit incl. 2 persons and electricity | £ 16.80 - £ 26.50 |
| extra person | £ 4.95 - £ 8.95 |
| child (3-14 yrs) | free - £ 5.90 |
| dog | £ 4.00 - £ 4.95 |

Minimum charges apply at peak times.
*See advertisement on page 26.*

For latest campsite news visit
# alanrogers.com

## Newquay
### Treloy Touring Park

Newquay TR8 4JN (Cornwall) T: 01637 872063. E: treloy-tp@btconnect.com
alanrogers.com/UK0205

Just three miles from the wonderful beaches around Newquay, yet peacefully located away from the crowds, Treloy is a pretty park. Family owned and run, there are 197 pitches, many level, some slightly sloping, all with 16A electricity (new system) and 20 fully serviced. All are used for touring units and caravans which are attractively interspersed with shrubs and form a pleasant landscape feature. Elsewhere hydrangea edge the roads around the more open pitches and the new trees have grown well. St Mawgan, the RAF air sea rescue base and Newquay's airport are nearby, but there is little disturbance. There is an hourly bus service to Newquay from the park entrance which means the coast and beaches can be enjoyed without taking the car. On return to Treloy there is the Park Chef and the Surfrider's Bar for meals and drinks. If you do not fancy the beach there is a pool on the park. This is a real family park providing for all ages.

### Facilities

Two new toilet blocks, one with showers, the other with toilets and washbasins only. Baby room with two large sinks. En-suite facilities for disabled visitors (key). Laundry. Gas. Shop with all necessities. Bar (20/5-15/9). Pleasant café with a good reputation and including breakfast (20/5-1/9). Swimming pool (walled and gated). Play areas and field with goal posts. Nature trail. Family entertainment such as magic shows, bingo, folk and rock music. Off site: Fishing 1 mile. Golf 0.5 miles. Riding and boat launching 3 miles. Other beaches such as Watergate Bay, Mawgan Porth and Porth beach are a short car ride.

Open: 20 May - 15 September.

### Directions

From A39 St Columb Major take the B3059 for Newquay. Park is signed after about 4 miles.
O.S.GR: SW858625. GPS: 50.432867, -5.0125

### Charges guide

| | |
|---|---|
| Per unit incl. 2 persons and electricity | £ 13.75 - £ 21.45 |
| extra person | £ 5.00 - £ 7.35 |
| child (3-14 yrs) | £ 3.00 - £ 4.45 |
| dog | £ 1.00 - £ 2.50 |

See advertisement on page 26.

## Newquay
### Trevella Caravan Park

Crantock, Newquay TR8 5EW (Cornwall) T: 01637 830308. E: holidays@trevella.co.uk
alanrogers.com/UK0170

One of the best known and respected of Cornish parks with its colourful flowerbeds (a regular winner of a 'Newquay in Bloom' award), Trevella is also one of the first to fill up and has a longer season than most. Well organised, the pitches are in a number of adjoining meadows, most of which are on a slight slope. Of the 250 pitches for touring units (any type), some 200 can be reserved and these are marked, individual ones. Over 200 pitches have electricity (10A), with 59 serviced pitches (with hardstanding, electricity and TV hook-ups, water, waste water), some extra large with sewage drain as well. Trevella is essentially a quiet family touring park. The accent is on orderliness and cleanliness with on-site evening activities limited, although Andy's Kitchen offers good home-cooked food. Access is free to two fishing lakes (permits from reception); with some fishing instruction and wildlife talks for youngsters in season. There is a pleasant walk around the lakes, which are a haven for wildlife and a protected nature reserve. It is also possible to walk to Crantock beach but check the tides first.

### Facilities

Kept very clean, three blocks provide good coverage with individual washbasins in private cabins for ladies, hairdressing room and baby room. Laundry. Freezer pack service. Well stocked supermarket (Easter-Oct). Café (including breakfast) and takeaway. Heated outdoor pool. Games room. Separate TV room. Crazy golf. Large adventure playground. Play and sports area. Pets corner. Fishing. Off site: Shuttle bus service to Newquay in high season. Nearest beach is 0.5 miles on foot, 1 mile by car and Newquay is 2 miles. Pubs and restaurants at Crantock, 1 mile. Riding 1 mile, golf 3 miles

Open: Easter - 31 October.

### Directions

To avoid Newquay leave A30 or A392 at Indian Queens, straight over crossroads with A39 and A3058, left at A3075 junction and first right at camping sign. O.S.GR: SW802598.
GPS: 50.3973, -5.096133

### Charges guide

| | |
|---|---|
| Per person | £ 4.65 - £ 8.20 |
| child (3-14 yrs) | £ 1.50 - £ 5.75 |
| pitch incl. electricity | £ 5.75 |
| service pitch | £ 9.75 - £ 13.75 |

Families and couples only.
See advertisement on page 27.

For latest campsite news visit
## alanrogers.com

## Newquay
### Monkey Tree Holiday Park

Rejerrah, Newquay TR8 5QR (Cornwall) T: 01872 572032. E: enquiries@monkeytreeholidaypark.co.uk
alanrogers.com/UK0165

Monkey Tree covers 56 acres and boasts an impressive entrance and smart reception. There are 500 pitches with 450 for touring units and 50 caravan holiday homes to rent in their own area. The pitches in the original part of the park benefit from mature hedging which offers a degree of privacy which the newer ones lack, but all have been planted with individual hedges. The pitches are of a good size and most have electricity (13/16A). Serviced pitches with hardstanding are being developed including some extra large pitches which include the use of private facilities in the toilet block. During the holiday season there is much going on at Monkey Tree. All the family should find something to keep them happy. For the little ones there is a morning Kid's Club, for older children there are adventure playgrounds, well fenced for safety, trampolines, bouncy castles and an amusement arcade and pool tables. For everyone there is an outdoor heated pool, paddling pool and a sauna. The club and restaurant are popular with entertainment for children in the early part of the evening, and bingo, karaoke, disco and cabaret acts follow. Themed weekends are organised early and late in the season, with Halloween being especially popular. Venturing off the park there are wonderful beaches, a range of watersports to enjoy and places such as the Eden Project and Flambards a must to visit.

### Facilities
The original block (refurbished) supplements two new modern timber blocks with heating, providing for all needs including facilities for babies and disabled visitors. Private en-suite facilities for use with the super pitches. Laundry. Motorcaravan services. Gas supplies. Shop (mornings only in low season). Club with entertainment, bar and restaurant (main season and B.Hs). Takeaway (high season). Outdoor pool and paddling pool (Whitsun-end Sept). Trampolines (supervised, with charge). Bouncy castles. Three adventure play areas. Amusement arcade. Fishing lakes. Caravan storage. Off site: Golf, riding, boat launching and sailing 5 miles.

Open: All year.

### Directions
Follow A30 ignoring all signs for Newquay. At Carland Cross with windmills on the right, carry straight over following signs for Perranporth. After 1 mile turn right at Boxheater Junction on B3285 signed Perranporth and Goonhavern. Follow for 0.5 miles then turn right into Scotland Road for 1 mile to park on the left. O.S.GR: SW801546. GPS: 50.352218, -5.091659

### Charges guide

| | |
|---|---|
| Per person | £ 3.75 - £ 6.20 |
| child (3-14 yrs) | free - £ 3.75 |
| pitch incl. electricity | £ 3.50 |
| incl. services | £ 7.50 - £ 10.50 |

## Newquay
### Newquay Holiday Park

Newquay TR8 4HS (Cornwall) T: 01637 871111. E: enquiries@parkdean.com
alanrogers.com/UK0200

Part of the Parkdean Group, Newquay Holiday Park lies peacefully on a terraced hillside only just outside the town, two miles from the beaches and town centre. Its main feature is an attractively laid out group of three heated swimming pools with a giant water slide (lifeguards in attendance) and 'green' sunbathing areas overlooked by a terrace for cool drinks. With a large proportion of caravan holiday homes (for let), there are still two fields used for touring units. These provide 187 marked pitches in hedged fields, some sloping, marked out by lines on ground but with nothing between them. Electricity (16A) is available. Family entertainment is provided each night with live music, discos etc. in the site's Fiesta Club which also has a bar, TV lounge and games room with pool and snooker tables.

### Facilities
Two good sized, modern toilet blocks include a unit for disabled visitors and baby bath. An extra block is opened for the main season when facilities may be under pressure. Launderette. Well stocked self-service shop (gas from reception). Bar/lounge with Sky TV. New café/restaurant with all day food also 'pub grub' in evenings. Outdoor pool complex with slide (and lifeguards). Pitch and putt and crazy golf. Playground for little ones and adventure play area for older children. Children's club. Recreation field. Amusement arcade.

Open: Easter - October.

### Directions
Park is east of Newquay on A3059 road 1 mile east of junction with A3058. O.S.GR: SW853626. GPS: 50.4225, -5.0245

### Charges guide

| | |
|---|---|
| Per unit incl. 4 persons | £ 7.00 - £ 27.00 |
| incl. services | £ 10.00 - £ 30.00 |
| extra person (over 3 yrs; up to 4 people) | £ 2.00 - £ 4.00 |
| dog | £ 2.50 |

# Newquay

## Porth Beach Tourist Park

Porth, Newquay TR7 3NH (Cornwall) T: 01637 87653. E: info@porthbeach.co.uk

alanrogers.com/UK0235

The park is just across the road from Porth Beach with its beautiful bay, sandy shoreline and rock pools. Situated in a small, rural valley with a gentle stream to one side you can enjoy the ducks and the wildlife. The 182 good sized grass pitches stretching up the valley in parallel lines accessed by tarmac roadways are level, marked by tram lines and back on to open fencing. Most have 16A electricity, and a few have hardstandings. A well equipped toilet block is to be found half way up, heated in cold weather and air conditioned in warmer times. Watergate Bay is just around the corner, and Newquay a couple of miles down the road, so if you are a surfer you will be in paradise. For walkers, Porth Headland and the South West Coastal path offer some outstanding views.

| Facilities | Directions |
|---|---|
| One modern, heated and fully equipped toilet block. Baby bath and facilities for disabled visitors. Launderette. Children's play area. Mobile homes to rent. Off site: Golf, riding and boat launching 1.5 miles. | From Newquay take the B3276 to Padstow. Site about half a mile on right. GPS: 50.426071, -5.0534 |

**Open: 5 March - 31 October.**

**Charges guide**

| | |
|---|---|
| Per unit incl. 2 persons and electricity | £ 12.00 - £ 39.00 |

*See advertisement on page 25.*

---

# Padstow

## Padstow Touring Park

Padstow PL28 8LE (Cornwall) T: 01841 532061. E: mail@padstowtouringpark.co.uk

alanrogers.com/UK0430

Padstow Touring Park has wonderful views over the surrounding countryside. Originally open fields, bushes and shrubs have grown to break up the gently sloping fields. There are 150 pitches, most with 10A electricity and some with hardstanding. Some have access to private, en-suite facilities. The site can accommodate motorhomes up to 34 ft. Padstow itself is a mile away, either by public footpath through the fields (20-30 minutes) or by bicycles on the road. A bus service passes (the site is a request stop) and reception holds timetables. Rick Stein's restaurant or bistro may tempt you – and there are many others in Padstow.

| Facilities | Directions |
|---|---|
| Three toilet blocks, including one new with underfloor heating, en-suite shower rooms, facilities for disabled visitors and a family room. Exclusive washrooms for use with some pitches. Full laundry facilities. Reception/shop for gas, camping equipment and provisions. Play area. WiFi access. Off site: Nearest beach is at Padstow, others are within 2 miles. Access to the Camel Trail cycle route. Riding or fishing 2 miles. Golf 5 miles. | The park is situated on the main A389 road into Padstow, on the right about 1 mile before the town. If towing or in a motorhome avoid A389 between Wadebridge and St Issey; instead take B3274, suitable for large units. O.S.GR: SW912739. GPS: 50.52705, -4.949183 |

**Open: All year.**

**Charges guide**

| | |
|---|---|
| Per unit incl. 2 persons | £ 13.50 - £ 18.50 |
| extra person | £ 2.00 - £ 4.50 |

---

# Pentewan

## Pentewan Sands Holiday Park

Pentewan, Saint Austell PL26 6BT (Cornwall) T: 01726 843485. E: info@pentewan.co.uk

alanrogers.com/UK0250

Pentewan Sands is a popular, well managed family park with an ideal position right beside a wide sandy private beach. A busy, 32-acre holiday park with lots going on, there are 501 touring pitches, 401 with electricity, and 120 caravan holiday homes for hire. The good sized pitches are on level grass with nothing between them. They are marked and numbered by frontage stones, mostly in rows adjoining access roads. A good heated pool with a paddling pool is beside the Beach Club. This area was due to be rebuilt providing new indoor pools, a lap pool, a fun pool, a gym, 'kids' zone' and new bar and restaurant. A full entertainment programme, beach activities, scuba diving, windsurfing courses and a club for children are organised.

| Facilities | Directions |
|---|---|
| Four main toilet blocks, maintained by individual cleaners. Two bathrooms, baby room and facilities for disabled campers. Laundry room. Motorcaravan service point. Shop, bistro and fast food (Easter-mid Sept). Bars, bar meals (Easter-mid Sept, limited hours off season). Entertainment programme. Swimming pools (supervised, open Whitsun-mid Sept). Playground. Games room. Tennis. Bicycle hire. Gas. Dogs are not accepted. Off site: Riding and golf 2 miles. Bicycle hire 0.5 miles. | From St Austell ring road take B3273 for Mevagissey. Park is 3.5 miles, where the road meets the sea. O.S.GR: SX018468. GPS: 50.288283, -4.78575 |

**Open: 1 April - 31 October.**

**Charges guide**

| | |
|---|---|
| Per unit incl. 2 persons and electricity | £ 13.55 - £ 29.50 |
| extra person | £ 2.99 - £ 5.00 |
| child (3-15 yrs) | £ 1.20 - £ 3.75 |

Sea front pitch plus 10-20%.

---

For latest campsite news visit

# alanrogers.com

# Penzance
## Wayfarers Camping & Caravan Park

Relubbus Lane, Saint Hilary, Penzance TR20 9EF (Cornwall) T: 01736 763326. E: elaine@wayfarerspark.co.uk
**alanrogers.com/UK0065**

Wayfarers is a neat and tidy garden-like park reserved for adults only in rural Cornwall. Sheltered by perimeter trees and consisting of two finely mown fields interspersed by shrubs and palm-like trees, 30 places are available for caravans (up to 23 ft. single axle), motorcaravans (up to 22 ft) and tents, plus four holiday caravans to rent. All have 16A electricity, with hardstanding available on 24. Should you enjoy walking you can follow the River Hayle down to St Erth. There are many more suggestions with maps and a good display of leaflets in the information room, including a star chart. The owners Elaine and Steve live on site and make you very welcome maintaining the park to a high standard. Do look at the dolls house in the shop. Built by Elaine's father, the detail and furniture are amazing. The Lizard and Lands End with the Minnack Theatre wait to be explored and St Michael's Mount is only two miles away.

### Facilities

The modern toilet block is fully equipped. Ladies have a wash cubicle and there are two smart en-suite shower rooms (key system). Fully equipped laundry. Dishwashing sinks in the house. Shop stocks basics. No twin-axle caravans. Dogs are not accepted. Off site: Two pubs with food in Goldsithney 1 mile. Fishing 1 mile. Golf 1.5 miles. Riding 1 mile. Bicycle hire 2 miles. Boat launching 5 miles. Beach 2 miles. Sailing 5 miles.

Open: May - September.

### Directions

Following the A30 Penzance road take the A394 Helston road after the St Ives turning. Follow for 1 mile then turn left on the B3280 and pass through Goldsithney village and site is 1 mile further on left. O.S.GR: SW559314. GPS: 50.133167, -5.416833

### Charges guide

| | |
|---|---|
| Per unit incl. 2 persons and electricity | £ 15.00 - £ 21.00 |
| extra person | £ 5.00 |

# Penzance
## Bone Valley Caravan & Camping Park

Heamoor, Penzance TR20 8UJ (Cornwall) T: 01736 360313. E: enquiries@bonevalleycandcpark.co.uk
**alanrogers.com/UK0018**

A small garden-like park tucked away at the back of Penzance, Bone Valley has five caravan holiday homes to let and 17 touring pitches. There is also room for a few tents tucked behind hedges and all is accessed by a circular roadway. The park is surrounded by tall trees and the fresh water in the small stream comes straight off the moors (good for keeping bottles cold). The philosophy of its owner can be summed up by his words, 'use your common sense and there is no need for rules and regulations'. A bus leaves from the village every half hour to Penzance but it only takes about 25 minutes to walk.

### Facilities

The small toilet block is traditional in style, bright and cheerful. Washing machine, dryer with large sink. Reception carries some emergency supplies. Simple meals served in a pleasant room with TV/radio and small library. Kettle, tea, coffee and sugar provided with welcome drink on arrival. Off site: Village has shops, pub etc. Beach, boat launching, bicycle hire and fishing 1.5 miles.

Open: All year.

### Directions

Take the A30 from Penzance and at second roundabout take fourth exit signed Madron. Take fourth turn right into Joseph's Lane signed Gulval, then next left signed Bone Valley. Park is 600 yards on the left. O.S.GR: SW461318. GPS: 50.13414, -5.5526

### Charges guide

| | |
|---|---|
| Per person | £ 3.00 |
| child (under 15 yrs) | free |
| pitch | £ 4.00 - £ 6.00 |
| electricity | £ 3.00 |

For latest campsite news visit
**alanrogers.com**

## Perranporth

### Perran Sands Holiday Park

Perranporth TR6 0AQ (Cornwall) T: 01872 573551. E: nick.cook@bourne-leisure.co.uk
alanrogers.com/UK0135

An amazing site on grassy sand dunes with over 1,100 pitches in total (350 for touring units), so numerous mobile homes are dotted amongst the dunes. It is a village in its own right, with all the facilities that you could need - shops, restaurants, bars and ample entertainment. A magnificent sandy beach is just over the next dune, popular with surfers, but for something a little more relaxing there are indoor and outdoor heated pools on site, both with lifeguards. To get around the site, you will need the Perran Puffer road train. The dedicated touring area has its own wardens and a separate reception in high season. Pitches are on sandy grass, marked by fencing, some level, some sloping, many with rabbit holes, 280 have 10A electricity and a few hardstandings. It is possible to hire tents and yurts. The entertainment centre is the heart of the site and is a short walk from the camping area. If you take advantage of everything on offer you won't need to leave the site, but the surfing paradise of Newquay is probably worth a visit and the Eden Project is not to be missed.

#### Facilities

Three basic toilet blocks (no electrical points) with two family rooms with facilites for babies and campers with disabilities. Launderette. Supermarket with bakery and off licence. Gift shop. Café/bar and grill with terrace. Fish and chips, Burger King, Papa John's takeaway pizza. Sports bar. Heated indoor fun pool with flume and heated outdoor pool (28/5-3/9). Multisports court. Mini ten-pin bowling. Amusement arcade. Pool tables. Surf school (equipment hire). Two family show/entertainment bars (one open outside July/Aug). Kids' club for all ages. Soft play area. Play land. Road train. Accommodation to hire. WiFi. Bus service. Off site: Fishing 2 miles. Newquay 8 miles. Eden Project 24 miles.

Open: 1 April - 31 October.

#### Directions

From Goonhaven take road for Perranporth. Site entrance on right before going down the hill. GPS: 50.359357, -5.143635

#### Charges guide

| | |
|---|---|
| Per unit incl. 2 persons and electricity | £ 8.00 - £ 61.00 |
| extra person | free - £ 2.00 |
| dog | £ 3.00 |

## Polruan-by-Fowey

### Polruan Holidays Camping & Caravanning

Polruan-by-Fowey PL23 1QH (Cornwall) T: 01726 870263. E: polholiday@aol.com
alanrogers.com/UK0190

Polruan is a rural site in an elevated position on the opposite side of the river to Fowey, 200 metres from the Coastal path. With 47 touring pitches and ten holiday caravans to let, this is a very pleasant little site. The holiday homes are arranged in a neat circle, with a central area for some touring units, including seven pitches with gravel hardstanding and electricity, one fully serviced. The remaining touring pitches are in an adjacent field with 8 electricity hook-ups, which is part level for motorcaravans and part on a gentle slope for tents. There are marvellous sea views, but it could be a little exposed when the wind blows off the sea. A raised picnic area gives more views across the estuary to Fowey. This is a nice little park in a popular tourist area, within walking distance (downhill all the way, and vice versa!) of the village, where there are various hostelries and a passenger ferry to Fowey. A member of the Countryside Discovery group.

#### Facilities

The fully equipped, heated, sanitary block has modern, controllable showers, large enough for an adult and child. Laundry room and dishwashing sinks. Motorcaravan service facilities. Range of recycling bins. Reception (with a small terrace) doubles as a shop for everyday needs. Gas. Drinks machine and freezer for ice packs. Tourist information and bus timetables (for Looe, etc). Sloping field area with swings for children. Max. 2 dogs. Off site: Coastal path 200 m. Fishing 0.5 miles. Riding or bicycle hire 3 miles. Golf 10 miles.

Open: Easter - 1 October.

#### Directions

From main A390 at East Taphouse take B3359 towards Looe. After 5 miles fork right signed Bodinnick and ferry. Watch for signs for Polruan and site to left. Follow these carefully along narrow Cornish lanes to site on right just before village. O.S.GR: SX133509. GPS: 50.32759, -4.62515

#### Charges guide

| | |
|---|---|
| Per unit incl. 2 persons and electricity | £ 14.00 - £ 20.00 |
| extra person | £ 3.00 - £ 5.00 |
| child (2-15 yrs) | £ 1.00 - £ 3.00 |
| dog | £ 1.00 - £ 2.00 |

No credit cards.

## Redruth

### Tehidy Holiday Park

Harris Mill, Illogan, Redruth TR16 4JQ (Cornwall) T: 01209 216489. E: holiday@tehidy.co.uk

alanrogers.com/UK0115

A traditional style, family park, Tehidy offers 30 touring pitches, 24 mobile homes to rent and six bungalows. Set on a wooded hillside with a stream at the bottom, there is direct access to a woodland walk alive with primroses and bluebells in springtime. The pitches are terraced where necessary and some are hedged, with others part fenced and with views across the countryside. All have 10A electricity and there are a few with hardstanding. The nearest beach is at Portreath which has a deep rock pool for swimming at low tide. The owners live on site and are constantly looking for ways to improve the site and to provide a peaceful and relaxing environment. Whilst the grass is neatly cut, the banks are left for nature to develop. There is a request bus stop outside the entrance for Truro, St Ives and Newquay. This is surfing country but you can also windsurf at St Stithian's reservoir. Tehidy Country Park (250 acres of woodland) is nearby, together with Tehidy Golf Club.

| Facilities | Directions |
|---|---|
| Modern fully equipped toilet block. Laundry facilities. Reception with shop area. Games room and tourist information. Play area with small trampoline. Picnic tables. Woodland walk. Local takeaway delivery. Pub and restaurant within walking distance. WiFi. Dogs are not accepted. Off site: Beach 2.5 miles. Golf 1 mile. Bicycle hire 1 mile. Riding 2.5 miles. Sailing 4 miles. | Leave A30 at exit for Redruth, Porthtowan and Portreath. Follow further signs for Porthreath and pick up signs to site. O.S.GR: SW681433. GPS: 50.244939, -5.252935 |

Open: March - November.

**Charges guide**

| Per unit incl. 2 persons and electricity | £ 15.00 - £ 20.00 |
|---|---|
| extra person | £ 2.00 |

*See advertisement on page 25.*

## Redruth

### Lanyon Holiday Park

Loscombe Lane, Four Lanes, Redruth TR16 6LP (Cornwall) T: 01209 313474. E: info@lanyonholidaypark.co.uk

alanrogers.com/UK0016

Lanyon's location is a pleasant surprise after the somewhat grey landscape found in parts of the tip of Cornwall. Tucked away down a lane, the holiday caravans are attractively situated with hedged touring fields beyond. A neat tarmac road curves around to reception, the pub and an indoor swimming pool. There are 25 large hedged touring pitches around the edge of two level fields and room for around 40 tents in high season in a separate field. A large play area for children is overlooked by the roof top terrace of the bar. This is a pleasant, nice and relaxed destination for a family holiday with something for everyone and splendid views across the surrounding countryside to the sea. Lanyon is well positioned for travel to the north and south coasts. The nearest beach is at Porthreath, although the park itself offers a small heated pool and meals are available in the pub. The holiday homes include 26 that are privately owned and 18 available to rent.

| Facilities | Directions |
|---|---|
| Three fully equipped toilet blocks, the one attached to reception with heating. The other two are of Portacabin type but well maintained. Showers may be in short supply at peak times. Laundry room. Bar serving meals (22/5-5/9). Heated indoor pool (10 x 4 m. Apr-Oct). Games room. Play area and trampoline. Off site: Riding, fishing and bicycle hire 2 miles. Golf 5 miles. Beach 5 miles. Watersports at St Stithian's reservoir 1 mile. | From southwest side of Redruth take B3297 Helston road. After 1 mile enter Four Lanes village. Pass two shops then take second right into Loscombe Lane. Follow to park on right. O.S.GR: SW683387. GPS: 50.20292, -5.24554 |

Open: Easter - 31 October.

**Charges guide**

| Per unit incl. 2 persons and electricity | £ 14.00 - £ 22.00 |
|---|---|
| extra person | £ 4.00 - £ 8.00 |
| child (2-15 yrs) | £ 2.00 - £ 4.00 |
| dog | £ 1.00 - £ 2.00 |

Minimum stay 5 nights in high season.

For latest campsite news visit

alanrogers.com

# Redruth

## Globe Vale Holiday Park

Radnor, Redruth TR16 4BH (Cornwall) T: 01209 891183. E: info@globevale.co.uk

alanrogers.com/UK0114

A family run, well maintained, 13-acre site, in countryside where the tin mine chimneys are a stark reminder of the past. The Owen family have worked hard in the past few years to upgrade the site. A number of mobile homes can be found in the first part of the site amidst a mix of trees and shrubs. A further neatly grassed and sheltered area has serviced pitches on hardstanding. Two large, open fields with wonderful countryside views and Cornish stone walls have some 100 touring pitches around the edges with a central open space. Reception, in the centre of the site, is part of the Owens' home. A very pleasant bar open in peak periods has a popular patio area and does food and takeaways.

### Facilities

Smart, well equipped Portaloo toilet facilities. Facilites for disabled campers, ramped access. Laundry room. Bar, restaurant, takeaway. Chidren's play area. Caravans to hire. Off site: Bicycle hire 2 miles. Beach 3 miles. 9-hole golf course, riding, boat launching, fishing, sailing all 5 miles.

Open: All year.

### Directions

Heading west on A30 take Redruth/Porthtowan exit, then take Porthtowan exit at roundabout and follow site signs. GPS: 50.257212, -5.218644

### Charges guide

| | |
|---|---|
| Per unit incl. 2 persons and electricity | £ 10.00 - £ 22.00 |
| extra person | £ 2.00 |

---

# Relubbus

## River Valley Country Park

Relubbus, Penzance TR20 9ER (Cornwall) T: 01736 763398. E: rivervalley@surfbay.dircon.co.uk

alanrogers.com/UK0060

River Valley is a quiet park set in the 18 acres of a partly wooded, peaceful river valley. It offers a mix of 106 timber lodges, caravan holiday homes and 40 touring pitches. The large, well spaced touring pitches are in small meadows or natural clearings. Most are clearly defined with shrubs, hedges or trees and 15A electrical connections are available. The caravan holiday homes and lodges, some privately owned, are in more or less separate areas, beside the river at the far end of the park or on the hillside at the back. A fence separates the park from the river and there is a pleasant walk for 2.5 miles alongside it, popular for walking dogs. St Michael's Mount is only three miles and can be reached by footpath. This is a very special park, very well run by Brian and Eileen Milsom. A member of the Surf Bay Leisure Group.

### Facilities

Three well maintained toilet blocks include family shower rooms. Some private cabins for ladies and make-up room with hair dryers. Separate laundry facilities and baby bath. Motorcaravan service point. Shop and takeaway (Easter-Sept). Off site: Bicycle hire 5 miles. Riding, fishing, beach and golf 3 miles.

Open: 31 March - 27 October.

### Directions

From A30 at St Michaels Mount roundabout, take A394 towards Helston. At next roundabout take B3280 to Relubbus. In about 3 miles in village turn left just over a small bridge. O.S.GR: SW566320. GPS: 50.142906, -5.412685

### Charges guide

| | |
|---|---|
| Per unit incl. 4 persons and electricity | £ 15.00 - £ 32.00 |

---

# Saint Agnes

## Beacon Cottage Farm Holidays

Beacon Drive, Saint Agnes TR5 0NU (Cornwall) T: 01872 552347. E: beaconcottagefarm@lineone.net

alanrogers.com/UK0125

Amazing views greet you as you arrive at Beacon Farm. The stark remains of Wheal Coates tin mine stand out against the cliffs, and views over the sea stretch for 25 miles – as far as St Ives. A mixed beef and arable farm, Beacon has its own home-bred herd of cows and calves. The buildings and the impressive stone walls are extremely well maintained. One large, sloping field and a smaller one enjoy sea views, but can be less sheltered than the pitches in smaller paddocks. There are 70 pitches of varying sizes, 42 with 10A electricity. This is a truly popular area with walkers and birdwatchers. A ten minute walk takes you to Chapel Porth beach, an unspoilt sandy cove offering excellent swimming and surfing, with caves and rock pools to explore. St Agnes with good shops and restaurants is 1.5 miles.

### Facilities

Good stone built toilet blocks are fully equipped and include a family room. Baby bath and changing mat. Laundry room. Fresh supplies are kept in reception (papers, milk, bread and eggs). Fish and chip van calls once a week. Play area with adventure type equipment. Off site: Fishing and beach 0.5 miles. Riding 1.5 miles. Bicycle hire 2 miles. Golf 3 miles.

Open: Easter/1 April - 30 September.

### Directions

From the A30 travelling west take B3277 (signed St Agnes) at Chiverton roundabout. At mini-roundabout approaching St Agnes, turn left for Chapel Porth and follow brown Beacon Cottage Farm signs. O.S.GR: SW705503. GPS: 50.30567, -5.2249

### Charges guide

| | |
|---|---|
| Per unit incl. 2 persons and electricity | £ 18.50 - £ 24.50 |
| extra person | £ 3.00 - £ 4.50 |

---

For latest campsite news visit

**alanrogers.com**

## Saint Austell
### Carlyon Bay Caravan & Camping Park
Bethesda, Carlyon Bay, Saint Austell PL25 3RE (Cornwall) T: 01726 812735. E: holidays@carlyonbay.net
alanrogers.com/UK0290

Tranquil open meadows edged by mature woodland, well cared for by the Taylor family who live on site, provide a beautiful holiday setting with the nearest beach five minutes walk from the top gate. The original farm buildings have been converted and added to, providing an attractive covered, central area with a certain individuality of design which is very pleasing. Pitches are in five spacious areas and allow for a family meadow and a dog free meadow (high season only). There are 115 marked pitches with electricity (10/16A), some with hardstanding and eight have full services. All are on flat, terraced or gently sloping grass with flowers and flowering shrubs or edged with trees. The impressively tiled toilet blocks are of good quality and design. In addition to the attractive kidney shaped pool and paddling pool there is now a large rectangular pool (also heated) within a walled and paved area which is excellent for sunbathing. This forms part of the central area at the heart of the site and complete with tables and chairs it is the place to enjoy family entertainment in high season. There is also a pleasant family pub and Kidsworld for children within walking distance.

### Facilities
Three individually designed, modern toilet blocks (one heated) provide a full range of comfortable facilities for all your needs. Fully equipped laundry room. Modern reception with little shop. Takeaway (May-mid Sept). Heated pools (Whitsun-Sept). TV lounge. Crazy golf. Play areas. Eden Project tickets. Off site: Pub 1 mile. Bus service on main road. Golf. Riding 3 miles. Bicycle hire 4 miles. Sailing 2 miles. Boat launching 5 miles. Buses to St Austell and Fowey from entrance. Eden Project 2 miles.

Open: Easter/1 April - end September.

### Directions
From Plymouth direction on A390, pass Lostwithiel and 1 mile after village of St Blazey, turn left at roundabout beside Britannia Inn. After 400 yds turn right on a concrete road and right again at site sign. O.S.GR: SX053526. GPS: 50.34085, -4.737217

### Charges guide
| Per unit incl. 2 persons | |
|---|---|
| and electricity | £ 14.00 - £ 28.00 |
| extra person | £ 4.00 - £ 5.00 |

Camping Cheques accepted.

Practical Caravan TOP 100 PARKS Regional winner 2006

*Carlyon Bay caravan & camping park*

- Award winning family park 2 miles from Eden Project
- Up to 180 touring pitches (no statics) • Footpath to large sandy beach
- Close to championship golf course • Heated swimming & paddling pool
- Set in over 30 acres of meadows and mature woodlands
- Ben's Play World for kids nearby • Pool, table-tennis and crazy-golf

For colour brochure call: **01726 812735**
www.carlyonbay.net e-mail:holidays@carlyonbay.net

## Saint Austell
### Heligan Park
Saint Ewe, Saint Austell PL26 6EL (Cornwall) T: 01726 843485. E: info@heliganpark.co.uk
alanrogers.com/UK0410

A peaceful, attractive park in a mature garden setting, Heligan Park complements its sister site, Pentewan Sands, with its busy beach life and many activities. One can enjoy the mature trees and flowering shrubs here which have been further landscaped to provide an attractive situation for a number of holiday homes (17 to rent). These face out over a part of the Lost Valley of Heligan, with the touring pitches below on sloping grass, some terraced and others in a more level situation (some with handstanding) amongst trees and shrubs. In all, there are 100 good sized touring pitches, 80 with 16A electricity. Part of this park's boundary actually edges The Lost Gardens of Heligan.

### Facilities
Fully equipped and well kept, the modern, heated toilet block includes a unisex room with full bath and small size bath. Extra showers in separate block. Fully equipped laundry room. Small shop (Easter-14/09). Adventure playground. Off site: Beach/sailing 1.5 miles. Riding 2 miles, golf 3.5 miles. Bicycle hire/boat launching. Lost Gardens of Heligan next door.

Open: Mid January - end November.

### Directions
From St Austell ring road take B3273 for Mevagissey. After 3.5 miles, pass Pentewan Sands, continue up the hill and turn right following site signs. Park is on left just before reaching Heligan Gardens. O.S.GR: SW999464. GPS: 50.288833, -4.812083

### Charges guide
| Per unit incl. 2 persons | |
|---|---|
| | £ 10.70 - £ 24.95 |
| extra person | £ 1.05 - £ 4.20 |

For latest campsite news visit
# alanrogers.com

## Saint Austell

### Meadow Lakes

Hewas Water, Saint Austell PL26 7JG (Cornwall) T: 01726 882540. E: info@meadow-lakes.co.uk
alanrogers.com/UK0415

Meadow Lakes is a well equipped park set in 56 acres of rolling Cornish countryside of woodland and lakes and is a wonderful place for a family holiday. The level grassy or hardstanding touring pitches here are of a good size, most with electrical connections. They are arranged around the central farm buildings which house all the amenities, including playbarn, games room and shop. Also available are the heated swimming pool, four coarse fishing lakes (each stocked with a different range of fish), pets corner (small animals and donkeys), outdoor play area and WiFi internet. Lodges, caravans and chalets are available to rent. The park managers encourage a happy and friendly atmosphere.

#### Facilities

New sanitary building containing three en-suite units per sex. Launderette. Shop. Heated swimming pool (28/5-5/9). Indoor and outdoor play areas. Tennis. Fishing (free). Play areas. Pets corner. WiFi (free). Off site: Nearest beach 4 miles. Golf (18-hole) 3 miles. Riding and bicycle hire 4 miles. Shipwreck rescue and heritage centre 5 miles. The Lost Gardens of Heligan 4 miles. Eden Project 8 miles.

Open: 19 March - 31 October.

#### Directions

Site is 4 miles west of St Austell. Take the A390 and then fork left to join the B3287 and the site is 1 mile further on the left. O.S.GR: SW965484. GPS: 50.30075, -4.85708

#### Charges guide

| | |
|---|---|
| Per unit incl. 2 persons and electricity | £ 15.00 - £ 24.00 |
| extra person | £ 5.00 |
| child (3-12 yrs) | £ 3.50 |
| dog (1st free) | £ 2.00 |

### Meadow Lakes — St Austell, Cornwall

Meadow Lakes is situated in 56 acres of beautiful Cornish countryside, close to St Austell & many of Cornwall's top tourist attractions.

Level grassy and also brickpaved hardstanding pitches available, most with electrical connection. New caravan & lodge holiday homes for sale.

4 coarse fishing Lakes, Outdoor heated swimming pool, Pets corner, Indoor & outdoor play areas.

www.meadow-lakes.co.uk
info@meadow-lakes.co.uk
01726 882540

## Saint Ives

### Polmanter Tourist Park

Halsetown, Saint Ives TR26 3LX (Cornwall) T: 01736 795640. E: reception@polmanter.com
alanrogers.com/UK0050

A popular and attractively developed park, Polmanter is located high up at the back of St Ives, with wonderful sea and country views. The Osborne family has worked hard to develop Polmanter as a complete family base. Converted farm buildings provide a cosy bar lounge with conservatory overlooking the heated swimming pool. The 250 touring pitches (no caravan holiday homes) are well spaced in several fields divided by established shrubs and hedges giving large, level, individual pitches with connecting tarmac roads. There are grass and hard-standing multi-serviced pitches with electricity, water, waste water and TV point, serviced pitches with 16A electricity and non-serviced tent pitches. It is a busy park with a happy atmosphere within 1.5 miles of St Ives. A footpath leads from the park (20 minutes downhill) or there is a bus service from the park in high season (hourly, 10.00-23.00). A member of the Best of British group.

#### Facilities

Three fully equipped toilet blocks can be heated and include en-suite family rooms. Facilities for disabled visitors. Baby room. Fully equipped laundry. Motorcaravan service point. Well stocked shop. Bar with food and family area (Whitsun-mid Sept). Takeaway. Heated swimming pool (Whitsun-mid Sept). Some entertainment (peak season). Tennis. Putting. Play area. Sports field. Games room. Off site: Golf 1 mile. Fishing, riding, bicycle hire and boat launching within 2 miles. Indoor pool and leisure centre at St Ives. Note: dogs are banned from the St Ives beaches in high season.

Open: 1 April - 31 October.

#### Directions

Take A3074 to St Ives from the A30 and then first left at a mini-roundabout taking 'Holiday Route' (B3311) to St Ives (Halsetown). At T-junction turn right for Halsetown, right at the Halsetown Inn then first left. O.S.GR: SW509392. GPS: 50.196183, -5.491017

#### Charges guide

| | |
|---|---|
| Per unit incl. 2 persons | £ 16.00 - £ 33.00 |
| extra person | £ 3.50 - £ 7.50 |
| child (3-15 yrs) | £ 2.50 - £ 6.00 |
| dog (max. 2) | £ 1.00 - £ 3.00 |

Camping Cheques accepted.

## Saint Ives
### Trevalgan Touring Park

Saint Ives TR26 3BJ (Cornwall) T: 01736 792048. E: recept@trevalgantouringpark.co.uk
alanrogers.com/UK0040

Trevalgan is owned by the same family that owns Ayr Holiday Park. It is a quiet, traditional style of park, located on the cliffs 1.5 miles west of bustling St Ives. It is a truly rural location where you can enjoy spectacular views and an abundance of flora and fauna. There are 120 clearly marked pitches (88 with 16A electricity and some with water as well) in two level fields edged by Cornish stone walls – it could be a little exposed on a windy day. The park is very popular with walkers, with direct access to the coastal path. A member of the Countryside Discovery group.

**Facilities**

A fully equipped toilet block includes a baby room and facilities for disabled visitors. Motorcaravan service point. Small shop (in reception). Mobile shop calls daily. Gas supplies. Games field, adventure play area. Purpose built games room with TV and coffee machine. Off site: Fishing 3 miles, bicycle hire 8 miles, riding and golf within 2 miles. Regular bus service to St Ives and back (June-mid Sept). As well as the coastal path, a path leads to St Ives across the fields (30-40 minutes).

Open: 1 May - 30 September.

**Directions**

Approach site down a narrow Cornish lane from the B3306 St Ives - Lands End road, following sign. O.S.GR: SW490400. GPS: 50.20769, -5.51882

**Charges guide**

| Per unit incl. 2 persons | |
|---|---|
| and electricity | £ 17.50 - £ 29.50 |
| extra person | £ 3.50 - £ 5.25 |
| child (5-16 yrs) | £ 2.00 - £ 2.75 |
| dog | £ 1.50 - £ 2.50 |

RAC  AA

*For a more rural experience*

'A touring park just 2 miles from St.Ives town centre.
Beautiful scenery, new facilities, serviced pitches, summer bus service to town.
Ideal for families, walkers, cyclists - explore St.Ives and West Cornwall.'

www.trevalgantouringpark.co.uk  Telephone: 01736 792048

## Saint Ives
### Little Trevarrack Holiday Park

Laity Lane, Carbis Bay, Saint Ives TR26 3HW (Cornwall) T: 01736 797580. E: info@littletrevarrack.co.uk
alanrogers.com/UK0035

Little Trevarrack is a traditional Cornish park covering 20 acres, with wonderful views from the top of the site across St Ives bay towards Hayle and the surrounding countryside. It is owned by Neil, son of the owners of Polmanter Park, and Annette Osborne and has a smart, large reception and entrance. There are 234 pitches, in five open fields (the top ones with gentle slopes), 153 with 10A electricity and 15 with water and drainage as well. Bushes and hedging have grown to provide individual pitches and give a continental appearance to the park. A smart, heated, outdoor pool also provides a paddling pool and sunbathing area. Landscaped and fenced, a new play area is alongside. Carbis Bay with its safe sandy beach is ideal for families with young children and is less than a mile away. In high season a bus runs hourly into St Ives. This is a developing park which will provide a quiet, peaceful base from which to explore St Ives and the southern tip of Cornwall.

**Facilities**

The large, central toilet block is modern and well equipped. Baby room and facilities for disabled visitors in the reception building. Laundry. Heated swimming and paddling pools (27/5-12/9). Games room. Internet access and WiFi. Play area and play field. Wild flower field with paths for dog walking. Max. 2 dogs. No kites allowed. Early and late arrivals area. Off site: Golf and riding 2 miles. Bicycle hire 4 miles. Beach and fishing 1 mile. Dogs are banned from the St Ives beaches in high season.

Open: 1 April - 30 September.

**Directions**

Follow signs for St Ives and take A3074 to Carbis Bay. Site is signed on left opposite junction to Carbis Bay beach. Follow road for 150 yds, cross small crossroads and site is the second turn on the right. O.S.GR: SW52737. GPS: 50.187233, -5.470833

**Charges guide**

| Per unit incl. 2 persons | |
|---|---|
| and electricity | £ 16.50 - £ 27.25 |
| extra person | £ 3.50 - £ 7.00 |
| child (3-15 yrs) | £ 2.50 - £ 5.00 |
| dog (max. 2) | £ 2.00 - £ 3.00 |

For latest campsite news visit
**alanrogers.com**

## Saint Ives

### Ayr Holiday Park

Higher Ayr, Saint Ives TR26 1EJ (Cornwall) T: 01736 795855. E: recept@ayrholidaypark.co.uk

alanrogers.com/UK0030

Ayr Holiday Park has an unparalleled position overlooking St Ives Bay and Porthmeor beach and is a popular, well cared for site. On first arrival it may seem to be all caravan holiday homes, but behind them is a series of naturally sloping fields with marvellous views providing a total of 90 pitches, of which 40 are for touring caravans and motorcaravans. These pitches are on grass, all with 16A electricity and several fully serviced. An extra field for tents is open in July and August. A stylish toilet block provides excellent facilities in a colourful and modern design. There is direct access to the coastal footpath.

**Facilities**

The excellent toilet block includes two family shower rooms and facilities for baby changing and disabled visitors. Wetsuit showers. Fully equipped laundry room. Motorcaravan point. Games room with TV, hot drinks and snack machines. Adventure play area. Max. 1 dog, contact site first. Off site: Spa shop nearby. Tate Gallery and beaches within walking distance. Leisure centre with indoor pool nearby. Golf 1 mile. Riding 2 miles. Sea and coarse fishing 2-3 miles.

Open: All year.

**Directions**

From the A30 follow signs for St Ives for heavy vehicles (not town centre). After 2 miles join the B3311 and then the B3306 1 mile from St Ives. Still heading for St Ives turn left at mini-roundabout following camping signs through residential areas. Park entrance is 600 yds. at Ayr Terrace. O.S.GR: SW515388. GPS: 50.21261, -5.48928

**Charges guide**

| | |
|---|---|
| Per unit incl. 2 persons and electricity | £ 12.75 - £ 30.50 |
| extra person | £ 1.75 - £ 6.00 |

## Saint Just

### Roselands Caravan & Camping Park

Dowran, Saint Just, Penzance TR19 7RS (Cornwall) T: 01736 788571. E: info@roselands.co.uk

alanrogers.com/UK0025

Roselands is a small, family owned park situated on the Cornish moors overlooking the village of St Just and with marvellous views of the sea and countryside around Lands End. In all there are 14 holiday homes to let, 17 level grassy touring pitches (all with 16A electricity) and some provision for tents. The owner's home provides a bar and conservatory, reception and a small shop. The conservatory acts as a community family room with games, internet facility and tourist information with a play area outside and a games room nearby. This area is very popular with walkers and birdwatchers.

**Facilities**

Small traditional toilet block, fully equipped and can be heated. Laundry facilities. Small shop for basics and gas. Bar with bar food served in conservatory (all year). TV and internet access. Play area. Games room. Bicycle hire. Off site: Fishing and Golf 1 mile. Riding 1 mile. Beach and surfing 2 miles at Sennen Cove. Boat launching 5 miles. Lands End and Cape Cornwall. Minack Outdoor Theatre.

Open: 1 January - 31 October.

**Directions**

Take the A3071 from Penzance for St Just. Follow for 5.5 miles and 0.5 miles before St Just turn left at sign for site. O.S.GR: SW386302. GPS: 50.11323, -5.658

**Charges guide**

| | |
|---|---|
| Per unit incl. 2 persons incl. electricity | £ 8.00 - £ 10.00 |
| | £ 10.00 - £ 12.50 |
| extra person | £ 2.00 |
| child (under 5 yrs) | £ 1.00 |

## Saint Mabyn

### Glenmorris Park

Longstone Road, Saint Mabyn PL30 3BY (Cornwall) T: 01208 841677. E: info@glenmorris.co.uk

alanrogers.com/UK0230

The beaches of North Cornwall and the wilds of Bodmin Moor are all an easy drive from Glenmorris Park. The park is being gradually improved and carefully maintained by the Hayman family and it provides a spacious and relaxed atmosphere. There are 80 level pitches, 60 with 16A electricity, on well drained and well mown grass with 20 hardstandings. There are some caravan holiday homes to let. A pleasant, sheltered outdoor pool is an added attraction. There is no bar, but the local village inn has a good reputation for food.

**Facilities**

The fully equipped modern toilet block includes an en-suite unit per sex. Laundry. Heated outdoor swimming pool and paddling pool (late May-early Sept), surrounded by a sheltered, paved and grass sunbathing areas. Good, fenced adventure play area with bark safety base. Play area for small children. Games room. Caravan storage. Off site: Fishing, riding or golf 3 miles, bicycle hire 5 miles.

Open: 1 April - mid October.

**Directions**

From Bodmin or Wadebridge on A389, take B3266 north signed Camelford. At Longstone turn left signed St Mabyn and brown camping sign. Site is 400 yds. on right. Ignore all other signs to St Mabyn. O.S.GR: SX053732. GPS: 50.5278, -4.745183

**Charges guide**

| | |
|---|---|
| Per person | £ 4.00 - £ 5.50 |
| child (3-15 yrs) | £ 1.25 - £ 1.50 |
| electricity (16A) | £ 3.30 |

## Saint Martins by Looe

### Polborder House Caravan & Camping Park

Bucklawren Rd, St Martins by Looe PL13 1QS (Cornwall) T: 01503 240265. E: reception@polborderhouse.co.uk

alanrogers.com/UK0320

Polborder House is a lovely site which may appeal to those who prefer a quiet, well kept little family site to the larger ones with many on-site activities. With good countryside views, up to 36 touring units can be accommodated on well tended grass. Pitches are marked with some hedging between pairs of pitches to give privacy and most have electrical connections (16A). There are several hardstandings and 17 serviced pitches. The new owners, Amanda and Dale Byers, live on the park and are most helpful. The nearest beach is 20-25 minutes' walk from a gate in the corner of the park. This is a good area for walking with links to the coastal path through Duchy woodland.

### Facilities

The refurbished, fully equipped, heated sanitary block (key entry) includes a baby room, fully equipped laundry room, and three covered sinks outside for dishwashing. En-suite toilet unit for disabled visitors has a ramped approach. Rubbish is recycled. Shop (all season) for gas and basics, and some camping accessories. Toddler's play area. Hut with tourist information. Off site: Fishing, golf and boat launching within 2 miles. Riding 6 miles. Restaurant 500 m. Diving school at Seaton, scuba centre and fishing trips at Looe. Seaton 2 miles, Looe 2.5 miles.

Open: All year.

### Directions

Park is less than half a mile south of the B3253. Turn off 2 miles east of Looe and follow signs to park and Monkey Sanctuary at junctions; care is needed with narrow road. O.S.GR: SX283555.
GPS: 50.377217, -4.4185

### Charges guide

| Per unit incl. 2 persons | |
|---|---|
| and electricity | £ 12.50 - £ 22.50 |
| extra person | £ 4.00 - £ 6.50 |
| child (5-16 yrs) | £ 2.00 - £ 4.00 |
| dog | £ 1.00 |

Less 10% for senior citizens for booked stays over 7 nights.

## Saltash

### Dolbeare Caravan & Camping Park

Saint Ive Road, Landrake, Saltash PL12 5AF (Cornwall) T: 01752 851332. E: reception@dolbeare.co.uk

alanrogers.com/UK0440

Ian and Chris are now the proud owners of this small, but well kept park. Dolbeare is in a rural setting (but very easily accessible from the main A38) and consists of a large, rectangular field of neat grass edged with trees and sloping slightly at the top, connected by a gravel road, and a camping paddock. All 66 pitches are on hardstanding and have 16A electricity connections. An extra field provides the camping paddock and can also be used for rallies. Part of it is set aside for a games field with a dog walk being developed at the top of the park. A new low level adventure play area has been added, along with giant chess and Connect 4 games. At reception, leaflets are provided on 'Where to Eat', 'Where to Walk' and 'Suggestions for what to do' with a good supply of tourist information and maps. Dog kennels nearby can provide day care from £3.50, but the drawback is that there could be some noise depending on season and wind direction. This is a very usefully situated park said to be 20 minutes from everywhere – Plymouth, beaches, several National Trust properties, Dartmoor and Bodmin Moor, and more. A member of the Best of British group.

### Facilities

The fully equipped heated toilet block to one side of the field. Indoor dishwashing sinks. Laundry next to reception. Fridge and freezer in camping field. Motorcaravan services. Reception doubles as a small shop for basics including gas (limited hours out of main season). Site barrier (card system with £5 deposit). Off site: Fishing and riding 3 miles. Golf 5.5 miles. Nearest beach 8 miles.

Open: All year.

### Directions

After crossing the Tamar Bridge into Cornwall, continue on A38 for a further 4 miles. In Landrake village turn right following signs and site is 0.75 miles on the right. O.S.GR: SX366616.
GPS: 50.43064, -4.30551

### Charges guide

| Per unit incl. 2 persons | |
|---|---|
| and electricity | £ 13.20 - £ 18.60 |
| extra person | £ 3.50 |
| child (5-16 yrs) | £ 2.25 |

See advertisement on page 26.

## Truro

### Cosawes Park

Perranarworthal, Truro TR3 7QS (Cornwall) T: 01872 863724. E: info@cosawes.com

alanrogers.com/UK0185

Cosawes is set in a beautiful wooded valley where there are woodland and river walks and the park offers a quiet and relaxing holiday. The Fraser family have owned the site for many years and the recent upgrading of the facilities is excellent, particularly for a site that is open all year. Cosawes offers 25 large, serviced pitches on gravel hardstandings, each on its own fenced space. These are particularly popular with motorcaravan owners and very useful for twin-axle vans. This still leaves around 35 grass pitches which are slightly sloping, some with electricity. A separate large residential area is private and away from the touring section. The situation of the park makes it good for visiting both the north and south coasts. Falmouth with its maritime museum is well worth visiting, whilst the north coast is popular for its surfing beaches. Saint Ives, Lands End and the unique Lizard peninsula are all within easy reach.

### Facilities

Modern new block beside the new serviced pitches provides 2 en-suite family rooms also good for disabled visitor. Toilets, laundry and dishwashing facilities are downstairs, upstairs are showers and washbasins in cubicles. Another older block is near reception. Dog walking field. WiFi (charged). Walks from site.

Off site: Golf and bicycle hire 5 miles. Sailing and boat launching 3-5 miles. Beach at Falmouth 7 miles. Two pubs within walking distance. Supermarket 3 miles.

Open: All year.

### Directions

Site is midway between Truro and Falmouth. Approaching from Truro via A39, after village of Perranarworthal, site is signed to the left and is 300 yds up the lane on the left. Use the second entrance. O.S.GR: SW768375.

GPS: 50.197026, -5.128319

### Charges guide

| Per unit incl. 2 persons and electricity | £ 13.00 - £ 15.00 |
|---|---|
| hardstanding, serviced pitch | £ 16.00 - £ 18.50 |
| extra person | £ 2.00 |
| child (5-16 yrs) | £ 1.00 |

## Welcome to Cosawes Touring & Camping Park...

Secluded and quiet. Cosawes nestles in a beautiful 100 acre sheltered valley near the village of Perranarworthal in South West Cornwall. The 2 acre campsite is able to cater for 45 tents and 25 caravans/motorhomes on well kept grass pitches or spacious fully serviced hardstandings. Our new shower and toilet block are heated and have free showers, hair dryers and vanity cubicles with an adjoining launderette equipped with washing machine, tumble dryer, iron and board and fridge freezer. There is also an under cover washing up facility along with 2 superb disabled and young family shower/toilet rooms, baby change and baby bath also available. Conveniently situated between the Cathedral City of Truro and the picturesque harbour-side town of Falmouth. Open all year round, campers benefit from the natural shelter of the surrounding woodland and valley in the worst of the winter weather and a sun-trap during the warm summer months. Dogs welcome provided they are kept under strict control. Nearby attractions:

- Water sports
- Golf course
- Fishing on site
- Horse riding
- Plenty of country walks
- Cycle hire
- Cultural and historical attractions
- Local Produce
- Asda Supermarket (24hr)
- Pubs offering good food and drink

**01872 863724**
(9am-1pm Mon-Fri)
info@cosawes.com
www.cosawestouringandcamping.co.uk

For latest campsite news visit
**alanrogers.com**

## Truro
### Porthtowan Tourist Park

Mile Hill, Porthtowan, Truro TR4 8TY (Cornwall) T: 01209 890256. E: Admin@PorthtowanTouristPark.co.uk

alanrogers.com/UK0014

This delightful and sheltered park is set a mile back from the pretty seaside village of Porthtowan, a haven for surfers but enjoyed by families who can explore the rock pools and coves. The beach has Blue Flag status. In an Area of Outstanding Natural Beauty, tall chimney stacks, stark against the sky, remain a reminder of the tin mining for which this area of Cornwall was once renowned. This is now a peaceful spot with plenty of space on the park and tall trees surrounding the three camping fields. There are 80 pitches around the edges of the fields, on level grass and half with 10A electricity. There are a few hardstandings. The park is attractively laid out with tarmac roads and flowering shrubs. The facilities were spotless when we visited in high season. There is a recycling box for odds and ends left behind by holidaymakers but of potential use to future visitors. A large adventure type play area in the centre of the large top field is popular. There is a waiting list for seasonal pitches and caravan storage. The Coast to Coast Tramway trail passes within half a mile of the site. The Newquay - Saint Ives bus stops in the village.

### Facilities

Modern, fully equipped toilet block with two en-suite family rooms also suitable for disabled visitors. Shop in reception. Games room with tourist information. Adventure type play area. Fish and chip van calls Wednesday teatimes. Bicycle hire by arrangement. Off site: Nearest beach 1 mile. Riding 200 yds. Fishing and golf 8 miles.

Open: 1 April - 30 September.

### Directions

From the A30 take exit for Redruth, Porthtowan and Portreath and follow signs for Porthtown for 2 miles. At T-junction turn right up hill to park on the left just past a restaurant. O.S.GR: SW694463. GPS: 50.27374, -5.23768

### Charges 2011

| Per unit incl. 2 persons | |
|---|---|
| and electricity | £ 12.00 - £ 20.00 |
| extra person | £ 4.00 |
| child (3-16 yrs) | £ 2.50 |
| dog | free - £ 1.00 |

## Truro
### Summer Valley Touring Park

Shortlanesend, Truro TR4 9DW (Cornwall) T: 01872 277878. E: res@summervalley.co.uk

alanrogers.com/UK0510

Summer Valley is a quiet and mature, but very pleasant, small rural park suitable for visiting both the north and south coast of Cornwall. South facing, the park consists of a large well kept grass area with reception and facilities to one side. A tarmac road circles this and mature trees edge the whole site providing shelter but still allowing rural views. Caravans go on the central area which slopes gently and is divided down the centre with more mature trees and shrubs. The pitches around the perimeter area are semi-divided by shrubs and used more for tents. There is provision for 60 units of all types, but only 50 are used, 45 with electricity connections (10/16A). A pleasant little sitting room provides a small library and tourist information, useful for campers in inclement weather. A small, wooded area at the bottom of the park is ideal for dog walking. The owners live on site and provide a warm welcome. A Countryside Discovery site.

### Facilities

A good quality, solid toilet block is well maintained with ladies to the left and men to the right, plus unisex showers. Washbasins in cabins and one shower/toilet en-suite per sex. Laundry facilities. Campers' rest room with library. Reception/licensed shop (basics) with freezer pack service (reduced hours out of main season). Gas supplies. Small play area hidden in a corner but part of the central area is left for ball games. Off site: Village of Shortlanesend within walking distance with post office and pub. Fishing 2.5 miles. Golf 3 miles. Riding 5 miles. Bicycle hire 2.5 miles. Perranporth beach 6 miles (dogs are allowed away from the village end).

Open: 31 March - 31 October.

### Directions

From Truro take B3284 north, signed Perranporth. Follow for 2.5 miles and site is signed on left just through the village of Shortlanesend. O.S.GR: SW 800479. GPS: 50.29098, -5.08823

### Charges guide

| Per unit incl. 2 persons | |
|---|---|
| | £ 12.00 - £ 15.00 |
| extra person | £ 3.00 |
| child (3-16 yrs) | £ 2.00 |
| electricity | £ 3.00 |

For latest campsite news visit
**alanrogers.com**

## Truro

### Penrose Farm Touring Park

Goonhavern, Truro TR4 9QF (Cornwall) T: 01872 573185. E: penroseholidays@hotmail.co.uk
alanrogers.com/UK0140

Penrose Farm, owned and run by the Welch family, has a quiet and comfortable atmosphere on the edge of the village of Goonhavern. The park is level and sheltered, with the pitches spread over five fields with flower beds and bushes set amongst them. These colourful flowers and those at the entrance give the park a neat and well cared for feel. There are over 100 pitches with 10A electricity, many with hardstanding, water and drainage, plus a few seasonal places and some privately owned caravan holiday homes. A play area will amuse children and the family are now offering a simple café menu, including breakfast. It is only a short walk to the village and its popular pub, and buses to Newquay stop in the village. The superb beach at Perranporth is only 2.5 miles away. To retain the quiet family image, there are no plans for bars or entertainment, and only couples and families are welcome.

**Facilities**

The fully equipped and refurbished toilet block is well maintained and includes four en-suite family rooms. Facilities for disabled visitors. Well equipped laundry. Small shop. Gas supplies. Takeaway incl. breakfast. Playground. Caravan storage. Off site: Fishing or riding 0.5 miles, golf 1 mile.

Open: 1 April - 31 October.

**Directions**

Take A30 from Exeter past Bodmin and Indian Queens. Just after wind farm take B3285 to Perranporth. Park is on the left as you enter Goonhavern village. O.S.GR: SW790535. GPS: 50.340133, -5.106567

**Charges guide**

| | |
|---|---|
| Per unit incl. 2 persons and electricity | £ 12.00 - £ 21.00 |
| incl. services | £ 14.00 - £ 25.00 |
| extra person (5 yrs and over) | £ 3.00 - £ 3.50 |
| dog | free - £ 2.00 |

Families and couples only.

MOTORHOMES
TENTS
CARAVANS

PENR SE
HOLIDAY PARK

Goonhavern, (Nr. Perranporth,) Truro, TR4 9QF
TEL: 01872 573 185 - Web: www.penroseholidaypark.com

## Truro

### Carnon Downs Caravan & Camping Park

Carnon Downs, Truro TR3 6JJ (Cornwall) T: 01872 862283. E: info@carnon-downs-caravanpark.co.uk
alanrogers.com/UK0180

Carnon Downs is an excellent all year park run personally and enthusiastically by Simon Vallance, a very forward thinking owner. It has been thoughtfully laid out in a series of fields covering 20 acres so that all pitches back onto attractive hedging or areas of flowering shrubs and arranged to provide some pleasant bays or other, more open grass areas. Gravel roads connect the 150 pitches, most with electricity (10/16A) and over 70 with hardstanding. Of these 55 are serviced, with the newer ones being exceptionally large and surrounded by young shrubs. On arrival you will receive a warm welcome, a neatly presented layout plan of the park and a touring information pack. This includes comprehensive details on walks and cycle paths leading from the park. Some of the park's amenities are to be found in the round-house next to the TV and information room. The round-house used to house the donkeys that turned the mill which once operated on the site! Although one side of the park is next to the A39 road, it is well screened with a band of mature woodland so noise should be minimal. This quiet, quality family park is well situated to explore the tip of Cornwall. Affiliated to the Caravan Club.

**Facilities**

Two excellent modern, light and airy, heated blocks include en-suite units and dishwashing and facilities for the disabled. Another well maintained block, also heated, includes some washbasins in cubicles and showers (unisex). Three good family bath/shower rooms, one suitable for use by disabled visitors or families. Mother and toddler room, two baby sinks and full sized bath. Two laundries with freezers. Motorcaravan service point (ask at reception). Good adventure-type play area. Caravan storage. Off site: Pub/restaurant 100 yds across the road. Fishing 5 miles. Riding or bicycle hire 2 miles. Golf 1 mile.

Open: All year.

**Directions**

From Truro take A39 Falmouth road. After 3 miles, the park entrance is directly off the Carnon Downs roundabout. O.S.GR: SW805406. GPS: 50.22529, -5.08012

**Charges guide**

| | |
|---|---|
| Per unit incl. 2 persons and electricity | £ 18.50 - £ 25.50 |
| extra person | £ 3.50 |
| child (5-16 yrs) | £ 3.00 |
| all-service hardstanding | £ 2.00 |

## Truro
### Trethem Mill Touring Park
Saint Just-in-Roseland, Saint Mawes, Truro TR2 5JF (Cornwall) T: 01872 580504. E: reception@trethem.com

alanrogers.com/UK0090

The Akeroyd family are proud of their park, work hard to keep it really well maintained and have been recognised for their commitment to high standards. They aim to attract couples and families who seek peace and tranquillity, and can manage without a bar and on-site entertainment. Trethem is a 'strictly touring' park with 84 pitches all with electricity, 60 with hardstanding and TV connections and 21 with water and waste water. All pitches are large, most on slightly sloping ground, some terraced, with the lower field more level and sheltered. All are individual or in bays, divided by hedging (some still growing) giving your own area. There is a comfortable and spacious feel as the park covers 11.5 acres, about half of which provides a dog and nature walk and recreation area. There is a circular tarmac access road and careful landscaping. The area around reception is particularly pretty where a small watermill has been built amongst the flowers and visitors are invited to make use of the herb garden. St Mawes, just three miles away, is a very popular, pretty village on the Roseland peninsula, which is itself an Area of Outstanding Natural Beauty. At Trethem Mill you can be sure of a warm welcome and it is ideally placed for sailing, walking the coastal path around the peninsula, visiting the gardens of Trelissick or Heligan, or simply lazing on the nearby beaches. A member of the Best of British group.

### Facilities
The well equipped central toilet block is kept spotlessly clean and is heated in cooler weather. En-suite facilities for disabled visitors which can double as a family room. Baby room (under 4s). Reception/shop, only small but well stocked and licensed. Freezer for ice packs (free). Motorcaravan services. Well equipped adventure playground (closed at 21.00). Large field for ball games. Extra field for dog walking. WiFi throughout park. Off site: Fishing 1.5 miles. Beach, sailing, boat launching 2 miles. Bicycle hire 2 miles. Golf 6 miles. Riding 8 miles.

Open: 1 April - 3 October.

### Directions
From Tregony follow A3078 to St Mawes. About 2 miles after passing through Trewithian, watch for caravan and camping sign. O.S.GR: SW863264. GPS: 50.19003, -5.00096

### Charges guide

| Per unit incl. 2 persons and electricity | £ 16.00 - £ 27.00 |
|---|---|
| extra person | £ 5.00 |
| child (3-14 yrs) | £ 4.00 |
| dog | £ 1.00 |

Englands Best..
NATIONAL WINNER
Caravan Park of the Year
enjoyEngland Excellence Awards 2010

**trethem mill**
TOURING PARK
★★★★

St Just In Roseland   Cornwall   TR2 5JF

www.trethem.com
Tel: 01872 580504

## Truro
### Killiwerris Camping & Caravan Park
Penstraze, Chacewater, Truro TR4 8PF (Cornwall) T: 01872 561356. E: killiwerris@aol.com

alanrogers.com/UK0012

Tucked down a Cornish lane, Killiwerris is a rare find. It has been developed from a large garden and the field surrounding the house into a small and delightful touring park which provides 20 good sized pitches for caravans and motorcaravans. Of these, 17 are semi-separated either by low fencing or hedging, and all with hardstanding in the front field with flowering shrubs sheltered by Monteray pines and other indigenous trees. The birds love it, as do adult humans – the park is 'adult only' so it is very peaceful. Three further pitches are found in the back field. Electricity (10/16A) is available for all the pitches with water points between two. The park is now owned by the Ashurst family and being centrally situated five miles from the city of Truro and four from the coastal village of St Agnes, this is an ideal base to explore the Cornish countryside.

### Facilities
A small heated toilet block provides for all needs with one shower each for men and women and ladies having one toilet/washbasin cubicle. Grab rails for disabled visitors. Separate laundry room. Max. 2 dogs. Off site: Bus stop 8 minutes level walk. Chacewater village (shop, pub, etc) 1 mile. Beach 4.5 miles. Fishing 2 miles. Golf 2 miles. Riding 1.5 miles. Bicycle hire 2-3 miles.

Open: Easter - end October.

### Directions
Using the A30 in the direction of Penzance, exit at Chiverton Cross roundabout (this is large roundabout 28 miles west of Bodmin signed for Truro and St Agnes). Take third exit for Blackwater and in 500 yds turn left into Kea Down Road. Park is 1 mile on right. O.S.GR: SW753455. GPS: 50.2655, -5.155

### Charges guide

| Per unit incl. 2 persons, electricity and awning | £ 12.00 - £ 16.00 |
|---|---|
| extra person | £ 3.50 |
| dog (max. 2) | £ 0.50 |

No credit cards.

For latest campsite news visit
alanrogers.com

## Truro

### Silverbow Park

Goonhavern, Truro TR4 9NX (Cornwall) T: 01872 572347.
alanrogers.com/UK0120

Silverbow has been developed by the Taylor family over many years and they are justifiably proud of their efforts. They believe Silverbow is a way of life and staying is an experience – they have certainly created a relaxed and tranquil atmosphere seeking to encourage couples and young families (teenagers are not accepted). Hard work, planting and landscaping has provided a beautiful environment set in 21 acres. There are 90 generous touring pitches, which include 69 even larger 'super' pitches in a newly developed area, with electricity, water and drainage. Many are on a slight slope with some attractive views. There are also 15 park-owned, high quality leisure homes. Much free space is not used for camping, including an excellent sports area with two grass and two all-weather tennis courts, as well as wild meadow and wooded areas ideal for walks. A natural area with ponds has been created to encourage wildlife (Silverbow was the first in Cornwall to gain the coveted '5-year Bellamy Gold' award for conservation). The park is 2.5 miles from the long, sandy beach at Perranporth (30 minutes walk away from traffic) and six miles from Newquay.

#### Facilities

Two good toilet blocks include private cabins, four family shower/toilet rooms, two accessible for wheelchairs, and a bath on payment. Laundry room. Motorcaravan services. Free freezer service. Shop for basics (mid May-mid Sept). Covered, heated swimming pool and small paddling pool (mid May-mid Sept) gated and sheltered by high surrounding garden walls. Games room. Adventure playground. Play field. Tennis. Off site: Gliding, riding and fishing nearby. Concessionary green fees are available at Perranporth golf club. Pub within walking distance.

Open: Early May - end September.

#### Directions

Entrance is directly off the main A3075 road 0.5 miles south of Goonhavern. O.S.GR: SW781531. GPS: 50.336567, -5.120633

#### Charges guide

| | |
|---|---|
| Per unit incl. 2 persons | £ 10.00 - £ 20.00 |
| extra person under 50 yrs | £ 3.00 - £ 6.00 |
| extra child (2-12 yrs) or adult over 50 yrs | £ 2.50 - £ 4.50 |
| full service pitch incl. electricity | £ 6.00 |
| dog | free - £ 1.50 |

Children over 12 yrs with or without parents not accepted. Discounts available.

## Truro

### Chacewater Park

Cox Hill, Chacewater, Truro TR4 8LY (Cornwall) T: 01209 820762. E: enquiries@chacewaterpark.co.uk
alanrogers.com/UK0010

For those who want to be away from the hectic coastal resorts and to take advantage of the peace and quiet of an 'adults only' park, this will be an excellent, value-for-money choice. Chacewater has a pleasant rural situation and the site is run with high levels of care and attention by Richard Peterken and his daughters, Debbie and Mandy. It provides 100 level touring pitches, all with 10A electricity and 80 with hardstanding, in two large field areas (slight slope) edged with trees or in small bays formed by hedges. There are 29 serviced pitches (electricity, water, and drainage connections) and an area for dog owners. The modern reception is not at the entrance but through the park to one side in a pleasant courtyard area. Truro is only five miles away, and there is a good choice of beaches north or south within five to ten miles. A bus stop is only 100 yards from the entrance.

#### Facilities

The main toilet block provides well equipped showers and two en-suite units. Laundry room. Second fully equipped block near reception providing roomy showers open direct to outside. Gas supplies. Icepack service. Library in reception. Only adults are accepted (over 30 yrs). Max. 1 dog, contact site first. Off site: Golf, riding and bicycle hire, all within 3 miles. Bus stop 100 yds. Cornish tramways/railway coast to coast trail to walk or cycle nearby.

Open: 1 May - 30 September.

#### Directions

From the A30 about 28 miles west of Bodmin take A3047 signed Scorrier and continue under bridge to roundabout and take left towards St Day. Continue for 500 yards turning right at the crossroads onto the B3298 signed St Day and continue for 1 mile. Turn left at the crossroads and continue for 0.75 miles, then turn left at the crossroad with blue camping sign (by Truro Tractors). Chacewater Park is the next right. O.S.GR: SW742439. GPS: 50.250802, -5.172557

#### Charges guide

| | |
|---|---|
| Per unit incl. 2 persons and electricity | £ 14.00 - £ 17.00 |
| dog (max. 1) | £ 1.00 |

Weekly rates for pre-booked pitches. Discounts for senior citizens.

# Wadebridge

## The Laurels Holiday Park

Padstow Rd, Whitecross, Wadebridge PL27 7JQ (Cornwall) T: 01209 313474. E: info@thelaurelsholidaypark.co.uk
alanrogers.com/UK0505

This is a small park in a garden-like setting of which the managers Edna and Ray are very proud. It is very well maintained and provides 32 level pitches with 16A electricity. Some have hardstanding and some are extra large. Neat hedging marks the pitches and the central area with shrubs and plants is kept clear for enjoyment. A good play area for children is well fenced from the A39 which could be the cause of some road noise. The Camel Trail for walking or cycling is close and follows the estuary from Wadebridge to Padstow. A bus stops outside the site.

### Facilities

Well kept fully equipped toilet block. Laundry. Facilities for drying wetsuits. Freezer and communal fridge. Play area with trampoline. Off site: Shops 1 mile. Beach 4 miles. Riding, bicycle hire, boat launching 3 miles. Fishing 5 miles. Camel Trail (walking/cycling).

Open: Easter - 31 October.

### Directions

The Park is half a mile from the Royal Cornwall Showground, at the junction between the A39 and A389 Padstow Road, at Whitecross, 2 miles from Wadebridge. O.S.GR: SW958716.
GPS: 50.50827, -4.88192

### Charges guide

| | |
|---|---|
| Per unit incl. 2 persons and electricity | £ 14.00 - £ 22.00 |
| extra person | £ 4.00 - £ 8.00 |
| child (2-15 yrs) | £ 2.00 - £ 4.00 |
| dog | £ 1.00 - £ 2.00 |

# Wadebridge

## Trewince Farm Holiday Park

Saint Issey, Wadebridge PL27 7RL (Cornwall) T: 01208 812830
alanrogers.com/UK0500

A well established and popular park, Trewince Farm is four miles from Padstow has been developed around a dairy farm with magnificent countryside views. Careful landscaping with flowering shrubs and bushes makes this an attractive setting. There are 35 caravan holiday homes discreetly terraced, some privately owned, some to let. Two touring areas on higher ground provide both hardstanding and level grass pitches with a sheltered tent area. Over half of the 120 touring pitches have electricity (10A) and 34 have water and drainage. The park's main feature is an excellent walled and heated swimming pool with paddling pool, and paved sunbathing area. Farm rides and Cornish pasty suppers in the barn are organised in high season.

### Facilities

Two fully equipped, well maintained toilet blocks include washbasins in cabins, hair care rooms, dishwashing under cover and laundry rooms. Also children's room with bath (20p) and facilities for disabled visitors. Well stocked shop (all season) by reception. Fish and chip van calls twice weekly, a butcher once a week. Swimming pool. Play area. Games room. Crazy golf. New fishing lake. Off site: Riding 3 miles. Golf and bicycle hire 3.5 miles. Beach 4.5 miles. Pubs and restaurants in nearby village of St Issey. Camel Trail nearby for walking or cycling (goes to Padstow).

Open: 23 March - 31 October.

### Directions

From Wadebridge follow A39 towards St Columb and pick up the A389 for Padstow. Site signed on left in 2 miles. Follow for short distance to park entrance on right. O.S.GR: SW937715.
GPS: 50.571937, -4.913213

### Charges guide

| | |
|---|---|
| Per unit incl. 2 persons incl. electricity | £ 9.00 - £ 14.00 £ 10.00 - £ 15.50 |
| hardstanding, drainage and electricity | £ 11.00 - £ 16.00 |
| extra person | £ 3.50 |
| child (3-15 yrs) | £ 1.85 - £ 2.90 |

For latest campsite news visit
alanrogers.com

## Ashburton

### River Dart Country Park

Holne Park, Ashburton TQ13 7NP (Devon) T: 01364 652511. E: info@riverdart.co.uk

alanrogers.com/UK0950

The park is marketed as 'River Dart Adventures', where campsite and adventure experiences are enjoyed by old and young from all over Europe. It does become busy at weekends and school holidays with supervised activities for seven year olds and upwards, such as climbing and canoeing. The camping and caravanning area is in open parkland overlooking the woods and is mainly on a slight slope with some shade from mature trees. There are 185 individual pitches of very reasonable size, marked by lines on the grass, some slightly sloping, with 105 electrical connections (10/16A) and 12 hardstandings. Once part of a Victorian estate with mature woodland on the edge of Dartmoor in the beautiful Dart valley, the park and its activities are now open to the general public on payment. It features a variety of unusual adventure play equipment (for example, a giant spider's web) arranged amongst and below the trees; Lilliput Land for toddlers, Jungle Fun, and woodland streams and a lake with a pirate ship for swimming and inflatables, fly fishing and marked nature and forest trails – all are free to campers except fishing. There is a new Commando assault course and falconry displays are organised in high season (Thursdays).

### Facilities

The woodland amenity block has been refurbished. A new 'Biomass heating system' provides hot water throughout. Washbasins in cubicles, baby facilities, laundry, freezer, en-suite unit for disabled visitors (access by key), family bathroom and drying room. Motorcaravan service point. Shop, restaurant, bar, Sunday carvery and takeaway (all 1/4-25/9). Large TV and games room. Indoor climbing room (some of these open all year for the activities on offer). Small, heated swimming pool (1/4-25/9). Tennis. Max. two dogs per pitch. Off site: Bicycle hire or riding 4 miles. Golf 6 miles.

Open: 1 April - 30 September.

### Directions

Signed from the A38 at Peartree junction, park is about 1 mile west of Ashburton, on the road to Two Bridges. Disregard advisory signs stating 'no caravans' as access to the park is prior to narrow bridge. O.S.GR: SX734701. GPS: 50.51698, -3.78869

### Charges guide

| | |
|---|---|
| Per unit incl. 2 persons and electricity | £ 19.00 - £ 26.50 |
| extra person (over 3 yrs) | £ 6.15 - £ 7.15 |
| dog (max. 2) | £ 3.00 |

Camping Cheques accepted.

For latest campsite news visit

## alanrogers.com

## Axminster

### Hawkchurch Country Park

Hawkchurch, Axminster EX13 5UL (Devon) T: 01297 678402. E: enquiries@hawkchurchpark.co.uk

alanrogers.com/UK1725

Although just four miles from the historic seaside town of Lyme Regis and two miles from Axminster itself, Hawkchurch Park enjoys a peaceful, rural situation with wonderful views over the Axe Valley. The park is set on a sloping hillside with a number of camping areas and is edged at the back with tall mature trees. In total there are just over 390 pitches with around 100 occupied by seasonal units in their own area and another section of 33 privately owned mobile homes. A further five are available to let. Most of the touring pitches have been levelled and have either concrete or gravel hardstanding, 208 have 16A electricity. Tent pitches are on grass and mostly in their own fields. A pleasant bar/restaurant has limited hours out of the main season. When we visited, a play area and games room were due to be added. The village of Hawkchurch is around a mile away with narrow roads and is best avoided when towing.

| Facilities | Directions |
|---|---|
| Two traditional, modernised toilet blocks, and one newer block near the tenting area. All are fully equipped and one is heated. Family washroom and baby changing unit. Washing machines. Shop for basics in reception. Bar/restaurant open weekends and on demand out of main season. Dog walking area. Possible to arrange bicycle hire on site. Off site: Beach at Lyme Regis and Charmouth both 4 miles. Golf at Seaton (15 mins drive). Forde Abbey, a former Cistercian Abbey now acclaimed for its award winning gardens. Take a ride alongside the River Axe on the open-top tramway at Seaton.<br><br>Open: 15 February - 4 January. | The best route to avoid narrow roads is to leave the A35 between Charmouth and Axminster at the Hunters Lodge pub and travel north on the B3165 for 1.5 miles. At Wareham Cross signpost follow sign to left for Hawkchuch and site almost immediately on left. O.S.GR: SY344985. GPS: 50.7824, -2.930506 |

Charges guide

| Per unit incl. 2 persons and electricity | £ 12.00 - £ 18.00 |
|---|---|
| tent pitch | £ 9.50 - £ 14.00 |
| extra person | £ 2.50 - £ 3.00 |
| child (0-16 yrs) | free - £ 2.00 |

A peaceful and tranquil caravan park only 10 minutes from the coast in beautiful East Devon

darwin holiday parks

- Convenience shop
- Licensed bar & restaurant
- Children's play area
- Rally facilities
- Mains electricity
- Waste disposal point
- Seasonal Pitches

Pet Friendly

To book: 01297 678 402 or www.hawkchurchpark.co.uk

## Axminster

### Andrewshayes Caravan Park

Dalwood, Axminster EX13 7DY (Devon) T: 01404 831225. E: info@andrewshayes.co.uk

alanrogers.com/UK1252

The Lawrences have been developing the park for over 50 years so it is well established, with visitors returning every year. As the farm has wound down, extra fields have been added providing 230 pitches in total. As the site is on the side of the valley with wonderful views across to the Blackdown Hills, most of the pitches have been terraced with central or circular access roads. One field has mainly seasonal vans, another has 60 privately-owned mobile homes, another 20 available to rent and the rest are for touring. The 150 touring pitches (some with hardstanding) have 10A electricity and most have water and waste water. The environment is important and hedge rows are left natural.

| Facilities | Directions |
|---|---|
| Two fully equipped toilet blocks (one recently built), with family rooms and facilities for disabled visitors. Launderette. Microwave. Bar (weekend evenings only low season). Takeaway (mid July-end Aug). Shop in reception for basics and Calor gas. Play area for younger children. Games room with video machines, pool table and soft ball pit. TV room. Off site: Fishing 2 miles. Golf 5 miles. Riding and beach 6 miles. Bus for Lyme, Exeter and Bridport.<br><br>Open: mid March - 31 October. | From Axminster following the A35 towards Honiton for 3 miles. Watch carefully for site sign at 'Taunton Cross' signposted Dalwood and Stockland. Park entrance 150 yds. GPS: 50.782995, -3.069477 |

Charges guide

| Per unit incl. 2 persons and electricity | £ 15.00 - £ 26.00 |
|---|---|
| extra person | £ 1.50 - £ 2.50 |
| dog | £ 1.50 - £ 2.50 |

For latest campsite news visit
## alanrogers.com

## Barnstaple

### Greenacres Touring Caravan Park

Bratton Fleming, Barnstaple EX31 4SG (Devon) T: 01598 763334
alanrogers.com/UK0700

A neat, compact, rural park on the edge of Exmoor, Greenacres is managed and run alongside, but separately from, the farm owned by the family. Drive through the farm access to the park (clearly signed) – you will need to go back and call at the house to book in. No tents are taken. The site has 30 very large, well drained pitches (all with 16A electric hook-ups) with connecting gravel paths to the road – in theory you can get to your unit without stepping on the grass. The top area is level, the lower part next to the beech woods is semi-terraced to provide six hardstandings and some hedged places. There are marvellous views outside the beech hedge that shelters the site. To the west of Exmoor, the park is very suitable for the coast at Ilfracombe and Combe Martin, or for exploring the moor. The family has opened up a woodland walk through newly planted trees and across the fields to a secluded valley picnic area beside a stream to take advantage of the marvellous views and surroundings. The West Country cycle way passes within a mile of the park and the area is the setting for the classic novel, 'Lorna Doone'.

#### Facilities

The neat, clean toilet block with showers (1M, 1F) on payment (20p). Units for disabled visitors (and general use in peak times). Laundry room, with sink, spin dryer, iron and board, and dishwashing room. Washing lines provided. Gas supplies. Tourist information kiosk. Area for children with football and volleyball nets and swings, separated by a Devon bank from the 2-acre dog exercise field. Off site: Fishing 3 miles. Riding 6 miles. Golf 12 miles. Pubs, restaurants and takeaways within 3 mile radius.

Open: Easter/1 April - 19 October.

#### Directions

From North Devon link road A361 (M5, exit 27) turn north at South Molton onto A399. Continue for 9 miles, past turning for Exmoor Steam Centre and on to Stowford Cross. Turn left towards Exmoor Zoological Park and Greenacres Farm is on the left. O.S.GR: SS660404. GPS: 51.147633, -3.917517

#### Charges guide

| | |
|---|---|
| Per unit incl. 2 persons and electricity | £ 9.00 - £ 13.00 |
| extra person (over 7 yrs) | £ 1.75 - £ 2.50 |
| dog | free |

No credit cards.

## Braunton

### Lobb Fields Caravan & Camping Park

Saunton Road, Braunton EX33 1HG (Devon) T: 01271 812090. E: info@lobbfields.com
alanrogers.com/UK1140

Lobb Fields has two camping areas providing 180 pitches on sloping grass, with a few hardstandings. Twelve pitches are reserved for seasonal caravans, and 98 have 16A electricity hook-ups. A third field is open for campers for 28 days only in high season. The pitches are marked and grass roads lead to the amenities. As the two toilet blocks are at the very bottom or very top of the fields, some up and down walking is inevitable. Lobbs Fields may be close to many holiday activities, but it is also a peaceful retreat for those wanting a quiet holiday. Braunton village, Saunton Sands, the famous Tarka Trail for cycling, Baggy Point for walking, the biosphere at Braunton Burrows (one of only 13 similar special reserves in the country), Marwood Gardens, and windsurfing and water skiing on the Taw estuary are just some of the many attractions within a short distance of Lobb Fields. If you just want to sit and relax, then the pitches at the park offer views of the Taw estuary and Saunton, as well as magnificent sunsets.

#### Facilities

Two elderly toilet blocks (one in each field) have all the usual facilities. Two family/baby rooms. Laundry. Cleaning and maintenance can be variable. The lower block can be heated and has good facilities for disabled visitors. Hair dryers and irons available from reception (£5 returnable deposit). Takeaway (all season). Play area. Surf shop. WiFi. Off site: Nearest shops less than a mile. Fishing, golf, riding and bicycle hire 1 mile. Boat launching 1.5 miles.

Open: 29 March - 29 October.

#### Directions

Take A361 Barnstaple to Braunton road, then the B3231 (signed Croyde) to Braunton. Park is 1 mile from Braunton on the right - take care through Braunton as roads are quite narrow and busy. O.S.GR: SS474370. GPS: 51.11165, -4.181233

#### Charges guide

| | |
|---|---|
| Per unit incl. 2 persons | £ 9.00 - £ 21.00 |
| prime pitch | £ 12.00 - £ 26.00 |
| extra person | £ 3.00 - £ 6.00 |
| dog | £ 1.00 - £ 2.00 |

For latest campsite news visit
**alanrogers.com**

# Braunton

## Hidden Valley Touring & Camping Park

West Down, Ilfracombe EX34 8NU (Devon) T: 01271 813837. E: relax@hiddenvalleypark.com

alanrogers.com/UK0710

The owners, the Legg family, run this aptly named family park to high standards. In a sheltered valley setting between Barnstaple and Ilfracombe, beside a small stream and lake (with ducks), it is most attractive and is also convenient for several resorts, beaches and the surrounding countryside. The original part of the park offers some 67 level pitches (standard, large, super and premium pitch options) on three sheltered terraces. On hardstanding, all have electricity (16A) and TV connections (leads for hire), with a water point between each pitch. Kingfisher Meadow, a little way from the main facilities and reached by a tarmac road, provides a further 58 pitches. These are entirely on grass (so suitable for campers with tents) and all have electricity, water, drain and TV hook-up. Two good adventure play areas have wooden equipment and safe bark surfaces (one near a fast flowing stream which is fenced). There is a well stocked, licensed shop, a coffee shop serving breakfast and light lunches. Essentially, this is a park for those seeking good quality facilities in very attractive, natural surroundings, without too many man-made distractions – apart from some traffic noise during the day time. It provides a relaxed setting with woodland walks direct from the site.

### Facilities

Two modern, heated toilet blocks are tiled and have non-slip floors. Some washbasins in cubicles, some en-suite with toilets in the Kingfisher Meadow block. Bathroom. Baby room. Complete facilities for visitors with disabilities. Laundry facilities. Motorcaravan service facilities. Gas supplies. Shop. Coffee shop. Play areas. Dog exercise area. Caravan storage. WiFi in coffee shop. Off site: Fishing and golf 2 miles. Bicycle hire 4 miles. Beach 4.5 miles. Riding 5 miles.

Open: All year.

### Directions

Park is on A361 Barnstaple - Ilfracombe road, 3.5 miles after Braunton. O.S.GR: SS499408. GPS: 51.146533, -4.14555

### Charges guide

| | |
|---|---|
| Per unit incl. 2 persons | £ 15.00 - £ 40.00 |
| extra person | £ 3.00 - £ 5.00 |
| child (2-15 yrs) | £ 2.00 - £ 4.00 |
| dog | £ 1.00 - £ 2.00 |

Discounts for over 50s.

## Brixham

### Galmpton Park

Greenway Road, Galmpton, Brixham TQ5 0EP (Devon) T: 01803 842066. E: galmptontouringpark@hotmail.com
**alanrogers.com/UK0850**

Within a few miles of the lively amenities of Torbay, Galmpton Park lies peacefully just outside the village of Galmpton, overlooking the beautiful Dart estuary just upstream of Dartmouth and Kingswear. A family park, now under new ownership, with 120 pitches (60 marked for caravans) which are arranged on a wide sweep of grassy, terraced meadow with some hedging. Each pitch has its own wonderful view of the river. Situated on the hillside, some parts have quite a slope, but there are flatter areas (the owners will advise and assist). There are 90 electrical connections (10A) and 23 pitches have water and drainage. Galmpton is a quiet and simple park (gates closed 23.15-07.30) in a most picturesque setting, within easy reach of all the attractions of South Devon. A member of the Countryside Discovery group.

**Facilities**

A central toilet block provides clean facilities including three washbasins in cabins, an attractive under 5's bathroom (key), baby unit and hair care areas. En-suite unit for disabled visitors. Dishwashing room with laundry facilities. Reception/shop sells basics including gas. Bread to order. Adventure play equipment. Max. 2 dogs (not accepted 16/7-30/8). Motorhomes over 21 ft. are not accepted. Torches useful. Off site: Local pub is 5 minutes walk. Bus 15 minutes walk on main road. Beach at Broadsands 2 miles. Paignton Zoo 4 miles. Golf 1 mile. Fishing, bicycle hire and boat launching 3 miles.

**Open:** Easter - 28 September.

**Directions**

Take A380 Paignton ring road towards Brixham until junction with the Paignton - Brixham coast road. Turn right towards Brixham, then second right into Manor Vale Road. Continue through the village, past the school and site is 500 yds. on the right. O.S.GR: SX885558. GPS: 50.391650, -3.568070

**Charges guide**

| | |
|---|---|
| Per unit incl. 2 persons and electricity | £ 14.70 - £ 19.50 |
| with water and drainage | £ 17.50 - £ 24.50 |
| extra person | £ 3.50 |
| child (5-16 yrs) | £ 2.50 |

## Brixham

### Hillhead Caravan Club Site

Hillhead, Brixham TQ5 0HH (Devon) T: 01803 853204
**alanrogers.com/UK0845**

Hillhead is set in 22 acres of beautiful Devon countryside. Originally developed in the 1960s within what is now a coastal protection area two miles from Brixham, the park has benefited from a £3 million redevelopment and offers a full entertainment programme in peak season. Hillhead has 239 pitches, all with electricity, and many with fine views. Amenities are to a uniformly high standard, notably the main complex based around an attractive courtyard, and housing a shop, bar, games room and restaurant. The children's play area is outstanding with a range of imaginative items including a large, wooden fort.

**Facilities**

The two new, well maintained sanitary blocks, each with 3 private family bathrooms (key from reception) and facilities for disabled visitors. Laundry facilities. Motorcaravan service point. Shop. Bar and restaurant. Swimming pool (heated May-Sept) with children's pool. Large play area. Skateboard ramp. Games room. TV. Games field. Dog walking area. WiFi. Off site: Beach and coastal path 2 miles. Bus stop at site entrance. Golf (18 holes) and riding 2 miles. Bicycle hire 2.5 miles. River Dart boat trips. Paignton, Torquay and Brixham.

**Open:** March - January.

**Directions**

Site is well signed from the A379 Paignton - Dartmouth road and is located on the B3205 (Slappers Hill Road). Entrance is on the left after 400 yards. O.S.GR: SX904534. GPS: 50.369621, -3.544816

**Charges guide**

| | |
|---|---|
| Per person | £ 5.00 - £ 9.00 |
| child (5-16 yrs) | £ 1.80 - £ 4.50 |
| pitch incl. electricity (non-member) | £ 12.20 - £ 17.50 |

For latest campsite news visit
**alanrogers.com**

## Chudleigh

### Holmans Wood Holiday Park

Harcombe Cross, Chudleigh TQ13 0DZ (Devon) T: 01626 853785. E: enquiries@holmanswood.co.uk

alanrogers.com/UK0940

Close to the main A38 Exeter - Plymouth road, with easy access, this attractive, neat park makes a sheltered base for touring south Devon and Dartmoor. The hedged park is arranged on well kept grass surrounding a shallow depression, the floor of which makes a safe, grassy play area for children. Many attractive trees are growing and the park is decorated with flowers. In two main areas and accessed by tarmac roads, there are 116 level pitches (including a number of seasonal pitches) and 25 smart mobile homes in a private area. There are 100 pitches with electrical hook-ups (10A) and 70 with hardstanding, electricity, water and drainage. There may be some traffic noise to the west of the park.

| Facilities | Directions |
|---|---|
| The single, good quality toilet block includes facilities for babies and disabled visitors. Laundry room. Play area. Caravan storage. Woodland and meadow walks. Dogs are not accepted. Off site: Pub/restaurant nearby in Chudleigh village. Spar shop 5 minutes walk. Bus stop outside gate. The beach and Dartmoor are 7 miles and Haldon Forest for walks is 2 miles. Sunday market at Exeter Racecourse (2 miles). Fishing 1 mile. Golf or riding 4 miles. | From Exeter on A38 Plymouth road, 0.5 miles after racecourse, take Chudleigh exit. Park is immediately on the left. From Plymouth turn off the A38 for Chudleigh/Teign Valley, then right for Chudleigh. Continue through the town and park is 1 mile. O.S.GR: SX882811. GPS: 50.61985, -3.582833 |

Open: Mid March - end October.

Charges guide

| Per unit incl. 2 persons and electricity | £ 17.00 - £ 22.00 |
|---|---|
| extra person | £ 2.00 - £ 3.50 |

## Combe Martin

### Newberry Valley Park

Woodlands, Combe Martin EX34 0AT (Devon) T: 01271 882334. E: relax@newberryvalleypark.co.uk

alanrogers.com/UK0685

Newberry Valley Park is set in a delightful semi-wooded valley that slopes down towards the rugged North Devon coast, close to the village of Combe Martin. Three wide terraces and several sheltered fields provide 95 good sized touring pitches with views to the hills. These vary from paved, fully serviced pitches with picnic tables to simple grass areas suitable for tents. Combe Martin with its small beach and rock pools is a ten minute walk from the site around a small headland. The site provides an atmosphere of peace and tranquillity, except perhaps at high season. The toilet block is centrally located and the reception area houses a small shop and tourist information. A choice of restaurants and larger shops is available in Combe Martin. A lovely on-site lake provides fishing (licence available at reception).

| Facilities | Directions |
|---|---|
| Central modern toilet block with all the usual facilities including those for disabled visitors. Washing and drying machines. Children's play area. Fishing (licence available). Small shop in reception. Motorcaravan service point. Off site: Beach 0.25 miles. Shops/restaurants in Combe Martin 0.5 miles. Golf 5 miles. Riding 8 miles. Ilfracombe with boat trips to Lundy Island (bookable on site) 5 miles. Lynton and Lynmouth 10 miles. | From Barnstaple take the A39 towards Lynton and Lynmouth; follow signs to Combe Martin and Ilfracombe. Drive through Combe Martin towards Ilfracombe, climb hill at seaward end of town and site is on the left. From the A361 (exit 27 off M5) at South Molton take the A399 to Combe Martin and Ilfracombe. Site is 20 miles on this road, through Combe Martin. GPS: 51.204191, -4.042599 |

Open: 1 March - 31 October.

Charges guide

| Per unit incl. 2 persons and electricity | £ 14.00 - £ 35.00 |
|---|---|
| extra person | £ 3.00 - £ 5.00 |
| child (2-15 yrs) | £ 2.00 - £ 4.00 |

## Crediton

### Yeatheridge Farm Caravan Park

East Worlington, Crediton EX17 4TN (Devon) T: 01884 860330. E: yeatheridge@talk21.com
alanrogers.com/UK1060

Yeatheridge is a friendly, family park with riding, fishing lakes, and indoor pools. Based on a 200-acre farm, nine acres have been developed over many years into an attractive touring park. Around the site there are views of the local hills and Dartmoor away to the south, and Exmoor lies to the north. The touring area is very neat and tidy with a spacious feel as units are sited around the perimeter or back onto hedges, leaving open central areas. The 85 numbered pitches are flat, gently sloping or on terraces and are sufficiently large, 80 with electricity. Seasonal units take 25 pitches and there are four caravan holiday homes. You can explore three woodland walks ranging from 1 to 2.5 miles and the banks of the River Dalch. There are two deep coarse fishing lakes (bring your own rod), the top one offering family fishing and the lower one for serious fishing (age 14 or over and free of charge). Horse riding is available on site (best to bring your own hat) with hour-long and park rides available. The ponies and goats are also popular with adults and children alike. The owners, Geoff and Liz, are constantly upgrading the park (recently opening a new reception and amenity building) and they try to make everyone feel at home.

#### Facilities

Two toilet blocks provide family rooms, washbasins in cubicles, showers and facilities for babies. En-suite room for disabled visitors. Laundry. Motorcaravan service point. Shop. Bar, restaurant and snack bar (hours vary acc. to season). Unsupervised indoor swimming pools, toddlers' pool and water slide (10.00-20.00). Fenced play area with fort for under 10s (parental supervision). Football field. TV room. Games room. Fishing. Riding.

Open: 15 March - 3 October.

#### Directions

Park is off B3042 Witheridge - Chawleigh (not in East Worlington). From M5 exit 27 onto A361 to Tiverton. Turn left onto A396 for 0.5 miles then right on B3137 almost to Witheridge, then left on B3042 for 3 miles to site, well signed down concrete road on left. O.S.GR: SS770114. GPS: 50.8887, -3.7501

#### Charges guide

| | |
|---|---|
| Per unit incl. 2 persons and electricity | £ 10.55 - £ 18.30 |
| extra person | £ 3.00 |
| dog (first two) | £ 1.00 |

**Yeatheridge Farm** *Caravan & Camping Park*
NEW ON-SITE RESTAURANT
**01884 860330**
*www.yeatheridge.co.uk*
If you are a country lover, there is everything to interest you here.
2 ½ miles of wood & riverside walks. If you wish to explore beautiful Devon, then there could not be a better location.

## Croyde

### Ruda Holiday Park

Parkdean Holidays, Croyde EX33 1NY (Devon) T: 01271 890671. E: rudatouring@parkdeanholidays.com
alanrogers.com/UK1150

Ruda Holiday Park is a recent addition to Parkdean Holidays, now comprising 12 parks in Scotland, Wales and southwest England. It is right beside a Blue Flag beach and has 312 camping and touring pitches in two distinct areas. A large camping area divided into four sections is reserved for tent campers and small motorcaravans (there are some electricity hook-ups around the perimeter and it is served by two clean toilet blocks). Touring caravan and motorcaravan pitches, all with 16A connections, are in a separate field across the road and have direct access to the beach. Here, the toilet facilities are modern with coded entry to stop day visitors using them. A central complex (away from the camping fields) houses a supermarket, laundry, food outlets, and all of the entertainment clubs and bars. There is plenty of walking on the sand dunes and around the park, and Croyde Bay is renowned for surfing.

#### Facilities

Two clean blocks in the camping fields provide toilets, showers with preset controls, and communal washbasins. A separate bathroom with toilet is accessible to wheelchairs (key from reception), but has no aids for visitors with disabilities. A third, modern building provides all facilities in the touring field. Dishwashing and laundry facilities. Bar, restaurant, snack bar and takeaway. Amusement arcade. Cascade Tropical pool. Adventure playground. Tennis court. Sports field. Fishing lake. Supermarket, boutique and hire centre. Surfing equipment for hire. Direct access to sheltered beach. Dogs are not accepted. WiFi. Off site: Golf 3 miles. Bicycle hire 8 miles. Lundy Island excursion.

Open: March - November.

#### Directions

From Barnstaple, take A361 signed Braunton and Ilfracombe. At Braunton, take sharp left (narrow road) towards Croyde (signed) and follow the road all the way to the beach. Entrance to Ruda is on the right. O.S.GR: SS561331. GPS: 51.135183, -4.2352

#### Charges guide

| | |
|---|---|
| Per unit incl. 4 persons | £ 13.50 - £ 37.50 |
| pitch with services | £ 17.50 - £ 41.50 |

Prices are for pitch and up to four persons; maximum of eight persons per pitch.

For latest campsite news visit
**alanrogers.com**

## Cullompton

### Forest Glade Holiday Park

Cullompton EX15 2DT (Devon) T: 01404 841381. E: enquiries@forest-glade.co.uk

alanrogers.com/UK1000

Forest Glade, owned and run by the Wellard family, is set in the Blackdown Hills (designated an 'Area of Outstanding Natural Beauty'), deep in mid-Devon away from the hectic life on the coast. A sheltered site set amongst woodland with extensive walking without using your car, there are 80 level touring pitches, 68 of which have 10/16A electricity connections, 4 have full services and 42 have hardstanding. Touring caravans must book in advance and the easiest route for them will be explained then (phone bookings accepted). Although set in the country, the beaches of East Devon are a fairly easy drive away. There is a small heated, covered pool with a paddling pool, sauna and patio area outside, and a large games room (up a flight of steps, so not suitable for visitors with disabilities). There is also a soft play area for children. The surrounding 300 acres of forest makes this a nature and dog lover's paradise (dogs are accepted). The owners have also developed a nature trail and wildlife pond.

**Facilities**

There is one main toilet block, heated in cold weather, with some washbasins in cubicles. Separate suite for visitors with disabilities. Laundry. Facilities for babies. Extra facilities of Portacabin style with toilets, washbasins and showers are at the swimming pool. Drain for motorhome tanks. Shop including gas, bread and pastries with a takeaway (open evenings except Sunday). Microwave in campers' kitchen. Adventure play area with access to woodland. Games room. Swimming pool (free). Sauna (on payment). All weather tennis court. Separate area for ball games. WiFi. Caravan storage. Off site: Fishing and riding 1.5 miles. Golf 6 miles. Beach 17 miles.

Open: Mid March - end October.

**Directions**

Park (at the top of a steep hill) is 5.5 miles from the M5 exit 28. Take A373 for 3 miles, turning left at camp sign, just past thatched pub on right, towards Sheldon. Park is on left after 2.5 miles. This access is not suitable for touring caravans owing to a steep hill - phone the park for alternative route details. O.S.GR: ST101073. GPS: 50.857833, -3.277517

**Charges guide**

| Per unit incl. 2 persons | |
| --- | --- |
| and electricity | £ 13.50 - £ 18.00 |
| extra person | £ 6.00 |
| child (4-18 yrs) | £ 1.50 - £ 3.00 |

## Dartmouth

### Little Cotton Caravan Park

Dartmouth TQ6 0LB (Devon) T: 01803 832558. E: enquiries@littlecotton.co.uk

alanrogers.com/UK0835

This lovely, family run park on the outskirts of Dartmouth is ideally situated for exploring this attractive area of South Devon. Well tended and immaculate, the 7.5-acre park is open and grassy. On level and gently sloping ground, it is situated on a hilltop and has views across the other fields. There are 95 pitches, all with electricity and mostly level with some hardstanding available. The park is divided into four areas with one dedicated to rallies. A dog walking area is to one side. Barbecues are allowed off the ground. Located next to the Dartmouth park and ride, it is easy to get into Dartmouth.

**Facilities**

The modern, heated toilet block is centrally situated. It is very clean, light, airy and warm. Some washbasins are in cubicles. Free showers are preset. Excellent facilities for disabled visitors. Laundry facilities. Unisex baby room. Well stocked shop in reception. Bread and sandwiches to order. Freezer. Off site: Dartmouth Castle and the steam railway can be easily accessed by ferry. Beach, fishing and boat launching 2 miles. Golf 3 miles.

Open: 15 March - 31 October.

**Directions**

Park is on the outskirts of Dartmouth on the A3122 opposite Sainsburys. From Totnes take A381 (Kingsbridge) and turn left at Halwell on A3122. Site is on right just before entering Dartmouth. O.S.GR: SX857508. GPS: 50.345106, -3.607606

**Charges guide**

| Per unit incl. 2 persons | |
| --- | --- |
| and electricity (16A) | £ 14.75 - £ 20.00 |
| extra person | £ 2.00 - £ 3.00 |

For latest campsite news visit

alanrogers.com

# Dartmouth

## Woodlands Grove Caravan & Camping Park

Blackawton, Dartmouth, Totnes TQ9 7DQ (Devon) T: 01803 712598. E: holiday@woodlandsgrove.com
alanrogers.com/UK0840

Woodlands is a pleasant surprise – from the road you have no idea of just what is hidden away deep in the Devon countryside. There has been sympathetic development of farm and woodland to provide a leisure centre, which is open to the public and has a range of activities and entertainment appealing to all ages. The camping and caravan site overlooks the woodland and the leisure park, taking 350 units on three sloping, grassy fields, the original terraced one maturing well. One of the others has been fully terraced to provide groups of four to eight flat, very spacious pitches (90% with 10A electricity and a shared water tap, drain and rubbish bin). The newest field has 120 pitches (with electricity) designed with a more open feel to provide space for larger groups or rallies. Children (and many energetic parents too!) will thoroughly enjoy a huge variety of imaginative adventure play equipment, amazing water coasters, toboggan runs, the new Sea Dragon Swing Ship, a white knuckle monster, the Avalanche and much more, hidden amongst the trees. Those more peacefully inclined can follow woodland walks around the attractive ponds. The Empire of the Sea Dragon, an indoor play centre, provides marvellous wet weather facilities comprising five floors of play areas and amazing slides. With a two night stay, campers on the touring park are admitted free of charge to the leisure park. A popular touring park, early reservation is advisable. A member of the Best of British group.

### Facilities

Three modern, heated toilet blocks, include private bathrooms (coin-operated, 20p) and 16 family shower cubicles. Two laundry rooms. Freezer for ice packs. Baby facilities. The leisure park café provides good value meals and a takeaway service for campers. Café opening hours and camping shop (with gas and basic food supplies) vary according to season and demand. TV and games room. Dogs are accepted on the campsite but not in the leisure park (kennels available). Caravan storage.
Off site: The charming town of Dartmouth and the South Hams beaches are near. Fishing 4 miles. Golf 0.5 miles. Riding 5 miles. Beach 4 miles.

Open: Easter - 1 November.

### Directions

From A38 at Buckfastleigh, take A384 to Totnes. Before the town centre turn right on the A381 Kingsbridge road. After Halwell turn left at Totnes Cross garage, on A3122 to Dartmouth. Park is on right after 2.5 miles. O.S.GR: SX813521. GPS: 50.357898, -3.675001

### Charges guide

| | |
|---|---|
| Per unit incl. 2 persons and electricity | £ 16.50 - £ 24.00 |
| extra person over 2 yrs | £ 7.50 |
| awning or extra small pup tent | £ 2.75 |
| large tent/trailer tent (120 sq.ft. plus) extra | £ 2.75 |
| dog (contact site first) | £ 2.75 |

Free entry to leisure park for stays 2 nights or more.

## Dawlish
### Leadstone Camping
Warren Road, Dawlish Warren, Dawlish EX7 0NG (Devon) T: 01626 864411. E: info@leadstonecamping.co.uk
alanrogers.com/UK1095

Leadstone provides traditional camping at its best in a series of hedged grass fields, sloping in parts, in a natural, secluded bowl. In a designated Area of Outstanding Natural Beauty, the beach and sand dunes of Dawlish Warren are only a half mile walk. The area can get somewhat frenzied in peak holiday times but Leadstone provides a haven of peace and tranquillity. Owned by the same family since 1974, the Leadstone welcome is personal and the site is totally relaxed. In all, there are 137 pitches, 102 with 16A electricity. A regular bus service passes the gate every 15 minutes. The toilet facilities are centrally situated, but of the Portacabin variety. This is due to the site's situation on the seaward side of the Warren road where it is subject to Coastal Preservation regulations (it must be possible to move buildings within 24 hours). However, the provision is good under the circumstances, if somewhat short on toilets. Extra toilet pods are brought in for peak times. The site is only open for a short season, but is popular and well run. Dawlish Warren is renowned for its good weather and average temperatures of over 70 degrees Farenheit are not uncommon.

#### Facilities
Fully equipped, centrally located Portacabin style provision is well kept. Unisex showers (20p for 5-6 minutes). Washing machines. Basic supplies and gas from reception. Play area with real tractor. WiFi. Off site: Beach with shops, cafés, etc. at Dawlish Warren 0.5 miles. Golf 0.5 miles. Bicycle hire 2 miles. Riding 5 miles. Boat launching 7 miles.

Open: 10 June - 4 September.

#### Directions
From Exeter follow the A379 Teignmouth road (M5 exit 30). After Starcross watch for left turn to Dawlish Warren and site is on right after 0.5 miles. O.S.GR: SX973780. GPS: 50.59396, -3.45162

#### Charges guide
| | |
|---|---|
| Per unit incl. 2 persons and electricity | £ 16.50 - £ 24.50 |
| extra person | £ 6.50 - £ 8.50 |
| child (3-14 yrs) | £ 2.50 - £ 3.00 |

## Dawlish
### Lady's Mile Holiday Park
Exeter Road, Dawlish EX7 0LX (Devon) T: 01626 863411. E: info@ladysmile.co.uk
alanrogers.com/UK1010

Lady's Mile is a popular, large family touring park that caters well for children. It has extensive grassy fields (with some trees for shade), in addition to the main, landscaped camping area which is arranged in broad terraces. There are 486 good sized pitches, mostly marked by lines but with nothing between them, most with electricity (10A) and some with water and hardstanding. To one side of the park there are also some caravan holiday homes to let. It is a 20 minute walk to a good sandy beach at Dawlish Warren and ten minutes to Dawlish beach, but the park also has a good sized, free outdoor swimming pool with a 200 ft. plus slide, a paddling pool and a paved surround plus a super heated indoor pool (20 x 10 m) with 100 ft. flume and separate paddling pool (both with lifeguards). A large and attractive bar complex has a family area overlooking the indoor pool and a daily entertainment programme caters for all ages. A new soft play area has been developed for children with a café/snack bar for parents.

#### Facilities
Four toilet blocks of various ages are of a good standard and well spaced around the park, with an additional shower block. Facilities for disabled visitors. Four family bathrooms (50p). Dishwashing sinks under cover. Two launderettes. Supermarket. Fish and chip takeaway. Bars. Entertainment programme. Restaurant and carvery (half-board option available). Café with pizzeria and snack bar (all Easter-mid Sept). Indoor (Easter-Oct) and outdoor (May-Sept) pools. Adventure play area. New soft play area. Games room. Winter caravan storage. WiFi throughout. Off site: Golf, riding and bicycle hire 1 mile. Fishing 3 miles. Bus stop on main road.

Open: All year.

#### Directions
Park is 1 mile north of Dawlish with access off the A379 (Exeter-Teignmouth) road. O.S.GR: SX969778. GPS: 50.59525, -3.459467

#### Charges guide
| | |
|---|---|
| Per unit incl. 2 persons and electricity | £ 11.50 - £ 30.00 |
| extra person over 2 yrs | £ 1.00 - £ 3.50 |
| dog | £ 1.50 - £ 3.50 |

Low season special offers.
Low season discount for OAPs.

For latest campsite news visit
alanrogers.com

# Dawlish

## Cofton Country Holidays

Starcross, Dawlish EX6 8RP (Devon) T: 01626 890111. E: info@coftonholidays.co.uk
alanrogers.com/UK0970

A popular and well run family run park, Cofton is 1.5 miles from a sandy beach at Dawlish Warren. It has space for 450 touring units on a variety of fields and meadows with beautiful country views. Although not individually marked, there is never a feeling of overcrowding. The smaller, more mature fields, including a pleasant old orchard for tents only, are well terraced. While there are terraces on most of the slopes of the larger, more open fields, there are still some quite steep gradients to climb. There are some 450 electrical connections (10A), 16 hardstandings and 14 'super' pitches. One area has 66 park-owned holiday homes for let or to buy. A well designed, central complex overlooking the pool and decorated with flowers and hanging baskets, houses reception, a shop and off-licence and a bar lounge, the 'Cofton Swan', where bar meals are available (all Easter-end October). A family room and bar are on the first floor of this building and there is an outdoor terrace and some light entertainment in season. The adjacent, supervised, kidney-shaped heated pool with paddling pool has lots of grassy space for sunbathing. Coarse fishing is available in five lakes on the park. The adjoining 50 acres of woodland provides wonderful views across the Exe estuary and a woodland trail of two miles to Dawlish Warren.

### Facilities

Six toilet blocks, well placed for all areas, one of very high standard. Facilities for disabled visitors and babies. Hair dryers. Two launderettes. Gas available. Ice pack hire. Bar lounge serving snacks. TV. Shop (1/4-28/10). Fish and chip shop also serving breakfast (1/4-30/10). Swimming pool (overall length 100 ft. open Spr.B.H-mid Sept). Games room. Adventure playground in the woods overlooking the pools and two other well equipped play areas. Coarse fishing (from £ 25 per rod for 7 days, discount for senior citizens outside July/Aug). Caravan storage. Seasonal pitches available. Off site: Beach and boat launching 1.5 miles. Woodland walks/pub 0.5 miles. Golf 3 miles. Riding 5 miles. Bicycle hire in Dawlish.

**Open:** All year.

### Directions

Access to the park is off the A379 road 3 miles north of Dawlish, just after Cockwood harbour village. O.S.GR: SX965797. GPS: 50.6126, -3.460467

### Charges guide

| | |
|---|---|
| Per unit incl. 2 persons and electricity | £ 13.00 - £ 27.50 |
| hardstanding pitch | £ 16.50 - £ 29.50 |
| serviced pitch | £ 19.50 - £ 33.50 |
| extra person (over 2 yrs) | £ 2.50 - £ 4.75 |

Small discount for Senior Citizens outside peak season .

*See advertisement on the back cover.*

For latest campsite news visit
**alanrogers.com**

## Dawlish
### Peppermint Park
Warren Road, Dawlish Warren, Dawlish EX7 0PQ (Devon) T: 01626 863436. E: info@peppermintpark.co.uk
alanrogers.com/UK1090

Now part of the Park Holidays group, Peppermint Park is a green oasis in a popular holiday area. Extensive, green, sloping fields edged with mature trees have been partly terraced to give level pitches for caravans and some more informal areas that cater for tents. There are 90 holiday homes (many privately owned but some to rent) along with timber lodges to rent close to a small fishing lake. There are 75 touring pitches, 60 with 16A electricity, which are marked and numbered. Tarmac roads thread through the site giving easy access to all areas. Visitors staying at Peppermint Park can use all the facilities at nearby Dawlish Sands and Golden Sands, also part of the Park Holidays Group. Dawlish Warren's safe Blue Flag beaches and its associated pleasure complex are within walking distance (700 yds) making it ideal for families. For others, there is the adjacent coastal footpath or the city of Exeter (seven miles) with its cathedral, museums and historic Quay complex. A passenger ferry operates from Starcross (two miles) across the estuary to Exmouth during high season. Dawlish Warren nature reserve is adjacent and includes an 18-hole links golf course.

### Facilities
Two fully equipped sanitary blocks can be heated. Two units (WC, washbasin and shower) for disabled visitors. Baby room. Laundry (washing machines, dryers and free irons). Shop with gas. Adventure playground on a hill. Field for ball games. Small coarse fishing lake (£5 for adult day ticket). WiFi throughout. Off site: Golf at Dawlish Warren (18-hole links course), 9-hole course at Starcross. Riding and bicycle hire 2 miles. Sailing and boat launching 5 miles.

Open: 1 March - 31 October.

### Directions
Leave the M5 at exit 30 and take A379 Dawlish road. Pass through Starcross (7 miles) then turn left to Dawlish Warren just before Dawlish. Continue for 1.5 miles down hill and park is on left in 300 yards. O.S.GR: SX978788. GPS: 50.599367, -3.446967

### Charges guide
| | |
|---|---|
| Per unit incl. 2 persons and electricity | £ 8.00 - £ 27.00 |
| extra person (2 yrs and over) | £ 2.00 - £ 4.00 |
| dog | £ 2.00 - £ 4.00 |

## Dawlish
### Golden Sands Holiday Park
327

Week Lane, Dawlish Warren EX7 0LZ (Devon) T: 01626 863099. E: goldensands@ParkHolidaysUK.com
alanrogers.com/UK1085

Dawlish is a deservedly popular South Devon resort. Golden Sands is one of the three Park Holidays sites in this area. There is some up-and-down walking to access a good range of facilities. There are only 28 touring pitches at Golden Sands, most with 16A electricity. Accommodation is mainly provided in mobile homes and chalets for rent. Evening entertainment is to a high standard and is organised nightly in peak season. Leisure facilities include indoor and covered swimming pools and an amusement arcade. There is also a dining area (with takeaway food). Dawlish Warren can be accessed on foot and is home to an important nature reserve. The Warren is the main roost for the wildfowl and wading birds of the Exe estuary. By way of contrast, Powderham Castle dates back over 600 years and is the home of the Earl of Devon. This part of Devon is well known for the quality of its beaches and there is a wide choice of fine sandy beaches close at hand.

### Facilities
Basic toilet block with washbasins and preset showers. Facilities for disabled visitors (but quite hilly ground to access). Laundry facilities. Shop. Bar. Restaurant. Indoor and outdoor swimming pools. Playground. Entertainment and activity programme (including children's club). Mobile homes and chalets for rent. Off site: Beach within walking distance. Golf 1 mile. Riding 4 miles. Dawlish (shops and restaurants). Crealy Adventure Park. Dawlish Warren.

Open: 1 March - 31 October.

### Directions
Leave the M5 at exit 30 and take the A379 to Dawlish. Drive through Starcross and continue on the A379 for about 2 miles. Golden Sands is signed to the left 1 mile before reaching Dawlish. GPS: 50.596267, -3.456316

### Charges guide
| | |
|---|---|
| Per unit incl. 2 persons and electricity | £ 8.00 - £ 27.00 |

## Drewsteignton
### Woodland Springs Touring Park

Venton, Drewsteignton EX6 6PG (Devon) T: 01647 231695. E: enquiries@woodlandsprings.co.uk
alanrogers.com/UK1250

Hidden away in a corner of the Dartmoor National Park, Woodlands Springs is a haven of peace and tranquillity. Set in a dip, it is sheltered by woodland with some views across the rural countryside. It provides 77 fairly level, grass pitches (44 with hardstanding) and 69 with electricity (10A), with a circular gravel access road and a central toilet block. Small shop and off licence, bread is baked daily. A large field provides good dog walking. The resident owners provide a warm welcome on this quiet park that only accepts adults. With 600 miles of public right-of-way on Dartmoor, there is plenty to keep walkers busy. Over 50 species of birds have been seen on the park over the last few years so it would also be a good base for bird watching.

### Facilities

Toilet block includes full facilities for disabled campers. Chemical disposal. Dog kennels for rent. Off site: Fishing 3 miles. Riding 5 miles. Golf 9 miles. Castle Drogo and the Mythic Gardens nearby.

Open: All year.

### Directions

From M5 exit 31 follow the A30 towards Okehampton. After 15 miles at Whiddon Down junction turn on A382 Moretonhampstead road. Stay on A382 for 0.5 miles then left at roundabout. After 1 mile turn left at brown caravan sign, then left and park is 150 yds down drive. O.S.GR: SX694911. GPS: 50.706417, -3.850667

### Charges guide

| | |
|---|---|
| Per unit incl. 2 persons and electricity | £ 18.00 - £ 21.00 |
| extra person | £ 3.00 |

---

## Exeter
### Webbers Caravan & Camping Park

Castle Lane, Woodbury, Exeter EX5 1EA (Devon) T: 01395 232276. E: reception@webberspark.co.uk
alanrogers.com/UK1100

Set in a lovely location in East Devon, with rural views, this family run park has developed over 20 years to one that can boast spacious, modern facilities, yet still retain its relaxed, rural atmosphere. The 115 marked, grass pitches are large, with the majority being level and a few gently sloping. Some of the higher pitches have marvellous views across the Exe river valley. There are 100 electricity connections (10/16A). The park is surrounded by fields and visitors can watch the wildlife and grazing sheep from a fenced walk around the park perimeter. Within the park is a pets' paddock with a friendly donkey, Shetland pony and goats. A short drive takes you to the two miles of glorious sand at Exmouth or the delightful pebble beach at Budleigh Salterton. Woodbury Common for excellent heathland walks is just over a mile away whilst, for a little city life, Exeter is also nearby. A member of the Countryside Discovery and Best of British groups.

### Facilities

There are three modern toilet blocks, one is a light and airy building with four family shower rooms, a bathroom (£1) and a unit for disabled visitors (WC, shower and washbasin). Laundry facilities. Unusual in terms of number, are seven chemical disposal points, located at each water point (and adequately separated). Motorcaravan service point. Small shop at reception for essentials. Ice pack service. Gas supplies. Play area and games field. All year caravan storage. Off site: Woodbury village within walking distance with excellent pub/restaurant, post office, etc. Exeter 6 miles. Fishing or golf (Woodbury Park Golf Club) 1 mile. Riding 4 miles. Bicycle hire or boat launching 5 miles.

Open: April - October.

### Directions

From M5 exit 30 take A3052 (Sidmouth) for 5 miles and turn right at Halfway Inn. From A30, Daisymount exit, take B3180 for 3 miles to Halfway Inn and go straight across at crossroads. All routes then follow B3180 (Budleigh Salterton/Exmouth). After 2 miles turn right into lane (signed Woodbury, golf and caravan parks). Follow downhill for 1 mile to park on left just before Woodbury village. O.S.GR: SY017874. GPS: 50.678083, -3.392017

### Charges guide

| | |
|---|---|
| Per unit incl. 2 persons and electricity | £ 12.00 - £ 18.00 |
| extra person (over 3 yrs) | £ 3.00 |
| pup tent | £ 2.00 |

Min. booking of 4 nights in high season.

For latest campsite news visit
**alanrogers.com**

## Exmouth

### Devon Cliffs Holiday Park

Haven Holidays, Sandy Bay, Exmouth EX8 5BT (Devon) T: 01395 226226

alanrogers.com/UK1260

Haven Holiday's flagship park, Devon Cliffs at Exmouth, is a very large, vibrant holiday resort, complete with its own almost private sandy beach. There are over 1,600 caravan holiday homes here (400 for hire). They are arranged in avenues on the attractively landscaped, hilly site around a central complex full of top class amenities. Overlooking this complex is a small, modern touring area providing 43 very neat pitches for caravans and motorcaravans, a good toilet block and its own warden. Fully serviced (electricity, aerial point, water and drain), each pitch has areas of gravel, concrete and grass. Tents are accepted in high season on another area of the park with a second toilet block. Comprehensive and very lively, the excellent amenities include an indoor and outdoor, multi-level pool complex, a spa centre, sports facilities and coaching, evening entertainment programme, a huge noisy hall with amusements and games, and much more. For families with children who need entertaining, this park is ideal. There is a good supermarket and plenty of options for eating in or out. Sandy Bay has a safe, sandy beach with lifeguards in high season and at high tide is only accessible from the park. An hourly bus takes visitors to Exmouth and its resort facilities and larger sandy beach.

### Facilities

Very neat and clean toilet facilities with open washbasins, preset showers and hairdryers. Excellent room for visitors with disabilities. Good family bathroom. Launderette. Shopping arcade. Sonny Jim's buffet and grill, two café bars, fish and chips, Burger King, pizzas, Starbucks Coffee. Two indoor 'show bars'. Indoor and outdoor pool complex (outdoor 22/5-31/8). Spa centre. Sports facilities. Amusements hall. Evening entertainment and clubs for children. Adventure play areas. Beach (lifeguards in high season). Tents accepted 24/7-4/9. Off site: Exmouth centre 2.5 miles with hourly bus. Bicycle hire 2.5 miles. Golf and riding 6 miles.

Open: 20 March - 2 November.

### Directions

From the M5 take exit 30, then the A376 signed Exmouth. On the outskirts of the town (just after a garage), turn left at traffic lights following signs for Budleigh Salterton, Littleham, Sandy Bay and the park. O.S.GR: SY033805.
GPS: 50.615645, -3.366387

### Charges guide

| | |
|---|---|
| Per unit incl. up to 4 persons and services | £ 17.00 - £ 46.50 |
| extra person | £ 2.00 - £ 3.00 |

## Ilfracombe

### Watermouth Cove Holiday Park

Ilfracombe EX34 9SJ (Devon) T: 01271 862504. E: info@watermouthcoveholidays.co.uk

alanrogers.com/UK1257

This park is set in a lovely position, being at the side of a stream as it flows into the harbour and sea at Watermouth Cove. It has its own private beach from where there are lovely views across the sea to Hangman's Hill. Part of the park is arranged on the fairly level valley floor, whilst the tent area is on the side of the private headland with beautiful views of the coast from the higher ground. Electricity hook-ups (10A) are available. Children will enjoy fishing from the rocks, there is an adventure play area and during high season activities are organised for them. A heated outdoor pool is open from May to September. During the peak season and at weekends at other times, entertainment is arranged in the bar. A shop in the reception area stocks a wide range of supplies including bread, milk and camping gas. There is lighting in the park but a torch is useful for the tent area. There are no sanitary facilities for disabled visitors and the paths down to the beach and on the hillside are probably not easily accessible.

### Facilities

New heated facilities are provided in good quality Portacabin style units arranged in a U-shape with decking and seating joining them together. Showers are preset, have non-slip bases and a glass partition. The camping field has its own basic toilets. Laundry. Drinks machines, one providing hot drinks. Shop. Bar, restaurant and takeaway (weekends only in low season). Heated outdoor pool (May-Sept). Play area and activities for children (high season). Beach access. Sea kayaks for hire. Fishing. Entertainment. Off site: Ilfracombe is nearby, Lynton and Lynmouth, Exmoor and Combe Martin within easy reach. Coastal roads and paths are numerous. Boat launching 0.5 miles.

Open: End March - end October.

### Directions

From M5 exit 27 follow signs for Barnstaple A361. At South Molton roundabout turn right signed A399 and continue for 16 miles following signs to Combe Martin. Go through Combe Martin on A399. After 2 miles Watermouth Cove is signed on the right. O.S.GR: SS557482. GPS: 51.212484, -4.071298

### Charges guide

| | |
|---|---|
| Per unit incl. 2 persons | £ 12.50 - £ 32.00 |
| incl. services | £ 15.50 - £ 35.00 |
| extra person | £ 2.00 |
| child (under 8 yrs) | free - £ 1.00 |

For latest campsite news visit
**alanrogers.com**

## Ilfracombe

### Hele Valley Holiday Park

Hele Bay, Ilfracombe EX34 9RD (Devon) T: 01271 862460. E: holidays@helevalley.co.uk

alanrogers.com/UK1145

Hele Valley is a well-established park which has been in the same family for over 30 years. Located a mile from Ilfracombe in a wooded valley, it is only a few minutes walk from Hele Bay beach. Here, quaint coves and coastal paths reveal a genuine smuggler's cave. Apart from the 80 attractively laid out caravan holiday homes (20 for rent), the park caters for tents, motorcaravans and smaller caravans only because of the difficult access. Some 50 pitches are set in two lush green fields surrounded by trees and hedges. Being in a valley, some of the pitches are terraced. Eight dedicated gravel pitches for motorcaravans have electricity and water and 50 for tents (12 large ones) have hook-ups. This is a great centre for touring North Devon with Lynmouth, Porlock (Lorna Doone country), Exmoor, the pretty market town of Barnstaple and Great Torrington, famous for Dartington Glass. Nature lovers can enjoy walks on Exmoor or along the coast, including the Tarka Trail and, for bird watchers, Lundy Island is but a boat ride away (trips from Ilfracombe). A path leads from the park to nearby Chambercombe Manor (open to the public) with its association with Lady Jane Grey, a tunnel and a mysterious visitor.

#### Facilities

The bright, airy and modern toilet block (access by key with deposit required) provides a mixture of open and enclosed washbasins, plus long mirrors and free hairdryers. Showers have glass doors. Separately, a deluxe baby room, complete with pretty frieze and chiming mobiles and a well-fitted unit for disabled visitors. Two good adventure play areas and a play field. Parents must keep children away from the steep-sided stream running the length of the park. Off site: Minimarket, pubs and cafés 5 minutes walk. Fishing, sea fishing, sailing, many shops in Ilfracombe 1 mile. Beach and golf 400 yards. Riding 4 miles. Bus service in main road.

Open: 1 April - 31 October.

#### Directions

From Ilfracombe, take A399 east towards Combe Martin. With Ilfracombe swimming pool on the left, proceed down the hill for a further 400 m. and, at brown Hele Valley sign, take sharp right turn (easier to approach from Combe Martin). Go down steep road and continue to T-junction (right-angled and narrow). Turn right to the park. From Combe Martin follow A399 west for 8 miles, past golf course on left. Continue down hill then left at the brown Hele Valley sign and as above. O.S. GR: SS533474.
GPS: 51.205404, -4.101202

#### Charges guide

| Per unit incl. 2 persons | |
|---|---|
| and electricity | £ 22.00 - £ 30.00 |
| extra person | £ 4.00 - £ 6.00 |
| child (3-14 yrs) | £ 3.00 - £ 5.00 |
| dog | £ 3.00 - £ 4.00 |

## Ilfracombe

### Napps Touring Holiday Park

Old Coast Road, Berrynarbor, Ilfracombe EX34 9SW (Devon) T: 01271 882557. E: info@napps.fsnet.co.uk

alanrogers.com/UK1120

Set in an idyllic location in North Devon, this popular, family-run site offers peace and quiet on site, with plenty to see and do off site. A path just outside the gates leads down to a private beach with safe bathing; although it is only 200 yards to the gate, there are 200 steps down to the beach so it is not suitable for wheelchair users. Combe Martin and Ilfracombe beaches are also close by. The 200 touring pitches, most with views of Watermouth Bay, are terraced and spacious, 87 are serviced with electricity, water tap and waste point, and another 78 have a 16A hook-up. An outdoor heated swimming pool with shallow section for children is unsupervised, but there is a terrace with table and chairs for non-swimmers to watch or enjoy a meal from the Bistro. Light entertainment is organised during the high season. The local pub (300 yards away) offers snacks, a beer garden, restaurant and entertainment.

#### Facilities

Two modern toilet blocks include open plan washbasins, showers and family wash cubicles. Laundry. Licensed shop. Gas supplies. Bar with terrace and entertainment during high season. Restaurant (open mornings and evenings). Takeaway. Heated outdoor pool with paddling pool and small toddlers' slide. Tennis. Ceramic studio for children. Games room. Adventure play area. Caravan storage. Off site: Beach and fishing 200 yds. Golf and boat launching 1.5 miles. Bicycle hire and riding 5 miles. Coombe Martin 1.5 miles. Ilfracombe 3.5 miles.

Open: 1 March - 31 October.

#### Directions

Leave M5 at exit 27, take A361 to South Molton and then A399 to Combe Martin. Site is 1.5 miles west of Combe Martin on the A399 (signed).
O.S.GR: SS559475. GPS: 51.208517, -4.064083

#### Charges guide

| Per unit incl. 2 persons | |
|---|---|
| and electricity | £ 10.00 - £ 26.00 |
| extra person over 10 yrs | £ 1.00 - £ 4.00 |
| child (5-10 yrs) | £ 1.00 - £ 3.00 |
| dog | £ 1.00 - £ 2.00 |

For latest campsite news visit

**alanrogers.com**

## Ilfracombe
### Stowford Farm Meadows
Berry Down, Combe Martin, Ilfracombe EX34 0PW (Devon) T: 01271 882476. E: enquiries@stowford.co.uk
alanrogers.com/UK0690

Stowford Farm is a friendly, family park set in 500 acres of the rolling North Devon countryside, available for recreation and walking, yet within easy reach of five local beaches. The touring park and its facilities have been developed in the fields and farm buildings surrounding the attractive old farmhouse and provide a village like centre with a comfortable spacious feel. There are 710 pitches on five slightly sloping meadows separated by Devon hedges of beech and ash. The numbered and marked pitches, some with hardstanding, are accessed by hard roads, most have electricity (10/16A) and there are well placed water points. The Old Stable Bar offers entertainment in high season including barn dances, discos, karaoke and other musical evenings. There is also much for children to do, from the indoor heated pool and under cover mini-zoo (Petorama) where they can handle many sorts of animals (on payment), to the wide range of organised activities on offer. In low season some facilities may only open for limited hours. Stowford provides plenty to keep the whole family occupied without leaving the park, including woodland walks and horse riding from the park's own stables. However, it is also a good base for exploring the North Devon coast and Exmoor. A new development of 40 very smart holiday lodges with wonderful views has been added to the park.

### Facilities
Five toilet blocks, each with a resident warden, are fully equipped and provide good, functional facilities, including laundry facilities and dishwashing. The newest block (in field 5) has underfloor heating and facilities for disabled visitors. Better facilities for disabled visitors, and private family washrooms are beside reception. Well stocked shop. Good value takeaway with restaurant area. Bars and entertainment in season. Indoor pool (22 x 10 m; heated Easter-Oct) at a small charge. Riding. 18-hole pitch and putt. Crazy golf. 'Kiddies kar' track (all charged). Games room. Large play area. Games and activities organised in high season. WiFi. ATM. Woodland walks. Max. 2 dogs (in separate areas). Summer parking and winter caravan storage. Caravan centre with sales, workshop, accessories and repair centre. Rallies accepted. Off site: Fishing and boat launching 4 miles. Bicycle hire 10 miles.

Open: All year.

### Directions
From Barnstaple take A39 towards Lynton. After 1 mile turn left on B3230. Turn right at garage on A3123 and park is 1.5 miles on the right. O.S.GR: SS565438. GPS: 51.174983, -4.05475

### Charges guide
| | |
|---|---|
| Per unit incl. 2 persons and electricity | £ 9.40 - £ 28.00 |
| extra person | free - £ 4.50 |

Low and mid season discounts for over 50s.

## Ilfracombe
### Sandaway Beach Holiday Park
Combe Martin Bay, Berrynarbor, Ilfracombe EX34 9ST (Devon) T: 01271 866766
alanrogers.com/UK0695

Sandaway Beach is set in a commanding position on the beautiful North Devon coast and is close to the charming fishing village of Combe Martin. The town is on the western edge of Exmoor National Park and offers all facilities including sea fishing trips. The park has a touring area for 20 caravans or motorcaravans, 12 of which have electricity, water and drainage. There are also two fields for tents at the far end of the park with wonderful coastal views. The remainder of the pitches are for rented caravan holiday home accommodation. Families will enjoy exploring the wild coast with its small coves and rocky cliffs which are accessible from the park. The park is steep with terraced areas for the holiday homes. The slightly sloping grass field for touring units is central to the facilities and each pitch is numbered but not divided. A small private beach is accessed through the camping fields. The South West Coastal Path goes past the park and there are many other hiking and walking paths in the area.

### Facilities
The single toilet block is downhill from the touring field and may pose difficult access for disabled visitors. There are clean hot showers and two private cubicles. The tent areas have their own toilets. Shop. Bar, restaurant and takeaway. Lovely heated outdoor pool with views to the coast. Enclosed play area. Kids' club. Off site: Bus stop at the gate for visiting Combe Martin and Ilfracombe (4 miles). Boat launching and riding 2 miles. Golf 6 miles. Shops, restaurants, cafes, fishing at Combe Martin and Ilfracombe.

Open: 15 March - 1 November.

### Directions
From A361 turn north at South Molton onto the A399 towards Ilfracombe and Combe Martin. Drive through Combe Martin and up steep hill towards Ilfracombe. Park is on the right side one mile out of town. Entrance is tight, especially from Combe Martin direction. O.S.GR: SS571472. GPS: 51.206393, -4.044642

### Charges guide
| | |
|---|---|
| Per unit incl. 2 persons | £ 24.00 - £ 45.00 |

See advertisement on page 16.

For latest campsite news visit
**alanrogers.com**

# escape to the
# stowford
# life

**Stowford Farm Meadows** is a family owned, award winning touring **caravan and camping site** close to Combe Martin, North Devon

**SPECIAL OFFERS** available during low & mid season check our website for vouchers

**FACILITIES INCLUDE**
Indoor Heated Swimming Pool • Horse Riding Centre • Mini Indoor Zoo • Woodland Walks • 18 Hole Fun Golf • Restaurants & Bars • Fun Packed Activities • Fantastic Family Entertainment

Stowford also includes a **Caravan Sales Centre and Accessory Shop** as well as the opportunity to purchase your very own **luxury holiday lodge**.

**To save your place or request a brochure call our** Booking Hotline

# 01271 882476

*Combe Martin North Devon EX34 0PW*

www.**stowford**.co.uk

## Kingsbridge
### Higher Rew Caravan & Camping Park

Malborough, Kingsbridge TQ7 3BW (Devon) T: 01548 842681. E: enquiries@higherrew.co.uk

alanrogers.com/UK0826

The Squire family have developed this rural park over the last 50 years on their farm which is located about a mile up a single track lane from South Sands, near Salcombe. South Sands is ideal for boating, sailing and windsurfing as well as providing safe bathing. A ferry runs to Salcombe town. The five miles of estuary which stretches between Salcombe and Kingsbridge is a local nature reserve famed for its unique marine habitats and its bird watching opportunities. You can travel the length of it by the 'Rivermaid' ferry. The rural views from the park are amazing but you have to climb a little higher to see the sea. The coastal path can be reached by footpaths from the park. There used to be a dairy herd on the farm but the buildings are now used to provide camping facilities which include a covered play area for children under 11 years. For older children there is a play barn with table tennis, skittle alley and a pool table. A tennis court is available to hire. A large, sloping, open field has been terraced to provide 90 grass pitches, 60 of which have 16A electricity.

**Facilities**

Good quality toilet facilities, with unisex showers in a separate, light and airy part with the laundry and dishwashing sinks. Showers are metered (20p for 4 mins). Freezer for ice packs. Tourist information. Reception with shop for basics and some camping bits (open main season). Play area. Tennis court. Skittle alley. Caravan storage. Hogroast on Thursdays at 18.00 (high season). Fish and chip van calls at certain times. Off site: Beach, fishing and sailing 1 mile. Boat launching 3 miles. Riding 5 miles. Golf 4-5 miles.

Open: Easter - October half term.

**Directions**

Park is clearly signed from Malborough. Follow signs to Soar for 1 mile. Turn left at Rew Cross, then first right for Higher Rew. Take care with single track roads, although there are passing places.
O.S.GR: SX73381. GPS: 50.230174, -3.805647

**Charges guide**

| | |
|---|---|
| Per unit incl. 2 persons and electricity | £ 14.00 - £ 21.00 |
| extra person | £ 2.00 - £ 4.00 |

No credit cards.

HIGHER REW
Higher Rew Camping and Touring Caravan Park
Malborough, Kingsbridge, Devon, TQ7 3BW
Email: enquiries@higherrew.co.uk Tel: 01548 842681
*Higher Rew is a family run park in an area of outstanding natural beauty close to the beautiful Salcombe Estuary. We have, over many years, created a relaxed caravan and camping park for your enjoyment.*

## Kingsbridge
### Karrageen Caravan & Camping Park

Bolberry, Malborough, Kingsbridge TQ7 3EN (Devon) T: 01548 561230. E: phil@karrageen.co.uk

alanrogers.com/UK0825

Karrageen is to be found in a wonderful area of Devon, near Kingsbridge and Salcombe, with a mixture of rolling countryside, hidden coves, cliff tops and sandy beaches. You can walk, sail, surf or just relax and enjoy the wonderful scenery. This is a small family park run personally by the Higgin family situated in the hamlet of Bolberry, one mile up the lane from Hope Cove. The main camping field slopes gently with either sea or rural views. It has been terraced with hedging to provide 70 grassy pitches with 54 electricity connections (10A). There are some 20 places specifically designed for touring caravans. A number of caravan holiday homes to let complete the provision in a separate field which houses the modern toilet block. Hope Cove with sandy beaches and rock pools is a mile down the single track road.

**Facilities**

Modern toilet block includes two curtained washbasins for privacy. Showers are metered (20p). En-suite provision for disabled visitors doubles as a family shower room. Parent and baby room. Laundry room. Separate dishwashing (metered as it is spring water, 20p). Freezer for ice packs. Shop including some basic camping equipment. Fresh baguettes and croissants daily. Calor and camping gas. Takeaway (evenings only, last orders 19.00). No play area as such but two open areas for ball games. Off site: Fishing, boat launching and beach 1 mile. Golf 3 miles. Riding 6 miles. Salcombe, sailing Mecca and fishing port with sandy beaches 3.5 miles. Kingsbridge, ancient market town 6 miles.

Open: Easter - 29 September.

**Directions**

Travelling south from Exeter on A38, take the A3121 (signed Ermington and Modbury). Follow signs to Kingsbridge and Salcombe. At Malborough, turn sharp right through the village, following signs for Bolberry for 0.6 mile. Turn right to Bolberry then after 0.9 miles the park is on right. On the left is a concrete drive to Karrageen House and reception.
O.S.GR: SX692391. GPS: 50.23929, -3.84004

**Charges guide**

| | |
|---|---|
| Per unit incl. 2 adults and 2 children | £ 13.00 - £ 27.00 |
| extra person | £ 1.00 - £ 5.00 |
| electricity | £ 2.00 - £ 3.00 |

No credit cards.

For latest campsite news visit
# alanrogers.com

## Kingsbridge

### Bolberry House Farm Caravan & Camping

Bolberry, Malborough, Kingsbridge TQ7 3DY (Devon) T: 01548 561 251. E: enquiries@bolberryparks.co.uk
alanrogers.com/UK0824

Five generations have farmed the land at Bolberry and the present owner's grandfather started the campsite in a field on top of the hill; this main field enjoys marvellous views of the surrounding countryside and out to sea. There are breathtaking sunsets, and even shooting stars – 15 were seen the evening we visited. This is a traditional campsite, which caters for all units in three fields connected by grass paths with some up and down walking – this is a small price to pay for the views! There are around 100 pitches with extra allowed in the peak period, well spaced around the edges of fairly level fields with plenty of central space for children to play. Seventy five have 10A electricity. There are a few static vans to let in a separate area. However, it is not just the situation which makes this site special, but the warm welcome from Fiona and Elaine who run it. There is no reception; the sisters meet all their visitors personally and provide them with comprehensive information and are real ambassadors for this wonderful area – nothing is too much trouble for them. They believe they live in a magical place and want their visitors to share it – especially families, who can enjoy a bucket-and-spade holiday at Hope Cove, or couples enjoying a walking holiday. The coastal path is close by and many other walks can be enjoyed. The sisters are like walking Tourist Information centres, with knowledge accumulated by their family over several centuries. Take time to see the model village near the farmhouse built by their father.

#### Facilities

Two dated toilet blocks fully equipped. Coin operated showers (20p). Laundry. Play area. Small van open in mornings sells basics. Fish and chip van (Sun). Hog roast (Weds. all main season). Four different takeaways will deliver to site. Hope Cove Holiday weekend (events, entertainment etc) last weekend in Aug. Off site: Hope Cove with sandy beach 1 mile. Coastal paths half a mile. Pubs, farmhouse teas all within walking distance. Fishing 1 mile. Salcombe with its creeks for sailing and watersports and safe sandy beaches 3 miles.

Open: Easter - end September.

#### Directions

From Totnes follow A381 bypassing Kingsbridge via Chuchstow, following signs for Salcombe. At Malborough turn sharp right through village. Follow signs for Bolberry until you come to park on right. GPS: 50.238221, -3.831081

#### Charges guide

| | |
|---|---|
| Per unit incl. 2 persons | £ 12.00 - £ 23.00 |
| extra person | £ 3.00 - £ 4.00 |
| electricity (10A) | £ 2.50 - £ 3.00 |
| dog | free - £ 1.00 |

**Bolberry House Farm**
NR. SALCOMBE · SOUTH DEVON
Friendly, family run park in a very beautiful and unspoilt coastal area.
An ideal base.
Tel: (01548) 561251
Email: enquiries@bolberryparks.co.uk
www.bolberryparks.co.uk

## Little Torrington

### Smytham Manor Leisure

Smytham Manor, Great Torrington EX38 8PU (Devon) T: 01805 622110. E: info@smytham.co.uk
alanrogers.com/UK1065

A family owned, rural retreat of 25 acres, Smytham Manor is hidden away in its own valley some ten miles south of Bideford and 18 miles north of Okehampton. Part landscaped with neat grass and magnificent trees, the house is to one side of the valley with some privately owned mobile homes, and more to the other side, with pretty gardens. Tents have space in the walled garden where the swimming pool is situated and caravans go on terraced grass opposite. There is room for 45 units, of which 44 can have 16A electricity connections. Some pitches have gravel hardstanding. Lower down, the valley becomes more natural and wooded, with a series of lakes and a path leading down to the Tarka trail which can be explored on foot or by bike. Three smart, wooden chalets are available to let and another houses the bar and reception.

#### Facilities

Very smart, heated toilet block with every modern facility, including provision for disabled visitors which double as a baby room. Bar with terrace overlooking the valley (open evenings, weekends only low season). Milk, bread and daily essentials at reception. Swimming pool (solar heated May-Sept). Adventure playground. Games room. Walks from site. Off site: Fishing, golf and bicycle hire 2 miles. Riding 4 miles. Beach 8 miles. Boat launching/sailing 9 miles. Great Torrington 2 miles. Tarka Trail.

Open: March - October.

#### Directions

From Bideford follow A386 Okehampton road through Great Torrington. Turn right to park after 2 miles. From A30 pick up A386 south of Okehampton and go north for 18 miles towards Great Torrington. O.S.GR: SS484163. GPS: 50.925141, -4.157663

#### Charges guide

| | |
|---|---|
| Per unit incl. 2 persons and electricity | £ 13.50 - £ 24.00 |
| extra person (over 5 yrs) | £ 2.00 - £ 3.00 |

## Lynton

### Channel View Caravan & Camping Park

Manor Farm, Barbrook, Lynton EX35 6LD (Devon) T: 01598 753349. E: relax@channel-view.co.uk

alanrogers.com/UK0680

Channel View is a quiet, family run park in a sunny, south-facing position overlooking Lynton and Lynmouth. The gently sloping ground provides fairly level pitches which are mostly on hardstandings. The park is divided into two areas, an open area that is sheltered by bushes and trees and one that is more exposed but has views. There are 15 serviced pitches with electricity, water and a drain, and 60 with electricity (16A). The grass is well cared for and there is site lighting, although a torch would be useful. There is a café on the site that also offers takeaways.

**Facilities**

The modern and very clean toilet and shower block is partly tiled. Showers are free (there are three steps down to the ladies showers from the toilets). Baby changing/family washroom. Facilities for disabled visitors (Radar key). Laundry with washing machines, dryers and iron. Café. Small shop. Play area. Off site: Lynton and Lynmouth, Exmoor and the Doone Valley are nearby. Many walks can be started from the site. Riding 1 mile. Fishing 1 mile. Golf 15 miles. Beach 2 miles.

Open: 15 March - 15 November.

**Directions**

Take the A399 from Ilfracombe. Turn left on the A39 and continue past the turn for Lynton to site on the left after 2 miles. It is not advisable to approach from Lynton and Lynmouth. O.S.GR: SS724482. GPS: 51.21800, -3.82930

**Charges guide**

| | |
|---|---|
| Per unit incl. 2 persons | £ 10.00 - £ 15.00 |
| incl. electricity | £ 12.00 - £ 14.00 |
| extra person | £ 3.00 - £ 4.00 |
| child (6-16 yrs) | £ 1.00 - £ 3.00 |

## Modbury

### Moor View Touring Park

California Cross, Modbury PL21 0SG (Devon) T: 01548 821485. E: info@moorviewtouringpark.co.uk

alanrogers.com/UK0820

Moor View has a gently sloping position with terraced, individual, level pitches with marvellous views across to the Dartmoor Tors. This is a park in a lovely corner of Devon, run personally by the enthusiastic owners, Edward and Liz Corwood. A member of the Countryside Discovery group and an 'adults only' park. It provides 68 pitches of varying size, connected by hardcore roads. All are on hardstanding with 10A electricity, water and drainage. Bushes and shrubs planted between the pitches are growing well giving the park a very attractive appearance.

**Facilities**

Traditional style, heated and well maintained toilet facilities accessed from a courtyard area, providing all necessary facilities including a laundry room and sink, and covered dishwashing sinks. Shop. Takeaway in season (to order, 18.30-20.30). TV room. WiFi. Off site: A local country pub is within walking distance. The small town of Modbury is 3 miles. Golf and bicycle hire 5 miles. Fishing 6 miles. Nearest beach is 15 minutes away.

Open: All year.

**Directions**

Just past Woodpecker Inn leave the A38 at Wrangaton Cross, signed Ermington, Modbury and Yealmpton. Turn left and straight on at crossroads signed Modbury, Kingsbridge for 3 miles to California Cross. Leave garage on left and follow towards Modbury (B3207). Park is 0.5 miles on left. O.S.GR: SX705533. GPS: 50.363691, -3.817444

**Charges guide**

| | |
|---|---|
| Per unit incl. 2 persons | £ 11.95 - £ 21.95 |
| extra person | £ 4.00 |

## Mortehoe

### Warcombe Farm Camping Park

Station Road, Mortehoe EX34 7EJ (Devon) T: 01271 870690. E: info@warcombefarm.co.uk

alanrogers.com/UK0725

This park is set in a quiet position on a hill above Woolacombe. It is a large, fairly open site on gently sloping land. There are 250 level or fairly level pitches, some secluded, others extra large with hardstanding and electricity, and others fully serviced. Shrubs and trees help to divide some of the pitches. Two hardstanding pitches are designed to provide facilities and access for disabled campers. In total, 160 pitches have electricity hook ups (16A). Fishing is permitted in the lake with free lessons sometimes available for those who want to learn.

**Facilities**

Two modern toilet blocks are spotlessly clean, with free preset showers. En-suite facilities in one block. Family bathrooms and facilities for disabled visitors (coded locks). Laundry with washing machines, dryers and iron. Motorcaravan services. Shop. Takeaway (weekends only in low season). Play area. Fishing. Torches useful. Off site: Woolacombe beach is 1.5 miles. Public footpaths and cycle trails (the Tarka Trail is on the doorstep). Riding and golf 1 mile. Bicycle hire 4 miles.

Open: 15 March - 31 October.

**Directions**

Approaching from Barnstaple on A361 follow signs for Ilfracombe. At Mullacott Cross (10 miles from Barnstaple) turn left and follow B3343 for Woolacombe. After 1.8 miles turn right for Mortehoe. Park is the first on the right in 500 yards. O.S.GR: SS477457. GPS: 51.190441, -4.180639

**Charges guide**

| | |
|---|---|
| Per unit incl. 2 persons | £ 14.00 - £ 31.00 |
| extra person | £ 4.00 |

For latest campsite news visit
**alanrogers.com**

## Newton Abbot
### Parkers Farm Holiday Park

Higher Mead Farm, Newton Abbot TQ13 7LJ (Devon) T: 01364 654869. E: parkersfarm@btconnect.com
alanrogers.com/UK0960

Well situated with fine views towards Dartmoor, Parker's Farm is a modern touring site on a working farm. Close inspection reveals a unique chance to experience Devon country life at first hand, with pigs, sheep, goats, calves and rabbits to feed and touch. The 100 touring pitches are set directly above the farm buildings on broad terraces giving groups of flat pitches, all with good views across the valley (over the A38 which may give some road noise). Hardstandings are available and electricity (12A) is provided throughout. Trees and hedges have matured nicely on the terraces, with many more planted. Caravan holiday homes are available to hire. In addition the Parker family has added a family bar which provides entertainment during the main season (live singers, family bingo, children's entertainers) and a restaurant using locally sourced ingredients. Farm walks and tractor rides are tremendously popular and take place three evenings a week in high season, on request at other times. Parker's Farm provides a warm welcome – in the words of one camper, 'You come here and feel you belong'.

### Facilities

Two modern, fully equipped toilet blocks provide two family shower rooms. Baby bathroom. En-suite room for disabled visitors. Laundry. Shop (Easter-mid Oct). Restaurant, comfortable bar with family room (Easter, then Whitsun-mid Sept) and entertainment. Games room. Indoor play and TV area. Large outdoor play area. Trampolines. 6 acres of fields for dog walking. Caravan storage. Caravan holiday homes to hire. Rallies welcome. American motorhomes accepted by prior arrangement. Off site: Bicycle hire 5 miles. Golf 4 miles. Riding 5 miles. Coast 12 miles.

Open: Easter - 31 October.

### Directions

From Exeter on A38, 26 miles from Plymouth, turn left at Alston Cross signed Woodland Denbury. Site is 400 yards. O.S.GR: SX757702.
GPS: 50.527646, -3.723459

### Charges guide

| | |
|---|---|
| Per unit incl. 2 persons | £ 7.00 - £ 17.00 |
| incl. electricity | £ 9.00 - £ 19.00 |
| extra person | £ 3.00 |
| child (3-15 yrs) | £ 2.00 |
| dog | £ 1.50 |

## Newton Abbot
### Lemonford Caravan Park

Bickington, Newton Abbot TQ12 6JR (Devon) T: 01626 821242. E: info@lemonford.co.uk
alanrogers.com/UK0980

Lemonford is a well run, neat and tidy site for all ages and families on the southern edge of the National Park, some three miles from both Ashburton and Newton Abbot. Personally run by the Ayres family, it is nicely landscaped with a mix of trees and shrubs and covers 7.5 acres. Although close to the main road, it is set in a sheltered, peaceful dip bordered by the pretty River Lemon. There are 87 touring pitches (around 40 used as seasonal pitches) on level grass and grouped in four areas with some new fully serviced pitches available. Most pitches have 10A electricity (some 16A), over 55 have hardstanding. A good pub is within walking distance, along the banks of the river. There is a number of holiday homes in the centre of the touring area, and in separate areas at the back of the site with some available to rent. With well mown grass and smart, trimmed hedges the park is well cared for. Some of the fully serviced pitches will accommodate large RV's.

### Facilities

Two modern toilet blocks. The newer one can be heated and provides some large private cabins, a ladies' bathroom (£1 payment) and a family bathroom with facilities for disabled visitors. Laundry facilities. Shop. Gas supplies. Freezer service. Play area. No commercial vehicles are accepted. Off site: Pub within walking distance. Golf 2 miles. Riding and bicycle hire 3 miles. Fishing 4 miles. Leisure pool in Newton Abbot.

Open: All year.

### Directions

Travelling from Exeter, turn off A38 Plymouth road at A382 (Drumbridges) exit signed Newton Abbot, Bovey Tracey, Mortonhampstead. At roundabout take third exit to Bickington. Continue for 3 miles and park is on left at the bottom of the hill. From Plymouth, take A383 (Goodstone) exit, cross A38 and take first left to Bickington to site on right. O.S.GR: SX793723. GPS: 50.5391, -3.704

### Charges guide

| | |
|---|---|
| Per unit incl. 2 persons and electricity | £ 12.00 - £ 18.50 |
| extra person | £ 2.50 - £ 3.00 |

For latest campsite news visit
**alanrogers.com**

# Newton Abbot

## Ross Park

Park Hill Farm, Newton Abbot TQ12 5TT (Devon) T: 01803 812983. E: enquiries@rossparkcaravanpark.co.uk

alanrogers.com/UK0910

Ross Park continues to impress us with the care and attention to detail and the amazing floral displays which are a feature of the park and must be seen to be appreciated. These are complemented by the wide variety of shrubs which form hedging for most of the pitches to provide your own special plot, very much as on the continent. Many pitches have wonderful views over the surrounding countryside and for those who prefer the more open style, one small area has been left unhedged. The park covers 31 acres but 21 acres are managed specifically as conservation areas providing a haven for wildlife which visitors can enjoy. The owners, Mark and Helen Lowe, are rightly proud of their park and strive to provide quality facilities and maintain standards. The New Barn provides a comfortable lounge, a mezzanine bar with bar snacks and a restaurant with extra seating in the conservatory which is home to some exotic and colourful plants. An orchard area alive with daffodils in the spring and a conservation area with information on wild flowers and butterflies, and with extended views, completes these environmentally considered amenities. The kitchen garden provides vegetables for the restaurant and plants for the park. Barn dances are organised on Sundays in high season. This is a well cared for park worthy of consideration. A member of the Best of British group.

### Facilities

Seven well equipped, heated en-suite units, one with baby facilities, two suitable for disabled visitors. Extra en-suite rooms built to a very high standard with underfloor heating. Further separate shower, washbasin and toilet facilities. Laundry room. Utility room with dishwashing, freezer and battery charging. Dog shower. Motorcaravan services. Recycling bins. Reception with licensed shop. Gas supplies. Bar, bar snacks and restaurant with à la carte menu (all Apr-end Oct, plus Christmas and New Year). New conservation and tourist information room. Games room (table tennis, snooker, pool). 7-acre park area for recreation. Separate area for dog walking. Croquet green. Badminton. Volleyball. Large well equipped playground. WiFi. Caravan storage. Bus stop on main road. Off site: Dainton Park 18-hole golf course is adjacent. Fishing 3 miles. Riding 1 mile. Beach 6 miles.

Open: All year excl. January and February.

### Directions

From A381 Newton Abbot - Totnes road, park is signed towards Woodland at Park Hill crossroads and Jet filling station. O.S.GR: SX845671. GPS: 50.491940, -3.634240

### Charges guide

| | |
|---|---|
| Per unit incl. 2 persons | £ 12.00 - £ 23.95 |
| incl. electricity | £ 13.00 - £ 24.95 |
| extra person | £ 3.25 - £ 5.30 |
| child (4-16 yrs) | £ 1.50 - £ 3.00 |

Christmas packages available.
No credit cards.

# Newton Abbot

## Woodville Caravan Park

Totnes Road, Ipplepen, Newton Abbot TQ12 5TN (Devon) T: 01803 812240. E: info@woodvillepark.co.uk

alanrogers.com/UK0915

A lovely little site for 'adults only', Woodville is in a sheltered situation, attractively laid out with a wide variety of shrubs and trees. There are 26 pitches all with hardstanding and 16A electricity. They are accessed by a circular roadway which provides a central lawned area. A caravan storage area is to one side. This is a quiet site with few services, although the park is adjacent to a garden centre which also sells food and drinks. Dainton Park golf course is directly opposite and Ipplepen village is within walking distance and has three pubs. The owners live on the site and take a pride in their park.

### Facilities

A fully equipped toilet block also provides a separate unit for visitors with disabilities. Washing machine and freezer. Vans selling fish and chips and eggs call weekly. Wooden chalet with tourist information doubles as reception open for an hour or two each morning. Off site: Shop and golf course adjacent. Three pubs within walking distance. Bus service on main road. Riding 3 miles. Fishing 5 miles. Beach and boat launching 7 miles.

Open: 1 March - 2 January.

### Directions

From Newton Abbot follow A381 Totnes road for about 3 miles. Site is on the right just after Fermoys Garden Centre. The site gate is kept closed. O.S.GR: SY296913. GPS: 50.49505, -3.62965

### Charges guide

| | |
|---|---|
| Per unit incl. 2 persons and electricity | £ 13.50 - £ 18.25 |
| extra person | £ 4.00 - £ 5.00 |
| pet | £ 0.50 |

For latest campsite news visit
**alanrogers.com**

## Newton Abbot

### Dornafield

Two Mile Oak, Newton Abbot TQ12 6DD (Devon) T: 01803 812732. E: enquiries@dornafield.com
alanrogers.com/UK0880

The entrance to Dornafield leads into the charming old courtyard of a 14th-century farmhouse giving a mellow feeling that is complemented by the warm welcome from the Dewhirst family. Having booked in, continue down the lane (with a tree-covered bank alive with wild flowers) to the Buttermeadow, a tranquil valley providing 75 individual pitches on flat grass, separated by grassy ridges and in some places, wild rose hedges. You pass the walled Orchard, secluded and cosy for tents. Or take the road up the hill to Blackrock Copse with large luxury pitches with all facilities including a chemical disposal point and cleverly concealed TV connections. Electricity points are 10A. Whilst having been carefully designed, the environment remains natural. Both Buttermeadow and Blackrock have super, well maintained, woodland adventure play areas and all pitches in these areas have all-weather surfaces. The reception, shop, tourist information/ecology room have been sympathetically converted from farm outbuildings, with the games room from the old milking parlour, complete with stalls. Dornafield is a member of the Caravan Club's Affiliated Site scheme, with both members and non-members made welcome. The rural situation is delightful and, being away from the coast and without any evening activities, it is a haven for those seeking a quiet, restful holiday. A park that is well worth consideration and a member of the Best of British Group.

**Facilities**

Both modern toilet blocks are excellent and heated, with some washbasins in cubicles and comfortable roomy showers, but the new block up the hill could be said to be 'state of the art' with underfloor heating and a heat recovery system. Both blocks have facilities for disabled visitors and babies. Laundry rooms. Shop (13/3-2/01). Gas supplies. All-weather tennis court. 7 acres for dog walking. Games room. Play areas. WiFi. All year caravan storage. Half-mile walk to main road for bus stop. Off site: Local inn 0.5 miles. Fishing 2.5 miles. Golf 1 mile.

Open: 13 March - 2 January.

**Directions**

Park is northwest of A381 Newton Abbot - Totnes road. Leave A381 at Two Mile Oak Inn, opposite garage, and turn left at crossroads after about half a mile. Entrance is on the right. O.S.GR: SX848683. GPS: 50.50032, -3.63717

**Charges guide**

| | |
|---|---|
| Per unit incl. 2 persons and electricity | £ 14.00 - £ 27.00 |
| extra person | £ 3.50 - £ 7.00 |
| child (5-16 yrs) | £ 1.50 - £ 3.50 |

## Okehampton

### South Breazle Holidays

Bratton Clovelly, Okehampton EX20 4JS (Devon) T: 01837 871752. E: louise@southbreazleholidays.co.uk
alanrogers.com/UK0785

Tucked away down a half mile long Devon lane is a rather special campsite. Purpose built by Steve and Louise, who own and run South Breazle farm, the site is spacious with large pitches around the edge of a well mown field, accessed by a circular roadway. Pitches are marked with young hedging and all named e.g. Badgers's Den or Squirrel's Secret. Yes, you may spot a squirrel in the magnificent tall trees which edge the field but do not block the views across the rolling Devon countryside. In all there are 29 large pitches (180 sq.m), 23 with 16A electricity and water, and some with hardstanding. There are places for backpackers as well. Reception with pots of herbs outside the door keeps local foodstuffs. Nearby Roadford lake offers opportunities to fish, canoe, surf, birdwatch or just follow the nature trail.

**Facilities**

Comfortable toilet block, with facilities for children and disabled visitors. Washing machine and dryer. Shop for basics and local products. Fun fountain. Games field. Walks from site. Free WiFi on every pitch. Barbecues off the ground are permitted. Dogs are not accepted (working farm). Caravan Storage. Off site: Roadford lake 2 miles fishing etc. Watersports centre 4 miles (far side of lake). Bicycle hire (can be delivered). Riding 10 miles. Golf 15 miles.

Open: 1 March - 31 October.

**Directions**

Exit A30 at Stowford Cross. Follow signs for Roadford Lake. At top of hill (1 mile) turn right. signed Bratton Clovelly then take second left signed Germansweek. South Breazle Holidays signed first right and follow down lane to site. GPS: 50.70007, -4.20982

**Charges guide**

| | |
|---|---|
| Per unit incl. 2 persons, electricity and water | £ 15.00 - £ 19.00 |
| extra person | £ 3.00 - £ 3.50 |
| child (5-16 yrs) | £ 1.50 - £ 2.00 |

For latest campsite news visit
**alanrogers.com**

## Paignton
### Beverley Park

Goodrington Road, Paignton TQ4 7JE (Devon) T: 01803 661978. E: info@beverley-holidays.co.uk

alanrogers.com/UK0870

Beverley Park is an amazing holiday centre catering for every need. It has been developed and run by the Jeavons family for over 50 years to very high standards. It is popular, busy and attractively landscaped with marvellous views over Torbay. The pools, a large dance hall, bars and entertainment, are all run in an efficient and orderly manner. The park has 190 caravan holiday homes and 23 lodges, mainly around the central complex. There are 179 touring pitches in the lower areas of the park, all reasonably sheltered, some with views across the bay and some on slightly sloping ground. All pitches can take awnings and 87 have 16A electricity (15 m. cable), 38 have hardstanding and 42 are fully serviced. Tents are accepted and a limited number of tent pitches have electrical connections. The park is open all year and reservations are essential for caravans in high season. Entertainment is organised at Easter and from early May in the Starlight Cabaret bar. There are indoor and outdoor pools, each one heated and supervised. The Oasis fitness centre provides a steam room, jacuzzi, sunbed and an excellent fitness room. A member of the Best of British group.

### Facilities

Good heated toilet blocks include roomy showers, some with washbasins en-suite. Baths (charged). Unit for disabled visitors. Facilities for babies. Laundry. Gas supplies. Motorcaravan service point. Shop (29/3-29/10). Restaurant, bars and takeaway (all Easter, 30/4-29/10, and Oct. half-term). Heated pools (outdoor 28/5-4/9, indoor all year). Fitness centre. Tennis. Crazy golf. Playground. Pool and games machines. Soft play area. Dogs not accepted. Off site: Minibus to Paignton. Fishing, bicycle hire, riding and golf within 2 miles.

Open: All year.

### Directions

Park is south of Paignton in Goodrington Road between A379 coast road and B3203 ring road and is well signed on both. O.S.GR: SX882584. GPS: 50.413533, -3.568667

### Charges guide

| | |
|---|---|
| Per unit incl. 2 persons and electricity | £ 15.10 - £ 32.30 |
| tent pitch incl. 2 persons | £ 12.60 - £ 28.20 |
| extra person | £ 4.70 |
| child | £ 3.50 |

## Paignton
### Widdicombe Farm Tourist Park

The Ring Road, Compton, Paignton TQ3 1ST (Devon) T: 01803 558325. E: info@widdicombefarm.co.uk

alanrogers.com/UK0900

Widdicombe Farm is an 'adults only' park, just three miles from Torquay and with easy access from the A380, well situated for the Torbay area. There are 200 numbered pitches, 160 with electricity (10A) of which most have hardstanding and 48 are fully serviced. Situated on a hillside and surrounded by farmland, the pitches are on terraces with open views across the countryside. Many trees and shrubs have been planted and there are tarmac access roads and steps linking the terraces. There may be some background traffic noise but it is not too intrusive. The site has a relaxed, friendly feel.

### Facilities

Three older style toilet blocks are kept very clean. The original heated block near reception includes facilities for disabled visitors, dishwashing area and laundry room. Shop. Restaurant and bar with entertainment (all Easter, then Spring B.H-mid Sept). Certain breeds of dog are not accepted. Caravan storage. Off site: Bus stop outside entrance. Beach 2.5 miles. Golf 1.5 miles. Fishing 2 miles. Bicycle hire and boat launching 2.5 miles.

Open: 20 March - 17 October.

### Directions

From Newton Abbot take A380 south for about 5 miles. On outskirts of Torquay turn right at roundabout onto ring road. Site is well signed. O.S.GR: SX874641 GPS: 50.467081, -3.586797

### Charges guide

| | |
|---|---|
| Per unit incl. 2 persons and electricity | £ 10.80 - £ 22.50 |
| extra person | £ 3.50 - £ 4.00 |

## Paignton

### Whitehill Country Park

Stoke Road, Paignton TQ4 7PF (Devon) T: 01803 782338. E: info@whitehill-park.co.uk

alanrogers.com/UK0860

Whitehill Country Park is beautifully situated in rolling Devon countryside, just 2.5 miles from the nearest beaches. Extending over 40 acres, a definite sense of space characterises this park and ten acres of ancient woodland are available for walks and attract a great deal of wildlife. Whitehill is a friendly park with 320 large grassy pitches which are located in separate fields around the site with evocative names, such as Nine Acres, Sweethill and Coombe Meadow. Most pitches have 16A electrical connections (15 m. cable). Around 60 pitches are used for caravan holiday homes. A new upmarket development of wooden lodges is now completed in Nine Acres field with views across the rural landscape. These luxurious homes are for private ownership and more may be added. The park was once a stud farm, now the stables and stone farm buildings are used for the wide range of park facilities providing a craft centre for children to try their hand at pottery and painting, and even hair braiding. There is also an amusement barn with various video games, amusement machines, pool tables and table tennis not to mention the Hayloft bar (with satellite TV), a café and an extensive decking area for outside eating. There is even a disco hidden in one of the barns. An outdoor pool, woods to explore and cycling and walking trails to follow, not to mention various play areas, make a marvellous holiday venue for all the family.

**Facilities**

Well equipped toilet blocks have private washing facilities for ladies and facilites for disabled visitors. Laundry. Gas supplies. Good shop. Bar. Disco. Café/takeaway (24/5-1/9). Swimming and paddling pools (heated 21/5-1/9). Three play areas. Electronic games, pool tables. Children's craft centre. Children's nature trail. Walking and cycle maps in reception. Dogs and other pets are not accepted. Off site: Fishing and golf 2 miles. Paignton 2.5 miles. Beach 3 miles. Riding 4 miles.

Open: Easter - 30 September.

**Directions**

Turn left at The Parkers Arms off the A385 Paignton to Totnes road, signed Stoke Gabriel. Site is 1 mile along this road. O.S.GR: SX857587.
GPS: 50.417867, -3.609

**Charges guide**

| | |
|---|---|
| Per unit incl. 2 persons and electricity | £ 14.60 - £ 26.90 |
| tent pitch incl. 2 persons | £ 12.70 - £ 23.40 |
| extra person | £ 4.00 |
| child | £ 3.00 |

## Paignton

### Byslades International Touring Park

Totnes Road, Paignton TQ4 7PY (Devon) T: 01803 555072. E: info@byslades.co.uk

alanrogers.com/UK0865

Byslades is a large, well maintained touring park covering 23 acres on the side of a valley. The site is cut into terraces on the steepest slopes, so that most of the pitches are level. Many of the pitches (grass and hardstanding) have a lovely view across the valley to the fields on the other side. There are 190 pitches, around 100 with electricity (10/16A). There is a security barrier at the entrance to the park and CCTV has been installed. An all-weather tennis court is on the site.

**Facilities**

Two modern toilet blocks are kept very clean, with some washbasins in private cubicles and free showers. Facilities for disabled visitors (key access). Baby changing facilities in the Ladies. Laundry. Motorcaravan waste disposal. Basic essentials kept in reception. Tennis, Play area. Facilities at sister park next door open to Byslade's guests. Off site: Bus stop near park entrance. Fishing ajacent. Beach 3 miles.

Open: 15 March - 31 October.

**Directions**

Leave the A38 near Buckfastleigh (A384) or near South Brent (A385) signed for Totnes. Leave Totnes on the A385 signed for Paignton and the site is about 3 miles from Totnes on the left. O.S.GR: SX845597.
GPS: 50.42997, -3.61702

**Charges guide**

| | |
|---|---|
| Per unit incl. 2 persons | £ 11.00 - £ 20.00 |
| extra person (over 3 yrs) | £ 3.00 |

For latest campsite news visit
## alanrogers.com

# Plymouth

## Riverside Caravan Park

Leigham Manor Dr, Marsh Mills, Plymouth PL6 8LL (Devon) T: 01752 344122. E: office@riversidecaravanpark.com

alanrogers.com/UK0810

As you leave the A38 for Plymouth and negotiate the Marsh Mills roundabout you can have no idea that there is a lush green touring park tucked away from the modern, out-of-town shopping units in a quiet green valley. Part of the park is being developed to provide a residential area alongside the river Plym which has therefore meant a reduction in the number of touring pitches. However, there are still some 150 spaces available for touring, 80 of which have electricity (10A) and many are on hardstanding. There are also a number of grass pitches for tents. Hidden behind a high, evergreen hedge are an attractive swimming pool and children's pool. A play area is nearby and a pleasant restaurant with bar and games room provide welcome facilities and entertainment in high season. Over 30 years ago this park was a corn field but, with careful development by its owner, it now provides a welcome oasis from which to explore Dartmoor, to enjoy the amazing views from Plymouth Hoe or even to overnight quietly before catching the ferry to France. The wooded valley sides give way to level grass where the trees and shrubs planted all those years ago have matured to give a park-like feel. The River Plym runs down one side of the site but it is carefully fenced.

### Facilities

Three modern, fully equipped toilet blocks include cubicles with toilets and washbasins. Laundry room. Motorcaravan service point. Gas supplies. Some basics are kept in reception (more in high season). Bar, restaurant and takeaway (B.Hs and high season) with entertainment included. Heated swimming pool (end May-12 Sept). Games room with TV. Play area. Off site: Fishing possible in River Plym (licence required). Sea fishing 3.5 miles. Bicycle hire and boat launching 3.5 miles. Golf and riding 5 miles. Beach 10 miles. Dry ski slope, supermarket and retail park within walking distance. Bus stop 10 minutes.

Open: All year.

### Directions

From the A38 Marsh Mills roundabout for Plymouth take the third exit. After a few yards turn left following caravan signs, then right alongside the River Plym to the park. O.S.GR: SX518576.
GPS: 50.398167, -4.087333

### Charges guide

| | |
|---|---|
| Per unit incl. 2 persons and electricity (10A) | £ 14.00 - £ 24.00 |
| tent pitch without electricity | £ 10.50 - £ 18.00 |
| extra person | £ 5.00 |
| child (0-16 yrs) | free - £ 2.50 |
| dog (max. 2) | £ 2.50 |

Our family owned and run touring park offers an established, level parkland setting just 3 miles from Plymouth City Centre (including The Hoe and Barbican) and within easy reach of Dartmoor, Cornwall and the beautiful South Hams coastline. Local supermarket, pubs and park and ride are all within a 15min walk.

Facilities include:
♦ Laundry and ironing room with hair drying facilities
♦ Bar, restaurant, takeaway, games room and TV room (Easter and Summer only)
♦ Heated swimming pool (Summer only)

Riverside Caravan Park, Leigham Manor Drive, Plymouth, PL6 8LL
www.riversidecaravanpark.com  office@riversidecaravanpark.com  Telephone: (01752) 344 122

# Sidmouth

## Oakdown Touring & Holiday Caravan Park

Weston, Sidmouth EX10 0PT (Devon) T: 01297 680387. E: enquiries@oakdown.co.uk

alanrogers.com/UK1020

Oakdown is a very attractive, well planned park which has been run by the Franks family since 1972. The family and their team continue to work hard, making developments in keeping with the environment. The park has easy access, beautiful floral displays and a spacious feeling. There are 100 level touring pitches arranged in landscaped bays, screened by a wide range of trees and shrubs and linked by a circular road. All have 10/16A electricity, all have hardstanding and many have water and drainage. An additional touring area near the golf course, Beech Grove, provides a further 50 large pitches with hedging and 16A electricity. There is also a new, fully equipped toilet block here. This park is an excellent choice for visitors, especially those with disabilities. A member of the Best of British Group.

### Facilities

The original, heated central toilet block has well maintained facilities. One private cabin for ladies. Two unisex family bathrooms double as units for disabled visitors. Laundry facilities plus free freezer and microwave. New facilities include a room for families and disabled visitors, and a laundry area. Motorcaravan service point. Café/shop selling essentials and snacks (mid May-mid Sept). Internet room. Fax service. TV room. Two excellent adventure play areas and castle. Lake. Dew pond. No cycling, skate-boarding or kite flying is permitted. Caravan storage. Off site: Riding 6 miles. Golf course adjacent. Swimming 1 mile. Beach 2 miles.

Open: 17 March - 7 November.

### Directions

Turn south off the A3052 (Exeter - Lyme Regis) road between Sidford and Colyford, 2.5 miles east of the A375 junction and park is on left.
O.S.GR: SY167902. GPS: 50.7056, -3.18063

### Charges guide

| | |
|---|---|
| Per unit incl. 2 persons and electricity | £ 15.20 - £ 22.00 |
| with water and drainage | £ 20.50 - £ 27.50 |
| extra person (5 yrs and over) | £ 3.00 |
| dog | £ 2.30 |
| Less 80p for senior citizens in low season. | |

For latest campsite news visit
**alanrogers.com**

## Sidmouth
### Salcombe Regis Camping & Caravan Park

Salcombe Regis, Sidmouth EX10 0JH (Devon) T: 01395 514303. E: contact@salcombe-regis.co.uk
alanrogers.com/UK1110

On the edge of Salcombe Regis village, 1.5 miles from Sidmouth and less than a mile from the sea, Salcombe Regis Park covers 16 acres of land. It is surrounded by farmland with views of the combe and the sea beyond. The focal point of the main camping area is a large 'village green' where the play area and pitch and putt are located. The reception and pitches are arranged around the green, all connected by a tarmac road. The 110 pitches are level and have their own water supply, with 98 electricity hook-ups (16A). A 25 minute walk across fields takes you to a small secluded beach, although the walk there is fairly steep – we are told there are 129 steps that take you down to the beach! There are many footpaths and coastal walks nearby, protected by the National Trust, and with views of Sidmouth and Weston Mouth. Sidmouth town, originally a small fishing town but now a seaside resort, is host to the annual International Folk Festival, where for one week in summer the town is filled with folk artists from all over the world.

| Facilities | Directions |
|---|---|
| The traditional style toilet block (to one side of the site and a longer walk for some) is kept spotlessly clean by the resident wardens and includes a bathroom for families and disabled visitors. Shop at reception selling basic supplies and local produce. Dishwashing area under cover. Laundry room with washing machines, dryers and ironing board. Motorcaravan service point. Play area. Pitch and putt. Caravan storage. Torches useful. Off site: Fishing, bicycle hire and golf 1.5 miles. Riding 3 miles. Sidmouth and beach 1.5 miles.<br><br>Open: Easter - 28 October. | Park is well signed on the A3052 Exeter - Lyme Regis road. From the east, take first left after Donkey Sanctuary. From the west proceed up the hill out of Sidford. Do not take first road signed Salcombe Regis, but take the next right at top of hill. Follow road round to site on left after golf range. O.S.GR: SY149892. GPS: 50.695717, -3.205367 |

**Charges guide**

| | |
|---|---|
| Per unit incl. 2 persons and electricity | £ 16.00 - £ 22.00 |
| extra person | £ 4.00 |
| child (5-15 yrs) | £ 2.60 |

Tranquil setting with excellent touring facilities Ideal base for exploring rural East Devon. Superb walking country

**Within walking distance of the sea & famous Donkey Sanctuary**

Ten Luxuriously equipped Rose Award leisure homes for hire. Situated ½ OFF main A3052 Exeter to Lyme Regis coast road. Spacious level sites with some views. Hardstanding with individual taps/soakaways, available for Tourers/Motor caravans at no extra cost. Heated amenity block.

**SALCOMBE REGIS**
CAMPING & CARAVAN PARK
Sidmouth, Devon
EX10 0JH

**Tel: (01395) 514303**
**Fax: (01395) 514313**
**www.salcombe-regis.co.uk**
**E-mail:**
**contact@salcombe-regis.co.uk**
**FREE colour brochure**

---

## South Molton
### Riverside Caravan & Camping Park

Marsh Lane, North Molton Road, South Molton EX36 3HQ (Devon) T: 01769 579 269
E: relax@exmoorriverside.co.uk  alanrogers.com/UK0745

A very impressive purpose-built campsite beside the River Mole, all the 44 pitches at this park have hardstanding, 16A electricity connection, water, drainage and a TV aerial socket. Neat grass, tarmac roads and growing trees and hedges contribute to the attractive, overall impression. The heated toilet block gleams, and a particular feature is the chemical disposal point, which has its own special house with a washbasin, and is tiled (would they were all like that!) The owners, Joy and Nicky Penfold, are not resting on their laurels and have developed fishing lakes with specimen carp down by the river and a play area on the opposite bank. The ancient market town of South Molton is a mile away and a bus stops outside the site entrance. Exmoor is on hand to explore, as are the North Devon resorts of Woolacombe, Ilfracombe, Combe Martin and Lynton, not to mention the surfing paradise of Croyde Bay.

| Facilities | Directions |
|---|---|
| Modern, fully equipped and heated toilet block accessed by code. Facilities for disabled visitors. Laundry room. Shop (limited hours in low season). Play area planned. Fishing. Caravan storage. Swimming in river. Off site: Riding 2 miles. Golf 5 miles. Boat launching and beach 12 miles.<br><br>Open: All year. | From M5 exit 27 take the North Devon Link road A361. Near South Molton watch for site sign (direction North Molton). O.S.GR: SS723270. GPS: 51.03086, -3.81871 |

**Charges guide**

| | |
|---|---|
| Per unit incl. 2 adults and 2 children | £ 10.00 - £ 18.00 |
| incl. electricity | £ 14.00 - £ 17.00 |
| extra person | £ 6.00 |
| large motorcaravan | £ 24.00 - £ 29.00 |

For latest campsite news visit
**alanrogers.com**

## Tavistock

### Langstone Manor Holiday Park

Moortown, Tavistock PL19 9JZ (Devon) T: 01822 613371. E: web@langstone-manor.co.uk

alanrogers.com/UK0802

Situated on the southwest edge of Dartmoor, this holiday park has been developed in the grounds of the old Langstone Manor house. The touring pitches are tucked into various garden areas with mature trees and flowering shrubs, or in the walled garden area with views over the moor. In all there are 42 level grass pitches which vary in size (30 with 10A electricity). A new camping area is popular and has been terraced with open views over farmland and the moor. You pass through a number of holiday caravans on the way to reception and the touring pitches where you will also find some holiday cottages and flats for rent. The 'pièce de résistance' is the unexpected traditional bar and restaurant in the Manor House, complete with a terrace that catches the evening sun. Open in high season and on demand in low season, it has an open fire (if needed) and games room. Approaching over a short section of the moor, you realise how well Langstone Manor is situated to explore Dartmoor by foot, by car or on bike (the park has direct access). The market town of Tavistock is three miles away and there is a wealth of National Trust houses and gardens to visit nearby.

#### Facilities

The toilet block is set to one side of the walled garden area, fully equipped and well maintained. Showers on payment (20p tokens from reception or bar). Fully equipped laundry room. Changing mat for babies in the ladies. Basic supplies kept in reception (order bread the day before). Bar/restaurant with terrace. Games room. Play area. Off site: Leisure centre and pool 2 miles. Golf 1 mile. Fishing 2 miles. Bicycle hire 3 miles. Boat Launching 10 miles. Sailing 15 miles.

Open: 15 March - end October.

#### Directions

From Tavistock take B3357 Princetown road. After about 2 miles turn right at crossroads (site signed). Pass over cattle grid onto moor and follow site signs. O.S.GR: SX524738. GPS: 50.5449, -4.084167

#### Charges guide

| | |
|---|---|
| Per unit incl. 2 persons and electricity | £ 16.00 - £ 19.00 |
| extra person | £ 4.00 |
| child (3-11 yrs) | £ 3.00 |
| dog | free |

DIRECT ACCESS ONTO MOOR - DARTMOOR'S BEST KEPT SECRET

**Langstone Manor Holiday Park**
CAMPING & CARAVANS

TEL/FAX: +44 (0)1822 623 371
www.langstone-manor.co.uk

CAMPING PODS NOW AVAILABLE

## Tavistock

### Woodovis Park

Woodovis House, Gulworthy, Tavistock PL19 8NY (Devon) T: 01822 832968. E: info@woodovis.com

alanrogers.com/UK0805

Woodovis Park is set in the grounds of Woodovis House, owned in the 19th century by a mine captain in the days when the valley had a thriving copper mining industry. It nestles in a sheltered wooded position covering 14 acres, by the edge of the Tamar Valley on the borders of Devon and Cornwall. John and Dorothy Lewis have been running Woodovis Park since 1999, helped by their very welcoming staff. There are 50 good sized pitches, all with 10A electricity. You have a choice of grass, all weather and 'super' pitches (with water, waste and TV hook-ups ). Split over two fields and landscaped inbetween are 35 caravan holiday homes. The whole area is sheltered by thick hedges and woodland but in places you can see across the valley to Cornwall. An indoor pool with spa pool and infrared sauna are a welcome attraction. The approach to the site is down a tree-lined lane with passing places. This is a peaceful spot with some nice touches, run to a very high standard. A member of the Best of British group.

#### Facilities

Fully equipped and heated toilet block. Bathroom (coin operated) is useful for disabled visitors or those with babies. Family cubicles. Toilet for disabled visitors at the pool. Fully equipped laundry. Motorcaravan service point. Shop for basics with off licence in reception. Indoor heated swimming pool (no swimming alone), spa and sauna. Games room. Fenced play area. Minigolf. Archery and 'water-walking' (weekly during school holidays). WiFi. Off site: Pub with restaurant within walking distance. Fishing 1.5 miles. Golf, riding and bicycle hire 3 miles. Canoeing and tree walking 3 miles. Boat launching 6 miles. Tavistock 4 miles. Dartmoor 6 miles.

Open: 27 March - 30 October.

#### Directions

From Tavistock follow A390 for Liskeard. After 3 miles turn right at Gulworthy roundabout signed Chipshop, Lamerton and Caravan Park. After 1 mile entrance is signed on left. O.S.GR: SX431743. GPS: 50.548867, -4.21585

#### Charges guide

| | |
|---|---|
| Per person (over 5 yrs) | £ 7.00 |
| pitch incl. electricity | £ 5.00 - £ 20.00 |
| awning | £ 2.00 |

For latest campsite news visit
**alanrogers.com**

## Tavistock

### Harford Bridge Holiday Park

Peter Tavy, Tavistock PL19 9LS (Devon) T: 01822 810349. E: enquiry@harfordbridge.co.uk

alanrogers.com/UK0790

Harford Bridge has an interesting history – originally the Wheal Union tin mine until 1850, then used as a farm campsite from 1930 and taken over by the Royal Engineers in 1939. It is now a quiet, rural, mature park inside the Dartmoor National Park. It is bounded by the River Tavy on one side and the lane from the main road to the village of Peter Tavy on the other, with Harford Bridge, a classic granite moorland bridge, at the corner. With 16.5 acres, the park provides 120 touring pitches well spaced on a level grassy meadow with some shade from mature trees and others recently planted; 52 pitches have electrical hook-ups and 11 have 'multi-services', five with hardstanding. Out of season or by booking in advance you may get one of the delightful spots bordering the river (these are without electricity). Some holiday caravans and chalets are neatly landscaped in their own area. At the entrance to the park a central grassy area is left free for games, which is also used by the town band, village fete, etc. While the river (unfenced) will inevitably mesmerise youngsters, a super central play area on a hilly tree knoll will claim them. In early summer there are chicks to watch, horses to make a fuss of and the park ducks are a feature. With its own and the local history, plus its situation, this is a super place to stay.

### Facilities

The single toilet block is older in style but fully equipped and well kept, with free hot water and showers all year. Facilities for disabled visitors and babies. Good laundry and drying room. Freezer. Motorcaravan service point. Games room with table tennis and separate TV room. Play area. Tennis court (free). Two communal barbecue areas. Fly fishing (by licence, £3/day, £10/week). WiFi (vouchers). Off site: Bicycle hire, riding and golf, all within 2.5 miles. West Devon cycle way (Route 27) and it is possible to cycle into Tavistock. Tavistock market twice monthly. Bus stop on main road.

Open: All year.

### Directions

Two miles north of Tavistock, off A386 Tavistock - Okehampton road, take the road to Peter Tavy. O.S.GR: SX504768. GPS: 50.5713, -4.114

### Charges guide

| | |
|---|---|
| Per unit incl. 2 persons and electricity | £ 14.75 - £ 19.75 |
| with full services | £ 16.25 - £ 21.50 |
| extra person | £ 5.50 |
| child (3-16 yrs) | £ 2.70 |

For latest campsite news visit
**alanrogers.com**

## Tavistock
### The Old Rectory Caravan & Camping Park

Gulworthy, Tavistock PL19 8JA (Devon) T: 01822 832927. E: info@tamarvalleycamping.co.uk
alanrogers.com/UK0795

The Old Rectory is a neat little park where hedging provides bays to give you your own space and shelter. You can share the larger bays with friends or family. The hedging will be taken down a foot or two in the Autumn to allow more enjoyment of the panoramic views across to Dartmoor. All the pitches are on grass, (eight having 10A electricity) with space for 11 caravans or motor homes and 20 tents. Four camping pods are available to rent if you have no tent or caravan. A small toilet block will be enlarged next year to double the facilities. There is no reception office, you simply contact the owners by phone when you arrive. Children will enjoy watching the miniature Shetland ponies; hopefully in the future they may be able to pull a little cart to give rides. Chickens wander in the orchard, the pedigree pigs look very contented and campers have a good supply of eggs, sausages and bacon! A three-acre field is available for rallies or events and ball games and a secure compound provides caravan storage for up to 40 units. The market town of Tavistock on the edge of Dartmoor is just three miles away. There may be some road noise from the A390 during the day.

**Facilities**

Small, fully equipped toilet block. Washing machine and dryers. Dishwashing sink under cover. Small freezer for ice blocks. Wash bay to clean down bikes or wet suits etc. Eggs, bacon and sausages for sale. Caravan storage. Camping pods to rent. Off site: Nearby activities include canoeing on Tamar river, tree surfing, mountain biking, or walking on Dartmoor. Bicycle hire and golf 2 miles. Fishing 3 miles. Boat launching 4 miles. Horse riding 5 miles.

Open: All year.

**Directions**

From Tavistock follow A390 for Liskeard. After 3 miles turn left at Gulworthy roundabout signed Bere Alston. Site on left past school and church hall. GPS: 50.532675, -4.190927

**Charges guide**

| | |
|---|---|
| Per unit incl. 2 persons and electricity | £ 12.00 - £ 16.00 |
| extra person (over 5 yrs) | £ 4.00 - £ 5.00 |
| dog | £ 1.00 |

## Old Rectory
### Caravan and Camping Park

This small family run park is nestled in a quiet, idyllic setting on the border of Devon and Cornwall. Close to Dartmoor National Park.

www.tamarvalleycamping.co.uk • info@tamarvalleycamping.co.uk • tel. +44 (0)1822 832 927

## Teignmouth
### Coast View Holiday Park

Torquay Road, Shaldon, Teignmouth TQ14 0BG (Devon) T: 01626 872392. E: info@coastview.co.uk
alanrogers.com/UK1080

On the coast road between Teignmouth and Torquay with magnificent views over Lyme Bay, this family run park has a section of caravan holiday homes and chalets, with the touring area higher on the hillside. There are 18 pitches with hardstanding and 16A electricity, and a number with water in a further area. A level area is kept for motorcaravans. Over 100 pitches for tents are on part sloping, part terraced grass on the hillside with adequate protection from the prevailing southwest winds and marvellous views. To the right of the park entrance is an attractive indoor swimming pool, and an entertainment area comprising a clubroom with a bar. Bar meals, snacks and takeaway food are served here. Entertainment is organised each evening, as are activities in the mornings for children. All these facilities are open all season. The park is conveniently located for the beach (1.5 miles) and the coastal footpath is adjacent. Torbay is five miles away. A bus service stops at the gates. Good for holidaymakers of all ages, this park offers superb views with a range of facilities.

**Facilities**

The modern toilet block is spacious with free hot showers and open washbasins, and includes a baby room. Laundry facilities. Licensed shop for basic provisions. Indoor pool and children's pool. Clubroom with bar, restaurant, takeaway, games room and TV room. Full entertainment programme and themed weekends. Adventure playground and indoor soft play area. Crazy golf. Off site: Beach 1.5 miles. Fishing and golf 1 mile. Riding 3 miles.

Open: 15 March - 31 October.

**Directions**

From A380 Exeter - Newton Abbot road, take the A381 to Teignmouth. On entering town turn right over Shaldon Bridge on B3199 for Torquay. Park is on right in about 1.5 miles. O.S.GR: SX932714. GPS: 50.53455, -3.503167

**Charges guide**

| | |
|---|---|
| Per unit incl. up to 5 persons and electricity | £ 19.00 - £ 29.00 |
| fully servced hardstanding pitch | £ 26.00 - £ 39.00 |
| dog | £ 2.50 |

For latest campsite news visit
alanrogers.com

## Tiverton

### Minnows Touring Caravan Park

Sampford Peverell, Tiverton EX16 7EN (Devon) T: 01884 821770
alanrogers.com/UK0750

Minnows is an attractive, neat small park with views across the Devon countryside, separated from the Grand Western canal by hedging. Easily accessible from the M5, it is an ideal touring centre for Devon and Somerset, for cycling, walking, fishing or canoeing (own landing stage), or simply for breaking a long journey. A small, neat park, open for eight months of the year, it provides 59 level pitches all with 16A electricity and hardstandings for all weather, four with water and a drain. A further 3.5 acres have been added to the park providing space for larger pitches, a grass tent area, and a play area. The village of Sampford Peverell, with pub and farm shop, is only a half mile walk via the towpath, with Tiverton 7.5miles. There are 12 miles of level walking on the towpath or one can take a trip on a horse-drawn barge. The site is also on the Sustran cycle route (route 3). Tiverton Parkway railway station is less than one mile, and buses run from the village to Tiverton. Coarse fishing permits for the canal are available from reception. A Caravan Club affiliated site, non-members are also very welcome. There could be some road noise from the adjacent A361.

#### Facilities

A fully equipped and well maintained, heated toilet block with pressurised showers. Facilities for disabled visitors and babies. Laundry with washing machine, dryer and ironing. Motorcaravan service point. Gas supplies. Shop. Newspaper delivery arranged. Play area. Bicycle hire (delivery to site). American RVs accepted (up to 36 ft), advance booking necessary. All year caravan storage. Site gates closed 21.00 and locked 23.00-07.30. Off site: Boat slipway, golf driving range and 9-hole course 400 yds, full course 4 miles. Riding 6 miles.

Open: 7 March - end October.

#### Directions

From M5 junction 27 take A361 signed Tiverton. After 600 yds take first exit signed Sampford Peverell. After 100 yds. turn right at roundabout and cross bridge over A361 to second roundabout. Go straight ahead and park is immediately ahead. From North Devon on A361 go to M5 junction 27 and return back up the A361 as above.
O.S.GR: ST042148. GPS: 50.925017, -3.364517

#### Charges guide

| Per unit incl. 2 persons | |
|---|---|
| (non member) | £ 12.70 - £ 18.40 |
| child | £ 1.30 - £ 2.50 |

Credit cards accepted for £10 or more.

## Woolacombe

### Golden Coast Holiday Park

Station Road, Woolacombe EX34 7HW (Devon) T: 01271 870343. E: goodtimes@woolacombe.com
alanrogers.com/UK1075

The Golden Coast Holiday Park is part of the Woolacombe Bay Holiday Parks group that includes Woolacombe Bay, Twitchen Park and Easewell Farm. Golden Coast's main interest is a range of brick-built bungalows, lodges and apartments, plus a variety of caravan holiday homes, all of good quality and well equipped. However, two touring areas also provide 101 pitches, all with electricity and about half with all-weather hardstanding. There are indoor and outdoor pools, spa facilities, a cinema and a range of sports facilities for active visitors. Guests at the park can enjoy extensive entertainment and nightly cabaret and a programme of daily activities is arranged for adults and children. A shuttle bus runs between the four parks and to the beach several times a day (it costs £3 per person per holiday). A visit to the Old Mill Inn should not be missed; it serves bar meals, and has an excellent beer garden with adventure play area for the children. The range of amenities and facilities at this large park will suit families looking for a lively holiday filled with activities and entertainment.

#### Facilities

The toilet block is unisex with recently upgraded facilities and was clean at the time of our visit. Washing machine and dryer. Large, well stocked supermarket, boutique and beauty salon. Indoor and outdoor swimming pools, outdoor flume, sauna and solarium. Bar, club, Old Mill Inn, restaurant and takeaway. Floodlit tennis court. Adventure playgrounds. Snooker. Games room. Soft play area. Ceramics studio. Learn to swim classes. 9-hole golf course. Indoor and outdoor bowls, 10-pin bowling. Nightly entertainment and cabaret. Activities and clubs for children. Fishing. Woodland walks. WiFi. Dogs are not accepted. Off site: Woolacombe beach is about 2 miles. For walkers there is the coastal path. Amenities at sister parks available to all visitors, with shuttle bus. Golf, riding and bicycle hire 0.5 miles.

Open: 12 February - 26 November.

#### Directions

From Barnstaple, take A361 (signed Braunton and Ilfracombe). Turn left on B3343 (signed Woolacombe) and follow the road towards the town. The park is on the left near the top of the hill. O.S.GR: SS480435. GPS: 51.1725, -4.172767

#### Charges guide

| Per caravan or motorcaravan | |
|---|---|
| incl. services | £ 15.75 - £ 57.75 |
| | £ 20.00 - £ 60.00 |
| tent, per person | £ 5.25 - £ 19.00 |
| tent, per child (5-15 yrs) | £ 2.60 - £ 9.50 |

See advertisement on page 79.

## Woolacombe

### Woolacombe Bay Holiday Park

Sandy Lane, Woolacombe EX34 7AH (Devon) T: 01271 870343. E: goodtimes@woolacombe.com

alanrogers.com/UK1070

Woolacombe Bay Holiday Park, and its sister site Golden Coast Holiday Park nearby, are well known sites providing a range of holiday accommodation from caravan holiday homes to luxury lodges, apartments and villas, with many on-site amenities including pools, restaurants and bars, and providing a wide range of entertainment. A camping section at the Woolacombe Bay park caters for tents and trailer tents only, so touring visitors can enjoy all the activities and entertainment of both parks. Partly terraced out of the hillside and partly on the hill top with some existing pine trees but with many more trees planted for landscaping, the site has magnificent views out across the bay. Marked and numbered pitches have been provided on grass for 150 tents, 97 with electricity (10/16A). All should be level, having been terraced where necessary and they are connected by gravel roads. Some up-and-down walking is needed for the toilet block. A bus service (small charge) runs between the two parks, the third and fourth parks in the group (Twitchen Park and Easewell Farm) and the beach during the main season, although there is a footpath to the beach from the site. The three larger parks have varied entertainment programmes and children's clubs and Woolacombe Bay also boasts a health spa and beauty suite.

### Facilities

A smart central toilet block has excellent facilities, including en-suite shower and washrooms and separate toilets, baby facilities, and also a sauna and steam room. Laundry rooms. Two units for disabled visitors. Bars, restaurant and entertainment. Supermarket. Indoor (heated) and outdoor pools with flumes and slides. Sauna and gym. Beauty and holistic treatments. Wide range of sporting activities. Tennis. ATM. Dogs are welcome at Woolacombe Bay but not at Golden Coast. New caravan holiday homes (2009). Off site: Fishing and riding 1 mile. Beach 1 mile.

Open: 11 May - end September.

### Directions

Take A361 Barnstaple - Ilfracombe road through Braunton. Turn left at Mullacott Cross roundabout towards Woolacombe then right towards Mortehoe. Now follow the camping signs by turning left and park is on the left. O.S.GR: SS469443. GPS: 51.177117, -4.191317

### Charges guide

| | |
|---|---|
| Per person (tents only) | £ 5.25 - £ 19.00 |
| child (5-15 yrs) | £ 2.60 - £ 9.50 |
| dog (camping only) | £ 1.50 - free |

## Woolacombe

### Twitchen Park

Mortehoe, Woolacombe EX34 7ES (Devon) T: 01271 870848. E: goodtimes@woolacombe.com

alanrogers.com/UK0730

Set in the grounds of an attractive Edwardian country house, Twitchen Park is owned by Woolacombe Bay Holiday Parks. Its main concern lies in holiday caravans and apartments, although it also provides marked pitches, all for touring units, at the top of the park, with some views over the rolling hills to the sea. With a more recently developed touring field, they include 228 pitches with 16A electricity, many with tarmac hardstanding (not always level), mostly arranged around oval access roads in hedged areas. Further non-electric pitches are behind in two open, unmarked fields which are sloping (blocks are provided, stored in neat wooden boxes next to water points). A smart, modern entertainment complex incorporates a licensed club and family lounge with snacks, a restaurant, teenage disco room, cartoon lounge, outdoor pool and smart indoor pool complex. Twitchen is very popular for families with children. If they become bored, there are always the excellent beaches nearby with a footpath down to the sea. All the facilities of Golden Coast and Woolacombe Bay Holiday Parks and Easewell Farm are free to visitors at Twitchen, with a bus (small charge) running regularly between the four parks and to the beach.

### Facilities

There are two toilet blocks, one of which is new and provides family bathrooms and saunas. Dishwashing and laundry facilities at each block plus a good modern launderette at the central complex. Motorcaravan service point. Shop and takeaway. Club, bars, restaurant and entertainment for adults and children, day and evening. Outdoor pool (heated mid May-mid Sept). Attractive indoor pool with sauna, paddling pool, fountain and a viewing area. Putting green. Games rooms. Good adventure play area. ATM. American motorhomes are accepted (up to 30 ft). Off site: Beach 1 mile. Golf 1 mile. Fishing, riding and bicycle hire 2 miles.

Open: Easter- end October.

### Directions

From Barnstaple take A361 towards Ilfracombe and through Braunton. Turn left at Mullacott Cross roundabout towards Woolacombe and then right towards Mortehoe. Park is on the left before village. O.S.GR: SS465451. GPS: 51.184683, -4.1977

### Charges guide

| | |
|---|---|
| Per caravan or motorcaravan | £ 15.75 - £ 57.75 |
| incl. services | £ 20.00 - £ 60.00 |
| tent (per person) | £ 5.25 - £ 19.00 |
| tent - child (5-15 yrs) | £ 2.60 - £ 9.50 |
| dog | £ 1.50 |

Special offers available.

For latest campsite news visit
## alanrogers.com

# Love Holidays?
# Love Woolacombe Bay

## ooking for a getaway you'll fall in love with?

ur award winning Holiday Parks set in Devon's breathtaking countryside
ext to Woolacombe's 3 miles of golden Blue Flag sandy beach. Sea view
amping, Touring & Supersite Pitches plus Luxury Lodges & Holiday Homes.

**OOLAC●MBE BAY**
HOLIDAY PARKS · NORTH DEVON

ll **0844 770 0363** or book online 24/7 **www.woolacombe.com/ar**

# Woolacombe
## Easewell Farm Holiday Park

Mortehoe, Woolacombe EX34 7EH (Devon) T: 01271 870343. E: goodtimes@woolacombe.com

alanrogers.com/UK0720

Near the sandy beaches of Woolacombe, Easewell Farm is now part of the Woolacombe Bay Holiday Park group who own the Woolacombe Bay, Golden Coast and Twitchen parks. A shuttle bus runs between the four parks and to the beach (tickets £3 per person per holiday). This is a traditional style touring park which during the day is a hive of activity, but the nights are quiet and peaceful. The largest of the camping fields is sloping with superb views across the headland to the sea. Two smaller fields are terraced and one area has upgraded hardstandings with new landscaping. Together they provide 330 pitches, 207 with electricity (16A) and 20 also with TV and water connections. Pea-shingle all-weather hardstandings have been added. Also available are a lovely four bedroom farmhouse (sleeping ten), a pretty two bedroom cottage (five beds) and a caravan holiday home. The shop is well stocked (gas available), there is a takeaway and restaurant and an attractive bar with patio overlooking a small duck pond. The park has its own very well maintained nine-hole golf course which is popular and has reduced fees for campers. One of the huge redundant farm buildings has been put to excellent use: divided into three areas, it provides table tennis and pool, a skittle alley and two lanes of flat green bowling with changing rooms. Walks to the local village and along the coastal path are easy from the site and a bus to Ilfracombe and Barnstaple stops 100 yards from the entrance.

### Facilities

The central toilet block has been regularly upgraded and can be heated. Two washbasins in the ladies have hoses for hair washing, controllable showers (no dividers). Small area with baby bath facilities. Laundry. These facilities are arranged around the farmhouse area and include a very well equipped unit for disabled visitors with everything in one large room including a hairdryer. Motorcaravan service point. Shop. Bar. Restaurant and takeaway. Golf. Small heated indoor swimming pool is well used, as are games and TV rooms. Fenced play area with bark base. Indoor skittle alley. Max. 1 dog, not accepted in high season. Off site: Fishing or riding 1 mile. Bicycle hire 3 miles. Tarka Trail for walking and riding. Boat trips to Lundy Island.

Open: End March - end October.

### Directions

From Barnstaple, take A361 Ilfracombe road through Braunton. Turn left at Mullacott Cross roundabout on B3343 to Woolacombe, turning right after 2-3 miles to Mortehoe. Park is on right before village. O.S.GR: SS465455. GPS: 51.1853, -4.198933

### Charges guide

| | |
|---|---|
| Per caravan or motorcaravan | £ 15.00 - £ 55.00 |
| incl. services | £ 19.00 - £ 57.50 |
| tent (per person) | £ 5.00 - £ 18.30 |
| tent - child (5-15 yrs) | £ 2.50 - £ 9.15 |
| dog | £ 1.50 |

See advertisement on page 79.

# Woolacombe
## Woolacombe Sands Holiday Park

Beach Road, Woolacombe EX34 7AF (Devon) T: 01271 870569. E: lifesabeach@woolacombe-sands.co.uk

alanrogers.com/UK0735

With sea views and within walking distance of Woolacombe's lovely sandy beach, this family park has been terraced out of the valley side as you drop down into the village. Apart from its smart entrance, it has been left natural. The pond and stream at the bottom are almost hidden with gated access to the National Trust fields across the valley. The 200 terraced level grass pitches, all with 16A electricity, are accessed by gravel roads with some good up-and-down walking needed to the toilet blocks (may be difficult for visitors with disabilities). Some 50 mobile homes and 14 bungalows are in the more central area, and tents tend to be placed on the bottom terraces. The park boasts both indoor and outdoor pools (accessed by code) with a full-time attendant. Above the indoor pool is a very pleasant conservatory seating area with great views, and an outside seating area adjacent. Evenings see Woolly Bear emerge from his 'shack' to entertain the children, with adult family entertainment later. A plus factor is the fact that all facilities open when the site opens. A path leads from the site to the beach via the car park and the walk is said to take 15 minutes.

### Facilities

Four basic toilet blocks with good hot water are spread amongst the terraces. The newer shower block has separate toilets opposite. Shop. Self-service food bar providing good value meals and breakfast (main season and B.Hs). Two bars and full entertainment programme. Heated indoor and outdoor pools both with paddling pool areas. Fenced play area on bark with plenty of equipment. Ball area with nets. Crazy golf. 'Kingpin' bowling. Off site: Beach 15 minutes walk or 0.5 miles. Riding next door. Golf, bicycle hire and freshwater fishing 0.5 miles.

Open: 1 April - 30 October.

### Directions

Follow A361 from Barnstaple through Braunton towards Ilfracombe. At Mullacott Cross roundabout turn left for Woolacombe (B3343). Site clearly signed on left as you go down the hill into the village. O.S.GR: SS468436. GPS: 51.17145, -4.191833

### Charges guide

| | |
|---|---|
| Per person (incl. electricity) | £ 5.00 - £ 15.00 |
| child (4-15 yrs) | £ 2.50 - £ 7.50 |
| dog | £ 5.0 |

For latest campsite news visit
## alanrogers.com

For latest campsite news visit
alanrogers.com

# Bath

## Newton Mill Camping Park

Newton Road, Bath BA2 9JF (Somerset) T: 01225 333909. E: enquiries@newtonmillpark.co.uk

alanrogers.com/UK1460

In a peaceful valley, two miles from the centre of the historic city of Bath and with direct access to the local cycle track network, Newton Mill is an excellent base from which to explore the city and the area. The site accepts 105 tents and also has 90 caravan pitches (with 30 long stay) which are located at the other end of the valley. All of these have hardstandings, 16A electricity and satellite TV hook-ups. This end of the park is closest to the main Bristol - London railway line, not visually obtrusive but occasional rail noise may be noticeable. The site has been created around an old mill, the bar and restaurant now occupying part of the original building, and there is a modern timber chalet style reception building with a small, well stocked shop. The restaurant (open evenings all year) serves good value, speciality meals. Breakfasts are available (weekends Easter-October, daily in summer). The tent meadow is in an elevated position, or alternatively you may prefer the paddock, a small field alongside the stream, in a car-free zone with a separate parking area.

### Facilities

Two new heated toilet blocks provide excellent modern facilities with some washbasins in cubicles, free hot showers, bathrooms (on payment), baby rooms and a good suite for disabled campers. Launderette. Basic motorcaravan service point. Shop, bar, restaurant with garden seating area. Play area. Boules court. Fishing. Off site: Bus service into Bath runs every ten minutes from Twerton village which is a ten-minute walk. Nearby Bristol and Bath Railway Path (a traffic-free cycle way) links to the West Bath Riverside Path, and Kennet and Avon towpath.

Open: All year.

### Directions

Site is 2 miles west of Bath city centre, about 1 mile southeast of the roundabout where the A4 meets the A39. From the north take M4 exit 19, turn on to M32 and almost immediately take A4174 (Avon ring road) for 7.5 miles to the A4. Turn left towards Bath and after 5 miles at second roundabout, take exit signed Newton St Loe. Entrance is on the left after 1 mile. O.S.GR: ST713647. GPS: 51.378133, -2.410817

### Charges guide

| | |
|---|---|
| Per unit incl. 2 persons and electricity | £ 22.00 - £ 28.00 |

# Bishop Sutton

## Bath Chew Valley Caravan Park

Ham Lane, Bishop Sutton BS39 5TZ (Somerset) T: 01275 332127. E: enquiries@bathchewvalley.co.uk

alanrogers.com/UK1510

A small, secluded garden site for adults only, Chew Valley has been developed with much tender love and care by the Betton family and is now affiliated to the Caravan Club. Caravans are sited on neat lawns amongst colourful beds of flowers and cars are tucked away on the nearby car park, providing a tranquil and restful atmosphere. An area of woodland is adjacent with an enclosed dog walking area called Puppies' Parade. There are neat hardstandings for all pitches and 27 spacious, fully serviced pitches, all with 16A electricity. This park will particularly appeal to garden and nature lovers. Next to reception there is a good library with tourist information. A member of the Best of British group.

### Facilities

The heated toilet block provides separate en-suite units, each with WC, basin and shower. One unit has facilities for disabled visitors. Utility room with sinks, spin dryer and ironing facilities; washing machine and tumble dryer for service washes only. Freezer. Motorcaravan service point. Internet access and WiFi. Max. 2 dogs. Off site: Village 100 yds. Supermarkets 15 minutes drive. Fishing 1 mile. Golf 5 miles. Riding 8 miles. Beach 15 miles.

Open: All year.

### Directions

From Bath on A368 turn right opposite Red Lion pub in Bishop Sutton. Continue past small track to the left (50 yds) for a further 50 yds. Park entrance is on the left with neat, clear entrance. O.S.GR: ST584599. GPS: 51.336583, -2.597183

### Charges guide

| | |
|---|---|
| Per unit incl. 2 persons and electricity | £ 22.00 - £ 26.00 |

## Bridgwater

### Mill Farm Caravan & Camping Park

Fiddington, Bridgwater TA5 1JQ (Somerset) T: 01278 732286

alanrogers.com/UK1306

On the edge of the village of Fiddington, in a countryside location at the foot of the Quantock Hills, Mill Farm is just seven miles from Bridgwater and four miles from the sea. This is an extensive and popular family holiday site with three main fields, each taking 50-60 units with a toilet block, a playground and a plentiful supply of water points. Extra fields are opened for the peak season allowing a total capacity of around 275 units, all with electricity connections (10A). The site has a large swimming pool complex with indoor and outdoor pools, free to campers. There is a licensed riding school, rowing boats on the little lake and organised daytime activities in high season, including treasure hunts, relay races and games tournaments. A well stocked mini-market provides all the usual items. American motorhomes are accepted, motorcyclists are at the management's discretion. Mill Farm is a good family holiday base, very much child orientated with a wide range of activities to keep them happy.

**Facilities**

Three toilet blocks include facilities for disabled visitors (Radar key), one washbasin in cubicle for each sex, bathrooms (on payment) and baby rooms. The blocks come under pressure in peak seasons when a fourth is opened. Launderette. Shop (all year). Large club room with bar, takeaway (weekends and peak seasons), games room and family entertainment (high season). Heated indoor pool with whirlpool and paddling pool (Easter - 10/11) and two outdoor pools with giant waterslide (15/5-15/9). Both pools unsupervised, but monitored by CCTV. Pony riding, canoe hire, and trampolining (charge). Off site: Golf 3 miles. Beach 4 miles. Fishing 4 miles.

Open: All year.

**Directions**

From M5 exit 23 or 24, turn west and pass through Bridgwater and continue on the A39. After 6 miles turn right towards Fiddington. Continue through narrow lane with passing places for 1 mile to site entrance. Park where instructed on the long entry driveway, and report to reception.
O.S.GR: ST217407. GPS: 51.16, -3.120517

**Charges guide**

| | |
|---|---|
| Per unit incl. 2 persons and electricity | £ 16.00 - £ 23.00 |
| extra person | £ 2.00 - £ 4.00 |
| child (2-14 yrs) | £ 1.00 - £ 3.00 |
| dog | £ 1.00 - £ 2.00 |

## Bridport

### Bingham Grange Touring & Camping Park

Melplash, Bridport DT6 3TT (Dorset) T: 01308 488234. E: enquiries@binghamgrange.co.uk

alanrogers.com/UK1770

Bingham Grange is an attractive, purpose built park for adults only. In a pleasant, rural situation two miles from the market town of Bridport, there are views seaward towards West Bay and inland across Beaminster Downs and Pilsdon Hill. The park provides an area of individual pitches with 10A electricity and over 75 hardstandings, nicely landscaped with shrubs and trees growing between the pitches, plus an open sloping field overlooking the valley with 26 serviced pitches and space for tents. A path is provided to the river which links with the main footpaths for Bridport (20 minutes).

**Facilities**

Well equipped toilet block, with underfloor heating with a separate, fully equipped room for the less able with ramped access and 5 luxury shower units (also with washbasin and 4 with WC). Laundry room with microwave and freezer. Reception keeps simple supplies. Restaurant serving home cooked food seems to be very popular. Gas available. Only adults (over 18 yrs) are accepted. Off site: Sea fishing and golf 3 miles.

Open: March - end October.

**Directions**

At the roundabouts on the A35 road, on east side of Bridport, follow signs for Beaminster on A3066. After about 2 miles watch for site entrance on the left.
O.S.GR: SY482963. GPS: 50.765076, -2.740911

**Charges guide**

| | |
|---|---|
| Per unit incl. 2 persons and electricity (10A) | £ 15.00 - £ 23.00 |
| extra person | £ 5.00 |

For latest campsite news visit

# alanrogers.com

## Bridport

### Highlands End Holiday Park

West Dorset Leisure Holidays, Eype, Bridport DT6 6AR (Dorset) T: 01308 422139. E: holidays@wdlh.co.uk
alanrogers.com/UK1750

On slightly sloping ground with superb open views, both coastal and inland, Highlands End is quietly situated on the Dorset Heritage Coastline. A path in front of the park runs along the cliff top and then leads down to a shingle beach a little further along. It is a good quality park with 180 caravan holiday homes, mostly privately owned, and 195 touring pitches in two areas nearest to the sea – one has to travel through the holiday homes to reach them. The field for tents has 73 pitches, ten with electricity and the field for touring is all electric with 45 pitches also having water, drainage and hardstanding. A further area is used for tents in high season. A modern, attractive building houses a lounge bar, excellent good value restaurant with takeaway facility, family room and games room with some musical evenings in high season. The park's amenities also include an excellent, air-conditioned indoor heated pool, a tennis court and a nine-hole pitch and putt (all charged). The park is run to high standards and is a member of the Best of British group.

#### Facilities

Two good quality toilet blocks near the touring sections are well maintained and can be heated. Some washbasins in cubicles with toilets, large, roomy showers. Covered dishwashing sinks and a dishwashing room. En-suite facilities for disabled visitors. Baby care room. Laundry room. Motorcaravan service point. Well stocked shop (opening times vary), including gas supplies. Bar and restaurant/takeaway (evenings and Sunday lunch). Tennis (charged). Indoor pool (20 x 9 m), gym, sauna/steam room. Games room. 9-hole pitch and putt. Excellent adventure play area. All facilities open all season. Internet access (charged). Off site: Beach 0.5 miles. Bicycle hire and golf 2 miles. Fishing 3 miles.

Open: 20 March - 8 November.

#### Directions

Follow Bridport bypass on A35 around the town and park is signed to south (Eype turning), down narrow lane. There is a new exit road. O.S.GR: SY452914. GPS: 50.725333, -2.777

#### Charges guide

| | |
|---|---|
| Per unit incl. 2 persons and electricity | £ 14.50 - £ 24.00 |
| all services and hardstanding | £ 16.25 - £ 26.25 |
| extra person | £ 4.00 - £ 5.00 |
| child (4-17 yrs) | £ 3.00 |
| dog (max. 2) | £ 3.00 |

**Highlands End and Golden Cap** Holiday Parks
Tel: 01308 422139 Email: holidays@wdlh.co.uk
Eype, Bridport, Dorset DT6 6AR
www.wdlh.co.uk
A World Heritage Coastline on your doorstep
WEST DORSET LEISURE HOLIDAYS

## Bridport

### Golden Cap Holiday Park

Seatown, Chideock, Bridport DT6 6JX (Dorset) T: 01308 422139. E: holidays@wdlh.co.uk
alanrogers.com/UK1740

Golden Cap, named after the adjacent high cliff (the highest in southern England) which overlooks Lyme Bay, is only 150 m. from a shingle beach at Seatown and is surrounded by National Trust countryside and the Heritage Coastline. The park is arranged over several fields on the valley floor, sloping gently down towards the sea. It is in two main areas, having once been two parks, each separated into fields with marvellous views and providing 108 touring pitches. All have electricity and 30 also have hardstanding with drainage and gravel awning area. An extra sloping tent area is used for peak season (torch useful), although it is a five minute walk from here to the toilet blocks and shop. There are 219 caravan holiday homes in their own areas. A small but attractive lake is used for coarse fishing and the heated indoor pool and gym at Highlands End (under the same ownership, three miles away) is open for campers at Golden Cap on payment. Beaches are nearby; sea fishing, boat launching, riding or fossil hunting are possible in the area, plus good walks including access to the coastal path.

#### Facilities

The modern toilet block is of good quality with spacious shower cubicles (some with toilet and washbasin). Facilities for disabled visitors. Baby room. Two other smaller blocks around the park. Laundry room. Motorcaravan service point. Useful and well stocked shop. Gas supplies. Small play area. American motorhomes are not accepted. WiFi throughout (charged). Off site: Bus stop in village 10 minutes walk. Pub nearby. Beach 150 yds. Golf 2 miles. Bicycle hire, boat launching 3 miles.

Open: 20 March - 8 November.

#### Directions

Turn off A35 road at Chideock, 3 miles west of Bridport, at sign to Seatown opposite church. Park is less than 1 mile down narrow lane. O.S.GR: SY423919. GPS: 50.715333, -2.821667

#### Charges guide

| | |
|---|---|
| Per unit incl. 2 persons and electricity | £ 14.50 - £ 24.00 |
| extra person | £ 3.00 - £ 5.00 |
| all service pitch | £ 16.75 - £ 26.50 |
| pitch with sea view | £ 21.00 - £ 31.00 |

For latest campsite news visit
alanrogers.com

## Bridport

### Freshwater Beach Holiday Park

Burton Bradstock, Bridport DT6 4PT (Dorset) T: 01308 897317. E: office@freshwaterbeach.co.uk
**alanrogers.com/UK1780**

Parks run by and for families, with direct access to their own private beach are rare in Britain and this one has the added advantage of being in beautiful coastal countryside in West Dorset. The site is next to the sea and a beach of fine pebbles, sheltered from the wind by pebble banks and has been run by the same family for the last 40 years. The River Bride edges the park and joins the sea here. Approached by a fairly steep access road, the park itself is on level, open ground. The 500 plus touring pitches, 400 with 10A electricity, are on an open, undulating grass field connected by tarmac or hardcore roads. Caravan pitches (10 x 11 m) are marked and evenly spaced in lines. Some tent pitches are in the main field, with others well spaced on a terraced field. In separate areas there are 260 caravan holiday homes, with 60 for hire. This lively holiday park has an extensive range of facilities which include an outdoor pool, a good value licensed restaurant, a main bar and two further small bars with an evening entertainment programme in season. Daytime entertainment caters for all ages – don't miss the donkey derby! Footpaths lead to the thatched village of Burton Bradstock or West Bay. The overall impression is of a large, busy holiday park with a friendly reception and happy atmosphere. Units over 23' long can have extra space at no extra cost during non-peak periods. Subject to planning permission a brand new leisure complex is planned with indoor pools, bowling alley and roof top bar.

### Facilities

Two fully equipped toilet blocks serve the caravan fields plus a newer block in the tent field. Facilities for disabled visitors (Radar key), and a baby care room (key system). Laundry and dishwashing sinks. Launderette. Bars with entertainment and evening shows. Licensed restaurant (weekends only in late season; closed Mon. all season). Three bars. Supermarket and takeaway. Heated and supervised outdoor swimming and paddling pools (25/5-25/9) with lessons. Games room, music, TV, amusements and soft drinks bar. Activities for children. Two play areas. High season pony trekking (stables on site). Internet café and WiFi (charged). Off site: Bus stop on main road. Golf course 0.5 miles. Abbotsbury 8 miles.

Open: 17 March - 12 November.

### Directions

Park is immediately west of the village of Burton Bradstock, on the Weymouth - Bridport coast road (B3157). O.S.GR: SY980898.
GPS: 50.70500, -2.73867

### Charges guide

| | |
|---|---|
| Per unit incl. up to 6 persons, car and awning | £ 14.00 - £ 37.00 |
| extra person, car or boat | £ 2.00 |
| electricity | £ 2.00 |
| small tent incl. 2 persons walking or cycling | £ 5.00 - £ 17.00 |
| dog | £ 2.50 |

Single sex groups not admitted.

For latest campsite news visit
**alanrogers.com**

## Bristol

### Baltic Wharf Caravan Club Site

Cumberland Road, Bristol BS1 6XG (Somerset) T: 01179 268030

alanrogers.com/UK1440

This excellent Caravan Club site in Bristol's redeveloped dockland, is well laid out and maintained to a high standard. It is screened from the road by a high wall with a boatyard on one side and residential apartments on the other, with access via a lockable gate to the Baltic Wharf dockside. The view across the dock towards Clifton village and Bristol is unique and you can even glimpse the suspension bridge. Accessed by a circular tarmac road, the 55 pitches are on stone chippings and are ideal for all year round use (steel pegs are sold at reception). All have electricity (16A) and TV aerial points (reception is poor). Awnings are prohibited on 16 pitches to meet fire regulations. It is a 30 minute walk to the city centre, a daily ferry runs throughout the year or there's a regular bus service. This is a popular site in a popular location so advance booking is essential. Arrive between 12.00 and 20.00.

#### Facilities

The toilet block provides good clean facilities including controllable showers and washbasins in cubicles (heated in winter). Good facilities for disabled visitors, plus toilets and showers for the walking disabled in the main block. Fully equipped laundry room. Motorcaravan service point. Dogs are welcome but there is no dog walk. Wardens live on the site. No units over 28 ft. Off site: Fishing and boating (permits from Harbour Master's office) 400 yards.

Open: All year.

#### Directions

From M5, J18, take A4 (signed Bristol West). Follow signs for Historic Harbour and SS Great Britain under Clifton Suspension Bridge and through Hotwells (about 5.5 miles). Cross Dock bridge and site is 500 yds. on left. O.S.GR: ST574721. GPS: 51.446533, -2.61425

#### Charges guide

| | |
|---|---|
| Per person | £ 5.10 - £ 6.90 |
| child (5-16 yrs) | £ 1.50 - £ 3.00 |
| pitch (non-member) | £ 12.15 - £ 15.50 |

## Burnham-on-Sea

### Holiday Resort Unity

328

Coast Road, Brean Sands, Burnham-on-Sea TA8 2RB (Somerset) T: 01278 751235. E: admin@hru.co.uk

alanrogers.com/UK1575

Holiday Resort Unity offers something for everyone, from young children to the young at heart. Apart from the extensive on-site amusements and entertainment programme, campers can also use the swimming pools, funfair and other leisure pursuits at the adjoining Brean Leisure Centre (owned by the same family), some free of charge and others by paying a small fee. Three large touring fields provide pitches that are flat and open, mostly grass but some on concrete hardstandings (for RVs and motorcaravans up to 30 ft, contact site). Most pitches have 16A electricity hook-ups. A separate warden looks after each camping field. New ready-erected 'Euro tents' and a substantial number of caravan holiday homes are available for rent. Access to the five-mile stretch of sandy beach is via a footpath opposite the site entrance. Fishing (with a licence) is permitted from Unity Lake in the Yellow Field. RJ's is a club with bars, food and nightly entertainment for the whole family. There is plenty of choice for either a sit-down meal (including the Sunday roast) or a takeaway.

#### Facilities

Three good toilet blocks include en-suite bathrooms. Some toilets and washbasins are adapted for visitors with disabilities (radar key). Well equipped laundries. Motorcaravan service point. Recycling station. Well stocked shop. Gas exchange. RJ's Club, Sarah's Pantry, Alan's fish and chip bar and Treaure Brean Chinese takeaway. Large adventure play area. Buster's Work Out Gym, Sally's sun beds. Monday market. All facilities open in high season, most open mid season and at weekends in low season. Torches advisable at night. Max. 2 dogs. Bus and land-train services vary according to season. Off site: Beach 100 m. Walking access from park to Brean Leisure Centre. Riding, cycling, cinema, walks, golf all within walking distance from park.

Open: 10 February - 20 November.

#### Directions

From M5 exit 22, follow signs for Burnham-on-Sea (B3140), Berrow and Brean. Holiday Resort Unity is on right along the main street of Brean – it is well signed. Take care as road through Berrow and Brean is rather narrow. O.S.GR: ST290539. GPS: 51.280483, -3.012217

#### Charges guide

| | |
|---|---|
| Per unit incl. 4 persons and electricity | £ 10.00 - £ 36.00 |
| extra person | £ 3.50 |
| dog | £ 3.00 |

# Burnham-on-Sea

## Northam Farm Touring Caravan Park

Brean Sands, Burnham-on-Sea TA8 2SE (Somerset) T: 01278 751244. E: enquiries@northamfarm.co.uk
alanrogers.com/UK1570

Brean has been a popular holiday destination for decades and many large campsites have evolved. Northam Farm, owned by the Scott family, is one of them. It is a large family park with good facilities and an ongoing programme of improvements. Of the 750 pitches, 300 are for seasonal units and these are separated from the four touring fields. Pitches are well established and many have block paved hardstanding. There are two play areas for youngsters, a playing field, bicycle track and football pitch for teenagers, and fishing on the lake for adults. The owners and staff are always available to help visitors enjoy their stay. A monthly newsletter is published giving details of what's on both on and off site. About 500 yards down the road is The Seagull, which is also owned by Northam Farm. Here you will find an excellent restaurant, bar and nightly live entertainment, even during the low season. Just down the road is Brean Leisure Park with its swimming complex, funfair, golf and much more.

### Facilities

Three good toilet blocks, well maintained and within reasonable distance of all pitches, provide ample toilets, washbasins and spacious showers (50p). Bathrooms (£1). Baby room. Rooms for visitors with disabilities (radar key access). Laundry. Motorcaravan service point. Dog shower and two exercise areas. Licensed shop well stocked with food and holiday accessories. Snack bar/takeaway. Free entry to live entertainment at The Seagull. Games room. Two play areas. Playing field. Fishing lake. Caravan workshop for repairs and servicing. Caravan storage. Dogs are not accepted in some of the fields. A bus stops at the park entrance. Off site: Beach 200 m. across road. Burnham-on-Sea 4 miles. Weston-Super-Mare 8 miles. Golf, bicycle hire and riding 0.5 miles.

Open: March - October.

### Directions

From M5 junction 22 follow signs to Burnham-on-Sea, Berrow and then Brean. Continue through Brean and Northam Farm is on the right, half a mile past Brean Leisure Park. O.S.GR: ST297556. GPS: 51.2949, -3.010167

### Charges guide

| | |
|---|---|
| Per unit incl. 2 persons and electricity | £ 7.75 - £ 24.00 |
| extra person | £ 2.00 - £ 2.50 |
| child (0-15 yrs) | £ 1.00 |
| dog, awning, fishing | free |

One of the most sought after touring parks in Somerset

Northam Farm
Brean Sands  Where the sea meets the countryside

Telephone:- 01278 751244 Fax:- 01278 751150
enquiries@northamfarm.co.uk | www.northamfarm.co.uk

# Burnham-on-Sea

## Warren Farm Holiday Centre

Brean Sands, Burnham-on-Sea TA8 2RP (Somerset) T: 01278 751227. E: enquiries@warren-farm.co.uk
alanrogers.com/UK1580

Warren Farm is a popular venue for family campers who want the beach, fun and entertainment. With over 1,000 pitches, the park is divided into several fields, with touring and seasonal pitches kept well apart; Sunnyside, part of Warren Farm, is about 200 yards further down the road and has its own warden. Access roads are wide and all the 565 touring pitches are grassy and level, with 16A electric hook-ups. There are no hardstandings so motorhomes may have difficulties in extremely wet weather. Play equipment is located in a line through the centre of the camping fields which may be a little noisy. Ranch-style wooden fences break up the fields. Couples usually park around the perimeter overlooking fields and views of the Mendip Hills. A fabulous play barn incorporates an indoor play centre, bowling alley, bouncy tractor, ball pit, large-screen television, and electronic games.

### Facilities

Several toilet blocks provide WCs, showers (on payment) and mostly communal washbasins. The larger blocks have hairdressing stations and laundry facilities. All have facilities for babies. Facilities for disabled visitors in all the fields. A warden looks after each block. Motorcaravan service point. Two shops, snack bar and Chinese takeaway at Sunnyside. Fish bar. Beachcomber Inn. Play equipment for toddlers. Play barn with play centre, bowling alley, large-screen TV, and electronic games. Fishing lake. Bicycle hire. No dogs in field six. WiFi. Off site: Golf and riding 1.5 miles. Bus stop outside gate.

Open: April - October.

### Directions

Leave M5 at junction 22 and follow the B3140 to Burnham-on-Sea, then to Berrow and Brean. Continue through Brean and Warren Farm is on the right about 1.5 miles past Brean Leisure Park. O.S.GR: ST297564. GPS: 51.302483, -3.009833

### Charges guide

| | |
|---|---|
| Per unit incl. 2 persons and electricity | £ 9.50 - £ 19.50 |
| extra person | £ 2.00 |
| dog | free |

For latest campsite news visit
**alanrogers.com**

## Burnham-on-Sea

### Home Farm Holiday Park & Country Club

Edithmead, Burnham-on-Sea TA9 4HD (Somerset) T: 01278 788888. E: SITE@hfhp.co.uk

alanrogers.com/UK1480

Home Farm is neatly and attractively laid out covering 44 acres, and is convenient for those using the M5. There are 780 level pitches in total including 180 privately owned holiday homes and a number of seasonal units. These are laid out on level grass, all clearly marked and accessed by tarmac roads. They are divided into various sections, one of which is an area specifically for those with dogs. The 183 pitches with hardstanding include 20 serviced pitches for RVs and motorcaravans. Electrical connections (10A) are available everywhere. A large, modern outdoor pool with paved surrounds and a paddling section is neatly walled and an indoor pool and leisure centre opened in 2009.

**Facilities**

Two main, heated, refurbished toilet blocks. Bathrooms (key with £5 deposit). Baby room. Laundry. Facilities for disabled visitors. Shop (April-end Nov). Club house with TV and entertainment. Restaurants and takeaway (Apr-Oct). Bar (all season). Outdoor pool (May-Sept). New leisure centre with pool, gym, sauna and massage (charged). Play area. Fishing lake. Internet access and WiFi. Off site: Golf 2 miles. Riding 3 miles. Beach 3 miles.

Open: 10 February - 6 January.

**Directions**

Home Farm is 400 yards from M5 exit 22 and the A38. It is signed from the B3140 into Burnham-on-Sea. O.S.GR: ST328493.
GPS: 51.23875, -2.964167

**Charges guide**

| | |
|---|---|
| Per unit incl. 2 persons, electricity and awning | £ 9.25 - £ 28.00 |
| extra person | £ 3.25 - £ 5.50 |
| child (4-17 yrs) | £ 1.75 - £ 4.75 |

---

## Chard

### Alpine Grove Touring Park

Forton, Chard TA20 4HD (Somerset) T: 01460 63479. E: stay@alpinegrovetouringpark.com

alanrogers.com/UK1415

This peaceful and green site is owned by Richard and Helen Gurd who go the extra mile to ensure you enjoy your stay here. The pitches vary in size (90-120 sq.m) and are on flat ground served by gravel roads giving easy access. Some informally marked pitches are tucked away in dense foliage and are very private. Electricity (10A) is supplied to 38 of the 40 touring pitches. All the standard facilities are near reception, including a free fenced and heated swimming pool (10x5 m). A play area is provided for children under the canopy of mature trees. Torches are essential at night.

**Facilities**

A clean, modern sanitary building provides all usual facilities. Family bathroom has facilities for disabled campers. Shop for basics. Heated swimming pool, play area and WiFi (charged). Dog sitting service (charged). Washing machine and dryers. Play area with trampoline (outside). Planned walks and some day activities. Two log cabins for hire. Bicycle hire. Off site: Supermarket and ATM at Chard. Fishing, golf and a wildlife park all 2 miles. Forde Abbey 2.5 miles. Beaches 25 mins. Riding by site.

Open: 14 March - 30 September.

**Directions**

From M5 exit 25 take the A358 signed Cricket St Thomes Wildlife Park and Chard. From Chard take the Forton road where the site is well signed. From the A35, take A358 via Axminster to Chard, and then Forton. Ignore GPS and approach through Chard. O.S.GR: ST342068. GPS: 50.85779, -2.93597

**Charges 2011**

| | |
|---|---|
| Per unit incl. 2 persons and electricity | £ 13.00 - £ 19.50 |
| incl. 6 persons | £ 21.00 - £ 35.50 |

---

## Charmouth

### Monkton Wyld Farm Caravan Park

Monkton Wyld Fm, Scotts La, Charmouth DT6 6DB (Dorset) T: 01297 631131. E: holidays@monktonwyld.co.uk

alanrogers.com/UK1730

Monkton Wyld Farm has pitches for both the independent camper and members of The Camping & Caravanning Club. The park prides itself on its conservation efforts and the space and landscaping provided; each pitch backs onto a hedge or flower bed. There are 130 pitches with 16A electricity and 120 are hardstanding. The family runs the two sites together, with the reception and the shop on the Club side. Both sites have matured into attractive, comfortable, garden-like parks, with trees and flowering shrubs such as hydrangea and lavender creating a colourful, scented backdrop.

**Facilities**

Two well built, heated toilet blocks are fully equipped. Family room with baby changing facilities (can also be accessed by wheelchairs). Laundry area. Gas supplies. Shop (Easter-end Sept). Takeaway (May-Aug). Play areas. Caravan storage. Caravan storage and holiday homes for sale. Off site: Fishing and riding 2 miles. Bicycle hire, golf and boat launching 3 miles. Shops and local pubs within 1 mile. Charmouth and Lyme Regis 3 miles (buses leave from just along the road to both towns).

Open: 13 March - 2 November.

**Directions**

Park is signed on A35 between Charmouth and Axminster, about 2.5 miles west of Charmouth. Turn right at Greenway Head (B3165 signed Marshwood) and park is on the left. Don't go to Monkton Wyld hamlet - the road is very steep. O.S.GR: SY329966. GPS: 50.765333, -2.9525

**Charges guide**

| | |
|---|---|
| Per unit incl. 2 persons | £ 18.50 - £ 30.50 |
| extra person | £ 7.50 - £ 10.00 |

For latest campsite news visit
**alanrogers.com**

## Charmouth
### Wood Farm Caravan Park

Axminster Road, Charmouth DT6 6BT (Dorset) T: 01297 560697. E: holidays@woodfarm.co.uk
alanrogers.com/UK1760

Wood Farm is an excellent, family run park, maintained to high standards and with an indoor swimming pool. On sloping, well landscaped ground, it has splendid rural views across the Marshwood Vale. There are 196 pitches for touring units, all with 10A electricity of which 25 are for tents on a grassy, terraced field. The standard pitches are neat, level all-weather pitches with hardstanding, electricity (10A) and TV connections, and provision for awnings. Some are divided by neat, box-like leylandii hedging, some are terraced. There are 57 'premium' pitches with water, waste water and TV connections. Around 80 caravan holiday homes are in separate areas. Excellent provision is made for disabled visitors, although there is considerable up and down walking due to the terrain. Situated on the western side of Charmouth beside the A35 (some road noise may be expected), the park is only a mile or two from Lyme Regis and its beaches. This area is now part of England's first natural World Heritage site, the Jurassic Coast. Wood Farm is part of the Caravan Club's 'affiliated' scheme (non-members are also very welcome). A member of the Best of British group.

### Facilities

Four modern, well equipped toilet blocks can be heated and include some washbasins in cubicles, en-suite family rooms charged). Excellent facilities for disabled visitors. Baby changing unit. Two laundry rooms. Motorcaravan service point. Shop by reception. Conservatory cafe with sun terrace and viewing area for the swimming pool serving food all day and supper on 2/3 nights per week. Fish and chip van several times weekly. Good heated indoor pool (charged). Recreation hall. Internet access. Bridge club. Outdoor draughts. Outdoor tennis court. Play field. Two coarse fishing ponds (carp, rudd, roach, tench, perch) adjacent – day and weekly tickets (licence required from park). Off site: Golf 1 mile. Riding 4 miles. Beaches and shops 1 and 2 miles.

Open: 1 April - 31 October.

### Directions

Park is 0.5 miles west of Charmouth village with access near the roundabout at the A35 and A3052 (Lyme Regis) junction. O.S.GR: SY356940.
GPS: 50.74216, -2.91588

### Charges guide

| | |
|---|---|
| Per person | £ 4.50 - £ 6.50 |
| child (5-16 yrs) | £ 2.00 - £ 5.00 |
| pitch incl. 10A electricity | £ 6.00 - £ 12.50 |
| 'premium' pitch | £ 11.50 - £ 18.00 |
| pup tent, dog, extra car | £ 2.00 |

Weekly offer in low and mid season.

* Breathtaking countryside views
* Superb indoor swimming pool
* Idyllic fishing ponds
* Tennis court
* 'Offshore' Cafe

TEL: (01297) 560697

WOOD FARM
CHARMOUTH · DORSET

www.woodfarm.co.uk

## Charmouth
### Newlands Caravan Park

Charmouth DT6 6RB (Dorset) T: 01297 560259. E: enq@newlandsholidays.co.uk
alanrogers.com/UK1810

Newlands is well situated on the Jurassic Coast, the first natural World Heritage site in England. A family owned park, it is run with care and enthusiasm, occupying a prominent position beside the road into Charmouth village with rural views southwards to the hills across the valley. The terrain is terraced in two fields to provide over 200 well spaced places for touring units, some for seasonal units and over 80 for caravan holiday homes (some for hire). The mainly sloping tent field also has super views towards the sea and Lyme Regis. Electricity (10A) is provided on 160 pitches and 30 have hardstanding, water and drainage. Other accommodation includes around 80 mobile homes, 36 privately owned, smart pine lodges, apartments and motel rooms. All the facilities are located in a modern building to one side of the wide tarmac entrance. The club bar opens each evening and lunch times to suit, and also serves food.

### Facilities

Two modern, heated toilet blocks provide roomy showers. Covered dishwashing areas and laundry rooms. Baby room. Well stocked shop (Mar-Nov). Licensed club bar (limited hours Nov-Mar). Restaurant (18.00-21.00. Mar-Nov plus Xmas/New Year) including takeaway. Outdoor heated pool (supervised in high season; the entrance is key coded). Indoor pool and jacuzzi (small charge, closed Dec/Jan). Indoor and outdoor play areas. Entertainment. Internet access. Off site: Beach 0.5 miles. Fishing 1 mile.

Open: 5 February - 1 December.

### Directions

Approaching from Bridport leave the A35 at first sign for Charmouth at start of the bypass and site almost directly on your left. O.S.GR: SY373935.
GPS: 50.7385, -2.889833

### Charges guide

| | |
|---|---|
| Per unit incl. up to 6 persons and awning | £ 13.00 - £ 29.00 |
| incl. electricity | £ 16.00 - £ 33.00 |
| fully serviced pitch | £ 19.00 - £ 37.00 |
| dog (max. 2) | £ 1.00 - £ 4.00 |

For latest campsite news visit
**alanrogers.com**

## Cheddar
### Bucklegrove Caravan & Camping Park
Wells Road, Rodney Stoke, Cheddar BS27 3UZ (Somerset) T: 01749 870261. E: info@bucklegrove.co.uk
alanrogers.com/UK1550

Bucklegrove is set right in the heart of Somerset on the southern slopes of the Mendip Hills and close to the tourist attractions of Cheddar Gorge, Wookey Hole, and Wells. The 120 touring pitches, 90 of which have 10A electricity connections, are split between two fields joined by a woodland walk. The top slightly undulating field is more suitable for tents and caravans, while the lower field with some short hardstandings is a little more level and would be suitable for caravans and smaller motorcaravans (under 7 metres). The play area (for under 14s) has a safety surface and includes a multiplay unit, slide and spring riders. Campers also have a games room, a heated indoor swimming pool and separate children's pool. Adjoining the pool is a licensed bar with terrace providing simple bar menus and low-key entertainment mainly during high season or depending on the number of campers on site. A new development includes four privately owned lodges.

#### Facilities
Two toilet blocks house all the usual amenities including some washbasins in cubicles and some spacious showers. The larger, heated block near reception also provides bathrooms (£1) with baby facilities and a room for visitors with disabilities. Laundry rooms. Freezer for ice packs. Well stocked shop. Indoor swimming pool and paddling pool with terrace bar. Games room. Play area. Dogs are accepted in certain fields. WiFi (charged). Off site: Riding 2 miles. Golf 3 miles. Fishing 5 miles. Beach at Weston-Super-Mare 12 miles. Wookey Hole 2 miles, Wells Cathedral 4 miles, Cheddar 7 miles. A bus to Wells and Cheddar stops at the park entrance.

Open: 1 March - 14 December.

#### Directions
Take A371 Wells to Cheddar road. Park is on right about 1 mile past Westbury village. Take care as the road between Wells and Cheddar is rather narrow through some of the villages. O.S.GR: ST490496. GPS: 51.243317, -2.7323

#### Charges guide
| | |
|---|---|
| Per unit incl. 2 persons and electricity | £ 15.00 - £ 27.00 |

#### BUCKLEGROVE CARAVAN, CAMPING & HOLIDAY PARK
Family run holiday park, set amidst the stunning Somerset countryside in the heart of the West Country.
Level secluded pitches with the finest facilities and the best views on the Mendips.
FREE indoor pool, showers, dishwashing and hot water.
Luxury Holiday Homes to let and for private ownership.
Tel: 01749 870261 or email via the website www.bucklegrove.co.uk
Midway between the Cathedral city of Wells and Cheddar Gorge on the A371 at Rodney Stoke, Nr Cheddar. BS27 3UZ

## Cheddar
### Cheddar Bridge Touring Park
Draycott Road, Cheddar BS27 3RJ (Somerset) T: 01934 743048. E: enquires@cheddarbridge.co.uk
alanrogers.com/UK1545

Within easy walking distance of Cheddar village, this is an adult only (over 18 yrs) park. A compact site, there are 50 pitches, mostly on level grass, with 45 electric hook-ups (16A) and 15 gravel hardstandings. A separate area for 20 tents is on the river bank, with its own toilet facilities. Six caravan holiday homes are now also available to rent. Reception keeps basic supplies and gas cylinders. Cream teas are available (that you prepare yourself) and profits go to charity. The site access is over a fairly narrow bridge with low stone walls, passable for double axle caravans, but more difficult for large motorhomes. Cheddar village has a small supermarket with ATM, garage, pubs, restaurants and a leisure centre with an indoor pool. Cheddar Gorge is a little further and would make a good day's hike with a packed lunch, without the problems of parking a vehicle in the Gorge itself where most parking is on payment.

#### Facilities
Attractive heated sanitary block (close to site entrance, some distance from most of the pitches) with washbasins in cubicles, large showers, and family bathroom with shower over the bath. Utility room with dishwashing and laundry sinks, and washer/dryer. Hot water is restricted to 07.00-12.00 and 16.00-21.00. Fishing. Off site: Cheddar Gorge and village. Swimming pool 0.5 miles. Golf 3 miles. Riding 3 miles.

Open: 1 March - end October.

#### Directions
Site entrance is about 100 yards south of village on A371, on right hand side, next to Football Club. O.S.GR: ST461530. GPS: 51.27315, -2.774583

#### Charges guide
| | |
|---|---|
| Per unit incl. 2 persons and electricity | £ 10.00 - £ 19.00 |
| tent incl. 2 persons | £ 10.00 - £ 17.00 |
| extra person | £ 3.00 |
| dog | £ 1.00 |
| Special offers available. | |

## Cheddar

### Broadway House Caravan & Camping Park

Cheddar BS27 3DB (Somerset) T: 01934 742610. E: enquiries@broadwayhouse.uk.com
**alanrogers.com/UK1410**

A well maintained park offering a range of facilities on continental lines, Broadway is now part of the Darwin Group. Occupying a gently sloping area at the foot of the Mendips near Cheddar Gorge, the park takes over 300 touring units of all types. From the entrance, after an area of neat caravan holiday homes and a separate area of luxury timber lodges, a series of touring areas graduates upwards, culminating in a tent and overflow rally field. The central access avenue is lined by trees with the groups of pitches on either side separated by ranch style fencing or hedging. All pitches have 16A electricity and 47 on gravel hardstanding have water and drainage. This park aims to cater for the normal active family – single sex groups are actively discouraged. There is a secluded, walled, heated pool (60x25 ft) and paddling pool (open Easter-September; unsupervised) with grass sunbathing area and shade from silver birches. A BMX track, adventure play areas and crazy golf will also help to keep children entertained. A nature trail leads from the park – Cheddar Wood is a site of special scientific interest.

**Facilities**

The large, purpose built toilet block at the start of the touring area has a good provision of showers, plus eight private cabins. Behind are 10 family shower units. Extra facilities with bathroom (coin operated) and a unit for disabled visitors are near reception, with a 'portacabin' type unit (no showers) in the top tent field. Baby room. Launderette. Motorcaravan service point. Shop. Bar and café. Swimming pool. Adventure playground. BMX track. Games room. Lodges and caravan holiday homes to rent. Off site: Buses pass the gate to/from Bristol, Weston-super-Mare and Wells. Fishing 0.5 and 5 miles.

**Open:** March - November.

**Directions**

From M5 exit 22 follow brown tourist signs towards Cheddar. Park entrance is on the A371 between Axbridge and Cheddar. O.S.GR: ST449547. GPS: 51.288214, -2.792303

**Charges guide**

Not available. Contact the park

## Chippenham

### Plough Lane Caravan Site

Plough Lane, Kington Langley, Chippenham SN15 5PS (Wiltshire) T: 01249 750146
E: enquiries@ploughlane.co.uk **alanrogers.com/UK1680**

Catering for adults only, this is a good example of a well designed, quality, modern touring site. The 50 pitches (all for touring units) are attractively laid out over four acres, access roads are gravel and the borders are stocked with well established shrubs and trees. The pitches are half grass, half hardstanding and all have electricity (16A), with 25 having full services. The site entrance has a barrier system for security. This site is an ideal base for visiting Bath and the Cotswolds, Avebury and Stonehenge.

**Facilities**

The sanitary building is heated, spacious, light and airy, and has all the usual facilities including some washbasins in cubicles, with a hairdressing area for ladies. Separate en-suite room for disabled visitors with ramp access. Dishwashing under cover. Fully equipped laundry. Max. 2 dogs per unit, a gravel dog path is provided. This park is for adults only (over 18 yrs). Off site: Supermarket, two public houses, and two garages (both with gas) less than 1 mile.

**Open:** Easter - October.

**Directions**

From M4 junction 17 turn south on A350 for 2 miles, then left at traffic lights where site is signed. From Chippenham head north on A350 (towards M4), approaching traffic lights (signed for site and Kington Langley) you need the right hand lane. O.S.GR: ST914764. GPS: 51.486367, -2.1257

**Charges guide**

| | |
|---|---|
| Per unit incl. 2 persons | £ 18.50 - £ 20.50 |
| extra person (max. 2 extra) | £ 5.00 |
| No credit cards. | |

## Chippenham

### Piccadilly Caravan Park

Folly Lane West, Lacock, Chippenham SN15 2LP (Wiltshire) T: 01249 730260. E: piccadillylacock@aol.com

alanrogers.com/UK1660

Piccadilly Caravan Park is set in open countryside close to several attractions, notably Longleat, Bath, Salisbury Plain, Stourhead, and Lacock itself. You will receive a warm welcome from the owner at this small, quiet family owned park that is beautifully kept. Well kept shrubs, plants and trees have been landscaped to give the impression of three separate areas and create a very pleasant ambience. There are 40 well spaced, clearly marked pitches, 12 of which have hardstanding, and two good areas for tents. Electrical connections (10A) are available on 34 pitches. A bus service runs from Lacock village to Chippenham (entry to the Chippenham museum and Heritage centre is free of charge). Lacock Abbey was once the home of Henry Fox-Talbot, pioneer of photography, and there is a museum in the village.

### Facilities

The one toilet block is well maintained and equipped, should be adequate in size for peak periods and can be heated in cool weather. Laundry room with baby changing facilities. Ice pack service. Small, bark-based playground and a large, grass ball play area. Limited gas supplies. Papers can be ordered. Off site: Fishing 1 mile. Bicycle hire 6 miles. Riding 4 miles. Golf 3 miles.

Open: Easter/1 April - October.

### Directions

Park is signed west off A350 Chippenham - Melksham road (turning to Gastard with caravan symbol) by Lacock village. 300 yds. to park. O.S.GR: ST911683. GPS: 51.4138, -2.129683

### Charges 2011

Per unit incl. 2 persons and electricity £ 18.00

No credit cards.

## Dulverton

### Exe Valley Caravan Site

Bridgetown, Dulverton TA22 9JR (Somerset) T: 01643 851432. E: paul@paulmatt.fsnet.co.uk

alanrogers.com/UK1590

Occupying a prime position in a wooded valley alongside the River Exe, within the National Park, Exe Valley Caravan Site is ideally situated for visiting the Doone Valley, Tarr Steps, Dulverton and many other beautiful venues in the area. This four acre 'adult only' campsite is owned and managed by Paul and Christine Matthews. Set beside the River Exe or the millstream, there are 50 large pitches (mostly grass but with some hardstandings at the top end), of which 41 have 10A electricity and TV hook-ups (cable provided on loan). Reception forms part of the owner's home which is an old mill, complete with water wheel and grindstones that are in working order. Open for visits every Sunday at 10.00, CCTV has been installed so campers may watch the bat colony in the loft from a screen in the mill. A small shop run by a village co-operative stocks local produce and crafts. Fly fishing along the River Exe is possible from the site or at Wimbleball Reservoir just over four miles away. This part of Somerset is a haven for walking, cycling, pony trekking, or as a place to just sit and relax.

### Facilities

The toilet block houses the usual facilities and an en-suite room for disabled visitors (short steep ramp to enter). Excellent laundry with domestic washing and drying machines, plus a microwave (free). Motorcaravan service point. Small shop. Bicycle hire. Gas supplies. Free fly fishing. WiFi. This is an adult only park. Off site: Riding 4 miles. Golf 12 miles. Pub at Bridgetown. Winsford village has a general stores and tea rooms.

Open: 18 March - 17 October.

### Directions

Bridgetown is roughly midway between Dunster and Tiverton on the A396. As you enter Bridgetown from Tiverton, look for site sign and turn left on minor road. Site is 100 yards on the right. O.S.GR: SS923332. GPS: 51.0882, -3.53875

### Charges guide

| | |
|---|---|
| Per unit incl. 2 persons, electricity and TV hook-up | £ 11.00 - £ 17.00 |
| extra person | £ 4.00 |
| awning | £ 1.00 |
| dog | £ 1.00 |

No credit cards.

For latest campsite news visit
alanrogers.com

## Glastonbury

### The Old Oaks Touring Park

Wick Farm, Wick, Glastonbury BA6 8JS (Somerset) T: 01458 831437. E: info@theoldoaks.co.uk

alanrogers.com/UK1390

The Old Oaks, an 'adults only' park, is tucked below and hidden from the Tor, in a lovely secluded setting with views across to the Mendips. The grounds are kept immaculate and there is a great deal of attention to cleanliness throughout. In total there are 100 large pitches in a series of paddocks, the majority with 16A electricity, hardstanding and several are fully serviced (including sewerage). Mainly backing on to hedges, they are attractively arranged and interspersed with shrubs and flowers in a circular development or terraced with increasing views. A quiet orchard area, a separated hedged paddock for camping and a larger field with chemical disposal facilities complete the provision.

**Facilities**

The heated toilet block, converted from the old stables, is of excellent quality and well equipped. Neatly paved outside, it has digital security locks (a public footpath from the Tor passes through the farm). Some washbasins are in cubicles. Two en-suite rooms and a bathroom (£1). Disabled visitors have two rooms. Laundry room. Motorcaravan service facilities. Licensed shop selling local produce and bread (pre-ordered). Library room. Bicycle hire (with helmets). Fishing. Adults only accepted (18 yrs and over). Off site: Riding 5 miles. Golf 6 miles.

Open: All year.

**Directions**

Park is north off A361 Shepton Mallet - Glastonbury road, 2 miles from Glastonbury. Take narrow unclassified road signed Wick for 1 mile and park is on the left. O.S.GR: ST521394. GPS: 51.152633, -2.6803

**Charges guide**

| Per unit incl. 2 persons | |
|---|---|
| and electricity | £ 18.00 - £ 23.00 |
| with full services | £ 20.00 - £ 26.00 |
| extra person | £ 5.00 |
| dog | £ 1.50 |

## Lyme Regis

### Shrubbery Caravan & Camping Park

Rousdon, Lyme Regis DT7 3XW (Dorset) T: 01297 442227. E: info@shrubberypark.co.uk

alanrogers.com/UK1720

Three miles south of historic Lyme Regis in a good situation to explore the Jurassic Coast, this well cared for park has distant views of the surrounding countryside. There are 120 generous pitches with more than enough room to pitch for most units. On slightly sloping, neatly cut grass which undulates in places, they are accessed by tarmac roads and all have 10A electricity. The pitches back on to well cut shrubs or the perimeter trees. A modern reception area is welcoming and stocks basic supplies and local provisions. This is a comfortable park where couples and families with young children are welcomed.

**Facilities**

Excellent heated toilet blocks, the newest (part of the reception building) with en-suite units, bathroom and laundry facilities. Two further blocks nearer the top of the park, fully equipped and well maintained. Facilities for disabled visitors. Simple shop at reception. General store at adjacent fuel station. Play area. Crazy golf.
Off site: Beach and boat launching 3 miles. Fishing 1 mile. Golf 3 miles. Riding 5 miles

Open: 1 April - 31 October.

**Directions**

From the A35 near Axminster follow the A358 towards Seaton. At T-junction turn left on A3052 signed Rousdon and Lyme Regis. Site entrance is on the left a few yards after Rousdon Garage. O.S.GR: SY298913. GPS: 50.71734, -2.99521

**Charges 2011**

| Per unit incl. 2 persons | |
|---|---|
| and electricity | £ 14.50 - £ 19.50 |

## Malmesbury

### Burton Hill Caravan Park

Arches Lane, Malmesbury SN16 0EH (Wiltshire) T: 01666 826 880. E: audrey@burtonhill.co.uk

alanrogers.com/UK1665

The owners of this park, Audrey and Warren Hateley, tend it with pride. It is a flat, grassy site surrounded by hedges, with open views across farmland on the outskirts of historic Malmesbury. There are 28 numbered touring pitches each with 16A electricity, 8 more for tents also with electricity and 8 without hook ups. It is a short walk (10-15 minutes) along the river bank to the town, its shops, Abbey House Gardens, Abbey and 15th century market place. Within easy travelling distance are the towns of Bath, Chippenham, Tetbury, Trowbridge and Bradford-on-Avon.

**Facilities**

Modern, well equipped and well maintained toilet block with free hot water. Separate well equipped facilities for disabled visitors. Washing machine. Off site: Malmesbury also has a new sports centre and swimming pool. Golf 6 miles.

Open: 1 April/Easter - 31 October.

**Directions**

From M4 exit 17 follow A4129 towards Cirencester for 5 miles. At approach to Malmesbury at international caravan sign, turn left into Arches Lane, and follow signs. If you miss the turning carry on to roundabout return and turn right into Arches Lane. O.S.GR: ST933866. GPS: 51.579083, -2.097321

**Charges guide**

| Per unit incl. 2 persons and electricity | £ 18.00 |
|---|---|

For latest campsite news visit

**alanrogers.com**

## Martock

### Southfork Caravan Park

Parrett Works, Martock TA12 6AE (Somerset) T: 01935 825661. E: southforkcaravans@btconnect.com

alanrogers.com/UK1420

Don't be put off by the address which is historic – this was once a 17th century flax mill. Michael and Nancy Broadley now own and run this excellent, modern, well drained site just outside the lovely village of Martock. With 27 touring pitches on grass with a gravel access road (21 with 10A electrical hook-ups and 2 with water and waste water), it is an orderly, quiet park on two acres of flat, tree lined meadow near the River Parrett. All the expected facilities are close to the entrance and as the owners live on the premises, the park is open all year. Most things are available, including an NCC approved caravan repairs/servicing centre. Despite the rural setting, the A303 trunk road is just five minutes away. This area of South Somerset contains much of interest, including gardens, historic houses and sites, the Fleet Air Arm Museum, Haynes Motor Museum and Cricket St Thomas Wildlife Park. Information about access to many cycle routes and numerous walks, including the Parrett Trail, is available from reception.

### Facilities

The heated well maintained toilet block is fully equipped and includes some washbasins in cabins. Laundry room with washing machine and dryer. Shop and limited off-licence with gas and comprehensive camping accessories. Play area. Off site: Fishing (with licences) on the River Parrett a few yards from the park. Golf 5 miles. Bicycle hire 8 miles. Riding 10 miles. Pubs with good food in South Petherton and Martock, less than 2 miles in each direction.

Open: All year.

### Directions

From A303 between Ilchester and Ilminster turn north at the roundabout signed for South Petherton. At T-junction in middle of village, turn right towards Martock. Park is at Parrett Works midway between the two villages (about 1.5 miles from South Petherton). O.S.GR: ST446187.
GPS: 50.965367, -2.789817

### Charges guide

| | |
|---|---|
| Per unit incl. 2 persons | £ 9.00 - £ 13.00 |
| incl. electricity (10A) | £ 11.50 - £ 15.50 |
| extra person | £ 1.75 |
| child (under 5 yrs) | free |
| dog | £ 1.00 |

## Minehead

### Burrowhayes Farm Caravan & Camping Site

West Luccombe, Porlock, Minehead TA24 8HT (Somerset) T: 01643 862463. E: info@burrowhayes.co.uk

alanrogers.com/UK1370

This delightful park with riding stables on site, is on the edge of Exmoor. The stone packhorse bridge over Horner Water beside the farm entrance sets the tone of the park, which the Dascombe family have created over the last forty years having previously farmed the land. The farm buildings have been converted into riding stables with escorted rides available (from Easter). Touring and tent pitches are on partly sloping fields with marvellous views or a flatter location in a clearing by the river, while 20 caravan holiday homes are in a separate area. Electrical hook-ups are available (16A), although some require long leads (25 m). Six new fully serviced pitches have been added. With walking, bird watching, plenty of wild life to observe, pretty Exmoor villages and Lorna Doone country nearby there is much to do. Children can ride, play in the stream or explore the woods at the top of the site. Limited trout fishing is available in Horner Water (NT permit) alongside the park.

### Facilities

The heated toilet block provides controllable hot showers, one washbasin cubicle for each sex, hairdressing and shaving areas, laundry room, unit for disabled visitors and babies, and an indoor dishwashing room. A second older block is opened in high season with extra WCs and washbasins. Motorcaravan service point. Well stocked shop doubles with reception (from 1/4). Riding stables. Dogs must be kept on leads at all times and exercised off site. Off site: Beach 2 miles. Fishing 2 miles. Bicycle hire 5 miles. Golf 6 miles. Minehead 5 miles. Local pub 20 minutes' walk.

Open: 15 March - 31 October.

### Directions

From A39, 5 miles west of Minehead, take first left past Allerford to Horner and West Luccombe. Site is on right after 400 yards. O.S.GR: SS899461.
GPS: 51.203533, -3.5778

### Charges guide

| | |
|---|---|
| Per unit incl. 2 persons and electricity | £ 12.50 - £ 17.50 |
| extra person | £ 4.00 - £ 5.00 |
| child (3-15 yrs) | £ 2.00 - £ 2.50 |
| dog | free |

# Minehead

## Halse Farm Touring Caravan & Camping Park

Winsford, Minehead TA24 7JL (Somerset) T: 01643 851259. E: ar@halsefarm.co.uk
alanrogers.com/UK1360

A truly rural park with beautiful, moorland views, you may be lucky enough to glimpse red deer across the valley or be able to see ponies and foals grazing outside the main gate which is adjacent to the moor. Two open, neatly cut fields (level at the top) back onto traditional hedging and slope gently to the middle and bottom where wild flowers predominate. One field provides electricity points (10A) and is used for motorcaravans and caravans, the other is for tents. There is no reception – you leave your unit by the toilet block and walk down to the farm kitchen to book in.

### Facilities

The central toilet block is heated, well equipped and maintained. It includes a toilet, washbasin and shower for visitors with disabilities, washing machine, dryer and iron, and tourist information. Gas is available at the farm. Play equipment. Off site: Riding 2 miles. Fishing 4 miles. Bicycle hire 5 miles. Tarr Steps and Barle Valley 3 miles. Winsford village 1 mile.

Open: 18 March - 1 November.

### Directions

Turn off A396 Tiverton - Minehead road for Winsford (site signed). In Winsford village turn left in front of the Royal Oak (not over ford) and uphill for 1 mile (go slowly round the sharp bend at the bottom). Cross cattle grid onto moor and turn immediately left to farm. Caravans should avoid Dulverton - keep to the A396 from Bridgetown (signed). O.S.GR: SS898342. GPS: 51.097717, -3.579983

### Charges guide

| | |
|---|---|
| Per unit incl. 2 persons | £ 14.50 - £ 16.50 |
| extra person | £ 6.00 - £ 7.00 |

# Minehead

## Westermill Farm

Exford, Minehead TA24 7NJ (Somerset) T: 01643 831238. E: info@westermill.com
alanrogers.com/UK1301

This superbly located farm campsite can be found nestling in a valley beside the River Exe. The working farm provides four meadows, all without electricity, and is ideal for 'back to basics' style touring. Uniquely, open fires are permitted in one field with logs being available to purchase. You can marvel at the wildlife, wander around the working farm and sample the farm's own produce in the shop, which also stocks basic provisions. Walking maps can be found at reception which is located in the old dairy.

### Facilities

The unheated toilet block houses the usual facilities including showers and washbasins and hot water is provided by solar energy. Laundry facilities. Farm shop (End May - early Sept). Gas supplies. Facility for freezer packs (20p). Fishing in the River Exe. The river is also used for bathing. Off site: Bicycle hire 6 miles. Riding 15 miles. Village 2.5 miles. Beach 15 miles.

Open: All year.

### Directions

Leave Exford on Porlock Road with Post Office on right. At Y fork turn left, down single track road. Farm is 2 miles on right. Do not use Sat Nav. GPS: 51.145631, -3.682158

### Charges guide

| | |
|---|---|
| Per person | £ 5.00 |
| child | £ 3.00 |
| car | £ 2.50 |

No credit cards.

# Salisbury

## Church Farm Caravan & Camping Park

Sixpenny Handley, Salisbury SP5 5ND (Wiltshire) T: 01725 553005. E: churchfarmcandcpark@yahoo.co.uk
alanrogers.com/UK1655

Sixpenny Handley is a Saxon hilltop village and St Mary's church dates back some 900 years. From the site you can hear the bells and the chimes of its clock. Church Farm, a stone's throw from the village centre, offers 35 partly-sheltered, level, spacious pitches including some hardstandings, all with 16A electricity, arranged around the perimeter of two fields, plus another field for tents. It is in an Area of Outstanding Natural Beauty and the views and many walks are an absolute delight. Not forgetting the hundreds of tumuli and prehistoric remains, there are many places for the visitor to discover the delights around this junction of Dorset, Hampshire and Wiltshire.

### Facilities

New spacious multi-function building houses reception, a seasonal café/bar, and up-to-date heated toilet facilities. Dedicated room for disabled campers. Baby changing. Laundry with washing machine and dryer. Freezer for ice packs. Gas supplies. Motorcaravan service point. Play area. Two holiday caravans for rent. Off site: The Roebuck Inn offers a varied menu. Tennis courts (hire equipment from site). Golf 4 miles. Riding 5 miles. Fishing 10 miles.

Open: All year.

### Directions

To avoid the village centre, 1 mile south of Handley Hill roundabout on A354 turn towards Sixpenny Handley, then right by the school and site is 300 yds by the church. O.S.GR: ST996173. GPS: 50.955317, -2.006883

### Charges guide

| | |
|---|---|
| Per unit incl. 2 persons | £ 15.75 - £ 16.75 |
| extra person | £ 6.50 - £ 7.00 |

For latest campsite news visit
**alanrogers.com**

## Salisbury

### Greenhill Farm Caravan & Camping Park

New Road, Landford, Salisbury SP5 2AZ (Wiltshire) T: 01794 324117. E: info@greenhillholidays.co.uk

alanrogers.com/UK1640

Located on the northern edge of the New Forest National Park, this park occupies 14 acres out of a total of 50 acres of beautiful forest owned by the family. It is an uncommercialised hideaway and has two distinctive areas: the 'adult only' area, fenced, gated and set around two small lakes, one of which is reserved for coarse fishing; and the family area, with a playground, views over the meadow, sightings of deer and a generally open aspect. There are 160 pitches in total, with 50 for tents in a separate hill-top meadow with views over the nearby forest and its own fishing lake. The remainder are for tourers with some seasonals and a number of hardstandings. All pitches are level and with 16A electricity.

### Facilities

New toilet block planned; in the interim, 'portacabin' style units of varying ages provide facilities. No dedicated facilities for disabled visitors. Laundry with washing machine and dryer. Reception/shop. Gas supplies. Takeaway in high season in Family Area. Bicycle hire. Coarse fishing lakes (£3.60 per rod per day). Grazing for horses. Torches useful. Off site: Landford village has a post office/general store (15 minutes walk). Golf 3 miles. Riding 4 miles. Local attractions include Paultons Park, Breamore House and the New Forest. Several pubs serving meals are close by and a bus stop outside the site entrance provides services to Salisbury and Southampton.

Open: All year.

### Directions

From M27 exit 2 take A36 north towards Salisbury for about 6 miles. Pass through West Wellow and after passing a B.P. garage on left, take next left into New Road, and continue for 0.9 miles to entrance on the left. O.S.GR: SU264184. GPS: 50.96445, -1.62575

### Charges guide

| | |
|---|---|
| Per unit incl. 2 persons, awning and electricity | £ 15.00 - £ 16.50 |
| tent incl. 2 persons | £ 9.00 - £ 13.00 |
| extra person | £ 3.50 |
| child | £ 2.00 - £ 3.50 |

## Shepton Mallet

### Batcombe Vale Campsite

Batcombe Vale, Shepton Mallet BA4 6BW (Somerset) T: 01749 831207. E: gary.butler1@virgin.net

alanrogers.com/UK1540

Set in a secluded valley with fields gently rising around it, contented cows grazing with watchful buzzards cruising above and views across the distant hills, this is a very special place. Descending slowly down the steep, narrow drive you see the pitches, attractively set and terraced where necessary, in an oval with the lakes below. The grass is left natural around the 32 pitches (20 have 10A electricity) and paths are mown where needed. Batcombe Vale House is an attractive, mellow building covered with wisteria, to one side of the valley overlooking the lakes and the 'wilder' landscape. Trees and shrubs have been skilfully placed to enhance the natural environment providing a range of colours and shapes. Designated an Area of Outstanding Natural Beauty, there are 120 acres around the valley where you are welcome to wander and picnic in the fields – a haven for wild flowers, birds and butterflies. For those who fish, two of the lakes have carp and tench up to 18 lbs but you must have a current licence. If you tire of the views and the fishing there is a range of circular walks from the site or you can potter about in one of the four free rowing boats. There are many places to visit nearby, from Glastonbury with the Tor, to Cheddar Gorge and the Caves.

### Facilities

The small rustic toilet block covered in honeysuckle meets all needs, including a freezer (ice packs only) and dishwashing sinks. Groundsheet awnings must be lifted daily. Fishing. Caravan storage. One dog per pitch is welcome (no dangerous breeds). Bed and breakfast available in Batcombe Vale House. Off site: Golf, riding and bicycle hire 5 miles. Bruton (for shops, etc.) 2 miles. Launderettes at Shepton or Frome.

Open: Easter - end September.

### Directions

Bruton is south of Shepton Mallet and Frome and north of Wincanton where the A359 intersects the B3081. Access to the site must be via Evercreech or Bruton (B3081), then follow the brown and white camping signs. Access drive is steep. O.S.GR: ST684376. GPS: 51.136467, -2.453167

### Charges guide

| | |
|---|---|
| Per unit incl. 2 persons and electricity | £ 19.85 |
| extra person | £ 4.85 |

No commercial vehicles or motorcycle 'packs'. Family groups only. No credit cards.

For latest campsite news visit
**alanrogers.com**

## Shepton Mallet

### Greenacres Camping

Barrow Lane, North Wootton, Shepton Mallet BA4 4HL (Somerset) T: 01749 890497
E: stay@greenacres-camping.co.uk  alanrogers.com/UK1490

Greenacres is a rural site in the Somerset countryside for tents, trailer tents and small motorcaravans only. Hidden away below the Mendips and almost at the start of the 'Levels', it is a simple green site – a true haven of peace and quiet. The grass is neatly trimmed over the 4.5 acres and hedged with mature trees, though there is a view of Glastonbury Tor in one direction and of Barrow Hill in the other. All of the 40 pitches are around the perimeter of the park, leaving a central area safe for children to play. At the south side if the site, 7 pitches have electricity hook-ups (10/16A) and are ideal for those without children or birdwatchers.

#### Facilities

The central wooden toilet block is simple but perfectly acceptable and kept clean. Hot showers are accessed directly from the outside. No shop but a van calls in high season with local produce (pre-ordered). Play equipment, football, badminton net and play house. The park office (and bicycle hire), is across the lane. New cabin with fridges and freezers for campers' use (free), library and tourist information. Free WiFi. Dogs are not accepted. Off site: North Wootton (under 1 mile) with large pub/restaurant and a vineyard. Fishing and riding nearby.

Open: April - September.

#### Directions

From A39 Glastonbury - Wells road turn east at Brownes Garden Centre and follow camping signs. From A361 Glastonbury - Shepton Mallet road follow camp signs from Pilton or Steanbow. (Roads are narrow with few passing places).
O.S.GR: ST553416. GPS: 51.172367, -2.641883

#### Charges guide

| | |
|---|---|
| Per person | £ 8.00 |
| child (4-14 yrs) | £ 2.50 |
| electricity | £ 3.50 |

## Sparkford

### Long Hazel Park

High Street, Sparkford, Yeovil BA22 7JH (Somerset) T: 01963 440002. E: longhazelpark@hotmail.com
alanrogers.com/UK1500

Pamela and Alan Walton are really enthusiastic about their neat, small, beautifully kept, 'adult only' park in the Somerset village of Sparkford where they will make you most welcome. This level, landscaped park is surrounded by attractive beech hedging, silver birches and many other ornamental trees and the park has a relaxed, comfortable feel. It provides 50 touring pitches for all types of units with electrical hook-ups (16A), 30 pitches with hardstanding, some extra long with grass lawns at the side, and the entrance has been widened for easier access. Part of the park is being developed with pine holiday lodges for private ownership or rent.

#### Facilities

The refurbished toilet block is clean, well equipped and heated. Well planned en-suite facilities for visitors with disabilities. Washing machine and dryer. Motorcaravan waste water discharge. Gas supplies. Long hardstanding pitches suitable for large motorhomes. Off site: Bus service. Spar shop, post office and McDonalds 400 yards. Village inn 100 yds. Riding and fishing 8 miles. Golf 5 miles.

Open: All year.

#### Directions

At roundabout on A303 take road into village of Sparkford and park is signed on the left 100 yds before the Inn. O.S.GR: ST604263.
GPS: 51.0344, -2.568633

#### Charges guide

| | |
|---|---|
| Per unit incl. 2 persons and electricity | £ 20.00 - £ 25.00 |
| extra person | £ 4.00 |

## Taunton

### Quantock Orchard Caravan Park

Crowcombe, Taunton TA4 4AW (Somerset) T: 01984 618618. E: member@flaxpool.freeserve.co.uk
alanrogers.com/UK1350

Quantock Orchard, nestles at the foot of the Quantock hills in quiet countryside, close to many of the attractions of the area. Attractively developed, mature apple trees, recently planted trees, shrubs and pretty flower beds with a nice use of heathers, make a pleasant environment. The clock tower on the wooden sanitary block and a dove cote at the entrance add interest. With access from fairly narrow gravel roads, there are 69 touring pitches, part separated by growing shrubs and hedging, of which 40 are for tents. Of various sizes, all touring pitches have 15A electricity and 30 have hardstanding.

#### Facilities

The central, heated sanitary block is very well maintained. Microwave. Laundry facilities. Facilities for disabled visitors but no shower. Well stocked licensed shop includes camping accessories and local produce. Mountain bike hire (some with buggies for children). Swimming pool (May-Sept). Leisure suite. Games room, Sky TV. Fenced safe-based play area. Caravan storage (Oct- Mar). Holiday homes for hire. Off site: Pubs serving meals 3 miles.

Open: All year.

#### Directions

Park is west off A358 road (Taunton - Minehead), about 1 mile south of Crowcombe village.
O.S.GR: ST140363. GPS: 51.1084, -3.22645

#### Charges guide

| | |
|---|---|
| Per unit incl. 2 persons and electricity | £ 13.00 - £ 25.00 |
| extra person | £ 5.00 |

For latest campsite news visit
**alanrogers.com**

## Taunton
### Lowtrow Cross Caravan Site
Upton, Wiveliscombe, Taunton TA4 2DB (Somerset) T: 01398 371199. E: info@lowtrowcross.co.uk

alanrogers.com/UK1355

Lowtrow Cross is a small adults only park situated just inside Exmoor National Park and ideal for owners of well-behaved dogs. It is quietly located on a hillside giving lovely views north towards the Brendon Hills. There are 18 pitches, three occupied by caravan holiday homes (two for hire) and six seasonal, and all the remaining touring pitches are hardstanding with grass surround, with electricity (16A) and TV socket. An adjacent meadow with stunning views over the rolling countryside can be used for tents. Although there is no bar or restaurant on site there is Lowtrow Cross Inn at the gate with local cask beers and excellent food. Lowtrow Cross is well situated for walking, cycling, riding and fishing in the beautiful Exmoor countryside with its wide variety of wildlife. Close by Haddon Moor, with its own herd of ponies and buzzards overhead, overlooks Wimbleball Lake where one can enjoy a variety of water based activities and nature trails. Clatworthy Reservoir is also convenient for walking and fishing, but dogs are not permitted here. Not far away are Dunster Castle, Porlock and the West Somerset Steam railway. The area is well known for its cider and there is a museum of cider-making at Taunton.

### Facilities
Traditional heated, well equipped, toilet block but no facilities for disabled visitors. Excellent laundry room. Freezer and microwave. Small shop in reception selling basic foodstuffs; milk, bread, free range eggs, frozen meals, local produce, toiletries and Calor gas. Tourist information. Maps for sale and book exchange. Off site: Lowtrow Cross Inn at gate. Garage 750 m. Excellent fishing and boating 3 miles. Golf and riding 10 miles.

Open: March - October.

### Directions
From M5 junction 25 follow signs for Minehead (A358) through Taunton, then 5 miles from Taunton turn west (left) on B3224 signed Raleigh Cross. Shortly after passing Raleigh Cross Inn turn south on B3190 signed Bampton. Site is on right in 4 miles just before Upton village. O.S.GR: ST007292. GPS: 51.053342, -3.419923

### Charges guide
| | |
|---|---|
| Per unit incl. 2 persons and electricity | £ 14.00 - £ 19.00 |
| extra adult | £ 4.00 |
| dog | free |

**Lowtrow Cross**
Upton, Nr. Wiveliscombe, Taunton Somerset, TA4 2DB
A small, quiet, adults only site set in a secluded area on the edge of Exmoor National Park
Email: info@lowtrowcross.co.uk
www.lowtrowcross.co.uk
* Spotless facilities
* Electric/TV hook ups
* Hardstandings
* Laundry
* Microwave/Freezer
* Small shop
* Wi Fi
* Tourist info
* Dogs Welcome free
Tel: (01398) 371199

---

## Taunton
### Waterrow Touring Park
Wiveliscombe, Taunton TA4 2AZ (Somerset) T: 01984 623464. E: waterrowpark@yahoo.co.uk

alanrogers.com/UK1520

Beside the River Tone in a pretty part of South Somerset, Tony and Anne Taylor have enthusiastically developed Waterrow into a charming, landscaped touring park for adults only. Nestling in a little sheltered valley, it is very peaceful and possible for an overnight stop (just over 30 minutes from M5) or ideal as a base for exploring nearby Exmoor and the Brendon Hills. There are 48 touring pitches, most of which are on level hardstandings, including five with full services. All have electricity (16A), spring and mains water are available and TV aerial points have been installed (your own lead is required, sometimes quite long). A small area has been set aside for tent campers. A member of the Best of British group.

### Facilities
A modern, clean toilet unit, well fitted out and with heating, provides WCs and washbasins, some in curtained cubicles. New heated shower block. Facilities for disabled visitors (key). Laundry facilities. Motorcaravan service point. Limited provisions are available in reception. Regular watercolour painting and drawing courses are run (May-Oct) at the in-house studio. Additional fly fishing holidays can be arranged at certain times. WiFi (charged). Caravan storage with 'store and stay' system. Site is not suitable for large American motorhomes. Max. 2 dogs. Luxury holiday home for hire. Off site: Fishing 5 miles. Golf 7 miles. Bicycle hire 10 miles. Riding 12 miles. Wiveliscombe 3 miles.

Open: All year.

### Directions
From M5 exit 25 take A358 (signed Minehead) round Taunton for 4 miles, then at Staplegrove onto the B3227 for 11.5 miles to Wiveliscombe where straight over at lights to Waterrow (still on B3227). Park is on left shortly after the Rock Inn. Do not use satellite navigation for this site as it takes you on roads unsuitable for caravans. O.S.GR: ST052250. GPS: 51.0165, -3.352717

### Charges guide
| | |
|---|---|
| Per unit incl. 2 adults and electricity | £ 14.00 - £ 23.00 |
| full services, plus | £ 5.00 |
| extra person | £ 5.00 |
| dog (max. 2) | £ 1.20 |

For latest campsite news visit
# alanrogers.com

## Taunton

### Cornish Farm Touring Park

Shoreditch, Taunton TA3 7BS (Somerset) T: 01823 327746. E: info@cornishfarm.com

alanrogers.com/UK1340

This neat little park, which opened for its first full season in 2006, is on level ground and conveniently located close to the M5 motorway. There are 49 pitches, all with 10A electricity, of which 25 are on gravel hardstanding. Most pitches are accessed from a gravel road (one-way system) with plenty of fresh water taps, site lighting and some picnic tables. A separate area for tents is close to the toilet block. Light power cables cross the site and there is some background motorway noise. Maximum length for motorhomes is 30ft, unless by prior arrangement with the wardens. With its old apple trees this park makes a very pleasant stop-over. Off to the left are the barns that house the Van Bitz workshops producing security systems for motorcaravans. The centrally situated, modern toilet block is maintained to a high standard and includes under-floor heating, designed by the owners who are campers and caravanners themselves. There are no other facilities on the park but a cycle path and a footpath will take you into Taunton town centre. Taunton, the county town of Somerset, is worth a visit with its Castle, museum, a variety of livestock and produce markets and an annual flower show.

**Facilities**

One central block has under-floor heating and modern fittings and you can listen to the local radio. Large dual purpose room providing facilities for disabled visitors and small children. Laundry room. Motorcaravan service point. Camping supplies for sale and plenty of tourist information available. On-site PC repair facility. WiFi throughout site (free). Off site: Village pub and shops are a short walk away. Level cycle/footpath into Taunton (2 miles) which has a castle, museum, and markets. Tesco Express 1 mile. Golf 2 miles. Bicycle hire 2 miles.

Open: All year.

**Directions**

From M5 exit 25 follow signs for Taunton. At first set of lights (Creech Castle) turn left (Corfe B3170). Take third left into Ilminster Road (Corfe). Right at roundabout (Blackbrook Way), left at next roundabout and follow to T-junction (B3170). Turn right then next left. Take second left and cross motorway. Site entrance is after bridge on the left. O.S.GR: ST 234 219. GPS: 50.99200, -3.09257

**Charges guide**

| | |
|---|---|
| Per unit incl. 2 persons and electricity | £ 13.00 - £ 15.00 |
| extra person | £ 2.00 - £ 3.00 |

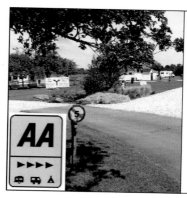

## Luxury Camping in the Heart of Somerset

Cornish Farm Touring Park, Shoreditch, Taunton TA3 7BS Tel: 01823327746 **www.cornishfarm.com**

"The best we've ever seen" - a frequent comment from happy customers about our facilities. Level gravelled hard standings. Only two miles away from town centre. Follow Racecourse signs from M5 or town centre until you pick up Cornish Farm brown signs. Rallies welcome. Large well equipped fully tiled and heated family/disabled shower room. Book exchange. Laundry room. Washing-up area. Low energy dusk to dawn lights for your security and safety.

## Warminster

### Longleat Caravan Club Site

Warminster BA12 7NL (Wiltshire) T: 01985 844663

alanrogers.com/UK1690

What a magnificent situation in which to find a caravan park, amidst all the wonders of the Longleat Estate including the Elizabethan House, gardens designed by Capability Brown and the Safari Park. Visitors can roam the woodlands and enjoy the views, watch the wildlife and marvel at the azaleas, bluebells, etc. according to the season or listen to the occupants of the Safari Park. The site itself is well managed by Caravan Club wardens. There are 165 generous pitches, all with 16A electricity.

**Facilities**

Two heated toilet blocks provide washbasins in cubicles, controllable showers and a vanity section with mirrors and hairdryers. Baby/toddler room, suite for disabled visitors, laundry and dishwashing room and a family room with a DVD player. Two motorcaravan service points. Play area. Office is manned 09.00-17.30 and stocks basic food items. Late arrivals area with hookup. Off site: Longleat House and its attractions. Frome 7 miles.

Open: March - November.

**Directions**

The main entrance to Longleat which caravans must use is signed from the A362 Frome - Warminster road near where it joins the A36 Warminster bypass. Follow the Longleat House route through the toll booths for 2 miles then caravan club signs for 1 mile. O.S.GR: ST806434. GPS: 51.1907, -2.278517

**Charges guide**

| | |
|---|---|
| Per person | £ 5.10 - £ 6.90 |
| pitch (non-member) | £ 5.15 - £ 8.50 |

For latest campsite news visit

**alanrogers.com**

## Wells
### Cheddar, Mendip Heights Camping & Caravanning Club Site
Priddy, Wells BA5 3BP (Somerset) T: 01749 870241. E: cheddar@campingandcaravanningclub.co.uk
alanrogers.com/UK1430

Now owned by the Camping & Caravanning Club, Mendip Heights is a well kept site half a mile from the village. There are tranquil views across the Mendip fields which are characterised by dry stone walling. It has a simple charm with field margins left natural to encourage wildlife and nest boxes in the mature trees edging the three fields which comprise the site. These provide space for 90 units on mostly slightly sloping short grass with 67 electric hook-ups (16A), 36 with hardstanding.

**Facilities**

The refurbished toilet block with all facilities is bright, cheerful and heated. Two family rooms (one with high and low toilet and shower). Facilities for disabled visitors. Laundry facilities. Motorcaravan service point. The reception/licensed shop doubles as the village shop. Fresh bread and pastries are baked each morning (advisable to pre-order). Off site: Two traditional village pubs within walking distance (0.5 miles). Bicycle hire and golf 5 miles. Fishing 6 miles, riding 2 miles.

Open: 1 March - 15 November.

**Directions**

From M5 exit 21 take A371 to Banwell. Turn left on A368, right on B3134 and right on B3135. After 2 miles turn left at camp sign. From M4 westbound exit 18, A46 to Bath, then A4 towards Bristol. Take A39 for Wells and right at Green Ore traffic lights on B3135; after 5 miles turn left at sign. O.S.GR: ST522518. GPS: 51.2636, -2.685383

**Charges guide**

| | |
|---|---|
| Per person | £ 7.70 - £ 11.10 |
| pitch incl. electricity (non-member) | £ 10.50 |

## Westbury
### Brokerswood Country Park
Brokerswood, Westbury BA13 4EH (Wiltshire) T: 01373 822238. E: info@brokerswoodcountrypark.co.uk
alanrogers.com/UK1630

This countryside campsite is located in an 80 acre country park, with ancient broadleaf woodland, plenty of marked walks, a woodland railway which also runs 'Santa Specials' (bookings taken from 1 August). The campsite has 65 pitches arranged around an open meadow area, served by a gravel roadway, with low level site lighting. There are 25 hardstanding pitches, and 44 electric hook-ups (10A). Although fairly recently laid-out, the site is maturing well. American RVs and other large units should use the coach entrance and they (and all arrivals after 18.00) are asked to phone ahead.

**Facilities**

Two well insulated and heated, timber clad buildings are at one end of the site. Some washbasins in cubicles, large, controllable hot showers. Family rooms (on payment). Fully equipped suite for disabled visitors with ramped approach and alarm. Laundry and ironing facilities. Motorcaravan services. Gas available. Milk, bread, newspapers to order from reception/shop. Café serving all day. Takeaway food service during August. Fishing. Cycling allowed on site but not in Country Park. Ready erected tents for hire. Off site: Golf 6 miles.

Open: All year.

**Directions**

From Trowbridge take A361 south for 2 miles, turning left (east) at Southwick, and follow signs to Country Park. O.S.GR: ST840524. GPS: 51.270283, -2.231417

**Charges guide**

| | |
|---|---|
| Per unit incl. 4 persons and electricity | £ 14.00 - £ 29.00 |
| extra person (1 yr or over) | £ 3.75 |
| dog | £ 1.00 |

## Weymouth
### Sea Barn & West Fleet Holiday Farms
Fleet Road, Fleet, Weymouth DT3 4ED (Dorset) T: 01305 782218. E: enquiries@seabarnfarm.co.uk
alanrogers.com/UK1830

Sea Barn and West Fleet are located just half a mile apart in delightful countryside overlooking the Fleet Lagoon, Chesil Bank and Lyme Bay which are all part of the Jurassic coast. Only tents, trailer tents and motorcaravans with tents and awnings are accepted. The parks share some facilities. An outdoor pool and clubhouse are at West Fleet, along with the new smart toilet block. Both have their own reception with well stocked shops. Sea Barn is quieter and popular over a longer period with spectacular views, whereas West Fleet attracts families. Both are popular with birdwatchers, walkers and fishermen.

**Facilities**

Traditional simple toilet blocks, brightly painted and clean. New block at both sites with en-suite room for disabled visitors and two bathrooms (free). Laundry facilities at both sites. Heated pool at West Fleet (May-Sept). Bigger shop offering wider range at West Fleet which also has the Club House (evenings), in reality an open ended barn and outdoor area which works well (home produced steaks the speciality). Family entertainment. Adventure play area. Off site: Access to South West Coastal path. Fishing.

Open: March - October.

**Directions**

From Weymouth take the B3157 coast road for Abbotsbury. Pass Chickerell and turn left at mini-roundabout to Fleet. Pass church on right and continue to top of hill. Sea Barn is to the left, West Fleet to the right. O.S.GR: SY626805. GPS: 50.62539, -2.53865

**Charges guide**

| | |
|---|---|
| Per unit incl. 2 persons and electricity | £ 14.00 - £ 23.00 |
| extra person | £ 4.00 - £ 5.00 |

For latest campsite news visit
**alanrogers.com**

# Weymouth

## Bagwell Farm Touring Park

Chickerell, Weymouth DT3 4EA (Dorset) T: 01305 782575. E: ar@bagwellfarm.co.uk
alanrogers.com/UK1820

A friendly, welcoming, family park, Bagwell Farm is situated between Weymouth and Abbotsbury, close to Chesil Beach. In a valley, yet with an open aspect, there are 320 numbered touring pitches, some taken up by seasonal units. There are 260 electricity connections (10A) and 25 serviced pitches (16A). Some of the terraced pitches have beautiful views of Chesil Bank and the sea. In addition there is a traditional camping field with a campers' shelter. An attractive bar has been converted from farm buildings where meals are served. This is open at weekends only in mid-season and daily in high season. Steaks are a speciality! A patio overlooks a good pets corner (also open to the public).

### Facilities

There are three toilet blocks (one year-round block is fully heated) with free showers. Coin-operated launderette and family bathrooms. Wet suit wash. Very well stocked shop that is open all day. Bar (Easter-Oct). Camper's shelter and communal barbecue. Off site: Situated on the Jurassic Coastline within easy reach of Weymouth and its sandy beach. Many activities available nearby including walking, sailing, diving and exploring the beautiful Dorset countryside.

Open: All year.

### Directions

Park is 3 miles west of Weymouth. Follow the B3157 from Weymouth towards Bridport. Park is 1 mile west of Chickerell on the B3157. The entrance is on the brow of a hill – care is needed. O.S GR: SY627816. GPS: 50.63088, -2.51999

### Charges guide

| | |
|---|---|
| Per unit incl. 2 persons and electricity | £ 13.50 - £ 26.00 |
| extra person | £ 5.00 |
| child (2-15 yrs) | £ 1.50 |
| dog | £ 1.00 |

# Weymouth

## East Fleet Farm Touring Park

Fleet Lane, Chickerell, Weymouth DT3 4DW (Dorset) T: 01305 785768. E: enquiries@eastfleet.co.uk
alanrogers.com/UK1800

East Fleet Farm has a marvellous situation on part level, part gently sloping meadows leading to the shores of the Fleet, with views across to the famous Chesil Bank with the sea beyond. This park has been developed by the Whitfield family within the confines of their 300 acre organic arable farm in keeping with its surroundings, yet with modern amenities. It is maturing well as bushes and trees grow. The 400 pitches back onto hedges and are a comfortable size so there is no feeling of crowding. Of these, 280 are level and marked with 10/16A electric hook-ups, 100 also have hardstanding. The terraced bar with views over the Fleet was converted from the barn and features original beams and brickwork. Part of the World Heritage Jurassic Coast, the Fleet is a lagoon renowned for its wildlife and popular with bird watchers. The busy resort of Weymouth with its safe bathing beaches and many watersports facilities is only 3 miles away (bicycle hire and boat launching possible). In peak season a regular bus service runs to Weymouth and the nearby Abbotsbury Swannery and Gardens.

### Facilities

Two fully equipped toilet blocks include family rooms. The newest one is very smart in a Norwegian log cabin. En-suite unit for disabled visitors. Laundry room. Motorcaravan service point. Reception plus shop with basic groceries, bread, papers and gas. Bar serving food with terrace (Easter-Sept). Games room. Fenced play area (remember, elsewhere this is a working farm). Games field. Nature watch boards. Off site: Riding and golf 2 miles. Access to the Fleet and coastal path.

Open: 15 March - 31 October.

### Directions

Park is signed at traffic lights on B3157 Weymouth - Bridport road, about 3 miles west of Weymouth beside Territorial Army base. Fleet Lane has been widened with plenty of passing places and speed bumps (20 mph). O.S.GR: SY639798. GPS: 50.61927, -2.50040

### Charges guide

| | |
|---|---|
| Per unit incl. 2 persons | £ 8.00 - £ 18.00 |
| incl. electricity | £ 12.00 - £ 22.50 |
| extra person | £ 1.00 - £ 4.50 |
| child (5-12 yrs) | £ 0.25 - £ 0.50 |

Rich in maritime herita
and historical attractic
the Southern region
comprises tranquil
English countryside
boasting picture-postcarc
villages, ancient cities and tov
formidable castles and grand state
homes, coupled with a beautiful
coastline and lively seaside resorts

**THIS REGION INCLUDES: EAST DORSET, HAMPSHIRE, ISLE OF WIGHT, OXFORDSHIRE, BERKSHIRE AND BUCKINGHAMSHIRE**

The south coast is a popular holiday destination for those looking for a beach holiday. Seaside resorts include Swanage, and Bournemouth, with its seven miles of golden sand. Also along this coastal stretch is Durdle Door, a natural arch that has been cut by the sea, and Europe's largest natural harbour at Poole Bay. Nearby, the Isle of Purbeck is not actually an island, but a promontory of low hills and heathland that juts out below Poole Harbour. Across the water is the Isle of Wight, easily reached via a short ferry trip across the Solent. Rural Southern England comprises green rolling hills and scenic wooded valleys, with numerous walking and bridle paths passing through picturesque villages with quintessential English pubs. The New Forest, well known for its wild roaming ponies, is a distinctive, peaceful retreat. The River Thames weaves its way through the Thames basin and Chilterns area, passing charming riverside villages, castles, stately homes and beautiful countryside, including that around Oxford. This city of dreaming spires has lovely scenic walks, old university buildings to explore, plus a huge selection of restaurants, pubs and shops. Along the river you can go punting, hire a rowing boat, or take one of the many river-boat trips available.

### Places of interest

*East Dorset:* Monkey World in Wareham; village of Cerne Abbas, with Cerne Giant.

*Hampshire:* historic Winchester; Portsmouth, home of the Mary Rose; Southampton maritime museum.

*Isle of Wight:* Cowes; Sandown with Dinosaur Isle; Shipwreck Centre in Ryde; Smuggling Museum in Ventnor; Carisbrooke Castle in Newport.

*Oxfordshire:* Blenheim Palace; Didcot Railway Centre; historic market town of Chipping Norton.

*Berkshire:* Windsor, with Legoland, Windsor Castle; Reading.

*Buckinghamshire:* Bletchley Park near Milton Keynes; county town of Aylesbury; Beaconsfield, once home to Enid Blyton, and now housing the world's first model village.

### Did you know?

The Cerne Giant is thought to have represented a pagan god dating back to pre 13th century.

Gosport is home to one of the worlds largest sundials covering 40 metres.

T.E Lawrence 'Lawrence of Arabia' was a fellow of All Souls College in Oxford and lived in Dorset.

Remains of over 20 species of dinosaur have been recovered on the Isle of Wight.

The annual Olney Pancake Race in Bucks has been running since around 1445.

Author Charles Dickens was born in Portsmouth, the house where he was born is now a museum.

Windsurfing was invented on Hayling Island by Peter Chilvers in 1958.

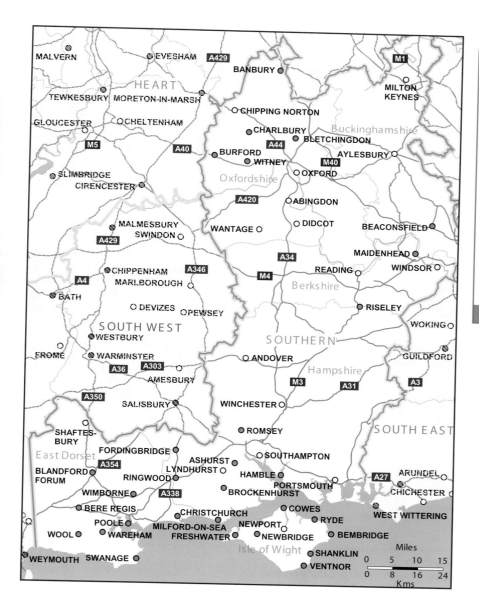

## Maps and campsite listings

For this 2011 guide we have changed the way in which we list our parks and also the way in which we help you locate the parks within each region.

We now include a map immediately after our Introduction to that region. These maps show the towns near which one (or more) of our featured parks is located. Within each regional section of the guide, we list these towns and the park(s) in that vicinity in alphabetical order.

You will certainly need more detailed maps for navigation, for example the Ordnance Survey road atlas. We provide O.S. references and G.P.S. coordinates for each park to assist you. Our three indexes will also help you to find a park by its reference number and name, by region and park name, or by the town where the park is situated.

## Ashurst

### Forest Holidays Ashurst

Forest Holidays, Lyndhurst Road, Ashurst SO40 7AR (Hampshire) T: 02380 292097
E: info@forestholidays.co.uk **alanrogers.com/UK2300**

Forest Holidays is a partnership between the Forestry Commission and the Camping & Caravanning Club. An attractive site, Ashurst is on the fringe of the New Forest, set in a mixture of oak woodland and grass heathland which is open to the grazing animals of the Forest. Smaller than the Hollands Wood site (23 acres), it provides 280 pitches, 180 of which have been gravelled to provide semi-hardstanding; otherwise you pitch where you like, applying the 20 ft. rule on ground that can be uneven. There are no electricity connections. Some noise must be expected from the adjacent railway line.

**Facilities**

The single well kept central toilet block (may be under pressure in main season) provides everything necessary, including hairdryers and a well equipped unit for visitors with disabilities. Good laundry room. Motorcaravan service point. Camping accessories and charcoal available. Torches useful. Dogs are not accepted. Off site: Shops and local buses within a five minute walk. Golf 4 miles.

Open: 26 March - 27 September.

**Directions**

From Southampton, follow A35 west through village of Ashurst, continue over railway bridge and site is 200 yards on left. O.S.GR: SU344099.
GPS: 50.88810, -1.52846

**Charges guide**

| | |
|---|---|
| Per unit incl. 2 persons | £ 10.00 - £ 26.50 |
| extra person | £ 4.25 - £ 8.50 |
| child | £ 2.25 - £ 4.25 |

## Banbury

### Bo Peep Caravan Park

Aynho Road, Adderbury, Banbury OX17 3NP (Oxfordshire) T: 01295 810605. E: warden@bo-peep.co.uk
**alanrogers.com/UK2610**

Set amongst 85 acres of farmland and woodland, there is an air of spacious informality about this delightful, friendly park which blends perfectly with the surrounding views. Warm Cotswold stone buildings, dovecotes and extensive planting of trees, shrubs and hedges enhance the natural environment of the park. There are 104 numbered pitches all with 16A electricity for caravans and motorhomes in several areas, each with a different character. A separate four acre field for tents provides a further 40 pitches, including four electricity points. One area provides eight gravel hardstandings.

**Facilities**

The original toilet block has been supplemented by a larger, purpose-built unit, all very clean and heated. Large showers and hairdryers. Laundry rooms. Motorcaravan service point. Low level lighting. Excellent small shop with off-licence, gas and basic supplies. Information centre with armchairs and internet access. Fishing. Caravan storage. Caravan cleaning area. Off site: Golf 1 mile. Riding 10 miles. Banbury 3 miles. Blenheim Palace 15 miles. Silverstone 16 miles. Day trips to Stratford-upon-Avon and Warwick.

Open: 14 March - 26 October.

**Directions**

Adderbury village is on the A4260 Banbury - Oxford road. From the north on the M40 use exit 11, the A422 (Banbury) then the A4260. At traffic lights in Adderbury turn on B4100 (Aynho). Park is signed 0.5 miles on the right (0.5 mile drive). From the south on the M40 use exit 10 onto the A43, then the B4100 (Aynho and Adderbury). O.S.GR: SP480348. GPS: 52.01585, -1.299433

**Charges guide**

| | |
|---|---|
| Per unit incl. 2 persons | £ 16.00 - £ 19.00 |
| No credit cards. | |

## Banbury

### Barnstones Caravan & Camping Park

Great Bourton, Banbury OX17 1QU (Oxfordshire) T: 01295 750289
**alanrogers.com/UK2600**

Three miles from Banbury, this small, neat park provides an excellent point from which to explore the Cotswolds, Oxford and Stratford-upon-Avon. There are 49 level pitches of which 44 have gravel hardstanding with a grass area for awnings (only breathable groundsheets are allowed) and electricity (10A); 20 of these are fully serviced. Shrubs, flowers and an oval tarmac road convey an attractive, tidy impression throughout. The park provides a pleasant environment for couples and young families, but it is near the main road, so some traffic noise is to be expected.

**Facilities**

The good toilet block is small, but very clean, heated and well maintained. It is quite adequate for the number of people it serves. Good tiled, adjustable showers. Laundry rooms. Freezer. Gas supplies. Good enclosed play area. Boules. American motorhomes accepted by prior arrangement. Off site: Pub 150 yds. Nearest shop 1 mile. Supermarket, fishing, bicycle hire, golf and riding, all within 3 miles.

Open: All year.

**Directions**

From M40 take exit 11 for Banbury. Follow signs for Banbury and Southom. On the two small roundabouts follow signs for Southom and Great Bourton. At third roundabout turn right on A423, Southom is 2.5 miles. Turn right (Great Bourton) and Crofedy and site is almost immediately on the right. O.S.GR: SP454454. GPS: 52.104966, -1.338868

**Charges 2011**

| | |
|---|---|
| Per unit incl. 2 persons | £ 12.00 - £ 14.00 |
| No credit cards. | |

For latest campsite news visit
**alanrogers.com**

## Beaconsfield

### Highclere Farm Country Touring Park

Newbarn Lane, Seer Green, Beaconsfield HP9 2QZ (Buckinghamshire) T: 01494 874505
E: highclerepark@aol.com  alanrogers.com/UK2750

Only 25 miles from London and 12 miles from Windsor, this is a peaceful park that backs onto fields and woodland. Originally developed around a working farm, the owners continue to keep chickens. There are 95 level pitches all with 10A electricity. Of these, 60 with gravel hardstanding are reserved for caravans and motorcaravans, the remainder being mainly used for tents. The atmosphere is friendly but informal, with reception doubling as a small shop supplying freshly laid eggs. At the top of the park is an open play area and a footpath leading to walks in the surrounding fields.

#### Facilities

The toilet and shower block is fully equipped and can be heated. Large showers (20p). Unit with toilet and washbasin for disabled campers. Baby changing. Two new units (in former stables) provide extra luxury facilities including showers at 50p. Launderette. Fridge and freezer. Basic shop in reception. Play area. Off site: Inn serving food 0.25 miles. Golf 0.5 miles. Riding 2 miles. Bicycle hire 3 miles. Fishing 8 miles.

Open: All year excl. February.

#### Directions

From M40 exit 2 follow signs for Beaconsfield at first roundabout. Then A355 towards Amersham and in 1 mile turn right signed Seer Green and Jordans following signs to park. From the north on M25 take exit 18 to Little Chalfont, B4442 to Chalfont St Giles, through village and park is 1.25 miles.
O.S.GR: SU977927. GPS: 51.625617, -0.590867

#### Charges guide

| | |
|---|---|
| Per unit incl. 2 persons | £ 17.50 - £ 21.50 |

## Bembridge

### Whitecliff Bay Holiday Park

Hillway, Whitecliff Bay, Bembridge PO35 5PL (Isle of Wight) T: 01983 872671. E: holiday@whitecliff-bay.com
alanrogers.com/UK2510

Whitecliff Bay is a very large complex divided by a road, with a holiday home and chalet park on the right hand side, and a touring site on the left hand side. The large touring site is on a sloping hillside with commanding views over the surrounding countryside. The 659 pitches are spread over three fields, the top and second fields are terraced, but field three (the only one in which dogs are permitted in low season only) is quite level. Half of the pitches have electric hook-ups (16A), and there are around 44 gravel hardstandings, 12 in the top field, the remainder in lowest field. There are 13 individual hedged multi-serviced pitches available, so book early. On the opposite side of the lane, in the holiday home park, you will find all the main entertainment and leisure facilities. These include The Culver Club with a bar and evening entertainment, several snack bars and takeaways, supervised swimming pools (indoor and outdoor), a sauna and sunbed, small gym and soft 'playzone' (under eights). Close to the outdoor pool a very steep path leads down to a sandy beach, where there is a small café.

#### Facilities

Three sanitary units, one on the lower part of the site. The other two are fairly close together, not far from reception. Showers (on payment) and a suite (with shower) for disabled visitors. Laundry. Motorcaravan service point. Small shop. Playground. At the holiday home park: Launderette, hairdresser and second larger shop. The Culver Club. Snack bars. Swimming pool (18 x 18 m, Whitsun-end Aug). Indoor fun pool, small gym, a soft play zone (under eights). Dogs only accepted in lower field outside 20/7-31/8. Fully equipped tents to rent. Off site: Golf 5 miles. Bicycle hire 4 miles. Riding 2 miles.

Open: 30 March - 1 November.

#### Directions

Bembridge is at the eastern end of the island. From the A3055 between Ryde and Sandown, turn east at Brading on B3395 for about 2 miles passing the Airfield and Propeller Club, fork right (site signed). Follow signs to site, first entry on right is static area, touring entrance is on left immediately after.
O.S.GR: SZ635865. GPS: 50.67498, -1.09606

#### Charges guide

| | |
|---|---|
| Per unit incl. 2 persons | £ 9.85 - £ 17.35 |
| incl. electricity | £ 13.15 - £ 21.25 |
| incl. full services | £ 16.15 - £ 25.50 |
| extra person | £ 2.85 - £ 6.70 |

For latest campsite news visit
**alanrogers.com**

## Bere Regis
### Rowlands Wait Touring Park
Rye Hill, Bere Regis BH20 7LP (Dorset) T: 01929 472727. E: enquiries@rowlandswait.co.uk

alanrogers.com/UK2050

Rowlands Wait is in a designated Area of Outstanding Natural Beauty and part of the park is officially of Special Scientific Interest. The top of the park, edged by mature woods (full of bluebells in spring) is a haven for tents (and squirrels) with marvellous views and provides 30 pitches in three descending fields. The rest of the park is a little more formal – and nearer to the central toilet block. Most pitches back on to hedging or trees and they are generally level. There are 71 pitches in total with 23 seasonal pitches. Many walks are possible from the park with information leaflets available from reception. It is also possible to walk into the village of Bere Regis. The owners Ivor and Stevie Cargill are keen to welcome nature lovers who enjoy bird watching, walking, and cycling. Sightings of various owls and two pairs of buzzards have been reported on the park. The park is a member of the Countryside Discovery group and is open in winter by arrangement. Rallies are welcome.

**Facilities**

The refurbished toilet block is fully equipped. New family room and facilities for disabled visitors. Laundry room. Recycling bins. Shop (reduced hours in low season) providing basic essentials and a freezer for ice packs. Play area. Games room. Bicycle hire arranged. Torch useful. Off site: Village (10 minute walk) with shops, two pubs, etc. plus a bus service for Dorchester and Poole. Golf 3 miles. Fishing 5 miles. Riding 9 miles.

Open: All year (31 October - 16 March by arrangement).

**Directions**

Park is about 0.5 miles south of Bere Regis on the road to Wool. O.S.GR: SY842933.
GPS: 50.743683, -2.22405

**Charges guide**

| | |
|---|---|
| Per unit incl. 2 persons | £ 11.00 - £ 14.00 |
| incl. electricity | £ 13.00 - £ 16.00 |
| extra person | £ 3.00 - £ 4.00 |
| child (under 16 yrs) | £ 1.50 - £ 2.50 |
| dog | £ 1.00 - £ 2.00 |

## Blandford Forum
### The Inside Park Touring Caravan & Camping Park
Blandford Forum DT11 9AD (Dorset) T: 01258 453719. E: mail@theinsidepark.co.uk

alanrogers.com/UK2070

The Inside Park is set in the grounds of an 18th century country house that burned down in 1941. Family owned and carefully managed alongside an arable farm, this is a must for those interested in local history or arboriculture and it is a haven for wildlife and birds. The nine acre camping field, a little distant, lies in a sheltered, gently sloping dry valley containing superb tree specimens – notably cedars, with walnuts in one part – and a dog graveyard dating back to the early 1700s under a large Cedar of Lebanon. In total there are 125 spacious pitches, 90 with electricity (10A) and some in wooded glades. The six acres adjoining are the old pleasure gardens of the house. The reception/toilet block and games room block are respectively the coach house and stables of the old house. No vehicle access to the park is allowed after 22.30 (there is a separate late arrivals area and car park). Extensive, marked walks are provided through the farmland and a guide is available in the shop.

**Facilities**

The toilet block provides some washbasins in cubicles, comfortably sized showers and facilities for disabled visitors and mothers and babies. Laundry room. Shop with basics, gas and camping provisions. Spacious games room. Safe based adventure play area. Day kennelling facilities for dogs. Mountain bike course. Winter caravan storage. Off site: Blandford leisure and swimming centre (temporary membership possible) 2 miles. Fishing and riding 2 miles. Golf 3 miles. Beach 25 miles.

Open: Easter - 31 October.

**Directions**

Park is about 2 miles southwest of Blandford and is signed from roundabout junction of A354 and A350 roads. O.S.GR: ST864045.
GPS: 50.841333, -2.19515

**Charges guide**

| | |
|---|---|
| Per unit incl. 2 persons and electricity | £ 17.20 - £ 21.00 |

For latest campsite news visit
alanrogers.com

## Bletchingdon
### Greenhill Farm Caravan & Camping Park
Bletchingdon OX5 3BQ (Oxfordshire) T: 01869 351600. E: info@greenhill-leisure-park.co.uk
alanrogers.com/UK2590

On a working farm in a rural setting, this is a newly established site. The approach is a half mile gravel track down into the valley, past recently planted woodlands, fields and the farm. The reception office with a shop and tourist information is located in the farmhouse. A gravel path continues round the park giving access to 61 pitches, all with 16A electricity and 25 with hardstanding. Growing trees and hedges partition the site and screen the water stands. An adjacent field is available for rallies and there is a second smaller field for tents. Continuing developments include two fishing lakes (carp, roach, bream and tench).

**Facilities**

Two new toilet blocks, one in a converted barn with ramp access for facilities for disabled visitors and families. Separate laundry room. Shop (April-Sept). Play area with assault course and basketball hoop. Fishing lakes. Games room which can also be used for meetings. Pets are not accepted 1/3-1/10. Caravan storage. Off site: Golf 2 miles. Boat launching and canal walks 1 mile.

Open: All year.

**Directions**

From M40 exit 9 take A34 to Newbury and Oxford. After 5 miles turn left on B4027 signed Bletchingdon. After 2.5 miles park is on left just past the village. O.S.GR: SP488177. GPS: 51.85754, -1.29142

**Charges 2011**

Per unit incl. 2 persons and electricity £ 15.00 - £ 18.00

## Brockenhurst
### Forest Holidays Hollands Wood
Forest Holidays, Lyndhurst Road, Brockenhurst SO43 7QH (Hampshire) T: 01590 622967
E: info@forestholidays.co.uk alanrogers.com/UK2310

Forest Holidays is a partnership between the Forestry Commission and The Camping & Caravanning Club. This is a large, spacious 168 acre secluded site in a natural woodland setting (mainly oak). It is set in the heart of the New Forest, with an abundance of wildlife. The site is arranged informally with 600 level unmarked pitches but it is stipulated that there must be at least 20 feet between each unit. There are no electrical connections and traffic noise is possible from the A337 which runs alongside one boundary. Brockenhurst village is only half a mile away, where there are shops for supplies and gas.

**Facilities**

Three refurbished toilet blocks provide all necessary requirements, including for disabled visitors and babies. Good laundry room. All these may be under pressure at peak times. Motorcaravan services. Freezer packs and charging of batteries (fee). Maps and guides. Barbecues allowed (off ground). Milk stocked. Barrier closed 22.30-07.00. Night security. Torches essential. Off site: Bicycle hire and riding 2 miles. Golf 3 miles.

Open: 26 March - 27 September.

**Directions**

Site entrance is on east side of A337 Lyndhurst - Lymington road, 0.5 miles north of Brockenhurst. O.S.GR: SU303034. GPS: 50.83655, -1.56952

**Charges guide**

Per unit incl. 2 persons £ 10.00 - £ 26.50
extra person £ 4.25 - £ 8.50
child £ 2.24 - £ 4.25

Discounts for families, backpackers, disabled guests and senior citizens.

## Burford
### Wysdom Touring Park
The Bungalow, Burford School, Burford OX18 4JG (Oxfordshire) T: 01993 823207
alanrogers.com/UK2620

You'll have to go a long way before you find anything else remotely like this site! The land is owned by Burford School and the enterprising caretaker and his wife, caravanners themselves, suggested that they create this wonderful place to raise money for the school (£41,000 raised in 2008/9). Beautifully maintained, it really is like stepping into their own private garden. This 'adults only' park is screened from the main school grounds by trees and provides 25 pitches (6 seasonal), separated by hedges, all with electricity (16A) and some have their own tap. Tents are accepted for short stays by arrangement.

**Facilities**

The heated sanitary building is clean and well maintained with two unisex showers (30p token) – there may be a queue at peak times. (Max. 2 dogs per pitch). Tennis courts. Off site: Burford is yards away with its famous hill full of antique shops, old coaching inns and all those 'interesting' shops it is so much fun rooting about in. Burford Golf Club is next door.

Open: All year (excl. 14 December - 5 January).

**Directions**

From roundabout on A40 at Burford, take A361 towards Lechdale on Thames. Park is a few yards on right signed Burford School. Once in drive watch for narrow entrance to site on right in about 100 yards. O.S.GR: SP250115. GPS: 51.801983, -1.639367

**Charges 2011**

Per unit incl. 2 persons and electricity £ 10.00 - £ 14.00

## Charlbury

### Cotswold View Caravan & Camping Park

Enstone Road, Charlbury OX7 3JH (Oxfordshire) T: 01608 810314. E: bookings@cotswoldview.co.uk

**alanrogers.com/UK2580**

On the edge of the Cotswolds and surrounded by fine views, this well-run family park offers a warm welcome. Originally a working farm, the touring park and self catering country cottages are situated amongst 54 acres of farmland. Wide gravel or tarmac roads ensure easy access to the 125 pitches (all with 10A electricity) in the ten acre touring area. The park has been thoughtfully separated by hedges into different areas to enable those with children to be close to play areas, and quieter areas for those wanting to enjoy the peaceful surroundings. The small reception also serves as a licensed shop selling freshly baked bread and homemade cakes. Farmhouse breakfasts (ordered the night before) are served in the farmhouse itself with B&B also offered. Extensive tree planting has been undertaken to create well defined and maintained grass trails in the forest. There is also a farm trail where small animals, pigs, sheep and donkeys in enclosures can be observed. Convenient for touring the Cotswolds, there is also a good train service for day trips to London.

### Facilities

Two well maintained heated toilet blocks provide washbasins in cubicles, showers, two family shower rooms (free), bathrooms (50p) and hairdryers. Good units for disabled visitors. Baby changing area. Laundry facilities. Motorcaravan service point. Shop and off-licence. Bar. Play areas. Games room. Tennis. Outdoor chess and draughts. Skittle alley. American motorhomes accepted. Security barrier (£5 deposit). Off site: Fishing 1 mile. Golf 7 miles. Riding 10 miles. Boat launching 1 mile.

Open: Easter/1 April - 31 October.

### Directions

From A44 Oxford - Chipping Norton road, take B4022 to Charlbury, just south of Enstone. Park is 2 miles on left. O.S.GR: SP365210. GPS: 51.886167, -1.4708

### Charges guide

| | |
|---|---|
| Per unit incl. 2 persons and electricity | £ 15.00 - £ 19.50 |
| extra person | £ 2.25 |
| child (6-16 yrs) | £ 2.00 |
| dog | free |

## Christchurch

### Grove Farm Meadow Holiday Park

Meadowbank Holidays, Stour Way, Christchurch BH23 2PQ (Dorset) T: 01202 483597

E: enquiries@meadowbank-holidays.co.uk   **alanrogers.com/UK2130**

Grove Farm Meadow is a quiet, traditional park with caravan holiday homes and a small provision for touring units. The grass flood bank which separates the River Stour from this park provides an attractive pathway. The river bank has been kept natural and is well populated by a range of water birds. It is popular with bird watchers and there is fishing in the river. There are just under 200 caravan holiday homes (75 for hire), sited in regular rows. For touring units there are 41 level pitches, all clearly numbered with electricity (10A), backing on to fencing or hedging and accessed by tarmac roads. There are 21 fully serviced with hardstanding, shingle base for awnings and chemical disposal point (the other grass pitches share service points). The impressive modern reception has a good collection of tourist information. The Littledown Centre, said to be the south coast's premier leisure facility is nearby. Bournemouth is ten minutes by car, Christchurch just five.

### Facilities

The well kept toilet block provides a bathroom for each sex (50p). Separate toilet and washbasin with ramped access for disabled visitors. Baby room. Spin dryer, iron and board and washing lines provided. Launderette near reception. Well stocked shop (limited hours in low season). Games room with pool table and electronic games. Adventure play area beside the river bank. Fishing (permits from reception). Dogs or other pets are not accepted. Off site: Golf 0.5 miles. Large supermarket 1.5 miles. Beach, boat launching and sailing 2 miles. St Catherine's nature reserve.

Open: 1 March - 31 October.

### Directions

From A388 Ringwood - Bournemouth road take B3073 for Christchurch. Turn right at the first roundabout and Stour Way is the third road on the right. O.S.GR: SZ136946. GPS: 50.750336, -1.807938

### Charges guide

| | |
|---|---|
| Per 'luxury' pitch incl. 2 persons and electricity | £ 14.00 - £ 27.00 |
| large pitch | £ 11.50 - £ 23.00 |
| standard pitch (no awnings) | £ 8.50 - £ 17.50 |
| extra person over 5 yrs | £ 1.00 - £ 2.00 |
| extra car or boat | £ 1.00 - £ 2.00 |

## Cowes
### Waverley Park Holiday Centre
51 Old Road, East Cowes PO32 6AW (Isle of Wight) T: 01983 293452. E: sue@waverley-park.co.uk
alanrogers.com/UK2530

This pleasant, small, family owned site is set in the grounds of an old country house which was once frequently visited by Dr Arnold, the subject of 'Tom Brown's Schooldays'. The owners have now terraced the grass area for touring units. This has created 31 large and level, well spaced, fully serviced hardstanding pitches all with outstanding views over the Solent. The remaining 14 caravan pitches share a sloping grass area with tents – these have no electricity. To one side there are 75 private and rental holiday homes. At the bottom of the park a gate leads onto the promenade and the pebble beach which is popular with sailors and windsurfers. The site, just five minutes from the East Cowes ferry terminal, is an ideal vantage point for Cowes Week, and has good views of the ocean liners sailing in and out of Southampton. A chain ferry across the Medina River operates between East Cowes and the famous West Cowes with its altogether better shops and tourist attractions.

### Facilities
At the top of the park, a toilet block provides the usual facilities, including some spacious cubicles with washbasins en-suite. Good suite for disabled visitors with baby changing. Basic chemical disposal point in the static area. Laundry facilities. Heated outdoor pool and paddling pool with sun terrace. Club with restaurant and bar serving good value meals, plus family entertainment in season (Whitsun-early Sept). Small adventure style playground. Games room. Boats accepted by prior arrangement – public slipway nearby. Off site: Tennis courts nearby. East Cowes, with its basic shops and services is within walking distance. Bus stop in East Lewes.

Open: All year.

### Directions
Immediately after leaving Southampton - Cowes car ferry, take first left, then right into Old Road, and park entrance is 300 yds on left. O.S.GR: SZ505958. GPS: 50.76088, -1.28366

### Charges guide
Per unit incl. 2 persons
and electricity                        £ 15.00 - £ 21.00
During Cowes Week min. pitch fees apply (£12.00 - £14.50). Packages incl. ferry travel and other offers available.

## Cowes
### Thorness Bay Holiday Park
Thorness Bay, Cowes PO31 8NJ (Isle of Wight) T: 01983 523109. E: holiday.sales@park.resorts.com
alanrogers.com/UK2520

Spread over a large area of rural down and woodland that slopes down to the beach at Thorness Bay, this is a large site with more than 500 holiday homes. The touring area has around 90 pitches, most with electricity (16A) including 27 multi-serviced pitches on gravel hardstandings with electricity, water, drain and TV points. These and some grass pitches are on terraces served by tarmac roads. The remainder are on sloping open grassland either divided by ranch style rails or in an open tent area, and all have views of the surrounding countryside. The main activity centre is located in the holiday home area, a short walk from the touring site. Outdoor sporting activities on-site include a multisport court, soccer, archery, and fencing. The indoor pool provides snorkelling, scuba diving and adult only swimming sessions. There is evening entertainment for all the family.

### Facilities
New toilet block providing showers, WCs and washbasins. Suite for disabled visitors. Baby changing. Laundry facilities. Shop. Indoor pool. Indoor playroom for small children. Adventure playground. Multisport court. Children's club. Off site: The beach is easily accessed from the main entertainment complex. All the attractions of the Island are within easy day-trip distances. Riding within 1 mile. Golf 4 miles.

Open: Easter - 29 October.

### Directions
Thorness Bay is southwest of Cowes. From East Cowes ferry follow signs to Newport. Follow A3054 (Yarmouth). Continue for about 2.5 miles to crossroads, turning right (north) to Thorness Bay. After about 2 miles, on sharp right hand bend, turn left, site signed. O.S.GR: SZ452926. GPS: 50.731133, -1.360467

### Charges guide
Per unit incl. electricity and
up to 6 persons                        £ 6.00 - £ 30.00
tent pitch                             £ 3.00 - £ 27.00
hardstanding pitch, plus                        £ 5.00
dog                                    £ 1.00 - £ 3.00

For latest campsite news visit
**alanrogers.com**

## Fordingbridge
### Sandy Balls Holiday Centre

328

Godshill, Fordingbridge SP6 2JZ (Hampshire) T: 0845 2702248. E: post@sandy-balls.co.uk

alanrogers.com/UK2290

Sandy Balls sits high above the sweep of the Avon river near Fordingbridge, amidst woodland which is protected as a nature reserve. It well deserves the entry it has maintained in these guides for over 30 years and continues to improve and develop. Very well run and open all year, the 120 acre park has many private holiday homes as well as 26 caravan holiday homes and 117 lodges for rent. The touring areas have 233 marked and hedged serviced pitches, for caravans and tents on part-hardstanding and part-grass, with 16A electricity and TV connections. In August there is an additional unmarked tent area. In winter only 50 pitches are available. A woodland leisure trail allows wild animals and birds to be observed in their natural surroundings and the attractions of the New Forest are close at hand. The heart of this holiday centre is the architecturally designed multi-million pound 'village'. With its traffic-free piazza, here are the bistro, pub, Guest Services bureau, gift shop, cycle shop, small supermarket and leisure club, all designed to blend in with the forest surroundings and provide space to relax and meet friends. A member of the Best of British Group.

### Facilities

Three refurbished toilet blocks have under-floor heating and washbasins in cubicles. One 'portacabin' style unit remains as an overflow in the tent field. Toilets for disabled visitors and baby facilities. Excellent central launderette. Motorcaravan service point. Entertainment (high season only). Outdoor pool (25/5-30/8). Indoor pool (66x30 ft). Well equipped gym, jacuzzi, steam room, sauna and solarium. Tempus therapy centre. Games room. Adventure playground and play areas. Soft play area. Clay modelling tuition and story telling. Tepees and tents for rent. River fishing (permit). Riding stables. Bicycle hire. Archery. Dogs only allowed on certain fields. Off site: Golf 6 miles. Beach 20 miles.

Open: All year.

### Directions

Park is well signed 1.5 miles east of Fordingbridge on the B3078 O.S.GR: SU168147.
GPS: 50.930267, -1.7602

### Charges guide

| Per unit incl. 2 persons | |
|---|---|
| and electricity | £ 10.00 - £ 37.00 |
| extra person | free - £ 3.50 |
| child (12-17 yrs) | free - £ 2.00 |
| child (3-11 yrs) | free - £ 1.50 |
| dog | free - £ 3.00 |

## Fordingbridge

### Hill Cottage Farm Camping & Caravan Park

Sandleheath Road, Alderholt, Fordingbridge SP6 3EG (Hampshire) T: 01425 650513
E: hillcottagefarmcaravansite@supanet.com  alanrogers.com/UK2360

This established, modern site is set in 47 acres of beautiful countryside on the Dorset and Hampshire border. The 35 pitches, all on hardstandings with electric hook-ups (16A), water taps and drainage are arranged around a circular gravel roadway. Secluded and sheltered, they have views across the surrounding countryside. A field, also with electric hook-ups, alongside the camping area is used for tents and rallies, and has space for ball games and a small playground. Also on site there are two small lakes for coarse fishing, and there are many woodland walks in the area. Overall this site is more suitable for adults and younger children – it is not really designed for active teenagers.

**Facilities**

A large modern barn-style building provides excellent heated facilities. Laundry room. Facilities for disabled visitors and babies. Facilities for tent pitches. First floor games room with full size snooker table, two pool tables and darts board, plus a separate function room. Motorcaravan services. Shop. Playground. WiFi. Shepherd's hut for hire. Off site: Village centre with pub, church, Post Office and store is a 20 minute woodland walk. Local attractions include Rockbourne Roman Villa, Cranborne Chase, The Dolls Museum at Fordingbridge, Salisbury, and Ringwood with its Wednesday market.

Open: 1 March - 30 November.

**Directions**

From Fordingbridge take B3078 westwards for 2 miles to Alderholt. On entering the village, at left hand bend, turn right towards Sandleheath (site signed) and site entrance is about 300 yards on the left. O.S.GR: SU120130.
GPS: 50.919017, -1.832783

**Charges guide**

Per unit incl. 2 persons
and electricity                          £ 17.00 - £ 27.00
extra person                             £ 5.00
child (0-15 yrs)                         £ 2.00 - £ 4.00
dog                                      £ 1.00

## Freshwater

### Heathfield Farm Camping

Heathfield Road, Freshwater PO40 9SH (Isle of Wight) T: 01983 407822. E: web@heathfieldcamping.co.uk
alanrogers.com/UK2500

Heathfield is a pleasant contrast to many of the other sites on the Isle of Wight, in that it is a 'no frills' sort of place, very popular with tenters, cyclists and small camper vans. Despite its name, it is no longer a working farm. A large, open meadow provides 60 large, level pitches, 50 with electricity (10A). Two small fenced areas provide traffic free zones for backpackers and cyclists' tents. There is no shop as you are only eight minutes walk from the centre of Freshwater. The site overlooks Colwell Bay and across the Solent towards Milford-on-Sea and Hurst Castle. A play field for ball games also has two picnic tables and two barbecues, and there is a wild flower meadow with the perimeter mown for dog walking. It is ideal for visiting attractions on the western side of the island including Totland and Freshwater Bays, The Needles and Old Battery, Compton Down, and Mottistone Manor Garden. The Military road which runs from Freshwater Bay to St Catherine's Point gives spectacular coastal views.

**Facilities**

The main toilet unit is housed in a modern, ingeniously customised, Portacabin type unit including one washbasin cubicle for ladies and a baby room. Showers have two pushbutton controls, one for pre-mixed hot water, the other for cold only. A second similar unit has WCs and washbasins in cubicles, plus facilities for disabled visitors. Laundry facilities. Motorcaravan service point. Gas supplies. Ice pack service. Play field. Bicycle hire arranged. No commercial vehicles are accepted. Gate locked 22.30-07.00. Off site: Bus stop 200 m. Beach 0.5 miles. Fishing 0.5 miles. Golf 1.25 miles. Riding 3 miles.

Open: 1 May - 30 September.

**Directions**

From A3054 north of Totland and Colwell turn into Heathfield Road where site is signed. Site entrance is on right after a short distance. O.S.GR: SZ336879.
GPS: 50.68940, -1.52704

**Charges 2011**

Per unit incl. 2 persons
and electricity                          £ 12.00 - £ 19.00
Min pitch fee July/Aug £17.

**Heathfield Farm Camping** www.heathfieldcamping.co.uk
Heathfield Rd., Freshwater, **Isle of Wight** PO40 9SH
Proprietors Mike & Doreen Haslin    Tel: 01983 407822
• Peaceful family park          • Touring & tents
• Magnificient views            • Excellent washing facilities
• Close to beach & bus route    • Two miles Yarmouth & The Needles
*Located in the peaceful West Wight with easy access to spectacular coastal and download walks.*

Southern England

For latest campsite news visit
**alanrogers.com**

111

## Hamble

### Riverside Holidays

Satchell Lane, Hamble, Southampton SO31 4HR (Hampshire) T: 023 8045 3220
E: enquiries@riversideholidays.co.uk  alanrogers.com/UK2315

What makes Riverside so special is its location; close to the River Hamble, Mecca for the international yachtsman. The site is family-owned and covers five acres surrounded by trees and hedges; it has 123 pitches of which 77 are level for touring caravans and tents with 53 electricity hook-ups (16A). The remaining pitches are used for lodges and residential and static caravans on slightly rising ground, but so well spaced and with plenty of grass they are not too obtrusive. A warden-run log cabin reception, with tourist information, including local bus and rail times, is at the entrance. Hamble village, one mile away, with its cobbled streets, pubs and restaurants, is famed the world over for its association with yachting. This is an ideal base for the Southampton Boat Show, Cowes Week and its very own Hamble Week Regatta. On the marina adjacent to the site, a mere two minutes walk, is Oyster Quay with a bar and restaurant overlooking hundreds of yachts worth millions.

### Facilities

A brand new 'lodge' contains the sanitary facilities, including family and baby changing rooms. The old 'portacabin' style unit has been kept for busy periods. Small laundry room alongside. All these facilities could be under pressure in high season. Bicycle hire. Caravan storage. Off site: Buses and trains 1 mile. Fishing, sea fishing, sailing, supermarket, 1 mile in village. Riding 3 miles. Golf 4 miles. You can catch a small ferry across to Warsash on the other bank or take a boat up to the Upper Hamble Country Park. The New Forest, Winchester and Portsmouth are nearby.

Open: 1 March - 31 October.

### Directions

From M27 exit 8 follow signs for Hamble. Take the B3397 with Tesco on the left, continue 1.9 miles through traffic lights until Hound roundabout. After 50 yds turn left into Satchell Lane (signed Mercury Marina) and site is on left in 1 mile.
O.S. GR: SU484082. GPS: 50.868835, -1.313586

### Charges year

| Per unit incl. 2 persons and electricity | £ 15.00 - £ 32.00 |
|---|---|
| extra person | £ 3.50 |
| child (4-16 yrs) | £ 2.50 |
| dog | £ 2.50 |

Camping Cheques accepted.

## Maidenhead

### Hurley Riverside Park

Hurley, Maidenhead SL6 5NE (Berkshire) T: 01628 824493. E: info@hurleyriversidepark.co.uk

alanrogers.com/UK2700

On the banks of the Thames, not far from Henley-on-Thames, you will find the picturesque village of Hurley where some buildings date back to 1086. Just outside the village is Hurley Riverside Park providing facilities for holiday homes, touring units and moorings for boats. The touring area is flat and separated into smaller fields. With the pitches arranged around the outside of each field and the centre left free, the park has a spacious feel. There are 138 touring pitches with 10A electricity including 12 fully serviced on long hardstandings. A camping field provides a further 62 pitches including six electric hook-ups. A very popular park, there is also a large rally field. You can enjoy walks along the banks of the Thames or visit the various pubs and restaurants in the village for a good meal and a pint. A new nature trail has been installed along the length of the Touring Park and there are large riverside picnic grounds alongside the Thames. Nearby Windsor has its famous castle or for younger members of the family, Windsor is the home of Legoland. At Henley you can watch the regatta. Alternatively, you can just relax in the peaceful settings of the site.

#### Facilities

Nature trail, riverside picnic grounds, slipway and fishing in season. Discounted tickets for Legoland Windsor, Thorpe Park and Chessington are available from reception. Three wooden toilet blocks (raised on legs) include a very good new unisex block with private bathrooms (shower, washbasin, toilet). The other blocks have been renovated and are well equipped. Separate shower and toilet facilities for disabled visitors. Baby area. Laundry. Motorcaravan service point. Shop at reception. Fishing. WiFi. Temporary moorings. Off site: Golf 5 miles. Riding 10 miles. Legoland at Windsor, Thorpe Park.

Open: 1 March - 31 October.

#### Directions

From M4 exit 8/9 take A404M towards Wycombe. After 3 miles take A4130 (Henley). Go down steep hill (Hurley village signed on right) - ignore this turning and take next right (site signed from here).
O.S.GR: SU825838. GPS: 51.5466, -0.8248

#### Charges guide

| | |
|---|---|
| Per unit incl. 2 persons | £ 11.00 - £ 21.00 |
| full services | £ 15.00 - £ 24.00 |
| extra person | £ 2.00 |
| child (5-17 yrs) | £ 1.50 |
| dog | £ 2.00 |

## Milford-on-Sea

### Lytton Lawn Touring Park

Lymore Lane, Milford-on-Sea SO41 0TX (Hampshire) T: 01590 648331. E: holidays@shorefield.co.uk

alanrogers.com/UK2280

Lytton Lawn is the touring arm of Shorefield Country Park, a nearby holiday home park and leisure centre. Set in eight acres, Lytton Lawn provides 135 marked pitches. These include 53 'premier' pitches (hardstanding, 16A electricity, pitch light, water and waste water outlet) in a grassy, hedged area – this section with its heated toilet block is open for a longer season. The rest of the pitches, all with electricity, are in the adjoining, but separate, gently sloping field, edged with mature trees and hedges and with a further toilet block. The larger reception and well stocked shop make this a good, comfortable, self sufficient site. Visitors to Lytton Lawn are entitled to use the comprehensive leisure facilities at Shorefield itself (2.5 miles away). These include a very attractive indoor pool, solarium, sauna and spa, fitness classes and treatments, all weather tennis courts, outdoor pools, restaurant facilities including a bistro (Easter-November), and entertainment and activity programmes. These are of a very good standard and mostly free (extra charges are made for certain activities).

#### Facilities

Two modern toilet blocks are well fitted. Washing machine and dryer. Baby changing. Facilities for disabled visitors (Radar key). Motorcaravan service point. Shop (Easter - end October). Small fenced play area and hedged field with goal posts. Euro tents for rent. Off site: Village pub 10 minutes walk. Golf, riding, coarse fishing (all within 3 miles), sailing, windsurfing and boat launching facilities (1.5 miles). The New Forest, Isle of Wight, Bournemouth, Southampton and the beach at Milford on Sea are nearby.

Open: All year excl. 3 January - 4 February.

#### Directions

From M27 follow signs for Lyndhurst and Lymington on A337. Continue towards New Milton. Lytton Lawn is signed at Everton; Shorefield is at Downton.
O.S.GR: SZ293937. GPS: 50.73497, -1.61803

#### Charges 2011

| | |
|---|---|
| Per unit incl. 6 persons and electricity | £ 12.00 - £ 36.00 |
| premier pitch incl. water, drainage and TV connection | £ 14.50 - £ 39.50 |
| dog | £ 1.50 - £ 3.00 |

*See advertisement on page 125.*

## Newbridge
### The Orchards Holiday Caravan & Camping Park

Newbridge, Yarmouth PO41 0TS (Isle of Wight) T: 01983 531331. E: info@orchards-holiday-park.co.uk
alanrogers.com/UK2450

In a village situation in the quieter western part of the island, The Orchards Holiday Park, a park for all seasons, has panoramic views of rolling countryside and the Solent. The park's neat 11 acre touring area has 164 marked pitches for tents, caravans and motorhomes, broken up by apple trees, mature hedges and fences. All pitches have electricity, 62 have hardstandings and 22 are 'all service' pitches, also with hardstanding. A meeting room is suitable for small rallies. A separate area contains 64 caravan holiday homes. The Orchards is a good base from which to explore the island and there are two beaches within five miles. The scenic harbour of Yarmouth is 5 minutes away, as are the attractions of Fort Victoria and Chessil Pottery, with bird watching at Newtown Creek. Osbourne House is 20 minutes away. There are walking and cycling routes from the park with leaflets available from reception. The park is part of the Caravan Club's affiliated scheme. A member of the Best of British group.

### Facilities

An excellent new facilities centre provides 24 shower and washbasin cubicles, a family bathroom, 2 family shower rooms, fully accessible facilities, spacious laundry and ironing area, walkers' drying room, baby changing room, campers' kitchen area and indoor washing up area all with underfloor heating. Shop. Gas supplies. Indoor heated pool (Feb-Dec). Outdoor heated pool (May-Sept). Licensed coffee shop. Takeaway (mid Mar-Sept). Play areas. TV and amusements rooms. Off site: Bus stop at entrance. Membership for village social club. Discount available at Freshwater Bus stop at entrance.

Open: All year excl. 3 January - 15 February.

### Directions

Park is in Newbridge village, signed north from B3401 (Yarmouth - Newport) road.
O.S.GR: SZ411878. GPS: 50.687967, -1.419967

### Charges guide

| | |
|---|---|
| Per unit incl. 2 persons and electricity | £ 16.00 - £ 30.00 |
| extra person | £ 4.50 - £ 6.50 |
| child | £ 2.00 - £ 5.00 |

No pitch fee for hikers or cyclists.
Packages incl. ferry travel - ring park for best deal.
Camping Cheques accepted.

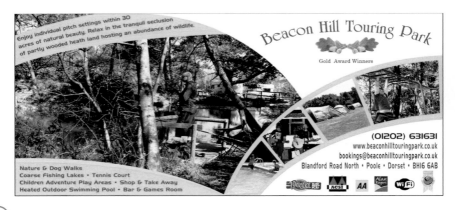

## Poole

### Pear Tree Holiday Park

Organford Road, Holton Heath, Poole BH16 6LA (Dorset) T: 01202 622434. E: enquiries@peartreepark.co.uk
alanrogers.com/UK2110

Pear Tree is a neat, landscaped and well cared for park welcoming families with young children and couples only. Set in 7.5 acres, with mature trees and views across to Wareham Forest, there are 154 pitches in total, of which around 90 are for touring with hardstanding, electricity (10A), water and drainage. Only breathable groundsheets are permitted for awnings. The tent area is a tranquil, secluded spot with many mature trees. Reception, incorporating tourist information and a small shop supplying milk, bread, gas and other basics, is at the entrance. The gates (with key) are closed at dusk, although latecomers are admitted. A large, hedged, separate play field for younger children has swings, a climbing frame, trampolines and ball games area. There is a walk from the back of the park into Wareham Forest.

#### Facilities

The main heated toilet block (opened by key and recently refurbished) provides some washbasins in cubicles, baby changing unit (two new family rooms with Belfast sink baby bath and a 'wet room' for disabled visitors. Separate small block near the tent area. All is kept spotlessly clean. Shop (basics only). Play area. All year caravan storage. Off site: A bus service stops outside for Wareham (2.5 miles) or Poole (5 miles). The Clay Pipe Inn 500 m. Bicycle hire 0.5 miles. Golf 2.5 miles. Riding 5 miles. Beach 9 miles.

Open: 1 March - 31 October.

#### Directions

From the A351 (Wareham - Poole) road, turn west at traffic lights in Holton Heath (signed Organford and Sandford Caravan Park). Park is on left after about 550 m. past Sandford Park and the Clay Pipe Inn. O.S.GR: SY940915. GPS: 50.724033, -2.086967

#### Charges guide

| | |
|---|---|
| Per unit incl. 2 persons and electricity | £ 17.00 - £ 23.00 |
| extra person | £ 5.00 - £ 6.00 |
| child (5-16 yrs) | £ 2.00 |
| dog | £ 2.50 |

A perfect touring caravan park in beautiful Dorset, located minutes from a variety of sandy beaches

pear tree holiday park

darwin holiday parks

- Convenience shop
- Local pub just a short walk away
- Children's play area
- Mains electricity
- Seasonal Pitches
- Waste disposal point

Pet Friendly

To book: 01202 622 434 or www.peartreepark.co.uk

## Poole

### Beacon Hill Touring Park

Blandford Road North, Poole BH16 6AB (Dorset) T: 01202 631631. E: bookings@beaconhilltouringpark.co.uk
alanrogers.com/UK2180

Beacon Hill is located in a marvellous, natural environment of partly wooded heathland, with certain areas of designated habitation for protected species such as sand lizards and the Dartford Warbler, but there is also easy access to main routes. Wildlife ponds encourage dragonflies and other species but fishing is also possible. Conservation is obviously important in such a special area but one can ramble at will over the 30 acres with the hilltop walk a must. Grassy open spaces provide 170 pitches, 151 with 10A electricity, on sandy grass which is sometimes uneven. Of these, 50 are for tents only and a few are seasonal. The undulating nature of land and the trees allows for discrete areas to be allocated for varying needs, for example young families near the play area, families with teenagers close to the bar/games room, those with dogs near the dog walking area, and young people further away. A wide range of facilities includes an open air pool. It is well situated for beaches, Poole harbour and ferries for France.

#### Facilities

Two fully equipped toilet blocks include facilities for disabled visitors. Laundry facilities. Well stocked shop at reception. Coffee bar and takeaway (main season). Bar (July/Aug, B.Hs, half-terms). Heated swimming pool (mid May-mid Sept). All weather tennis. Adventure play areas with hideaway. Games room. TV room. Internet (WiFi). Fishing (charged). Off site: Poole harbour and ferries 3 miles. Riding 2 miles. Bicycle hire 3 miles.

Open: 17 March - end September.

#### Directions

Park is about 3 miles north of Poole. Take the A350 (Blandford) at roundabout where A350 joins A35. Park signed to right after about 400 yards. O.S.GR: SY977945. GPS: 50.74953, -2.03446

#### Charges guide

| | |
|---|---|
| Per unit incl. 2 persons | £ 13.50 - £ 35.00 |
| extra person | £ 3.50 - £ 6.50 |
| child (3-15 yrs) | £ 2.50 - £ 3.00 |
| dog | £ 1.00 - £ 1.50 |

For latest campsite news visit
## alanrogers.com

## Poole
### South Lytchett Manor Caravan & Camping Park
Dorset Road, Lytchett Minster, Poole BH16 6JB (Dorset) T: 01202 622577. E: info@southlytchettmanor.co.uk
alanrogers.com/UK2120

Joanne and her husband are rightly proud of what they have achieved in three years at South Lytchett Manor. It has an unusual situation on parkland either side of what was once one of the driveways to the manor itself with impressive gates at the entrance. The access to the manor (it is now a school) is now closed off but there is room for 150 pitches in meadows or bays or beside the roadway. All are level, of a good size, with TV connections and have electricity, and 54 have hardstanding, water and waste water. They are neatly landscaped with rural views. There is extra provision for tents on meadowland to one side. The manor was occupied by the Americans in the last war and some 500 tanks were once camouflaged down the tree-lined avenue. The shop seems to provide everything including eggs from chickens on site which happily peck away in their own enclosure. A path from the site leads to the Courtyard Centre with Craft Shop and Café and Lytchett Minister itself is within walking distance down the road. The site has an arrangement with the local pub for special meal 'deals' and local takeaways will deliver to the site. There is much to explore on the Isle of Purbeck and the Jurassic Coast. Joanne and David have really tried hard to meet all your needs and they and their staff make you very welcome.

### Facilities
Three modern fully equipped toilet blocks with four en-suite family rooms and facilities for disabled visitors. Motorcaravan service point. Laundry. Well stocked shop with off licence and gas. Games room. Play area. Playing field. Woodland walk. Dog walk. Tourist Information Centre. Internet and WiFi. Bicycle hire. Off site: Regular bus service passes site entrance for nearby Poole or Weymouth. Shops, pubs, ATM 1 mile. Beach and sailing 2 miles. Golf, fishing and riding 3 miles. Ferry port 3 miles.

Open: 1 March - 2 January.

### Directions
At the roundabout at the end of the dual carriageway on the A35 to the west of Poole turn north on the B3067 to Lytchett Minster. Go through village and site is on the left half a mile past the church. O.S.GR: SY966934. GPS: 50.73959, -2.05542

### Charges guide
| | |
|---|---|
| Per unit incl. 2 persons and electricity | £ 15.00 - £ 27.00 |
| extra person | £ 4.50 - £ 7.50 |
| child (3-14 yrs) | £ 2.00 - £ 4.00 |
| dog | free - £ 1.00 |

## Ringwood
### Shamba Holidays

Ringwood Road, Saint Leonards, Ringwood BH24 2SB (Hampshire) T: 01202 873302
E: enquiries@shambaholidays.co.uk  alanrogers.com/UK2340

Shamba is a family run, very modern park, although the aim remains to create a relaxed, pleasant atmosphere. There are 150 pitches, most of which are used for touring units, 45 are on a seasonal basis and three new fields have been opened for tents (no electricity) for three weeks in August. Surrounded by trees, the camping area is on flat, open grass with electricity (10/16A) available on all pitches. A Scandinavian style building forms the focal point and here you will find reception, a bar/restaurant, takeaway and a shop. The indoor swimming pool has walls and a roof which can be opened in good weather. The park's location is excellent for a short stop-over but well worth a longer stay for a family holiday. Bournemouth with its shops and beaches is eight miles, while the delights of the New Forest and Dorset are within easy reach.

### Facilities

Sanitary facilities with under-floor heating include modern showers, washbasins and toilets and family changing rooms. Baby rooms with bath and facilities for disabled visitors. Launderette. Motorcaravan service point. Bar with meals and takeaway. Indoor swimming pool (12x6 m, heated) and children's pool. Large play area. Amusements room. Adjacent field for dog walking and football/sports pitch. Off site: Riding 1 mile. Golf 2 miles. Fishing and bicycle hire 2.5 miles. Ringwood 2.5 miles. Moors Valley Country Park 1 mile. Beach 8 miles.

Open: 1 March - 31 October.

### Directions

Take the A31 westbound from Ringwood, after 3 miles, at second roundabout, turn back on yourself and after only 20 m. turn left at the park sign.
O.S.GR: SU104026. GPS: 50.825067, -1.853117

### Charges 2011

Per unit incl. 2 persons
and electricity £ 20.00 - £ 30.00
A minimum advance booking policy applies at peak periods.
Camping Cheques accepted.

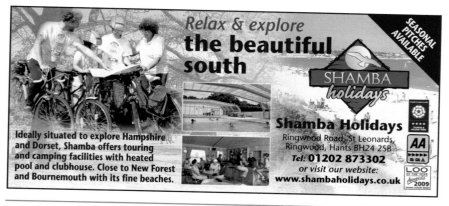

Relax & explore
the beautiful south

SHAMBA holidays

SEASONAL PITCHES AVAILABLE

Shamba Holidays
Ringwood Road, St Leonards,
Ringwood, Hants BH24 2SB
Tel: 01202 873302
or visit our website:
www.shambaholidays.co.uk

AA

Ideally situated to explore Hampshire and Dorset, Shamba offers touring and camping facilities with heated pool and clubhouse. Close to New Forest and Bournemouth with its fine beaches.

## Ringwood
### Red Shoot Camping Park

Linwood, Ringwood BH24 3QT (Hampshire) T: 01425 473789. E: enquiries@redshoot-campingpark.com
alanrogers.com/UK2350

Red Shoot is set on four acres of open, slightly sloping, level grass, in the heart of the New Forest. A simple, rural retreat with panoramic views of the surrounding countryside and forest, it is very popular in high season. There are 120 good sized pitches, 45 with electrical hook-ups (10A), served by a circular gravel road. There is no site lighting so a torch would be useful. The adjacent Red Shoot Inn (under separate ownership) serves hot or cold meals and brews its own real ales – Forest Gold and Tom's Tipple. There are ample opportunities for walking, cycling and naturalist pursuits in the area. Local attractions include watersports at the New Forest Water Park near Ringwood, a Doll Museum in Fordingbridge, cider making in Burley, and Breamore House just north of Fordingbridge.

### Facilities

The toilet and shower facilities have been upgraded to a high standard with underfloor heating, including a family shower room/baby bath and changing area. Well equipped laundry room. Good unit for disabled visitors. Very well stocked, licensed shop. Fenced adventure style playground. Off site: Fishing 5 miles. Riding 6 miles. Golf 7 miles. Beach 12 miles. Nearby Ringwood has a market on Wednesday.

Open: 1 March - 31 October.

### Directions

From A338 about 1.75 miles north of Ringwood, turn east (signed Linwood and Moyles Court). Follow signs, over a staggered crossroads, and continue straight on for another 1.75 miles to Red Shoot Inn. O.S.GR: SU188095. GPS: 50.883917, -1.7347

### Charges guide

Per unit incl. 2 persons
and electricity £ 19.00 - £ 28.00
extra person £ 7.00
child (3-14 yrs) £ 3.80

For latest campsite news visit
**alanrogers.com**

## Ringwood

### Forest Edge Holiday Park

229 Ringwood Road, Saint Leonards, Ringwood BH242SD (Hampshire) T: 01590 648331
E: holidays@shorefield.co.uk alanrogers.com/UK2285

This popular family park is part of the Shorefield Group. Offering 120 pitches for tents and touring holidays and eight caravan holiday homes, it is complemented by the leisure facilities available at Oakdene Forest Park (which is no longer taking any touring units). There is easy access to the level, marked pitches, each with 16A electricity hook-ups. The cheerful, flowery reception and well stocked shop help create a friendly and relaxed atmosphere. Picnic tables are dotted about the park giving it a country feel. A short walk through Hurn Forest (less than a mile) leads to Oakdene and its new clubhouse and entertainment centre. Visitors at Forest Edge may use the bar, restaurant, large pools, games room and other free entertainment which is ideal for families not wishing to travel too far. The location of Forest Edge is ideal for visiting Bournemouth (beaches, shops and shows), the New Forest and all the attractions of Dorset.

| Facilities | Directions |
|---|---|
| The toilet block provides clean but fairly standard facilities. Unit for disabled visitors. Baby area. These facilities may be under pressure in high season. Laundry in a separate room near the children's adventure play area. Gas supplies. Shop with off-licence. Heated outdoor swimming pool (Whitsun-Sept, weekends only plus school holidays). Football and netball court. Games room. Off site: Riding 1 mile. Fishing 1 mile. Golf 1 mile. Beach 7 miles.<br><br>Open: 4 February - 2 January. | Take the A31 westbound from Ringwood. After 3 miles and two roundabouts, turn left at the second roundabout into Boundary Lane (before reaching Oakdene). Site is signed. O.S.GR: SU105024. GPS: 50.82137, -1.84989 |

Charges 2011

| Per unit incl. 6 persons | |
|---|---|
| and electricity | £ 12.00 - £ 36.00 |
| dog | £ 1.50 - £ 3.00 |

*See advertisement on page 125.*

## Riseley

### Wellington Country Park

Riseley, Reading RG7 1SP (Berkshire) T: 01189 326444. E: info@wellington-country-park.co.uk
alanrogers.com/UK2690

Wellington Country Park is open to the general public on payment of an entry fee (entry for campers however, is included in your pitch fees) and many visit it for a day out. It contains children's play areas, slides, sand pits, nine-hole crazy golf, an animal farm and petting barn, miniature railway (£1 extra), four nature trails, a deer park and a host of play equipment to climb in and on. The camping site, and consequently your pitch, is situated within woodland which is part of 350-acre park. There are 72 pitches, 15 non-electric for tents, 57 with electricity hook-ups (6A). A few 'premium' pitches offer slightly more privacy. It is a beautiful setting within the woods and once the park closes at 18.30 to the general public, all is much quieter and all the facilities of the park are for campers only. You should aim to arrive before 18.00 when the main reception centre closes. Access to the site is through a locked gate (key from reception on check-in). The design of the site with individual pitches and some small groups all within woodland clearings gives a very rustic and relaxed ambience. A warden lives on the site.

| Facilities | Directions |
|---|---|
| The newly refurbished central toilet block provides modern style facilities including washbasins in cubicles and well equipped showers with good dry areas. Laundry. Shop stocks basics. Calor gas exchange. Country Park with nature walks, deer field, crazy golf and children's play areas and miniature railway (£1 extra). Family events are held all year round. Torch useful. Off site: Local shops, bars and entertainment including swimming, cinema, ice skating all within a short drive. Major attractions such as Legoland, Thorpe Park, Windsor etc. all within easy reach<br><br>Open: Early March - 9 November. | Park is signed at Riseley, off the A33 road between Reading and Basingstoke. From the M4 take exit 11 and park is 4 miles south off the second roundabout (signed). From the M3 use exit 8 and follow the A33 for 7 miles towards Reading. Turn right at the roundabout after the Wellington monument and park is at the next roundabout. O.S.GR: SU727628. GPS: 51.3592, -0.961167 |

Charges guide

| Per unit incl. 2 persons | £ 15.50 - £ 25.00 |
|---|---|
| extra person | £ 5.00 |
| child (3-15 yrs) | £ 4.00 |
| dog | £ 2.00 |

# Romsey

## Hill Farm Caravan Park

Branches Lane, Sherfield English, Romsey SO51 6FH (Hampshire) T: 01794 340402. E: gjb@hillfarmpark.com
alanrogers.com/UK2380

This 11 acre rural park is ideal for those seeking a quiet base but one that is within easy reach of all the main tourist attractions of Hampshire and Dorset. There are 120 pitches, of which 30 for seasonal units are located in a separate area. The touring area is a large open field surrounded by trees and hedges. All pitches are well marked, numbered and mainly level. All have electric hook-ups (6/10A), 20 pitches are fully serviced and some are available with hardstanding. Adding to the attractiveness of the site is a pitch and putt golf course, set in a sizeable and well landscaped area. For anyone interested in roses, nearby Mottisfont Abbey (National Trust) has a unique collection of old fashioned varieties and during the summer open-air plays, films and concerts take place here. The New Forest with Beaulieu Estate and National Motor Museum is just a short drive away. A trip to the Isle of Wight makes a good excursion – the ferry terminal is within a 30 minute drive.

### Facilities

Two very clean, traditionally built toilet blocks include washbasins, both open style and in cubicles, and controllable showers. Facilities for babies and disabled visitors. Motorcaravan service point. Shop in reception for gas supplies and basics. Bread and pasties are cooked on the premises. Tea rooms serving breakfast, lunch and afternoon tea (homemade cakes and desserts). Play area. Pitch and putt golf. Off site: Riding and fishing 3 miles. Bicycle hire 15 miles. Bournemouth and Southampton for shopping, leisure and family entertainment nearby. Golf 3 miles.

Open: 1 March - 31 October.

### Directions

From Romsey, drive north on the A27 for 3.5 miles, turning right into Branches Lane and site is a further 0.5 miles on right. O.S.GR: SU235300.
GPS: 51.00627, -1.57682

### Charges guide

| | |
|---|---|
| Per unit incl. 2 persons and electricity | £ 16.00 - £ 32.00 |
| extra person | £ 5.00 |
| child (4-16 yrs) | £ 2.00 - £ 4.00 |

Minimum booking requirement for B.Hs, July and August weekends.
No credit cards.

# Ryde

## Whitefield Forest Touring Park

Brading Road, Ryde PO33 1QL (Isle of Wight) T: 01983 617069. E: pat&louise@whitefieldforest.co.uk
alanrogers.com/UK2495

This family run park, opened in May 2007, has been sympathetically developed by the owners working closely with the Forestry Commission to maintain the natural beauty of the ancient woodland, Whitefield Forest. There is a mixture of well drained all-weather hardstanding and grass pitches (70 in total) all with 16A electricity hook up. Varying in size (100-170 sq.m), the pitches are level and sheltered with some on terraces. They are all suitable for tents, caravans and motorcaravans. There is good access to the park and the pitches. Some slight road noise is audible from a few pitches. The park is suitable for families and pre-teen children who want a peaceful relaxing holiday. The nearby towns of Ryde, Shanklin and Sandown provide evening entertainment.

### Facilities

The excellent well appointed heated toilet block has private cubicles, hairdryers and razor points. Family shower rooms. Baby changing and facilities for campers with disabilities. Laundry room with free ironing (iron from reception). Motorcaravan service point. Paperback book exchange. Adventure type play area with bark surface for children over 5 yrs. Suitable for American style motorhomes and twin axle caravans. Off site: Network of public footpaths from site. Supermarket, golf 800 yards. Riding, fishing, beach and boat launching 2 miles. Bicycle hire 2.5 miles.

Open: 1 April - 3 October.

### Directions

From Fishbourne and East Cowes follow A3054 to Ryde. Follow the A3055 to Brading. Site is 800 yds. on left (signed) after Tesco roundabout. From Yarmouth follow A3054 to Newport, then to Ryde. Follow the A3055 to Brading and as above. O.S.GR: SZ606894. GPS: 50.70044, -1.14572

### Charges 2011

| | |
|---|---|
| Per unit incl. 2 persons and electricity | £ 12.40 - £ 19.40 |

For latest campsite news visit
**alanrogers.com**

## Shanklin
### Ninham Country Holidays

Ninham, Shanklin PO37 7PL (Isle of Wight) T: 01983 864243. E: office@ninham-holidays.co.uk

alanrogers.com/UK2465

Ninham is an attractive, well maintained site tucked in a wooded valley, but only ten minutes drive to the bustling resort of Shanklin with its long, sandy beaches and good shops and restaurants. Two touring parks, one open all season, have spacious grass and gravel pitches, some open and some separated by hedges, with water and electrical hook-ups. There are two (unfenced) lakes for carp fishing, and numerous cycle paths, which can be used to access local amenities. Children will enjoy the heated outdoor pool, and the games room offers pool, table tennis and other activities. The site will appeal in particular to walkers and cyclists, who can take full advantage of the beautiful countryside. 'The Heights' leisure centre, just five minutes drive away, has pools, a jacuzzi, sauna, steam room and multi-gym.

### Facilities

Clean and well maintained toilet facilities are housed in two traditional buildings, and a Portacabin for use in high season. Washbasins have hot and cold water, showers are in separate cubicles and there are adequate electrical points for hairdryers etc. No special facilities for visitors with disabilities. Space for baby changing in main washing areas. Laundry facilities (token from reception). No shop, but supermarket nearby. Small outdoor pool (end May-Sept). Games room with TV for special events. Children's play areas. Course fishing. WiFi. Dogs welcome in one area. Mobile homes and self-catering houses to rent. Off site: Bus stop by entrance to Shanklin, Sandown and Newport. Leisure centre nearby.

Open: 30 April - 4 September.

### Directions

Site is off the A356 Newport - Sandown road. From Newport/Cowes direction, pass the park entrance and continue 400 m. to the Morrison's roundabout, and return to filter off left onto private drive. From Ryde - Fishbourne (AQ355), turn onto A3056 at Lake. Entrance is 1 km. on left after the Morrison's roundabout. Look for brown and white tourist signs to Ninham Farm. GPS: 50.640607, -1.192424

### Charges guide

| | |
|---|---|
| Per unit incl. 2 persons and electricity | £ 15.00 - £ 20.00 |
| extra person | £ 5.00 - £ 7.50 |
| child (3-13 yrs) | £ 3.00 - £ 4.50 |
| dog | £ 3.50 |

### THE PERFECT HOLIDAY DESTINATION

Unique country setting, just a 20 minute walk from the Island's favourite beach resort of Shanklin. Ninham is a private country park setting with a wooded valley and small fishing lake.

**NINHAM**
**COUNTRY HOLIDAYS**
Camping & Caravanning
Shanklin Isle of Wight PO37 7PL
01983 864243
www.ninham-holidays.co.uk
office@ninham-holidays.co.uk

- Heated outdoor pool
- Spacious pitches
- Electric hook-ups
- Fishing
- Walks / cycle trails
- Book online
- Ferry tickets issued

## Shanklin
### Lower Hyde Holiday Park

Landguard Road, Shanklin PO37 7LL (Isle of Wight) T: 01983 866131. E: holiday.sales@park-resorts.com

alanrogers.com/UK2475

This site is located on the edge of Shanklin, within walking distance of shops and services and only 1.5 miles from the beach. Lower Hyde is a large holiday park complex with around 200 caravan holiday homes for rent and 114 privately owned. The separate touring area has 115 well-spaced and numbered pitches, 85 with electric hook-ups (16A) of which 26 are fully serviced with hardstanding, water, drain, electricity and TV hook-up. This area is in an elevated position with good views over the surrounding countryside. The pitches are large and flat, easily accessed, with tarmac roads and low-level lighting. Landscaping is good, with much wildlife planting throughout. There is a permanent warden for the tourers. This is a lively site with a large stage area for discos and spectacular cabaret shows. With all the activities, lots of young staff, security personnel and lifeguards, it is excellent for a family holiday.

### Facilities

The new toilet block has WCs, open washbasins, showers, a family shower room and two bathrooms. Separate baby room. Suite for disabled visitors. Launderette. Shop. Bar. Restaurant and takeaway. Indoor and outdoor pools. Adventure playground. Children's clubs. Entertainment. Multisport court. Soccer. Archery. Fencing. Tennis. ATM. Off site: Fishing and boat launching 1.5 miles. Golf 2.5 miles. Riding and bicycle hire 5 miles.

Open: 2 April - 29 October.

### Directions

From East Cowes ferry terminal take A3021 for about 2.5 miles to roundabout and turn right on A3054 to Newport. From Newport take A3020 towards Sandown and Shanklin. After 1.5 miles (at Blackwater) continue straight on joining A3056 to Sandown. Keep on this road until you pass Safeway on the left, and shortly afterwards, turn right into Whitecross Lane (signed Landguard Camping). Keep straight on, past Landguard and site is on right after 1 mile. O.S.GR:SZ576817. GPS: 50.633317, -1.180983

### Charges guide

| | |
|---|---|
| Per unit incl. up to 6 persons | £ 3.00 - £ 32.00 |
| hardstanding | £ 5.00 |
| dog | £ 1.00 - £ 3.00 |

# Swanage

## Ulwell Cottage Caravan Park

Ulwell, Swanage BH19 3DG (Dorset) T: 01929 422823. E: enq@ulwellcottagepark.co.uk

alanrogers.com/UK2020

Nestling under the Purbeck Hills on the edge of Swanage, in the Dorset and East Devon Coast World Heritage Site, Ulwell Cottage is a family run holiday park with an indoor pool and a wide range of facilities. A good proportion of the park is taken by caravan holiday homes (140), but an attractive, undulating area accessed by tarmac roads is given over to 77 numbered touring pitches interspersed with trees and shrubs. All have electricity (16A) and 8 are fully serviced. The colourful entrance area is home to the Village Inn with a courtyard adjoining the heated, supervised indoor pool complex (both open all year and accessible to the public) and modern reception. The hill above the touring area, Nine Barrow Down, is a Site of Special Scientific Interest for butterflies and overlooks Round Down. It is possible to walk to Corfe Castle this way. With Brownsea Island, Studland Bay, Corfe village and the Swanage Railway close by, Ulwell Cottage makes a marvellous centre for holidays.

### Facilities

The modern, cheerful toilet block at the top of the site is heated and includes a unit for disabled visitors. An older block in the holiday home section has been converted to family rooms. Both are well equipped. Laundry room and baby sinks in the upper block. Well stocked shop with gas (Easter-mid Sept). Bar snacks and restaurant meals with family room. Takeaway (July/Aug). Indoor pool with lifeguard (times vary acc. to season). Playing fields and play areas. Off site: Beach 1 mile. Fishing and golf 1 mile. Bicycle hire, sailing and riding 2 miles.

Open: 1 March - 7 January.

### Directions

From A351 Wareham - Swanage road, turn onto B3351 Studland road just before Corfe Castle. Follow signs to right (southeast) for Swanage and drop down to Ulwell. Park is on right 100 yards after 40 mph. sign. O.S.GR: SZ019809.
GPS: 50.626460, -1.969403

### Charges guide

| | |
|---|---|
| Per unit incl. up to 6 persons | £ 18.50 - £ 36.70 |
| full services incl. hardstanding | £ 21.00 - £ 39.00 |
| extra tent, car or boat | £ 2.50 |

Less £2 for two persons only,
less £1 for three persons.

For a brochure call:
**01929 422823**
*website: www.ulwellcottagepark.co.uk*
*e-mail: enq@ulwellcottagepark.co.uk*

**Find a warm welcome** at this family run park in the Isle of Purbeck, an area of outstanding natural beauty and breath taking World Heritage coastline. Nearby sandy beaches, coastal walks and golf.
• **77 Touring Pitches** with hard standings, electric, water and drainage hook-ups and views of the surrounding hills
• **Superb meals** at the 'Village Inn' • Heated Indoor Pool •General Shop

---

# Swanage

## Swanage Coastal Park

Priestway, Swanage BH19 2RS (Dorset) T: 01590 648331. E: holidays@shorefield.co.uk

alanrogers.com/UK2000

With wonderful views over Swanage Bay and the Purbeck hills, Swanage Coastal Park is now part of Shorefield Holidays who own other parks in the New Forest. It offers a quiet holiday on the hills above Swanage with its lovely sandy beach (it is quite a steep climb up from the town). Over 100 holiday caravans are terraced up the hillside, of which two-thirds are privately owned. For touring units there are six hardstandings with 10A electricity, plus four grass pitches on a small plateau. The other 52 grass pitches are unnumbered without electricity. In nooks and crannies on various levels, they are separated by trees and shrubs. Swanage is at the start of the Jurassic Coast World Heritage Site and there is direct access to the coastal paths and to Durlston Country Park and Castle.

### Facilities

One older type toilet block at the bottom of the site is clean but basic. Laundry facilities. Dishwashing sinks. Play area. Membership of the Health and Fitness Club at the next door park allows use of the indoor pool, gym, sauna, solarium, bar and restaurant as paying customers (open all year). It also has a shop (open B.Hs. and high season). Off site: Beach and town 1 mile. Golf 3 miles. Bicycle hire, fishing and boat launching 1 mile. 'Hop on Hop off' bus allows you to explore the whole of the Jurassic Coast.

Open: 14 March - 30 October.

### Directions

From A351 Wareham - Swanage road turn right just after 'Welcome to Swanage' sign into High Street then immediately right again into Bell Street. At the top turn left into Priests Road then first right up hill towards Priestway. O.S.GR: SZ018783.
GPS: 50.60605, -1.974983

### Charges guide

| | |
|---|---|
| Per pitch | £ 7.50 - £ 15.00 |
| incl. electricity and hardstanding | £ 8.50 - £ 20.00 |
| dog | £ 1.50 |

*See advertisement on page 125.*

---

## Wareham

### Wareham Forest Tourist Park

North Trigon, Wareham BH20 7NZ (Dorset) T: 01929 551393. E: holiday@warehamforest.co.uk

alanrogers.com/UK2030

This peacefully located and spacious park, on the edge of Wareham Forest, has 200 pitches and is continually being upgraded by its enthusiastic owners, Tony and Sarah Birch. The focal point of the park is the modern reception and shop, located by the pools. Four main areas provide a wide choice of touring pitches from grass to hardstanding and luxury, all with 16A electricity. Tenters have their own choice of open field or pinewood. The site has provided direct access for walkers into the forest or the seven miles of the Sika cycle trail may be used. The lovely market town of Wareham is accessible by bike without having to use the roads. This park has an almost continental feel, with plenty of space. Even when it is busy, it is calm and peaceful in its forest setting. In low season you may be lucky enough to spot the herd of Sika deer which live in the forest. The park is well situated to explore the Dorset coast and Thomas Hardy country. A member of the Best of British Group.

### Facilities

Two well maintained toilet blocks are of a good standard with some washbasins in cubicles. Main block recently completely refurbised and both blocks are centrally heated. Facilities for disabled visitors. Well equipped laundry rooms. Motorcaravan service point. Small licensed shop with gas. Swimming pool (60x20 ft), heated 20/5-15/9. Large adventure play area. Barrier closed 23.00-07.00. Resident wardens on site. Caravan storage. WiFi. Off site: Cycle trail and walking in the forest. Bicycle hire and golf 3 miles. Fishing 5 miles. Riding 8 miles.

Open: All year.

### Directions

From A31 Bere Regis, follow A35 towards Poole for 0.5 miles and turn right where signed to Wareham. Drive for a further 1.5 miles. First park on the left as you enter forest. O.S.GR: SY899903. GPS: 50.721733, -2.156217

### Charges guide

| | |
|---|---|
| Per unit incl. 2 persons and electricity | £ 15.50 - £ 30.00 |
| 'superior' pitch fully serviced | £ 18.00 - £ 33.00 |
| extra person | £ 3.00 - £ 5.00 |
| child (5-15 yrs) | £ 2.00 - £ 3.75 |
| dog | free - £ 1.75 |

Couples and families only.

## Ventnor

### Appuldurcombe Gardens Holiday Park

Wroxall, Ventnor PO38 3EP (Isle of Wight) T: 01983 852597. E: info@appuldurcombegardens.co.uk

alanrogers.com/UK2480

Originally part of the grounds of an historic house, this pretty family holiday park is situated in 14 acres of beautiful countryside in the valley of Stenbury Downs and St Martin's Downs, close to the sandy beaches at Sandown, Shanklin and Ventnor. The camping field is set in a grassy meadow through which a stream meanders, with a tranquil seating area close by. With hard access roads, there are 100 spacious marked pitches for touring units and tents, 70 of which have electricity hook-ups (10A). The old walled orchard contains 40 good quality caravan holiday homes. Here also is the access friendly Orchard Lodge (all accommodation on one level with ramp access to outside), plus two self contained apartments. In an Area of Outstanding Natural Beauty, it is an ideal spot for bird watching and horse riding. For walkers and cyclists there is an excellent network of footpaths and cycle paths.

### Facilities

Two good toilet blocks (access by key) are fully tiled with free hot water throughout. Facilities for visitors with disabilities. Launderette. Shop (fresh baguettes baked daily) and café. Bar and family entertainment room. All amenities open from spring B.H. Large outdoor swimming pool and toddlers' pool (May-early Sept). Play area. Pitch and putt. Crazy golf. Off site: Fishing, golf, riding, bicycle hire, boat launching, beach, sailing, all within 2-3 miles.

Open: All year excl. mid December - mid January.

### Directions

Do not use Sat Nav instructions, road with restricted access nearby. From Newport take A3020 towards Shanklin and Ventnor. Travel through Blackwater, Rookley, Godshill and Sandford. At Whiteley Bank roundabout turn right towards Wroxhall (B3320). Pass Donkey Sanctuary and turn right into Appuldurcombe Road. Park entrance is second on the right, 150 yards along this road. O.S.GR: SZ548803. GPS: 50.61891, -1.22657

### Charges guide

| | |
|---|---|
| Per person | £ 5.00 - £ 7.50 |
| child (3-14 yrs) | £ 1.50 - £ 3.75 |
| serviced pitch | £ 2.50 |
| dog | £ 1.00 - £ 1.50 |

For latest campsite news visit

alanrogers.com

## Wimborne
### Merley Court Touring Park
Merley, Wimborne BH21 3AA (Dorset) T: 01590 648331. E: holidays@shorefield.co.uk
alanrogers.com/UK2080

Merley Court is the latest addition to the Shorefield Group and all aspects of this well planned, attractively landscaped park are constantly maintained to the highest of standards. Tarmac roads connect 179 touring pitches, 162 of which have 16A electricity, on neat lawns or one of the many hardstandings. This provision includes 20 serviced pitches with water, waste disposal and satellite TV. The entire park is interspersed with a variety of shrubs, plants and the odd ornamental urn. Some attractive tent pitches are to be found in a small wooded valley. A well furnished club complex provides a lounge bar where meals are available. There is also a snack bar, takeaway, large games room with pool tables and a family room leading onto a spacious sheltered patio. This in turn leads to the paved walled swimming pool area. There are woodland walks (including dog walks) directly from the site connecting to the disused railway line where nature has returned with an abundance of wild flowers, which in turn leads to Delph woods with designated nature trails. A member of the Best of British group.

### Facilities
Three heated toilet blocks, two with showers, are of good quality. Separate facilities for disabled visitors and babies. Dishwashing and laundry facilities. Motorcaravan service point. Shop with caravan accessories and gas. Café and takeaway. Bar with food (limited hours in low and mid season). Outdoor pool (30 x 20 ft) with children's section open Whitsun-early Sept. Tennis and short tennis courts. Table tennis. Play area. Games room with pool tables. Tourist information. Barrier card £5 deposit. Off site: Fishing, riding and golf all within 2 miles. Bicycle hire 5 miles. Poole 5 miles, Bournemouth 8 miles. Tower Park leisure and entertainment centre is nearby, Kingston Lacy House, Knoll Gardens, Brownsea Island and the Moors Valley Country Park are also near.

Open: All year excl. 3 January - 5 February.

### Directions
Site clearly signed at the junction of A31 and A349 roads (roundabout) on the Wimborne bypass.
O.S.GR: ST008984. GPS: 50.785733, -1.98525

### Charges 2011

| Per unit incl. 6 persons | |
|---|---|
| and electricity | £ 14.50 - £ 37.00 |
| all service pitch | £ 20.00 - £ 42.50 |
| dog | £ 1.50 - £ 3.00 |

No extra pup tent or awning.

## Wimborne
### Woolsbridge Manor Farm Caravan Park
Three Legged Cross, Wimborne BH21 6RA (Dorset) T: 01202 826369. E: woolsbridge@btconnect.com
alanrogers.com/UK2150

Close to the Moors Valley Country Park, this friendly, family run site is within easy reach of the south coast, the resorts of Christchurch, Bournemouth and Poole, and the ancient market town of Wimborne Minster. Entry is restricted to couples and families. The seven acre camping meadow has 101 large level pitches (51 seasonal) all with electricity (16A) and arranged on either side of a central tarmac road. Reception has a well stocked shop and a good selection of tourist information. The site is part of a working beef cattle farm, so parents should be aware of moving farm machinery and tractors. A cycleway/footpath crosses the fields to the Country Park – very safe for children – where amenities include coarse fishing, golf, steam railway, bicycle hire, a tea room and a country shop.

### Facilities
The neat, refurbished toilet block is well maintained and has ample facilities. Four newly built family rooms each with shower, WC, basin, handrails and ramped access provided for disabled visitors, babies and toddlers. Washing machine, dryer and ironing facilities. Shop. Gas. Playground. Fishing. American RVs accepted, advance booking appreciated. Torches useful. Caravan storage. Off site: Old Barn Farm inn and restaurant 400 m. Riding, golf and bicycle hire 0.5 miles. Boat launching and sailing 5 miles.

Open: Easter - 31 October.

### Directions
From Ringwood take A31 southwest to the large Ashley Heath roundabout (Junction of A31 and A338 to Bournemouth). Take left hand slip road up to roundabout, avoiding underpass, and turn right (north) onto unclassified road signed for Three Legged Cross, Ashley Heath, Horton and Moors Valley Country Park. Follow signs to Country Park (2 miles), pass the park entrance on right, continue for another 400 yards to campsite entrance (well signed on right). O.S.GR: SZ 099052.
GPS: 50.842982, -1.859982

### Charges guide

| Per unit incl. 2 persons | |
|---|---|
| and electricity | £ 15.50 - £ 20.50 |
| extra person | £ 5.50 - £ 6.00 |
| child (under 16 yrs) | £ 3.50 - £ 4.00 |
| dog | £ 1.50 - £ 2.00 |
| awning or extra car | £ 2.50 |

For latest campsite news visit
**alanrogers.com**

## Wimborne

### Wilksworth Farm Caravan Park

Cranborne Road, Wimborne BH21 4HW (Dorset) T: 01202 885467
E: rayandwendy@wilksworthfarmcaravanpark.co.uk  alanrogers.com/UK2060

First opened by the parents of the present owners, the careful and sympathetic development of Wilksworth continues with the aim of providing all the 'mod cons' yet remain in keeping with the environment. It is a spacious, quiet park, well suited for families with a heated outdoor pool which has been totally refurbished in a beautiful Spanish style. The rural situation is lovely, just outside Wimborne and around 12 miles from the beaches between Poole and Bournemouth. The park takes 65 caravans and 25 tents mainly on grass. All pitches have electricity, 10 also have water and drainage.

**Facilities**

The central, well equipped toilet block has under-floor heating, washbasins in cubicles, a family bathroom and a shower/bath for children with baby changing. Facilities for disabled visitors. Laundry room. Reception and shop (basics only, limited hours, Easter-30 Sept). Gas supplies. Coffee shop serving simple meals with takeaway service (weekends and B.Hs. only outside the main season). Heated 40x20 ft. swimming pool (May-Sept). Small paddling pool. Adventure play area. BMX track. Two tennis courts. Games room. Off site: Golf, fishing and riding 3 miles. Wimborne 1 mile. Beach 12 miles.

Open: Easter/1 April - 30 October.

**Directions**

Park is 1 mile north of Wimborne, west off the B3078 road to Cranborne. O.S.GR: SU010019. GPS: 50.8167, -1.9904

**Charges guide**

| Per unit incl. 2 persons | |
|---|---|
| and electricity | £ 14.00 - £ 24.00 |
| extra person | £ 3.00 |
| child | £ 2.00 |
| full services | £ 2.00 |
| dog | £ 1.00 |

No credit cards.

---

## Witney

### Lincoln Farm Park

High Street, Standlake, Witney OX29 7RH (Oxfordshire) T: 01865 300239. E: info@lincolnfarmpark.co.uk
alanrogers.com/UK2570

From its immaculately tended grounds and quality facilities, to the efficient and friendly staff, this park is a credit to its owner. Situated in a small, quiet village, it is well set back and screened by mature trees, with wide gravel roads, hedged enclosures, brick pathways and good lighting. All 90 numbered, level touring pitches are generously sized and have electrical connections (10/16A), 75 with gravel hardstanding and grass for awnings, and 22 are fully serviced (fresh and waste water, electricity and satellite TV). Gazebos or extra tents are not permitted on pitches. A member of the Best of British group.

**Facilities**

Two heated toilet blocks are well maintained and clean, with showers and washbasins in cubicles. Well equipped, separate unit for disabled visitors. Two family bathrooms (with baby bath and changing facilities). Laundry facilities. Motorcaravan service point. Shop (basics). Putting green and adventure play area. Indoor swimming pools. WiFi. Games room. Off site: Fishing (lake and river) 300 yds and 5 miles. Riding and water sports nearby. Golf 5 miles.

Open: 1 February - mid November.

**Directions**

Take A415 Witney - Abingdon road and turn into Standlake High Street by garage; park is 300 yds on the right. O.S.GR: SP396029. GPS: 51.7232, -1.428783

**Charges 2011**

| Per unit incl. 2 persons | |
|---|---|
| and electricity | £ 16.95 - £ 27.95 |

Low season offers.

---

## Wool

### Whitemead Caravan Park

East Burton Road, Wool BH20 6HG (Dorset) T: 01929 462241. E: whitemeadcp@aol.com
alanrogers.com/UK2090

The Church family continue to make improvements to this attractive little park which is within walking distance of the village of Wool, between Dorchester and Wareham. Very natural and with open views over the Frome Valley water meadows, it provides 95 numbered pitches on flat grass sloping gently north and is orchard-like in parts. The 76 touring pitches are well spaced, mostly backing onto hedges or fences and all have electrical connections. All roads are now tarmac. There are no caravan holiday homes but 20 pitches are seasonal. There may be some rail noise but this is not intrusive at night.

**Facilities**

The toilet block provides showers, private cubicles, a baby room, dishwashing and laundry sinks, washing machine and dryer. Shop (limited hours) with off-licence, gas supplies and information room/library. Games room with pool table and darts. Playground. Caravan storage. WiFi in games room. Off site: The Ship Inn is 300 yards. Riding, fishing and golf 3 miles. Bicycle hire 2 miles. Nearest beach is at Lulworth (4.5 miles).

Open: 15 March - 31 October.

**Directions**

Turn off main A352 on eastern edge of Wool, just north of level crossing, onto East Burton road. Site is 350 yards. on right. O.S.GR: SY841871. GPS: 50.68164, -2.22595

**Charges guide**

| Per unit incl. 2 persons | |
|---|---|
| and electricity (10A) | £ 11.75 - £ 18.50 |
| extra person (over 5 yrs) | £ 3.50 |

No credit cards.

For latest campsite news visit
**alanrogers.com**

Land of 1066, the South East is brimming with historical sights as castles, stately homes and cathedrals abound. It also boasts miles of footpaths and cycle routes through some of the best landscapes in England, passing chalk downland, wooded valleys and dramatic white-faced cliffs.

## THE SOUTH EAST COMPRISES: EAST SUSSEX, WEST SUSSEX, SURREY AND KENT

The chalk countryside of golden downland in Sussex offers many opportunities for an active holiday, from walking and cycling to more adventurous pursuits such as rock climbing or ballooning. Once an ancient forest, much of the Weald is now taken up with farmland, but some areas still remain, including Ashdown Forest, a walker's paradise with stunning views of the High Weald and South Downs. The many rivers of the county have cut their way through gaps in the chalk landscape, ending spectacularly in white cliffs on the coast. Here you will find the Regency resorts of Bognor Regis and Brighton, with its Royal Pavilion, famous pier and quirky shops. Often referred to as the 'Garden of England', Kent is a richly fertile region flourishing with hop gardens, fruit orchards and flowers. It is also home to the world renowned Canterbury Cathedral, several splendid castles, hidden towns, and quaint villages with oast houses. Surrey too boasts a rich heritage with numerous stately homes and National Trust sites plus large areas of ancient woodland. With a network of rivers, an enjoyable way to explore the beautiful countryside is by boat, stopping off at a riverside pub – or two!

### Places of interest

*East Sussex:* Eastbourne; Runnymede; Thorpe Park in Chertsey; Bexhill; historical towns of Hastings and St Leonards.

*West Sussex:* Chichester; Bognor Regis; Arundel, with castle; Littlehampton.

*Surrey:* Guildford castle and cathedral; Mole Valley; Royal Horticultural Society's gardens at Wisley; Chessington World of Adventures; Dorking, a renowned centre for antiques.

*Kent:* Leeds Castle and gardens, the oldest stately home in the country; Canterbury, a designated World Heritage Site; Dover, with museum and castle; traditional seaside resort of Folkstone; Hever Castle in Sevenoaks; market town of Maidstone; Isle of Thanet incorporating Margate, Broadstairs and Ramsgate.

### Did you know?

Hastings is home to Britain's first Norman castle, built by William the Conqueror.

Some of England's finest writers have found inspiration from living in Sussex – Rudyard Kipling, Sir Arthur Conan Doyle and A.A. Milne.

Bexhill housed one of the country's first cinemas and was the first to permit 'risqué' mixed sea bathing.

The world famous McLaren F1 racing team has its base in Woking.

Runnymede takes its name from the meadow where the Magna Carta, the great charter of English liberties, was sealed by King John in 1215.

## Ashford

### Broadhembury Caravan & Camping Park

Steeds Lane, Kingsnorth, Ashford TN26 1NQ (Kent) T: 01233 620859. E: holidaypark@broadhembury.co.uk

alanrogers.com/UK3040

In quiet countryside just outside Ashford and within easy reach of Dover, Folkestone and the Kent coast, this sheltered park is attractively landscaped. It takes 65 touring units of any type with several seasonal units and 25 caravan holiday homes (5 for hire) in separate areas. The well kept pitches are on level grass and backed by tall, neat hedges, with over 50 electricity connections (16A). In addition, 7 pitches are fully serviced and 8 more have double hardstanding plus a grass area for an awning. The welcome is friendly at this popular park and it is often full in the main season, with a good proportion of continental visitors, so reservation is advisable. Thoughtfully considered amenities include a very good toilet block, well equipped campers' kitchen and provision for children of all ages. Security arrangements are excellent – with coded entry through gates and onto park. For those who would like a trip to France, the International railway terminal is at Ashford (Paris in two hours) – take your passport. A member of the Best of British group.

### Facilities

The toilet block is well equipped including under-floor heating and is kept very clean. A new block is planned for 2011. Private cabins. High quality facilities for disabled visitors (can also be used as a family bathroom). Well equipped laundry room. Good campers' kitchen, fully enclosed with dishwashing sinks, microwaves, fridge and freezer, all free of charge. Motorcaravan service point. Well stocked shop (bread and papers to order) and comprehensive tourist information. Internet access. Pool room, games room with video games, table football and table tennis. Two play areas (one for children under 7 yrs) with wood-chip bases. Play field away from the touring area. Campers' herb garden. WiFi (charged). Dog exercise field – up to two dogs per pitch are accepted. Large units are accepted if pre-booked. Off site: Fishing 300 m. Golf 1 mile. Riding 2 miles. Beach 12 miles.

Open: All year.

### Directions

From M20 junction 10 take A2070. After 2 miles follow sign for Kingsnorth. Turn left at second crossroads in Kingsnorth village.
O.S.GR: TR010382. GPS: 51.10647, 0.86809

### Charges guide

| | |
|---|---|
| Per unit incl. 2 persons and electricity | £ 22.00 - £ 26.00 |
| extra person | £ 5.00 |
| child (5-16 yrs) | £ 2.00 - £ 3.00 |
| tent incl. 2 persons | £ 16.00 - £ 21.00 |

Less 10% for bookings of 7 nights or more.

For latest campsite news visit
## alanrogers.com

## Battle
### Crazy Lane Tourist Caravan Park
Crazy Lane, Sedlescombe, Battle TN33 0QT (East Sussex) T: 01424 870147. E: info@crazylane.co.uk
alanrogers.com/UK2960

This simple, neat two acre park has just 36 pitches arranged on grassy terraces, all with electricity (5/10A) and 4 with hardstanding. Many pitches are used by seasonal units so it may be best to phone to make sure space is available before travelling long distances. With easy access from the A21 (some background road noise), the park is set in the heart of '1066 country' with its historical links. Other local attractions within easy reach include the pretty village of Sedlescombe, a steam railway, an organic vineyard and the seaside at Hastings. This is an ideal park for couples.

**Facilities**

New solar heated toilet facilities are unisex providing excellent private rooms, each with WC, shower and washbasin. Laundry facilities. Shop at reception. Caravan storage. Off site: Golf 0.5 miles. Riding 2 miles. Fishing 3.5 miles. Bus stop and pub in the village. The fascinating towns of Battle and Rye, plus Hastings (6.5 miles) with its beaches, markets and Heritage Shipwreck Centre.

Open: March - October.

**Directions**

From the A21, 6 miles north of Hastings and 100 yards south of junction with B2244 (to Sedlescombe), turn right into Crazy Lane. Site is immediately on the right. O.S.GR: TQ782170. GPS: 50.92453, 0.53495

**Charges guide**

| Per unit incl. 2 persons and electricity | £ 16.00 - £ 20.00 |
| extra person over 8 yrs | £ 1.50 |
| dog | £ 1.00 |

No credit cards.

**Crazy Lane Tourist Park**
Whydown Farm, Crazy Lane, Sedlescombe Battle TN33 0QT East Sussex
Tel/Fax: +44 (0)1424 870147 • info@crazylane.co.uk

*WELCOME!*
*Gill and Ron Morgan would like to welcome you to Crazy Lane Tourist Caravan Park. This family-run park is in a quiet, secluded, sun-trapped valley in the heart of '1066' country within easy reach of beach and historical sites.*

## Bexhill
### Kloofs Camping & Caravan Park
Sandhurst Lane, Whydown, Bexhill-on-Sea TN39 4RG (East Sussex) T: 01424 842839
E: camping@kloofs.com  alanrogers.com/UK2955

This peaceful and rural park is situated in a quiet country lane with countryside views yet within easy reach of several well known towns on the East Sussex coast. Set in three acres, Kloofs is owned and run by Terry and Helen Griggs who have taken great care in making this a most attractive and well maintained park. There are 40 level, generously sized touring pitches divided into two areas, and a combination of grass and hardstanding make them suitable for all-weather touring. It is evident that considerable investment has been made to ensure visitors have a comfortable stay. The lower field, surrounded by hedging and trees offers some landscaped pitches which are divided by their own private trellised garden area, complete with picnic table. Pitches for caravans and motorcaravans are terraced, easy to access and surrounded by hedges and mature trees which provide shade. Most pitches have electric hook-ups and a water tap, some also have waste water drainage. Very large units would find the narrow lanes to the park a challenge.

**Facilities**

One main, centrally heated toilet block is modern and spotlessly clean. Washbasins in cubicles and spacious hot showers. Large shower room for families and good en-suite facility for disabled visitors (key from reception). The lower paddock service block is now complete offering additional toilet and shower facilities for both able and disabled visitors. Heated kitchen area. Washing machine, dryer, iron and board. Small shop in reception for basic requirements and camping gas. Wooden adventure style play area (fenced). Small library. Off site: Footpath from site to local village for pubs and other eating places 1.4 miles. Beach 2 miles. Bexhill-on-Sea 3 miles. Battle 6 miles. Hastings 8 miles. Eastbourne 11 miles. Watersports, golf, riding and fishing all nearby.

Open: All year.

**Directions**

From the north (Battle, Catsfield, Ninfield), take A269 and turn right into Pear Tree Lane, then right at crossroads. Sandhurst Lane is 300 m. on the left and site is signed a short way down on the right. From east (Hastings), take A259 to Little Common roundabout. Turn off right into Pear Tree Lane, then left at crossroads. Then as above. From west (Eastbourne), take A259 to Little Common roundabout. Turn left into Pear Tree Lane, then left at crossroads. Then as above. O.S.GR: TQ708090. GPS: 50.8560, 0.4271

**Charges 2011**

| 2 person, pitch incl. electricity and water | £ 23.00 - £ 31.00 |
| extra person | £ 6.50 |
| child (5-17 yrs) | £ 3.00 |

For latest campsite news visit
**alanrogers.com**

# Bexhill
## Chestnut Meadow Camping & Caravan Park
Ninfield Road, Sidley, Bexhill-on-Sea TN39 5JG (East Sussex) T: 01424 892361
E: info@chestnutmeadow.co.uk  alanrogers.com/UK2945

In a peaceful country location near Bexhill, with Hastings and rural East Sussex to explore close by, a family, long used to camping themselves, have developed this into an attractive park. The well-drained sheltered meadow is virtually surrounded by trees, with a glimpse of the sea. Flowers and shrubs enhance the entrance and buildings. The 79 large touring pitches (up to 150 sq.m) are marked by posts with numbered buckets which you can use for recycling. There are 74 with electricity (16A) and 22 have hardstanding below the grass, eight with their own water and drainage. They are well spaced, with the central area kept free for children to play and adults to gather and relax.

### Facilities
Excellent new, heated sanitary building. Shop with local produce at reception. Bar, café (good value, serving breakfast through to evening meal) and takeaway (all high season and weekends). Laundry. Games hall with snooker, pool, table tennis, air hockey, table football. Large, new, fenced play area. WiFi (free). Off site: International fishing lakes 4 miles. Golf 1 mile. Riding 1.5 miles. Drucillas Family Park 16 miles.

Open: Mid March - mid January.

### Directions
The park is northwest of Bexhill on the A269 Ninfield Road between Sidley and Ninfield, with a 110 yard long entrance drive. O.S.GR: TQ721101. GPS: 50.865412, 0.447312

### Charges guide
| | |
|---|---|
| Per unit incl. 2 persons and electricity | £ 21.00 - £ 24.00 |
| extra person | £ 2.00 - £ 2.50 |

Barrier card £10 deposit.

# Brighton
## Sheepcote Valley Caravan Club Site
East Brighton Park, Brighton BN2 5TS (East Sussex) T: 01273 626546
alanrogers.com/UK2930

Brighton is without doubt the South of England's most popular seaside resort and the Caravan Club's Sheepcote Valley Site is a first class base from which to enjoy the many and diverse attractions both in the town and this area of the south coast. A wide tarmac road winds its way through the site from reception, with gravel pitches on either side, leading to terraces with grass pitches on the lower slopes of the valley. The 169 pitches all have electricity (16A), 86 have hardstanding and 11 have water, drainage and TV sockets. Three grass terraces are for tents.

### Facilities
Two heated sanitary blocks include all washbasins in private cabins. In the main season a third timber-clad building provides additional services near the tent area. Well equipped room for wheelchair users, another one for walking disabled and two baby and toddler wash rooms. Laundry facilities. Motorcaravan service point. Gas available. Milk and bread from reception. Play area with safety base. Off site: Brighton is 2 miles with a bus service from the entry road. Large recreation grounds adjacent.

Open: All year.

### Directions
From the north (London) on M23/A23, join A27 (Lewes). Exit via slip road for B2123 (Falmer). At roundabout turn right on B2123. Continue for 2 miles then right at traffic lights into Warren Ave. After 1 mile left at traffic lights into Wilson Ave, crossing Racecourse. In 1.75 miles at foot of hill (before lights) turn left. Follow lane to site. O.S.GR: TQ341043. GPS: 50.820975, -0.097799

### Charges guide
| | |
|---|---|
| Per person | £ 5.00 - £ 6.90 |
| pitch(non-member) | £ 12.10 - £ 15.50 |

# Canterbury
## Canterbury Camping & Caravanning Club Site
Bekesbourne Lane, Canterbury CT3 4AB (Kent) T: 01227 463216. E: canterbury.site@thefriendlyclub.co.uk
alanrogers.com/UK3070

Situated just off the A257 Sandwich road, about 1.5 miles from the centre of Canterbury, this site is an ideal base for exploring Canterbury and the north Kent coast, as well as being a good stopover to and from the Dover ferries, and the Folkestone Channel Tunnel terminal. There are 200 pitches, 109 with electric hook-ups (10/16A) and, except at the very height of the season, you are likely to find a pitch, although not necessarily with electricity. Most of the pitches are on well kept grass with hundreds of saplings planted, but there are also 72 pitches with hardstanding (more are planned).

### Facilities
Two modern toilet blocks, the main one with a laundry room. Motorcaravan service point. Reception stocks a small range of essential foods, milk and gas. Excellent tourist information room. Play area with equipment on bark chippings. Off site: Shop 0.5 miles. Golf adjacent. Bicycle hire 2 miles.

Open: All year.

### Directions
From A2 take Canterbury exit and follow signs for Sandwich - A257. After passing Howe military barracks turn right into Bekesbourne Lane opposite golf course. O.S.GR: TR172577. GPS: 51.2769, 1.113533

### Charges guide
| | |
|---|---|
| Per person | £ 7.50 - £ 9.00 |
| pitch (non-member) | £ 7.00 |

For latest campsite news visit
# alanrogers.com

## Canterbury

### Yew Tree Park

Stone Street, Petham, Canterbury CT4 5PL (Kent) T: 01227 700306. E: info@yewtreepark.com

alanrogers.com/UK3060

Yew Tree Park is a small, quiet site located in the heart of the Kent countryside overlooking the Chartham Downs. Just 5 miles south of Canterbury and 8 miles north of the M20, it is ideally placed either to explore the delights of the ancient city or the many attractions of eastern and coastal Kent. Its nearness to the Channel ports also makes it useful for a night stop on the way to, or on return from, the continent. With some caravan holiday homes, the site also has 45 pitches for tourers and tents. The 20 with electricity (10A) are marked on mainly level grass either side of the entrance road, the remainder unmarked on a rather attractive, sloping area, left natural with trees and bushes creating cosy little recesses in which to pitch. There are mobile homes and apartments to rent. This neat, tidy park, created by resident proprietors Derek and Dee Zanders, makes an excellent base away from the hurly-burly of life where you can enjoy the rural scenery and also have the opportunity for walking, riding, visiting local places of interest or for cross-Channel excursions.

**Facilities**

Two brick-built sanitary blocks (one for each sex) can be heated. Washbasins (H&C) and four showers (on payment). Extra toilets on the edge of the camping area. Toilet/shower room for families and disabled visitors. Laundry and dishwashing sinks, plus a washing machine, dryer and iron. Gas supplies. Outdoor heated swimming pool (53x30 ft; June-Sept). Play area. WiFi. Torches may be useful. Dogs are not accepted. Off site: Pub (serving food) 100 m. Riding 4 miles. Golf 6 miles. Bicycle hire 5 miles. The County cricket ground is 4 miles.

Open: Easter - mid October.

**Directions**

Park is on B2068 Canterbury-Folkestone road. From south, take exit 11 from the M20. From Canterbury, ignore signs to Petham and Waltham on B2068 and continue towards Folkestone. From either direction, turn into road beside the Chequers Inn, turn left into park and follow road to owners' house/reception. O.S.GR: TR138507. GPS: 51.2168, 1.058183

**Charges guide**

| | |
|---|---|
| Per unit incl. 2 persons and electricity | £ 16.30 - £ 21.30 |
| extra person | £ 4.00 - £ 5.00 |
| child (2-16 yrs) | £ 2.00 - £ 2.75 |

## Chertsey

### Chertsey Camping & Caravanning Club Site

Bridge Road, Chertsey KT16 8JX (Surrey) T: 01932 562405

alanrogers.com/UK2810

This long-established site (1926) is splendidly located on the banks of the River Thames, only a few minutes walk from the shops and amenities of Chertsey. A flagship site for the Club, it was totally redeveloped a few years ago at a cost of over a million pounds. There are 200 pitches including 50 new serviced pitches with hardstanding and 16A electricity and 15 'super service' pitches which have TV aerial points, water and waste drainage. The work included a new road system, heated toilet blocks with facilities for disabled visitors, recreation hall and much more. There has been extensive landscaping and the existing Thames creek has been extended to flow through the site with marshland areas to support the local wildlife environment. When possible, energy saving devices have been used. Squirrels, rabbits and ducks abound and trees and plants create a pretty site with views across the water and towards Chertsey bridge. Unfortunately there is some road noise and, depending on flight paths, aircraft noise. The rail station for London is at Chertsey or Weybridge. Fishing is possible and canoes can be launched from the site.

**Facilities**

The well equipped toilet blocks can be heated and include washbasins in cabins and facilities for disabled visitors. Hairdryers. Laundry. Motorcaravan service point. Well stocked shop for essentials and gas (08.00-11.00 and 16.00-18.00). Recreation hall. Play area on bark. Fishing (adults £1.70, NRA licence needed). Short dog walk areas. Caravan storage. Torches are necessary. Off site: Bus service in Chertsey 1.5 miles. Trains in Weybridge 3 miles. Golf and bicycle hire 1 mile.

Open: All year.

**Directions**

Suggested: from M25 use junction 11. Turn left at roundabout on A317 towards Shepperton and continue to second set of traffic lights. Turn right then almost immediately left watching for green Club camp sign just before Chertsey bridge; the opening is narrow. O.S.GR: TQ052667. GPS: 51.38993, -0.48966

**Charges guide**

| | |
|---|---|
| Per person | £ 6.65 - £ 9.25 |
| child (6-18 yrs) | £ 2.45 - £ 5.30 |
| non-member pitch fee | £ 6.00 |

For latest campsite news visit

**alanrogers.com**

## Chichester

### Warner Farm Touring Park

Warner Lane, Selsey, Chichester PO20 9EL (West Sussex) T: 01243 604499. E: touring@bunnleisure.co.uk

alanrogers.com/UK2885

This site is a member of the Bunn Holiday Villages group, owners of several large holiday home parks which surround the pretty holiday town of Selsey. Warner Farm is a top quality touring park with 250 large grassy pitches, 165 of which have electrical connections. Pitches have a generally open aspect and there is a large area at the back of the site, the 'Artichoke Field', which offers an unmarked camping area, as well as providing picnic tables and barbecues. There are 35 serviced pitches with electricity, water and waste water. The site is modern and well maintained, and benefits from free access to the extensive leisure facilities on offer at the neighbouring holiday villages. These include the Oasis Pool and Leisure Complex with two indoor pools, a fun fair, a number of bars and restaurants and a lively 'top name' entertainment programme and kids' club. Surprisingly perhaps, the site retains a pleasant rural feel with plenty of space despite its proximity to the sea and the resort of Selsey.

**Facilities**

Modern toilet block with facilities for disabled visitors. Preset showers in large cubicles. Washing machines and dryers. Small shop. Play area. Multisport area. Communal barbecues, picnic area and dog walking area. Free shuttle bus to neighbouring parks. Off site: Nearest beach 900 m. Oasis Pool and Leisure Complex, indoor pools, fun fair, bars, restaurants, entertainment and kid's club. Bicycle hire. Tennis.

Open: 1 March - 30 October.

**Directions**

Head for Chichester on the A27. At the Whyke roundabout join the B2145 and follow signs to Selsey. At Selsey go across mini-roundabout and continue past entrance to Bunn Leisure. After next mini-roundabout take second right into School Lane, right again into Paddock Lane and then first left into Warner Lane. Follow signs to park.
O.S.GR: SZ846939. GPS: 50.73815, -0.79913

**Charges guide**

| | |
|---|---|
| Per unit incl. up to 4 persons and electricity | £ 19.50 - £ 33.50 |
| extra person | £ 7.50 |
| extra child (0-18 yrs) | £ 5.00 |
| dog | £ 3.00 |

## Chichester

### Chichester Camping & Caravanning Club Site

345 Main Road, Southbourne PO10 8JH (West Sussex) T: 01243 373202

alanrogers.com/UK2320

This small, neat site is just to the west of Chichester and north of Bosham harbour. Formerly an orchard, it is rectangular in shape with 58 pitches on flat, well mown lawns on either side of gravel roads. All pitches have 16A electricity, 42 with level hardstanding. Although the A27 bypass takes most of the through traffic, the site is by the main A259 road so there may be some traffic noise in some parts (not busy at night). Opposite the park are orchards through which paths lead to the seashore. Arrival must be before 20.00 unless prior arrangements have been made with the site manager.

**Facilities**

The well designed, brick built toilet block is of first class quality. Fully tiled and heated in cool weather, with facilities for visitors with disabilities (access by key). Laundry facilities. Gas supplies. WiFi (charged). No ball games permitted. Dogs can be walked in the lane opposite. Off site: Bicycle hire 1 mile. Fishing 5 miles, riding 6 miles.

Open: February - November.

**Directions**

Park is on A259 Chichester - Havant road at Southbourne, 750 yards west of Chichester Caravans. O.S.GR: SU774056.
GPS: 50.84498, -0.90299

**Charges guide**

| | |
|---|---|
| Per person | £ 7.10 - £ 9.15 |
| child (6-18 yrs) | £ 2.45 - £ 2.54 |
| pitch (non-member) | £ 6.46 |

For latest campsite news visit
**alanrogers.com**

## Chichester

### Lakeside Holiday Park

Vinnetrow Road, Chichester PO20 1QH (West Sussex) T: 0845 815 9775. E: lakeside@ParkHolidaysUK.com
alanrogers.com/UK2875

Located just outside the historic city of Chichester, this large site is a member of the Park Holidays group. This is a mecca for anglers with no fewer than 10 large fishing lakes. The site is set in 150 acres of Sussex countryside, but also within easy access of a sandy beach and the traditional resort of Bognor Regis. This is a lively site in peak season with a newly refurbished entertainment centre boasting a choice of bars and dining options. On-site amenities include a swimming pool, and a children's club (5-14 years) is organised in peak season. Chichester is an attractive city, with its 12th-century cathedral of particular interest. The city is also home to the Festival Theatre, one of England's flagship cultural centres. Bognor Regis was originally a smuggling village but it became popular as a holiday resort in the 19th century.

**Facilities**

Bar. Restaurant. Entertainment complex. Supermarket. Swimming pool. Fishing. Children's play area. Children's club. Tourist information. Mobile homes for rent. Off site: Nearby resort of Bognor Regis (good selection of cafés, restaurants and shops). Walking and cycle routes. Chichester (cathedral city).

Open: 1 March - 31 October.

**Directions**

From Chichester take the A27 towards Havant and Brighton. At the Bognor Road roundabout take the fourth exit onto Vinnetrow Road (Pagham), and you will reach the site. GPS: 50.823885, -0.75119

**Charges guide**

| | |
|---|---|
| Per unit incl. 2 persons and electricity | £ 9.00 - £ 24.00 |

## Dover

### Hawthorn Farm Caravan & Camping Site

Martin Mill, Dover CT15 5LA (Kent) T: 01304 852658. E: info@keatfarm.co.uk
alanrogers.com/UK3100

Hawthorn Farm is a large, relaxed park near Dover. Set in 27 acres, it is an extensive park taking 226 touring units of any type on several large meadows which could accommodate far more, plus 160 privately owned caravan holiday homes in their own areas. Campers not requiring electricity choose their own spot, most staying near the toilet blocks, leaving the farthest fields to those liking solitude. There are 112 pitches with electricity (10/16A), 46 of which are large and separated by hedges, the remainder in glades on either side of tarmac roads. There are 15 new hardstandings available. A well run, relaxed park with plenty of room, mature hedging and trees make an attractive environment. A torch would be useful. Being only 4 miles from Dover docks, it is a very useful park for those using the ferries and is popular with continental visitors. Close to the sea at St Margaret's Bay, it is a fairly quiet situation apart from some rail noise (no trains 23.30-05.30).

**Facilities**

Two heated toilet blocks are well equipped and of good quality. Facilities for disabled visitors. Baby room. Launderette. Motorcaravan services. Breakfast and other meals are served at the shop (all season). Gates close at 20.00 (22.00 in July/Aug), £10 deposit for card. Caravan storage. Off site: Riding 0.5 miles. Golf 3 miles. Bicycle hire, fishing and boat launching 4 miles. Martin Mill railway station 500 yds.

Open: 1 March - 31 October.

**Directions**

Park is north of the A258 road (Dover - Deal), with signs to park and Martin Mill where you turn off about 4 miles from Dover. O.S.GR: TR341464. GPS: 51.16855, 1.346333

**Charges guide**

| | |
|---|---|
| Per unit incl. 2 persons and electricity | £ 13.00 - £ 20.00 |
| unit over 7 metres with electricity | £ 20.00 - £ 25.00 |
| extra person | £ 3.00 |
| child (5-16 yrs) | £ 2.00 |
| dog | £ 1.50 |

Less 10% for 4 nights booked (and paid for on arrival).

## Eastbourne

### Bay View Park

Old Martello Road, Pevensey Bay BN24 6DX (East Sussex) T: 01323 768688. E: holidays@bay-view.co.uk

alanrogers.com/UK2920

This friendly beachside park is located at the end of a private road right beside the beautiful Sussex coast and its pebble beach and the park's own brand new nine-hole, par three golf course. Two separate areas of grass (some areas are a little uneven) are surrounded by low banks and hedges to give shelter if it is windy. Careful use of wooden fencing adds to the attractiveness, whilst also keeping the rabbits off the flowers. The 94 touring pitches (80 sq.m, most with 16A electricity and some with hardstanding) are neatly marked and numbered. Several caravan holiday homes for hire are positioned at the back of the park. The golf course clubhouse provides tea, coffee and snacks. Visitors can enjoy the attractions of Sussex, as well as swimming, fishing and windsurfing. This is an ideal park for a family beach holiday. A cycle path leads to Pevensey Bay and Eastbourne's new Sovereign Harbour marina with its shops, restaurants and cinema.

#### Facilities

Each area has toilet facilities, one a new, fully equipped block with private cubicles (shower, washbasin and WC) and facilities for babies and disabled visitors. Heated when required, both blocks are kept very clean. Fully equipped laundry room. Motorcaravan services. Well stocked shop (open long hours as the managers live on site). Golf (9-hole, par 3). Clubhouse for tea, coffee and snacks. Gas. Popular, fenced play area (ten years and under). Winter caravan storage. Off site: Sailing club. Sea fishing. Indoor swimming pool 1 mile.

Open: 1 March - 31 October.

#### Directions

From the A27/A259 roundabout at Pevensey take A259 through Pevensey Bay. Park and golf course are signed after 1 mile (private access road) to the left, 2 miles east of Eastbourne. O.S.GR: TQ648028. GPS: 50.79998, 0.33797

#### Charges guide

| | |
|---|---|
| Per unit incl. 2 persons and electricity | £ 19.50 - £ 22.00 |
| extra person | £ 2.50 |
| child (5-16 yrs) | £ 2.00 |
| dog | £ 1.00 |

Couples and families only.
No commercial vehicles, large vans or pick-ups.

| Tel: | 01323 768688 |
|---|---|
| Fax: | 01323 769637 |
| E-mail: | holidays@bay-view.co.uk |
| Web: | www.bay-view.co.uk |

**BAY VIEW PARK**
HOLIDAY HOMES, TOURING AND CAMPING

Award-winning caravan and camping park
next to the beach on Eastbourne's sunshine coast

## Eastbourne

### Fairfields Farm Caravan & Camping Park

Eastbourne Road, Westham, Pevensey BN24 5NG (East Sussex) T: 01323 763165
E: enquiries@fairfieldsfarm.com  alanrogers.com/UK2915

Part of a working, family-run farm, this is a simple peaceful park which is ideally located to enjoy the Sussex countryside and coast, just a short distance from Eastbourne. A single, rectangular meadow is split by a line of attractive silver birch trees and provides 66 large pitches, all but 4 with electricity connections. The farm and its rural landscape stretch towards the sea at Pevensey Bay and you can walk through the fields to the beach. Beyond the camping field there is a duck pond with grassy surrounds and picnic benches, pens with numerous small animals and pets and a pleasant walk to a fishing lake. Children are invited to feed the animals (with special food on sale). Within walking distance are the villages of Westham and Pevensey with a choice of pubs and restaurants, as well as Pevensey Castle which has a history spanning 16 centuries. Eastbourne has a promenade and beautiful beaches with a retail complex and cinema at the Sovereign Centre.

#### Facilities

The single, central toilet block is traditional in style and very clean. Toilet for disabled visitors. Laundry facilities. Farm shop. Small animals and pets. Fishing lake (licence required). Off site: Pubs, restaurants and fish and chip shop within walking distance. Beach 1.5 miles. Golf 4 miles. Eastbourne 5 miles.

Open: 1 April - 31 October.

#### Directions

From the roundabout junction of the A27 and A259 (Little Chef and petrol station) take exit to Pevensey and the Castle. Go around the castle walls and into Westham village. At end of high street turn left (B2191), over level crossing and park is on left. O.S.GR: TQ639041. GPS: 50.81358, 0.32448

#### Charges guide

| | |
|---|---|
| Per unit incl. 2 persons | £ 11.50 - £ 13.00 |
| incl. electricity | £ 15.00 - £ 16.50 |
| extra person | £ 3.00 |
| child (3-13 yrs) | £ 1.50 |
| dog | £ 1.00 |

# Folkestone
## Little Satmar Holiday Park
Winehouse Lane, Capel-le-Ferne, Folkestone CT18 7JF (Kent) T: 01303 251188. E: info@keatfarm.co.uk
alanrogers.com/UK3095

Capel-le-Ferne is a relatively little known seaside town midway between Dover and Folkestone. Little Satmar is a quiet site a short walk from the delightful cliff top paths which run between these towns and which offer fine views across the English Channel. The site is a member of the Keat Farm group and is located about a mile from the village. There are 61 touring pitches, 51 of which have electricity (10A). The pitches generally have a sunny, open setting, a few with rather more shade. Privately owned mobile homes occupy 78 pitches but these are quite separate from the touring field.

**Facilities**

Two toilet blocks (one in a 'Portacabin' style unit) are modern and kept very clean and the main block has now been fitted with heating. Washing and drying machines. Shop (with gas). Play area. For more than 1 dog per unit, contact park. Off site: Bus at end of lane to Dover and Folkestone. Port Lympne Zoo, seafront funpark nearby.

Open: 1 March - 31 October.

**Directions**

Leave A20 Dover - Folkestone road at Capel-le-Ferne exit and follow signs to the village. Site is clearly signed to right after about 0.75 miles. O.S GR: TR256393. GPS: 51.101917, 1.222933

**Charges guide**

| Per unit incl. 2 persons and electricity | £ 15.25 - £ 25.00 |
| extra person | £ 3.00 - £ 3.50 |

# Folkestone
## Black Horse Farm Caravan Club Site
385 Canterbury Road, Densole, Folkestone CT18 7BG (Kent) T: 01303 892665
alanrogers.com/UK3090

This neat, tidy and attractive 6 acre park, owned by the Caravan Club, is situated amidst farming country in the village of Densole on the Downs just 4 miles north of Folkestone, 8 west of Dover and 11 south of Canterbury. Accessed directly from the A260, the tarmac entrance road leads past reception towards the top field which has gravel hardstanding pitches with a grass area for awnings (possibly some road noise), past hedging to the smaller middle area with 8 hardstandings, then to the large bottom field which has been redeveloped to give 140 large pitches (including 15 for tents and some extra large for large motorhomes), all with electricity (16A).

**Facilities**

The carefully thought out and well constructed toilet blocks, one below reception and the other at the far end of the site, have washbasins in private cabins with curtains, good sized shower compartments, a baby room and facilities for disabled visitors, laundry and dishwashing facilities, all well heated in cool weather. Motorcaravan service point. Gas supplies. Play area. A fish and chip van calls on Thursdays (April-Sept). Caravan storage. Off site: Riding 1 mile. Golf and fishing 5 miles.

Open: All year.

**Directions**

Directly by the A260 Folkestone - Canterbury road, 2 miles north of junction with A20. Follow signs for Canterbury. O.S.GR: TR211418. GPS: 51.132617, 1.158483

**Charges guide**

| Per person | £ 4.10 - £ 5.60 |
| child (5-16 yrs) | £ 1.30 - £ 2.15 |
| pitch incl. electricity (non-member) | £ 11.50 - £ 14.20 |

# Folkestone
## New Beach Holiday Park
Hythe Road, Dymchurch TN29 0JX (Kent) T: 0845 815 9775. E: newbeach@parkholidaysuk.com
alanrogers.com/UK3085

330

New Beach Holiday Park is a member of the Park Holidays group. This is a popular family park located between Hythe and Dymchurch on Kent's south coast. This is a lively site in high season with a varied entertainment programme and a club for children (5-14 years). Evening entertainment is of a high standard and is organised on a nightly basis in peak season. Leisure facilities include a heated indoor swimming pool, an adventure playground and amusement arcade. Off site, Dymchurch is a lively resort, as well as a station on the famous Romney, Hythe and Dymchurch steam railway.

**Facilities**

Shop. Bar. Restaurant. Indoor swimming pool. Adventure playground. Amusement arcade. Entertainment and activity programme (including children's club). Tourist information. Mobile homes and chalets for rent. Off site: Dymchurch (shops and restaurants). Port Lympne Wild Animal Park. Romney Marsh.

Open: 1 March - 31 October.

**Directions**

Leave the M20 at exit 11 (Canterbury). At roundabout take third exit onto the B2068 (signed Hastings, Hythe). At roundabout take second exit onto Ashford Road (A20). Entering Newingreen at T-junction turn left onto Hythe Road (A261, signed Hythe). Enter Hythe and continue onto Scanlons Bridge Road (A2008). Turn right onto Dymchurch Road (A259) and New Beach is on the right. O.S.GR: TR139299. GPS: 51.043687, 1.027458

**Charges guide**

| Per unit incl. 2 persons | £ 9.00 - £ 24.00 |

South East England

For latest campsite news visit
**alanrogers.com**

135

## Guildford

### Horsley Camping & Caravanning Club Site

Ockham Road North, East Horsley KT24 6PE (Surrey) T: 01483 283273

alanrogers.com/UK2820

London and all the sights are only 40 minutes away by train, yet Horsley is a delightful, quiet unspoilt site with a good duck and goose population on its part lily covered lake (unfenced). It provides 130 pitches, of which 83 have 10A electrical connections and 42 are all weather pitches (most with electricity). Seventeen pitches are around the bank of the lake, the rest are further back in three hedged, grass fields with mostly level ground but with some slope in places. A new area has been developed in woodland. There is a range of mature trees and a woodland dog walk area (may be muddy).

**Facilities**

Two purpose built, heated toilet blocks with good design and fittings, with some washbasins in cabins, a Belfast sink and parent and child room with vanity style basin, toilet and wide surface area. Laundry room and new drying areas. Well designed facilities for disabled visitors. Small shop in reception. Play area. Fishing is possible from May (adult £5.20/children £2.60 per day, NRA licence required). Off site: Golf 1.5 miles. Riding 2 miles.

Open: March - October.

**Directions**

From M25 junction 10, in the direction of Guildford, after 0.5 miles take first left B2039 to Ockham and East Horsley, continuing through Ockham towards East Horsley. After 2 miles watch for brown site sign (not easy to see) and site is on right in 2.5 miles. O.S.GR: TQ083552. GPS: 51.28640, -0.44502

**Charges guide**

| | |
|---|---|
| Per person | £ 6.60 - £ 8.60 |
| non-member pitch fee | £ 6.00 |

## Heathfield

### Horam Manor Touring Park

Horam, Heathfield TN21 0YD (East Sussex) T: 01435 813662. E: camp@horam-manor.co.uk

alanrogers.com/UK2900

In the heart of the Sussex countryside, this rural touring park is part of (but under separate management from) Horam Manor which has a farm museum, nature trail and several fishing lakes. The 90 generously sized, numbered pitches, 54 with electricity, are on two open meadows. The area nearer reception has an undulating surface, the second field is flatter but slopes. Both areas are ringed with a variety of mainly tall trees. The whole park, back from the main Eastbourne to Tunbridge Wells road, is a haven of peace and tranquillity, although in high season it naturally becomes very busy.

**Facilities**

The well built toilet block (unheated) is fully equipped and is said to be cleaned four times daily. Some curtained cubicles. Family room (key access) with shower, washbasin, toilet and baby bath, suitable also for disabled visitors (not good for wheelchairs). Laundry. Gas supplies. Very simple fenced play area (under 12 yrs). WiFi. Off site: Horam Manor adjacent with café, fishing and riding. Shops and inns within walking distance. Tennis 200 yds. Golf within 1 mile. Brighton, Hastings and Eastbourne are within easy reach.

Open: 1 March - 31 October.

**Directions**

Horam is on the A267 between Tunbridge Wells and Eastbourne and entry to the park is signed at the recreation ground at southern edge of the village. O.S.GR: TQ577169. GPS: 50.931783, 0.240167

**Charges guide**

| | |
|---|---|
| Per unit incl. 2 adults, 2 children and electricity | £ 19.50 - £ 21.50 |
| extra person | £ 6.00 |
| extra child | £ 2.50 |

Accept credit cards.

## Horsham

### Honeybridge Park

Honeybridge Lane, Dial Post, Horsham RH13 8NX (West Sussex) T: 01403 710923

E: enquiries@honeybridgepark.co.uk  alanrogers.com/UK2940

This 15 acre park is situated amidst beautiful woodlands and countryside on the edge of the South Downs, within an Area of Outstanding Natural Beauty. Of the 150 pitches, 100 are for touring. Some are on hardstandings and all have electricity (16A). Some pitches are hedged for privacy, others are on slightly sloping grass, well spaced and generously sized. The reception building houses a licensed shop. A large wooden, adventure-style playground is provided for children away from the pitches, and simple family entertainment is organised on special occasions. A large games room provides darts, table tennis, pool, free use of many board games and a library.

**Facilities**

Modern toilet facilities are heated in cool weather and include spacious facilities for disabled visitors (Radar key). Laundry facilities. Motorcaravan service point. Licensed shop. Play area. Games room with library. Caravan for hire. Off site: Bus 0.5 miles. Pub/restaurant in nearby village. Old Barn Nurseries serves meals during the day. Horsham and Billingshurst are both 8 miles. Fishing 1 mile. Golf 10 miles. Riding 5 miles. Beach 10 miles.

Open: All year.

**Directions**

Two miles south of the junction of A24 and A272 at Dial Post, turn east by Old Barn Nurseries. Follow signs to site (about 0.5 miles). O.S.GR: TQ153183. GPS: 50.94864, -0.35274

**Charges guide**

| | |
|---|---|
| Per unit incl. 2 persons and electricity | £ 17.40 - £ 23.40 |
| extra person | £ 3.00 - £ 6.00 |

## Marden
### Tanner Farm Touring Caravan & Camping Park
Goudhurst Road, Marden TN12 9ND (Kent) T: 01622 832399. E: enquiries@tannerfarmpark.co.uk
alanrogers.com/UK3030

Tanner Farm is a top class, quality park, developed as part of a family working farm in the heart of the Weald of Kent. It is surrounded by orchards, oast houses, lovely countryside and delightful small villages and the owners are much concerned with conserving the natural beauty of the environment. The park extends over 15 acres, most of which is level and part a gentle slope. The grass meadowland has been semi-landscaped by planting saplings, etc. which units back onto, as the owners do not wish to regiment pitches into rows. There are 100 pitches, all with 16A electricity, 38 with hardstanding, 25 with a water tap and 12 with a waste water point also. Places are numbered but not marked, allowing plenty of space between units which, with large open areas, gives a pleasant, comfortable atmosphere. The park is a member of the Caravan Club's Affiliated Site scheme although non-members are also very welcome. A member of the Best of British and Countryside Discovery groups.

**Facilities**

Two heated, well cared for sanitary units include some washbasins in private cubicles in both units. Purpose built facilities for disabled visitors. Bathroom (£1 token) and baby facilities in the newer block (this block is not open Nov-Easter). Small launderette. Motorcaravan service point. Reception, shop and tourist information building (opening hours and stock limited in winter) with meeting/conference facilities in newly renovated barns. Gas supplies. WiFi in reception area. Off site: Riding and golf within 6 miles, leisure centres and sailing facilities near and good shopping facilities at Maidstone and Tunbridge Wells. Many National Trust attractions in the area (Sissinghurst, Scotney Castle, Bodiam Castle).

**Open:** All year.

**Directions**

Park is 2.5 miles south of Marden on B2079 towards Goudhurst. O.S.GR: TQ732417. GPS: 51.1471, 0.47482

**Charges guide**

| | |
|---|---|
| Per person | £ 4.70 - £ 6.20 |
| child (5-16 yrs) | £ 1.50 - £ 2.50 |
| pitch incl. electricity | £ 3.45 - £ 8.80 |
| tent pitch | £ 2.65 - £ 6.30 |

Only one car per pitch permitted.

## Paddock Wood
### The Hop Farm Touring & Camping Park
Maidstone Road, Paddock Wood TN12 6PY (Kent) T: 01892 838161. E: touring@thehopfarm.co.uk
alanrogers.com/UK3055

Set in 400 acres of the Garden of England, The Hop Farm is a popular family visitor attraction. There are plenty of activities to entertain children including adventure play areas (indoor and outdoor), a driving school, funfair rides, the Magic Factory and the Great Goblin Hunt. This is also the venue for many special events throughout the summer including music festivals, shows and other gatherings. To one side and overlooking all this activity and the attractive cluster of oasts is the touring park which provides over 300 grass and hardstanding pitches on flat, open fields. Electricity (16A) and water are available. There is also plenty more space for tents. The single toilet block is clean and provides straightforward, simple facilities. It would be supplemented by portacabin units when events bring extra campers. Entry to the visitor attraction is half price for caravanners and campers and here are the Shires Restaurant and the Happy Hopper's café. This park would suit those looking to enjoy the visitor attraction or attend one of the events.

**Facilities**

Brick built toilet block with open washbasins, preset showers (with curtain) and toilets. Further Portacabin style units when the park is full for events. Small shop for essentials. Restaurant and café at the visitor attraction (half price entry for campers). Dogs accepted but not permitted inside the visitor attraction. Activities and entertainment at the visitor attraction. Off site: Shops, restaurants and golf courses nearby.

**Open:** 1 March - 31 October.

**Directions**

The Hop Farm is located on the A228 near Paddock Wood. Follow the brown tourist signs from junction 4 of the M20 or junction 5 of the M25 onto the A21 south. O.S.GR: TQ674472. GPS: 51.200725, 0.39333

**Charges guide**

| | |
|---|---|
| Per unit incl. 4 persons and electricity | £ 16.00 - £ 20.00 |
| extra person (over 3 yrs) | £ 2.00 |
| dog | £ 1.00 |

## Redhill

### Alderstead Heath Caravan Club Site

Dean Lane, Merstham, Redhill RH1 3AH (Surrey) T: 01737 644629

alanrogers.com/UK2800

Alderstead Heath is a surprisingly rural site given that it lies just 25 minutes from central London by train. It is also well located for exploring the North Downs and is situated on the Pilgrim's Way. There are 150 pitches, all with 16A electrical connections. Most pitches are on well kept grass, but there are also 59 hardstandings. Given the proximity of the M25 and M23 motorways, there is a certain amount of background traffic noise in parts of the site. An attractive wooded area surrounds the site and concrete tracks there were laid during the war for tanks in preparation for the D-Day landings.

**Facilities**

Two well-maintained toilet blocks include a parent and toddler bathroom. The main block houses facilities for disabled visitors. Motorcaravan service point. Reception stocks a small range of essential foods, milk and gas. Small playing field. Good tourist information room. Off site: Golf 2 miles, Fishing 3 miles.

Open: All year.

**Directions**

Leave M25 at junction 8 and join A217 signed Reigate. Fork left after 300 yards (signed Merstham). After a further 2.5 miles turn left at T-junction and join the A23. After 500 yards turn right into Shepherd's Hill and after 1 mile turn left into Dean Lane. Site is on the right after 175 yards. O.S.GR: TQ290557. GPS: 51.283284, -0.138702

**Charges 2011**

| | |
|---|---|
| Per person | £ 4.10 - £ 5.60 |

## Sevenoaks

### Gate House Wood Touring Park

Ford Lane, Wrotham Heath, Sevenoaks TN15 7SD (Kent) T: 01732 843062
E: contact@gatehousewoodtouringpark.com  alanrogers.com/UK3120

This sheltered park has been created in a former quarry where all the pitches are on well drained grass. A spacious paved entrance with a new reception building and well stocked shop, leads on to the park itself. The 54 pitches are level and open with a few small trees, two brick built barbecue units, and 36 electric hook-ups (10A). A playground has swings, a seesaw and a slide, all set on a safety base, and the entire site is enclosed by grassy banks on three sides, with a wild flower walk around the top. Local attractions include Brands Hatch Circuit (four miles), the International Karting Circuit at Buckmore Park (seven miles), and the nearby Country Park at West Malling.

**Facilities**

Comprehensive toilet facilities are smart and well maintained, including a well equipped room which is designed for disabled visitors. The laundry and dishwashing room is at one end of the modern heated building. No dogs or other pets. Caravans/motorcaravans greater than 28 ft overall are not admitted. Commercial vehicles are not accepted. Off site: Within walking distance are three pubs and a good Cantonese restaurant. Trains run to London Victoria from Borough Green (2 miles). Golf 1 mile. Riding 3 miles. Fishing 7 miles.

Open: 1 March - 31 October.

**Directions**

From M26 junction 2a, take A20 eastwards towards Wrotham Heath and Maidstone. Just past junction with A25, and opposite the Royal Oak pub, turn left into Ford Lane, and park is immediately on left. O.S.GR: TQ630580. GPS: 51.300133, 0.345383

**Charges guide**

| | |
|---|---|
| Per unit incl. 2 persons and electricity | £ 16.00 - £ 18.00 |
| extra person | £ 3.50 |
| child (3-12 yrs) | £ 2.00 |
| No credit cards. | |

For latest campsite news visit
alanrogers.com

## Washington

### Washington Caravan & Camping Park

Old London Road, Washington RH20 4AJ (West Sussex) T: 01903 892869. E: washcamp@amserve.com
alanrogers.com/UK2950

Washington is a pleasant campsite to the north of Worthing with a bias towards tenting families. It provides just 21 hardstanding pitches for caravans or motorcaravans, and a large gently sloping grassy field with enough space for 80 tents. The 23 electric hook-ups (16A) are on slot meters (50p). There is some road noise from the A24. There is an equestrian centre adjacent to the campsite offering stabling and paddock facilities. There are excellent riding opportunities on the bridle paths of the South Downs Way. Local attractions (all with free admission, check opening times) include Highdown Chalk Gardens at Worthing, Nutbourne Vineyard near Pulborough, and Steyning Museum.

**Facilities**

A heated wooden chalet style building houses the sanitary facilities including spacious shower rooms (20p) and indoor dishwashing and laundry facilities. No on-site shop but eggs, bread, butter and milk can be obtained from the reception office. Drinks machine and freezer. Off site: Bus stop 200 yds in village. Eating out options include the local pub and a nearby restaurant. Beach 9 miles.

Open: All year.

**Directions**

Site entrance is just east of the junction of A24 and A283 at Washington, 6 miles north of Worthing. O.S.GR: TQ122134. GPS: 50.90875, -0.4056

**Charges guide**

| Per unit incl. 2 persons | £ 19.00 |
| extra person | £ 4.00 |
| tent | £ 6.00 |
| car | £ 5.00 |

## West Wittering

### Nunnington Farm Campsite

Rookwood Road, West Wittering PO20 8LZ (West Sussex) T: 01243 514013. E: nunningtonfarm@hotmail.com
alanrogers.com/UK2895

This no-frills, basic, family run farm site for touring units only can be found on the coast a mere seven miles from Chichester. There are 147 touring pitches, 77 with 15A electricity connections. The pitches are large, level and grassy, providing a comfortable feeling, even when the site is full. The safe, sandy beaches of The Witterings, only a mile away, make this an especially good venue for families in the holidays and a quieter one for off-season visitors. The easily accessible pets corner is an attraction for children of all ages. Visitors with tents are very welcome here and a second field is opened in busy periods, but with no electricity.

**Facilities**

Three rather dated but clean, central toilet blocks provide all facilities including showers in cubicles, open washbasins, baby bath, washing machines and ramped facilities for disabled visitors (key access). Gates closed 23.00-07.00. Off site: Local shops 300 yds. Bus service to Chichester every 30 minutes. Beach and boat mooring 1 mile. Bicycle hire 2 miles. Golf 3 miles.

Open: Easter - second week October.

**Directions**

From A27 at Chichester, take A286 signed The Witterings and continue to roundabout. Take second exit on B2179 for West Wittering and site is on left after 2 miles. O.S.GR: SZ785988. GPS: 50.78377, -0.88588

**Charges guide**

| Per unit incl. 2 persons | £ 13.00 - £ 18.00 |
| extra person | £ 2.00 |
| child (under 17 yrs) | £ 0.50 |

No credit cards.

## Kent holiday parks

Park Holidays
You might also like to consider...

For latest campsite news visit
**alanrogers.com**

## London

The largest city in Euro covering over 600 squa miles, London is jam packed with hundreds of magnificent museums impressive art galleries, historic buildings and monume beautiful parks, bustling shopping centres and markets; it really has something to offer everyone.

**WE HAVE CHOSEN FOUR PARKS WHICH HAVE EASY ACCESS TO CENTRAL LONDON, INCLUDING ONE IN HERTFORDSHIRE**

Despite its size, London is relatively easy to explore, largely thanks to the efficient underground service. Buses are also very useful and allow you to see the famous sights as you travel, in particular, the open-top tourist buses which ply the streets offer a good introduction to the city. Among London's many landmarks are the Tower of London, Trafalgar Square, Piccadilly Circus, Buckingham Palace, Big Ben and the Houses of Parliament, to name but a few! Running through the heart of London is the River Thames, dividing north and south; over the years many attractions, restaurants and chic bars have appeared along its banks. Being one of the most multicultural cities in the world, there is a huge choice of restaurants offering a diverse variety of cuisine; food markets are dotted all around the capital. Shopping is another major feature of the city, from the famous Harrods store and Harvey Nichols, to commercial Oxford Street and the street markets of Camden town and Portobello Road. If all the crowds become too much then head to one of London's beautiful parks such as St James' Park next to Buckingham Palace, or Hyde Park, where you can take a boat trip along the Serpentine.

### Places of interest

*London Eye:* world's highest observation wheel, reaching 450 feet. With 32 capsules, carrying 25 passengers in each, it offers breathtaking views.

*Madame Tussaud's:* huge collection of wax figures.

*Tate Modern:* contemporary art gallery housed in a transformed Bankside Power Station.

*Victoria & Albert Museum:* decorative art and design from around the world.

*Kew Gardens:* beautiful botanical gardens, with over 40,000 varieties of plants.

*London Dungeon:* a grisly house of horrors.

*Hampton Court Palace:* one the best palaces in Britain, with maze.

*British Museum:* houses a treasure trove of objects from all over the globe.

### Did you know?

One in eight of the UK population live in London and over 200 languages are spoken.

The London Underground dates back to 1863 when the first underground railway was opened, from Paddington to Farringdon Street. Today, 150,000 people an hour enter the Tube network.

Founded in 1753 the British Museum is the oldest public museum in the world.

With 345 steps to the top, the Monument marks the start of the Great Fire of London.

London has over 18,000 licensed taxis.

At over 900 years old, the Tower of London has been a palace, prison, treasury, arsenal and even a zoo. It is now home to the Crown Jewels, which have been housed there since the 14th century.

## Abbey Wood

Abbey Wood Caravan Club Site

Federation Road, Abbey Wood, London SE2 0LS (London) T: 020 8311 7708

alanrogers.com/UK3260

Situated close to Abbey Wood, it is hard to believe that this park is in London and the wardens have made every effort to create an attractive environment. There are 120 level caravan pitches all with 16A electricity and TV aerial connections. Of these, 64 have hardstandings. A large tent area provides an additional 100 pitches. Many pitches benefit from shade by mature trees. A secure fence around the perimeter is linked to close circuit TV cameras for security and just outside is a late arrivals area with electric and toilets; also protected by cameras. This park attracts many UK and overseas visitors as it offers a very good base from which to visit central London. A train service runs every 15 minutes from Abbey Wood station (5 minutes walk) to either Charing Cross or Cannon Street.

### Facilities

Three modern, fully equipped toilet blocks, two with under-floor heating, one designed to be open all year, include washbasins in cubicles, generous showers, baby/toddler washroom, laundry equipment and dishwashing sinks. Good private facilities for disabled visitors. Motorcaravan service point. Gas. Bread, milk and cold drinks from reception (high season). Play area. Good travel and information centre can provide tickets for travel and tourist attractions. Off site: Sports centre 1 mile. Golf 4 miles.

Open: All year.

### Directions

From east on M2/A2 or from central London: on A2 (third exit) turn off at A221 into Danson Road (signed Bexleyheath, Welling and Sidcup). Follow sign Bexleyheath to Crook Log (A207 junction); at traffic lights turn right and immediately left into Brampton Road. In 1.5 miles at traffic lights turn left into Bostal Road (A206); in 0.75 miles at traffic lights turn right into Basildon Road (B213); in 300 yds. turn right into McLeod Road, in about 0.5 miles at roundabout turn right into Knee Hill; in 100 yds. turn right (second right) into Federation Road. Site on left in 50 yds. From M25, north, west or south approach: leave at junction 2 onto A2 (signed London), then as above. O.S.GR: TQ472785. GPS: 51.48693, 0.11757

### Charges guide

| | |
|---|---|
| Per person | £ 4.90 - £ 6.60 |
| child (5-16 yrs) | £ 1.50 - £ 2.95 |
| pitch incl. electricity (non-member) | £ 11.80 - £ 15.35 |

Tent campers apply to site.

# Chingford

## Lee Valley Campsite

Sewardstone Road, Chingford, London E4 7RA (London) T: 020 8529 5689. E: scs@leevalleypark.org.uk

alanrogers.com/UK3250

This attractive site provides an excellent base from which to visit London, having both easy access to the M25 and excellent public transport links into the centre of London. Close to Epping Forest in the heart of the Lee Valley, this site is on a hillside overlooking the King George reservoir in a very pleasant and relaxed setting. Like its sister sites, it is understandably very popular with foreign tourers. With capacity for 200 units the site is mostly level, with several bush sheltered avenues and plenty of trees throughout providing shade. There are 20 pitches with tarmac hardstanding and 100 with electricity (10A). American motorhomes are not accepted. Just outside the gate is a bus stop (reception have full details of good value Travel Card schemes). The bus (no. 215) will take you to Walthamstow Central Underground station from where a frequent service runs to central London. Alternatively you can park at South Woodford or Chingford stations and use the train for London visits. Staff are very pleasant and helpful.

### Facilities

Three blocks offer good facilities (one is heated in low season), all recently totally refurbished. Good en-suite room for disabled visitors. Baby changing area. Laundry. Motorcaravan service point. Well stocked shop. Gas available. Playground. Off site: Fishing 500 yards. Shops within 2 miles. Riding 1 mile. 9-hole golf 1 mile, 18-hole golf 3 miles. Waltham Abbey 3 miles. River Lee Country Park and Epping Forest nearby.

Open: 1 April - 4 November.

### Directions

From M25 take exit 26 on A112 to Chingford and site is on right in 3 miles. From the A10 take the A110 (Chingford). After passing between reservoirs, at next traffic lights turn left on A112. Site is on the left after 2 miles. O.S. GR: TQ378970.
GPS: 51.653983, -0.006517

### Charges guide

| | |
|---|---|
| Per person | £ 6.45 |
| child (under 16 yrs) | £ 2.90 |
| electricity | £ 2.80 |
| dog | £ 1.65 |
| Min charge £8.60 per unit/night | |

# Crystal Palace

## Crystal Palace Caravan Club Site

Crystal Palace Parade, London SE19 1UF (London) T: 020 8778 7155

alanrogers.com/UK3270

The Caravan Club's site at Crystal Palace in south London provides easy access to the city centre and all its many attractions. The pitches are pleasantly arranged in terraces overlooking the ruins of the old Crystal Palace, its park and National Sports Centre. It is surprisingly quiet given its location (with the exception of police sirens and over-flying aircraft). In peak season advance booking is always necessary. Most pitches are on gravel hardstanding, so it is particularly useful for out of season stays. There are places for 126 caravans or motorcaravans, all with electricity (16A). Tents are placed on the site's well mown lawns near reception, where there are four additional electric points. The Crystal Palace park is extensive and provides open spaces for strolls or picnics and plenty of activities for children. The Sports Centre has two swimming pools, tennis and squash courts and gym facilities, with national events in a variety of sports to watch at certain times. An area at the site entrance should be used for arrivals after 20.00.

### Facilities

The main toilet block can be heated in cool weather with curtained washbasins for ladies. Another block provides basic unisex showers and toilets. Facilities for disabled visitors. Laundry room. Dishwashing sinks and rubbish bins. Motorcaravan service facilities. Gas available. Off site: Shops, pubs, etc. 400 yards. Many buses stop outside the site, including services to central London.

Open: All year.

### Directions

On A205 South Circular road travelling east, pass Dulwich College and golf course on right, turn right at traffic lights. Within 400 yards, at traffic lights, turn right into Sydenham Hill. In 350 yds. at roundabout turn left. Site is 1 mile opposite mini-roundabouts. Travelling west on A205 South Circular, immediately after passing under Catford railway bridge, keep left onto A212 (Crystal Palace). After 2.75 miles, site is on left. O.S.GR: TQ341724.
GPS: 51.42587, -0.07379

### Charges guide

| | |
|---|---|
| Per person | £ 4.90 - £ 6.60 |
| child (5-16 yrs) | £ 1.50 - £ 2.95 |
| pitch (non-member) | £ 11.80 - £ 15.35 |
| Tent campers apply to site. | |

For latest campsite news visit
## alanrogers.com

## Edmonton
### Lee Valley Camping & Caravanning Park

Meridian Way, Edmonton, London N9 0AR (London) T: 020 8803 6900. E: leisurecentre@leevalleypark.org.uk

alanrogers.com/UK3230

Certainly one of the only sites in this guide with a multiplex cinema just outside the gate, you are greeted here by a very attractive entrance with flower displays. The site offers 140 spacious level pitches, with hardstandings and 100 with electricity hook-ups. The pitches are well laid out around a large field and there is a tent area just behind two grassy mounds. The grass and gardens are well trimmed and kept very tidy. The site also offers hook-up points for tents. The adjacent sports complex is being rebuilt and will be used for the 2012 Olympics. The cinema complex incorporates a pizza restaurant, and from here you can hop on a bus to Edmonton Green or Ponders End station from where there is a regular service into central London (journey time around 40 minutes). The friendly site managers have detailed information about the various Travel Card schemes available. Alternatively, historic Waltham Abbey, Epping Forest and the 1,000 acre River Lee Country Park are all within easy access. This is a popular site, very well looked after and kept clean and tidy by site managers, this is a peaceful stop within easy reach of the city.

### Facilities

Two modern, heated toilet blocks include spacious showers and two large en-suite units for disabled visitors. Baby changing area. All facilities are accessed by combination locks. Dishwashing. Laundry. Motorcaravan service point. New barbecue area. Kitchen. Shop. Play area. badminton. Off site: Cinema at entrance. Supermarket 0.5 miles. Fishing 0.5 miles. Golf adjacent. Riding 4 miles.

Open: All year excl. Christmas, Boxing Day and New Year's Day.

### Directions

From M25 take exit 25. Follow signs for the city. At first set of traffic lights turn left (Freezywater). Continue on for about 6 miles. Follow signs for Lee Valley Leisure Complex. After roundabout (where A110 crosses), turn left at second set of traffic lights onto the complex. Follow site signs.
O.S.GR: TQ357940. GPS: 51.632383, -0.038383

### Charges guide

| | |
|---|---|
| Per unit incl. 2 persons and electricity | £ 17.70 |
| extra person | £ 7.10 |
| child (5-16 yrs) | £ 3.10 |
| Min. charge £ 9.60 | |

The East of England is a perfect mix of soft and gentle countrysid[e], ancient cities, historic[al] towns, and storybook villages. Its coastline is largely untouched and studd[ed] with nature reserves, ideal for bird-watching, while the traditiona[l] beach resorts offer old-fashioned seaside fun.

**THIS REGION INCLUDES THE COUNTIES OF ESSEX, SUFFOLK, NORFOLK, CAMBRIDGESHIRE, HERTFORDSHIRE AND BEDFORDSHIRE**

Bedfordshire and Hertfordshire are the smallest counties in the region, with peaceful canals, undulating countryside with chalk downs, and some of the greatest stately homes in the country. Essex is full of quaint villages with a smattering of old towns and traditional seasides resorts, including Colchester and Southend-on-Sea. The river Cam winds its way through Cambridgeshire; punting along the river in Cambridge is a good way to relax and take in the many famous university buildings that dominate the waterfront along the 'Backs'. Further along the river is the ancient cathedral city of Ely, once an island before the Fen drainage. The flat Fenland has a network of rivers and canals, ideal for narrowboat trips, as are the Norfolk Broads. Norfolk itself is very flat, sparsely populated and tranquil, popular with walkers and cyclists, while the numerous nature reserves attract a variety of wildlife. It also has a beautiful coastline; the seaside towns of Great Yarmouth and Hunstanton are major draws. This unspoilt coastline stretches into Suffolk, 'Constable Country'. Full of space, with picturesque villages set amongst lush green countryside, dotted with timbered cottages and ruined abbeys, the county is home to Newmarket, the horse racing capital of the world.

### Places of interest

*Essex:* Clacton-on-Sea; Walton-on-the-Naze, with nature reserve; Colchester, Epping; Chelmsford.

*Suffolk:* Ipswich; Felixstowe; Lowestoft; Bury St Edmonds; village of Clare with country park.

*Norfolk:* Norwich, seaside resort of Cromer; old fishing village of Sheringham, Sandringham Palace near King's Lynn; Banham Zoo.

*Cambridgeshire:* King's College and Chapel in Cambridge plus Fitzwilliam Museum; Peterborough; Imperial War Museum in Duxford; Huntingdon; Wildfowl & Wetland Trust near Wisbech.

*Hertfordshire:* St Albans; stately homes and gardens of Knebworth House and Hatfield House.

*Bedfordshire:* Bedford, Woburn with Abbey and safari park; Whipsnade Wild Animal Park; Shuttleworth Collection near Biggleswade.

### Did you know?

Newmarket has been recognised as the Headquarters of Racing for over 300 years.

The highest point of the East of England is the Dunstable Downs at 244 metres.

Colchester is Britain's oldest recorded town with Europe's largest Norman Castle keep.

The artist John Constable was born in 1776 in the village of East Bergholt. Nearby Flatford Mill, was portrayed in his most famous scene 'The Haywain'.

Peterhouse is the first Cambridge college, founded in 1284 by the Bishop of Ely.

Epping Forest was the haunt of the renowned highwayman, Dick Turpin.

## Aldeburgh
### Church Farm Holiday Park
Church Farm Road, Aldeburgh IP15 5DW (Suffolk) T: 01728 453433. E: aldeburgh@amberleisure.com
alanrogers.com/UK3350

This area of the Suffolk coast has always been a popular destination for visitors and Church Farm Holiday Park has an enviable location on the outskirts of Aldeburgh. The park includes a large area designated for caravan holiday homes as well as a separate touring area situated to the front of the park. The touring area provides 85 pitches for caravans and motorhomes (tents and trailer tents are not accepted). Pitches are separated by attractive hedging that blends in well with the natural environment. 62 pitches have access to 16A electricity, as well as own water taps and a shared waste outlet (one between two pitches). The park lies opposite a shingle beach (to the south of Thorpeness) and is adjacent to a nature reserve, a haven for birds and other wildlife. The town of Aldeburgh is only 15 minutes walk away, where there are many pubs, restaurants and takeaways. Fresh local seafood is also available along the seafront, seven days a week. The famous Aldeburgh lifeboat station is open to visitors and there are many other places of interest within easy reach. This is a quiet park with no facilities for children on site, but close to the beach and amenities in Aldeburgh.

### Facilities
The single toilet block has been fully upgraded with heating, free showers, toilets and washbasins (entry card with deposit). Access to the toilets and showers are via two steps, making it unsuitable for wheelchair users. However ambulant toilets are provided. Laundry room. Gas supplies. Off site: Bus service 0.5 - 1 mile. Shops, pubs, etc. 15 minutes walk. Beach 5 minutes walk. Fishing and bicycle hire 1 mile. Riding 6 miles.

Open: Easter - 31 October.

### Directions
On arrival at Aldeburgh, site is signed at roundabout in the direction of Thorpeness. Where road meets seafront, site is on left. From town centre follow road along seafront to site on left at end of town.
O.S.GR: TM465572. GPS: 52.15827, 1.60330

### Charges guide
| | |
|---|---|
| Per pitch incl. all persons | £ 20.00 - £ 24.00 |
| incl. services | £ 28.00 - £ 32.00 |

Cheques are not accepted.
Credit cards 2.5% surcharge.

For latest campsite news visit
**alanrogers.com**

## Banham

### Applewood Caravan & Camping Park

Banham Zoo, The Grove, Banham NR16 2HE (Norfolk) T: 01953 888370. E: info@banhamzoo.co.uk

alanrogers.com/UK3385

Applewood is a 13 acre touring park, adjacent to the famous Banham Zoo, the residents of which are the only thing that may disturb your relaxation while on this park (but they do not usually rise until 08.00). Visitors to the park receive a special price for admission to the Zoo. At weekends, one of Norfolk's largest car boot sales is held at the arena area alongside the site. Applewood has 100 pitches, 70 with electric hook-ups (10A). They are spread amongst thirteen areas, each separated by high, established hedges which offer privacy and seclusion. There is a large rally field and a function room. The Appleyard, two minutes walk from the park provides a Spar shop, Huckleberry's restaurant and gift shops. The village with its pub is also within walking distance.

#### Facilities

Two toilet blocks, one new and one refurbished provide good, clean and spacious facilities. Room for disabled visitors. Laundry. Motorcaravan service point. Accessory shop, rally field and function room. Gas supplies. Off site: Zoo and The Appleyard with shop and restaurant. Snetterton race circuit 3 miles. Norwich 15 miles.

Open: 13 February - 31 October.

#### Directions

From Attleborough on the A11 take B1077 to New Buckenham and Banham Zoo. Follow road to T-junction with B1113 and turn right signed Banham. Follow through village and park is on the left at top of hill. O.S.GR: TM058871. GPS: 52.44636, 1.02514

#### Charges guide

| | |
|---|---|
| Per person incl. electricity | £ 15.95 - £ 19.95 |

## Bury Saint Edmunds

### The Dell Caravan & Camping Park

Beyton Road, Thurston, Bury Saint Edmunds IP31 3RB (Suffolk) T: 01359 270121
E: thedellcaravanpark@btinternet.com alanrogers.com/UK3345

Close to the A14 and surrounded by farmland, this small touring site, four miles east of Bury St Edmunds, provides a convenient base to explore the nearby town and surrounding villages or as a stopover point. The current owners have created 60 spacious pitches within the main touring area, divided into two sections – one of which is reserved for adults only. All pitches have 10A electricity. A separate field with a further ten pitches situated under trees is available for contractors working locally, as well as any visitors who prefer shaded areas. The main touring field has some shade from well maintained hedges and the trees bordering the site. All pitches have access to the site's facilities. Food is available from local village pubs within two miles of the park. There is some noise from the nearby A14, especially to the south side of the park, but otherwise the site provides a quiet base for tourers to explore the area.

#### Facilities

Excellent and ample toilet and spacious shower facilities (free) are provided within a purpose built sanitary block. Ladies' toilets include a private bathroom and toilet. Family bathroom with bath, shower and baby changing facilities (charged). Separate toilet/shower for disabled visitors. Laundry room. Off site: Bus service to Bury St Edmonds from outside park. Fishing, golf and riding 3 miles. Local pubs and restaurants in Thurston and neighbouring villages.

Open: All year.

#### Directions

From the A14 take exit for Thurston and Beyton, 4 miles east of Bury St Edmunds. Follow signs to Thurston. Park is on the left, shortly after arriving at Thurston and signed from Beyton. O.S.GR: TL928640. GPS: 52.24053, 0.82437

#### Charges guide

| | |
|---|---|
| Per unit incl. 2 persons and electricity | £ 15.00 - £ 18.00 |

---

### Welcome to The Dell Caravan Park

The Dell is located in the heart of the idyllic Suffolk Countryside. Suffolk will spoil you with its space and peace, gently rolling countryside and picturesque villages with thatched, colourwashed cottages; scenes that inspired some of Britain's greatest painters. Suffolk also boasts a largely unspoiled 45 mile long coastline, much of it now managed for conservation and offering broad views, long walks, fine bird watching and charming seaside villages. Thurston is our local village (about 1 mile away) and has a fish and chips shop, a post office, general store, garage/ filling station, pub, hotel, vet and railway station that goes to Bury and Ipswich. The park is open all year round and has 55 widely spaced pitches situated on six acres of level ground, surrounded by trees and fields.

**Dell Touring Caravan & Camping Park**
Beyton Road, Thurston, Bury St Edmunds,
Suffolk. IP31 3RB
Tel: 01359 270121
Email: thedellcaravanpark@btinternet.com
www.thedellcaravanpark.co.uk

---

# Cambridge

## Highfield Farm Touring Park

Long Road, Comberton, Cambridge CB23 7DG (Cambridgeshire) T: 01223 262308
E: enquiries@highfieldfarmtouringpark.co.uk   alanrogers.com/UK3560

Situated five miles from Cambridge, this eight acre park is set in a delightfully quiet touring location yet close to major routes around Cambridge. The welcome is always warm from the friendly family owners. The facilities are of high quality and the grass and hedges are well cared for. Divided into five enclosures by conifer hedges, there are also shady glades for those who wish to retreat even further and one enclosure is reserved for those without children. Offering 60 numbered pitches for caravans or motorcaravans, and 60 for tents, pitching is around the outer edges. As a result, the park never looks crowded even when fully booked (which is frequently the case). All pitches have 10A electricity, 50 have gravel hardstanding, and most are level. A good dog walk is provided, which can be extended to a pleasant 1.5 mile walk, with seats, around the farm perimeter. A member of the Best of British group.

### Facilities

Three heated toilet blocks provide more than adequate coverage and good facilities, all very clean and well maintained. Baby room but no dedicated provision for disabled visitors, although one block has extra wide doors and easy access. Laundry room. Small play area. Good shop. Motorcaravan service point. Excellent tourist information room. Gates closed midnight to 07.30.
Off site: Comberton village 0.5 miles. Golf 2 miles. Fishing 3.5 miles. Cambridge 5 miles. Duxford War Museum and National Trust properties.

Open: 23 March - 31 October.

### Directions

From M11 exit 12, take A603 towards Sandy. After 0.5 miles turn right, B1046 to Comberton. Turn right just before village signed Madingley (also caravan sign). Site on right just north of village.
O.S GR: TL391571. GPS: 52.194981, 0.031103

### Charges 2011

| Per unit incl. 2 persons | |
|---|---|
| and electricity | £ 16.50 - £ 20.00 |
| extra person | £ 4.25 |
| child (5-16 yrs) | £ 2.75 |
| dog | £ 1.00 |

No credit cards.

Highfield Farm Touring Park

A warm welcome awaits you at our popular award winning park with its excellent facilities, set in peaceful farming countryside. It is close to the historic University City of Cambridge, the Imperial War Museum, Duxford and ideally suited for touring East Anglia.

Comberton, Cambridge CB23 7DG Tel/Fax: 01223 262308
www.highfieldfarmtouringpark.co.uk

## Clacton-on-Sea

### Homestead Lake Park

Thorpe Road, Weeley, Clacton-on-Sea CO16 9JN (Essex) T: 01255 833492
E: lakepark@homesteadcaravans.co.uk  alanrogers.com/UK3300

This well laid out, 25 acre park was opened in 2002. It is hidden from the road at the rear of Homestead Caravans sales areas and workshops in the countryside of the Tendring district, at Weeley near Clacton. It offers 50 fully serviced, hardstanding pitches on gently sloping ground overlooking a fishing lake and recently built holiday lodge accommodation on the other side of the lake. Tents accepted for short stays only on a limited number of pitches. The park makes an ideal spot to stay either for fishing, for a relaxing weekend, or as a base for touring this part of Essex. A special area has been added to allow wheelchair users to fish. You could even arrange for your caravan to be serviced or repairs to be made while you stay. Homestead also has a large accessories superstore and café, where breakfast is recommended as a start to your day.

### Facilities

The toilet block offers clean and spacious facilities including an en-suite unit for disabled visitors. Baby changing facilities. Coffee shop/café and snack bar. Fishing lake. Woodland walks. Caravan sales, workshops and accessory shop. A large rally field is also available. Off site: The site is ideally situated for visiting the many attractions of this holiday area. The towns of Clacton-on-Sea, Frinton, Harwich and Brightlingsea are all within a 10-mile radius and the heart of 'Constable' country, with Flatford Mill and Dedham, is a short drive away.

Open: 1 March - 31 October.

### Directions

From Colchester take A120, then A133 signed Clacton. At roundabout, turn left on B1033 into Weeley and site and showrooms are on left just past council offices. O.S GR: TM149225.
GPS: 51.85989, 1.12021

### Charges guide

| | |
|---|---|
| Per unit incl. 2 persons and electricity | £ 15.00 - £ 22.00 |
| extra person | £ 4.00 |
| child (under 18 yrs) | £ 2.00 |
| dog | £ 2.00 |

## Colchester

### Fen Farm Caravan & Camping Site

East Mersea, Colchester CO5 8FE (Essex) T: 01206 383275. E: fenfarm@talk21.com
alanrogers.com/UK3290

Tents were first pitched at Fen Farm in 1923 and since then the park has 'grown rather than developed' – something of which owners Ralph and Wenda Lord and their family are proud. The 65 touring pitches are all unmarked, on level grass and within three fields that have a spacious feel to them. An area for over 80 holiday homes is separate and screened from the touring area. All pitches have 10A electricity connections and three have hardstanding and are fully serviced. A limited number of touring pitches are available on the smaller field, with outstanding views and direct access to the beach. This is an attractive well laid out site with trees and two ponds. The site provides facilities for launching boats from the seashore and it is popular with water skiers and windsurfers. Jet skis are not allowed. There are also many opportunities for walking, either inland or along the beach.

### Facilities

The toilet block in the main touring field includes a family room and shower/toilet for disabled visitors. Laundry room. Mobile shop calls with basic supplies from local shop (daily high season, weekends low season). Mobile shop for papers, bread and milk (weekends in summer). Gas supplies. Play area. Caravan and boat storage. WiFi (charged). Off site: Shop 1.5 miles. 'Pick your own' fruit farm and tea room. Shops, pubs, restaurants and banks in West Mersea.

Open: 19 March - 31 October.

### Directions

From Colchester, take B1025 to Mersea Island. After crossing causeway, take left fork to East Mersea. Follow road for 2.75 miles to 'Dog and Pheasant' pub. Site entrance is next right. NB: Access across the causeway onto Mersea Island is restricted at high tide. O.S.GR: TM058144.
GPS: 51.78996, 0.98460

### Charges guide

| | |
|---|---|
| Per pitch | £ 20.00 - £ 25.00 |
| awning | free |
| extra car | £ 5.00 |

# Cromer

## Woodhill Park

Cromer Road, East Runton, Cromer NR27 9PX (Norfolk) T: 01263 512242. E: info@woodhill-park.com
alanrogers.com/UK3500

Woodhill is a seaside site with good views and a traditional atmosphere. It is situated on the cliff top, in a large, gently sloping, open grassy field, with 300 marked touring pitches. Of these, 210 have electricity (16A), 7 are fully serviced and many have wonderful views over the surrounding coastline and countryside. A small number of holiday homes are available with magnificent sea views. Although the site is fenced there is access to the cliff top path which takes you to the beach. It is possible locally to take a boat trip to see the seals off Blakeney Point. Nearby attractions include the Shire Horse Centre at West Runton and the North Norfolk Steam Railway.

### Facilities

There are all the usual facilities you would expect including toilets, showers, hairdryers, baby changing, laundry and washing up sinks as well as a toilet and shower for the disabled. You can also make use of the family bathroom, with a bath, shower, toilet, sink and baby changing unit and three other family shower rooms, all with toilets and sinks providing families with both privacy and security. Green technology plays a major role with solar panels added to one of the blocks roof to heat the water. Well stocked shop (19/3-31/10). Large adventure playground and plenty of space for ball games. Crazy golf. Giant chess and golf course adjacent. Off site: Beach 0.5 miles. Fishing 1 mile. Bicycle hire, golf and riding 2 miles.

Open: 19 March - 31 October.

### Directions

Site is beside the A149 coast road between East and West Runton. O.S.GR: TG190420. GPS: 52.93307, 1.27664

### Charges guide

| | |
|---|---|
| Per unit incl. 2 persons and electricity | £ 15.00 - £ 18.00 |
| extra person | £ 2.50 |
| child (4-16 yrs) | £ 1.00 |
| dog | £ 2.00 - £ 3.50 |

# East Harling

## The Dower House Touring Park

Thetford Forest, East Harling NR16 2SE (Norfolk) T: 01953 717314. E: info@dowerhouse.co.uk
alanrogers.com/UK3390

Set on 20 acres in the heart of Britain's largest forest on the Suffolk and Norfolk borders, The Dower House provides quiet woodland walks and cycle ways, with an abundance of wildlife. David and Karen Bushell, owners for many years, continue to upgrade the facilities without compromising the park's natural features. There are 160 really large pitches with electricity available (10A). Most are level, although given the forest location there are a few tree roots. A fourth field provides 60 pitches for tents. Six pitches for visitors with mobility problems are linked by a path to the main facilities.

### Facilities

Two toilet blocks. A small, refurbished one near the entrance and a larger one with a baby room. A separate building houses the showers (five for each sex) and a unit for disabled visitors. Dishwashing room. Laundry facilities. Separate licensed shop doubling as reception and open daily in the season, on request at other times. Gas supplies. Information room. TV and quiet rooms (no games machines). New heated outdoor swimming pool (31/5-1/9, under 15s must be with an adult). Paddling pool. Caravan storage. Torches necessary. Off site: Fishing nearby 1.5 miles.

Open: 19 March - 3 October.

### Directions

From A11 (Thetford - Norwich) road, 7 miles from Thetford, turn right on B1111 towards East Harling. Turn right at church and right at T-junction; park is on right. From A1066 Thetford-Diss road take left fork signed East Harling. Ignore signs for Forestry Commission site and park is next on left. Follow long drive (unmade road) for about 1 mile - keep speed down. O.S GR: TL969853. GPS: 52.42829, 0.89631

### Charges guide

| | |
|---|---|
| Per unit incl. 2 persons | £ 11.95 - £ 20.95 |
| incl. electricity | £ 15.25 - £ 24.50 |
| extra person | £ 4.00 |

For latest campsite news visit
**alanrogers.com**

## Fakenham

### The Old Brick Kilns Caravan & Camping Park

Little Barney Lane, Barney, Fakenham NR21 0NL (Norfolk) T: 01328 878305. E: enquiries@old-brick-kilns.co.uk
alanrogers.com/UK3400

This is a tranquil, family run park and a friendly, helpful atmosphere prevails. The park's development on the site of old brick kilns has resulted in land on varying levels. This provides areas of level, well drained pitches (e.g. the Dell, the Orchard) all of which are on hardstanding. There are 65 pitches in total, all with electricity (16A), including a newer area with serviced pitches. Banks around the park and a wide range of trees and shrubs provide shelter and are home for a variety of wildlife. There are garden areas, including a butterfly garden, and a conservation pond is the central feature. Drinking water is supplied by a 285 ft. bore and excellent roofed service areas provide water and waste disposal. Amenities include a large, comfortable bar area and restaurant, open at weekends. and as the park is 8 miles from the coast, it is ideally situated to explore North Norfolk. A member of the Best of British group.

### Facilities

Smart, heated toilet blocks provide very good, clean facilities with washbasins in curtained cubicles. Baby room. Facilities for disabled visitors (unisex; Radar key). Laundry room. Motorcaravan service point. Good shop with gas supplies. Bar/restaurant (weekends) with patio area outside with barbecue. TV and games room. Giant chess. Small library. Fenced play area. Fishing (purpose-built platforms). Internet access. B&B also available. Strictly no arrivals until after 13.00. Caravan storage. Off site: Riding 6 miles. Golf 5 or 8 miles. Thursford collection 2 miles.

Open: All year excl. 7 January - 1 March.

### Directions

From Fakenham take A148 Cromer road. After 6 miles, at Thursford, fork right on B1354 Melton Constable road. In 300 yds, turn right, signed Barney, and then first left along a narrow country lane with passing places, for 0.75 miles.
O.S.GR: TG004332. GPS: 52.85804, 0.97583

### Charges guide

| Per unit incl. 2 persons | |
|---|---|
| and electricity | £ 14.50 - £ 18.50 |
| 'super pitch' plus | £ 2.50 - £ 3.50 |
| extra person | £ 3.00 |
| child (up to 15 yrs) | £ 1.00 - £ 2.00 |
| dog (max. 2) | £ 0.75 |

## Great Yarmouth

### The Grange Touring Park

Ormesby St Margaret, Great Yarmouth NR29 3QG (Norfolk) T: 01493 730306. E: info@grangetouring.co.uk
alanrogers.com/UK3490

The appearance of this family touring site is that of a garden, with hanging baskets, flower beds, bluebells and daffodils under the trees in spring, all carefully tended by the resident wardens. There are 70 level pitches with electricity (16A), 13 with hardstanding, and 10 pitches for tents, all arranged on well trimmed grass with tarmac access roads. Adjacent to the campsite is The Grange – a free house offering meals, beers and real ale, plus children's play equipment (open all year). The site owner also has a holiday campsite at Hemsby (4 miles) with its own wide sandy beach, which guests at The Grange are welcome to use. The nearest beach is a mile away and local attractions include Caister Castle and Motor Museum and Norfolk Rare Breed Centre. Great Yarmouth Centre with many attractions and The Broads are within 5 miles.

### Facilities

A modern, heated toilet building is spacious and well maintained, housing all the usual facilities including free showers. Baby room in the ladies'. Laundry room with washing machine and dryer. Washing lines are provided at the rear of the building. Gas supplies. Swings for children. Internet café and WiFi (£3 per hour or per 24 hours if using own computer). Three family/disabled visitors rooms/cubicles and a motorcaravan service point have been added. Off site: Bus service 250 yds. Beach, shops and supermarket 1 mile. Riding 2 miles. Golf 3 miles. Fishing 4 miles. Great Yarmouth 5 minutes drive.

Open: Mid March - early October.

### Directions

Site is just north of Great Yarmouth. Entrance is just south of the roundabout at the northern edge of the Caister bypass. O.S.GR: TG512141.
GPS: 52.66812, 1.71097

### Charges guide

| Per unit incl. up to 4 persons | |
|---|---|
| and electricity | £ 14.00 - £ 20.00 |
| extra person | £ 3.50 |
| child (under 5 yrs) | free |
| dog | free - £ 3.50 |

For latest campsite news visit
**alanrogers.com**

## Great Yarmouth
### Clippesby Hall

Clippesby, Great Yarmouth NR29 3BL (Norfolk) T: 01493 367800. E: holidays@clippesby.com
alanrogers.com/UK3485

Set in the heart of the Broads National Park this is a spacious, high quality park where you can be sure of a warm welcome from the Lindsay family who have lived in the Hall for many years. Clippesby offers the choice of pitching amongst the shady woodland, on the gently sloping lawns of the Hall with colourful mature trees and shrubs or in a new area, 'The Meadow' which offers fully serviced pitches with hardstanding. The 100 pitches are well spaced and clearly numbered (70 have 10A electricity). Children can roam at will in safety, and parents can relax at this beautiful park. Facilities include a sunken grass tennis court, a play area, a timber adventure playground, a football pitch and family golf with a seaside theme. There is also a small, heated swimming pool with a separate paddling pool. The Muskett Arms with a comfortable family bar and a sheltered courtyard outside, provides fresh, home-cooked meals, music nights and other family entertainment. Susie's Coffee Shop has a good selection of food during the day. The Broads and Great Yarmouth close by are waiting to be explored.

### Facilities

Three timbered heated toilet blocks provide very clean, modern facilities. Some cabins with washbasin and WC. En-suite room for disabled visitors. Family room with bath and baby changing. Laundry. Gas. Shop (Easter-end Oct). Café and family bar/restaurant (early May-end Oct). Pizza takeaway. Small swimming pool and paddling pool (end May-end Sept). Adventure play area. Football. Bicycle hire. Max. 1 dog per pitch. Dog walk. WiFi (free). Off site: Bus service 1.5 miles. Fishing and boat launching 2 miles. Riding 3 miles. Golf, beach and sailing 5 miles. Great Yarmouth 7 miles. Norwich 15 miles. The Broads.

Open: 1 April - 31 October.

### Directions

From the A47 Norwich - Great Yarmouth road at Acle roundabout take exit for Filby (A1064). After 1.5 miles fork left on B1152 signed Potter Heigham. Take first left and park is 100 yards on the right. O.S.GR: TG423145. GPS: 52.67283, 1.58299

### Charges guide

| | |
|---|---|
| Per unit incl. 2 persons and electricity | £ 13.50 - £ 29.50 |
| extra person | £ 5.00 |
| child | £ 2.50 |
| dog (max. 1) | £ 3.50 |

## Great Yarmouth
### Rose Farm Touring Park

Stepshort, Belton, Great Yarmouth NR31 9JS (Norfolk) T: 01493 780896
E: myhra@rosefarmtouringpark.fsnet.co.uk  alanrogers.com/UK3382

This part of Norfolk is well known for its seaside attractions and the campsites which combine caravan holiday homes and touring pitches. Rose Farm caters for another type of camping holiday, offering space with the peace and tranquillity that you may not be expecting in this particular area! There are 120 pitches, 80 with electricity (16A). Spread over eight acres, the park is split into two separate fields. The first is large and open, surrounded by fencing and hedges, with pitches around the edge. It is very spacious with a very good toilet/shower block. The second field is long with pitching on either side. A new toilet/shower block here offers top quality facilities. Some hardstanding pitches are also available.

### Facilities

The two excellent blocks offer super facilities. The newer block is in Norwegian style, with a very modern fresh and spacious interior. Showers are good with changing space, washbasins are open or in cubicles. The laundry is in the first block along with an iron and ironing board. Facilities for disabled visitors. Adventure playground. TV room. Dog walk. Internet access. Off site: Fishing and golf 3 miles. Riding and bicycle hire 4 miles. Beach 5 miles.

Open: All year.

### Directions

From Great Yarmouth and Gorleston take the A143 signed Beccles and Diss. At dual carriageway (Bradwell) take immediate right to Burgh Castle, take next right, site on right in 25 yards. O.S.GR: TG486033 GPS: 52.57136, 1.66876

### Charges guide

| | |
|---|---|
| Per unit incl. 2 persons | £ 15.00 - £ 19.00 |
| No credit cards. | |

## Harleston
### Little Lakeland Caravan Park
Wortwell, Harleston IP20 0EL (Norfolk) T: 01986 788646. E: information@littlelakeland.co.uk
alanrogers.com/UK3480

This peaceful hideaway with its own fishing lake is tucked behind the houses and gardens that border the village main street. It is a traditional, mature little park with just 58 pitches. There are several caravan holiday homes and long stay units, but there should always be around 22 places with 10A electricity for touring units. The pitches are mostly individual ones separated by mature hedges and trees giving varying amounts of shade. Fishing in the attractive lake is free of charge and solely for the use of campers (bream, tench, roach, perch and carp). A member of the Countryside Discovery Group.

**Facilities**

A modern, heated toilet block provides washbasins in cubicles for ladies, and one for men. Laundry. En-suite room for disabled visitors. A further heated unit by reception provides a shower, WC and basin per sex and is used mostly in the colder months. Reception stocks gas and some basic essentials. Small play area. Fishing (max. 4 rods per unit). WiFi (charged). Off site: Bus 250 yds. Pub 500 yds. Golf and bicycle hire 4 miles. Riding 6 miles.

Open: 15 March - 31 October.

**Directions**

Approaching from Diss, leave A143 at roundabout signed Wortwell. Continue to village, pass 'The Bell' public house, a garage on the right, then turn right at first bungalow (Little Lakeland Lodge) watching carefully for signs. Site is down lane, 250 yards on right. O.S.GR: TM270850. GPS: 52.41628, 1.35282

**Charges guide**

| Per unit incl. 2 persons | £ 16.00 - £ 18.50 |

No credit cards.

## Hunstanton
### Searles Leisure Resort
South Beach Road, Hunstanton PE36 5BB (Norfolk) T: 01485 534211. E: bookings@searles.co.uk
alanrogers.com/UK3520

This is a high quality 'all-in' family holiday park on the North Norfolk coast offering everything for a great seaside family holiday. There is a beach within walking distance, a covered 'town plaza' including a sports bar, Chinese restaurant and American diner plus fish and chip bar, club house, pools, Country Club, golf course and driving range, fishing lakes and bowling greens; there should be something to entertain everyone. There are 823 pitches with 323 pitches for touring, 129 with 16A electricity. Some are on hardstanding and fully serviced with others on grass. There is an open area reserved for tents.

**Facilities**

Three large, modern, clean toilet blocks with washbasins and toilets in cubicles. Facilities for disabled visitors. Baby room. Laundry. Food hall. Restaurants, bars and cafés. Hair and beauty salon. Indoor and outdoor heated swimming pools. Gym. Tennis. Soft play area. Golf (9-hole course, driving range and putting course). Fishing lake. Bowling green. Bicycle, pedalo hire. WiFi. Off site: Nearest beach 400 yds. Hunstanton 0.5 miles.

Open: All year, excl. 25th December.

**Directions**

From King's Lynn take A149 north to Hunstanton. At first roundabout take B1161. After 0.3 miles cross roundabout (supermarket), site immediately on left. O.S.GR: TF670401. GPS: 52.93033, 0.48289

**Charges guide**

| Per pitch | £ 15.00 - £ 39.00 |
| fully serviced pitch | £ 17.00 - £ 53.00 |
| dog | £ 3.00 |

## Huntingdon
### Wyton Lakes Holiday Park
Banks End, Wyton, Huntingdon PE28 2AA (Cambridgeshire) T: 01480 412715. E: loupeter@supanet.com
alanrogers.com/UK3555

Wyton Lakes is a family run, adults only park with four well stocked fishing lakes, very close to the River Great Ouse, between Huntingdon and St Ives. There are 80 level pitches of medium size with 60 for caravans and motorhomes and 20 for tents. The tent pitches are on grass and have no electricity. The other pitches are mainly on hardstanding with gravel for awnings and all have electricity and a water tap. Most of the pitches border the lakes making fishing possible from the pitch. Well placed as a centre for touring, the park has easy access for large outfits. The old market towns of Huntingdon and St Ives are only three miles away and the delightful village of Houghton with its old mill, pub and riverside walks is just one mile. Just across the road is a large garden centre complete with restaurant and coffee shop.

**Facilities**

Heated toilet block with all necessary facilities including those for campers with disabilities. Coarse lake and river fishing on payment (carp, bream, tench, perch, roach and rudd, up to 30 lb). Riverside walks. Off site: Garden centre, restaurant and coffee shop opposite entrance. Interesting old village Houghton, pub, shop, National Trust Mill, riverside walks, 1 mile. St Ives, Huntingdon, 3 miles. Boat hire, golf 3 miles. Huntingdon Race Course 4 miles. Paxton Pits Nature Reserves, Hinchingbrooke Park.

Open: 1 April - 26 October.

**Directions**

From the A14 take exit 26 (St Ives). Take A1096 north towards St Ives. Turn left onto A1123, signed Huntingdon and site entrance is on the left in about 2 miles opposite garden centre. O.S.GR: TL269725. GPS: 52.33664, -0.13872

**Charges guide**

| Per unit incl. 2 persons and electricity | £ 15.00 |
| tent pitch incl. 2 adults | £ 12.00 - £ 14.00 |

Adults only (over 18 yrs). No credit cards.

For latest campsite news visit
**alanrogers.com**

## Ipswich

### Westwood Park Caravan Park

Old Felixstowe Road, Bucklesham, Ipswich IP10 0BW (Suffolk) T: 01473 659637
E: westwoodcaravanpark@bt-connect.co.uk  alanrogers.com/UK3335

This new park opened in Easter 2007 and has been developed on land previously owned by the neighbouring farm. The park is situated between Felixstowe and Ipswich and is within easy reach of the River Deben and Woodbridge. The 90 level grass pitches are of varying size to accommodate both small and large caravans, motorhomes and tents. All pitches have 16A electricity. The planting of hedges should ensure separation of individual pitches as the park develops. Families are welcome and a grass area has been fenced off for football and other games at the far end of the park. A dog walking area has been created screened by shrubs along two sides of the park and a nature area to encourage local wildlife is also being developed.

#### Facilities

A brand new, but traditionally built, toilet block in the centre of the park includes facilities for disabled visitors (£5 deposit for key). Laundry. Purpose built reception provides local information and sells a limited range of provisions e.g. milk (plus bread and papers at B.Hs and high season). Recycling facilities planned. Grass play area for children. Off site: Free range eggs from a farm (short walk). Pubs serving meals in nearby Bucklesham and surrounding villages. Fishing 2 miles. Golf 4 miles. Beach 5 miles. Bus service to Ipswich nearby.

Open: All year excl. 16 January - 28 February.

#### Directions

Site is near Bucklesham. From the A12 (south) or A14(12) (north) take A14 towards Felixstowe. Continue for 5 miles and turn left signed Kirton, Bucklesham and Brightwell. Continue for about 1 mile: Park is on the right, immediately after Tenth Road on the left. O.S.GR: TN253411. GPS: 52.02316, 1.28389

#### Charges guide

| | |
|---|---|
| Per unit incl. 2 persons, 2 children and electricity | £ 18.00 - £ 20.00 |

---

## Ipswich

### The Oaks Caravan Park

Chapel Road, Bucklesham, Ipswich IP10 0BT (Suffolk) T: 01394 448837. E: oakscaravanpark@aol.com
alanrogers.com/UK3325

Situated between Felixstowe and Ipswich and with views over open farmland, this pleasant adult only touring park provides access to the surrounding countryside and towns, including the River Deben, Woodbridge and the Suffolk Heritage coast. Since opening in the summer of 2003, the park continues to attract many repeat visitors. Trees and shrubs planted around the perimeter and across the length of the site are now maturing, creating screening and shade for the 89 marked touring pitches. There are 79 electricity hook-ups and the well maintained grass pitches are laid out either side of an oval gravel path. A summer house in the centre contains local information, newspapers and a small patio area with tables and chairs where visitors can sit and read. The site provides a minibus service in the evenings to local pubs/restaurants (by prior arrangement).

#### Facilities

The single modern sanitary block provides bright and clean toilet and shower facilities, as well as a covered dishwashing area and motorcaravan point. Facilities for disabled visitors are planned. Gas is available at reception. Bicycle hire. Off site: Bus service outside park. Minibus service in the evenings by prior arrangement to nearby local pubs/restaurants, fish and chips Friday evenings. Riding 1 mile. Fishing less than 1 mile. Golf 4 miles. Beach 5 miles.

Open: 1 April - 31 October.

#### Directions

Site is situated between Bucklesham and Kirton. From the A12 (south) or A14(12) (north) take the A14 towards Felixstowe. Continue for 5 miles and turn left signed Bucklesham and Brightwell. Continue for 1 mile, past Tenth Road on the left, take next right signed Kirton and Newbourne. Park is on the right in 550 yds. O.S.GR: TM261411. GPS: 52.02210, 1.29913

#### Charges guide

| | |
|---|---|
| Per unit incl. 2 persons and electricity | £ 13.00 - £ 15.00 |
| tent incl. 2 persons | £ 12.00 |
| extra person | £ 2.50 |
| dog | free |

For latest campsite news visit
**alanrogers.com**

## Ipswich

### Orwell Meadows Leisure Park

Priory Lane, Ipswich IP10 0JS (Suffolk) T: 01473 726666. E: recept@orwellmeadows.co.uk
alanrogers.com/UK3315

This popular, family park is set on the edge of the Orwell Country Park near Ipswich with its many miles of walks and the famous Orwell Bridge with views of the Suffolk countryside. The park is run by David and Sally Miles and offers an ideal spot for a family holiday with an outdoor swimming pool and a good clubhouse with a bar, restaurant and a shop. Spacious pitches are around the edges of several separate meadows (surrounded on three sides by earth banks), all offering 16A electricity hook-ups. There is much to see and do in the area.

**Facilities**

The modern toilet block includes clean and spacious showers. It is kept to a very high standard. En-suite facilities for disabled visitors. Well stocked shop. Bar and restaurant. Outdoor pool. Play area. TV/family room. Max. two dogs per unit.

Open: March - January.

**Directions**

From A14 Ipswich bypass take Nacton/Ipswich exit (north of the A14) and follow signs for Orwell Country Park (narrow lane). Cross single track bridge over the A14 to the site entrance 20 yards on left. Follow signs past house/reception up hill and park on the left and walk back to reception.
O.S.GR: TM190408. GPS: 52.02044, 1.19161

**Charges guide**

| | |
|---|---|
| Per unit incl. 2 persons | £ 15.00 - £ 17.00 |

---

## Ipswich

### Low House Touring Caravan Centre

Bucklesham Road, Foxhall, Ipswich IP10 0AU (Suffolk) T: 01473 659437. E: low.house@btinternet.com
alanrogers.com/UK3310

Set in a sheltered 3.5 acres, this site has 30 level, grass pitches and an abundance of shrubs and flowers. The park has been divided into two areas bordered by mature trees and the grounds are well maintained. There are many different varieties of trees with a tree walk leading round two sides of the park. All the pitches have electrical connections (10/16A) and they back onto trees that provide plenty of shade and the opportunity to observe a range of wildlife. Low House lies between Felixstowe and Ipswich and would be a useful stopover for the Felixstowe port or Harwich.

**Facilities**

The older style, heated sanitary block is spotlessly clean with hot showers (50p). No on-site provisions but a supermarket is 2 miles (towards Ipswich). Frozen goods can be stored. Small, secure play area. Pet area with rabbit, hens and guinea fowl. Off site: Good bus service to Ipswich stops nearby. Pub in Bucklesham village (1.5 miles) and other good pubs nearby. Golf 2 miles. Fishing 3 miles.

Open: All year.

**Directions**

Turn off A14 (was A45) Ipswich ring road (south) via slip road onto A1156 (Ipswich East). Follow road over bridge crossing over the A45 and almost immediately turn right (no sign). After 0.5 miles turn right (Bucklesham). Site is on left after 400 yards.
O.S.GR: TM225423. GPS: 52.03402, 1.24507

**Charges guide**

| | |
|---|---|
| Per unit incl. 2 adults, 2 children and electricity | £ 14.00 - £ 20.00 |
| extra person | £ 3.00 |

No large commercial vehicles. No credit cards.

---

## Kings Lynn

### The Garden Caravan Site

Barmer Hall, Syderstone, Kings Lynn PE31 8SR (Norfolk) T: 01485 578220. E: nlmason@tiscali.co.uk
alanrogers.com/UK3460

In the quiet Norfolk countryside, this imaginative touring park is a sun trap set in an enclosed walled garden. Sheltered from the winds by the high walls, visitors can relax in peace and tranquillity. Attractive mature trees, shrubs and climbers provide shade at various times of the day. The Mason family run the site in a relaxed way and the atmosphere is superb. There are 30 pitches, all with electricity (16A) and TV hook-up, but little shade. Some are slightly sloping and will require blocks. Reception is housed in a small kiosk (not always manned, so pitch yourself and pay later).

**Facilities**

The single toilet block (heated) has all the usual facilities including a toilet and washbasin for campers with disabilities. Dishwashing sinks, spin dryer and iron. No shop, but gas (not Camping Gaz), ices, soft drinks and fresh, free range eggs are available. Off site: Bicycle hire 4 miles. Riding 6 miles. Golf 10 miles. Norfolk Lavender, Langham Glass or the Thursford collection of steam engines and mechanical organs.

Open: 1 March - 1 November.

**Directions**

About 6 miles west of Fakenham leave the A148 and take B1454 signed Docking and Hunstanton. After 3 miles turn right Barmer Hall (site signed). Road marked 'unsuitable for motor vehicles' but continue for 0.3 miles. Beyond Hall turn left to site.
O.S.GR: TF814336. GPS: 52.86414, 0.69116

**Charges guide**

| | |
|---|---|
| Per unit incl. 2 persons | £ 17.50 - £ 19.50 |

No credit cards.

For latest campsite news visit
alanrogers.com

## Lowestoft
### Kessingland Beach Holiday Park

Kessingland, Lowestoft NR33 7RN (Suffolk) T: 01502 740636
E: holidaysales.kessinglandbeach@park-resorts.com  alanrogers.com/UK3370

Set near the most easterly point in the UK, this park offers all you need for that total family holiday experience, including bowling, pool tables, an amusement arcade and indoor and outdoor swimming pools. If you so wish you need never leave Kessingland Beach until your holiday ends. There is evening entertainment, as well as a selection of bars and restaurants. Although mainly a large park for static caravan holiday homes, there is a touring area to the west of the park with quite spacious pitching. Electricity hook-ups are available. The toilet block is older in style but has been refurbished. There is much to see and do here on the Suffolk coast, in nearby Lowestoft and further along the coast in Great Yarmouth, as well as nearby Oulton Broad.

#### Facilities
The toilet block has been refurbished, but access is unsuitable for wheelchairs. Laundry. Shop. Bars, restaurants, fish and chips. Entertainment complex. Indoor and outdoor swimming pools. New all-weather sports court. Adventure play area. Tennis courts. Amusements. Crazy golf. Bicycle hire. Off site: Beach and sea fishing 100 yds. Golf and riding 3 miles.

Open: 20 March - 26 October.

#### Directions
From Lowestoft, north, on A12 ignore first turning to Kessingland village and continue along A12 to next roundabout. Take left turning on roundabout signed Kessingland Beach. From A12 south, turn right at roundabout signed Kessingland Beach. At beach take sharp right continuing along to park entrance (narrow road). O.S.GR: TM535859.
GPS: 52.40715, 1.72470

#### Charges guide

| | |
|---|---|
| Per caravan or motorcaravan incl. electricity | £ 6.00 - £ 29.00 |
| tent pitch | £ 3.00 - £ 26.00 |
| dog | £ 1.00 - £ 3.00 |

## Mundesley-on-Sea
### Sandy Gulls Caravan Park

Cromer Road, Mundesley-on-Sea NR11 8DF (Norfolk) T: 01263 720513
alanrogers.com/UK3410

This is a super, adults only clifftop hideaway on the outskirts of Mundesley-on-Sea. One of the only clifftop parks with space for touring units on this coastline, there are panoramic views from every pitch. All 35 pitches have electricity and TV aerial hook-ups. Some are on hardstanding, others are slightly sloping on grass (chocks advised). Primarily a caravan holiday home park, there are units to rent. Facilities are excellent and well maintained. Access to the Blue Flag beach is via a large tarmac ramp. The village of Mundesley is only a mile away with a nine-hole golf course and a wide variety of shops and pubs. There is much to see and do in this area of Norfolk with a steam railway further along the coast. North Walsham is within easy reach and has a good array of shops and supermarkets.

#### Facilities
The toilet block is modern and spacious offering large shower rooms and open washbasins, all kept very clean. Facilities for disabled visitors planned. Shops, pubs and restaurants nearby. Off site: Village 1 mile. Tennis, boat launching, riding and golf nearby.

Open: March - November.

#### Directions
Site is 1 mile north of Mundesley (4 miles south of Cromer) on the main coast road.
O.S.GR: TG302373. GPS: 52.88457, 1.42074

#### Charges guide

| | |
|---|---|
| Per unit incl. up to 4 persons and electricity | £ 12.00 - £ 21.00 |

For latest campsite news visit
**alanrogers.com**

## North Walsham

### Two Mills Touring Park

Yarmouth Road, North Walsham NR28 9NA (Norfolk) T: 01692 405829. E: enquiries@twomills.co.uk

alanrogers.com/UK3420

Two Mills is a quiet site for adults only. Set in the bowl of a former quarry, the park is a real sun trap, both secluded and sheltered, with bird song to be heard at all times of the day. Neatly maintained with natural areas, varied trees, wild flowers and birds, the owners, Barbara and Ray Barnes, want to add their own touches to this popular park. Following the purchase of an adjacent field, there are now 81 level pitches for tourers, including 56 serviced pitches (patio, water and waste water drainage), 48 all weather gravel. All are generously sized and have electricity (10/16A). This is a good centre from which to explore the north Norfolk coast, the Broads or for visiting Norwich and a footpath from the park joins the Weavers Way. A member of the Best of British group.

### Facilities

Neat, clean central toilet block can be heated and includes some washbasins in cabins, en-suite facilities for disabled visitors, laundry and dishwashing rooms. Small shop at reception. TV room with tea and coffee facilities. Dogs are accepted by arrangement only. Only adults are accepted. Off site: Hotel/pub 100 yds. Town 20 minutes walk. Fishing or golf 5 miles. Bicycle hire 1.5 miles. The coast is 5 miles.

Open: All year excl. 2 January - 1 March.

### Directions

From A149 Stalham - North Walsham road, watch for caravan sign 1.5 miles before North Walsham (also signed White Horse Common). The road runs parallel to the A149 and site is on right after 1.25 miles. From North Walsham take Old Yarrmouth road past hospital, and park is on left after 1 mile. O.S.GR: TG292287. GPS: 52.80384, 1.40360

### Charges guide

| | |
|---|---|
| Per unit incl. 2 persons and electricity | £ 15.00 - £ 19.00 |
| full service pitch | £ 16.00 - £ 21.50 |
| extra person | £ 3.50 |
| dog (by arrangement) | £ 0.75 |
| Senior citizen discounts. | |

## Norwich

### Deer's Glade Caravan & Camping Park

White Post Road, Hanworth, Norwich NR11 7HN (Norfolk) T: 01263 768633. E: info@deersglade.co.uk

alanrogers.com/UK3455

In 2003, David and Heather Attew decided that they had an area that would make a superb setting for a caravan park and that they could give up farming. In early 2004 after much hard work, they opened this top quality park and it has since developed into a very popular site. Not far from the Norfolk Broads and close to the East Anglian coast, the park is open all year round. There are 125 level pitches (some with hardstandings), all with 16A electricity and 100 with TV aerial points. New hedging between pitches is becoming established. Internet access is possible from all the pitches. Amenities are of a high standard and include two toilet blocks, a play area, small shop and a popular, well stocked fishing lake. As its name suggests, you would not be surprised to wake and see deer wandering on this park and in the surrounding woodland areas. If you do miss them, a short walk will take you to Gunton Park where deer are bred and wander in herds.

### Facilities

Two spacious new toilet blocks are of a high standard and include vanity style washbasins for ladies, a room for disabled visitors and families, dishwashing room and a laundry. Motorcaravan service point. Licensed shop (all year). Play area. Fishing lake (charge). Bicycle hire. Caravan valet service. Free minibus to local tavern. Off site: Bus service under 1 mile. Pub 1.5 miles. Woodland walks. Riding 2 miles. Beach, golf 5 miles.

Open: All year.

### Directions

From Norwich take A140 towards Cromer and 5 miles after Aylsham turn right towards Suffield Park (White Post Road). Park is 0.5 miles on the right. O.S.GR: TG214340. GPS: 52.85781, 1.28765

### Charges guide

| | |
|---|---|
| Per person | £ 5.00 - £ 7.50 |
| child | £ 1.75 - £ 2.75 |
| awning | £ 1.75 |
| dog | £ 1.00 |
| Family deals available. | |

## Norwich

### Little Haven Caravan & Camping Park

The Street, Erpingham, Norwich NR11 7QD (Norfolk) T: 01263 768959. E: patlhaven@tiscali.co.uk
alanrogers.com/UK3450

Within easy reach of the coast and the Broads, this is an attractive, peaceful little site with good facilities. Only adults are accepted. There are 24 grassy pitches, all with electricity (16A) and 6 with hardstanding. They are arranged around the outside of a gravel access road with a central lawn and decorative pergola, a neat little garden and a seating area. There is no shop, but two pubs serving food and traditional ales are within walking distance. An ideal base for cycling and walking (the Weavers Way footpath is within half a mile) or just relaxing. Also close by is magnificent Blickling Hall.

**Facilities**

The well maintained toilet unit is heated and includes spacious hot showers and a covered dishwashing and laundry area. Facilities for disabled visitors are planned. Gas available. Site is unsuitable for American motorhomes. Note: This is an adults only park. Off site: Bus service on the main A140 road. Riding 1 mile. Fishing 3 miles. Bicycle hire 5 miles. Beach 6 miles. Golf 10 miles. The market town of Aylsham.

Open: 1 March - 31 October.

**Directions**

From A140 Cromer - Norwich road, going south towards Aylsham and 3 miles south of Roughton, past the Horseshoes pub and Alby crafts, take first turning right signed Erpingham 2 miles (narrow road). Site is 175 yards on right. O.S.GR: TG190320. GPS: 52.84208, 1.27090

**Charges guide**

| | |
|---|---|
| Per unit incl. 2 persons, electricity | £ 11.00 |

No credit cards.

## Peterborough

### Ferry Meadows Caravan Club Site

Ham Lane, Peterborough PE2 5UU (Cambridgeshire) T: 01733 233526
alanrogers.com/UK3580

Three miles from bustling Peterborough and closer still to the East of England Showground, the immaculate Ferry Meadows is an ideal family holiday site occupying 30 acres of the 500 acre Nene Country Park. Open all year the site provides 252 pitches (16A electricity) – 160 grass pitches on one side of the park, informally laid out in small groups and surrounded by a variety of mature trees, and 94 gravel hardstandings just across the road for caravans and motorcaravans.

**Facilities**

Two modern, well appointed and heated toilet blocks are of the usual high standard, with en-suite facilities for disabled visitors in one block. Baby/toddler washroom. Laundry room. Motorcaravan service point. The office stocks basic provisions. Tourist information room. Good play areas. TV socket and lead. WiFi in one area. Off site: Wheelchair hire in Nene Park. Steam railway 500 yards. Bus service 800 yards. Nearest shops 1 mile. Restaurants within 0.5 miles. Peterborough, lido, night clubs and supermarkets 3 miles.

Open: All year.

**Directions**

From south on A1, do not turn onto A1139, but turn left, 1 mile on, at next junction (signed Showground) and immediately left onto A605 (Peterborough). Straight on at three roundabouts, signed Nene Park. At fourth roundabout turn left into Ham Lane, signed Nene Park. Site is 300 yards beyond level crossing. From the east follow Nene Park signs around Peterborough onto the A605 and then site. O.S.GR: TL151972. GPS: 52.56053, -0.30593

**Charges guide**

| | |
|---|---|
| Per person | £ 4.70 - £ 6.20 |
| pitch (non-member) | £ 11.90 - £ 14.80 |

## Pidley

### Stroud Hill Park

Fen Road, Pidley PE28 3DE (Cambridgeshire) T: 01487 741333. E: stroudhillpark@btconnect.com
alanrogers.com/UK3575

Open all year round for adults only, Stroud Hill Park is a well-designed, high quality park; a credit to its owners, David and Jayne Newman. Developed from the farmland where David grew up, the park has been landscaped to create a terraced effect and now incorporates a large fishing lake (well stocked with carp, tench, bream, rudd and roach) plus a superb tennis court. There are 60 large, slightly sloping pitches, of which 44 are hardstanding, fully serviced with electricity (16A), fresh water and drainage. Affiliated to the Caravan Club, non-members are equally welcome.

**Facilities**

Toilets and spacious en-suite shower facilities are located in the main building along with a well equipped room for disabled visitors. Laundry room. Vegetable preparation area. Small, licensed shop stocks basic provisions, local produce, gas and camping accessories. Attractive bar and café/restaurant. Fishing (£5 per day). All-weather tennis. Off site: Golf course, ten-pin bowling and paintball adjacent to site. Riding 0.5 miles. Peterborough, Cambridge, Ely, Huntingdon and St Ives all within reach.

Open: All year.

**Directions**

Leave A1 near Huntingdon, take A14 east. Leave A14 at A141, signed March. In Warboys turn at roundabout, turn right on B1040 signed Pidley. In Pidley turn left just beyond church, Fen Road. Site is about 1 mile on right. O.S.GR: TL335787. GPS: 52.38926, -0.03966

**Charges guide**

| | |
|---|---|
| Per unit incl. 2 persons and electricity | £ 23.50 - £ 26.00 |
| extra person | £ 2.50 |

## Sheringham
### Kelling Heath Holiday Park
Weybourne, Holt, Sheringham NR25 7HW (Norfolk) T: 01263 588181. E: info@kellingheath.co.uk
alanrogers.com/UK3430

Not many parks can boast their own railway station and Kelling Heath's own halt on the North Norfolk Steam Railway gives access to shopping in Holt or the beach at Sheringham. Set in 250 acres of woodland and heathland overlooking the north Norfolk coast, this spacious holiday park offers freedom and relaxation with 300 touring pitches, all with 16A electricity (some are fully serviced) in four different zones. Pitching is good on quite firm, level grass (no hardstanding). Together with 384 caravan holiday homes (36 to let, the rest privately owned), they blend into the part-wooded, part-open heath. A wide range of facilities provides activities for all. 'The Forge' has an entertainment bar, an adult only bar and a family room, with comprehensive entertainment. 'Fitness Express' provides an indoor pool, spa pool, sauna, steam rooms and gym. An adventure playground with assault course is near. The central reception area is attractively paved to provide a 'village store' and an open air bandstand where one can sit and enjoy the atmosphere. The park's natural environment allows for woodland walks, a nature trail and cycling trails, and a small lake for fishing (permit holders only). Other amenities include two hard tennis courts, a small, outdoor heated fun pool and play areas (some rather hidden from the pitches).

### Facilities
Three toilet blocks serve the touring pitches, one heated and with a conservatory providing covered access all year to disabled visitors. Baby room. All blocks have a few washbasins in private cubicles, baby baths and, in season, a nappy disposal service. Laundry facilities. Shop. Gas supplies. Bar, restaurant and takeaway. Indoor leisure centre with pool (19x9 m), gym, etc. with trained staff (membership on either daily or weekly basis). Outdoor pool (main season). Adventure play area. Tennis. Fishing. Bicycle hire. Entertainment programme. Torches useful. Off site: The Norfolk coast, Felbrigg Hall, the Walsingham Shrine and the Norfolk Broads National Park are nearby.

Open: 10 February - 12 December.

### Directions
On A148 road from Holt to Cromer, after High Kelling, turn left just before Bodham village (international sign) signed Weybourne. Follow road for about 1 mile to park O.S.GR: TG117418. GPS: 52.92847, 1.13663

### Charges guide
| | |
|---|---|
| Per unit incl. electricity | £ 17.25 - £ 35.00 |
| with full services | £ 22.50 - £ 37.50 |
| dog (max. 2) | £ 3.00 - £ 5.00 |
| awning | £ 2.00 - £ 5.00 |

Min. 7 day stay in high season.
No single sex groups.

Escape the normal routine...

## Sheringham
### Woodlands Caravan Park
Holt Road, Upper Sheringham NR26 8TU (Norfolk) T: 01263 823802
E: enquiries@woodlandscaravanpark.co.uk  alanrogers.com/UK3435

This pleasantly wooded caravan park is set in the beautiful surroundings of North Norfolk's protected heathland, next to Sheringham Park (National Trust). There are many lovely walks all around the area, including one to the beach (1.5 miles). The park is within easy reach of Holt, Cromer and Sheringham, with the major bird watching areas of Blakeney, Cley and Salthouse also within 30 minutes drive. There are 225 touring pitches in two main areas for caravans and motorcaravans (tents are not accepted).

### Facilities
Three well maintained toilet blocks provide good facilities and include facilities for disabled visitors, baby changing and laundry. Well stocked shop. Gas. Lounge bar and family bar with entertainment most weekends. Leisure Club with indoor pool, gym, sauna. etc. Off site: Golf and bicycle hire 1.5 miles. Fishing and riding 3 miles.

Open: March - October.

### Directions
From Cromer on the A148 towards Holt, pass signs for Sheringham Park and site is on right just before Bodham village. From Holt on A148 just after Bodham, site is on left, well signed.
O.S.GR: TG130409. GPS: 52.92363, 1.19444

### Charges guide
| | |
|---|---|
| Per unit incl. electricity | £ 15.50 - £ 18.50 |

For latest campsite news visit
**alanrogers.com**

## Swaffham

### Breckland Meadows Touring Park

Lynn Road, Swaffham PE37 7PT (Norfolk) T: 01760 721246. E: info@brecklandmeadows.co.uk
alanrogers.com/UK3470

Open all year, this compact, adult only park offers peace and tranquillity yet only ten minutes' walk from the historic market town of Swaffham. The site makes a good base to explore East Anglia and the local area with a wide range of diverse attractions. There are 45 average sized pitches, 25 on hardstanding and the remainder on fairly level, neat grass; all have 16A electricity hook-ups. There are two main roads close to the park but well established hedges and trees help minimise any noise. There is a small shop selling basic supplies, ices and drinks with a good library.

**Facilities**

The modern, well cared for toilet block provides all the usual facilities, including spacious showers and facilities for disabled visitors. Laundry room. Gas supplies. WiFi. Off site: Swaffham with a range of shops, bars, restaurants, museums, Saturday market 0.5 miles. Bicycle hire 1 mile. Golf 2 miles. Riding 4 miles. Fishing 5 miles. Iceni village. Gooderstone Water Gardens.

Open: All year.

**Directions**

Park is 0.5 miles west of Swaffham on Low Road (old A47). Entrance on right just beyond garage. O.S.GR: TF809094. GPS: 52.65115, 0.67687

**Charges guide**

| Per unit incl. 2 persons and electricity | £ 11.75 - £ 13.75 |
| extra person | £ 3.00 |

No credit cards.

## Wisbech

### Parklands Caravan & Camping Park

Sutton Road, Four Gotes, Wisbech PE13 5PH (Cambridgeshire) T: 01945 420505
E: enquiries@parklandsholidays.co.uk alanrogers.com/UK3585

A small, quiet, secluded family run site occupying five acres of level grassland on the borders of Cambridgeshire, Lincolnshire and Norfolk. The site is surrounded by tall conifers giving shelter from the wind. There are 58 good sized, level grass pitches, with 56 for touring and 50 have 10A electricity. The pitches are separated by low hedges and a few trees giving little shade but some will get some shade from the high conifer hedging surrounding the site. Access is easy for large outfits. There is a shop, small swimming pool, and a bar serving takeaway food to order. No charcoal barbecues.

**Facilities**

Small heated toilet block with good sized adjustable showers and facilities for campers with disabilities. Washing machine. Small heated swimming pool, corner spa, sunbathing area (Apr-Sept). Shop with bread and newspapers to order. Bar/takeaway food/breakfast rolls (weekends only in low season). Games/TV/entertainment room. Play area. Putting green. Evening music (weekends low season). Off site: Lake and river fishing nearby. Golf course with restaurant. Market town of Wisbech. Many walks and cycle routes.

Open: 15 March - 15 October.

**Directions**

Parklands is on A1101 between Wisbech and Long Sutton. From Wisbech go north to Four Gotes. Site is on right 800 yds. after entering village. O.S.GR: TF451172 GPS: 52.732953, 0.14698

**Charges guide**

| Per unit incl. 2 persons and electricity | £ 14.60 - £ 18.80 |
| extra person | £ 3.00 - £ 5.00 |
| child | £ 2.00 - £ 3.00 |

## Woodbridge

### Moat Barn Touring Caravan Park

Dallinghoo Road, Bredfield, Woodbridge IP13 6BD (Suffolk) T: 01473 737520
alanrogers.com/UK3330

Mike Allen opened this small touring park in April 2000 on the Suffolk Heritage Cycle Route, and also the Hull - Harwich National Cycle Route. The main touring area is bordered by established hedging and incorporates a circular roadway. The park currently provides 25 level grass pitches, all with electricity (10A), and there are plans to extend the number of pitches to 34. The park is popular with both walkers and cyclists and provides a tranquil environment to explore nearby Woodbridge and surrounding areas. There is limited provision for large units (e.g. American motorhomes). There are no facilities for children.

**Facilities**

The well equipped sanitary block can be heated. A separate unit houses a dishwashing sink. Motorcaravan service point. Bicycle hire. Laundry and shop planned. Off site: Nearby pub serving food. Public footpath.

Open: 1 March - 15 January.

**Directions**

Park is midway between Woodbridge and Wickham Market. From A12 take turning signed Bredfield (left from south, right from north). At village pump in Bredfield turn right and follow road past public house and church. Continue through S-bends and, after 200 yards, site entrance is on left, just after farm buildings. O.S.GR: TM270537. GPS: 52.13510, 1.31710

**Charges guide**

| Per unit incl. 2 persons and electricity | £ 15.00 |

## Woodbridge
### Run Cottage Touring Park
Alderton Road, Hollesey, Woodbridge IP12 3RQ (Suffolk) T: 01394 411309. E: contact@run-cottage.co.uk
alanrogers.com/UK3322

This small and very attractive 20 pitch site in the heart of unspoilt Suffolk countryside offers an opportunity to explore many of the local attractions on Suffolk's 'Heritage Coast'. Facilities on the site are limited but certainly adequate and the resident owners, Michele and Andy Stebbens are always available to ensure that you have an enjoyable stay. The site is open all year round and all pitches have 10A electricity, with 6 on hardstanding. This is a popular site and advance booking is strongly recommended. Local attractions include Sutton Hoo, Orford Castle and Framlingham Castle. The market town of Woodbridge is only 6 miles away. Within a short drive are the pretty coastal towns of Southwold, Dunwich, Orford and Aldeborough.

| Facilities | Directions |
|---|---|
| New, well finished sanitary block is easily accessed and is well equipped. Reception contains a comprehensive selection of tourist leaflets and details of local attractions. Off site: Excellent pubs and restaurants within 1 mile. Riding 1 mile. Beach, fishing and bicycle hire 1.5 miles. Golf 5 miles.<br><br>Open: All year. | From A12 (Ipswich - Lowestoft) turn right at roundabout at Melton onto A1152 (Bawdsey, Orford). In 1.5 miles, at roundabout, turn right onto B1083 (Bawdsey, Hollesley). Within 0.75 miles take left fork to Hollesley. At Duck Corner cross road, turn right and continue through village to site on the left, 100 yds past Red Brick Bridge. Note: Do not follow sat nav directions. O.S.GR: TM351442. GPS: 52.04503, 1.42683 |

**Charges 2011**

| | |
|---|---|
| Per unit incl. 2 persons and electricity | £ 16.00 |
| extra person (over 3 yrs) | £ 2.50 |
| dog (max. 2) | free |

Run Cottage Touring Park,
Alderton Road, Hollesey,
Woodbridge, Suffolk. IP12 3RQ
Tel: 01394 411 309
Website:http://www.run-cottage.co.uk
Email: contact@run-cottage.co.uk

Close to the town of Woodbridge we are a small family run touring park with 20 pitches. Set in a 2.5 acre parkland setting with a large pond and views over open farmland, we offer peace and tranquility. A place to escape the hustle and bustle of today's busy lifestyle.

- All electric hook ups
- Six all weather caravan pitches
- Open all year
- Two acre dog exercise area
- Toilet & shower block
- Chemical disposal point
- Tourist information area
- 1.5 miles from shingle beach
- Village shop & pub within easy walking distance

## Woodbridge
### The Moon & Sixpence
Newbourne Road, Waldringfield, Woodbridge IP12 4PP (Suffolk) T: 01473 736650
E: info@moonandsixpence.eu  alanrogers.com/UK3320

This excellent site offers 60 large touring pitches that are positioned in the centre of an established and very spacious caravan holiday home park. The site is extremely well maintained and all the 60 touring pitches are equipped with 5A electricity, TV point, water tap and a drain. In the centre of the site and easily accessible to all, is an unsupervised lake with a sandy beach. An area at one end of the lake is set aside for 10 pitches for adults only, all with views of the lake. Quiet is essential from 9 pm. There is an excellent bar and restaurant that offers a good range of dishes, with 'specials' at weekends. The site boasts good leisure facilities with three tennis courts and a nine hole compact golf course. These, together with other recreational facilities, are positioned at the rear of the site and do not affect those looking for a peaceful holiday break in the unspoilt Suffolk countryside.

| Facilities | Directions |
|---|---|
| Exceptionally well finished, centrally placed unisex sanitary block consists of 11 fully equipped private rooms containing a selection of WCs, washbasins and showers and baths. No specific facilities for disabled visitors but access to the block is via a ramp. Laundry facilities. Well stocked shop. Bar and restaurant (main season). TV room. Two adventure play areas. Dog walk trails. Lake with beach. Tennis. Golf. Off site: Boat launching 2 miles. Fishing 2 miles, bicycle hire and riding 5 miles.<br><br>Open: 1 April - 31 Ocotber. | From the A12 (Ipswich - Lowestoft) turn right at roundabout, towards Waldringfield and follow signs to site. After one and a half miles, turn left at Waldringfield Golf Club to site, less than one mile on the left. O.S.GR: TM260457. GPS: 52.06252, 1.29858 |

**Charges 2011**

| | |
|---|---|
| Per person (over 2 yrs) incl. unit and services | £ 9.00 - £ 16.00 |
| dog | £ 1.00 |
| Min. charges apply. Max. length 6.5 m. | |
| Max. age of unit 15 yrs. | |

For latest campsite news visit
## alanrogers.com

Spanning central England, from the ancient borders of Wales on the west across to Lincolnshire on the east coast, the Heart of England is rich in glorious rolling countryside, magnificent castles, fine stately houses and beautiful gardens.

**THE REGION COMPRISES LINCOLNSHIRE, RUTLAND, NORTHAMPTONSHIRE, NOTTINGHAMSHIRE, WEST MIDLANDS, DERBYSHIRE, STAFFORDSHIRE, LEICESTERSHIRE, WARWICKSHIRE, HEREFORDSHIRE, WORCESTERSHIRE, GLOUCESTERSHIRE & SHROPSHIRE**

The charming and diverse countryside of the Heart of England includes: the Lincolnshire Wolds, with the dramatic open landscape of the Fens; the ragged crags, dales and moorland of the Peak District National Park in Derbyshire and Staffordshire; the heathered hilltops of Shropshire; the famous Sherwood Forest, in the heart of Nottinghamshire; and the miles of lush green countryside of Herefordshire, dotted with black and white timber houses. Rutland Water is a mecca for watersports and the whole region offers superb opportunities for walking, cycling and more daring activities such as rock climbing and caving. The Cotswolds to the west of the region is the largest Area of Outstanding Natural Beauty in England and Wales. Here you will find many traditional English villages, with charming country pubs and cottage gardens. Another significant feature of the region are the rivers and canals. Passing pretty towns and villages, a large canal network threads its way through the area, weaving through the Lincolnshire Fens, past the waterside bars and restaurants of Birmingham and along to estuaries of the rivers of Severn and Avon.

### Places of interest

*Lincolnshire:* Belvoir Castle near Grantham.

*Rutland:* market towns of Oakham and Uppingham.

*Northamptonshire:* Silverstone; Althorp House.

*Nottinghamshire:* Nottingham Castle.

*West Midlands:* Birmingham; Cadbury World.

*Derbyshire:* Bakewell; Buxton; Chatsworth House.

*Staffordshire:* Alton Towers; Stoke-on-Trent.

*Leicestershire:* Snibston Discovery Park; Twycross Zoo.

*Warwickshire:* Warwick Castle; Stratford-upon-Avon.

*Herefordshire:* Hereford Cathedral.

*Worcestershire:* West Midland Safari Park.

*Gloucestershire:* Sudeley Castle; Cheltenham.

*Shropshire:* Shrewsbury and Whitchurch.

### Did you know?

Herefordshire is one of the largest apple cider producers in the world.

The World Toe Wrestling Championship, held every June in Wetton, is a registered international sport.

The hollow trunk of the 'Mighty Tree' in Sherwood Forest is reputedly where Robin Hood and his Merry Men hid from the Sheriff of Nottingham.

Quite different from the more familiar tart, the Bakewell pudding was first created in the 1860s.

Rutland is the smallest county in Britain, measuring just 16 miles by 16 miles.

The Peak District contains over 50 reservoirs, including Ladybower, where the bouncing bomb used in World War II was tested.

For latest campsite news visit

**alanrogers.com**

## Ashbourne
### Woodland Caravan Park
Snelston Hall, Ashbourne DE6 2ET (Derbyshire) T: 01335 346 120
alanrogers.com/UK3860

Set in woodland within the privately owned grounds of Snelston Hall, this site presents a charming, tranquil haven for those seeking a leafy retreat. The 900-acre estate has walks on private and public footpaths. The 52 pitches, constructed from local limestone are level, each with electric hook-up. Expect to see shafts of light falling on irregularly arranged pitches allowing a sense of privacy within the tall trees that give the site its name. These trees help screen out low level traffic noise, which is much reduced at night. Modern, clean, toilet blocks are tastefully coloured to blend with the surroundings. Woodland Caravan Park is situated just a few miles south of the Peak District National Park and the market town of Ashbourne with shops and restaurants. It has good facilities on site for dog walkers. An enclosed area allows dogs to be let off the leash, although the site restricts access to certain breeds. Motorcycle enthusiasts may also enjoy nearby Darley Moor, a small independent motorcycle racing circuit with a limited number of meets (visitors should check dates). At most times, visitors can relax in the woodland setting; those who enjoy walking can access some of the footpaths on the estate. The owners will supply good maps of the various walking routes at reception.

Facilities

One modern, clean, toilet block (key access) with room for visitors with disabilities. Ample lighting on site. Water is within easy reach of each pitch. Laundry. Kitchen area with microwave. Separate, enclosed area for dog walking (breeds restricted). Reception offers advice on waymarked walks and allows access to the large private estate. Site has eco-friendly water handling. Motorcaravan services – ask at reception for help with grey waste. Off site: Darley Motorcycle Circuit 1 mile. Local Spa town of Ashbourne 4 miles. Tissington Trail with bicycle hire 5 miles. Peak District National Park 6 miles. Carsington reservoir 11 miles.

Open: 22 March - 30 September.

Directions

Leave the A50 at Sudbury and take A515 signed Ashbourne. Follow road for approximately 7 miles. Just before Darley Moor Motor Cycle Circuit (on your right) turn left (signposted Snelston and Woodland Caravan Park) and turn almost immediately right into Woodland Park. GPS: 52.98102, -1.7531

Charges guide

| | |
|---|---|
| Per unit incl. 2 persons and electricity | £ 12.00 - £ 20.00 |
| extra person | £ 2.00 |

## Ashbourne

### Rivendale Caravan & Leisure Park

330

Buxton Road, Alsop-en-le-Dale, Ashbourne DE6 1QU (Derbyshire) T: 01335 310311
E: enquiries@rivendalecaravanpark.co.uk  **alanrogers.com/UK3850**

This unusual park has been developed in the bowl of a hill quarry which was last worked over 50 years ago. The steep quarry walls shelter three sides with marvellous views over the Peak National Park countryside to the south. A wide access road passes the renovated stone building which houses reception, a shop, bar and a café/restaurant. It gently climbs to a horseshoe shaped area providing 136 pitches some of which are rather small but most are of a generous size with 16A electricity. The pitches are a mixture of hardstanding and grass, and are divided by shrubs. A further, open, marked grass area is accessed by hardcore roads. All the pitches are within easy reach of the central stone-built toilet block which is in keeping with the environment and thoughtfully provided with underfloor heating. The park takes up about 11 acres and a further 26 acres belong to the owners with certain parts suitable for walking – a must to appreciate the Derbyshire countryside with its dry stone walls, wild flowers and a little more of the quarry history. The park is situated almost on the Tissington Trail for walking or off road cycling and linking with the High Peak and Monsal Dale Trail. Other spectacular walks and cycle rides run along the Manifold, Wye and Dove valleys.

**Facilities**

First rate toilet facilities include some washbasins in cubicles for ladies, and an excellent en-suite room for disabled visitors. Laundry room. Glass and paper recycling bins. Shop (all essentials). Bar (evenings) and café with home-made and local food (open mornings, lunch and evenings, both with limited opening in low season). Packed lunches from reception. Special events monthly and games in main season. Hot tubs for hire, delivered to your pitch. WiFi. For rent on the park are 4 B&B rooms (more planned as part of an indoor pool and spa development), a luxury caravan holiday home and a yurt (6 persons). Off site: Bicycle hire and riding 5 miles. Sailing and boat launching 8 miles. Fishing and golf 10 miles. Alton Towers 35 minutes drive.

Open: All year excl. 9 January - 2 February.

**Directions**

Park is 7 miles north of Ashbourne on the A515 to Buxton, on the eastern side of the road. It is well signed between the turnings east to Alsop Moor and Matlock (A5012), but take care as this is a very fast section of the A515. O.S.GR: SK161566. GPS: 53.106383, -1.760567

**Charges guide**

| | |
|---|---|
| Per unit incl. 2 persons and electricity | £ 14.50 - £ 19.00 |
| extra person | £ 2.50 |
| child (4-15 yrs) | £ 2.00 |
| dog | £ 1.00 |

Camping Cheques accepted.

## Ashbourne

### Callow Top Holiday Park

Buxton Road, Sandybrook, Ashbourne DE6 2AQ (Derbyshire) T: 01335 344020. E: enquiries@callowtop.co.uk
**alanrogers.com/UK3855**

Situated just north of the market town of Ashbourne, Callow Top nestles within an elevated country setting. The park's location makes it well placed to allow visitors to explore the picturesque villages, bustling market towns and the many attractions of the Peak District. It is ideal for both walking and cycling holidays. Spread over seven separate areas, there are 200 flat pitches of which 100 are for touring units. Those on hardstanding have 10A electricity, the grass pitches have no power supply. Water points tend to be rather scarce. Some of the pitches are rather small and on these, cars are parked away from the pitch. There are also cottages and caravan holiday homes for rent.

**Facilities**

Three heated toilet blocks (only one open in low season) provide unisex showers (20p). Toilet for disabled visitors. Laundry room. No motorcaravan service point. Calor gas. Shop. Inn/restaurant. Snack bar and takeaway. Heated swimming and paddling pools (May-Sept). Bicycle hire. Games room. Play area. Entertainment (w/ends and high season). Fishing. Winter caravan storage. Off site: Golf 1.5 miles. Riding 3 miles. Ashbourne (supermarket etc) 1 mile. Carsington Water 4 miles. Alton Towers 10 miles.

Open: 15 March - 6 November.

**Directions**

At Sandybrook, 0.5 miles north of Ashbourne, turn left off the A515 (Ashbourne - Buxton) into site road. Site is signed. O.S.GR: SK179483. GPS: 53.02693, -1.74646

**Charges guide**

| | |
|---|---|
| Per unit incl. 2 persons | £ 16.50 - £ 21.50 |
| incl. hardstanding and electricity | £ 20.00 - £ 27.00 |
| extra person | £ 2.50 |
| child (4-16 yrs) | £ 1.50 |

For latest campsite news visit
**alanrogers.com**

# Bishop's Castle

## The Green Caravan Park

Wentnor, Bishop's Castle SY9 5EF (Shropshire) T: 01588 650605. E: karen@greencaravanpark.co.uk
alanrogers.com/UK4440

Remotely situated in a pleasant valley, in a designated Area of Outstanding Natural Beauty, and sandwiched between the Stiperstones and The Long Mynd, the Green would make an ideal base for some serious walking; a footpath to the Stiperstones passes through the site. The 15-acre site is delightful, and is divided into several fields. There are 160 pitches, taking 41 seasonal units, and around 20 holiday homes, with approximately 140 pitches for tourists (41 with 16A electric hook-ups). The main field has some hardstandings. The East Onny is a small, shallow river which runs through the site.

### Facilities

One main sanitary block, rather austere in appearance, built into the side of a large barn. However it provides adequate and plentiful facilities with spacious hot showers (coin operated) and laundry facilities, but there is no dedicated unit for disabled visitors. Small shop in new reception building. Playground. Off site: Four pubs within 3 miles, one next door. Fishing 3 miles. Riding 4 miles. Bishops Castle with museums. Leisure Centre.

Open: Easter - 31 October.

### Directions

From Shrewsbury take A49. Right turn at Marsh Brook. At the T-junction turn right onto the A489 for 5 miles. Turn right at the brown campsite sign. Site immediately after The Inn on the Green.
O.S.GR: SO381933. GPS: 52.53375, -2.91375.

### Charges guide

| | |
|---|---|
| Per unit incl. 2 persons and electricity | £ 13.50 - £ 15.00 |
| extra person | £ 3.00 |

# Bridgnorth

## Stanmore Hall Touring Park

Stourbridge Road, Bridgnorth WV15 6DT (Shropshire) T: 01746 761761. E: stanmore@morris-leisure.co.uk
alanrogers.com/UK4400

This attractive park is situated in the former grounds of Stanmore Hall, where the huge lily pond, fine mature trees and beautifully manicured lawns give a mark of quality. There are 135 generously sized pitches, 130 with 16A electricity including 30 hardstanding 'super' pitches with TV connections. Also available are 23 'standard' pitches, but most are on grass. Some pitches are reserved for adult only use (over 18 years). Access and internal roads are tarmac; site lighting is adequate and reassuring. The park is a member of the Caravan Club's managed under contract scheme but non-members are also very welcome. A size restriction of 30ft exists for motorcaravans.

### Facilities

The upgraded, centrally-heated sanitary block is accessed by key. Facilities are excellent and provide washbasins in cubicles and a room for disabled visitors and baby care. Full laundry facilities. Motorcaravan service points. A well-equipped shop stocking camping and caravan accessories. A TV booster system is available. Play area. Dogs are limited to two per unit. Off site: Fishing at Bridgnorth 1.5 miles. Golf and Riding 2 miles.

Open: All year.

### Directions

Site is 1.5 miles from Bridgnorth on the A458 (signed Stourbridge). If using satnav approach from Bridgnorth only. O.S.GR: SO744922.
GPS: 52.52715, -2.378617

### Charges guide

| | |
|---|---|
| Per unit incl. 2 persons and electricity | £ 21.50 - £ 24.30 |
| extra person | £ 2.20 - £ 6.30 |

# Buxton

## Longnor Wood Holiday Park

Newtown, Longnor, Buxton SK17 0NG (Derbyshire) T: 01298 83648. E: info@longnorwood.co.uk
alanrogers.com/UK3980

A secluded rural location, deep in the heart of the Peak District, Longnor Wood is an adult only park (over 18 yrs) and an ideal environment for a relaxing break from the outside world. It is a good base for walking, red deer and bird watching (barn owls) and serious cycling – the area is very hilly. There are 47 touring pitches plus an additional 13 pitches for holiday homes. Pitches are level, some on small terraces, all with 10A electric hook-ups. There are 17 with multi-services (electricity, water, waste water and TV connections) and 40 on half hardstanding and half grass.

### Facilities

The single heated building has modern facilities and includes cubicles with a toilet and washbasin and spacious showers. Freezer for ice packs and a microwave oven (donations to charity). Laundry facilities. Reception stocks basic requirements. Gas supplies. Putting green. Badminton. Boules. Dogs accepted, max. 2 per unit. RVs accepted by appointment. WiFi. Off site: Markets in Buxton and Leek. Dove Dale and the Manifold Valley. Arbor Low Stone Circle. Riding 4 miles. Fishing 5 miles. Bicycle hire 6.5 miles. Golf 8 miles.

Open: All year excl. 11 January - 28 February.

### Directions

Longnor village is on the B5053, about 6 miles south of Buxton. At crossroads in village square, turn right. Take left turn after 1.25 miles and then immediately right. Also signed from the A53 between Leek and Buxton, turning next at the Winking Man pub. O.S.GR: SK072640. GPS: 53.17086, -1.90042

### Charges guide

| | |
|---|---|
| Per unit incl. 2 persons and electricity | £ 21.00 |
| serviced pitch incl. 2 persons | £ 23.00 |
| tent incl. 2 persons | £ 15.00 - £ 19.00 |
| extra person | £ 6.00 |

For latest campsite news visit
## alanrogers.com

## Buxton

### Clover Fields Touring Caravan Park

1 Heath View, Harpur Hill, Buxton SK17 9PU (Derbyshire) T: 01298 78731. E: cloverfields@tiscali.co.uk

alanrogers.com/UK3845

Stephen and Jan Redfern are more than happy to welcome you to their family owned park which, from 1st February 2011, will be for adults only (over 18yrs). It is located on the outskirts of the beautiful spa town of Buxton within easy reach of the magnificent Peak District National Park. You will be able to relax here in the 'away from it all' atmosphere. There are just 25 pitches divided by low hedges, part hardstanding and part grass, all with 16A electricity, a water tap and a barbecue. There is a little noise from the adjacent road. The site has its own animals which are happy to be spoiled! As well as a resident donkey and ponies, there are also rabbits, lambs, hens, geese and ducks and a wildlife pond.

**Facilities**

The toilet and shower block is modern and clean. Facilities for disabled visitors. Gas supplies. Laundry room. Motorcaravan service point. Small shop selling essentials, home made jam and chutney and caravan accessories. Newspapers and milk delivered to your pitch. Small library. Torches recommended. Off site: Supermarket in Buxton. Golf 3 miles. Riding 6 miles. Bicycle hire 6 miles.

Open: All year.

**Directions**

From Buxton, at Harpur Hill just to the southeast, turn right off the A515 (Buxton - Ashbourne) onto the B5053. Turn immediately right towards Harpur Hill. Site is 0.5 miles on the left. O.S.GR: SK075704. GPS: 53.23066, -1.8878

**Charges 2011**

| | |
|---|---|
| Per unit incl. 2 persons | £ 16.00 - £ 18.00 |

No credit cards.

## Buxton

### Lime Tree Park

Dukes Drive, Buxton SK17 9RP (Derbyshire) T: 01298 22988. E: info@limetreeparkbuxton.co.uk

alanrogers.com/UK3840

A select park with high quality, modern facilities, Lime Tree is in a convenient, edge of town location that makes a very good base for touring the Peak District. There are 99 pitches including 36 seasonal, 28 privately owned mobile homes and 12 caravan holiday homes to rent. The 64 with 10A electricity (hardstandings available) and an area for tents (some terracing but mainly sloping ground) are on the two upper terraces which have the best views but are slightly more exposed. Below are areas set aside for late arrivals and the mobile homes. There is a small shop for gas, caravan spares and basic groceries.

**Facilities**

A modern toilet building serves the caravan and motorcaravan area, including some washbasins in cubicles, controllable showers, a baby room and a family room with facilities for disabled visitors. The refitted original unit serves the tent area. Both units can be heated. Laundry facilities. Motorcaravan service area. Shop. Basic play area. Games/TV room. Off site: Pub just around the corner. Swimming, riding and golf 1 mile. Fishing, bicycle hire, sailing and boat launching 5 miles. Supermarket in Buxton.

Open: 1 March - 31 October.

**Directions**

Park is on outskirts of Buxton and is signed from A515 Buxton - Ashbourne road 1 mile south of town. From town, immediately after hospital bear sharp left into Dukes Drive, go under railway viaduct and site is on the right. From south watch out for sharp turn right at foot of hill (signed in advance). O.S.GR: SK069725. GPS: 53.250230, -1.896673

**Charges guide**

| | |
|---|---|
| Per unit incl. 2 persons and electricity | £ 20.00 |
| extra person | £ 3.00 - £ 6.00 |

## Cirencester

### Hoburne Cotswold

Broadway Lane, South Cerney, Cirencester GL7 5UQ (Gloucestershire) T: 01285 860216
E: enquiries@hoburne.co.uk alanrogers.com/UK4100

Since this park is adjacent to the Cotswold Water Park, those staying here will have easy access to the varied watersports available. On the park itself there is a lake with pedalos for hire. The wide range of other amenities includes outdoor and indoor heated swimming pools and an impressive, large indoor leisure complex. There are 189 well marked touring pitches for any type of unit, all with hardstanding (only fairly level) and a grass surround for awning or tent. Pitches are of a good size but with nothing between them, and little shade; all have electricity (some need long leads). Part of the Hoburne group.

**Facilities**

Four small toilet blocks are clean and well maintained with preset showers and background heating. Baby changing facilities. Basic facilities for disabled visitors. Launderette. Supermarket. Indoor leisure complex including pool with flume, spa bath, sauna, detox, steam room and mini-gym. Outdoor pool (mid May-early Sept). Clubhouse with bar, food and entertainment and free WiFi. Football. Tennis. Adventure playground. Crazy golf. Fishing lake. Animals are not accepted. Off site: Swindon and Cheltenham.

Open: March - October.

**Directions**

Three miles southeast of Cirencester on the A419, turn west towards Cotswold Water Park at new roundabout on bypass onto B4696 signposted South Cerney. continue past Water Park for 1.5 miles. Road to campsite is on the right. O.S.GR: SU055957. GPS: 51.66018, -1.91910

**Charges guide**

| | |
|---|---|
| Per unit incl. max. 6 persons and electricity | £ 15.45 - £ 34.75 |

For latest campsite news visit

## alanrogers.com

## Cleethorpes

### Thorpe Park Holiday Centre

Humberston, Cleethorpes DN35 0PW (Lincolnshire) T: 01472 813395

alanrogers.com/UK3655

Thorpe Park is a Haven Holiday Park at Cleethorpes on the north Lincolnshire coast. The touring site, although part of one of the largest caravan parks in Europe, is neat and compact. There are 69 landscaped 'Euro' pitches with brick-built hardstandings, electricity, water and drain and a further 55 in an open area, most with electricity available. There is direct access to the beach from one corner of the site and the park's main entertainment complex is a short walk away. A shuttle 'train' will take you to more distant parts of the park, including a nine-hole golf course.

### Facilities

Two modern toilet blocks. The one in the main area has pushbutton showers, open style washbasins and an excellent room for disabled visitors and families (with a bath). The newer, smaller block has fairly basic showers and open washbasins. Motorcaravan services. Fish and chips. Supermarket. Laundry. Bicycle and buggy hire. Entertainment complex, Heated indoor pool and outdoor flumes and 'lazy river'. Play area. Crazy golf. Climbing wall. Tennis. Fishing lakes. Roller rink. 9-hole and family golf courses. Off site: Riding, sailing and boat launching 1 mile. Shops and restaurants within 1 mile.

Open: Easter - 2 November.

### Directions

Cleethorpes is 2 miles southeast of Grimsby and 60 miles east of Doncaster. From M180 take A180 to Grimsby, turn south on A16 towards Louth, then east on A1098 to Humberston and follow signs for Pleasure Island and Holiday Parks. Park is to right at roundabout. O.S.GR: TA328059. GPS: 53.5347, 0.00412

### Charges guide

| | |
|---|---|
| Per unit incl. up to 4 persons | £ 10.00 - £ 86.00 |
| extra person | £ 2.00 - £ 3.00 |

## Coleford

### Forest Holidays Christchurch

Bracelands Drive, Christchurch, Coleford GL16 7NN (Gloucestershire) T: 01594 837258

E: fod.site@forestholidays.co.uk  alanrogers.com/UK4160

Set high above the Wye Valley, a partnership between the Forestry Commission and the Camping and Caravanning Club, Forest Holidays makes a perfect family holiday destination. With 280 unmarked pitches (240 for touring), this 20-acre site occupies an open grassy area in the heart of the Forest of Dean. There are seven hardstandings and 102 pitches with electrical hook-ups (10A). A new reception will include a shop, cafétéria and ranger station. An accessory shop/bicycle hire and WiFi are planned for 2011. Symonds Yat Rock is within walking distance with spectacular views over the Wye Valley.

### Facilities

Two fairly modern sanitary units with spacious, well equipped showers, some vanity style basins with dividers. Laundry facilities. Units for disabled visitors and baby changing in both blocks. Adventure playground on bark. No specified dog walk, but trails and footpaths surround the site. Limited television and mobile reception. Off site: Fishing and swimming 1 mile. Coleford 1.5 miles. Golf 2 miles. Ross-on-Wye 8 miles. Riding 10 miles.

Open: All year.

### Directions

From Monmouth take the A4136 east for 5 miles turning north at crossroads at Pike House Inn and site is on the left after 0.5 miles. From centre of Coleford take road towards Monmouth, turning right to Symonds Yat and Berry Hill (site signed). O.S.GR: SO569129. GPS: 51.813333, -2.62735

### Charges guide

| | |
|---|---|
| Per unit incl. 2 persons | £ 13.00 - £ 20.00 |
| extra person | £ 4.25 - £ 6.25 |

## Coventry

### Hollyfast Caravan Park

Wall Hill Road, Allesley, Coventry CV5 9EL (Warwickshire) T: 02476 336411

E: sales@hollyfastcaravanpark.co.uk  alanrogers.com/UK4075

Hollyfast is situated in beautiful countryside on the outskirts of Coventry, part of the park being set within a lovely woodland area giving peace and tranquillity all year round. Located on the Birmingham side of Coventry, this means a short drive into the centre of Coventry and a fifteen minute drive to Birmingham's National Exhibition Centre. You will receive a friendly welcome and be directed to a very clean and well spaced site with 40 pitches of varying sizes with 16A electricity connections. You may be asked to park your car on a nearby car park. Rallies are welcome and a club house is provided for these groups.

### Facilities

The modern toilet block provides simple clean facilities with good sized showers (3 per sex) and open washbasins. Toilet and shower for disabled campers. Games room. Club house for rallies. Deposit for barrier (£25). Off site: The local area has shops, three pubs (hot and cold food), a golf course and a riding centre. Bus stop 1 mile for Coventry. Interesting British Road Transport museum. Birmingham, Stratford upon Avon.

Open: All year.

### Directions

From M1/M45 (or the M40/A46, or M69/A46) take A45 (Birmingham). Turn right on A4114 and follow camping signs. After turning by White Lion pub, site is 0.5 miles on the left. From north take M6 north of Birmingham or M1 north (Nottingham) follow M42 to NEC, A45 (Coventry) and onto A4114 and as above. O.S.GR: SP303831. GPS: 52.44588, -1.55572

### Charges guide

| | |
|---|---|
| Per unit incl. 2 persons | £ 15.00 - £ 19.50 |

For latest campsite news visit

**alanrogers.com**

## Ellesmere

### Fernwood Caravan Park

Lyneal, Ellesmere SY12 0QF (Shropshire) T: 01948 710221. E: enquiries@fernwoodpark.co.uk

alanrogers.com/UK4380

Fernwood is set in an area known as the Shropshire Lake District – the mere at Ellesmere is the largest of nine meres – and the picturesque Shropshire Union Canal is only a few minutes' walk. The landscaped park is tranquil and presented to a very high standard, the natural vegetation blending harmoniously with trees and shrubs. In addition to 164 caravan holiday homes, with one unit for hire, there are 30 touring pitches (caravans, motorcaravans and trailer tents only) in several well cut, grassy enclosures (including 30 seasonal long stay). All pitches have electricity (10A) and six also have water and drainage.

| Facilities | Directions |
|---|---|
| The small toilet block for tourers has background heating for cooler days and includes some washbasins in cabins and facilities for disabled visitors. There are plans to include baby changng facilities. Basic motorcaravan services. Laundry room, also additional sanitary facilities. Shop (1/4-30/10, hours vary). Coarse fishing lake. Off site: Shrewsbury, Oswestry and Chester. | Park is just northeast of Lyneal village, signed southwest off the B5063 Ellesmere - Wem road, 1.5 miles from junction of the B5063 with the A495. O.S.GR: SJ452338. GPS: 52.899167, -2.816017 |

**Open:** 1 March - 30 November.

**Charges guide**

| | |
|---|---|
| Per unit incl. 2 persons and electricity | £ 20.00 - £ 29.00 |

## Evesham

### Ranch Caravan Park

Honeybourne, Evesham WR11 7PR (Worcestershire) T: 01386 830744. E: enquiries@ranch.co.uk

alanrogers.com/UK4180

This quiet, attractive caravan park set in the Vale of Evesham covers an area of 50 acres of flat, partly undulating, hedged meadows. The park lies between Bidford-on-Avon and Broadway and is only half an hour's drive from Stratford. The park takes 120 touring units – caravans, motorcaravans or trailer tents, but not other tents. The spacious pitches are not marked but the staff help to position units. All have electrical connections (10A) and there are 20 hardstandings including eight fully serviced pitches (electricity, TV, water and drainage). There are 193 caravan holiday homes in their own section.

| Facilities | Directions |
|---|---|
| Two very well appointed, modern sanitary blocks with free hot showers and heating, one of which includes facilities for disabled visitors, plus baby changing area. Laundry facilities. Motorcaravan service point. Shop. Clubhouse (weekends only in early and late season) offering wide range of good value meals with entertainment arranged throughout the season. Heated pool (55x30 ft; spring B.H. - mid Sept). Gym and sauna (charged). Games room with TV. Playground. Tents are not accepted. Off site: Riding and bicycle hire 2 miles. Fishing 4 miles. Golf 6 miles. | From A46 Evesham take B4035 towards Chipping Campden. After Badsey and Bretforton before Weston Subedge pass over the old railway bridge, turn left at the crossroads to Honeybourne. Park is through village on left before station. O.S.GR: SP112444. GPS: 52.09722, -1.83124 |

**Open:** 1 March - 30 November.

**Charges guide**

| | |
|---|---|
| Per unit incl. 2 persons and electricity | £ 20.00 - £ 25.50 |
| incl. water and drainage | £ 23.50 - £ 29.00 |
| extra person (over 5 yrs) | £ 3.25 - £ 4.25 |

## Grantham

### Woodland Waters

Willoughby Road, Ancaster, Grantham NG32 3RT (Lincolnshire) T: 01400 230888
E: info@woodlandwaters.co.uk alanrogers.com/UK3765

This attractive holiday park occupies 70 acres of woodland, gently sloping grassland and lakes, with the caravan park itself taking up about 20 of them. The site has 120 pitches although only 60 are regularly used (all with 10A electricity and water taps nearby). There is a rally field of 20 pitches with hook-ups, plus areas for camping and those not requiring hook-ups. The land slopes gently down to the 14 acre lake and the pitches nearer the water are more level, although probably not suitable for those with younger children since there is no fencing. Reception is housed in a neat modem building at the entrance to the park. Fishing tickets are sold and tourist information is available. Some aircraft noise is possible.

| Facilities | Directions |
|---|---|
| A single, modern, heated toilet block is well maintained and kept clean. Washbasins (in cubicles for ladies) and free showers (controllable for ladies, pushbutton for men). A second block provides extra facilities. Small laundry room. Motorcaravan service point. Bar and restaurant with takeaway. Play area. Fishing. Off site: Shop and trains in village 1 mile. Go-karting and paintball 1 mile. Golf 3 miles. Riding 6 miles. | Ancaster is 8 miles northeast of Grantham and 19 miles south of Lincoln. The park entrance is off the A153 Grantham - Sleaford road, 600 yards west of the junction with the B6403 High Dyke road (Ermine Street). O.S.GR: SK973437. GPS: 52.98053, -0.54698 |

**Open:** All year.

**Charges guide**

| | |
|---|---|
| Per unit incl. 4 persons | £ 16.50 - £ 18.50 |
| extra person | £ 2.00 |

For latest campsite news visit
**alanrogers.com**

## Grantham

### Wagtail Country Park

Cliff Lane, Marston, Grantham NG32 2HU (Lincolnshire) T: 07814 481088. E: info@wagtailcountrypark.co.uk
alanrogers.com/UK3775

There has been a small campsite here for many years, but the new owner has transformed the appearance of the original camping area alongside an attractive little fishing lake and is in the process of creating a new, larger lake with additional pitches and facilities. There are currently just 11 pitches all with electricity, on gravel hardstanding and separated by raised flower beds or timber beams. The new development will offer (for 2011) a further 20 pitches, including a couple on grass and 10 fully serviced with water and drainage. There will also be five privately owned wooden chalets.

#### Facilities

Two small heated buildings provide spacious controllable showers and open-style washbasins. A new heated toilet block with full facilities is planned including a unit for disabled visitors and laundry facilities. Motorhome service point. Security barriers plus overnight pitch for late arrivals. Calor gas. Secure caravan storage. Fishing (£3 per person). No special provision for children and lake not fenced. Off site: Shopping Outlet and Garden Centre 3 miles. Golf 5 miles. Belton House 5 miles. Grantham 6 miles. Riding 7 miles. Newark 14 miles.

Open: All year.

#### Directions

Site is off the A1 between Grantham and Newark. Turn east towards Marston at filling station 1.2 miles north of Gonerby Services, Grantham and 8 miles south of Newark. In 500 yards turn right into Green Lane towards Barkston, then right again in 0.75 miles into Cliff Lane where park is signed. GPS: 52.961229, -0.667269

#### Charges guide

| | |
|---|---|
| Per unit incl. 2 persons and electricity | £ 15.00 |
| extra person | £ 1.00 |

No credit cards.

---

## Halesowen

### Clent Hills Camping & Caravanning Club Site

Fieldhouse Lane, Romsley, Halesowen B62 0NH (West Midlands) T: 01562 710015
alanrogers.com/UK4040

Conveniently close to Birmingham and only a couple of miles or so off the M5/M42 intersection, this site is a real surprise in terms of being quiet and peaceful and very pretty with good views. Its only disadvantage is that it is on sloping ground, but the present, very helpful holiday site managers are happy to assist in pitching anyone who has a problem in getting level (mainly motorcaravanners); in fact, there are some level pitches and these are all earmarked for motorcaravans. The 95 pitches are all of a good size, 74 with electrical connections (10/16A) and 17 with hardstanding.

#### Facilities

The central sanitary toilet block can be heated and provides the latest facilities, including washbasins in cabins, hairdryers, baby room and a toilet and shower for disabled visitors. It was spotless when last visited. Laundry facilities. Small play area with rubber safety surface. Gas supplies. Caravan storage. Off site: Riding 1 mile. Fishing 3 miles. Golf 7 miles.

Open: March - November.

#### Directions

From M5 junction 4 take A491, branch right to Romsley on B4551 and watch for site signs in Romsley village by shops. Site is on left. O.S.GR: SO955795. GPS: 52.41469, -2.06814

#### Charges guide

| | |
|---|---|
| Per person | £ 4.90 - £ 7.25 |
| child (6-18 yrs) | £ 2.15 |
| non-member pitch fee | £ 5.65 |

---

## Henley-in-Arden

### Island Meadow Caravan Park

The Mill House, Aston Cantlow, Henley-in-Arden B95 6JP (Warwickshire) T: 01789 488273
E: holiday@islandmeadowcaravanpark.co.uk  alanrogers.com/UK4090

This peaceful, traditional, family run site is in a rural location, surrounded by the River Alne and its mill race. A good base for walking, cycling and bird watching, it has 80 pitches in total, with 56 holiday homes (4 for rent) located around the perimeter. The 24 touring pitches are on the spacious, central grassy area of the site, all have 10A electric hook-ups. Only environmentally friendly groundsheets are permitted. Note: The site is on an island with obvious hazards for small children. There is an excellent playground in the village centre (five minutes walk via footpath across Mill Meadow).

#### Facilities

Two sanitary units, both heated. The original provides adequate WCs and washbasins for men, and the more modern unit has been provided for women, with a separate access shower unit for the men, and a suite for disabled visitors on one end. Laundry facilities. Good coarse fishing. Off site: The village has its own 'club' (campers welcome) and the local pub serves a range of meals. Golf 3 miles, riding 4.5 miles, bicycle hire 6 miles. Warwick Castle. Stratford-upon-Avon. Buses from village to Alcester and Stratford, including a late night service.

Open: 1 March - 31 October.

#### Directions

From A46 (Stratford-Alcester) follow signs for Mary Arden's House. At Wilmcote follow signs to Aston Cantlow and site. O.S.GR: SP136598. GPS: 52.23549, -1.80265

#### Charges guide

| | |
|---|---|
| Per unit incl. 2 persons and electricity | £ 17.50 |
| extra person | £ 2.00 |
| child (5-12 yrs) | £ 1.00 |
| tent (2 man) | £ 14.00 |

Gazebos only by prior arrangement. No credit cards.

For latest campsite news visit
**alanrogers.com**

# Hereford

## Lucksall Caravan & Camping Park

Mordiford, Hereford HR1 4LP (Herefordshire) T: 01432 870213. E: karen@lucksallpark.co.uk

alanrogers.com/UK4310

Set in 17 acres and bounded on one side by the River Wye, and over 90 acres of woodland on the other, Lucksall has 120 large, well spaced and level touring pitches, all with 16A electricity and 65 with hardstanding. The river is open to the site with lifebelts and safety messages in evidence. Canoes are available for hire or bring your own (launching facilities); fishing permits may be obtained from reception. A large, fenced playground and a large grassy area for games are provided. A well stocked shop selling a variety of goods is in reception (a mini market is within 1.5 miles) and a café is planned for 2011. A member of the Countryside Discovery group.

### Facilities

Three centrally heated toilet blocks provide top of the range facilities, a separate unit with ramped entrance for disabled campers. Laundry room. Dishwashing area. Family room. WiFi. Only breathable groundsheets are permitted. Off site: Golf 5 miles. Bicycle hire 9 miles. Sustrans cycle route nearby.

Open: 1 March - 30 November.

### Directions

Between Mordiford and Fownhope, 5 miles southeast of Hereford on B4224, the park is well signed. O.S.GR: SO571355. GPS: 52.02302, -2.63052

### Charges guide

| | |
|---|---|
| Per unit incl. 2 persons | £ 16.00 - £ 22.00 |
| extra person (over 17 yrs) | £ 3.00 - £ 3.50 |
| small 3 man tent | £ 13.00 - £ 20.00 |

# Horncastle

## Ashby Park

West Ashby, Horncastle LN9 5PP (Lincolnshire) T: 01507 527966. E: ashbyparklakes@aol.com

alanrogers.com/UK3680

Ashby Park is a pleasant, well run site located in 70 acres of former gravel pits that now provide seven attractive fishing lakes. There is a series of clearings occupied by privately owned caravan holiday homes and by 77 touring pitches. Most are on grass, but some have hardstanding. All have access to electricity (16A) and 12 super pitches also have hardstanding, water tap and waste water drain. Lakeside pitches will no doubt appeal to anglers, whereas families with young children will probably prefer to be further away from the lakes, which are inevitably unfenced. This is a peaceful site in an interesting area.

### Facilities

Three toilet blocks are well maintained and equipped, with open style washbasins and controllable showers; all hot water is metered (20p). Good facilities for disabled visitors. Laundry room. Limited dishwashing (in the new block – a long walk from lakeside pitches). Motorcaravan service point. Fishing (day ticket £4.50). Off site: Golf 0.5 miles. Riding 5 miles. Sailing and lakeside beach 6 miles. Seaside beaches 20 miles. Horncastle 2 miles.

Open: 1 March - 30 November.

### Directions

Horncastle is 20 miles east of Lincoln on the A153 Sleaford - Louth road. Turn west off the A153, 1.6 miles north of the town along Docking Lane and follow signs to site in 0.8 miles. O.S.GR: TF251724. GPS: 53.233293, -0.122426

### Charges guide

| | |
|---|---|
| Per unit incl. 2 adults and 2 children | £ 11.50 |
| incl. electricity | £ 15.00 |
| serviced pitch | £ 18.50 - £ 20.00 |

# Leek

## Glencote Caravan Park

Station Road, Cheddleton, Leek ST13 7EE (Staffordshire) T: 01538 360745. E: canistay@glencote.co.uk

alanrogers.com/UK3970

Nestled in the Churnet Valley, three miles south of the market town of Leek, a pleasant stay awaits you at this, well-managed, family run park of six acres. Each of the 74 level touring pitches, accessed via tarmac roads, has grass and a paved hardstanding, electrical connections (16A) and a dedicated water supply. Pretty flowerbeds, trees and varied wildlife make a very pleasant environment. Alongside a fenced coarse fishing pool is a grass play area and this whole corner is enclosed by banks with an abundance of attractive shrubs and flowers.

### Facilities

The clean toilet block is centrally situated and can be heated. Facilities include one private cabin for ladies, a combined shower and toilet for disabled visitors, a small laundry room, two dishwashing sinks and one vegetable preparation sink under cover. Gas supplies. Max. 2 dogs per unit. Wifi (charged) covers site. Information centre and small library. Off site: Small supermarket and post office in Cheddleton 0.5 miles. Variety of inns, including the canalside Boat Inn, within walking distance. Golf 4 miles. Bicycle hire 5 miles. Riding 10 miles.

Open: 1 February - end December.

### Directions

Park is signed off A520 Leek - Stone road, 3.5 miles south of Leek on northern edge of Cheddleton Village. O.S.GR: SJ982524. GPS: 53.06994, -2.02901

### Charges guide

| | |
|---|---|
| Per unit incl. 2 persons and electricity | £ 22.00 |
| extra person | £ 5.00 |
| child (5-16 yrs) | £ 2.50 |
| dog | £ 1.00 |
| Min. stay of 3 nights at B.Hs. | |

For latest campsite news visit
alanrogers.com

## Leominster

### Townsend Touring & Caravan Park

Townsend Farm, Pembridge, Leominster HR6 9HB (Herefordshire) T: 01544 388527
E: info@townsend-farm.co.uk  alanrogers.com/UK4345

This is a modern, family run campsite hidden in a natural dip next to a working farm, but within a short walk of Pembridge. With tarmac roads, good site lighting, well spaced pitches and a drive-over motorcaravan service point, plenty of open space and a small fishing lake (with ducks and completely unfenced). There are 60 pitches in total, 23 with gravel hardstanding, the remainder on grass, and all have access to electricity hook-ups (16A), water and drainage. Reception is at the Farm Shop by the entrance, stocking a wide variety of fresh fruit, vegetables and eggs; a butchery section has farm produced meats. New for 2010 were three standard and one jumbo sized pods for rent. Pembridge, known as the jewel in the crown of the Black and White Village trails, holds its Farmers' Market on the first Saturday of each month. Occupied since before the Magna Carta, every street contains medieval buildings which, in any other location, would be individual attractions in themselves. Ideal for eating out, shopping or just having a drink. A member of the Best of British group.

#### Facilities

A modern sanitary building with blown air heating, is accessed through a foyer with tourist information and public telephone. It is surrounded by wide decking with ramps giving easy access for wheelchairs to all facilities including the dishwashing area and laundry room. Inside are spacious controllable showers, some washbasins in cubicles, a suite for disabled guests, family bathroom and baby changing facilities. Off site: Riding and bicycle hire 0.5 miles. Kington 5 miles. Leominster 7 miles. Golf 7 miles.

Open: 1 March - 15 January.

#### Directions

Site is beside the A44, 7 miles west of Leominster. Site is just inside the 30 mph. speed limit on the eastern edge of Pembridge village.
O.S.GR: SO385580. GPS: 52.21792, -2.88845

#### Charges guide

| Per unit incl. 2 persons, | |
|---|---|
| electricity, water and drainage | £ 14.00 - £ 25.00 |
| extra person | £ 5.00 |
| child (5-15 yrs) | £ 2.00 |
| dog | £ 2.00 |

## Ludlow

### Westbrook Park

Little Hereford, Ludlow SY8 4AU (Shropshire) T: 01584 711280. E: info@bestparks.co.uk
alanrogers.com/UK4390

A beautifully kept, traditional, quiet touring campsite in a working cider apple orchard, Westbrook Park is bordered on one side by the River Teme and is within walking distance of the village and pub. There are 60 level pitches with 16A electric hook-ups, gravel or concrete/gravel all-weather hardstandings with water and waste water drain. Some pitches have semi-shade, others have none. All the pitches at Westbrook have recently been upgraded. The new spacious, hardstanding pitches, with new and improved electricity supply, TV aerial, water and waste water have been very well received. Satellite TV hook-ups are available to all pitches. A footpath along the river bank in one direction leads to the Temeside Inn which serves hot meals. There is a pleasant riverside walk and dog walk in the other direction.

#### Facilities

A modern, timber-clad, heated toilet block provides spacious hot showers (coin-operated), washbasins in curtained cubicles, a basic laundry room and dishwashing sinks. Full facilities for disabled visitors (WC and basin). Gas supplies. Playground (fenced, woodchip base). Fishing (£4 per day). Riverside walks. No gazebos. No cycling. Only well-behaved dogs accepted. Off site: The Temeside Inn does not accept payment by cards but has a cash point. Burford House Gardens. Croft Castle. Market towns of Tenbury Wells, Leominster, and Ludlow, famed for its restaurants. Golf 3 miles. Riding and bicycle hire 5 miles.

Open: 1 March - 30 November.

#### Directions

From A49 midway between Ludlow and Leominster, turn east at Woofferton on A456 (Tenbury Wells, Kidderminster). After 2 miles turn right just before river bridge and Temeside Inn. Turn left after 150 yds. Park is on left. Access roads are narrow.
O.S.GR: SU547679. GPS: 52.307377, -2.665815

#### Charges guide

| Per unit incl. 2 persons | |
|---|---|
| and electricity | £ 17.00 - £ 23.00 |
| extra person | £ 4.00 |
| child (5-12 yrs) | £ 2.00 |
| dog | £ 1.00 |

For latest campsite news visit
## alanrogers.com

## Lutterworth
### Stanford Hall Caravan Park

Stanford Road, Swinford, Lutterworth LE17 6DH (Leicestershire) T: 01788 860387
E: stanfordpark@yahoo.co.uk **alanrogers.com/UK3890**

This picturesque and tranquil site is ideally situated for an overnight stop where you are guaranteed a warm welcome and a pleasant stay. Formerly a Caravan Club site, it is set in the rural grounds of the Stanford Hall Estate, just a mile from the M1. There are 123 pitches (30 of which are seasonal), 80 on grass and 43 on hardstanding, all with 16A electricity. There are no shower or toilet facilities on the park, so your unit must be self contained. The site experiences high levels of repeat bookings so you are advised to contact them in advance of busy weekends to avoid being disappointed. Dogs are welcome but must be kept on a lead on the main site. A designated dog walk has been established through part of the estate woodland. Visitors staying on site (for two nights or more) receive free admission to the grounds of Stanford Hall during normal opening times, except on certain event days. There is a small charge for admission to the house.

**Facilities**

There are no toilets or shower facilities on site which means each unit must be totally self-contained. Tents are not accepted. A small shop sells basics. Newspapers can be ordered daily. Motorcaravan services. Picnic tables. Information room. Off site: Supermarkets and banks in Lutterworth. Warwick Castle 25 miles. NEC, Birmingham 30 miles. Stratford Upon Avon 35 miles. Silverstone, Rockingham and Mallory Race Circuits and Althorpe are all within easy reach. Good location for walking and fishing. Jurassic Walk and the Grand Union Canal nearby.

Open: All year.

**Directions**

From the north on M1 and from M6 leave at exit 19 and at roundabout take first exit, signed Swinford, and follow signs for Stanford Hall. Site is on the left on Stanford Road. From east on A14, at the junction with M1 roundabout, take exit to Swinford. From south on the M1, leave at exit 18 onto A428, A5 north and then follow signs for Stanford Hall. O.S.GR: SK820133. GPS: 52.406493, -1.149361

**Charges guide**

| | |
|---|---|
| Per unit incl. 2 adults, 2 children and electricity | £ 12.00 |
| extra person | £ 1.50 |
| dog | free |

**STANFORD HALL CARAVAN PARK**

- This picturesque and tranquil site is set in the rural Grounds of the Stanford Hall Estate
- Open all year
- Great location for Walkers, Twitchers and Fishing with Jurassic Walk and the Grand Union Canal close by
- Call Charlotte or Eddie on 01788 860387 or e-mail us at stanfordpark@yahoo.co.uk

## Malvern
### Kingsgreen Caravan Park

Kingsgreen, Berrow, Malvern WR13 6AQ (Worcestershire) T: 01531 650272
**alanrogers.com/UK4190**

An attractive, welcoming and well kept site with views of the Malvern Hills, Kingsgreen is in a lovely rural location. An ideal site for adults who like the quiet life, there are no amusements for children. The surrounding countryside is ideal for walking or cycling, and the small, fenced fishing lakes on the site are well stocked (£4 per day). There are 45 level, grass and gravel pitches, all with electricity (13A), plus an additional area for tents. Some old orchard trees provide a little shade in parts. The site is 7 miles from the market town of Ledbury with its half timbered buildings. A barrier is closed at all times. The site is within easy driving distance of Malvern, with its Elgar Trail, the Three Counties Showground, Cheltenham and Gloucester, the Cotswolds and the Forest of Dean. Tewkesbury, famous for being the site of one of the bloodiest and final battles of the War of the Roses, with its 12th-century Abbey is only ten miles away.

**Facilities**

Modern heated toilet facilities (key on deposit) provide hot showers (25p token from reception) and a separate unit for disabled visitors (WC and washbasin). No baby changing facilities. Laundry room with coin-operated washing machine and dryer. Gas. Fishing. Off site: Nearest shop and pub 1.5 miles. Riding 3 miles. Golf 5 miles.

Open: 1 March - 31 October.

**Directions**

From M50 exit 2, take A417 towards Gloucester, then first left, where site is signed, also signed the Malverns, back over the motorway. Site is 2 miles from the M50. O.S.GR: SO767338. GPS: 52.00211, -2.33929

**Charges guide**

| | |
|---|---|
| Per unit incl. 2 persons and electricity | £ 14.50 - £ 17.50 |
| extra person over 2 yrs | £ 1.50 |
| dog | £ 1.50 |

No credit cards. VAT not included.

For latest campsite news visit
**alanrogers.com**

## Market Rasen

### Walesby Woodlands Caravan Park

Walesby, Market Rasen LN8 3UN (Lincolnshire) T: 01673 843285. E: walesbywoodlands@talk21.com
alanrogers.com/UK3660

Surrounded by mature Forestry Commission woodland, this small family-run, no frills touring park is mainly very peaceful (if the wind is in a certain direction trains may be heard in the distance). The owners, Paul and Christine Burrows will make you very welcome. There are 60 well spaced pitches, 52 with 10A electricity, marked out in a single, mainly flat, grassy field divided by a central gravel road and with a double row of trees providing useful visual screening. About a mile away is the small town of Market Rasen, but further afield and within easy driving distance, are Lincoln, the east coast including Skegness and, of course, the Lincolnshire Wolds.

#### Facilities

The single, heated toilet block (£5 deposit charged for the key) is spacious and ample for the site. Pushbutton showers and open style washbasins. Toilet facilities for disabled visitors. Laundry room. Some basic supplies kept in reception. Coffee shop open at busy weekends. Bicycle hire. No kite flying (overhead wires). Winter caravan storage. Off site: Golf 1.5 miles. Riding 2 miles. Fishing 3 miles. Shops, supermarkets, pubs and restaurants 1-2 miles. Racecourse 2 miles. Beach 20 miles.

Open: 1 March - 31 October, plus Christmas/New Year.

#### Directions

Market Rasen is on the A46, 17 miles northeast of Lincoln. Park is just over a mile northeast of the town. Take the B1203 towards Tealby, then turn left about half a mile along Walesby Road on the left and is signed from all the main approach roads to town. O.S.GR: TF117907. GPS: 53.40135, -0.321

#### Charges guide

| Per unit incl. 2 persons and electricity | £ 16.00 - £ 18.00 |
| extra person | £ 2.00 |

---

## Matlock

### Lickpenny Touring Park

Lickpenny Lane, Tansley, Matlock DE4 5GF (Derbyshire) T: 01629 583040. E: lickpenny@btinternet.com
alanrogers.com/UK3815

This spacious caravan park on a hill above Matlock has 122 terraced pitches, all on hardstandings (no tents) and with electricity (16A). Of these, 100 are touring pitches, 27 of which are fully serviced and 22 are seasonal. There are rows of mature trees and pitches are large and separated by shrubs and bushes. The enthusiastic owners have taken full advantage of the fact that this was previously a market garden and are continuing to work hard to maintain high standards and improve facilities. Recreational grassy areas and flower borders are well tended, whilst the top corner has been kept as woodland.

#### Facilities

Two well equipped, heated toilet blocks include free controllable showers and some washbasins in cubicles. Good facilities for disabled visitors. Family room with small bath, toilet and washbasin. Laundry room. Motorcaravan services. Security barrier with keypad access at all times. Off site: Bus service from end of the road. Woodland walk to garden centre with restaurant 200 yards. Riding 1 mile. Fishing 3 miles. Golf 4 miles. Bicycle hire 6 miles.

Open: All year.

#### Directions

From M1 exit 28, follow signs for Matlock on A38, A61 and A615. After 5 miles on A615 turn north on Lickpenny Lane to site (signed). From Matlock take A615; after Tansley fork left on B6014 (Clay Cross) and turn right at top of hill after garden centre. O.S.GR: SK339598. GPS: 53.134533, -1.490483

#### Charges guide

| Per unit incl. 2 persons | £ 15.00 - £ 21.00 |
| extra person | £ 5.00 |

---

## Meriden

### Somers Wood Caravan Park

Somers Road, Meriden CV7 7PL (Warwickshire) T: 01676 522978. E: enquiries@somerswood.co.uk
alanrogers.com/UK4070

Somers Wood is a quiet, peaceful park, attractively situated amongst pine trees. This is a very pleasant park which only accepts adults and does not take tents. It is especially useful for those visiting the various shows at the NEC when it can get very busy. From the reception building at the entrance, an oval gravel road provides access to 48 pitches, all on hardstanding and with 10A electricity hook-ups. Areas of woodland, carpeted with flowers in summer, surround the site and partition it into small intimate areas that create a rural feel. A member of the Best of British group.

#### Facilities

The central, heated, completely refurbished (private cabins), sanitary block is fully equipped, and a facility for the disabled has been added. Shower cubicles are especially large. Two dishwashing sinks on the veranda area. Laundry service at reception. WiFi on payment. Off site: Local shops and restaurant less than 1 mile and visitors also welcome to use the bar and restaurant at the golf club next door.

Open: All year.

#### Directions

From M42 exit 6 (NEC) take A45 towards Coventry. Keep in left lane down to roundabout and exit on A452 (signed Leamington/Meriden), then turn left into Hampton Lane at the next roundabout. Site is signed with golf and fishing centres on the left. O.S.GR: SP228819. GPS: 52.43930, -1.66947

#### Charges guide

| Per unit incl. 2 persons | £ 20.00 - £ 23.00 |
| extra person | £ 3.00 |

For latest campsite news visit
**alanrogers.com**

## Moreton-in-Marsh

### Moreton-in-Marsh Caravan Club Site

Bourton Road, Moreton-in-Marsh GL56 0BT (Gloucestershire) T: 01608 650519

alanrogers.com/UK4130

This excellent, busy, but rural, site located in mature woodland in the heart of the Cotswolds offers what one would hope for from a camping holiday. Only 250 yards from the town, there is ample choice for food and pubs. The site has 183 pitches, all with electricity (16A) and TV sockets, 173 with hardstanding. An outfit limit of 8.2 metres for motorhomes and caravans exists. Milk and ice-cream are available from reception. Adjacent to a dog exercise field is an updated play area, crazy golf and a boules pitch. In an adjoining field there is plenty of room for ball games. Kite flying is not allowed because of low power cables. Tents are not accepted.

**Facilities**

The two main toilet blocks have been renovated and offer excellent facilities. A separate toilet block exists with disabled toilet and baby room containing a small toilet and bath with seat for children. Large laundry. Play area. Boules. WiFi (charged). Off site: Shops, pubs and restaurants 400 yards. Golf 7 miles. Nearby are the Cotswold Falconry Centre, Hidcote Manor Gardens, Snowshill Manor and the Rollright Stones.

Open: All year.

**Directions**

From Evesham on A44, site on left after Bourton-on-the-Hill village, 150 yards before town sign. From Moreton-in-Marsh take A44 towards Evesham and site is on right in 150 yards past Wellington museum. O.S.GR: SP200323. GPS: 51.98875, -1.710833

**Charges guide**

| | |
|---|---|
| Per person | £ 5.00 - £ 6.90 |
| pitch incl. electricity (non-member) | £ 12.10 - £ 15.50 |

## Newark

### Orchard Park

Marnham Road, Tuxford, Newark NG22 0PY (Nottinghamshire) T: 01777 870228

E: info@orchardcaravanpark.co.uk  alanrogers.com/UK3950

This well established family run touring and caravan park has been created in an old fruit orchard in a quiet location, yet is very convenient for the A1. It has a friendly feel, with just 65 pitches, all with electricity (10A), 34 with hardstanding and 20 occupied by seasonal units. There is also a spacious camping field with good views. Reception is at the owner's house with a nearby cabin with information on attractions including Sundown Adventureland, Laxton Medieval village and Victorian Times, Rufford Abbey, Clumber Park, Sherwood Forest and the Robin Hood Centre.

**Facilities**

The heated toilet block has pushbutton showers, open style washbasins and a well equipped room for disabled visitors. Laundry facilities. Small shop with basics and gas. Picnic area. Excellent children's adventure trail and nature walk. Apples, pears and blackberries can be picked in season. WiFi available on most of site (£4 per weekend). Off site: Pub 0.5 miles, shops 1 mile. Riding 3 miles. Fishing 4 miles. Bicycle hire and golf 10 miles.

Open: March - October.

**Directions**

The park lies to the east of the A1. Leave at signs for Tuxford and turn east on A6075 towards Lincoln (A57), continue through village and turn south towards Marnham for 0.5 miles. Site is on right 0.5 miles after railway bridge (well signed). O.S.GR: SK750710. GPS: 53.2296, -0.8695

**Charges 2011**

| | |
|---|---|
| Per unit incl. 2 persons | £ 17.00 - £ 20.00 |
| extra person | £ 4.00 |

## Newark

### Milestone Caravan Park

Great North Road, Cromwell, Newark NG23 6JE (Nottinghamshire) T: 01636 821244

E: enquiries@milestonepark.co.uk  alanrogers.com/UK3945

Situated just off the A1 north of Newark, Milestone has a good deal more to offer than simply a stopover option. Its 91 good-sized, level touring pitches all have electricity (16A) and nearby water points. Grass pitches are available, but most are all-weather in a variety of locations. Five are outside the barrier for those in transit (although key access is always available), then comes a pleasantly landscaped area and finally terraces overlooking an attractive fishing lake. An embankment built to muffle traffic noise provides a pleasant grassed walk with views across an adjoining lake and the surrounding countryside. This is a Caravan Club affiliated site.

**Facilities**

Two heated toilet blocks provide pushbutton showers and open-style washbasins (may be under pressure at busy times). Excellent en-suite facilities for disabled visitors. Laundry facilities. Motorcaravan service points. Fishing (£3 a day). Lakeside cabin. Off site: Large fishing lake adjacent. Village has shop, small brewery and buses to Newark. Riding and boat launching 3 miles. Golf 5 miles. Bicycle hire at Sherwood Forest 12 miles.

Open: All year.

**Directions**

From the south on A1, 3.7 miles after A46 junction, take slip road to Cromwell and site is on the left after the village. From the north on A1, 9 miles after Markham Moor junction, take slip road for Cromwell, turn right over bridge and right again to site. O.S.GR: SK798620. GPS: 53.1494, -0.8077

**Charges guide**

| | |
|---|---|
| Per unit incl. 2 persons | £ 14.60 - £ 20.20 |
| extra person | £ 4.80 - £ 6.20 |

For latest campsite news visit

**alanrogers.com**

## Newark

### Smeaton's Lakes Touring Caravan & Fishing Park

Great North Road, South Muskham, Newark-on-Trent NG23 6ED (Nottinghamshire) T: 01636 605088
E: lesley@smeatonslakes.co.uk  alanrogers.com/UK3940

This 82 acre site is really ideal for anglers, with four fishing lakes (coarse, carp and pike) and river fishing on the Trent. There are 130 pitches of which 100 have electricity connections (16A). Non-anglers might choose this park if visiting antique fairs or events at nearby Newark Showground, or Newark town (1 mile) with its castle, air museum and various weekly markets. During your stay, you might visit Southwell Cathedral, Sherwood Forest, Clumber Park or Lincoln with its castle and cathedral.

**Facilities**

Two toilet blocks (with keypad access) are heated and include a good unit for disabled visitors, but no laundry room. Laundry and dishwashing sinks are outside. Reception keeps gas, soft drinks, dairy produce, etc. and newspapers can be ordered. On-site concessions for lake and river fishing. Entry barrier with key access. Security cameras and night-time height barrier (about 6 ft). Off site: Bus stop at the end of the entry lane – buses run into Newark twice hourly until 10 pm. Riding and boat launching 2 miles. Golf 3 miles.

Open: All year.

**Directions**

From south on A1, take A46 west (signed Newark, then Leicester) and turn north on A6065/A616 towards South Muskham. From southwest (M1/A46) turn north off Newark bypass on A6065/A616 as above. From north on A1 leave B6325 (Newark) continue south through South Muskham and follow signs for Newark. GPS: 53.0936, -0.820667

**Charges guide**

| | |
|---|---|
| Per unit incl. 2 persons and electricity | £ 15.00 - £ 18.00 |
| extra person | £ 3.00 |

---

## Oakham

### Greendale Farm Caravan & Camping Park

Pickwell Lane, Whissendine, Oakham LE15 7LB (Rutland) T: 01664 474516. E: enq@rutlandgreendale.co.uk
alanrogers.com/UK3904

This is a delightful little adult only park set in rolling countryside, ideal for those seeking peace and tranquillity. It is very eco-friendly and extremely well appointed for such a small site. There are only 13 pitches, all with electricity, so it is worth checking availability! Reception, the shop and the toilet facilities are housed in a modern building adjoining the owners' house. The shop is well stocked with essentials and local produce. Cooked breakfasts are available on Sundays. It also has one of the most comprehensive information displays we have seen on any campsite. No arrivals before 13.00.

**Facilities**

Each of the two rooms of the toilet block has a power shower, WCs and two washbasins (cubicles for the ladies). All is beautifully appointed and immaculately kept. Washing machine, tumble dryer and spin dryer. Small open air swimming pool (6x3 m; £1 charge), heated by solar-panels, with summer house. Two bicycles for hire. WiFi (charged). Off site: Village with bus service 0.5 miles. Supermarket in Oakham 4 miles. Fishing 3 miles. Riding 4 miles. Golf 8 miles. Sailing, bird-watching, walking, cycling (and bicycle hire) and fishing at Rutland Water 8 miles. Barnsdale Garden 8 miles.

Open: 15 April - 30 September.

**Directions**

Whissendine is just off the A606 Oakham - Melton Mowbray road. Approach park from this road and NOT through the village. From Oakham ignore first turning to Whissendine, continue 2 miles and turn right at campsite sign. From Melton ignore first two turnings to Whissendine; turn left after Rutland sign (at campsite sign). Park is on right in 0.6 mile. O.S.GR:SK819133. GPS: 52.711833, -0.788617

**Charges guide**

| | |
|---|---|
| Per unit incl. two adults and electricity (10/16A) | £ 17.00 - £ 22.00 |
| extra person | £ 4.00 |

---

## Peterchurch

### Poston Mill Caravan Park

Peterchurch HR2 0SF (Herefordshire) T: 01981 550225. E: info@poston-mill.co.uk
alanrogers.com/UK4300

Set in pleasant undulating farmland in the heart of the Golden Valley, Poston Mill Park is a mile from the delightful village of Peterchurch. It is an ideal location for relaxation or exploring. There are currently 43 touring pitches set on level grass or hardstanding with mature trees around the perimeter of the park. All pitches are fully serviced with electricity, water and TV connections, and a new area has been set aside for tents. You can enjoy a walk along one side of the park, edging the River Dore. Adjoining the park is 'The Mill' licensed restaurant and a general store. A member of the Best of British group.

**Facilities**

One central sanitary block with a smaller, refurbished block near the holiday home area which includes private cubicles. Units for disabled visitors and families. Laundry rooms. Motorcaravan service point. Play area. Pitch and putt. Tennis. Golf driving range. Games room. Winter caravan storage. Off site: Riding 3 miles. Bicycle hire 10 miles. Fishing and walking.

Open: All year.

**Directions**

Park is 1 mile southeast of Peterchurch on the B4348 road. O.S.GR: SO356371. GPS: 52.02832, -2.9388

**Charges guide**

| | |
|---|---|
| Per unit incl. 2 persons | £ 17.00 - £ 23.00 |
| extra person | £ 4.00 |
| Min. charge at B.Hs. 5 nights. | |

For latest campsite news visit

**alanrogers.com**

## Ripley

### Golden Valley Caravan & Camping Park

Coach Road, Golden Valley, Ripley DE55 4ES (Derbyshire) T: 01773 513881
E: enquiries@goldenvalleycaravanpark.co.uk  **alanrogers.com/UK3865**

Golden Valley Caravan & Camping Park is located in the beautiful hamlet of Golden Valley alongside the Cromford Canal in the Amber Valley area of the Peak District. The site is situated within 26 acres of historic woodland which was once a thriving industrial centre for coal, iron foundries and canal workers on the adjacent Canal. This secluded woodland site has just 40 pitches on grass or hardstanding for motorcaravans and caravans. There are 24 with independent water supply, electrical connection and mains drainage. There are also two wooded areas for tents and a communal barbecue area. A small fishing pond is available containing carp and it is visited by kingfishers, dragonflies and ducks. The pond is securely fenced to avoid access by young children. There is a great deal of interest in the area including the Midland Railway centre (reduced fares for campers) and many footpaths and cycle ways, including the Cromford canal towpath, and of course throughout the magnificent Peak District National Park.

**Facilities**

A centrally positioned, heated utility block provides free showers and toilets, facilities for disabled visitors, a laundry room, heated jacuzzi, an indoor playroom and a gym. Bar and café (July/Aug and weekends). Fishing pond. Woodland walks. Play area. Tourist information. Off site: Midland Railway Centre. Denby Pottery. Derby 7 miles. Nottingham 15 miles. Walking and cycling in the Peak District National Park.

Open: All year.

**Directions**

Leave the M1 at exit 26 and follow signs for Matlock and Ripley (A610). Upon arrival at Codnor, turn right at the traffic lights and then first right onto the Alfreton Road. After a further 2 miles turn left before passing the Newlands Inn to join Coach Road. Site entrance is on the left. O.S.GR: SK424512. GPS: 53.05669, -1.37267

**Charges guide**

| Per unit incl. 2 persons | |
|---|---|
| and electricity | £ 20.00 |
| extra person | £ 5.00 - £ 10.00 |
| child (1-16 yrs) | £ 3.00 |
| dog | £ 2.00 |

## Ross-on-Wye

### Broadmeadow Caravan & Camping Park

Broadmeadows, Ross-on-Wye HR9 7BW (Herefordshire) T: 01989 768076. E: broadm4811@aol.com
**alanrogers.com/UK4320**

Ross-on-Wye town centre is within easy walking distance of this modern, spacious park, complete with open views and its own fishing lake. The approach to the site is very unusual, passing through an industrial estate, but eventually you will arrive at a well laid out and pleasant site with facilities of the highest quality. There are 150 large pitches on a mixture of hardstanding and level, open grass; the site is especially good for tents. Each set of four pitches has a service post with water, drain, electricity points (16A) and lighting. There may be some traffic noise from the A40 relief road. Seasonal pitches are now available. The market town of Ross-on-Wye is centrally placed for touring Herefordshire, the Wye Valley or the Forest of Dean. The town itself has many facilities such as an indoor pool, putting greens and tennis courts. Plus, of course, lots of good places to eat and drink. Shopping is excellent with a general market held on Thursdays and Saturdays and a Farmers' Market once a month.

**Facilities**

Two fully equipped, modern sanitary blocks with baby rooms, family bathrooms each with WC, basin and bath, and a comprehensive unit for disabled visitors. Dishwashing room and laundry at each block. Basic motorcaravan service point. Entrance barrier and keypad exit system. Small part-fenced playground. Fenced fishing lake (coarse fishing £7.50 per rod per day - fishing licence not available at reception). Off site: Supermarket 200 m. Bicycle hire in town. Golf 3 miles. Riding 8 miles.

Open: Easter/1 April - 30 September.

**Directions**

From A40 relief road turn into Ross at roundabout, take first right into industrial estate, then right in 0.5 miles before supermarket, where site is signed. O.S.GR: SO610240. GPS: 51.91657, -2.57489

**Charges guide**

| Per unit incl. 2 persons | |
|---|---|
| and electricity | £ 11.25 - £ 13.75 |
| extra person | £ 4.25 |
| child (2-9 yrs) | £ 2.75 |
| dog | £ 1.50 |

## Shrewsbury
### Oxon Hall Touring Park

Welshpool Road, Shrewsbury SY3 5FB (Shropshire) T: 01743 340868. E: oxon@morris-leisure.co.uk
alanrogers.com/UK4430

Oxon Hall is a purpose-built park, well situated for visiting Shrewsbury. Under the same ownership as Stanmore Hall (UK4400) the site has been developed to a very high standard with mature trees and shrubs providing some shade and shelter. Of the 120 pitches only 105 are in use for tourers, all of which have electric hook-ups (16A), 65 are full service pitches (fresh and waste water facilities, TV hook-up), the others being either grass or with hardstanding. An area is set aside as an adults only section. Some pitches for RV-style units have 32A electric hook-ups. A member of the Best of British group.

**Facilities**

Toilet facilities here are first rate with washbasins in cubicles, ample showers, baby room and facilities for disabled visitors (all due to be refurbished in 2011). Laundry facilities. Shop selling camping accessories and basic provisions. Some of the pitches are quite a distance from the facilities. Motorcaravan service point. Up to two dogs per pitch. Off site: Supermarket and pub within walking distance. Golf, riding and fishing nearby.

Open: All year.

**Directions**

From junction of A5 and A458, west of Shrewsbury, follow signs for Oxon 'park and ride'. Park is signed just 0.5 miles from junction. O.S.GR: SJ457134. GPS: 52.71540, -2.804917

**Charges guide**

| | |
|---|---|
| Per person | £ 6.30 - £ 6.70 |
| child (5-15 yrs) | £ 2.20 |
| standard grass pitch | £ 9.00 - £ 10.90 |

---

## Shrewsbury
### Beaconsfield Farm Caravan Park

Battlefield, Shrewsbury SY4 4AA (Shropshire) T: 01939 210370. E: mail@beaconsfield-farm.co.uk
alanrogers.com/UK4410

Just north of the historic market town, a drive of half a mile through open fields leads to this purpose-designed park for adults only (21 years). It is neatly laid out in a rural situation, with a well stocked trout fishing lake and a small coarse pool forming the main feature. The ground has been levelled and grassed to provide 80 well-spaced pitches, all have 10A electricity connections, of which 50 are 'super' hardstanding pitches. Two further areas accommodate 49 caravan holiday homes. The park is well lit with a circular tarmac access road, beyond a security barrier. A member of the Best of British Group.

**Facilities**

Heated toilet facilities (£2.50 key deposit) are of excellent quality, with roomy, pre-set showers and hairdryers. Excellent unit for disabled visitors. Laundry facilities. Motorcaravan services. Restaurant. Indoor heated swimming pool with daily open sessions (£3 per person, incl. steam room) and to hire privately at other times. Small library. WiFi. Only two dogs per unit are accepted. Dog exercise area off site. An adult only park. Car hire available. Luxury lodges and static caravans for hire. Off site: Bicycle hire and golf 2 miles. Riding 7 miles.

Open: All year.

**Directions**

Site is north of Shrewsbury off the A49 Whitchurch road. In the village of Hadnall, turn right opposite the New Inn at camping sign towards Astley and park entrance is 400 m. on right, Continue down 800 m. narrow access road with passing places. O.S.GR: SJ525195. GPS: 52.770917, -2.704817

**Charges guide**

| | |
|---|---|
| Per unit incl. 2 persons | £ 18.00 - £ 22.00 |
| extra adult | £ 4.00 |

Last arrivals 19.00 (20.00 Fridays).

---

## Skegness
### Skegness Sands Touring Site

Winthorpe Avenue, Skegness PE25 1QZ (Lincolnshire) T: 01754 761484. E: info@skegness-sands.com
alanrogers.com/UK3730

This very well organised touring site is part of a much larger caravan holiday home park, but has its own entrance. It is a modern, well appointed site adjacent to the promenade and beach. There are 85 pitches, all level and with electricity (16A); 45 are grass and 37 have gravel hardstandings, 4 of which are fully serviced. Site lighting is good throughout and there are regular security patrols. The gate to the promenade is kept locked at all times, campers getting a key. The site is a Caravan Club Affiliated Site, members and non-members are all made welcome.

**Facilities**

The good quality, heated toilet block includes washbasins in curtained cubicles plus three family shower rooms with WC and washbasin and a well equipped room for disabled visitors. Laundry room. Gas supplies. Hairdressing salon. Indoor heated swimming pool (spring B.H-30 Sept; charged). Small modern playground. Off site: Well stocked shop/post office 500 m. Bus service to Skegness and Ingoldmells 500 m. Fishing 1 mile. Golf 2 miles. Bicycle hire 2.5 miles.

Open: All year.

**Directions**

Site is off the A52 Boston - Skegness - Mablethorpe road, 1.75 miles north of Skegness town centre. Turn east opposite 'Garden City' pub with Winthorpe Avenue and site entrance is on the left at far end of road. New arrivals please contact site if unable to arrive before 17.00. O.S.GR: TF570640. GPS: 53.1668, 0.3495

**Charges guide**

| | |
|---|---|
| Per person | £ 4.60 - £ 6.35 |
| pitch | £ 4.80 - £ 15.10 |

---

For latest campsite news visit
**alanrogers.com**

## Sleaford

### Low Farm Touring & Camping Park

Spring Lane, Folkingham, Sleaford NG34 0SJ (Lincolnshire) T: 01529 497322. E: lowfarmpark@sky.com

alanrogers.com/UK3770

This quiet secluded park is a lovely spot either just to relax or to tour the Lincolnshire countryside. Jane and Nigel Stevens continue to work hard to make this site a pleasant place to stay and have a well laid out park offering good quality facilities which are very clean and tidy. The site offers 36 touring pitches with electricity hook-ups (10A) and a field for tents and small rallies. Some hardstandings are available. The site is on the edge of the village of Folkingham with a pub (serving food) and a couple of small shops. There are some pleasant walks around the village which is set in attractive Lincolnshire countryside. Larger shops and places of interest are in and around Bourne (9 miles), Sleaford (10 miles), Grantham (14 miles), Lincoln and Peterborough (both 26 miles).

**Facilities**

Central, well maintained toilet block with controllable free showers and open style washbasins. Washing machine. Reception is at the owners' house but nearby is a tourist information room with toilets. Large field where children can play (also sometimes used by tenters).
Off site: Fishing 2 miles. Golf 6 miles. Riding 7 miles.

Open: Easter - 30 September.

**Directions**

Folkingham is 26 miles south of Lincoln on the A15 to Peterborough, 2 miles south of the roundabout junction with the A52 (Nottingham, Grantham - Boston). Park is on southern edge of village; at foot of hill at campsite sign, turn west and site is at end of lane. O.S.GR: TF070333. GPS: 52.88685, -0.411167

**Charges guide**

| | |
|---|---|
| Per unit incl. 2 persons and electricity | £ 12.00 - £ 16.00 |
| extra person | £ 3.00 |
| child | £ 1.50 |

No credit cards.

---

## Slimbridge

### Tudor Caravan & Camping Park

Shepherds Patch, Slimbridge GL2 7BP (Gloucestershire) T: 01453 890483. E: info@tudorcaravanpark.co.uk

alanrogers.com/UK4170

This attractive, peaceful campsite is adjacent to the Gloucester - Sharpness Canal. Located behind the Tudor Arms public house, a gate clearly identifies the entrance and reception is up a short path on the left. There are many trees and hedges, particularly surrounding the site, so the canal is not visible. Attractively laid out on two separate fields, there are 75 pitches, all with electric hook-ups (16A), and 35 with hardstanding. The old orchard is for long stay or adult only units, with gravel hardstandings, and the more open grassy meadow for family touring units. There is also a rally field beyond the meadow. The adjacent pub has a restaurant and bar (2009 CAMRA award winner) and just across the road, beside the canal, is a café and shop where boats and bicycles can be hired. This is a delightful, peaceful park with plenty to offer: walking, fishing and boating, not to mention ornithology as the Wildfowl and Wetlands Centre founded by Sir Peter Scott at Slimbridge is only 800 yards away.

**Facilities**

The toilet building (can be heated in winter) is located to one side of the orchard and provides all the usual facilities including pushbutton hot showers. A second, high quality shower block with underfloor heating provides large shower cubicles, private washing cubicles, baby changing room and facilities for disabled visitors. Laundry. Gas available. Some site lighting but a torch would be useful. Gate locked 22.30-07.00. Off site: Meals at the Tudor Arms pub. Shop and cafe in boatyard opposite the site (Easter-Sept), also serves breakfasts. Fishing adjacent. Towpath walks. Berkeley Castle, Frampton and Stroud.

Open: All year.

**Directions**

From A38 by the junction with A4135 (Dursley), turn west, signed WWT Wetlands Centre Slimbridge. Continue for 1.5 miles turning left into car park of the Tudor Arms. Site entrance is at rear of car park. O.S.GR: SO728042. GPS: 51.735533, -2.395817

**Charges guide**

| | |
|---|---|
| Per unit incl. 2 persons and electricity | £ 16.50 - £ 19.50 |
| extra person | £ 2.00 |
| child (under 12 yrs) | £ 1.00 |

No credit cards.

## Spalding

### Foreman's Bridge Caravan Park

Sutton Saint James, Spalding PE12 0HU (Lincolnshire) T: 01945 440346. E: foremansbridge@btconnect.com
alanrogers.com/UK3750

Foreman's Bridge is a compact park occupying a large, level and grassy meadow surrounded by trees and high hedges which give it a very secluded feel. The park has 42 level pitches, of which 24 are now occupied by caravan holiday homes (7 for rent). The remainder are touring pitches, all with electricity (16A) and gravel hardstanding. Up to half of these are occupied on a seasonal basis. The park could be a useful base from which to explore the Fens and to visit Spalding, famous for its annual flower festival held at the beginning of May. At times there can be noise from military aircraft.

#### Facilities

The modern, brick-built toilet unit is spacious and kept clean, providing really large individual shower rooms with seats and washbasins (showers on payment). Laundry room. Gas. Fishing possible in the river running past the entrance. Bicycle hire. Two cottages to rent. Winter caravan storage. Off site: Small shop in village 1 mile. Golf 3 miles. Riding 8 miles. Coast 12 miles (The Wash); nearest beach 32 miles.

Open: 1 March - 15 January.

#### Directions

Sutton St James is 26 miles northeast of Peterborough and 17 miles west of Kings Lynn. From A17 Spalding - Kings Lynn road turn south on B1390 at Long Sutton towards Sutton St James for about 2 miles. Site entrance is on the left immediately after the bridge. O.S.GR: TF410198. GPS: 52.75785, 0.088

#### Charges guide

| | |
|---|---|
| Per unit incl. 2 persons and electricity | £ 14.00 |
| extra person | £ 3.00 |
| child | £ 2.00 |
| dog | £ 1.00 |

No credit cards.

## Stamford

### Tallington Lakes Camping & Caravanning

Barholm Road, Tallington, Stamford PE9 4RJ (Lincolnshire) T: 01778 347000. E: info@tallington.com
alanrogers.com/UK3760

This well maintained and attractive 160-acre site surrounds over 200 acres of clean, spring fed water that provides many watersport activities including water-skiing, jet-skiing, sailing, windsurfing, canoeing, pedalos and angling; along with a Pro Shop for water sports. In addition there is a 120 m. high, floodlit dry ski slope and a 15 m. tower for climbing and abseiling. Of the 338 pitches, 88 are in a separate area for touring and 46 have 10A electricity. They are level, in groups, separated by some hedging and are either on grass or hard standing. Some mature trees give a little shade. The two well appointed toilet blocks at each end of the site may be a considerable distance from some of the pitches. The bar/restaurant with attractive terrace overlooks the swimming pool and the lake beyond. Stamford, with its famous old coaching inns is only five miles away and Peterborough with many shops, parks and modern cathedral is only a few miles further. The surrounding area has much to offer, including the Stamford Museum, the beautiful Burghley House (known for its horse trials), Sacrewell Farm and Country Centre and the Nene Valley Railway. Lake swimming is not allowed.

#### Facilities

The heated sanitary unit has facilities for babies, small children and campers with disabilities. Additional WCs and showers (also used by the water skiers). Laundry and dishwashing facilities. Motorcaravan service point. Bar and restaurant. Swimming and paddling pools (charged). Climbing wall. Go-karting. Watersports. Fishing. Dry-ski slope, snowboard centre and tennis. Small, well fenced, adventure style playground. Off site: Bus stop 1 mile. Golf, riding and bicycle hire 5 miles. Stamford 5 miles. Peterborough 11 miles. Stamford Museum, Burghley House, Sacrewell Farm and Country Centre and the Nene Valley Railway.

Open: All year.

#### Directions

From A16, midway between Stamford and Market Deeping, just east of the railway crossing at Tallington, turn north into Barholm Road. Site entrance is on the right in 0.3 miles (site is signed). O.S.GR: TF099094. GPS: 52.67007, -0.37940

#### Charges guide

| | |
|---|---|
| Per unit incl. 2 persons and electricity | £ 20.00 - £ 30.00 |
| extra person | £ 5.00 |
| dog (max. 2 per unit) | £ 5.00 |

For latest campsite news visit
**alanrogers.com**

## Stoke-on-Trent

### The Star Caravan Park

Cotton, Alton Towers, Stoke-on-Trent ST10 3DW (Staffordshire) T: 01538 702219
alanrogers.com/UK3983

Just one mile from the main gate at Alton Towers, this is a family owned and orientated site and single sex groups of more than three people are not admitted; the emphasis here is the safety and comfort of families. The beautifully landscaped and maintained site offers grass pitches to accommodate any size and a number of all-weather hardstandings are available. Most pitches are equipped with electricity (10A) and some mobile homes are available for rent. The toilet blocks are immaculate and include an outstandingly equipped family room. A number of special amenities are available for disabled visitors. Alton Towers is undeniably the main attraction in the area, but the surrounding Staffordshire Moorlands are of great beauty and an efficient reception ensures that information for other attractions can be found. The site's owners are happy to recommend a number of pubs and restaurants in the vicinity which, they feel, offer particular quality and value. Dovedale is deservedly popular, a dramatic limestone ravine with much loved stepping stones across the tranquil river Dove. This is excellent walking country with numerous marked routes available. Tittesworth, Carsington and Rudyard Reservoirs are within easy reach offering boating opportunities.

#### Facilities

Modern, well-equipped and maintained, heated sanitary units with facilities for disabled visitors (reserved parking outside) and a parent and baby room. Motorcaravan services. Special places available for larger motorcaravans. Basic provisions available at reception. Laundry with industrial size washing machines and dryers. Good play area safety checked with advice from ROSPA. Large area for ball games. Dog walking area. WiFi (charged). Tourist information. Mobile homes for rent. Rally field available. Off site: Alton Towers nearby. Bicycle hire, golf 3 miles. Riding, fishing 4 miles. Walking and cycle tracks. Boat launching 18 miles. Staffordshire Moorlands. Stoke-on-Trent and Derby (both about 45 minutes drive).

Open: 27 March - 7 November.

#### Directions

Approaching from the east (Ashbourne) on A52, continue as far as Cauldron Low and then take the southbound B5417 and follow signs to the site (and Alton Towers). O.S.GR: SK064455. GPS: 53.00905, -1.901726

#### Charges guide

| | |
|---|---|
| Per unit incl. 2 persons and electricity | £ 12.00 - £ 30.00 |
| extra person | £ 6.00 |
| child (6-15 yrs) | free - £ 2.00 |
| dog | free - £ 2.00 |

With Alton Towers so near - only just over 1 mile away from the main gate, we are the number one choice for visitors who are looking for a great family-friendly, camping and caravan park experience that offers good value and clean facilities. We are close to Dovedale, the Peak District, Ashbourne, Derbyshire, Leek, Staffordshire, Cheadle and Uttoxeter.

The Star Caravan & Camping Park
Star Road, Cotton, Nr Alton Towers,
Stoke-on-Trent, Staffordshire,
ST10 3DW

01538 702219
(8.00 am - 8.00 pm)
www.starcaravanpark.co.uk

## Stourport-on-Severn

### Lickhill Manor Caravan Park

Lower Lickhill Road, Stourport-on-Severn DY13 8RL (Worcestershire) T: 01299 871041
E: excellent@lickhillmanor.co.uk alanrogers.com/UK4210

Lickhill Manor is a well managed touring and holiday site within easy walking distance of the town centre, accessed by a footpath along the River Severn. Opportunities exist for fishing and boating. The site is open for tourers all year and there are 120 touring pitches all with hook-ups (10A) of which seven are super pitches. A large 14-acre rally field with 68 hook ups is available for tourers. An attractive site with 124 holiday homes that are well screened from the touring areas and therefore not visually intrusive. There are two excellent play areas for children and a dog exercise field within the park. The site is well laid out, populated with native trees and shrubs and wildlife ponds.

#### Facilities

An additional sanitary building serves the touring pitches and complements the older unit at the far end of the park. This heated building provides good, modern facilities including a well equipped suite for disabled guests which doubles as a family washroom with facilities for baby changing. Drive over motorcaravan service point. Recycling bins. Gas supplies. Fishing permits are available from site shop. Off site: Stourport shops and pub 10 minutes walk. Riding 1 mile. Bicycle hire 3 miles. Golf 5 miles.

Open: All year.

#### Directions

From the A451 in Stourport take B4195 northwest towards Bewdley. After 1 mile turn left at crossroads (traffic lights), into Lickhill Road North where site is signed. O.S.GR: SO790730. GPS: 52.343404, -2.299088

#### Charges guide

| | |
|---|---|
| Per unit incl. 4 persons and electricity | £ 16.00 - £ 22.00 |
| 2 person tent | £ 12.00 |
| extra person over 2 yrs | £ 2.00 |

Weekly rates available.
Bank Holidays minimum 3 nights stay.

## Stratford-upon-Avon
### Riverside Caravan Park
Tiddington Road, Tiddington, Stratford-upon-Avon CV37 7AB (Warwickshire) T: 01789 292312
E: info@stratfordcaravans.co.uk  alanrogers.com/UK4080

On the bank of the River Avon, this spacious site has about 250 pitches in total, and about 100 privately owned mobile homes. The 125 touring pitches (no tents) are on level grass, all with electric hook-ups (16A). There is a small shop and cafe on site, which serves breakfasts and takeaways in addition to stocking a good selection of basic supplies. A clubhouse that incorporates a bar, playground, games room and TV room is on the adjacent Rayford Park which is under the same management. There is a possible flood risk during periods of inclement weather. A river taxi runs to Stratford.

**Facilities**

The main toilet unit has been re-fitted to modern standards and is bright and comfortable with central heating. Spacious pre-set showers, some washbasins in cubicles, with a child-size toilet and shower in the ladies. Facilities for disabled guests. Utility room with dishwashing and laundry facilities. Slipway and fishing on-site. Courtesy river launch to Stratford. Gas supplies. No commercial vehicles are accepted.

Open: 1 April - 31 October.

**Directions**

From Stratford take B4086 towards Wellesbourne. Site entrance is on left, after one mile, just before Tiddington village (ignore entrance to Rayford Park C.P). O.S.GR: SP219559. GPS: 52.20023, -1.68213

**Charges guide**

| | |
|---|---|
| Per unit incl. 2 persons and electricity | £ 15.00 - £ 18.00 |
| extra person | £ 1.50 |
| child (4-15 yrs) | £ 1.00 |

## Sutton-on-Sea
### Cherry Tree Site
Huttoft Road, Sutton-on-Sea LN12 2RU (Lincolnshire) T: 01507 441626. E: info@cherrytreesite.co.uk
alanrogers.com/UK3650

This is a delightful, tranquil, adult only site and is a fine example of a small, good value touring park. It is a 15-minute walk from a Blue Flag beach and a short drive from some of the attractive villages of the Lincolnshire Wolds. A very warm welcome awaits from Geoff and Margaret Murray whose attention to detail is evident everywhere. The site is level, the grass is neatly trimmed and well drained, and screening is provided by lines of evergreen hedging. There are 40 good sized touring pitches, all with 10A electricity and hardstanding (no tents) and ten with water and waste water drain.

**Facilities**

The brick-built toilet block, recently extended and refurbished to a high standard, can be heated and is immaculately kept. Controllable hot showers, hairdryers. En-suite unit for disabled visitors (Radar key). Combined dishwashing and laundry room with washing machine, spin dryer and tumble dryer. Neat reception and separate tourist information cabin. Gas. Off site: Riding adjacent. Shop and pub 0.6 miles. Beach 1.5 miles. Tennis, bowls and fishing 1.5 miles. Golf 2 miles.

Open: 4 March - 29 October.

**Directions**

Sutton-on-Sea is 15 miles north of Skegness and 40 miles east of Lincoln. The site is 1.5 miles south of the town on A52 coast road, with the entrance leading off a lay-by on the east. O.S.GR: TF518828. GPS: 53.29292, 0.28439

**Charges guide**

| | |
|---|---|
| Per unit incl. 2 persons and electricity | £ 17.00 - £ 23.50 |
| extra person | £ 3.50 |
| dog | £ 0.50 |

## Symonds Yat West
### Doward Park Camp Site
Great Doward, Symonds Yat West HR9 6BP (Herefordshire) T: 01600 890438. E: enquiries@dowardpark.co.uk
alanrogers.com/UK4360

The site, which was created around 1997 in a disused quarry, has matured into a very pleasant, peaceful little site, partially terraced, and in a sheltered location. The access roads and the physical proportions of the site make it suitable only for tents, trailer tents and campervans. This site is popular with couples, nature lovers, walkers and those with young families, but has nothing to offer teenagers. There is a children's play area in Bluebell Wood (unsupervised) at the top of the site with a rope swing and a climbing structure. Of the 27 pitches for touring (11 with 16A electricity), three are hardstanding for motorcaravans up to 23 feet in length, the remainder are on grass.

**Facilities**

A neat central building provides the usual facilities including refurbished hot showers. No designated area for disabled visitors, but toilet facilities have wide access. Dishwashing sinks and a freezer for ice packs. Small shop selling basic supplies. Service washing and drying facilities available. Torches are advisable. Off site: Variety of inns at both Symonds Yat West and East all offering meals. Fishing 1 mile. Shops and services in Monmouth 4 miles. Golf 4 miles. Bicycle hire 10 miles.

Open: 15 March - 31 October.

**Directions**

From A40 between Ross-on-Wye and Monmouth, turn for Symonds Yat West, and follow signs for Doward Park and Biblins. Turn into narrow lane for about 1 mile and site is on right, on sharp left hand bend. O.S.GR: SO548157. GPS: 51.838517, -2.657

**Charges guide**

| | |
|---|---|
| Per unit incl. 2 persons and electricity | £ 15.75 - £ 19.75 |
| extra person | £ 2.50 |

## Tattershall
### Tattershall Lakes Country Park

57 Sleaford Road, Tattershall LN4 4JG (Lincolnshire) T: 01526 348800. E: info@tattershall-lakes.com
alanrogers.com/UK3685

This extensive park with seven lakes of varying sizes is well kept, offers great opportunities for enthusiasts of watersports and fishing and is only a few hundred yards from the pleasant village of Tattershall. The touring fields are flat and rather featureless but with views across the main lake. There are 269 pitches, numbered but with no hedges or markings to separate them; 180 have electrical connections (16A) and 50 also have an individual tap and drainage, plus hardstanding. Fifty lodges and static caravans of varying styles are available for rent and a further 300 are privately owned. The lakeside clubhouse includes a coffee shop serving a variety of meals and snacks, a comfortable bar downstairs where the evening discos and other entertainment take place and, upstairs, another bar overlooking the lake. This houses electronic games, darts and TV, together with a spacious and comfortable lounge with widescreen satellite TV and a games room equipped with a full-size snooker table and two pool tables. A large pub and eatery is close to the park entrance and the nearby village has a number of small shops and pubs. RAF Coningsby is close by (so some daytime aircraft noise is inevitable).

### Facilities

Toilet block with preset showers and open-style washbasins will be under considerable pressure at busy times. En-suite unit for disabled visitors. Washing machines and dryers. A Portacabin provides eight very basic en-suite units (shower, toilet, washbasin), though access is not easy. Small, well-stocked shop, Coffee shop serving meals, snacks and takeaways. Two bars. TV and games rooms. Golf. Archery. Bicycle and pedalo hire. Fitness suite and indoor pool planned for 2011. Off site: Tattershall Castle 800 yards. Shops, pubs, restaurants 1 mile.

Open: 1 April - 31 October.

### Directions

Tattershall is 22 miles southeast of Lincoln on the A153 Sleaford/Horncastle road, 14 miles northeast of Sleaford. Park is on the western edge of the village between the River Witham and Tattershall Castle. GPS: 53.095794, -0.196799

### Charges guide

| | |
|---|---|
| Per unit incl. 6 persons and electricity | £ 5.00 - £ 23.00 |

## Tattershall
### Willow Holt Camping & Caravan Park

Lodge Road, Tattershall LN4 4JS (Lincolnshire) T: 01526 343111. E: enquiries@willowholt.co.uk
alanrogers.com/UK3675

Willow Holt is a pleasant park with plenty of potential. It will appeal, in particular, to fishing enthusiasts and to those who would like a quiet location from which to explore this interesting corner of Lincolnshire with its RAF associations. It covers some 25 acres of woodland and former gravel pits, with the camping areas on flat land alongside the large lake. There are 60 pitches occupied on a seasonal basis but a further 47 are available for touring units. All have 10A electricity and water taps close by. An area without electricity is available for tents.

### Facilities

The toilet block is small and must be under considerable pressure at busy times. Showers are preset and hot water is free to the open style basins. Motorcaravan service point. Laundry room with washing machines, dryers and iron/ironing board. No facilities for disabled visitors or for babies and young children. Free fishing (permit required). Off site: Golf and riding 2.5 miles. Tattershall 1.5 miles.

Open: 15 March - 31 October.

### Directions

Site is 1.5 miles north of town; from Market Place follow brown campsite sign along Lodge Road. Entrance is on left before junction with B1192 to Woodhall Spa. O.S.GR: TF201592. GPS: 53.116664, -0.206652

### Charges guide

| | |
|---|---|
| Per unit incl. 2 persons | £ 10.00 - £ 16.00 |
| extra person | £ 2.00 |

For latest campsite news visit
alanrogers.com

## Tewkesbury

### Croft Farm Water & Leisure Park

Bredon's Hardwick, Tewkesbury GL20 7EE (Gloucestershire) T: 01684 772321
E: enquiries@croftfarmleisure.co.uk  alanrogers.com/UK4150

Croft Farm is an AALA licensed Watersports Centre with Royal Yachting Association approved tuition available for windsurfing, sailing, kayaking and canoeing. The lakeside campsite has around 96 level pitches, with electric hook-ups (10A), but there are many seasonal units, leaving around 36 pitches for touriing, plus some tent pitches. There are 36 gravel hardstandings with very little shade or shelter. 'Gym and Tonic' is a fully equipped gymnasium with qualified instructors, sunbed and sauna. Sports massage, aromatherapy and beauty treatments are available by appointment. Activity holidays for families and groups are organised. Campers can use their own non-powered boats on the lake with reduced launching fees and there is river fishing. There are plans to include a launch ramp onto the river. Climb Bredon Hill (2 miles) for a panoramic view of the Severn and Avon Valleys. Places of interest include Bredon Barn, pottery and church, and the historic town of Tewkesbury with its Abbey, theatre and indoor swimming pool.

#### Facilities

A recently modernised building has excellent facilities with spacious hot showers, plus some dishwashing sinks. A heated unit in the main building is always open and best for cooler months; this provides further WCs, washbasins and showers, laundry and facilities for disabled visitors. Gas. Cafe/bar (Fri-Sun low season, daily at other times). Takeaway. Gym. Playground. River fishing. Barrier and toilet block key (£5 deposit). Fenced dog exercise area. WiFi in the clubhouse (free to visitors spending £5 or over). Off site: Pub opposite. Tewkesbury 1.5 miles. Golf 3 miles. Riding 8 miles.

Open: 1 March - 31 December.

#### Directions

Bredon's Hardwick is midway between Tewkesbury and Bredon on B4080. Site entrance opposite 'Cross Keys Inn'. From M5 exit 9 take A438 (Tewkesbury), at first lights turn right into Shannon Way. Turn right at next lights, into Northway Lane, cross motorway bridge. Turn left into housing estate and cross second bridge. At T-junction turn right on B4080, site is on left. O.S.GR: SO912353. GPS: 52.015967, -2.130267

#### Charges guide

| | |
|---|---|
| Per unit incl. 2 persons, electricity and awning | £ 16.00 |
| extra person (over 3 yrs) | £ 3.50 |
| dog | £ 1.00 |

## Tewkesbury

### Winchcombe Camping & Caravanning Club Site

Brooklands Farm, Alderton, Tewkesbury GL20 8NX (Gloucestershire) T: 01242 620259
alanrogers.com/UK4140

This is a popular, quiet site in a rural location, close to the Cotswold attractions. Some pitches surround a small coarse fishing lake, with others in a recently developed area of maturing bushes and shrubs with open views over the surrounding countryside. In total there are 80 pitches, 53 with electric hook-ups (16A) and 42 with gravel hardstanding. The reception building flanks a small gravel car park and late arrivals area which is approached from a tarmac drive. A number of lodges, an extended camping area and a new toilet block have been recently added.

#### Facilities

The main, heated sanitary unit is kept very clean and tidy, to an extremely high standard by the wardens. To the rear of the site is a small, portacabin style sanitary unit (also heated). Well equipped unit for disabled visitors. Laundry facilities. Gas supplies. Large recreation room. Small outdoor play area. WiFi throughout site. Off site: Several pubs and restaurants in the area. Golf 7 miles.

Open: 12 March - 15 January.

#### Directions

From M5 exit 9, take A46 Evesham road for 3 miles to Toddington roundabout, then the B4077 towards Stow-on-the-Wold for a further 3 miles to the site entrance. Ignore signs for Alderton village. O.S.GR: SP 007324. GPS: 51.9904, -1.990683

#### Charges guide

| | |
|---|---|
| Per person | £ 7.50 - £ 10.00 |
| child (5-16 yrs) | £ 2.60 - £ 2.80 |
| non-member pitch fee incl. electricity | £ 10.50 |

Mid and low season discounts for members over the age of 55.

## Woodhall Spa

### Glen Lodge Touring Park

Glen Lodge, Edlington Moor, Woodhall Spa LN10 6UL (Lincolnshire) T: 01526 353523

alanrogers.com/UK3692

This quiet, attractive and spacious site is ideal for couples and families who enjoy the rural lifestyle, yet it is only just over a mile from the thriving village of Woodhall Spa which retains much of its old-fashioned charm. All 35 pitches have hardstanding and 10A electricity hook-ups (one or two appeared to need long leads) and are served by shingle roads with some street lighting. The grass and flowerbeds are obviously tended by someone who enjoys gardening. In fact, the whole park has a much-loved feel. Behind the pitches, on one side of the park, is an attractive lawned area with trees and shrubs, whilst on the other side is a field where ball games are permitted. Woodhall Spa has two modern supermarkets and a good range of traditional shops, as well as tearooms, restaurants and pubs. There is also a delightful, old-style cinema called the Kinema in the Woods. Places to visit in the area include the Battle of Britain Memorial Flight, Tattershall Castle, Horncastle with its antiques centre and the city of Lincoln. Skegness is only 26 miles away.

### Facilities

The modern heated toilet block (key-pad access) is kept spotlessly clean with controllable showers, vanity style washbasins and piped music. En-suite facilities for disabled visitors. Washing machine and dryer. Off site: Pub serving good food 0.5 miles. Open air pool, tennis and bowls 1 mile. Shops in village 1.5 miles. Golf and fishing 2 miles. Tattershall Castle 5 miles. Riding 6 miles. Horncastle 6 miles.

Open: 1 March - 30 November.

### Directions

Woodhall Spa is 18 miles southeast of Lincoln. From mini-roundabout in village turn northeast towards Bardney on B1190 (Stixwould Road) past Petwood Hotel. In just over 1 mile at sharp left bend, turn right. Site is 300 yards on left. O.S.GR: TF189647. GPS: 53.166233, -0.22

### Charges guide

| | |
|---|---|
| Per unit incl. 2 persons and electricity | £ 15.00 |
| extra person (over 4 yrs) | £ 3.00 |
| dog | free |

No credit cards.

## GLEN LODGE TOURING PARK

Small family run park within a mile of Woodhall Spa, set in beautiful woodland surroundings. Heated toilet/shower block and utility room with washer, dryer and phone. A great combination of peace and tranquillity and yet within easy reach of the seaside town of Skegness. Discounts available Monday to Thursday for senior citizens.

**Edlington Moor, Woodhall Spa, Lincolnshire LN10 6UL ▪ Tel/Fax No. 01526 353523**

## Woodhall Spa
### Bainland Country Park

Horncastle Road, Woodhall Spa LN10 6UX (Lincolnshire) T: 01526 352903. E: bookings@bainland.co.uk
alanrogers.com/UK3690

A family park with many amenities, Bainland has 170 spacious, level pitches in hedged bays (120 touring pitches) grouped in circles and islands and linked by curving roads. There are 51 fully serviced pitches with hardstanding, honeycombed for awning, individual water, drainage and chemical disposal, 16A electricity and TV aerial hook-ups. The remainder of the pitches are either on gravel hardstanding or level grass, all with 10A electricity. The friendly reception is housed in a pleasant Swiss-style building together with the heated indoor pool and jacuzzi, a bistro and spacious bar area. These overlook the 18-hole, par 3 golf course and outdoor bowls area. Bainland is 1.5 miles from Woodhall Spa, with its old fashioned charm and Dambusters associations, yet deep in the heart of the Lincolnshire Wolds, surrounded by mature trees and with direct access to woods for walking dogs. A member of the Best of British Group.

### Facilities

Three modern, well equipped, heated toilet blocks including a baby room, unisex en-suite shower rooms, family bathroom, fully equipped unit for disabled visitors. Laundry room. Motorcaravan service points. Licensed shop (Feb-Dec). Bistro and bar (all year). Indoor pool (under 16s must be accompanied by an adult). Adventure playground. Trampolines. Crazy golf. Croquet. Games room. Soft play area. Floodlit tennis dome with 3-4 courts including badminton (the dome comes off in the summer). Par 3, 18 hole golf. Bowls. Leisure activities, including the pool, are individually booked and paid for at reception. Some entertainment in high season. WiFi (free). Winter caravan storage. Off site: Fishing and boat launching 3 miles. Sailing 5 miles. Tattershall Castle 5 miles. Riding and bicycle hire 6 miles.

Open: All year (in winter, 'super' pitches only).

### Directions

Woodhall Spa is 18 miles southeast of Lincoln. Entrance to park is off B1191 Horncastle road 1.5 miles northeast of the village centre and is clearly signed. O.S.GR: TF214637.
GPS: 53.158617, -0.183517

### Charges guide

| | |
|---|---|
| Per unit incl. 2 persons and electricity | £ 15.00 - £ 32.00 |
| serviced pitch, plus | £ 1.00 - £ 7.00 |
| extra person | £ 2.00 - £ 5.00 |
| child (5-12 yrs) | £ 2.00 - £ 3.00 |

Special rate for firework display (min. 2 nights, 4/5 Nov).
Discounts for senior citizens.

## Worksop
### Riverside Caravan Park

Central Avenue, Worksop S80 1ER (Nottinghamshire) T: 01909 474118
alanrogers.com/UK3920

A town centre touring park, adjacent to the Worksop cricket ground, this excellent site is attractive and surprisingly peaceful. Riverside is within easy walking distance of the town centre pedestrian precinct and shops, and the Chesterfield Canal runs close to its northern side offering delightful towpath walks or fishing (children would need to be watched). For those who cannot resist the thwack of leather on willow, this site is ideal. Of the 60 marked level pitches, 10 are seasonal and 43 are for touring, mainly on gravel hardstanding, 7 are on grass and some are separated by trees and low rails, and all have electric hook-ups (10A). There is good site lighting. Attractions in the area include Creswell Crags, Clumber Park, the Dukeries Cycle Trail, Thoresby Park and Gallery, Mr Straw's House, Rufford Mill Craft Centre and Country Park and Meadowhall Shopping Centre in Sheffield.

### Facilities

The single sanitary unit near reception can be heated and has all the usual facilities, although showers are on payment (20p). No laundry. Motorcaravan service point. Off site: Fishing 0.5 miles. Several golf courses 1 mile. Bicycle hire 4 miles. Squash and flat or crown green bowling nearby. Campers are made very welcome at the cricket ground clubhouse. One of Worksop's most interesting buildings, the medieval Priory Gatehouse, is open free of charge. Market days are Wednesday, Friday and Saturday.

Open: All year.

### Directions

Worksop is 7 miles west of the M1 at junction 30 and 4 miles east of the A1. Easiest approach is from A57/A60 roundabout west of the town – third roundabout from the A1. Turn east (at Little Chef) on B6024 towards town centre. Site is well signed. Turn left into Cricket Ground taking care at sharp left turn after bridge. Site entrance is to the left of clubhouse. O.S.GR: SK580790. GPS: 53.30600, -1.12867

### Charges guide

| | |
|---|---|
| Per unit incl. 2 persons, awning and electricity | £ 16.00 - £ 18.00 |

A beautiful and varied region of rolling hills and undulating moor Yorkshire has an histe past with a wealth of n attractions. Its landscape has inspired famous authors and been the setting for some of Britain's best-loved television programmes.

## THE REGION IS DIVIDED INTO NORTH, SOUTH, EAST AND WEST YORKSHIRE

The major attractions of this region are the parks: the Yorkshire Dales National Park is comprised of 680 square miles of unspoilt countryside with high fells, winding rivers, ancient castles and outstanding views of the surrounding landscapes; the Peak District is noted for its rocky peaks and limestone plateau; while the North York Moors National Park has miles of open, heather covered moorland and pretty villages in its valleys. These areas are ideal places for walking, cycling, horse riding and climbing. Or if you prefer to relax and take in the scenery, the North Yorkshire Moors Railway, starting at Pickering, is one of the many steam railways in the region. On the coast, traditional family resorts like Scarborough, Bridlington and Cleethorpes offer the holidaymaker a wide range of activities. Also by the sea is Kingston Upon Hull, a maritime city with powerful links to Britain's proud seafaring tradition, and the picturesque fishing port of Whitby, once home to Captain James Cook. Elsewhere in the region are the vibrant cities of York, with its wealth of ancient sites including the Minster, Leeds and Sheffield plus the busy market town of Doncaster.

### Places of interest

*North:* Harrogate; Wensleydale Creamery in Hawes; Jorvik Viking Centre in York; Lightwater Valley Theme Park, near Ripon; Castle Howard near York: Flamingo Land Theme Park and Zoo in Malton; Skipton Castle.

*South:* Hatfield Waterpark near Doncaster; Tropical Butterfly House and Wildlife Centre in Anston; Sheffield Ski Village, Europe's biggest artificial ski resort; Magna science adventure centre in Rotherham.

*East:* Bempton Cliffs RSPB Nature Reserve near Bridlington, England's largest seabird colony; market town of Beverly; Captain Cook Museum in Whitby; Scarborough Millennium.

*West:* Bolling Hall in Bradford; Royal Armouries Museum in Leeds; 'Brontë Country' and village of Haworth; Pontefract.

### Did you know?

The comedy series Last of the Summer Wine is filmed in the Pennine town of Holmfirth and its surrounding countryside.

York is the oldest city in Yorkshire, founded in AD71. The Minster is the largest Gothic Cathedral in Northern Europe.

Pontefract has been growing liquorice since medieval times, it is believed that Pontefract cakes were made by the monks for medicinal purposes.

The Tan Hill Inn is the highest pub in England at 528 metres above sea level.

Dick Turpin, the notorious 17th century highwayman, lived in Pontefract.

Rudston is said to be the oldest inhabited village in England, named after the Rood Stone, a mysterious 4000 year old monolith.

# Bridlington

## South Cliff Caravan Park

Wilsthorpe, Bridlington YO15 3QN (East Yorkshire) T: 01262 671051. E: southcliff@eastriding.gov.uk
alanrogers.com/UK4498

This traditional style caravan park is part of a large complex owned and operated by the East Riding of Yorkshire Council. There are 184 touring pitches, each with an electricity post (16A); 20 for tents, the remainder with hardstanding surrounded by grass or, in a few cases, extended to the road. Many of them lie back from the road, so access for larger units can be tricky when the site is full. Direct access to the seafront is through the vast caravan holiday home park and from there a 'land train' runs a mile along the shore to Bridlington. Here you can visit the historic old town, the harbour with its heritage museum, the Spa Theatre and Ballroom, Sewerby Hall and Gardens, and Leisure World. Further afield are Beverley with its Minster and racecourse, Flamborough Head, Spurn Point, Scarborough and even Pickering and the North York Moors.

### Facilities

Two toilet blocks (one traditional, one new) provide push button showers, open washbasins (a few in cubicles for ladies). Excellent en-suite units for disabled visitors. Three bathrooms with washbasins and baby changing facilities. No motorcaravan service point. Franchised facilities: launderette (washing machines and dryers). Well stocked shop (1/3-8/10); fish and chip shop (busy at times). Leisure complex (bar, restaurant, clubroom, games room) offering entertainment evenings in high season and monthly themed weekends (outside August). Dogs are not accepted (except assistance dogs). Off site: Golf 0.5 m. Beach (by car), riding, sailing, boat launching and bicycle hire 1 mile. Shops, pubs and restaurants within 2 miles.

Open: 1 March - 30 November.

### Directions

Bridlington is 40 miles east of York via the A166/A614. From M62 exit 37, take A614 to Bridlington. Before Carnaby turn east to join the A165 to Bridlington South. From the Humber Bridge take A164 to Beverley, then A165 to Bridlington. Site is signed from A165 at Wilsthorpe.
O.S.GR: TA166648. GPS: 54.0641, -0.2132

### Charges guide

| | |
|---|---|
| Per unit incl. up to 5 persons | £ 18.00 - £ 25.00 |

Discounts in low season and mid seasons.

For latest campsite news visit
**alanrogers.com**

# Driffield

## Thorpe Hall Caravan & Camping Site

Rudston, Driffield YO25 4JE (East Yorkshire) T: 01262 420393. E: caravansite@thorpehall.co.uk

alanrogers.com/UK4510

Just outside the village of Rudston, in the grounds of Thorpe Hall, this pleasant small touring park is 4.5 miles from the sea at Bridlington. Enthusiastically managed by Jayne Chatterton, it is set on flat grass, largely enclosed by the old kitchen garden wall. The 90 pitches are numbered and well spaced with 78 electrical hook-ups (16A) and TV connections. A separate area takes tents and there are no caravan holiday homes. There is always a chance of finding space, though it is best to book for bank holidays and peak weeks. Information sheets on a range of local walks are provided and Sir Ian Macdonald takes visitors on walks around the estate.

### Facilities

The solid, central toilet block has been completely refurbished and can be heated. Some washbasins are in cabins. Refurbished bathroom for disabled visitors and families with young children (deposit for key). Launderette. Large recycling area. Small shop with gas, essentials and local produce. Games room with pool table, table football and table tennis. TV room. Coarse fishing lake. WiFi. Off site: Bicycle hire, golf and boat launching at Bridlington 4.5 miles. Riding 2 miles. Footpath to the village.

Open: 1 March - 31 October.

### Directions

Site is by the B1253 road, 4.5 miles from Bridlington, on east side of Rudston. O.S.GR: TA105676. GPS: 54.093817, -0.3125

### Charges guide

| | |
|---|---|
| Per unit incl. 2 adults, 3 children and electricity | £ 15.00 - £ 29.00 |
| tent pitch incl. 2 persons | £ 11.00 - £ 25.00 |

Less 25% on booked stays of 7 days or more. Other discounts available.

# Harrogate

## Rudding Holiday Park

Follifoot, Harrogate HG3 1JH (North Yorkshire) T: 01423 870439. E: holiday-park@ruddingpark.com

alanrogers.com/UK4710

The extensive part wooded, part open grounds of Rudding Park are very attractive, peaceful and well laid out. One camping area is sloping but terraces provide level pitches in the very sheltered old walled garden. All 141 touring pitches have electricity (10/16A) and 49 'super pitches' are fully serviced. Further pitches are let on a seasonal basis and a separate area contains 96 owner-occupied caravan holiday homes and chalets. On the outer edge of the park is 'The Deer House', a family pub serving bar meals, open daily during bank holidays and school holidays, otherwise at weekends.

### Facilities

Two toilet blocks (heated when necessary and may be under pressure at peak times), some washbasins in cabins, baby room and bathroom. Laundry rooms. Facilities for disabled visitors. Motorcaravan service point. Shop (1/3-4/11, sometimes limited hours). Gas. Restaurant and bar. Heated outdoor swimming and paddling pools (25/5-30/8), supervised (extra charge). Adventure playground. Football pitch. Games room. Golf. Off site: Riding 1 mile. Fishing 2 miles.

Open: 1 March - 31 January.

### Directions

Park is 3 miles southeast of Harrogate, clearly signed north of the A658 and west of the A661. O.S.GR: SE333528. GPS: 53.97307, -1.49720

### Charges guide

| | |
|---|---|
| Per unit incl. 4 persons and electricity | £ 17.50 - £ 42.00 |
| extra person | £ 5.00 - £ 10.00 |
| child (5-16 yrs) | £ 3.00 - £ 7.00 |
| dog | £ 2.50 |

# Harrogate

## Ripley Caravan Park

Ripley, Harrogate HG3 3AU (North Yorkshire) T: 01423 770050. E: ripleycaravanpark@talk21.com

alanrogers.com/UK4630

Peter and Valerie House are the friendly, resident owners of Ripley Park, an 18 acre grass caravan park with an indoor heated pool. It accommodates 100 touring units and 40 caravan holiday homes on fairly level grass which undulates in parts. Connected by a circular gravel road, some pitches are marked, others carefully spaced (allowing the grass to recover). There are 130 electricity connections (10A) and 20 hardstandings (more have been added). The owners have planted 2,000 trees and these are developing well. A pond with ducks provides an attractive feature.

### Facilities

The central, attractively designed toilet block can be heated and provides smart facilities including washbasins in curtained cubicles, a baby bath and a separate unit with a shower for disabled visitors. Small laundry. Motorcaravan service point. Shop with gas. Games room with TV. Nursery playroom. Adventure play equipment. Heated indoor pool (£1 per person) and sauna. Winter caravan storage. Off site: Fishing, riding and golf 3 miles.

Open: Easter - 31 October.

### Directions

About 4 miles north of Harrogate, park access is 150 yds. down the B6165 Knaresborough road from its roundabout junction with the A61. O.S.GR: SE291601. GPS: 54.0369, -1.558833

### Charges guide

| | |
|---|---|
| Per unit incl. 2 persons and electricity | £ 14.00 - £ 16.50 |
| extra person | £ 4.00 - £ 5.00 |

For latest campsite news visit
## alanrogers.com

## Helmsley

### Foxholme Touring Caravan & Camping Park

Harome, Helmsley YO62 5JG (North Yorkshire) T: 01439 771904

**alanrogers.com/UK4580**

Foxholme is now an adult only park. With 60 pitches, many are individual ones in clearings in the coniferous plantation where the trees give shade and privacy (manoeuvring may be difficult on some of the pitches). Recent work has reduced the tree cover and a seven acre field provides further, more open grass pitches. All the pitches have electricity (6A, a few need long leads) and six have hardstanding. Some picnic tables are provided. There are 30 pitches for touring units, the remainder being taken by seasonal units. The site is managed by a warden, with limited reception opening times. Very basic provisions are kept. The park is set in quiet countryside and would be a good base for touring, being within striking distance of the moors, the coast and York. There are no on site activities. There is lighting, but a torch would be useful.

**Facilities**

The toilet block is an older style building and is clean but basic. Laundry facilities and a washing up area. Two further small blocks provide WCs only in other parts of the park. Motorcaravan service point. Caravan storage. Off site: The nearest shops are at Helmsley and Kirkbymoorside, both about 4 miles away, where there is also bicycle hire. Riding and golf also 4 miles.

Open: Easter - 31 October.

**Directions**

Turn south off the A170 between villages of Beadlam (to west) and Nawton (to east) at sign to Ryedale School, then 1 mile to park on left (passing another park on right). From east ignore first camp sign at turning before Nawton. From west turn right 400 yards east of Helmsley, signed Harome, turn left at church, go through village and follow camping signs. Sat nav postcode: YO62 7SD.
O.S.GR: SE661831. GPS: 54.23745, -0.990333

**Charges 2011**

| Per unit incl. 2 persons and electricity | £ 20.00 - £ 25.00 |
| --- | --- |

No credit cards.

---

# FOXHOLME TOURING CARAVAN PARK

## HAROME, HELMSLEY, NORTH YORKSHIRE YO62 5JG

### Telephone: (01493) 771 904, or (01493) 771 696

**AA 3 PENNANT - CARAVAN CLUB APPROVED - CAMPING CLUB APPROVED**

A quiet, rural site for touring vans, motor caravans and some tents. All pitches in well sheltered clearings in the 6 acres of 40 year old woodland. All weather roads, some hardstandings, luxury toilet block graded excellent by the AA, washbasins in cubicles, H&C showers, laundry room, small shop, gas exchange and mains electric hook-ups available.

**ADULTS ONLY   BEAUTIFUL COUNTRYSIDE
CLOSE TO THE NORTH YORK MOORS NATIONAL PARK**
*Please send stamp for brochure to G.C. Binks*

---

## High Bentham

### Riverside Caravan Park

High Bentham, Lancaster LA2 7FJ (North Yorkshire) T: 01524 261272. E: info@riversidecaravanpark.co.uk

**alanrogers.com/UK4715**

The pretty, tree lined approach to Riverside leads into an attractive park, owned by the Marshall family for over 40 years. Nestling in beautiful countryside, alongside the River Wenning, the park has easy access to the Yorkshire Dales and the Lake District. There are 49 marked, level grass touring pitches with 10A electricity and TV hook-ups. In addition there are 12 'super' pitches on tarmac. An area has been developed for 50 seasonal pitches on gravel. Located away from the touring area are 206 privately owned holiday homes. Tents are not accepted. The smart reception building includes a small shop an easy walk from the park. A member of the Best of British Group.

**Facilities**

The modern toilet block with under-floor heating is centrally situated. Washbasin cubicles. Unisex showers in a separate area. Toilet and shower room for disabled visitors (radar key) also doubles as a family shower room (charged). Motorcaravan services. Caravan storage. Outdoor play area. Family games room. The river can be used for fishing (permit from reception) swimming, and small boats. Off site: Golf and riding nearby.

Open: All year excl. 15-28 December.

**Directions**

Leave the M6 at exit 34, and head east on the A683 towards Kirkby Lonsdale. After about 5 miles take B6480 signed to High Bentham. At the Black Bull Hotel follow the caravan signs. The entrance is on the right after crossing the river bridge.
O.S.GR: SD662687. GPS: 54.11311, -2.51066

**Charges guide**

| Per unit incl. 2 persons | £ 18.75 - £ 24.25 |
| --- | --- |
| extra person | £ 4.50 |

---

# Hull

## Burton Constable Holiday Park & Arboretum

The Old Lodges, Sproatley, Hull HU11 4LN (East Yorkshire) T: 01964 562508. E: info@burtonconstable.co.uk
alanrogers.com/UK4500

This park is in the grounds of the stately home of Burton Constable, and consequently the entrance is most impressive – one of the gatehouses acts as reception and tourist information room. The 90 acre campsite is part of the 300 acre park which was landscaped by Capability Brown in the 18th century and, with well trimmed grass and hedges, it has a spacious feel. All 160 touring pitches have electricity, there is a separate field for tents and a large hardstanding area providing electricity, water and drainage for 6 motorcaravans. All the pitches overlook two small lakes (unfenced). Both of these are used for fishing (permits at reception), one for boating (bring your own, but no engines). Privately owned caravan holiday homes are quite separate and do not intrude.

### Facilities

Two heated toilet blocks – one older and small with unisex showers, the central newer block including a laundry room with baby changing. Well equipped room for disabled visitors (Radar key). Shop in the mobile home area. Bar with family room and tables outside overlooking the lakes. Good adventure play area. Off site: Sproatley (1 mile) has pubs, a shop and the occasional bus. Hull 7 miles. Golf 4 miles. Riding 3 miles.

Open: 1 March - 31 October.

### Directions

From south via the M62 or Humber Bridge, take the A63 into Hull, then follow signs to A165 Bridlington. On eastern outskirts of Hull follow B1238 signed Aldborough. At Sproatley, site is signed to left. From the north and Beverley, take A1035 to Hornsea. At roundabout with A165 (Hull - Bridlington) follow signs to Burton Constable for about 8 miles. Pass the Hall to Sproatley, then follow caravan signs.
O.S.GR: TA186357. GPS: 53.80265, -0.199

### Charges guide

| | |
|---|---|
| Per unit incl. 2 persons and electricity | £ 15.00 - £ 22.00 |
| extra person | £ 2.00 |

# Leyburn

## Constable Burton Hall Caravan Park

Constable Burton Hall, Leyburn DL8 5LJ (North Yorkshire) T: 01677 450428
E: caravanpark@constableburton.com alanrogers.com/UK4690

This tranquil park is in beautiful Wensleydale and the emphasis is on peace and quiet with wardens working to provide a relaxing environment. Being in the grounds of the Hall, it has a spacious, park-like feel to it. On part level, and some a little uneven, well maintained grass, the 120 pitches (40 for touring units) are of a good size and all have electrical connections (10A). There are no pitches for tents. There is no shop on site but nearby Leyburn will provide all your needs. Opposite the park entrance is the Wyvill Arms for bar meals. Ball games are not permitted on site and there is no play area. The gardens of the Hall are open to the public, with a collection of maples and terraced gardens developed by Mrs Vida Burton. The park is ideally placed for visiting the Northern Dales.

### Facilities

Two toilet blocks built of local stone and blending in with the local surroundings, have been refurbished recently, are well tiled, kept immaculately clean, and can be heated. Facilities for disabled visitors. Baby room. The former deer barn has been adapted for use as a laundry room and extra washrooms with basins for both men and women. Information leaflets and a few books for visitors can also be found here. Gas supplies. Gates closed 22.00-08.00. Off site: Irregular bus service from site gate. Fishing and golf within 5 miles.

Open: Late March - 31 October.

### Directions

Park is by the A684 between Bedale and Leyburn, 0.5 miles from the village of Constable Burton on the Leyburn side. O.S.GR: SE152907.
GPS: 54.3125, -1.754167

### Charges guide

| | |
|---|---|
| Per unit incl. 2 persons and electricity | £ 16.00 - £ 20.00 |
| extra person | £ 5.00 - £ 7.00 |
| child (5-16 yrs) | £ 3.00 |
| dog | free |
| No commercial vehicles. | |

**Constable Burton Hall Caravan Park**
01677 450428
caravanpark@constableburton.com
*This tranquil park is set in the beautiful grounds of the historic Constable Burton Hall, Wensleydale off the A684*

Constable Burton Hall Caravan Park, Leyburn, North Yorkshire, DL8 5LJ

For latest campsite news visit
alanrogers.com

## Malton
### Wolds Way Caravan Park

West Farm, West Knapton, Malton YO17 8JE (North Yorkshire) T: 01944 728463. E: info@ryedalesbest.co.uk
alanrogers.com/UK4545

Opened in 2004, this park is located along the top of the Yorkshire Wolds with super panoramic views across the Vale of Pickering to the North Yorks Moors. The one and a half mile tarmac and gravel track from the road to the park is well worth while to reach this peaceful location set amongst glorious countryside. There are 80 level pitches (50 for touring units), most with 16A electricity and some with water points. There are 34 pitches with hardstanding. Seating areas, picnic benches and barbecues are provided on the park. There are many footpaths and cycle ways in the area. As well as the obvious attractions of walking the Wolds Way national trail, the park is well placed for visiting all the local attractions which include Scarborough, Bridlington, Sledmere House and Scampston Hall.

### Facilities
A brand new toilet block is very well appointed and heated. Family bathrooms. Laundry facilities. Very large heated room with sinks, microwave, fridge/freezers, hot drinks machine, TV and tourist information. Room for disabled visitors. Reception also provides a small shop selling basic supplies. Play area and football field for children and many places to walk dogs. Caravan storage. A well equipped chalet for up to five people is available to rent. Off site: Bus stop 1 mile. Fishing 3 miles. Golf and riding 5 miles. Beach 15 miles.

Open: 1 March - 31 October.

### Directions
Park entrance is on the south side of the A64 York - Scarborough road, just past the B1258 turn off and it is well signed. O.S.GR: SE896744.
GPS: 54.16615, -0.654033

### Charges guide

| Per unit incl. 2 persons | |
|---|---|
| and electricity | £ 13.00 - £ 18.00 |
| extra person (over 15 yrs) | £ 4.00 |
| child (8-15 yrs) | £ 1.50 |
| awning | £ 1.50 |
| dog | free |

West Farm, West Knapton, Malton, North Yorkshire, YO17 8JE
Telephone/Fax 01944 728 463

www.ryedalesbest.co.uk

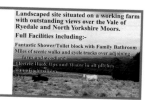

## Northallerton
### Cote Ghyll Caravan & Camping Park

Osmotherley, Northallerton DL6 3AH (North Yorkshire) T: 01609 883425. E: hills@coteghyll.com
alanrogers.com/UK4775

Jon and Helen Hill are working hard to maintain the good standard and make improvements to their park, and their efforts are evident. The site is set on a secluded hillside with the higher pitches terraced and the lower ones on a level grassy area, bordered by the small Cod Beck stream. Of the 80 pitches, 50 are for tourers. There are also 18 pitches used for caravan holiday homes and 30 are seasonal. All pitches have 10A electricity hook-ups, 12 are fully serviced. A simple site, Cote Ghyll is highly suited for lovers of peace and quiet, for bird watching or for more energetic hobbies such as cycling and walking. On the western edge of the North York Moors, cycle paths and footpaths lead almost from the site entrance and the three main long distance footpaths, the Lyke Wake walk, the Cleveland Way and the Coast to Coast, all pass close by. A 10 minute stroll takes you to the pretty and popular Osmotherley village, where there is a post office and general store, tea rooms and two pubs and a bistro selling reasonably priced meals.

### Facilities
Two heated toilet blocks, one new, provide free power showers, vanity style washbasins and hairdryers. Bathroom and facilities for babies and disabled visitors. Laundry room with washing machine, dryer, iron and board. Drying room. Motorcaravan service point. New reception and larger shop. Gas supplies. Play area. Caravan storage. Off site: Shop and pubs 10 minutes walk. Fishing 1 mile. Bicycle hire 6 miles. Golf and riding 8 miles. Mount Grace Priory 4 miles. Swimming pool and leisure centre 6 miles. Beach 18 miles.

Open: 1 March - 31 October.

### Directions
Osmotherley is east of the A19. Leave the A19 at A684 exit signed Northallerton and Osmotherely. Go to Osmotherley and site is at the northern end of the village, well signed. O.S.GR: SE460983.
GPS: 54.37643, -1.29166

### Charges guide

| Per unit incl. 2 persons | |
|---|---|
| incl. electricity | £ 14.00 - £ 17.50 |
| incl. full services plus | £ 16.00 - £ 19.50 |
| extra person | £ 4.50 |
| child (5-12 yrs) | £ 2.50 |
| | £ 1.00 |

## Northallerton

### Otterington Park

Station Farm, South Otterington, Northallerton DL7 9JB (North Yorkshire) T: 01609 780656
E: info@otteringtonpark.com alanrogers.com/UK4765

This family-owned, five-acre park is located on a former farm. Between Thirsk and Northallerton, in the Vale of York, it is ideally placed for visiting the Yorkshire moors and dales, along with local market towns, theme parks and stately homes. Predominantly, it is a flat grass site with gravel hardstanding for 40 touring pitches, with a separate paddock for a further 28 pitches, all with 16A electricity. Privately owned chalets and static caravans are located in an adjoining park, separated from the tourers by an old, well established, tall hedge. A family oriented park, there is a playground and grassy play areas for children. The owners have supplied good tourist information and local nature walks for visitors. There is coarse fishing in a well stocked, spring fed, one-acre lake located 200 m. from the site. The main London - Edinburgh railway line runs along one side of the holiday lodge and static park, so some minor train noise may be experienced.

**Facilities**

One purpose built, clean block in a heated building. Unisex en-suite style shower rooms with free showers. Facilities for disabled visitors. Family bathroom with a baby area. Laundry. Drinks/snacks vending machines in reception. Play area. Off site: Large supermarkets 4 miles. Local bus service to Thirsk and Northallerton run every 2 hours from park entrance (not Sunday). Several local country pubs serving meals within 1 mile. Fishing 250 yds. Riding 5 miles. Golf 3 miles.

Open: 1 March - 31 October.

**Directions**

From A1M join A684 for Leeming Bar and Morton-on-Swale. At roundabout bear right on A167 signed South Otterington and Topcliffe. At South Otterington crossroads (pub) turn left signed Thornton-le-Moor to park in 500 yards. O.S.GR: SE378881. GPS: 54.28771, -1.42046

**Charges guide**

| | |
|---|---|
| Per unit incl. 4 persons and electricity | £ 16.00 - £ 20.00 |

## Pickering

### Rosedale Caravan & Camping Park

Rosedale Abbey, Pickering YO18 8SA (North Yorkshire) T: 01751 417272. E: info@flowerofmay.com
alanrogers.com/UK4770

In a beautiful location below Rosedale Moor and on the edge of a popular village, this is a campsite that is highly suitable for walkers. The site itself has a wide entrance on the edge of the village and, as it is within the National Park, the buildings are in the local stone and in keeping with the area. The site is reasonably level, with 200 pitches, a few with hardstanding and with 28 electricity connections (10A). There are some caravan holiday homes (private) and seasonal touring pitches in their own areas, with the remainder used for touring caravans and motorcaravans. The majority have superb views of the surrounding hills. One field is set aside for tents only and many are sited near the river which runs along the edge of the park. The surrounding hillsides are a maze of public footpaths and these and nearby Cropton Forest can all be reached without using your car. In summer the Dales bus runs through the village, connecting several of the popular villages. The 13 mile Rosedale circuit follows the route of the old iron ore railway, giving magnificent views and reminders of bygone industries. There is a glass blower at the village blacksmiths and the Ryedale Folk Museum at Hutton-le-Hole is 3.5 miles away.

**Facilities**

Sanitary facilities with under-floor heating include free showers and hairdressing units. They may be under a little pressure when the site is very full and are a distance from some pitches. Facilities for disabled visitors and baby changing. Laundry facilities. Reception provides maps and a small selection of camping accessories, plus gas supplies. Games room with pool and video games. Large play area with space for ball games. Entrance barrier controlled by card (£10 deposit). Off site: The village has a general store with daily papers, a post office, bakery, pubs and a restaurant. 9-hole golf course (set on a picturesque hillside) 200 yards.

Open: Easter - 28 October.

**Directions**

Rosedale is signed from the A170, 2 miles west of Pickering. Site is in the village of Rosedale Abbey, 8 miles north of the A170. O.S.GR: SE725958. GPS: 54.35366, -0.88795

**Charges guide**

| | |
|---|---|
| Per unit incl. electricity and up to 4 persons | £ 18.00 - £ 25.00 |
| tent incl. up to 4 persons | £ 14.00 - £ 20.00 |

10% discount on pitch fee for weekly bookings.
*See advertisement on page 196.*

For latest campsite news visit
alanrogers.com

## Pickering

### Upper Carr Chalet & Touring Park

Upper Carr Lane, Malton Road, Pickering YO18 7JP (North Yorkshire) T: 01751 473115
E: info@uppercarrchaletandtouringpark.co.uk  alanrogers.com/UK4620

With a central location in the Vale of Pickering, Upper Carr is well placed for the many attractions the area has to offer. The enthusiastic manager is keen to develop it into a family-friendly park, introducing themed weekends and nature trails. The park is surrounded by a high, well trimmed hedge which protects it from the wind and deadens the road noise. Upper Carr's six acres provide 80 level pitches, 75 with 10A electricity and some with hardstanding. Seasonal units use 25 pitches. The picturesque village of Thornton Dale can be reached on foot or by cycle along the Upper Carr nature trail.

#### Facilities

The heated toilet blocks are dated (in chalet style buildings) but clean. There are plans for these to be updated. Showers are charged for. Baby changing facilities. Separate room with WC and washbasin for disabled visitors. Dishwashing sinks outside, but under cover. Laundry room. Motorcaravan service point. Small shop in reception supplies basic needs and gas. Good play area. Bicycle hire. Nature trail. Off site: Pub 100 yards. Golf (9-hole) or tennis adjacent to park. Riding 6 miles. Fishing 5 miles. Bus service passes entrance.

Open: 1 March - 31 October.

#### Directions

Travelling on the Pickering - Malton A169 road, park is on the left about 1.5 miles south of Pickering. O.S.GR: SE804815. GPS: 54.222967, -0.769

#### Charges guide

| | |
|---|---|
| Per unit incl. 2 adults, 2 children and electricity | £ 13.00 - £ 18.90 |
| extra person | £ 2.50 |
| extra child | £ 1.50 |

---

## Pickering

### Forest Holidays Spiers House

Cropton Forest, Cropton, Pickering YO18 8ES (North Yorkshire) T: 01751 417591. E: info@forestholidays.co.uk
alanrogers.com/UK4570

Forest Holidays is a partnership between the Forestry Commission and The Camping and Caravanning Club. The Spiers House site is set in a sunny clearing in the middle of Cropton Forest. It is an ideal location for a cycling or walking holiday without having to move your car. The site buildings, built in local stone, are set around a central courtyard with a pedestrian archway leading to the pitches. Sloping fields provide 150 pitches, which include 74 with 10A electricity and 19 with hardstanding (there are plans for more hardstanding pitches). Reception provides leaflets for way-marked walks in the forest.

#### Facilities

The tiled toilet block is spacious, if a little Spartan, with open plan washbasins and roomy, preset showers (refurbishment is planned). Unit for disabled campers. Dishwashing sinks under cover with free hot water, laundry room with washing machine, dryer and sinks (hot water charged). Well stocked shop. Large adventure playground and games field set under tall pines. Raised barbecues are permitted. Off site: Pub with home-brewed beer 1 mile. Riding 5 miles. Fishing 7 miles. Golf 12 miles.

Open: All year.

#### Directions

From the A170 Pickering head westwards towards Helmsley. Turn right signed Cropton and Rosedale (do not go into Cropton village). Forest and park signed after 4 miles. Entrance is via a 500 m. single track with passing places. O.S.GR: SE758918. GPS: 54.30765, -0.846267

#### Charges guide

| | |
|---|---|
| Per unit incl. 2 persons | £ 11.00 - £ 21.50 |
| extra person | £ 4.75 - £ 6.25 |
| extra child | £ 2.75 - £ 3.75 |

---

## Pickering

### Overbrook Caravan Park

Maltongate, Thornton-le-Dale, Pickering YO18 7SE (North Yorkshire) T: 01751 474417
E: enquiry@overbrookcaravanpark.co.uk  alanrogers.com/UK4534

Situated in the very pretty village of Thornton-le-Dale, Overbrook has been developed on the site of the old railway station. With the line dismantled, the station building now provides holiday cottages and the caravan park toilet facilities. This is a level site with 50 pitches (20 for tourers, the remainder used for seasonal units) arranged either side of a tarmac access road and backed by trees. All are on hardstanding and all have electricity connections (16A). Neither children nor tents are accepted at this adult only park. The owners will do all they can to assist you during your stay.

#### Facilities

The toilet and shower facilities are situated in the old station house. Laundry facilities. Gas supplies. No tents accepted. Children are not admitted. Off site: Village with bus stop, shops, pubs, fish and chips 800 yds. Bicycle hire 800 yds. Fishing 3 miles. Golf 5 miles.

Open: 1 March - 31 October.

#### Directions

Thornton-le-Dale is on the A170 Pickering - Scarborough road. In the village follow sign for Malton and park is 800 yds. on the left. O.S.GR: SE833821. GPS: 54.228533, -0.7229

#### Charges guide

| | |
|---|---|
| Per unit incl. 2 persons | £ 14.50 - £ 17.00 |
| extra person | £ 2.50 |
| No credit cards. | |

---

For latest campsite news visit
**alanrogers.com**

# Ripon

## Riverside Meadows Country Caravan Park

Ure Bank Top, Ripon HG4 1JD (North Yorkshire) T: 01765 602964. E: info@flowerofmay.com

**alanrogers.com/UK4760**

Riverside Meadows is a rural park, although the approach to it belies that fact. The short approach from the main road passes a row of houses and a factory, but once they are passed, the park opens up before you and you are once again back in the countryside. There are plenty of caravan holiday homes here but they are, on the whole, quite separate from the 64 touring pitches. These pitches, practically all with electrical hook-ups, are mainly on gently sloping grass with just a few hardstandings. A meadow separates the park from the River Ure, a favourite place for strolling and fishing (licences available). Close to Ripon is the Lightwater Valley theme park, and a little further are Fountains Abbey, Harrogate, Knaresborough, the Yorkshire Dales and Thirsk with its market and the James Herriot centre. There is lots to see and do on and off the park for both families and couples.

### Facilities

The tiled toilet block is quite new and includes a baby room, dishwashing room, a fully fitted shower room for disabled visitors. Laundry facilities. Shop. Bar with snacks. Games room. Well equipped play area. Indoor pool. Off site: Fishing, bicycle hire and riding 800 yds. Golf 1.25 miles. The delightful market town (city) of Ripon with its ancient cathedral is only 20 minutes walk.

Open: Easter - 31 October.

### Directions

At the most northern roundabout on the Ripon bypass (A61), turn onto the A6108 signed Ripon, Masham and Leyburn. Go straight on at mini-roundabout and park is signed on right. O.S.GR: SE317727. GPS: 54.15045, -1.515

### Charges guide

| | |
|---|---|
| Per unit incl. up to 4 persons and electricity | £ 18.00 - £ 25.00 |
| tent incl. up to 4 persons | £ 14.00 - £ 20.00 |

10% discount on pitch fee for weekly bookings.

*See advertisement on page 196.*

# Ripon

## Woodhouse Farm Caravan & Camping Park

Winksley, Ripon HG4 3PG (North Yorkshire) T: 01765 658309. E: woodhouse.farm@talk21.com

**alanrogers.com/UK4660**

This secluded family park on a former working farm, is only six miles from Ripon and about four from the World Heritage site of Fountains Abbey. It is a very rural park with a spacious feel and various pitching areas are tucked away in woodland areas or around the edges of hedged fields with the centre left clear for children. There are hard roads and most of the 160 pitches have 16A electricity. There are 56 acres in total, 17.5 devoted to the site and 20 acres of woodland for walking. The 2.5 acre fishing lake is a big attraction and provides a pleasant area for picnics or walks. The tastefully developed bar (daily) and restaurant (weekends only) offers reasonably priced menus. Woodhouse Farm has a quiet, secluded location from which many excursions can be made – the Yorkshire Dales of Nidderdale, Wharfedale, Wensleydale and Swaledale are all within easy reach. As in most parts of the Dales, the peace is occasionally disturbed by passing jets, but happily not very often.

### Facilities

The clean toilet block near the touring pitches has been upgraded and includes heating, roomy showers and some washbasins in cabins. Two bathrooms. Facilities for disabled visitors. Extra facilities are in the farm buildings along with a well equipped laundry, reception and shop. Gas supplies. Motorcaravan services. Bar (daily) and restaurant (weekends). Takeaway on request. New games room with TV. Excellent outdoor play equipment including climbing frames. Fishing (day tickets from reception). Mountain bike hire. Caravan storage. WiFi in reception. Off site: Twice daily bus service passes gate. Many attractive villages with inns supplying food and drinks. The small historic city of Ripon has a beautiful cathedral. Riding 3 miles. Golf 6 miles.

Open: Mid March - 31 October.

### Directions

From Ripon take Fountains Abbey - Pateley Bridge road (B6265). After about 3.5 miles turn right to Grantley and then follow campsite signs for further 1-2 miles. O.S.GR: SE241715. GPS: 54.137417, -1.634667

### Charges guide

| | |
|---|---|
| Per unit incl. 2 persons and electricity | £ 16.00 - £ 22.00 |
| extra person | £ 3.50 |
| child (under 16 yrs) | £ 1.00 |
| dog | £ 0.75 |

For latest campsite news visit
**alanrogers.com**

# Scarborough

## Lebberston Touring Park

Filey Road, Lebberston, Scarborough YO11 3PE (North Yorkshire) T: 01723 585723
E: info@lebberstontouring.co.uk  alanrogers.com/UK4780

Lebberston Touring Park is a quiet, spacious touring site and is highly suitable for anyone seeking a quiet relaxing break, such as mature couples or young families (although tents are not accepted). There is no play area or games room, the only concession to children being a large central area with goal posts, so teenagers may get bored. The park itself has a very spacious feel – it is gently sloping and south facing and the views are superb. There are 125 numbered pitches with 75 for touring units. All have 10A electricity and 25 are on hardstanding. The circular access road is tarmac, the grass is well manicured and the entrance is a mass of flowers. Reception is part of a farmhouse style new build, also the home of the owners and their young family.

### Facilities

Recently upgraded toilet blocks are of high quality and kept very clean. Large shower cubicles and washbasins in cubicles with curtains. Both blocks have dishwashing sinks and one has a family bathroom (20p). Good room for disabled visitors. Laundry with washing machine, dryer, spin dryer, iron and board. A key is supplied for the laundry and bathroom, with radar key access to the disabled shower room. Reception sells a few supplies, plus papers, ice cream and gas. Only breathable groundsheets are permitted. WiFi (charged). Off site: Hourly bus 5 minutes walk. Local pub within 5 minutes walking distance. Each new arrival is given details of parking in Scarborough including a parking disc.

Open: 1 March - 31 October.

### Directions

From A64 Malton - Scarborough road turn right at roundabout (MacDonald's, pub and superstore) signed B1261 Filey. Go through Cayton, Killerby and in 4.5 miles site is signed on the left (not easy to see). If you miss the turning to the park, continue to roundabout and turn around. O.S.GR: TA082823. GPS: 54.22650, -0.34709

### Charges guide

| Per unit incl. 2 persons | |
|---|---|
| and electricity | £ 15.00 - £ 25.00 |
| extra person | £ 1.50 |
| child (5-14 yrs) | £ 1.00 |
| full awning | £ 2.00 |

# Scarborough

## Saint Helens in the Park

Wykeham, Scarborough YO13 9QD (North Yorkshire) T: 01723 862771. E: caravans@wykeham.co.uk
alanrogers.com/UK4540

St Helens is a high quality touring park with pleasant views, set within 30 acres of parkland. The site is divided into terraces with trees screening each area (one of which is set aside for adults only) and the 250 mainly level pitches have a spacious feel. Electrical hook-ups (16A) are available on 240 pitches and also in the late arrivals area. Set on a hillside, the park's buildings are built in local stone and all is maintained to a high standard. The Downe Arms, a short stroll away, is known for its good food and family-friendly atmosphere. Scarborough is only five miles away with its beaches and summer shows, and buses pass the site gates.

### Facilities

Four heated toilet blocks are well equipped and maintained to a high standard. Some washbasins in cabins, free showers and baby baths. Unit for disabled visitors. Good central laundry room. Well stocked shop. Café and takeaway. Internet café. WiFi. Bicycle hire. Small games room. Tourist information cabin. Caravan storage. Off site: Nearby Wykeham Lakes offer fishing (trout and coarse), scuba diving, windsurfing and sailing (in your own boat), 1 mile. Golf and riding 2 miles.

Open: All year excl. 15 January - 13 February.

### Directions

Park access road leads off the A170 (Pickering - Scarborough) road in Wykeham village 2 miles west of junction with B1262. O.S.GR: SE963835. GPS: 54.238033, -0.500467

### Charges guide

| Per unit incl. 2 persons | |
|---|---|
| and electricity | £ 14.90 - £ 19.90 |
| extra person (over 3 yrs) | £ 1.50 |
| dog | £ 1.50 |

## Scarborough
### Flower of May Holiday Park

Lebberston Cliff, Scarborough YO11 3NU (North Yorkshire) T: 01723 584311. E: info@flowerofmay.com
**alanrogers.com/UK4520**

Situated on the cliff tops, 4.5 miles from Scarborough and 2.5 miles from Filey, Flower of May is a large, family owned park for both touring caravans and caravan holiday homes. The entrance to the park is very colourful and the reception office is light and airy. The park is licensed for 300 touring units and 184 caravan holiday homes (45 to hire, the remainder privately owned). The touring pitches are pretty level, arranged in wide avenues, mainly on grass and divided by shrubs. There are 223 with electricity (10A), including 200 'star pitches' with water and drainage also. The range of leisure facilities is grouped around reception. It includes an indoor pool with areas for both adults and children, a water flume and a jacuzzi. In the same building are two squash courts, 10 pin bowling, table tennis and amusement machines. The leisure centre is also open to the public (concessionary rates for campers) but during high season is only available to local regulars and the caravanners and campers on the park. There is a cliff walk to the beach but it is only suitable for the reasonably active – there is an easier walk down from a car park a mile away. Riverside Meadows at Ripon and Rosedale Country Caravan Park near Pickering are under the same ownership.

### Facilities

Three toilet blocks, all refurbished in a light and colourful style, are fully tiled with washbasins in both cabins and vanity style. Baby rooms. Facilities for disabled visitors. Well stocked and licensed shop near the leisure centre, as is the laundry room. Two modern bar lounges, one for families and one for adults only, with discos in season. Café and takeaway fish and chips. Games room with TV. Large adventure playground. Pay and play golf course (£5 a round). Indoor swimming pool. Skateboard ramps. Basketball. Dog exercise area, but numbers and breeds are limited (one per pitch). WiFi throughout the park. Off site: The Plough Inn near the park entrance offers good bar meals. Fishing, boat slipway and riding 2 miles. Bicycle hire 4 miles.

Open: Easter - 28 October.

### Directions

Park is signed from roundabout at junction of the A165 and B1261 from where it is 600 yds. O.S.GR: TA088836. GPS: 54.2292, -0.3425

### Charges guide

| | |
|---|---|
| Per unit incl. up to 4 persons | £ 18.00 - £ 25.00 |
| tent (no electricity) | £ 14.00 - £ 20.00 |
| child (under 3 yrs) | free |

10% discount on pitch fee for weekly bookings.

## Scarborough
### Cayton Village Caravan Park

Mill Lane, Cayton Bay, Scarborough YO11 3NN (North Yorkshire) T: 01723 583171
E: info@caytontouring.co.uk **alanrogers.com/UK4550**

Cayton Village Caravan Park can only be described as a gem. Just three miles from the hustle and bustle of Scarborough, it is a peaceful, attractive haven. Originally just a flat field with caravans around the perimeter, years of hard work have produced a park which is very pleasing to the eye and of which the owner, Carol, can be justly proud. The entrance is a mass of flowers. The 200 pitches are numbered and everyone is taken to their pitch; 190 of the touring pitches have electricity (many with hardstanding) and 90 are fully serviced pitches. The late arrivals area here also has electrical hook-ups. A short walk across the park takes you to Cayton Village which has a popular pub providing excellent meals, a post office, stores and a church, and Cayton Bay is half a mile away.

### Facilities

Three toilet blocks (key code locks) can be heated and have high quality tiling and fittings. Some showers are pre-set, others controllable. Two family shower rooms, family bathroom and baby facilities. Reception and shop with comprehensive range including gas and caravan spares. Adventure playground. Nature walk. Caravan storage. New playground catering for younger children (18 months-12 yrs). Off site: Fishing 0.5 miles. Bicycle hire 3 miles. Regular bus service from park entrance to Scarborough, Filey and Bridlington.

Open: 1 March - 31 October.

### Directions

From A64 Malton - Scarborough road turn right at roundabout (with McDonalds and pub) signed B1261 Filey. Follow signs for Cayton, in Cayton village take second left after Blacksmiths Arms down Mill Lane (at brown tourism sign) and park is 200 yds. on left. From roundabout to park is 2.25 miles. From A165 turn inland at Cayton Bay roundabout and park is 0.5 miles on right. O.S.GR: TA057837. GPS: 54.235733, -0.376117

### Charges guide

| | |
|---|---|
| Per unit incl. 2 persons, | |
| electricity and awning | £ 15.00 - £ 28.00 |
| incl. services and hardstanding | £ 19.00 - £ 30.00 |
| tent pitch without electricity | £ 12.00 - £ 20.00 |
| extra person | £ 1.00 |
| dog | £ 1.00 |

# FLOWER OF MAY

## *Magical Family Holidays*

# Discover the Beauty Surrounding Yorkshires Finest Holiday Parks

1723 584311

1765 602964

751 417272

347 810829

A choice of Holiday Parks situated at the Coast, on the Moors and in the Countryside of North Yorkshire.

Our well maintained Parks are superbly located within easy reach of North Yorkshires stunning landscapes and well known attractions.

Please send for our colour brochure –
**Flower of May,**
**Lebberston Cliff,**
**Scarborough, YO11 3NU.**

## 01723 584311

or e-mail us:
info@flowerofmay.com

## Relax, Explore and Enjoy!

### www.flowerofmay.com

## Scarborough

### Jasmine Park

Cross Lane, Snainton, Scarborough YO13 9BE (North Yorkshire) T: 01723 859240
E: enquiries@jasminepark.co.uk  alanrogers.com/UK4740

Jasmine is a very attractive, quiet and well manicured park with owners who go to much trouble to produce many plants to decorate a very colourful entrance. Set in the Vale of Pickering, the park is level, well drained and protected by a coniferous hedge. The 126 pitches (78 for touring units) are on grass, with electricity connections (10/16A) for all caravans and some tents. There is no play equipment for children, although a field is provided for games. Much tourist information is provided in a log cabin and the owners are only too happy to advise. This is an award-winning, peaceful park for a restful holiday. A member of the Countryside Discovery group.

**Facilities**

The heated toilet block has been refurbished to a high standard and is kept very clean. It includes a large room for families and disabled visitors containing a bath, shower, WC and washbasin (access by code). Laundry room with dishwashing sinks, washing machine, dryer and iron (hot water metered). Motorcaravan service point. Licensed shop selling essentials and gas. Caravan storage. WiFi. Off site: Bus service in village 0.5 miles. Riding 2 miles. Fishing and bicycle hire 5 miles.

Open: 1 March - 31 October.

**Directions**

Snainton is on the A170 Pickering - Scarborough road and park is signed at eastern end of the village. Turn down Barker's Lane and at small crossroads turn left and the Park is 230 yards on the left. O.S.GR: SE928813. GPS: 54.218583, -0.575567

**Charges guide**

| | |
|---|---|
| Per unit incl. 4 persons, electricity | £ 18.00 - £ 30.00 |
| extra person | £ 2.00 |
| child (under 14 yrs) | £ 1.00 |

## Scarborough

### Jacobs Mount Caravan Park

Stepney Road, Scarborough YO12 5NL (North Yorkshire) T: 01723 361178. E: jacobsmount@yahoo.co.uk
alanrogers.com/UK4590

Situated just two miles from the centre of Scarborough, on the edge of the Forge Valley National Park, Jacobs Mount is well placed to meet many holiday needs. The sea and the sand are the main attractions, but this is also on the doorstep of the North York moors and the Dalby Forest Drive. In addition to caravan holiday homes in separate areas of the park, there are 142 touring pitches, all with electricity. Of these 131 are fully serviced (water, drainage) on well spaced gravel hardstandings. In sunny locations, some pitches have good views. There is a bar with a pleasant lounge (no children).

**Facilities**

The heated toilet block is new and of a high standard. Washbasins in cubicles with WCs, large shower cubicles (free) and a family bathroom (metered hot water) and baby changing facilities. Separate unisex cubicles contain WC, washbasin and shower. Motorcaravan service point. Small shop in reception. Bar with bar meals and takeaway. Two play areas. Caravan storage. Max. two dogs per pitch. Off site: Scarborough centre and beach 2 miles. Golf, fishing and bicycle hire 2 miles. Riding 5 miles.

Open: 1 March - 6 November.

**Directions**

Entrance is on the A170 Pickering - Scarborough road, about 2 miles west of Scarborough (on the right as you start to drop down into the town). O.S.GR: TA021877. GPS: 54.267283, -0.43455

**Charges guide**

| | |
|---|---|
| Per unit incl. 4 persons and electricity | £ 11.00 - £ 19.50 |
| extra person (3 yrs and over) | £ 2.00 |
| dog (max. 2) | £ 2.50 |

## Selby

### The Ranch Caravan Park

Cliffe Common, Cliffe, Selby YO8 6EF (North Yorkshire) T: 01757 638984
E: contact@theranchcaravanpark.co.uk  alanrogers.com/UK4645

The Ranch Caravan Park is a small family run park set in six acres of woodland. All the pitches are on hardstanding with electricity connections and some also have water and a drain. Several pitches are most suitable for American RVs. This is a well maintained park with two areas of open grass surrounded by trees. There are gravel roads. A security gate at the entrance requires a £20 deposit for a key. A large hall with a bar, lounge area, dance area and entertainment opens on Friday and Saturday evenings and serves light meals; children are welcome if supervised.

**Facilities**

Heated toilet block with free showers, disabled wet room that doubles as a family room with baby bath and baby changing facilities. Laundry, with washer and dryer, outside drying area. Motorcaravan service point. Small play area. Off site: Selby 4 miles. York 12 miles. Fishing 2 miles. Golf and riding 15 miles.

Open: All year excl. 5 January - 5 February.

**Directions**

Leave M62 at exit 37 (Goole) and take A63 towards Selby. At Cliffe turn right and after 1 mile, turn left at crossroads. Park is 80 yards on the right. O.S.GR: SE663338. GPS: 53.79821, -0.99064

**Charges guide**

| | |
|---|---|
| Per unit incl. 2 persons and electricity | £ 15.00 |
| extra person | £ 1.50 |
| child (5-16 yrs) | £ 1.00 |

# Settle

## Knight Stainforth Hall Caravan & Camping Park

Little Stainforth, Settle BD24 0DP (North Yorkshire) T: 01729 822200. E: info@knightstainforth.co.uk
alanrogers.com/UK4720

In a very attractive setting, this park is located in the heart of the Yorkshire Dales, the whole area is a paradise for hill-walking, fishing and pot-holing and has outstanding scenery. The camping area is on slightly sloping grass, sheltered by mature woodland. There are 100 touring pitches, 50 with electricity (16A) and 10 with hardstanding, and a separate area contains 66 privately owned caravan holiday homes. A gate leads from the bottom of the camping field giving access to the river bank where the Ribble bubbles over small waterfalls and rocks and whirls around deep pools where campers can swim.

### Facilities

A modern, heated amenity block provides toilets and showers and includes some washbasins in cubicles. Facilities for disabled visitors and baby changing. Laundry facilities. Motorcaravan service point. Small shop. Games/TV room. Play area with safety base. Fishing (permit from reception). Security barrier. Deposit for key to toilet block and barrier £10. WiFi. Off site: Bicycle hire and golf 3 miles. Riding 6 miles. The Dales Falconry and Conservation Centre at Felzor.

Open: 1 March - 31 October.

### Directions

From Settle town centre, drive west towards Giggleswick. Ignore turning marked Stainforth and Horton, and after 200 yards turn right into Stackhouse Lane (signed Knight Stainforth). After 2 miles turn right at crossroads. O.S.GR: SD815671. GPS: 54.10025, -2.284833

### Charges guide

| | |
|---|---|
| Per unit incl. 2 persons | £ 12.00 - £ 15.00 |
| incl. electricity | £ 14.00 - £ 17.00 |
| extra person | £ 1.50 - £ 2.50 |

# Skipsea

## Skipsea Sands Holiday Park

Mill Lane, Skipsea YO25 8TZ (East Yorkshire) T: 0871 664 9812. E: skipsea.sands@parkresorts.com
alanrogers.com/UK4496

This well established holiday park is now owned by Park Resorts and is primarily dedicated to caravan holiday homes, of which there are 600 privately owned and 61 to rent. There is however a pleasantly laid out touring park occupying its own corner of the site and bordered by an attractive duck pond and a large playing area (both well fenced). The 91 marked, level pitches are separated by hedges and all have electricity (16A), water and drain; 18 also have sewage connections. The leisure facilities are outstanding and a full daily programme of activities and entertainment is offered for children and adults.

### Facilities

Two heated toilet blocks are fairly basic, with push button showers and open washbasins. En-suite facilities for disabled visitors are rather stark. Basic chemical disposal and motorcaravan service point. Washing machines and dryers. Well stocked shop. Bar, coffee shop and restaurant with takeaway. Leisure centre with sports hall, ten-pin bowling, heated indoor swimming pool, jacuzzi, sauna and steam room. Fitness centre with gym and sun bed. Games 'Kingdom' and 'Kids Zone'. Off site: Beach 0.25 m (on foot) or 4 miles (by car). Fishing 2 miles.

Open: Easter - 31 October.

### Directions

Skipsea is 20 miles northeast of Hull and 10 miles south of Bridlington. From the Humber Bridge or from the M62/A63 west of Hull, head north on the A164 to Beverley. Then take the A165 towards Bridlington and turn east on B1249 to Skipsea. In village, turn right then left to site (signed). O.S.GR: TA175565. GPS: 53.98957, -0.20716

### Charges guide

| | |
|---|---|
| Per unit incl. all services | £ 14.00 - £ 33.00 |
| tent pitch | £ 3.00 - £ 24.00 |
| dog | £ 1.00 - £ 3.00 |

# Skipton

## Howgill Lodge Caravan & Camping Park

Barden, Skipton BD23 6DJ (North Yorkshire) T: 01756 720655. E: info@howgill-lodge.co.uk
alanrogers.com/UK4750

Howgill Lodge is a traditional family park set in the heart of the Yorkshire Dales. Arranged on a sloping hillside, the terraced pitches have fantastic views. It is a small park catering for the needs of walkers, tourers and people who like to just relax. The whole area is a haven for both experienced walkers or the casual rambler, without having to move your car. All the pitches on the upper part of the park are on hardstanding and have electricity connections (10A), the lower ones are mainly on grass (40 in total). Picnic tables and chairs are provided. There are four mobile homes available to rent.

### Facilities

Heated toilet facilities are at the entrance, close to reception. Showers are large and adjustable (on payment). Fully equipped laundry room with four unisex showers also here. Two small blocks housing WCs are lower down the site for the convenience of tent campers. Shop. No play area. Fishing licences are available. Off site: Bus service within walking distance. Skipton 8 miles. Fishing 1 mile. Golf, riding and bicycle hire 7 miles.

Open: 1 April - 31 October.

### Directions

Turn off A59 Skipton - Harrogate road at roundabout onto B6160 Bolton Abbey, Burnsall road. At Barden Towers, bear right signed Appletreewick and Pateley Bridge. This road is fairly narrow for 1.25 miles (with passing places). Park is signed on right. O.S.GR: SE065593. GPS: 54.025767, -1.909833

### Charges guide

| | |
|---|---|
| Per unit incl. 2 persons and electricity | £ 17.00 - £ 21.00 |

# Skipton

## Wood Nook Caravan Park

Skirethorns, Threshfield, Skipton BD23 5NU (North Yorkshire) T: 01756 752412. E: enquiries@woodnook.net

alanrogers.com/UK4670

Wood Nook is a family-run park in the heart of Wharfedale, part of the Yorkshire Dales National Park. The access road is narrow for a short distance, so care should be taken. The site includes six acres of woodland with quite rare flora and fauna. Reception is in the farmhouse, as is the small shop. The gently sloping fields have gravel roads and provide 48 touring pitches with gravel hardstanding. All have electricity (10A) and nearby water and chemical disposal points. There is also room for 24 tents and there are some caravan holiday homes to let. The Thompson family are very friendly.

### Facilities

Converted farm buildings provide dated but clean sanitary facilities which can be heated. Washbasins in cubicles for ladies. Roomy showers (in another building – coin operated). Laundry facilities. Motorcaravan service points. Licensed shop for basics and gifts (from Easter). Gas. Small play area. American motorhomes are taken by prior arrangement. Internet access. WiFi (charged). Off site: Fishing and bicycle hire 2 miles. Riding 3 miles. Golf 9 miles. Leisure centre.

Open: 1 March - 31 October.

### Directions

Threshfield is 9 miles north of Skipton on the B6265. Continue through village onto B6160 and after garage turn left into Skirethorns Lane. Follow signs for 600 yds, keeping left up narrow lane, then turn right up track for 300 yds. The last 900 yds. is single track – on arrival phone to make sure it is clear. O.S.GR: SD974641. GPS: 54.07267, -2.04199

### Charges guide

| | |
|---|---|
| Per person | £ 3.00 |
| child (5-16 yrs) | £ 1.50 |
| serviced pitch | £ 9.00 |

# Wakefield

## Nostell Priory Holiday Park

Nostell, Wakefield WF4 1QE (West Yorkshire) T: 01924 863938. E: park@nostellprioryholidaypark.co.uk

alanrogers.com/UK4700

This tranquil, secluded woodland park is within the Nostell Priory estate and provides 40 touring pitches, in addition to 84 caravan holiday homes in a separate area. In a grassy, flat and sheltered area edged with mature trees and a gravel access road, all the touring pitches have electricity (5A) and hardstanding. The park's amenities are designed to blend into the environment and are built in rustic wood, including the sanitary block. The park is well cared for and the natural environment is encouraged so there is an abundance of birds and wildlife. Nostell Priory itself, with its collection of Chippendale furniture and attractive gardens, is well worth a visit.

### Facilities

The toilet block, although older in style, has been refurbished and includes some washbasins in cubicles (coded entry). Separate room for dishwashing. Laundry with two washing machines and a dryer (opening times on the door). Gas supplies. Play area (no ball games on site). Fishing. Up to two dogs are accepted. 'Cocoon' luxury tent for hire. Off site: Nearest shops 2 miles. Golf 5 miles. Boat launching 8 miles.

Open: 1 March - 31 October.

### Directions

Park entrance is off A638 Wakefield - Doncaster road, 5 miles southeast of Wakefield. Follow drive for 0.5 miles (rose nursery on left). Approaching from the south on A638, the site entrance is almost a mile past the entry to the Priory, on the right. O.S.GR: SE394181. GPS: 53.65495, -1.3985

### Charges guide

| | |
|---|---|
| Per unit incl. 2 persons and electricity | £ 11.00 - £ 19.50 |

# Wetherby

## Maustin Caravan Park

Kearby with Netherby, Wetherby LS22 4DA (North Yorkshire) T: 01132 886234. E: judith@maustin.co.uk

alanrogers.com/UK4755

A tranquil site for couples only, this well manicured park is set within the North Yorkshire National Park. It offers 25 well spaced pitches sited on grass, all with peaceful, scenic views of the surrounding area. Caravan holiday homes are in a separate area. A bowling club on the site offers membership to all visitors and competitions are held throughout the season. Relax in the comfortable lounge or in the tasteful bar and restaurant area. A covered terrace overlooks the bowling green. There is an information building providing books, DVDs, videos and games which you may borrow free of charge.

### Facilities

One heated, purpose built toilet block has luxury showers, free hairdryers and roomy toilet and washing cubicles, all with non-slip flooring. Designated facility for disabled visitors. Laundry room. Kitchen area with freezer. Milk, newspapers, etc. to order. Internet facilities. Off site: Riding 2 miles. Golf 4 miles.

Open: All year excl. February.

### Directions

From A1 North take exit 47 for Harrogate (A59), then after three roundabouts (9 miles) turn left on the A61 (Leeds). In 2 miles turn left (Kirkby Overblow) then right to Kearby and park. O.S.GR: SE331468. GPS: 53.91818, -1.49518

### Charges guide

| | |
|---|---|
| Per unit incl. 2 persons | £ 15.50 - £ 17.50 |
| extra person | £ 2.00 |

For latest campsite news visit
**alanrogers.com**

## Whitby
### Middlewood Farm Holiday Park

Middlewood Lane, Fylingthorpe, Robin Hood's Bay YO22 4UF (North Yorkshire) T: 01947 880414
E: info@middlewoodfarm.com  alanrogers.com/UK4532

Middlewood Farm is a level park, surrounded by hills and with views of the sea from some of the pitches. A short walk through the farm fields and wild flower conservation areas leads to the picturesque old fishing village of Robin Hood's Bay and the sea. The park has 30 touring pitches for caravans and motorcaravans with 10A electricity, 17 with hardstanding and the remainder on grass. There is space for around 130 tents in two areas with 12 electricity connections (10A) available and 30 caravan holiday homes to rent. A good beach is only ten minutes walk through the fields. The nearby village of Fylingthorpe with a post office, stores and a pub is a level walk. This is a very tidy farm park.

### Facilities

The central toilet block has clean facilities and is modern, heated and tiled with free showers. Another new block is planned. Fully equipped laundry room including iron and board. Facilities for babies and disabled visitors. One private family shower/toilet room to rent. Play area with bark base set amongst the tents. Off site: Shop and public transport in village 5 minutes walk. Sandy beach with fishing 0.5 miles. Boat launching 2 miles. Golf 7 miles.

Open: Easter - early November.

### Directions

From the A171 Scarborough - Whitby road turn right signed Robin Hood's Bay and Fylingthorpe (site signed). Just past the 30 mph sign bear right and after 100 yds. turn right into Middlewood Lane (site signed). From Whitby on the A171 turn left on the B1447 signed Robin Hood's Bay and Fylingthorpe. After 1.5 miles turn right signed Fylingthorpe and brown site sign. Follow for 1 mile to crossroads and shops and straight on to Middlewood Lane.
O.S.GR: NZ945045. GPS: 54.43012, -0.54670

### Charges guide

| | |
|---|---|
| Per unit incl. 2 persons and electricity | £ 14.00 - £ 25.00 |
| extra person | £ 3.00 |
| awning | £ 3.00 |
| dog | £ 2.00 |

## Whitby
### Sandfield House Farm Caravan Park

Sandsend Road, Whitby YO21 3SR (North Yorkshire) T: 01947 602660. E: info@sandfieldhousefarm.co.uk
alanrogers.com/UK4528

Although it is set on a hill in undulating countryside on the low cliffs near Whitby, this park provides 200 level pitches, all with electricity. There are 60 pitches for touring caravans, all on hardstanding, and these are mainly set to the front of the park giving wonderful views over the golf course and the sea. Tents are not accepted here. Whitby is only a mile away and a quarter of a mile walk down a gently sloping track from the park brings you to a two mile long sandy beach. From here it is a gentle stroll along the new promenade to Whitby harbour. Whitby offers a variety of attractions to interest all the family, from fishing trips and amusement arcades, to the Spa theatre, plus the famous fish and chips.

### Facilities

Two toilet blocks (one older, one new and very good) have free hot showers. Laundry room with washing machines, dryers and iron. No facilities for disabled visitors. Tents are not accepted. Off site: Shops 800 yards. Hourly bus service to town centre. Fishing 400 yds. Golf 200 yds. Boat launching 800 yds. Railway station 1 mile.

Open: 1 March - 31 October.

### Directions

From Whitby follow signs for Sandsend on the A174. The park is on the landward side of the road, opposite the golf course and well signed.
O.S.GR: NZ872117. GPS: 54.491717, -0.642767

### Charges guide

| | |
|---|---|
| Per unit incl. up to 4 persons and electricity | £ 15.50 - £ 18.50 |
| extra person | £ 2.00 |
| awning | £ 2.00 |
| dog (max. 2) | £ 1.00 |
| No credit cards. | |

## York
### Goose Wood Caravan Park

Sutton-on-the-Forest, York YO61 1ET (North Yorkshire) T: 01347 810829. E: enquiries@goosewood.co.uk

**alanrogers.com/UK4640**

A family owned park in a natural woodland setting, Goose Wood provides a quiet, relaxed atmosphere from which to explore York itself or the surrounding Yorkshire Dales, Wolds or Moors. The park has a well kept air and a rural atmosphere, with 100 well spaced and marked pitches, all with 16A electricity on hardstanding (four also have water and drainage). Tents are not accepted. For children, there is a 'super plus' adventure playground in the trees at one side of the park and for adults, a small coarse fishing lake and attractive, natural woodland for walking, plus a large scale chess set. A new health suite has been added with pool, sauna, hot tub and exercise machines. The park is popular with families in high season when it can be busy at weekends. A park and ride scheme for York operates from nearby all year, six days a week or there is a bus every two hours. The park is just over a mile from Sutton village.

**Facilities**

Tiled and heated, the modern toilet block is well maintained. An additional unit provides shower rooms, WC and washbasins in cubicles and extra dishwashing sinks. Full facilities for disabled visitors. Laundry room. Motorcaravan service point. Well-stocked shop (with gas). Fishing lake. Large adventure playground. Games room. Outdoor table tennis. Dogs (max. two per pitch), to be exercised in nearby woodland. WiFi throughout the park. No tents are accepted. Off site: Riding and golf 1 mile. Bicycle hire 6 miles. York 6 miles.

Open: February - December.

**Directions**

Park is 6 miles north of York; from the A1237 York outer ring-road take the B1363 for Sutton-on-the-Forest and Stillington, taking the first right after the Haxby and Wigginton junction and follow park signs. O.S.GR: SE595636. GPS: 54.05929, -1.09406

**Charges guide**

| | |
|---|---|
| Per unit incl. 4 persons and electricity | £ 15.00 - £ 25.00 |
| extra person | £ 3.00 |
| awning or extra pup tent (1 only) | £ 3.00 |

*See advertisement on page 196.*

## York
### Alders Caravan Park

Home Farm, Alne, York YO61 1RY (North Yorkshire) T: 01347 838722. E: enquiries@homefarmalne.co.uk

**alanrogers.com/UK4638**

Alders is located in the village of Alne, only nine miles from the centre of the ancient city of York. Carefully developed on a working farm in historic parkland, the drive to reach the pitches gives a real feeling of space. On reaching the 87 level pitches (25 for tourers, the rest for seasonal units), you will find an area of well trimmed grass and a pitch layout designed to give as much privacy and space as possible. Arranged in small bays, each group is named after a Yorkshire Abbey or Dale. Newly planted woodland with woodland walks and a water meadow with wild flowers enhance the wonderful peace and tranquillity. The site overlooks the village cricket pitch where you can watch summer matches or enjoy a drink at the club bar at weekends. This park would suit couples or young families (no play area). The village centre is only a short stroll away. Alders is also well placed for visiting the many attractions of the area, for example York, Harrogate and Castle Howard.

**Facilities**

The central toilet block is heated with family sized shower rooms, one also has a bath (£1 charge). A new block includes en-suite bathrooms with bath or shower, laundry and dishwashing facilities. Provision for disabled visitors. Gas is sold at reception (shop in the village). Off site: Floodlit tennis courts in the village. Fishing 2 miles. Golf 3 miles. Riding 4 miles.

Open: 1 March - 31 October.

**Directions**

From the north on the A19: after leaving Easingwold bypass take next right turn signed Alne. From the south (A19), 5 miles north of Shipton turn left at sign for Alne. In 1.5 miles at T-junction turn left and in about 0.5 miles, site is signed in the centre of the village. O.S.GR: SE496651. GPS: 54.08185, -1.24105

**Charges guide**

| | |
|---|---|
| Per unit incl. 2 persons and electricity | £ 14.00 |
| extra person | £ 2.50 |
| awning | £ 1.50 |

For latest campsite news visit
**alanrogers.com**

## York
### Moorside Caravan Park
Lords Moor Lane, Strensall, York YO32 5XJ (North Yorkshire) T: 01904 491208
alanrogers.com/UK4610

Strensall is only a few miles from York, one of England's most attractive cities and Moorside Adult Touring Park will provide a peaceful haven after a day's sightseeing. Children (under 16) are not accepted at this park. It will impress you with its pretty fishing lake, masses of flowers and the tranquillity (except for the odd passing daytime train). There are 57 marked pitches on neat well trimmed grass, most with electricity (5/10A) and 18 with paved hardstanding. The whole park is very well maintained making it a very pleasant environment. The small lake is well stocked for coarse fishing and the pitches bordering the lake are the most popular. York Golf Course is almost opposite the site entrance.

**Facilities**

The purpose built toilet block can be heated and houses immaculately kept facilities with washbasins in cubicles for ladies. One WC is suitable for use by disabled visitors. Fully equipped laundry room. Tourist information and books to borrow. Coarse fishing (£3 per day). Caravan storage. Off site: Strensall village with shops and places to eat is less than a mile. Golf 0.5 miles. Riding 3 miles.

Open: March - end October.

**Directions**

From A1237 York outer ring road follow signs for Earswick and Strensall. At Strensall follow Flaxton road. The park entrance is on the left past signs to Strensall village and York Golf Club. O.S.GR: SE647614. GPS: 54.042733, -1.011683

**Charges guide**

Per unit incl. 2 persons and electricity £ 13.00 - £ 16.50
No credit cards.

## York
### Golden Square Caravan & Camping Park
Oswaldkirk, Helmsley, York YO62 5YQ (North Yorkshire) T: 01439 788269
E: reception@goldensquarecaravanpark.com alanrogers.com/UK4560

Golden Square is a popular, high quality, family owned touring park. Mr. and Mrs. Armstrong are local farmers who have worked hard to turn an old quarry into a very attractive caravan park with a number of level bays that have superb views over the North York Moors. The 130 pitches are not separated but they do have markers set into the ground and mainly back on to grass banks. In very dry weather the ground can be hard and steel pegs would be needed (even in wet weather the park is well drained). All pitches have electricity (10A), 24 have drainage and six are 'deluxe' pitches (with waste water, sewage, electricity, water and TV aerial connection).

**Facilities**

Two heated toilet blocks have been refurbished and are of excellent quality, one with underfloor heating, with some washbasins in private cabins. Showers are free. Bathroom (£1) also houses baby facilities. Both ladies and men have full facilities for disabled visitors. Laundry facilities. Motorcaravan service point. Shop. Two excellent play areas. Games field and a barn with games. Bicycle hire. All year caravan storage. Off site: Riding 2 miles. Golf 3 miles. Fishing 5 milesl.

Open: 1 March - 31 October.

**Directions**

From York take B1363 to Helmsley. At Oswaldkirk Bank Top turn left on B1257 to Helmsley. Take second left turn signed Ampleforth to site. O.S.GR: SE605797. GPS: 54.209333, -1.073783

**Charges guide**

Per unit incl. 2 persons £ 14.00 - £ 20.00
extra person £ 2.00
extra child (5-14 yrs) £ 1.00
No credit cards.

## York
### South Lea Caravan Park
The Balk, Pocklington, York YO42 2NX (North Yorkshire) T: 01759 303467. E: info@south-lea.co.uk
alanrogers.com/UK4655

South Lea is situated just off the A1079 road near the delightful market town of Pocklington, about 12 miles from York. A well presented open park with 72 pitches set in 15 acres of flat grassland. Some are hardstanding and all have electricity (16A). The park is divided in to areas by shrubs and hedges, each named after a type of tree. Some areas are in the early stages of planting. The site is ideally positioned for touring the many places of interest in the surrounding area and is within reach of the coast. There is a public telephone box on site, and a large dog walking area.

**Facilities**

One toilet block (can be heated) with free showers and hairdryers. There are no facilities for campers with disabilities at present, but these are being planned. Dog showers. Calor Gas supplies. Off site: Pocklington nearby with shops and restaurants, a comprehensive leisure centre and pool. Local airfield for gliders, lessons and pleasure flight. Bus stop at site entrance.

Open: 1 March - 31 October.

**Directions**

Travelling from the west on the A1079 ignore the first turn off to Pocklington. Stay on the A1079 to signs for the campsite. The turning will be on the left and the site is a short distance down this road on the left. GPS: 53.914298, -0.773592

**Charges guide**

Per unit incl. 2 persons £ 13.50 - £ 16.50
No credit cards.

## North West England

The northwest region boasts a wealth of industrial heritage with undiscovered countrys... the vibrant cities of Manchester and Liverpo... the seaside resorts of Black... and Morecambe Bay, plus miles ... glorious coastline, home to a wide variety of bird species.

**THIS REGION INCLUDES: CHESHIRE, LANCASHIRE, MERSEYSIDE, GREATER MANCHESTER AND THE HIGH PEAKS OF DERBYSHIRE**

The miles of beautiful, North West countryside offers endless opportunities for recreation. For the more active, the peaceful plains of Cheshire are a walker's haven with endless trails to choose from. Lancashire is also good walking country, with way-marked paths passing through the outstanding forest of Bowland, which affords marvellous views over the Lake District in Cumbria and the Yorkshire Dales. Birdwatchers are catered for too, with the coast offering some of the best bird spotting activity in the country, most notably along the Sefton coast and around the Wirral Peninsula. The region's cities have their own charm. Manchester, with its fabulous shopping centres and vibrant nightlife, boasts a rich Victorian heritage; the maritime city of Liverpool has more museums and galleries than any other UK city outside London; Lancaster features fine Georgian buildings and an imposing Norman castle; while Chester is renowned for its medieval architecture and shopping galleries. And offering good, old-fashioned seaside fun is Blackpool. England's most popular seaside resort is packed full of lively entertainment and attractions, such as the white knuckle rides at the pleasure beach, amusement games on the pier and the observation decks in the famous Tower.

### Places of interest

*Cheshire:* Tatton Park in Knutsford; Chester Cathedral and Zoo; Cheshire Military Museum; Lyme Park stately home in Macclesfield; Beeston Castle; Boat Museum at Ellesmere Port.

*Lancashire:* Williamson Park, Castle and Leisure Park in Lancaster; Camelot Theme Park; Museum of Football in Preston; Morecambe Bay; Hoghton Tower and National Museum of Football in Preston.

*Merseyside:* Liverpool Football Club Museum and Tour Centre; The Beatles Story Museum; Speke Hall Garden and Estate; The Wirral Country Park; Williamson Tunnels Heritage Centre.

*Greater Manchester:* Imperial War Museum North; Manchester United Football Club Museum; The Lowry; Corgi Heritage Centre in Rochdale; Stockport Air Raid Shelter.

### Did you know?

The first public gallery to open in England was in Liverpool in 1877.

Lancaster Castle is infamous as host to the Pendle Witch trials in 1612.

The first passenger railway station was built in Manchester.

Hoghton Tower is where King James I knighted a loin of beef in 1617 – hence the name Sirloin.

To date 300 bird species have been recorded within the boundaries of Sefton.

Chester has the most complete set of city walls in Britain.

Opened in 1894, the Blackpool Tower was copied from the Eiffel Tower; the height to the top of the flagpole is 518 feet 9 inches.

## Maps and campsite listings

For this 2011 guide we have changed the way in which we list our parks and also the way in which we help you locate the parks within each region.

We now include a map immediately after our Introduction to that region. These maps show the towns near which one (or more) of our featured parks is located. Within each regional section of the guide, we list these towns and the park(s) in that vicinity in alphabetical order.

You will certainly need more detailed maps for navigation, for example the Ordnance Survey road atlas. We provide O.S. references and G.P.S. coordinates for each park to assist you. Our three indexes will also help you to find a park by its reference number and name, by region and park name, or by the town where the park is situated.

## Carnforth

### Old Hall Caravan Park

Capernwray, Carnforth LA6 1AD (Lancashire) T: 01524 733276. E: info@oldhallcaravanpark.co.uk
alanrogers.com/UK5271

In a woodland clearing, just five minutes drive from junction 35 of the M6, Old Hall Caravan Park is a gem. Approached along a tree-lined road, this secluded park offers peace and tranquillity. There are 38 touring pitches which are accessed from a circular roadway, all on marked and level hardstandings and with 16A electricity, water and drainage (shared between two pitches). TV hook-ups are available (free). Tents are not accepted. There are 220 privately owned holiday homes which are quite separate from the touring pitches. A new adventure play area is located in a wooded clearing and there are woodland walks for all to enjoy along with the birds and wildlife. A narrow river runs through the park. Tourist information is available from the reception building.

**Facilities**

The central sanitary block (combination lock) is very clean and is heated during cooler months. Vanity style washbasins and large controllable showers. Separate unit for disabled visitors doubles as a family room. Laundry facilities. Gas supplies. WiFi. Off site: Canal fishing 300 yds. Over Kellet 2 miles. Carnforth 3 miles. Historic Lancaster and the seaside town of Morecambe (15 minutes drive). Trough of Bowland, Yorkshire Dales and Grange-over-Sands (30 minutes drive).

Open: 1 March - 10 January.

**Directions**

From M6 exit 35 take link road signed Over Kellet. Turn left on B6254. At Over Kellet village green turn left signed Capernwray and follow for 1.5 miles. Park is on the right at the end of a 0.5 mile drive. O.S.GR: SD538718. GPS: 54.13958, -2.71357

**Charges guide**

| | |
|---|---|
| Per unit incl. electricity | £ 20.00 |

## Carnforth

### Bay View Holiday Park

A6 Main Road, Bolton Le Sands, Carnforth LA5 8ES (Lancashire) T: 01524 732854
E: info@holgatesleisureparks.co.uk alanrogers.com/UK5270

Previously two adjacent parks, Bolton Holmes and Detrongate, Bay View is being developed by the Holgate family into an excellent addition to their group. Situated on the coast north of Lancaster, the park is an ideal base for exploring the Lake District, North Yorkshire and the Forest of Bowland. The park is divided into several grassy, sloping fields and many of the pitches have stunning views over Morecambe Bay, others look towards the Lakeland Fells. It is a very open park with little shade. Of the 240 touring pitches, 192 have 6-15A electricity and 15 are fully serviced. There are also 100 pitches for caravan holiday homes. From the park there is direct access to the salt marshes and eventually the sea, although care must be taken in Morecambe Bay because of the quicksands. A safe way of crossing the bay is to join an organised walk led by the Queens Guide, Cedric Robinson. These take place on many weekends during the summer, and a list of dates is posted in reception.

**Facilities**

Three toilet blocks, one refurbished the others to follow. Facilities for disabled visitors. Good laundry. Motorcaravan service point. Small shop. Playground for younger children, large field for ball games. Games room. Future plans include a bar/restaurant. Off site: Fishing 200 yds. Golf and riding 3 miles. Canal cruises on Lancaster Canal. Leighton Moss RSPB nature reserve. Good shopping in nearby Lancaster and Kendal 15 miles.

Open: 1 March - 31 October.

**Directions**

From M6 exit 35 take the A601M to roundabout and follow signs to Morecambe. Continue through Carnforth and after mini-roundabout look for site sign in 500 yds on the right. O.S.GR: SD480692. GPS: 54.11602, -2.78791

**Charges guide**

| | |
|---|---|
| Per unit with 2 persons, car and electricity | £ 12.00 - £ 16.00 |
| extra person | £ 3.00 |
| child | £ 2.00 |
| dog | £ 1.00 |

For latest campsite news visit
**alanrogers.com**

## Carnforth

### Holgates Caravan Park

Middlebarrow Plain, Cove Road, Silverdale LA5 0SH (Lancashire) T: 01524 701508. E: caravan@holgates.co.uk
alanrogers.com/UK5350

This attractive, very high quality park is in an outstanding craggy, part-wooded, hillside location with fine views over Morecambe Bay. It takes 80 touring units, with 339 privately owned caravan holiday homes and 14 to rent located in woodland away from the touring pitches. With just 5 grassy pitches for tents (steel pegs required), the remaining large touring pitches are on gravel hardstandings, all with electricity (16A), free TV connection, individual drainage and water points. The main complex with reception and the entrance barrier, provides a well stocked supermarket, lounge bar, restaurant with good value meals and a terrace with views over the bay. There is also an indoor leisure centre. Children have a choice of two adventure playgrounds and plenty of space for ball games. Also on site is a small but challenging pitch and putt golf course. Everything is completed to the highest standards.

**Facilities**

Two modern, heated toilet buildings are fully equipped with top quality fittings and include some private cubicles with WC and washbasin. Excellent provision for disabled visitors with a reserved pitch and parking bay adjacent. Launderette. Shop. Gas supplies. Bar and restaurant. Indoor pool (17x17 m. with lifeguard) with spa pool, steam room and sauna. Well equipped gym (charged). Playgrounds. Games room. Pitch and putt course (£2 per person). Facilities are limited mid week in January and early February. Off site: Riding, cycling, golf and fishing all within 4 miles. Morecambe or Lancaster 12 miles. Kendal 15 miles. RSPB nature reserve at Leighton Moss.

**Open:** All year excl. 6 November - 21 December.

**Directions**

From traffic lights in centre of Carnforth take road to Silverdale under low bridge. After 1 mile turn left signed Silverdale and after 2.5 miles over level crossing, carry on and turn right at T-junction. Follow Holgates sign from here watching for left then right forks (narrow roads). O.S.GR: SD460755. GPS: 54.17615, -2.8359

**Charges guide**

| | |
|---|---|
| Per unit incl. 2 adults and all services | £ 30.00 |
| extra person | £ 8.00 |
| extra child (2-17 yrs) | £ 3.50 |
| awning or pup tent | £ 2.00 |

Minimum stays apply for all B.H weekends.

## Discover an ever-changing landscape

Discover the very best of British holidays in one of our award winning holiday parks and cottages. Situated in the unspoilt Cumbria Lancashire borders, nestled between the Coast and Lake District Mountains.

**Holgates**
Make the discovery

For all enquiries contact Holgates Caravan Parks
Telephone: 01524 701508 or Email: info@holgates.co.uk
Website: www.holgates.co.uk

## Lancaster

### Moss Wood Caravan Park

Crimbles Lane, Cockerham, Lancaster LA2 0ES (Lancashire) T: 01524 791041. E: info@mosswood.co.uk
alanrogers.com/UK5272

Moss Wood is a well established park set in a secluded rural location near the village of Cockerham. You can be sure of a friendly welcome from the park wardens Ian and Sandra when you arrive. A sheltered field has 25 touring pitches on level hardstandings (steel pegs required) with 16A electricity. Most also have water and drainage. Screened from the touring area by a high fence so not visually intrusive are 175 privately owned holiday homes. A purpose-built log cabin houses reception and a shop which sells basic supplies. Although there are passing places, the approach road to the park is narrow.

**Facilities**

New centrally located sanitary block (key entry) is kept spotlessly clean and provides vanity style washbasins and roomy, preset showers. Fully equipped facilities for disabled visitors. Laundry facilities. Adventure playground. Fishing lake (fenced). Woodland dog walking. Off site: Pubs at Cockerham 1 mile. Riding 3 miles. Beach 5 miles. Golf 6 miles. Garstang, seaside town of Morecambe and the Lune Valley all within easy reach.

**Open:** 1 March - 31 October.

**Directions**

Park is 1 mile west of Cockerham on the A588. Leave M6 at junction 33 joining the A6 southbound and follow signs for Cockerham. A588 is 4 miles. Site is signed on the left. O.S.GR: SD456498. GPS: 53.93788, -2.82087

**Charges guide**

| | |
|---|---|
| Per unit incl. 2 adults, 2 children and electricity | £ 18.00 - £ 23.00 |
| extra person | £ 3.00 |

## Lytham Saint Annes

### Eastham Hall Caravan Park

Saltcotes Road, Lytham Saint Annes FY8 4LS (Lancashire) T: 01253 737907. E: info@easthamhall.co.uk

alanrogers.com/UK5295

Eastham Hall is a well established, family run park set in rural Lancashire between the Victorian town of Lytham and the pretty village of Wrea Green. Entering by an electronic barrier system, one sees an area of 150 caravan holiday homes. Quite separate are around 173 pitches for touring units and seasonal rental on open plan, mostly level grass, with 10A electricity. Of these, there are 49 'super' pitches on hardstanding and grass with full services including 16A electricity. Tents are not accepted. A further 5 extra large pitches are on grass (units up to 28 feet can be taken). Mature trees border the park and shrubs and bushes separate the various areas. The reception is spacious with lots of tourist information and, at one end, is a large well stocked shop. The park has no bar or clubhouse, but Lytham is just five minutes by car or a pleasant twenty-minute walk. The flat terrain is also ideal for cycling.

### Facilities

Three toilet blocks are kept clean and are being updated to include solar panels for heating and private cubicles. Laundry. Excellent facilities for disabled visitors. Gas supplies. Well stocked shop. Adventure play area and large sports field. Barrier (£10 deposit). WiFi throughout park. Off site: Excellent pub in Wrea Green. Shops and restaurants in Lytham 2.5 miles. Blackpool 6 miles. Golf and riding 1 mile. Fishing 2.5 miles. Boat launching 2 miles. Local bus stops at entrance to park.

Open: 1 March - 31 October.

### Directions

From M55 take exit 3 and turn left for Kirkham. At roundabouts follow signs for Wrea Green and Lytham. Continue on B5259 passing Grapes pub and village green. After 1.5 miles cross level crossing (Moss Side) and park is 1 mile on left. O.S.GR: SD377290. GPS: 53.75375, -2.94225

### Charges guide

| | |
|---|---|
| Per unit incl. 1-4 persons | |
| and electricity | £ 15.00 - £ 28.00 |
| serviced pitch | £ 19.00 - £ 32.00 |
| extra person | £ 2.50 |
| child (5-11 yrs) | £ 1.00 |
| dog | £ 2.00 |

*Eastham Hall Caravan Park - a secluded tranquil Holiday Park*

This family run park is a lovely oasis of calm in beautiful rural surroundings. Only 1½ miles from the stylish Victorian town of Lytham, 2 miles from the pretty village of Wrea Green and 6 miles from Blackpool.

01253 737907 • info@easthamhall.co.uk • www.easthamhall.co.uk

Eastham Hall Caravan Park, Saltcotes Road, Lytham St Annes, Lancashire, FY8 4LS

Eastham Hall

## Northwich

### Lamb Cottage Caravan Park

Dalefords Lane, Whitegate, Northwich CW8 2BN (Cheshire) T: 01606 882302. E: info@lambcottage.co.uk

alanrogers.com/UK5240

This quiet, family run adult only park is set in the midst of the lovely Vale Royal area of Cheshire. Fifteen landscaped seasonal caravan pitches are followed by the touring area which has 41 large pitches, all with 16A electric hook-ups, gravel hardstandings, water and drainage. There are an additional 4 motorcaravan pitches with hardstanding and electricity. Only breathable groundsheets are permitted and tents are not accepted. Nearby are Delamere Forest with its walking and mountain biking trails, Whitegate Way walking trail, Oulton Park Motor Racing Circuit, castles at Peckforton and Beeston, and the city of Chester, which is 12 miles.

### Facilities

Toilet and shower facilities are housed in a custom built 'park home' style unit which includes washbasins in cubicles and facilities for disabled guests. Laundry room. Recycling of glass and paper. Calor gas stocked. Fenced dog walk (max. 2 dogs per unit permitted). Off site: Pub serving food under 1 mile. Riding 1.5 miles. Golf 2 miles. Supermarket 3 miles. Fishing 3 miles. Bicycle hire 4 miles.

Open: 1 March - 31 October.

### Directions

From M6 exit 19 take A556 towards Chester. After about 12 miles turn left at traffic lights (signed Winsford and Whitegate) into Dalefords Lane. Continue for about 1 mile and site entrance is on right between a white house and bungalow. O.S.GR: SJ614693. GPS: 53.218244, -2.578655

### Charges guide

| | |
|---|---|
| Per unit incl. 2 persons | |
| and electricity | £ 18.00 - £ 25.00 |

For latest campsite news visit
alanrogers.com

## Ormskirk

### Abbey Farm Caravan Park

Dark Lane, Ormskirk L40 5TX (Lancashire) T: 01695 572686. E: abbeyfarm@yahoo.com
**alanrogers.com/UK5280**

This quiet, well equipped, family park beside the Abbey ruins has views over open farmland. It is an ideal base for a longer stay with plenty of interest in the local area, including Ormskirk parish church, unusual for having both a tower and a spire. The park is divided into small paddocks, one of which is for privately owned seasonal units, one for tents, the others for touring units, plus a rally field for special events. The 60 touring pitches, all with electricity (16A), and 12 of which have water and waste water, are on neatly mown level grass, separated by small shrubs and colourful flower borders. Mature trees provide shade in parts. Amenities include a farm walk and a small, free lending library with a good stock of tourist information. A member of the Countryside Discovery group.

#### Facilities

The main toilet block is modern, heated and spotless, providing controllable hot showers. Dual purpose family bathroom that includes facilities for disabled visitors. The second smaller unit has individual shower/WC/washbasin cubicles. Laundry room. Small well stocked shop at reception, with a butcher calling twice weekly. Indoor games room. Small adventure playground and large field for ball games. Fishing lake (£2 per rod, per day). Off site: Local market on Thursday and Saturday. Southport beach and Pleasureland 10 miles. Wigan Pier, Aintree for the Grand National, Southport Flower Show and Martin Mere Nature reserve are within easy reach.

**Open:** All year.

#### Directions

From M6 junction 27 take A5209 (Parbold) road. After 5 miles turn left (just before garage) onto B5240, and then first right into Hob Cross Lane, following signs to site. O.S.GR: SD433099. GPS: 53.5698, -2.85665

#### Charges guide

| | |
|---|---|
| Per unit incl. 2 persons and electricity | £ 14.10 - £ 17.70 |
| extra person | £ 3.50 |
| child (5-15 yrs) | £ 2.00 |
| dog | £ 1.00 - £ 2.50 |

Less 10% for 7 nights booked on or before arrival.

---

## Preston

### Royal Umpire Caravan Park

Southport Road, Croston, Preston PR26 9JB (Lancashire) T: 01772 600257. E: reception@royalumpire.co.uk
**alanrogers.com/UK5290**

Royal Umpire is a spacious park near the coast and the M6 for overnight or longer stays. The entrance to the park is past a large grass area leading to the security barrier with reception immediately to the left, and slightly ahead is an unusual sunken garden area that is a pleasing feature. Comprising 60 acres, the park has 200 pitches, almost all with 10A electricity, but a few with 16A. About 75% of the pitches have gravel hardstanding, some with TV and water connections. Tarmac and gravel roads connect the various pitch areas. There is a shop within 100 yards and a good choice of pubs serving bar or restaurant meals nearby. A rally field can accommodate large groups and events.

#### Facilities

Two modern, heated, toilet blocks, one beside reception, the other centrally situated. Fully equipped laundry. Very good facilities for disabled visitors that are shared with baby facilities (entrance with key, £20 deposit). Adventure playground. Field area for ball games. Rally field. Dog exercise area. Off site: A short walk takes you to the nearby river for fishing and the conservation village of Croston. Shop and pubs nearby. Riding 2 miles.

**Open:** All year.

#### Directions

From north use M6 exit 28 joining A49 going south (parallel to M6) for 2 miles. Then right across M6 on A581 to Croston (4 miles). From the south use M6 exit 27 onto A5209 but immediately right on the B5250 and follow towards Eccleston, joining the A581 at Newtown (5 miles). Site is clearly signed with wide entrance east of Croston. O.S.GR: SD505189. GPS: 53.66669, -2.74827

#### Charges 2011

| | |
|---|---|
| Per unit incl. 2 adults, 2 children and electricity | £ 14.00 - £ 26.00 |

Less 10% for 7 nights pre-booked.
Mid-week stays less.

## Southport
### Willowbank Touring Park

Coastal Road, Ainsdale, Southport PR8 3ST (Mersey) T: 01704 571566. E: info@willowbankcp.co.uk

alanrogers.com/UK5360

Willowbank Park is well situated for the Sefton coast and Southport, set on the edge of sand dunes amongst mature, wind swept trees. Entrance to the park is controlled by a barrier, with a pass-key issued at the excellent reception building which doubles as a sales office for the substantial, high quality caravan holiday home development. There are now 87 touring pitches, 30 on gravel hardstandings, 24 on grass (all with 10A electricity) and a further 33 new pitches with 16A electricity. These are on grass hardstanding using an environmentally friendly reinforcement system. Tents, large units (longer than 8 m) and caravans of foreign manufacture are not accepted. The owners are very well supported on the touring side by the reception team which has considerable experience in managing the touring park. There could be some noise from the nearby main road. This is a good area for cycling and walking with the Trans Pennine Way being adjacent. The attractions of Southport with its parks, gardens, funfair and shopping are 4 miles away. The area is famous for its golf courses including the Royal Birkdale championship links.

### Facilities

The purpose built, heated toilet block (refurbished in 2010) is of a high standard including an excellent bathroom for disabled visitors, although the showers are rather compact. Baby room. Laundry. Motorcaravan service point. Play area. Field for ball games. Beauty treatments. Off site: Beach 1.5 miles. Golf and riding 0.5 miles. Fishing 4 miles. Bicycle hire 4.5 miles. Martin Mere nature reserve nearby.

Open: All year excl. February.

### Directions

Park is 4 miles south of Southport. From Ainsdale on A565 travel south for 1.5 miles to second traffic lights (Woodvale) and turn right into Coastal Road to site on left in 150 yds. From the south pass RAF Woodvale and turn left at second set of lights. O.S.GR: SD308108. GPS: 53.5888, -3.044

### Charges guide

| | |
|---|---|
| Per unit incl. 2 persons and electricity | £ 13.20 - £ 16.20 |
| hardstanding | £ 1.65 |
| extra person | £ 2.50 - £ 3.20 |
| dog (max. 2) | £ 1.30 |

Latest arrival time 21.00 hrs.

## Willowbank Touring Park

* 87 pitches available * Gravel Hardstanding * Grass
* Grass Hardstanding * All with electricity hook up
* Level park throughout * Luxury heated shower and toilet facilities * Laundry Dish washing room * Separate shower and toilet room with wheelchair access * Childrens' play area * Dog exercise area * Strictly no vans or commercial vehicles admitted to the park

*Early booking is essential for busy periods and special events such as the Flower Show and Air Show*

**Willowbank, Coastal Road, Ainsdale, Southport PR8 3ST**
**Tel: 01704 571566   Fax: 01704 571576   www.willowbankcp.co.uk**

For latest campsite news visit
**alanrogers.com**

## Southport

### Riverside Holiday Park

Southport New Road, Banks, Southport PR9 8DF (Lancashire) T: 01704 228 886
E: reception@harrisonleisureuk.com  alanrogers.com/UK5285

Situated by a busy road on the outskirts of the Lancashire coastal town of Southport, Riverside Holiday Park covers 80 acres and has a total of 620 pitches. Of these, 200 are for touring units and tents, 70 with electricity (10A), some with hardstanding. The park is level and open with little shade. A narrow unfenced river runs through the park where fishing in season is possible (licence required). Apart from an outdoor play area for younger children, most of the activities on the park centre around the indoor games room, with live entertainment, a pool room, and a large amusement arcade.

#### Facilities

Three heated toilet blocks (key entry) only one of which has showers. At busy times these could be stretched and cleaning is variable. Facilities for disabled visitors and babies. Laundry. Well stocked shop. Large bar with TV. Café. Games room. Pool room. Large amusement arcade. Play area. River fishing (with licence). Family club in high season with games, fancy dress, discos etc. Dog walking area. Bus route. WiFi in Café. Off site: Shops and botanical gardens in Southport, Splash World swimming complex, Martin Mere wetland wildlife reserve. Golf and riding (1 mile). Bicycle hire and beach (5 miles).

Open: All year excl. 1-13 February.

#### Directions

From the south, M6 junction 26 take M58 to the end, take A59 north towards Preston. From the north, M6 junction 31 take A59 south towards Liverpool/Southport. Both directions, just south of Tarleton, turn west on A565 towards Southport. Park on left in 3 miles. GPS: 53.666955, -2.901056

#### Charges guide

Per unit incl. electricity                 £ 17.00 - £ 25.00

---

## Thornton-Cleveleys

### Kneps Farm Holiday Park

River Road, Stanah, Thornton-Cleveleys FY5 5LR (Lancashire) T: 01253 823632
E: enquiries@knepsfarm.co.uk  alanrogers.com/UK5300

A well established park with top class modern facilities, Kneps Farm is still operated by the family who opened it in 1967. Next to Wyre Country Park, it makes an excellent base from which to explore the area. A VNPR operated barrier system flanks the reception building which also houses a well stocked shop. The 60 marked and numbered touring pitches are generally on hardstandings, 48 with electricity (16A), and all are accessed from tarmac roads. There are also some grassy pitches and a separate area with 50 caravan holiday homes (most privately owned). A path leads through a gate at the back of the site into the country park. Just down the lane is a public slipway and the Wyreside Ecology Centre. A list and map are provided of local services and amenities, including pubs, restaurants, takeaway, etc. Other local attractions include Marsh Mill Village with a restored windmill, the Freeport Shopping and Leisure village at nearby Fleetwood and several bird-watching sites around the estuary and country park.

#### Facilities

The large, centrally heated sanitary building is warm and inviting with ten individual family bathrooms, each providing a WC, basin and bath/shower. Separate toilet facilities with electric hand-wash units for men and women. Well equipped room for disabled visitors. Combined baby care/first aid room. Laundry room. Small well stocked shop. Small, fenced playground. Up to two dogs are accepted per unit. WiFi in reception area. Off site: Sailing 300 yds. Beach and golf 2.5 miles. Fishing 4 miles.

Open: 1 March - 15 November.

#### Directions

From M55 junction 3, take A585 towards Fleetwood. Turn left at traffic lights, then turn right at traffic lights by Shell station (for Thornton-Cleveleys), straight across next traffic lights, then right at the next roundabout by River Wyre Hotel. After one mile (past school) turn right at mini-roundabout into Stanah Road, continue across second mini-roundabout and eventually into River Road with site entrance ahead of you. Do not use sat nav. O.S.GR: SD350430. GPS: 53.87903, -2.98506

#### Charges guide

| | |
|---|---|
| Per unit incl. 2 adults, 2 children and electricity | £ 22.50 - £ 25.00 |
| tent incl. 2 adults, 2 children | £ 19.50 - £ 22.00 |
| adult couple | £ 14.50 - £ 19.00 |
| extra person | £ 3.25 - £ 3.75 |
| extra child | £ 2.50 - £ 3.00 |
| Special senior citizen rates. | |

With spectacular lakes undulating fells, impressive mountains and lush green valleys, Cumbria is ideal for those who wish to get away from it all and unwind in peaceful, natural surroundings, or for the more active who want to participate in a range of outdoor pursuits.

Cumbria is best known for the beautiful Lake District National Park, with the picturesque valleys and lakes of Windermere, Ullswater and Derwentwater, each with its own distinctive character. Windermere offers no shortage of watersports, whereas Ullswater mainly attracts peaceful sailing boats. While the Lake District is well known, there are also many quiet, undiscovered areas in the region including the wild, rugged moors of the north Pennines and the beautiful Eden Valley, an ideal place for a casual stroll along the riverside footpaths. The Western Lakes and Fells offer more tranquillity. Here the fells drop down to a long and spectacular coastline, with many undiscovered, quiet corners from Ennerdale and Esdale to the sandstone cliffs of St Bees Head, now part of a designated Heritage Coast. The Lake District Peninsulas along the southern coast of Cumbria also display beautiful scenery and are home to a cluster of ancient ruins such as Furness Abbey and the medieval castle, built by monks, on Piel Island. Rich in heritage, the historic city of Carlisle, which was sited on the Roman-built Hadrian's wall, boasts an impressive castle, Cumbria's only cathedral, a superb Victorian covered market and an array of speciality shops.

## Places of interest

*Barrow-in-Furness:* South Lakes Wild Animal Park; Dalton Castle; Furness Abbey; Piel Island.

*Carlisle:* 11th-century castle; Birdoswald Roman fort; Lanercost Priory.

*Ravenglass:* Muncaster Castle, an historic haunted castle and Headquarters of the World Owl Trust.

*Ulverston:* the world's only Laurel and Hardy museum.

*Kendal:* historic riverside town situated between the Lakes and Dales, famous for its mint cake and castle ruins.

*Lake Derwentwater:* lakeside theatre open all year hosting plays, music, dance, comedy and film.

*Windermere:* Steamboat Centre, a collection of Windermere's nautical heritage with boats on display; World of Beatrix Potter.

*Grasmere:* Dove Cottage and Wordsworth Museum.

## Did you know?

Cumbria has the steepest road in England, called the Hardknott Pass.

The Lake District was the inspiration for many poets, writers and artists, including William Wordsworth, Beatrix Potter and John Ruskin.

Ulverston is the birthplace of Quakerism and pole vaulting.

Bassenthwaite is the only real lake in the Lake District! All the others are either meres, (Windermere) or waters (Derwentwater, Coniston Water and Ullswater).

Stretching 73 miles, Hadrian's Wall was built by Romans in the second century.

## Ambleside

### Skelwith Fold Caravan Park

Ambleside LA22 0HX (Cumbria) T: 01539 432277. E: info@skelwith.com

**alanrogers.com/UK5520**

Skelwith Fold has been developed in the extensive grounds of a country estate taking advantage of the wealth of mature trees and shrubs. The 300 privately owned caravan holiday homes and 150 touring pitches are absorbed into this unspoilt natural environment, sharing it with red squirrels and other wildlife in several discrete areas branching off the central, mile long main driveway. Touring pitches (no tents) are on gravel hardstanding and metal pegs will be necessary for awnings. Electricity hook-ups (10A) and basic amenities are available in all areas. Youngsters and indeed their parents will find endless pleasure exploring over 90 acres of wild woodland and, if early risers, it is possible to see deer, foxes, etc. at the almost hidden tarn deep in the woods.

#### Facilities

Eight toilet blocks, well situated to serve all areas, have the usual facilities including laundry, drying and ironing rooms. Some blocks have facilities for disabled visitors. Well stocked, licensed shop. Motorcaravan service point. Battery charging, gas and caravan spares and accessories. Adventure play area. Family recreation area with picnic tables and goal posts in the Lower Glade. Off site: Ambleside village 2.5 miles. Pubs within walking distance. Fishing 200 m. Riding and sailing 3 miles.

Open: 1 March - 15 November.

#### Directions

From Ambleside take the A593 towards Coniston. Pass through Clappergate and on the far outskirts watch for the B5286 to Hawkshead on the left. Park is clearly signed 1 mile down this road on the right. Do not use sat nav to find this park.
O.S.GR: NY358028. GPS: 54.41715, -2.995283

#### Charges guide

| | |
|---|---:|
| Per pitch | £ 18.50 - £ 23.00 |
| incl. electricity | £ 21.50 - £ 26.00 |
| awning | £ 3.00 |

For latest campsite news visit

**alanrogers.com**

## Appleby-in-Westmorland

### Wild Rose Park

Ormside, Appleby-in-Westmorland CA16 6EJ (Cumbria) T: 01768 351077. E: reception@wildrose.co.uk

alanrogers.com/UK5570

Set in the Eden Valley within easy reach of the Lake District and the Yorkshire Dales, Wild Rose is a well known park. The entrance is inviting with its well mown grass, trim borders and colourful flower displays. It is immediately apparent that this is a much loved park, and this is reflected throughout the site in the care and attention to detail. There are 226 touring pitches all with electricity, however 105 also provide water and waste water, plus the site boasts on-site wardens to ensure that everything is always neat and tidy. Wild Rose deserves its excellent reputation, which the owners strive to maintain and improve. There are five distinct areas on the park providing a variety of pitches and services. Hazel Heights and Egglestone Tiers provide fully serviced 'super' pitches with hardstanding, Braithwaite Fold and the Chesters have pitches with electricity and shared water points. The grass area of Donkey's Nest provides pitches with shared electricity and water. There are also 263 privately owned caravan holiday homes and lodges plus five wooden wigwams. Nothing is overlooked here, from recycling bins, electric buggies to keep the noise down, 'sac-o-mat' special bags and bins in the dog walk to cycle racks placed around the park. A member of the Best of British group.

### Facilities

Three toilet blocks (two heated) of excellent quality and kept spotlessly clean. Most washbasins are in cubicles. Facilities for babies and for disabled visitors. Fully equipped laundry with lines and drying rooms. Motorcaravan service point. Exceptionally well stocked shop incl. gas (1/4-1/11). Licensed restaurant with takeaway and conservatory/coffee lounge (weekends only in low season). Outdoor pool (late May-Sept). Indoor playroom for under fives. TV room. Cinema room. Tennis. Off site: Fishing 2 miles. Golf and riding 3 miles.

Open: All year.

### Directions

Park is signed south off B6260 road 1.5 miles southwest of Appleby. Follow signs to park, in the direction of Ormside. O.S.GR: NY697165. GPS: 54.54893, -2.46422

### Charges guide

| | |
|---|---|
| Per unit incl. 2 persons and electricity | £ 18.00 - £ 32.50 |
| extra person (over 4 yrs) | £ 3.00 - £ 4.00 |
| dog | £ 1.50 |

Less 10% for 7 nights or more and for over 60s.

# Eden's caravanning paradise

Nestling in magnificent Eden - very close to the Lake District and the Pennines, Wild Rose Park is a multi-award winning park set in beautiful tranquil surroundings. This superb park includes over 220 designated camping and touring pitches, mini market, restaurant, laundrette, adventure playgrounds, outdoor pools, TV and Games Rooms... paradise!

Call or write for a FREE brochure:
Ormside, Appleby, Cumbria, CA16 6EJ.
017683 51077 reception@wildrose.co.uk

## www.wildrose.co.uk

## Arnside

### Hollins Farm Caravan & Camp Site

Far Arnside, Arnside LA5 0SL (Cumbria) T: 01524 701508. E: Info@hollinsfarm.co.uk

alanrogers.com/UK5595

Hollins Farm has been considerably improved since being taken over by the Holgate family just a year ago, without losing its appeal as a simple farm site. In a superb location overlooking Morecambe Bay, the park consists of several fields divided by trees. Of the 100 pitches, there are 40 for touring all with electricity (16A), water and TV connections, although large units may have difficulty negotiating the narrow country lanes. This is very popular walking country and leaflets may be obtained from reception. Visitors here are able to use the excellent facilities at the nearby Holgate Leisure Centre (charged).

### Facilities

Smart new portacabins house the toilets and showers, including facilities for disabled visitors. This site also now boasts fridge hire as well as caravan storage plus from 1/3 - 31/10 a site shop. In addition to this is a children's playground and TV room. Off site: Leighton Moss RSPB Nature reserve. Cross Bay walks. Golf 2 miles. Fishing 9 miles. Market town of Kendal 12 miles.

Open: 14 March - 31 October.

### Directions

From exit 35 of the M6 take the A601(M) and at first roundabout take second exit A6 North. In 2.5 miles take the left turn signed Yealand Redmayne, then follow site signs for Holgates. Hollins is 0.5 miles beyond Holgates. GPS: 54.18077, -2.84352

### Charges guide

| | |
|---|---|
| Per unit incl. 2 adults, 2 children and services | £ 21.00 - £ 29.00 |

For latest campsite news visit

## alanrogers.com

## Carlisle
### Green Acres Caravan Park
High Knells, Houghton, Carlisle CA6 4JW (Cumbria) T: 01228 675418. E: info@caravanpark-cumbria.com
alanrogers.com/UK5640

Green Acres is a small, family run park which from 2009 accepts only adults. Situated in beautiful, rural surroundings, yet only two miles from the M6/A74 it is perfect for an overnight stop or a longer stay to enjoy Cumbria, Hadrian's Wall and the delights of Carlisle city (4 miles away). The Browns have developed Green Acres into an attractive, well maintained and level touring park. There are 30 numbered pitches, all on large hardstandings, arranged in a semi-circle, with electricity connections (10A) and four serviced pitches (16A). Divided by a long beech hedge is a large camping field including on one side 12 new hardstanding 'super' pitches for seasonal letting.

| Facilities | Directions |
|---|---|
| Small, very clean toilet block with open style washbasins and coin operated showers (50p for 10 minutes). No facilities for disabled visitors. Laundry room in farm building. Car wash area. Caravan storage. Off site: Golf 3 miles. Fishing 8 miles. Riding and bicycle hire 10 miles. | Leave M6/A74 at junction 44 and take A689 for 1 mile. Turn left towards Scaleby (site signed) and site is 1 mile on left. O.S.GR: NY419615. GPS: 54.94505, -2.90728 |
| Open: 1 April - end October. | **Charges guide** |

Per unit incl. 2 persons
and electricity £ 13.00 - £ 17.00

## Kendal
### Ashes Exclusively Adult Caravan Park
New Hutton, Kendal LA8 0AS (Cumbria) T: 01539 731833. E: info@ashescaravanpark.co.uk
alanrogers.com/UK5650

The Ashes is a friendly, small, adult only park in an extremely peaceful setting in the rolling Cumbrian countryside, yet less than three miles from the M6, and only slightly further from Kendal. Thus it is not only a convenient night stop, but also a useful base from which to explore the Lake District and the Yorkshire Dales. A very tidy park, the central grass area is attractively planted with shrubs and bushes and there is an open vista (with little shade). There are 25 hardstanding gravel pitches, all with electrical connections (10A). These are neatly placed around the perimeter, with an oval access road. The whole area slopes gently down from the entrance, with some pitches fairly level and others with a little more slope (levelling system for caravans on all pitches). No tents are accepted other than trailer tents.

| Facilities | Directions |
|---|---|
| A small, purpose built stone building with a slate roof houses two unisex, heated shower rooms and the washing and toilet facilities. New facilities for disabled visitors. Laundry service. No shop. New electronic barrier. TV signal booster. WiFi. Off site: Mr and Mrs Mason have prepared a full information sheet with details of shopping, eating and many other local venues. Fishing 2 miles. Golf and riding 3 miles. Bicycle hire 4 miles. Kendal 4 miles. | From M6 junction 37 follow the A684 towards Kendal for 2 miles. Just past a white cottage turn sharp left at crossroads signed New Hutton. Site is on right in 0.75 miles at a left bend. Only approach and depart using this road. O.S.GR: SD560908. GPS: 54.313133, -2.675 |
| Open: 1 March - 6 November. | **Charges guide** |

Per unit incl. 2 persons £ 16.00 - £ 18.00
extra person (over 18s only) £ 4.50

## Kendal
### Waters Edge Caravan Park
Crooklands, Kendal LA7 7NN (Cumbria) T: 015395 67708. E: info@watersedgecaravanpark.co.uk
alanrogers.com/UK5645

Close to the M6 motorway, Waters Edge makes an ideal stop-over. However it is also well worth a longer stay, being centrally situated for visiting the Lake District and the Yorkshire Dales. Surrounded by farmland the park is long and narrow, with one road running down the centre and the pitches on either side. There are 26 level touring pitches, all with hardstanding. These are open and to the small side. At each end of the park there are 6 privately owned caravan holiday homes. There are no play areas for children, and parents of young children would need to be vigilant here, as there is a well signed but unfenced fast flowing stream.

| Facilities | Directions |
|---|---|
| Centrally located toilet block, although a little dated, is spotlessly clean with showers and washbasins in cubicles. Facilities for disabled visitors. Laundry. No motorcaravan service point. Shop. Bar with TV. Off site: Hotel serving food. Canal and boat trips. Kendal 15 minutes drive. | From M6 exit 36 take the A65 (east) signed Kirkby Lonsdale for 300 yds. At next roundabout take first exit signed Crooklands and Endmoor. Park entrance is about 1 mile on the right at Crooklands Motor Co. O.S.GR: SD536836. GPS: 54.24697, -2.7162 |
| Open: March - November. | **Charges guide** |

Per unit incl. electricity £ 13.50 - £ 19.50
tent £ 10.00

For latest campsite news visit
**alanrogers.com**

## Keswick
### Castlerigg Hall Caravan & Camping Park
Keswick CA12 4TE (Cumbria) T: 01768 774499. E: info@castlerigg.co.uk
alanrogers.com/UK5660

This well laid out park was started in the late 1950s by the Jackson family, who over the years have developed and improved the site whilst maintaining its character. Good use has been made of the traditional stone buildings to house the reception and shop, whilst another building houses a modern amenity block along with a really excellent campers' kitchen. Tarmac roads wend their way around the site to the separate tent area of 110 pitches. Gently sloping with some shelter, these pitches have fine views across Keswick, Derwentwater and the western Fells.

**Facilities**

The main toilet block is beautifully fitted out, fully tiled and heated, with showers, vanity style washbasins (2 in cabins) and hair care areas. Unit for disabled visitors (key). Baby area. Fully equipped laundry. Games room and campers' kitchen with microwave, toasters, kettle and hot plates. Two other toilet blocks are older in style but clean. Reception houses an internet point and a well stocked shop (with gas). Off site: Hotel/pub for meals adjacent to site. Fishing, golf, riding. bicycle hire, all 1.5 miles.

Open: Mid March - November.

**Directions**

From Penrith take the A66 towards Keswick and Cockermouth. Leave at first sign for Keswick (A591) and follow to junction (A5271). Turn left on A591 signed Windermere and after 1 mile, take small road on right signed Castlerigg and Rakefoot. Park entrance is on right after 400 yards. O.S.GR: NY282227. GPS: 54.5931, -3.112583

**Charges guide**

| | |
|---|---|
| Per unit incl. 2 persons | £ 16.95 - £ 20.00 |
| extra person (over 4 yrs) | £ 2.50 - £ 3.00 |

## Kirkby Lonsdale
### Woodclose Caravan Park
Kirkby Lonsdale LA6 2SE (Cumbria) T: 01524 271597. E: info@woodclosepark.com
alanrogers.com/UK5605

Woodclose is an established, nine acre park with new owners. Situated in the Lune Valley and just one mile from the market town of Kirkby Lonsdale, this park offers a peaceful and secluded setting catering for walkers, tourers and people who just want to relax. Access to the park is narrow, so care should be taken. The whole park has a very well cared for appearance with well mown grass, flowering tubs and neat hedges. The upper part contains many privately owned holiday homes with neat terraces built from local stone. Screened by a hedge and placed around the perimeter are several seasonal pitches with touring units being placed in the centre. These pitches are numbered and mostly level, some on hardstanding, some on grass, with 16A electricity and digital TV hook-ups. More seasonal pitches and holiday homes on the lower part of the park, again most attractively terraced with stone walling and paths. Reception is part of the well stocked shop which includes local produce and fresh baked bread; an information room is adjoining with tables and chairs and internet access (£1 per half an hour).

**Facilities**

Two toilet blocks, the main one central to the touring area. These facilities are all unisex in large, heated, individual rooms with toilets, washbasin and toilet or washbasin and shower, all well equipped and very clean. Well equipped laundry. The second block is in the lower part, again all unisex in cubicles. Facilities for disabled visitors. No motorcaravan service point. Shop. Small adventure play area. Bicycle hire. Internet access. Off site: Golf 1 mile. Fishing 7 miles. Beach 20 miles.

Open: 1 March - 1 November.

**Directions**

From M6 exit 36 take A65 to Kirkby Lonsdale. Site is off the A65 in 6 miles. O.S.GR: SD620781. GPS: 54.19835, -2.585017

**Charges guide**

| | |
|---|---|
| Per unit incl. 2 persons and electricity | £ 10.00 - £ 20.00 |
| extra person | £ 3.75 |
| child (5-16 yrs) | £ 2.00 |
| Book for 7 nights and receive 1 night free (high season only). | |

## Kirkby Stephen
### Pennine View Caravan & Camping Park
Station Road, Kirkby Stephen CA17 4SZ (Cumbria) T: 01768 371717
alanrogers.com/UK5600

Suitable for night halts or longer breaks to visit the Lake District or the Yorkshire Dales, Pennine View is a super small park, well managed and well maintained. With a very attractive rockery at the entrance, the whole site is very neat and tidy. Level, numbered pitches with gravel hardstanding are arranged around the perimeter with grass pitches in the centre. The pitches are of a good size (some being especially large) and are all are supplied with electricity hook-ups (16A). Pennine View was opened in 1990 and is built on reclaimed land from a former railway goods yard. One end of the park adjoins the River Eden. There are steps leading down huge to projecting stone slabs on the river bank (good for sunbathing). There are trout but a licence is needed for fishing.

### Facilities
Built of local stone, the modern toilet block is accessed by a digital keypad and includes individual wash cubicles and deep sink for a baby bath. Both ladies and men have large en-suite units for disabled visitors. Well equipped laundry room. Gas available. Play area. Off site: Nearby hotel offers bar meals. Kirkby Stephen 1 mile. Bicycle hire 300 m. Golf 4 miles.

Open: 1 March - 31 October.

### Directions
Park is on the A685 on the southerly outskirts of Kirkby Stephen (just under a mile from the town centre). Turn left at small site sign opposite the Croglin Castle hotel. Site is 50 yds. on right. O.S.GR: NY772075. GPS: 54.461667, -2.353367

### Charges guide
| | |
|---|---|
| Per person | £ 5.10 - £ 5.50 |
| child (4-15 yrs) | £ 2.00 - £ 2.50 |
| pitch | £ 5.00 - £ 6.00 |

## Penrith
### Flusco Wood Touring Caravan Park
Flusco, Penrith CA11 0JB (Cumbria) T: 01768 480020. E: info@fluscowoodtouringpark.co.uk
alanrogers.com/UK5670

Flusco Wood Caravan Park is still being developed but everything is to a very high standard. Set amongst woodland with the 12 touring pitches in bays, this park will meet the needs of those requiring a quiet holiday (with plenty of walks from the site) and also those travelling up or down the M6 looking for a quiet night's rest. All pitches are on hardstanding, with an area near reception with hardstandings for motorcaravans. Recent additions here include new log cabins (privately owned), with further planned. The area abounds with wildlife including deer and red squirrels, as well as many breeds of birds (we watched a woodpecker taking food from a bird feeder). Member of the Countryside Discovery group.

### Facilities
A log cabin style building houses very clean, heated facilities including pre-set showers and vanity style washbasins (1 cubicle). Large en-suite shower rooms for families or disabled visitors, one in the ladies' and one in the men's. Laundry, drying room and boot washing sink. Second log cabin serves as reception/shop with basic supplies, gas and daily newspapers. Grass area for ball games on bark. Grass area for ball games. Off site: Pub and P.O. stores 2 miles. Fishing, bicycle hire and golf 4 miles. Riding 5 miles.

Open: Easter/1 April - 29 October.

### Directions
From M6 take A66 towards Keswick. Go straight on at first roundabout, then third right at top of hill (signed Flusco, Recycling Centre, Pottery and caravan sign). After 0.5 miles road turns right up hill (narrow, so take care in large units), site is on left at the top. Site is 4 miles from M6. O.S.GR: NY457293. GPS: 54.655408, -2.841346

### Charges guide
| | |
|---|---|
| Per unit incl. 2 persons and electricity | £ 17.50 - £ 20.50 |
| extra person (over 6 yrs) | £ 3.00 |
| dog | £ 1.00 |

For latest campsite news visit
alanrogers.com

Cumbria

## Penrith
### Ullswater Caravan, Camping & Marine Park
Watermillock, Penrith CA11 0LR (Cumbria) T: 017684 86666. E: info@uccmp.co.uk
alanrogers.com/UK5635

Located within the Lake District National Park, Ullswater Caravan Park is centrally situated for touring the many attractions of this glorious area. It has 220 pitches, 58 for touring units, the rest used for holiday homes. All have 10A electricity, 50 also have water and drains. Some are situated very close to the bar and are also overlooked by mobile homes with little privacy. At the far end of the park other pitches are in a more wooded area. In between is a large grassy space for tents. There are occasional glimpses of the lake through the trees. Attractive holiday cottages are available for rent.

**Facilities**

Two toilet blocks, one refurbished the other a little dated and unheated. Facilities for babies and disabled visitors. Laundry. Shop with off-licence. Bar and games room open 8pm at busy times. Well equipped playground for younger children. Off site: Walks in the hills above the park. Steamer rides on the lake from Pooley Bridge 2 miles.

Open: 1 March - 14 November.

**Directions**

From M6 exit 40 take the A66 west signed Keswick. At first roundabout (Rheged) take second exit signed Ullswater on the A592. At T-junction turn right still on the A592 and after Breckenrigg Inn on the right, carry on downhill to sign for church. Turn right here and up to entrance on right in 800 yds.
O.S.GR: NY436229. GPS: 54.5978, -2.87482

**Charges guide**

| | |
|---|---|
| Per unit incl. 2 persons | £ 16.50 - £ 22.00 |
| extra person | £ 2.50 - £ 3.50 |

## Penrith
### The Quiet Site Caravan & Camping Park
Watermillock, Penrith CA11 0LS (Cumbria) T: 07768 727016. E: info@thequietsite.co.uk
alanrogers.com/UK5630

The Quiet Site is a secluded, family run park, operating as a carbon neutral company. It is situated on a hillside in the National Park with views over the fells and just 1.5 miles from Lake Ullswater. There are 100 unmarked touring pitches, most with hardstanding and 50 with electricity. Most have been terraced to provide level surfaces, but a few are very sloping. The camping area is very undulating. In a separate part of the park, screened by mature trees, are 23 privately owned caravan holiday homes. There are two cottages to rent and timber built 'camping pods' as an alternative to bringing your own tent.

**Facilities**

The toilet block provides pre-set showers and open style washbasins. Three bathrooms and two private shower rooms. Bathroom with facilities for disabled visitors. Baby area. Laundry facilities. Motorcaravan services. Well stocked shop at reception. Gas supplies. Bar (weekends only in low season). TV and games room. Adventure play area. Caravan storage. American motorhomes would find access very difficult. Off site: Fishing 1.5 miles. Riding and bicycle hire 3 miles. Golf 8 miles.

Open: All year (excl. 17 January - 28 February).

**Directions**

We advise not using GPS. From M6, exit 40, take A66 (Keswick) for 1 mile, then A592 signed Ullswater for 4 miles. Turn right at Lake junction, signed Windermere. After 1 miles turn right (at Brackenrigg Inn) and follow for 1.5 miles to site on right (large units should phone for an alternative route).
O.S.GR: NY431236. GPS: 54.604683, -2.882783

**Charges guide**

| | |
|---|---|
| Per unit incl. 2 persons, | £ 17.00 - £ 27.00 |
| Camping Cheques accepted. | |

## Penrith
### Lowther Holiday Park
Eamont Bridge, Penrith CA10 2JB (Cumbria) T: 01768 863631. E: alan@lowther-holidaypark.co.uk
alanrogers.com/UK5625

Sitting on the banks of the River Lowther this holiday park occupies 50 acres of rural, wooded parkland, home to the rare red squirrel. There are 400 caravan holiday homes and lodges around the park, together with 200 touring pitches. A proportion of these are taken by seasonal lets. Marked and numbered, on mostly level ground between mature trees, 70 have 10A electricity and hardstanding. A separate elevated grass area is available for tents. There is a small touring office with 24 hour security adjacent to the holiday home sales office. The Squirrel Inn is open all season and serves meals and takeaways.

**Facilities**

Two toilet blocks are central to the touring areas (key entry). Very clean, they provide large, preset showers. Fully equipped bathroom with baby changing. Drive through motorcaravan service. Well equipped laundry. Full facilities for disabled visitors. Licensed shop. Squirrel Inn with restaurant, terrace and games room. Play areas. Fly fishing on river (permit from office). Activity weekends. Live entertainment. Max. two dogs per unit. Off site: Golf, riding and bicycle hire 2 miles. Boat launching 4 miles.

Open: 7 March - 13 November.

**Directions**

From M6 exit 40 take A66 towards Scotch Corner for 1 mile. At roundabout take A6 south for 1 mile towards Shap. Lowther is on the right as you pass through village of Eamont Bridge.
O.S.GR: NY527264. GPS: 54.647667, -2.737017

**Charges guide**

| | |
|---|---|
| Per unit incl. 6 persons | |
| and electricity | £ 22.50 - £ 30.00 |

218

For latest campsite news visit
alanrogers.com

Penrith

## Cove Camping Park

Ullswater, Watermillock, Penrith CA11 0LS (Cumbria) T: 01768 486549. E: info@cove-park.co.uk
alanrogers.com/UK5620

Cove Camping is a delightful small site, some of the 50 pitches having great views over Lake Ullswater. A separate area behind the camping field holds 39 privately owned caravan holiday homes. The grass is well trimmed, there are ramps to keep speeds down to 5 mph. and the site is well lit. At the top of the park are 17 level pitches with electric hook-ups and hardstanding suitable for touring caravans and motorcaravans. The rest of the park is quite sloping. Rubbish bins are hidden behind wooden fencing, as are recycling bins. The park is well situated for walking, boating, fishing and pony trekking activities. The road up from the A592 is narrow, but a self imposed one way system is generally adhered to and the warden will advise on a different way to leave the site.

### Facilities

The tiled toilet block is immaculate and heated in cooler months, providing adjustable showers, some washbasins in cabins and, for ladies, a hairdressing area with stool and a baby changing unit. Foyer containing a freezer (free), and tourist information. Laundry with washing machine, dryer and an iron. Gas supplies. Small, grass based play area. Off site: Shop nearby. Fishing 1.5 miles. Riding 3 miles. Golf 6 mile. Bicycle hire 7 miles (will deliver).

Open: March - 31 October.

### Directions

We would advise using the following directions rather than GPS. From A66 Penrith - Keswick road, take A592 south, signed Ullswater. Turn right at Brackenrigg Inn (site signed) and follow road uphill for about 1.5 miles to park on left. This road is narrow so if you have a larger unit, telephone the park for advice about an alternative route. O.S.GR: NY431236. GPS: 54.604283, -2.881883

### Charges guide

| | |
|---|---|
| Per unit incl. 2 persons and electricity | £ 15.00 - £ 25.00 |
| tent incl. 2 persons | £ 10.00 - £ 22.00 |
| extra person (5 yrs and over) | £ 3.00 |
| dog | £ 1.00 |

No credit cards.

**Cove Park** "The Peaceful Park"

A small and quiet caravan and camping park in The Lake District. Pure tranquility and escapism. We are easy to find only 7 miles from junction 40 on the M6, yet in the very heart of the Northern Lakes overlooking Ullswater. AA

www.cove-park.co.uk
01768 486549

Penrith

## Waterfoot Caravan Park

Pooley Bridge, Penrith CA11 0JF (Cumbria) T: 01768 486302. E: enquiries@waterfootpark.co.uk
alanrogers.com/UK5610

Waterfoot is a quiet family park for caravans and motorcaravans only. It is set in 22 acres of partially wooded land, developed in the fifties from a private estate. The 146 private caravan holiday homes are quite separate from the 34 touring pitches. Lake Ullswater is only about 400 yards away and a half mile stroll through bluebell woods brings you to the village of Pooley Bridge. Waterfoot's touring pitches are arranged very informally in a large clearing. Most are level, there are some hardstandings and all have 10A electricity. The park no longer accepts American RVs. There is a bar in a large, imposing mansion, in the past a family home then a golf hotel. Public footpaths lead straight from the park. The regular lake steamer service calls at Pooley Bridge, the Ullswater yacht club is only 10 minutes drive and the market town of Penrith is 5 miles away. The historic house and gardens of Dalemain are a short walk.

### Facilities

The heated toilet block includes washbasins and preset showers in cubicles. New facilities for disabled visitors. Large, light and airy dishwashing room and fully equipped laundry. Small shop selling basics, gas and newspapers. Bar with strictly enforced, separate family room open weekend evenings in low season and every evening in high season. Large fenced field with play equipment to suit all ages and goal posts for football and a new play park. Off site: Fishing 0.5 miles. Riding 1.5 miles. Golf 5 miles. Pooley Bridge has a post office/general store, hotels and restaurants.

Open: 1 March - 14 November.

### Directions

Do not use GPS here - it directs outfits the wrong way, finishing up on farm tracks. Please use the following directions. From M6 junction 40, take A66 signed Keswick. After 0.5 miles at roundabout take A592 signed Ullswater and site is on right after 4 miles. O.S.GR: NY460245. GPS: 54.614017, -2.83115

### Charges guide

| | |
|---|---|
| Per unit incl. all persons and electricity | £ 17.50 - £ 27.50 |

Pay for 7 nights in one payment and receive 1 night free.

*See advertisement on page 216.*

For latest campsite news visit
**alanrogers.com**

Cumbria

## Penrith

### Westmorland Caravan Park

Tebay, Orton, Penrith CA10 3SB (Cumbria) T: 01539 711322. E: caravans@westmorland.com

alanrogers.com/UK5590

For caravans, motorhomes and trailer tents only, this is the ideal stopover for anyone heading either north or south, near the M6 motorway, but far enough away for the traffic noise not to be too disturbing. There are 80 level pitches on gravel, divided into bays of about six or seven units (25 are for touring units). All touring pitches have electricity (16A). The bays are backed by grassy banks alive with rabbits and birds – a long list in the office describes the large variety of birds to be seen on the site. There is good site lighting and a late arrivals area. The park is situated in beautiful countryside making it a good choice for spending an extra day or two in the area, although on-site facilities are limited.

| Facilities | Directions |
|---|---|
| The heated toilet block is basic but kept very clean and includes washbasins and showers. Bathroom for disabled visitors with ramped access. Family room. Laundry. Reception sells gas. Dog walk. Off site: Shops and restaurants five minutes walk away at the motorway service area. Fishing 2 miles. Golf 17 miles. Within 30 minutes drive are the market towns of Appleby, Penrith and Kendal. Boat rides on Ullswater. | From the M6, exit for Tebay Services (site signed) just north of junction 38. Site is accessible from the services travelling north or south. O.S.GR: NY607060. GPS: 54.4477, -2.606467 |

Open: 5 March - 12 November.

Charges guide

| | |
|---|---|
| Per unit incl. 4 persons and electricity | £ 17.00 - £ 20.00 |
| awning | £ 2.50 |

## Penrith

### Sykeside Camping Park

Brotherswater, Patterdale, Penrith CA11 0NZ (Cumbria) T: 01768 482239. E: info@sykeside.co.uk

alanrogers.com/UK5560

This small touring park is located in a really beautiful, quiet spot in the northern Lakes area (it is just 400 yards from Brotherswater). With views up the Dovedale valley, the park has 100 pitches in the valley floor, mainly for tents. There are 19 for motorcaravans on hardstanding, 16 of which have 10A electricity. Pitches are not marked and campers arrange themselves to best enjoy the superb views. A stone-built building, an original barn, near the entrance houses all the facilities. These include the recently extended and refurbished Barn End bar where meals are served. The site is surrounded by the fells and is ideal for active outdoor holidays with walking or climbing on the high hills.

| Facilities | Directions |
|---|---|
| The toilet block includes hot showers and has been refurbished, with a chemical disposal point added. Small launderette and dishwashing room. Self-service shop with camping equipment, gas and an ice-pack service, doubles as reception. Cosy, licensed bar and restaurant (daily in summer, weekends only in winter). Bunkhouse accommodation for 30 persons in various groupings. Fishing nearby. Off site: Bicycle hire 3 miles. Good sailing on Ullswater 4 miles. Riding 8 miles. Golf 10 miles. The Brotherswater Inn is adjacent (open all year). | From exit 40 of the M6 take the A66 in the direction of Keswick. At the first roundabout take A592 and follow signs for Ullswater and Glenridding, continue to Brotherswater and Sykeside is on the right of the A592. The entrance is just behind the Brotherswater Inn. O.S.GR: NY396005. GPS: 54.4985, -2.9255 |

Open: All year.

Charges guide

| | |
|---|---|
| Per tent incl. 2 persons and car | £ 10.00 - £ 23.00 |
| motorcaravan with 2 persons and electricity | £ 17.00 - £ 24.50 |

## Wigton

### The Larches Caravan Park

Mealsgate, Wigton CA7 1LQ (Cumbria) T: 01697 371379. E: thelarches@hotmail.co.uk

alanrogers.com/UK5510

Mealsgate and The Larches lie on the Carlisle - Cockermouth road, a little removed from the hectic centre of the Lake District, yet with easy access (and good views towards it) and to other attractions nearby. This family run, adults only park takes 73 touring units of any type, 42 of which have electricity (10A), water and drainage. Touring pitches are in different grassy areas with tall, mature trees, shrubs and accompanying wildlife. Some are sloping and irregular, others on marked hardstandings. There are currently a few holiday homes and there are plans to extend this area of the park.

| Facilities | Directions |
|---|---|
| Toilet facilities are clean but a little dated and provide en-suite facilities for both sexes. Washbasins for ladies are in cubicles, those for men set in flat surfaces. Separate unit for disabled visitors can be heated. Campers' kitchen. Laundry room. Small shop. Small indoor heated pool. Wildlife pond. Caravan storage. Off site: Riding 1.5 miles. Golf 3.5 miles. Bicycle hire 7 miles. Fishing 8 miles. | Park entrance is south off A595 (Carlisle - Cockermouth road) just southwest of Mealsgate. O.S.GR: NY206415. GPS: 54.763267, -3.2358 |

Open: 1 March - 31 October.

Charges guide

| | |
|---|---|
| Per unit incl. 2 persons | £ 12.50 - £ 14.90 |
| incl. electricity | £ 14.50 - £ 16.90 |
| extra person | £ 2.00 - £ 2.50 |
| No credit cards. | |

For latest campsite news visit
## alanrogers.com

# Wigton

## Stanwix Park Holiday Centre

Greenrow, Silloth CA7 4HH (Cumbria) T: 01697 332666. E: enquiries@stanwix.com

alanrogers.com/UK5505

Stanwix Park is a family run holiday park with absolutely everything anyone could want for a memorable holiday all year round. The park has 111 caravan holiday homes and chalets for rent, together with 212 which are privately owned. These are mostly located around the central complex. In addition at either end of the park, there are 121 fully serviced (10A electricity) pitches for touring units and tents, some on grass, some with hardstanding. A warm welcome awaits in the main reception, with lots of local and tourist information. Motorhomes over 8 m. accepted by prior arrangement. The indoor tropical leisure centre contains a 29 m. fun pool with slides, a steam room, sauna, spa, fitness gym and vertical sun shower (charge). The upper floor has the Sky Bar and Dunes Cabaret Bar (adults only) with the Sunset Inn licensed family club, all enjoying nightly entertainment and special themed weekends from November to March. A giant TV and snooker room are in the Gallery observation area with the Astro Bowling Centre (charged) and amusement arcade, with a soft play area to one side. Outside are a large, terraced pool, an adventure play area and minigolf, all screened by plants and shrubs.

### Facilities

The two heated sanitary blocks have been refurbished to a high standard, kept spotlessly clean and opened by combination lock. Large en-suite bathrooms, showers, vanity style washbasins and a unit in each for disabled visitors. Campers' kitchen. Fully equipped laundry. Gas sales. Well stocked shop (6/3-15/11). Restaurant with takeaway (all year). Bars with entertainment (6/3-15/11). TV and snooker room. Indoor leisure centre. Outdoor swimming pool (31/5-1/9). Ten-pin bowling. Amusement arcade. Soft play area. Minigolf. Tennis. Bicycle hire. Dogs max. 2. Off site: Silloth golf club. Beach 1 mile.

Open: All year.

### Directions

From the south, take exit 41 from the M6 and follow B5305 through Wigton to Silloth. From north on A74/M6 take exit 44 and the A595 and A596 to Wigton. On entering Silloth, turn left following signs for park. Entrance is on the right. O.S.GR: NY108525. GPS: 54.8614, -3.388333

### Charges guide

| | |
|---|---|
| Per person | £ 4.00 - £ 4.80 |
| child (under 5 yrs) | £ 2.60 - £ 3.10 |
| pitch | £ 12.40 - £ 15.50 |
| dog (max. 2) | £ 3.00 |

Many special offers and short break prices.

# Wigton

## Hylton Caravan Park

Silloth, Wigton CA7 4AY (Cumbria) T: 01697 332666. E: ericstanwix@stanwix.com

alanrogers.com/UK5506

Hylton Caravan Park is owned and managed by the Stanwix family and although it is only a short walk away from the livelier Stanwix Leisure Park, it is a peaceful haven for people who prefer the quiet life. The only activity is an adventure park for children which is not visible from the touring area. Divided by a circular road, the 170 privately owned caravan holiday homes are visible but not intrusive. There are 90 open plan, mostly level touring and tent pitches, all fully serviced and with 10A electricity. There is no shop on site as the town and Stanwix Holiday Park are both within walking distance.

### Facilities

A high quality toilet block is superbly fitted out and includes toilets, showers, vanity style washbasins, extra large bathrooms and a separate cubicle for disabled visitors. Fully equipped laundry. Gas sales. Max. 2 dogs per pitch. Off site: Bus stop 1 mile. Entertainment and amenities at Stanwix Park. Bowling. Windsurfing, boat launching and fishing 1 mile. Riding 7 miles.

Open: 1 March - 15 November.

### Directions

On entering Silloth, turn left following signs to Hylton Caravan Park. O.S.GR: NY114534. GPS: 54.868333, -3.39835

### Charges guide

| | |
|---|---|
| Per person | £ 4.00 - £ 4.80 |
| child (under 5 yrs) | £ 2.60 - £ 3.10 |
| pitch | £ 10.00 - £ 12.50 |

For latest campsite news visit

**alanrogers.com**

## Windermere
### Hill of Oaks Caravan Park

Tower Wood, Windermere LA12 8NR (Cumbria) T: 01539 531578. E: enquiries@hillofoaks.co.uk

alanrogers.com/UK5615

This park on the banks of Lake Windermere lives up to its name 'Hill of Oaks'. Set on a hillside in mature woodland, the park offers families a safe natural environment with nature walks through the managed ancient woodlands, as well as six jetties for boat launching and access to watersport activities (jet skis are not allowed). The road into the park passing the farmhouse is long, winding and narrow, so care should be taken especially with long outfits, reception being about half a mile from the entrance. Although the park is situated on Lake Windermere the touring pitches nestle within the trees, not actually by the lake. All 43 have electricity (16A), digital TV hook-up and hardstanding. Most are large enough to take a car and boat and three large super pitches also have water and a drain. Tents are not accepted at Hill of Oaks. The entrance barrier is open from 08.00 till dusk with a security code being provided for exit. The reception and shop selling basics with a tourist information room adjacent are on the lakeside in wooden chalet-type buildings with an abundance of hanging baskets and flowers. Privately owned caravan holiday homes have been built into the hillside on terraces and are quite unobtrusive, screened by hedges and trees.

### Facilities

The central tiled toilet block, recently refurbished, is very clean and heated. Vanity style washbasins, controllable showers and free hairdryers. Baby changing areas. Fully equipped laundry. Unit for disabled visitors (combination lock). Motorcaravan service point. Shop for basics. Two fenced play areas, one for toddlers and adventure type for over 5s. Picnic areas and nature trails. Fishing (licence required). Off site: Fell Foot Park and Gardens 1 mile, with rowing boat hire and ferry rides to Lakeside and Ambleside. Aquarium of the Lakes (3.5 miles) at Newby Bridge. Golf 4 miles. Riding and bicycle hire 6 miles.

Open: 1 March - 14 November.

### Directions

From M6 exit 36 head west on A590 towards Barrow and Newby Bridge. Follow A590 to roundabout signed Bowness and turn right on the A592 for about 3 miles. Site is signed on left. O.S.GR: SD384903. GPS: 54.30755, -2.9454

### Charges guide

| | |
|---|---|
| Per pitch | £ 10.00 - £ 24.00 |
| car | £ 1.00 |
| awning | £ 3.00 |
| boat | £ 5.00 - £ 10.50 |

See advertisement on page 216.

---

## Windermere
### Park Cliffe Camping & Caravan Estate

Birks Road, Windermere LA23 3PG (Cumbria) T: 01539 531344. E: info@parkcliffe.co.uk

alanrogers.com/UK5545

This beautiful park is situated in the heart of the Lake District National Park and is well managed and maintained, with welcoming staff. The 70 touring pitches are open and unshaded on gravel hardstanding, with electricity (10A), water and drainage. There are some seasonal units and three mobile homes available for hire. Tucked away in a valley are privately owned mobile homes. Two areas have been set aside for tents, one of which has electric hook-ups (steel pegs required). There is no automatic barrier, but the gates are closed to both campers and caravanners 23.00-07.30 with a warden on site for emergencies. A member of the Best of British group.

### Facilities

Two blocks of toilets and showers are heated and very clean. Full facilities for disabled visitors and excellent baby room. Four private bathrooms are available for hire (min. 3 days), and one by the hour (with refundable deposit). Laundry. Motorcaravan service point. Bar, restaurant and takeaway. Small well stocked shop. Games room. Large outdoor adventure play area is set secluded to one side of the tourers, not fenced as a public footpath runs through to Moor How. Off site: Fellfoot Country Park with boat launching (sail), walking, climbing, cycling and many other activities possible. Cruises on the lake.

Open: 1 March - 13 November.

### Directions

From M6 exit 36 take A590 to Newby Bridge. Turn right on A592 for 3.6 miles and turn right. Site is signed shortly on the right. Caravans and trailers must approach Park Cliffe from the direction of Newby Bridge on the A592. The park does not advise the use of sat nav to reach it. O.S.GR: SD391911. GPS: 54.312517, -2.9375

### Charges guide

| | |
|---|---|
| Per unit incl. 2 persons and electricity | £ 23.50 - £ 28.00 |
| extra person | £ 5.00 |
| child (5-17 yrs) | £ 2.50 |
| dog | £ 2.00 |

For latest campsite news visit
## alanrogers.com

The most northerly region of England, Northumbria is steeped in history, full of ancient forts and fairytale castles. The great outdoors offers limitless walking with plenty of trails stretching across moorlands and beaches, encompassing views of the beautiful scenery.

**THE REGION COMPRISES: NORTHUMBERLAND, DURHAM, TYNE AND WEAR, AND TEESIDE**

The 400 square mile Northumberland National Park is one of the most peaceful, remote places in England. With endless walks across moorlands and hills, it stretches south from the Cheviot Hills, through the Simonside Hills, to the crags of Whin Sill, where it engulfs a section of the historic Hadrian's Wall, built by the Romans to mark the northern limit of their empire. The Pennine Way was the country's first official long-distance path and is still the longest. At 268 miles, it stretches from the Peak National Park to the border. The coastline is not to be forgotten, with mile upon mile of deserted, sandy beaches, with resorts that still have an old fashioned feel to them, such as Whitley Bay, South Shields and Seaton Carew. The majestic castles of Bamburgh, and Dunstanburgh can be seen for miles along the Northumberland coast. Surrounded on three sides by the river Wear, the small, historic city of Durham is dominated by England's greatest Norman Cathedral. With cobbled medieval streets and restricted car access it is a popular place with visitors. Further north is the bustling city of Newcastle. Home to an array of cosmopolitan restaurants and bars, music venues, and fabulous architecture, it also boasts a lively nightlife.

## Places of interest

*Northumberland:* Bamburgh Castle; Alnwick Castle and gardens; Berwick-upon-Tweed; bird reserve on Farne Islands, home to large colony of grey seals; Hauxley Nature Reserve; Dunstanburgh Castle; Corbridge Roman sites at Hadrian's Wall.

*Durham:* Durham Castle and Cathedral; Barnard Castle, a ruined castle overlooking the River Tees; Diggerland at Langley Park; Harperley POW Camp.

*Tyne and Wear:* New Metroland, Europe's only indoor theme park within a large shopping complex; Newcastle with Life Science Centre, Discovery Museum and Castle Keep; Whitley Bay.

*Teeside:* Kirkleatham Owl Centre; Darlington Railway Centre and Museum; Guisborough Hall; Hartlepool Historic Quay and HMS Trinacomalee; Butterfly World in Stockton-on-Tees.

## Did you know?

Alnwick Castle is used as the setting of Hogwarts in the Harry Potter films.

Stretching from Wallsend to Bowness-on-Solway, Hadrian's Wall is 81 miles long; it is possible to walk the entire length.

Born in Northumbria in 1825, George Stephenson was the first person to design the steam engine that ran on wheels.

In the past 300 years Berwick has changed hands between the Scottish and the English no less than 13 times.

The Angel of The North is made up of 200 tonnes of steel and rises 20 metres from the ground.

Built in 1817, HMS Trinacomalee is the oldest ship afloat in the UK.

## Alnwick

### Dunstan Hill Camping & Caravanning Club Site

Dunstan Hill, Dunstan, Alnwick NE66 3TQ (Northumberland) T: 01665 576310

**alanrogers.com/UK5770**

Off a quiet lane between Embleton and Craster this is a rural site with a tree belt to shelter it from the north wind and access to the beach by a level footpath through the fields, across the golf course and past the ruins of Dunstanburgh Castle. This is just over a mile by car. With gravel access roads, the peaceful site has 150 level, well spaced pitches, 80 with 16A electricity. Reception is manned by very helpful managers and there is an area for outside parking and late arrivals at the entrance. This is a wonderful area to visit, with its unspoilt beaches and the whole area is steeped in history. This site is not suitable for large American motorhomes.

### Facilities

Two very clean and well maintained toilet blocks have some washbasins in cubicles, hairdryers (20p) and a washroom for children with deep sinks. Fully equipped facility for disabled visitors in one block, a laundry in the other. Small shop for gas and basic provisions. Bread and milk can be ordered and a mobile shop and the paper man visit. Fish and chip van on Fridays. Well stocked tourist information room. Small play area. Torches are useful. WiFi (charged). Off site: Beach, fishing and golf 1.5 miles. Riding 8 miles. Bicycle hire 10 miles.

**Open:** March - October.

### Directions

From A1 just north of Alnwick take B1340 or B6347 (further north) for Embleton. Site is signed in Embleton village. Avoid signs to Dunstanburgh Castle and follow those for Craster. Site is (south) on the left after about 0.5 miles. O.S.GR: NU236214. GPS: 55.4855, -1.6291

### Charges guide

| | |
|---|---|
| Per person | £ 5.80 - £ 8.90 |
| child (6-18 yrs) | £ 2.60 - £ 2.80 |
| non-member pitch fee | £ 10.50 |

For latest campsite news visit
**alanrogers.com**

## Bamburgh
### Waren Caravan & Camping Park
Waren Mill, Bamburgh NE70 7EE (Northumberland) T: 01668 214366. E: waren@meadowhead.co.uk
alanrogers.com/UK5750

Developed from 100 acres of undulating privately owned heath and woodland, Waren Park is a large, spacious family site with marvellous views over Northumberland's golden beaches and the sea. A large section of caravan holiday homes is separate from a self contained four acre touring area. Enclosed by sheltering banks, this provides 150 reasonably level pitches, 100 with 16A electrical connections. Wooden wigwams are also available. As well as the spacious grounds to wander in, there is much to see nearby from historic castles and the Farne Islands to the Cheviot Hills and miles and miles of sandy beaches. There is a dog walk along the top of the embankment with views along the coast. The well spaced pitches, with a play area in the middle, provide an open and uncrowded feel to this quiet site.

**Facilities**

The older toilet facilities have been refurbished to a high standard and include four family en-suite shower rooms, a family bathroom and facilities for disabled visitors. A newer block situated in a separate static holiday home section also provides good facilities. Laundry room. Dishwashing sinks. Motorcaravan service point. Licensed shop. Bar with terrace serving bar meals (all season). Gaming machine room with pool table. Patio area. Children's play park and playing fields. Splash pool (June-Sept). WiFi internet access. Off site: Beach 500 yds. excellent for birdwatching, unsuitable for bathing. Safe bathing beach 4 miles (Bamburgh). Golf and bicycle hire 2 miles. Riding 5 miles. Birdwatching opportunities nearby.

Open: 14 March - 31 October.

**Directions**

Follow B1342 from the A1 to Waren Mill towards Bamburgh. After Budle Bay turn right and follow signs. O.S.GR: NU154342.
GPS: 55.60045, -1.75487

**Charges guide**

| | |
|---|---|
| Per unit incl. 2 persons and electricity | £ 17.00 - £ 22.00 |
| extra person (over 5 yrs) | £ 3.00 |
| 1-man tent (no car) | £ 9.50 - £ 12.00 |
| dog | £ 3.00 |

Less 10% for bookings of 7 days or over.

## Barnard Castle
### Barnard Castle Camping & Caravanning Club Site
Dockenflatts Lane, Lartington, Barnard Castle DL12 9DG (Co. Durham) T: 01833 630228.
alanrogers.com/UK5720

Welcoming non-members and tents, the Camping and Caravanning Club site at Barnard Castle was opened in 1996. One side of the site is bordered by mature trees and further planting now gives privacy to individual pitches. There are 90 flat pitches, most on grass but including 12 hardstanding pitches (gravel base with room for both car and caravan and space for an awning on grass). There are 56 electrical hook-ups (16A). There is an attractive woodland dog walking area leading to a riverside footpath which takes you into Barnard Castle. There are many footpaths and walks in the area and numerous local attractions.

**Facilities**

The centrally located toilet facilities can be heated and are of good quality and kept spotlessly clean. Washbasins are in cubicles and free, controllable showers are roomy. Baby room. Fully equipped unisex unit for visitors with disabilities. Large laundry with washing machine, dryer, iron and sink, with outside lines. Small shop in reception area. Motorcaravan service point. Gas supplies. Central play area with rubber safety base. Caravan storage. WiFi (charged). Off site: Riding 200 m. Golf 2.5 miles. Fishing 4 miles. Bus service from end of lane.

Open: 30 March - 30 October.

**Directions**

Follow B6277 from Barnard Castle (towards Middleton in Teesdale) for 1 mile to Lartington. Turn left at club sign into narrow lane with passing places to site entrance on left (there is no need to go into Barnard Castle). O.S.GR: NZ025168.
GPS: 54.546883, -1.962583

**Charges guide**

| | |
|---|---|
| Per person | £ 5.80 - £ 8.90 |
| child (6-18 yrs) | £ 2.60 - £ 2.80 |
| non-member pitch fee | £ 10.50 |

For latest campsite news visit
**alanrogers.com**

## Barnard Castle

### Doe Park Touring Caravan Park

Cotherstone, Barnard Castle DL12 9UQ (Co. Durham) T: 01833 650302. E: info@doepark.co.uk

alanrogers.com/UK5710

The Lamb family will make you very welcome and personally take you to your pitch at Doe Park. The camping fields have a lovely open aspect with wonderful views and the 70 pitches are spacious with well mown grass, all with 10A electricity, over 40 with hardstanding. This is Hannah Hauxwell country and the Dales, less frequented than other upland areas, provide wonderful walking country; indeed part of the Pennine Way runs near this peaceful site. The park's reception is a new wooden cabin at the entrance to the pitch area and is well stocked with tourist information guides. The farm and park are close to where the River Balder joins the Tees at Cotherstone and the ancient oak wood beside the river is an SSSI (Site of Special Scientific Interest) for its insects and flowers, but is also a haven for birdwatchers. The farmhouse, formerly Leadgard Hall, is a mellow three storey, Grade II listed building with a history of its own. A bus service passes the park from Barnard Castle to Middleton and the village of Cotherstone is only half a mile with a post office and a restaurant, a pleasant walk by road or river bank.

**Facilities**

With toilet facilities at the farmhouse, two well kept blocks are closer to the pitches. Built in local stone, these are fully tiled with the newest one heated. Washbasins in cabins and adjustable showers. Well appointed unisex unit for disabled visitors. Small laundry. Eggs and milk are available from the farmhouse, plus gas supplies and battery charging. No play area but a large grass area in front of some of the pitches can be used for ball games. River fishing on site. Dogs and pets are accepted by arrangement only. Off site: Reservoirs (sailing, water skiing and fishing) 3 miles. Bicycle hire and golf 4 miles. Riding 2 miles. Local leisure centre with pool 4 miles.

Open: 1 March - 31 October.

**Directions**

Follow B6277 from Barnard Castle in direction of Middleton in Teesdale. The farm is signed on the left just after Cotherstone village (there is no need to go into Barnard Castle). O.S.GR: NZ005204. GPS: 54.578217, -1.99235

**Charges guide**

| | |
|---|---|
| Per unit incl. 2 persons and electricity | £ 13.50 - £ 16.00 |
| family rate (2 adults, 2 children and awning) | £ 16.50 - £ 19.00 |
| extra person (over 6 yrs) | £ 1.50 |
| full awning | £ 1.00 |

No credit cards.

## Belford

### South Meadows Caravan Park

South Meadows, Belford NE70 7DP (Northumberland) T: 01668 213326. E: g.mcl@btinternet.com

alanrogers.com/UK5755

South Meadows is set in the north Northumberland countryside, within walking distance of the village of Belford with its market cross and old coaching inn. Covering six acres of level grass, there are 150 hardstanding pitches, most with electricity (13A), water and TV aerial point. At present 60 pitches are available for touring units. A further area takes 50 tents. The manager is environmentally aware and encourages recycling. Determined that visitors have a relaxing holiday, he will site your caravan using his own towing equipment. There is an area especially for disabled visitors with wider paths and safety features including a 24 hour telephone directly to the manager's home on site. The park is pleasantly landscaped and two short walks lead into the adjacent Blue Bell woods with streams, wildlife and spring flowers. Just off the A1, this would be a convenient stopover but Northumberland is an undiscovered county with castles and stately homes, the Farne Islands, Holy Island and long golden beaches, and you would be made most welcome here for a longer stay. This attractive, well maintained park is already popular with couples and young families and booking is advised.

**Facilities**

The fully tiled toilet block is excellent, heated in cool weather, with washbasins in cabins and roomy showers (free). Three family shower rooms. An additional portacabin toilet block is open in one area for the summer months. Hairdryers. Full facilities for disabled visitors. Laundry with washing machines, dryers and iron plus a baby unit. Food preparation and cooking area. Coffee shop (weekends, incl. Sunday roast) and takeaway (daily until 16.00). Play area. Caravan storage and servicing. Off site: Village with pub and shops 0.5 miles. Golf 0.5 miles. Riding 3 miles. Beach 3 miles. Alnwick Castle of Harry Potter fame.

Open: All year.

**Directions**

Turn off A1 about 15 miles from Alnwick to Belford village and park is signed at the southern end. O.S.GR: NU115331. GPS: 55.590967, -1.822583

**Charges guide**

| | |
|---|---|
| Per unit incl. 2 persons and electricity | £ 15.00 - £ 30.00 |
| tent per adult | £ 6.00 - £ 14.00 |
| extra person | £ 5.00 - £ 11.00 |
| child (2-16 yrs) | £ 2.00 - £ 4.00 |

No credit cards.

## Berwick-upon-Tweed

### Ord House Country Park

East Ord, Berwick-upon-Tweed TD15 2NS (Northumberland) T: 01289 305288. E: enquiries@ordhouse.co.uk
**alanrogers.com/UK5800**

Ord House is a 40 acre park for 260 privately owned holiday homes and 74 touring caravan and tent pitches. The park has a very well cared for appearance throughout with well mown grass and colourful arrays of flowering bushes. Ord House itself, an 18th century mansion, has been tastefully converted to provide a bar, lounge bar and family room. The touring pitches, 67 with electricity (16A), are in small sections, from the secluded, walled orchard to the more open areas nearer the toilet blocks. There are 39 hardstanding pitches, each with electricity, water and drainage, 12 in the walled garden separated by shrubs and camomile lawns. At the entrance to the park an area with a few pitches is suitable for wheelchair users and close by is a small sanitary unit with WCs and showers plus a large, unisex, well appointed unit (Radar key). The whole site is wheelchair friendly with good access to the airy reception. Although there are many caravan holiday homes, they are not overwhelming and their presence does mean that other amenities can remain open all season. A member of the Best of British group.

**Facilities**

The main, modern toilet building is of excellent quality and cleanliness, very well maintained and can be heated. Two good large family bathrooms (with two showers, a bath, WC and washbasin). Two rooms for disabled visitors. Large well equipped laundry. Motorcaravan service point. Gas supplies. Bar, bar food and family room. Crazy golf. Draughts. Play area. Commercial vehicles are not accepted. Dogs are only accepted by prior arrangement. WiFi. Off site: Post office stores 50 yards from the entrance. Leisure centre with a pool 15 minutes walk. Beach 1.5 miles. Fishing 1.5 miles. Golf 2 miles. Riding 8 miles. Sea fishing can be booked in Berwick.

Open: All year.

**Directions**

From A1 Berwick bypass take East Ord exit and follow signs. O.S.GR: NT982515.
GPS: 55.75416, -2.03348

**Charges guide**

| | |
|---|---|
| Per unit incl. up to 4 persons and electricity | £ 16.50 - £ 26.50 |
| extra person (over 5 yrs) | £ 2.50 |
| tent pitch | £ 12.50 - £ 22.50 |
| dog | free - £ 1.50 |

Discounts for 1- and 2-man tents and for longer stays.

---

## Durham

### Grange Caravan Club Site

Meadow Lane, Durham DH1 1TL (Co. Durham) T: 01913 844778
**alanrogers.com/UK5705**

Fully refurbished and landscaped, this park offers 76 flat spacious pitches suitable for all units. Easy access to the A1M and the A690 make it an ideal stopover for those travelling north or south or for visiting the historic cathedral city of Durham, Beamish museum or Gateshead Metro centre. A coppice of mature trees and newly planted shrubs mask road noise and make an attractive dog walking area. The park has been redesigned with attention to detail in all areas offering pockets of privacy and a central area with picnic tables and benches. A purpose built central block offers spacious, heated, modern and clean facilities.

**Facilities**

The single toilet block is a heated building with free showers, hairdryers, and private cubicles. Laundry and food preparation area. Separate baby area and facilities for disabled visitors are via a key entry system. Shop in reception with limited supplies; bread, milk and newspapers to order. Gas. Secure caravan storage. WiFi (charged). Off site: Large supermarket 2 miles. Park and ride (07.00-19.00) into Durham city centre 800 yds. Local service buses run from Belmont and Carville.

Open: All year.

**Directions**

From A1M exit 62 turn left for Durham city (A690). After 20 yds. turn right (across dual carriageway A690) – a safer approach for large units, and continue along A690 to next exit about 2 miles and return on A690 left hand turn (signed just before A1M). O.S.GR: NZ302446.
GPS: 54.79513, -1.52935

**Charges guide**

| | |
|---|---|
| Per person | £ 4.80 - £ 6.20 |
| child (5-16 yrs) | £ 1.50 - £ 2.50 |
| pitch incl. electricity (non-member) | £ 12.00 - £ 14.80 |

For latest campsite news visit
## alanrogers.com

## Durham

### Strawberry Hill Caravan Park

Running Waters, Old Cassop, Durham DH6 4QA (Co. Durham) T: 01913 723457. E: info@strawberryhf.co.uk

alanrogers.com/UK5700

This park is owned and managed by Howard and Elizabeth who are experienced caravanners. They have terraced their site to offer panoramic views over the fields and woodland from all the pitches. The park is licensed to accommodate more units but the owners prefer to offer space to visitors by providing generous pitches on either grass or hardstanding. There are 50 touring pitches (with 16A electricity), including 10 on hardstanding, plus a separate terrace for tents. At present the new landscaping on the park offers limited shade. Nature corridors and the surrounding countryside make this a haven for nature lovers and visitors are encouraged to enjoy the tranquillity of the area. The owners supply good tourist information and details of local nature walks. The easy access to the A1M and the proximity of the historic cathedral city of Durham (3 miles) make this an ideal location for visiting local attractions. These include the Beamish museum, Gateshead Metro Centre and the historic Hartlepool Quays.

**Facilities**

The single toilet block can be heated and is kept immaculately clean. Free showers. Laundry. Facilities for disabled visitors incorporating a baby care area. Small but well stocked shop in reception. Gas. Off site: Country pub with meals 1 mile. Large hypermarket 3 miles. Riding 5 miles. Park and ride (07.00-19.00) into Durham city centre operates nearby. Buses (Durham - Hartlepool) from entrance.

Open: 1 March - 30 December.

**Directions**

From A1M exit 61 follow signs for Peterlee. At next roundabout take first left (A688). Straight on at next roundabout then right at the next (A181). Park is approx. 2 miles on the left as you go up a hill on a dual carriageway. O.S.GR: NZ338399. GPS: 54.75326, -1.47809

**Charges guide**

| Per unit incl. 2 persons | |
|---|---|
| and electricity | £ 15.50 - £ 17.50 |
| extra person | £ 4.00 |
| child (3-16 yrs) | £ 1.50 |

## Hexham

### Fallowfield Dene Caravan & Camping Park

Acomb, Hexham NE46 4RP (Northumberland) T: 01434 603553. E: info@fallowfielddene.co.uk

alanrogers.com/UK5810

Although only 2.5 miles from Hexham, Fallowfield Dene Caravan Park is very secluded, situated in mature woodland at the end of a no-through road. Set in woodland glades (formerly a Victorian lead mine), each with a Roman name (Hadrian's Wall is close), are 118 seasonal pitches and 32 touring pitches, all with 16A electricity. A further 10 tent pitches have been added, suitable for smaller tents, and a barbecue area with views of woodland and fields. The park entrance, with a new reception and shop, is neat, tidy and very colourful. There is no play area or games field, but the surrounding woods are a paradise for children. Fallowfield Dene itself is a network of tracks and there are footpaths from the site entrance. The site is a haven for wildlife with red squirrels, foxes and badgers to be seen. Hadrian's Wall is only a mile away, with Roman forts such as Housesteads Fort and Chesters being great attractions. The whole area abounds with well preserved Roman remains. Nearby, Hexham market town has its Border History museum, housed in the oldest purpose-built gaol in England, where one can learn about the Border Reivers. This site has a very friendly atmosphere.

**Facilities**

Brick built toilet blocks (one for each sex) are central and heated in cool weather. Well tiled and kept very clean, there are washbasins in cabins and free hairdryers. Separate, fully equipped room for disabled visitors. Laundry room with dishwashing sinks. Baby bath. Motorcaravan service point. Small shop for necessities, including gas. Barrier card £5 deposit. WiFi. Off site: Supermarkets and other shops at Hexham and Corbridge. Good restaurant five minutes walk. Fishing and riding 3 miles. Golf 5 miles.

Open: 14 March - 1 November.

**Directions**

From A69 Newcastle - Carlisle road, take the A6079 north signed Bellingham and Rothbury. At village of Acomb, site is signed to right. Follow site signs for about 1.5 miles. Then turn left down a single track road with passing places. O.S.GR: NY938676. GPS: 55.00166, -2.09470

**Charges guide**

| Per unit incl. 2 persons | |
|---|---|
| and electricity | £ 16.00 - £ 17.00 |
| extra person | £ 3.00 |
| child (5-15 yrs) | £ 1.50 |
| dog | £ 0.50 |

## Seahouses

### Seafield Caravan Park

Seahouses NE68 7SP (Northumberland) T: 01665 720628. E: info@seafieldpark.co.uk
alanrogers.com/UK5745

The park is situated just across the road from the sea and rock pools. The site has caravans to rent and pitches for 20 tourers (no tents). All the pitches have concrete bases, water, waste, sewerage and electricity (20A), but none has a sea view. A number of small gates give immediate access to Seahouses with its excellent range of shops and eating places. The large site is attractive with landscaped gardens, pools and a stream among the caravans and tourers. The private mobile homes are set apart from those available to rent. Its location in Seahouses makes it an ideal base for visiting the Farne Islands and many other interesting and historical places such as Alnwick Castle and gardens, Craster (kippers), Bamburgh and Lindisfarne on Holy Island. The fee includes free access to the Ocean Club facilities – a 20 metre swimming pool, children's pool, spa, steam room, sauna and fitness suite. There is a licensed coffee shop, a children's nature trail and outdoor play area.

### Facilities

The single toilet block is housed in an old building but is of the highest standard inside with a family bathroom, controllable showers with door and ample changing space. The block has heating, hair dryers (charged) and the latest in hand dryers. There is a well equipped baby room. The laundry has four sinks, three for dishwashing and one for clothes. All facilities are accessed by a code. Chemical disposal unit. Snack bar/takeaway. Swimming pool, children's pool, spa, steam room, sauna, fitness suite and coffee shop in adjacent Ocean Club. Children's play area. WiFi throughout. Off site: Immediate access to the town of Seahouses with all amenities, local transport, and various trips available from the harbour. A good beach at Bamburgh just along the coast.

Open: All year (excl. 10 January - 8 February).

### Directions

On entering Seahouses from the south take the road to Bamburgh and the site is on your left just past the road down to the harbour.
GPS: 55.583162, -1.657171

### Charges guide

| | |
|---|---|
| Per unit incl. 2 persons and electricity | £ 25.00 - £ 45.00 |
| extra person | £ 7.00 |
| child (2-15 yrs) | £ 4.00 |

---

## Stockton-on-Tees

### White Water Caravan Club Park

Tees Barrage, Stockton-on-Tees TS18 2QW (Teeside) T: 01642 634880.
alanrogers.com/UK5740

Being part of the multi-million pound development at the Tees Barrage, this pleasantly landscaped club site caters for all tastes, especially watersports enthusiasts. The Tees Barrage has transformed 11 miles of the Tees, providing clean, non-tidal water for many activities. The site itself provides 115 pitches, hedged with bushes, all with 16A electricity connections, and includes 21 fully serviced pitches set within bays and hedges (fresh water and waste disposal). The site is well lit, with a security barrier. The adjoining White-Water Course (Britain's largest purpose-built canoe course) provides facilities for both advanced and beginner canoeists, and hosts major national and international events.

### Facilities

The central, heated toilet block of high quality includes washbasins in cubicles, baby changing facilities and a well appointed unit for disabled visitors. Laundry room. Motorcaravan service point. Play area on fine gravel. Heated family room with TV and pool table for wet weather. Off site: Supermarket 6 minutes. Hotel near the entrance. Retail and leisure park, just across barrage bridge, with 14-screen cinema, 10-pin bowling, shops and fast food outlets. North Yorkshire Moors and the Hartlepool Historic Quay within 40 minutes drive. Fishing and bicycle hire 2 miles. Golf and riding 3 miles.

Open: All year.

### Directions

From A1(M1) take A66 for Darlington and follow until you pick up signs for Teeside Retail Park and the Tees Barrage. Cross railway bridge and the Barrage bridge, then first right to site on left in 400 yards. O.S.GR: NZ463194. GPS: 54.567733, -1.286567

### Charges guide

| | |
|---|---|
| Per person | £ 3.60 - £ 5.30 |
| child (5-16 yrs) | £ 1.30 - £ 2.00 |
| pitch incl. electricity (non-member) | £ 11.20 - £ 13.30 |

Tent campers apply to site.

Land of ancient myths and Celtic legends, Wales is a small and compact country boas a diverse landscape, from lakes and mountains rivers and valleys to beautiful coastlines and rolling wooded countryside. It offers superb opportunities for an active holiday.

Wales' biggest asset is undoubtedly its countryside, home to three National Parks that make up almost a quarter of the country's total area. Snowdonia National Park in the north combines dramatic mountain scenery with glacial valleys, lakes and streams, while in the south the Brecon Beacons boast mountains, moorlands, forests and wooded gorges with deep caves. The surrounding area of the Wye Valley on the borders with England is a designated Area of Outstanding Beauty; as is the Gower Peninsula, the Lleyn Peninsula, the Anglesey Coast and the Clwydian Range. The endless miles of largely unspoilt and beautiful Pembrokeshire coastline in the west has some of the finest long beaches in Europe, with pretty little bays plus the lively traditional seaside resorts of Tenby and Whitesand. Further inland is the secluded and pretty Gwaun Valley. The capital of Wales, Cardiff, has many attractions, including its newly developed waterfront, the Millennium Stadium. Castles can be seen all over Wales, ranging from tiny stone keeps to huge medieval fortresses; some of the best preserved are Caernarfon, Conwy and Harlech, all built by Edward I.

### Places of interest

*North:* Isle of Anglesey; Victorian School of 3Rs and Motor Museum at Llangollen; Victorian seaside resort of Llandudno; Colwyn Bay; Caernarfon Castle; Snowdon Mountain Railway at Llanberis.

*West:* Oakwood Park, Wales' only theme park; the National Botanic Gardens at Aberglasney; Dolaucothi Goldmines; historic, stone-walled Aberaeron.

*Mid:* Brecon Beacons National Park; the lakes of the Elan Valley; entertaining events all summer at Llanwrtyd Wells; the Centre for Alternative Technology near Machynllleth.

*South:* Merthyr Tydfil, the Iron Capital of the World; Caerphilly's truly massive medieval castle; Cardiff, capital of Wales; the Wye Valley and the Vale of Usk of the Welsh borderlands with Tintern Abbey.

### Did you know?

The origins of the Red Dragon flag may date back to the Roman period, when the dragon was used by military cohorts.

St David's in Pembrokeshire is Britain's smallest city by virtue of its Cathedral to the patron saint of Wales.

There are many sites in Wales linked to the legend of King Arthur: Castell Dinas Brân, near Llangollen, is reputed to be the resting-place of the Holy Grail.

Towering at 1085 metres Mount Snowdon is the highest mountain in England and Wales.

'The Dam Busters' was filmed on location in the Elan Valley.

The Welsh language is one of Europe's oldest languages and shares its roots with Breton, Gaelic and Cornish.

## Aberaeron

### Aeron Coast Caravan Park

North Road, Aberaeron SA46 0JF (Ceredigion) T: 01545 570349. E: enquiries@aeroncoast.co.uk

alanrogers.com/UK6280

Aeron Coast is a family holiday park with a wide range of recreational facilities, on the west coast of Wales. Although it has a high proportion of caravan holiday homes (200 privately owned), touring units of all types are provided for in two fields separated from the beach and sea by a high bank (although the best beach is on the south side of this traditional fishing village). Pitches are on level grass with all units regularly and well spaced in lines in traditional style. The main attraction of the park is its excellent provision for families, both in and out of doors. This includes two outdoor pools and a toddlers' pool (unsupervised) in a paved, walled area good for sunbathing, a tennis court and small half-court for youngsters, football and a sand pit with pirate ship. The indoor leisure area provides an under-5s room with slide, air-hockey, table tennis, pool and games machines and TV room. In high season activities are organised nightly free of charge in the large entertainment and disco room. In low season reception is open 10.00-14.00 – choose a pitch from the numbers on the board and return in the morning.

#### Facilities

Two modern toilet blocks offer excellent facilities including large family showers. Facilities for disabled visitors and babies are in one block. Basic motorcaravan service point. Heated swimming pools (1/6-15/9). Club house and bar (from Easter, 12.00-14.00 and from 19.00) with family room serving bar meals and takeaway in school holiday periods. Large entertainments room. Shop at the petrol station at the entrance. Only one dog per unit is accepted. Off site: Beach, fishing and boat launching 1 mile. A steam railway, craft centre, woollen mills and potteries can be visited locally.

Open: 1 March - 31 October.

#### Directions

Park is on northern outskirts of Aberaeron village with entrance on the right beside a petrol station. Brown sigpost. O.S.GR: SN461631.
GPS: 52.2445, -4.254917

#### Charges 2011

| | |
|---|---|
| Per unit incl. 4 persons and electricity | £ 15.00 - £ 25.00 |
| extra person (over 2 yrs) | £ 4.00 |
| dog | £ 1.00 |

## Abergele

### Hunters Hamlet Caravan Park

Sirior Goch Farm, Betws-yn-Rhos, Abergele LL22 8PL (Conwy) T: 01745 832237. E: huntershamlet@aol.com

alanrogers.com/UK6650

This small, family owned park is licensed for all units except tents (trailer tents are allowed). On a gently sloping hillside providing beautiful panoramic views, one area provides 15 well spaced pitches with hardstanding and 10A electricity, with access from a circular, hardcore road. A more recent area has been developed next to this of a similar design but with eight fully serviced 'super pitches' (water, waste water, sewage, TV and 16A electricity). Shrubs and bushes at various stages of growth enhance both areas. A natural play area incorporating rustic adventure equipment set amongst mature beech trees with a small bubbling stream is a children's paradise. Milk and papers can be ordered and the Hunters will do their best to meet your needs. The park is well situated to tour Snowdonia and Anglesey and is within easy reach of Llandudno and Rhyl.

#### Facilities

The heated toilet block has fully tiled facilities including showers en-suite with toilets for both sexes. A sunroom to the rear houses laundry and dishwashing (hot and cold), washing machine and dryer, iron and board, freezer and fridge. Family bathroom (metered) and basic toilet and shower facilities for disabled visitors. Play area. WiFi (free). All year caravan storage. Max. 2 dogs per pitch. Off site: Fishing and golf 2 miles. Riding 10 miles.

Open: 21 March - 31 October.

#### Directions

From Abergele take A548 south for almost 3 miles; turn onto B5381 in direction of Betws-yn-Rhos and park is on left after 0.5 miles. O.S.GR: SH929736.
GPS: 53.248833, -3.6068

#### Charges 2011

| | |
|---|---|
| Per unit incl. 2 persons incl. electricity | £ 17.00 - £ 22.00 |
| super pitch | £ 22.00 - £ 27.00 |
| extra person | £ 4.00 |
| child (at school) | £ 1.00 |
| Less £5 on weekly bookings. | |

## Abergele

### Ty Mawr Holiday Park

Towyn Road, Towyn, Abergele LL22 9HG (Conwy) T: 01745 832079. E: nikkie.lawrence@park-resorts.com

alanrogers.com/UK6655

Ty Mawr Holiday Park is located close to the many attractions of the North Wales Coast and the Snowdonia National Park. There are two areas for touring units, one on open meadows with facilities provided in excellent portacabin style units, the other in a more well established area with older, more traditional amenities near the playgrounds and entertainment complex. Both areas are flat with views of open countryside. There is some traffic noise from the road adjacent to the meadow. There is a large proportion of rental and privately owned caravan holiday homes which are neatly sited on well manicured grass pitches. It is an easy walk into the town of Towyn with seaside facilities, and Rhyl, some three miles along the coast, is a busy resort with a funfair and holiday amusements. Ty Mawr is ideal for families seeking plenty of holiday park type activities, with organised children's clubs for 5-16 year olds. The outdoor all-weather multisport courts and the playground are excellent facilities for younger family members and the whole family are catered for in the entertainment complex which provides mini ten-pin bowling, pool and darts. In the evening there are discos and live spectaculars. The heated indoor pool complete with flume is the venue for organised water-based activities.

### Facilities

Two well maintained, functional blocks which can be heated serve the main touring area with portacabin style units on the open meadows. They are regularly cleaned. Washbasins are open style, preset showers have curtains and hooks, but no seats. Baby rooms. Facilities for disabled visitors (key). Launderette. Ice pack service. Shop. Bar with meals, cafeteria and takeaway. Indoor pool. Multisport courts. Excellent play areas and children's clubs. Evening family entertainment. Off site: Beach 0.25 miles. Bicycle hire 0.5 miles. Golf, riding and boat launching 3 miles. Fishing 6 miles. The island of Anglesey and the historic towns of Conwy and Caernarfon are within easy reach.

Open: Easter - 30 October.

### Directions

Take the A55 in a westerly direction into North Wales and take exit for Abergele. Follow signs for A548 Rhyl towards Towyn. Shortly after Towyn turn right into site. O.S.GR: SH965791
GPS: 53.29867, -3.55442

### Charges guide

| | |
|---|---|
| Per pitch | £ 5.00 - £ 33.00 |
| incl. electricity | £ 8.00 - £ 36.00 |
| dog | £ 1.00 - £ 3.00 |

Units over 6 metres in length are charged for 2 pitches.

## Abergele

### Plas Farm Caravan Park

Plas-yn-Betws, Betws-yn-Rhos, Abergele LL22 8AU (Conwy)

You might also like to conside ...

## Aberystwyth

### Glan-y-Mor Leisure Park

Clarach Bay, Aberystwyth SY23 3DT (Ceredigion) T: 01970 828900. E: glanymor@sunbourne.co.uk

**alanrogers.com/UK6290**

Follow the road to Clarach Bay and on the seafront is Glan-y-Mor, a busy, holiday-style park with an enviable situation. On a wet day you may not wish to go far with the comprehensive leisure centre on site – it is open eight months of the year with reduced entry fee for campers. Although the balance of pitches is very much in favour of caravan holiday homes (3:1) which dominate the open park and bay, there are 50 touring pitches, 45 with electricity (10A) and 4 new 'super' pitches. They are rather small and are pressed together in two small sections on the lower part of the park.

**Facilities**

The heated toilet block is on the lower touring area with dishwashing facilities and laundry room, plus a toilet for disabled visitors. A Portacabin type block (high season only) is on the ridge ground. A suite including shower for disabled visitors is in a block in the upper static site, with further facilities at the leisure centre (RADAR key). Motorcaravan service point. Freezer pack service. Gas supplies. Supermarket. Play area. Swimming pool. Licensed restaurant and takeaway (from Easter). WiFi.

Open: 1 March - 31 October.

**Directions**

Clarach is signed west from the A487 (Aberystwyth - Machynlleth) in village of Bow Street (take care at narrow bridge). Follow signs over crossroads to beach and park. Access for caravans from Aberystwyth on B4572 is difficult.
O.S.GR: SN587841. GPS: 52.43625, -4.08025

**Charges guide**

| | |
|---|---|
| Per unit incl. up to 6 persons | £ 15.00 - £ 26.50 |
| dog (max. 2) | free - £ 2.00 |

## Amroth

### Little Kings Park

Amroth Road, Ludchurch, Narberth SA67 8PG (Pembrokeshire) T: 01834 831330
E: littlekingspark@btconnect.com  **alanrogers.com/UK5975**

This superb family run park has a number of attributes to make your stay both comfortable and memorable. There are stunning views over Carmarthen Bay to the Gower and on beyond to the coast of Somerset and North Devon. At night no fewer than seven lighthouses can be seen blinking out their warnings. A touring field provides 56 well spaced, large touring pitches all with 10A electricity, 21 with gravel hardstanding and fully serviced. An attractive playground is in the central open grass area. A further seven pitches are in a different area. There are 60 pitches for tents in an adjoining paddock.

**Facilities**

The two toilet blocks are modern and well equipped, including controllable hot showers (20p for 6 minutes 30p for 9), open style washbasins, a family shower room and a full suite for disabled campers. Laundry rooms. Shop with bakery. Takeaway, bar and restaurant with conservatory (evenings only; low season at B.Hs and weekends only). Covered swimming pool. Games room. Play area. Gas supplies. Off site: Nearest supermarket at Kilgetty 2.5 miles. Tenby and Pendine Sands both 7 miles. Fishing 1.5 miles. Riding 4 miles. Golf 8 miles.

Open: 1 March - 31 October.

**Directions**

Site is 5 miles southeast of Narberth. From the A477 Carmarthen to Pembroke road, 2 miles after Llanteg at petrol station, turn left towards Amroth, Wiseman's Bridge, Ludchurch. After 1 mile, at crossroads, turn right (signed Ludchurch, Narberth) and park is 800 m. O.S.GR: SN146093.
GPS: 51.751517, -4.6879

**Charges guide**

| | |
|---|---|
| Per unit incl. 2 persons | £ 16.00 - £ 24.00 |
| extra person (over 3 yrs) | free - £ 2.20 |

## Amroth

### Pantglas Farm Caravan Park

Tavernspite, Amroth SA34 0NS (Pembrokeshire) T: 01834 831618. E: pantglasfarm@btinternet.com

**alanrogers.com/UK5974**

A secluded, rural, family run park with a nice atmosphere, Pantglas Farm is four miles from the coast with extensive views over rolling countryside and down to the sea. Set in three gently sloping paddocks spread over 14 acres, there are 86 generously sized, fairly level pitches with electricity (10A), on gravel hardstanding. This is a popular and attractive site close to the main resorts but enjoying a more tranquil atmosphere. An on-site clubhouse also has a lounge with TV and a games room, with some simple entertainment activities arranged at Bank Holidays, weekends and in high season.

**Facilities**

Two toilet blocks (one can be heated) are of a good standard including large controllable showers and some washbasins in cubicles. Facilities for disabled campers include a Wet room. Laundry. Gas supplies. Battery charging and freezer pack services. Licensed clubhouse (evenings only every day for B.Hs and peak season, weekends only low season). Updated play area. Games field. Games room. TV lounge. Caravan and boat storage. Off site: Supermarket in Whitland 3 miles. Fishing 1 mile.

Open: March - third weekend in October.

**Directions**

From A477 Tenby - Pembroke road turn right at Red Roses crossroads to Tavernspite for 1.25 miles. At the village pump take the middle road and site is about 0.5 miles on left. O.S.GR: SN 176122.
GPS: 51.778317, -4.645417

**Charges guide**

| | |
|---|---|
| Per unit incl. 2 persons and electricity | £ 17.00 - £ 19.00 |
| extra person | £ 3.00 |

Wales

# Bala

## Glanllyn Lakeside Caravan & Camping Park

Llanuwchllyn, Bala LL23 7ST (Gwynedd) T: 01678 540227. E: info@glanllyn.com

alanrogers.com/UK6345

This 16 acre site lying alongside the southern end of Bala lake has 204 pitches. With around 40 seasonal units, this leaves 164 tourist pitches, 94 of which have electric hook-ups. In this location, virtually all the pitches have wonderful views of the lake or the surrounding mountain sides. The terrain is grassy, fairly open and level, but with natural terraces. There are around 19 individual hardstandings and a further hardstanding area by the beach is a favourite with motorcaravanners. The site is served by main tarmac access roads with speed bumps. The park is an ideal base for some serious walking.

### Facilities

A complex of three modern buildings (one can be heated and is used in low season) is located centrally at the rear of the site. Preset hot showers, hairdressing and shaver stations. Facilities for babies and suite for disabled visitors (key code access). Laundry room. Motorcaravan service point. Well stocked shop at reception (Easter-Oct). Freezer pack service. Gas supplies. Splendid, well fenced adventure style playground on bark surface. Only 2 dogs per unit permitted. Off site: Bus stops outside site gate. Snowdonia National Park. Riding 18 miles.

Open: Easter - mid October.

### Directions

From Bala take A494 southwest towards Dolgellau for about 3 miles, entrance is on left, on a right hand bend. O.S.GR: SH893324. GPS: 52.877667, -3.64665

### Charges guide

| | |
|---|---|
| Per unit incl. 2 persons and electricity | £ 16.00 - £ 20.00 |
| tent pitch incl. 2 persons | £ 12.00 - £ 16.00 |
| extra person | £ 3.00 - £ 5.00 |
| dog (max. 2) | £ 2.00 |

# Bala

## Pen-y-Bont Touring & Camping Park

Llangynog Road, Bala LL23 7PH (Gwynedd) T: 01678 520549. E: penybont-bala@btconnect.co.uk

alanrogers.com/UK6340

This is a pretty little park with 59 touring pitches, 42 of which have hardstanding. Connected by circular gravel roads, they are intermingled with trees and tall trees edge the site. Electricity connections (16A) are available, including 11 for tents, and there are 24 serviced pitches with hardstanding, electricity, water and drainage. There are also pitches for 25 seasonal units. The park entrance and the stone building that houses reception and the well stocked shop provide quite a smart image. With views of the Berwyn mountains, Pen-y-bont has an attractive and useful location being the closest park to Bala town.

### Facilities

The toilet block includes washbasins in cubicles and spacious hot showers. Two new cubicles with washbasin and WC. Separate laundry room and an en-suite unit for disabled visitors, that doubles as a baby room, operated by key (£2 deposit). Outside covered area with fencing and concrete floor for dishwashing sinks and bins. Motorcaravan service point. Shop. Bicycle hire. Caravan storage. WiFi. Off site: Fishing 200 yds. Boat launching, golf and riding 2 miles. Bala market on Mondays.

Open: 1 April - 31 October.

### Directions

Park is 0.5 miles southeast of Bala village on the B4391. Bala is between Dolgellau and Conwen on the A494. O.S.GR: SH932350. GPS: 52.901717, -3.590117

### Charges guide

| | |
|---|---|
| Per unit incl. 2 persons and electricity | £ 17.00 - £ 21.00 |
| tent pitch incl. 2 persons | £ 12.00 - £ 19.00 |
| extra person | £ 4.00 - £ 6.00 |
| dog | £ 1.00 |

# Barmouth

## Hendre Mynach Touring Caravan & Camping Park

Llanaber, Barmouth LL42 1YR (Gwynedd) T: 01341 280262. E: mynach@lineone.net

alanrogers.com/UK6370

A neat and tidy family park, colourful flowers and top rate facilities make an instant impression on arrival down the steep entrance to this park (help is available to get out if you are worried). Of the 240 pitches, 60 are for touring guests and are allocated in various areas, with substantial tenting areas identified. All 60 touring pitches are fully serviced with electricity, water taps and waste water. The beach is only 100 yards away but a railway line runs between it and the park. The railway can be crossed by pedestrian operated gates which could be a worry for those with young children.

### Facilities

Two toilet blocks, one modern and one traditional, both offer excellent facilities including spacious showers (free) and washbasins in cubicles. An extension to the traditional block has added a good unit for disabled visitors with ramp access. Motorcaravan service point. Well stocked shop incorporating a snack bar and takeaway (Easter-1/11). WiFi. Off site: Beach 100 m. Fishing and bicycle hire within 0.5 miles. Riding 5 miles. Golf 9 miles.

Open: All year excl. 10 January - 28 February.

### Directions

Park is off the A496 road north of Barmouth in village of Llanaber with entrance down a steep drive. O.S.GR: SH606171. GPS: 52.73300, -4.06618

### Charges guide

| | |
|---|---|
| Per unit incl. 2 persons | £ 16.00 - £ 29.00 |
| extra person | £ 4.00 |
| child (2-14 yrs) | £ 2.00 |
| first dog free, extra dog | £ 1.00 |

## Beddgelert

### Forest Holidays Beddgelert

Caernarfon Road, Beddgelert LL55 4UU (Gwynedd) T: 01766 890288. E: info@forestholidays.co.uk

alanrogers.com/UK6590

Forest Holidays is a partnership between the Forestry Commission and The Camping and Caravanning Club. This well equipped site is in the heart of Snowdonia, set in a marvellous, natural, wooded environment on the slopes of Snowdon. Well equipped and well managed, the site provides 240 pitches – tents in a semi-wooded field area and caravans amongst the trees with numbered hardstandings, and 105 places with 10/16A electricity. Tents may pitch where they like in their areas leaving six metres between units or there are six new grass pitches with electrical hook-ups for tents. Metal tent pegs may be best (available from the shop). There is abundant fauna and flora, tumbling streams and always something to watch from the cheeky squirrels to the smallest bird in Britain. Free maps of the forest walks are provided in reception and orienteering and fishing are possible. A bus service stops at the top of the entrance lane (two hourly for Caernarfon and Porthmadog).

**Facilities**

Two fully equipped modern sanitary toilet blocks clad in natural wood provide large, free hot showers (with good dry areas). Laundry equipment is in one block. A small unit provides extra washbasins and toilets in peak season and there is a toilet and washbasin for disabled visitors. Excellent drive-through motorcaravan service point. Well provisioned shop (Easter-end Sept). Adventure playground. Log cabin common room. Off site: Pub within walking distance (under 1 mile) and other eating places nearby. Bicycle hire within 500 yds. in forest.

Open: All year.

**Directions**

Site is clearly signed to the left 1 mile north of Beddgelert on the A4085 Caernarfon road. O.S.GR: SH579492. GPS: 53.02075, -4.119767

**Charges guide**

| | |
|---|---|
| Per unit incl. 2 persons | £ 8.00 - £ 20.50 |
| extra person | £ 4.25 - £ 6.25 |
| child (5-14 yrs) | £ 1.75 - £ 3.25 |

Discounts for families, disabled guests and senior citizens.

## Benllech

### Plas Uchaf Caravan & Camping Park

Benllech Bay, Benllech LL74 8NU (Isle of Anglesey) T: 01407 763012

alanrogers.com/UK6636

This spacious, family run, campsite is set in 16 acres of flat, well mown grass with some hardstandings. Within the park there are woodland walks and a play route for children to explore, an attractive play area with robust play equipment and a dog walk. All in an open, rural setting this park offers a safe haven for young families to enjoy. The pitches are set around the perimeter of six individual areas, each with picnic tables for communal use and all 110 touring pitches offer electricity (10/16A). Motorcaravans over 26 feet in length are not accepted. With five privately owned mobile homes in a separate field, this popular campsite is ideally located with a safe sandy beach a mile away and well positioned for exploring the island. Motor bikes, boats and jet skis cannot be accommodated.

**Facilities**

Three clean, traditional style sanitary blocks have separate facilities for men and women, with hot showers (charge), open style washbasins, hairdryers and small baths. Baby areas. No facilities for disabled visitors. Limited laundry. Large playing field, play equipment and dog walk. Freezer facilities. Off site: Shops, bars, restaurants, fishing, golf, sandy beach, riding and sailing all within 1 mile.

Open: 14 March - 14 October.

**Directions**

From the Britannia Bridge take the A5025. In Benllech turn left onto the B5108. After the fire station on left, turn first right and the park is signed. O.S.GR: SH509832. GPS: 53.32676, -4.23956

**Charges guide**

| | |
|---|---|
| Per unit incl. 2 persons and electricity | £ 13.00 - £ 18.00 |
| extra person (over 3 yrs) | £ 3.00 |
| dog | £ 0.50 |

No credit cards.

For latest campsite news visit
alanrogers.com

## Brecon

### Pencelli Castle Caravan & Camping Park

Pencelli, Brecon LD3 7LX (Powys) T: 01874 665451. E: pencelli@tiscali.co.uk

alanrogers.com/UK6040

Open all year round, this is a quality park with atmosphere and character which continues to improve. Set amidst the Brecon scenery, it offers excellent facilities in peaceful, rural tranquillity. The owners, Liz and Gerwyn Rees, have retained the country charm but have added an all embracing range of spacious, heated, luxury facilities, attractively enhanced by potted plants, etc. There are three touring fields. The 'Orchard' incorporates 15 fully serviced pitches with hardstanding, amongst shrubs, fruit trees and a stone cider mill. The 'Oaks' taking 20 caravans and tents and the 'Meadow' for 40 tents (with boot and bike wash) are bordered by majestic trees and the Monmouthshire and Brecon Canal. All the fields are level with neatly mown grass and tarmac access roads. The historic manor house, that dates back to 1583, is adjacent to arched barns that house an increasing collection of vintage farm machinery including carts and rare tractors.

**Facilities**

The toilet block is very well designed and includes some private cubicles, two large fully equipped rooms for families or disabled visitors incorporating double showers, baby changing and bath facilities, all humorously decorated for the young at heart. Laundry. Drying room. Planning shop. WiFi (free). Motorcaravan service point. Small shop. Playground and nature trail. Bicycle hire. Dogs not accepted. Off site: Royal Oak Inn with meals 100 m. Riding 2 miles. Golf and bicycle hire 5 miles.

**Open:** 30 December - 30 November.

**Directions**

From A40 south after Brecon bypass take the B4558 at signs for Llanfrynach and later Pencelli (narrow bridge). If travelling north on A40, approach via Tal-y-Bont. Site at south end of Pencelli. O.S.GR: SO095249. GPS: 51.914783, -3.317867

**Charges guide**

| | |
|---|---|
| Per unit incl. 2 persons | £ 15.60 - £ 25.60 |
| extra person | £ 6.50 - £ 11.00 |
| child (5-15 yrs) | £ 4.50 - £ 6.00 |

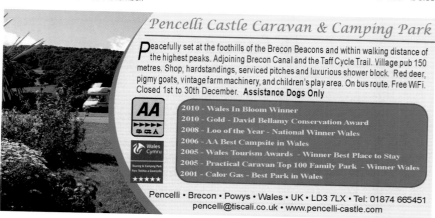

## Pencelli Castle Caravan & Camping Park

Peacefully set at the foothills of the Brecon Beacons and within walking distance of the highest peaks. Adjoining Brecon Canal and the Taff Cycle Trail. Village pub 150 metres. Shop, hardstandings, serviced pitches and luxurious shower block. Red deer, pigmy goats, vintage farm machinery, and children's play area. On bus route. Free WiFi. Closed 1st to 30th December. **Assistance Dogs Only**

**AA** ►►►►► ⌂ ⌘ 🛦

Wales Cymru
Touring & Camping Park
Parc Teithio a Gwersylla
★★★★★

2010 - Wales In Bloom Winner
2010 - Gold - David Bellamy Conservation Award
2008 - Loo of the Year - National Winner Wales
2006 - AA Best Campsite in Wales
2005 - Wales Tourism Awards - Winner Best Place to Stay
2005 - Practical Caravan Top 100 Family Park - Winner Wales
2001 - Calor Gas - Best Park in Wales

Pencelli • Brecon • Powys • Wales • UK • LD3 7LX • Tel: 01874 665451
pencelli@tiscali.co.uk • www.pencelli-castle.com

## Brynsiencyn

### Fron Caravan & Camping Park

Brynsiencyn, Anglesey LL61 6TX (Isle of Anglesey) T: 01248 430310. E: mail@froncaravanpark.co.uk

alanrogers.com/UK6635

A traditional, all touring campsite in a peaceful rural location, Fron has panoramic views over the surrounding countryside. From the entrance gate a tarmac drive passes through a two acre level grass paddock, which is reserved for 35 large tent pitches. The drive leads up to the old farmhouse which houses reception and a well stocked shop. Behind the farmhouse is another two acre sloping paddock with 40 caravan and motorcaravan pitches, five with hardstandings, and 57 electricity hook-ups (10A). By the farmhouse a heated swimming pool is well controlled by the owners and has a retractable roof.

**Facilities**

Toilet facilities are in three units of varying ages and designs located at both sides of the farmhouse. These include a unit for ladies with some basins in cubicles, good hot showers with dividers (20p), hairdryers, a baby area and a suite for disabled campers. Laundry with washing machine and dryer. Motorcaravan service point. Heated swimming pool (30x14 ft; May-Sept). Gas stocked. Max. 2 dogs per pitch. Torches useful. Off site: Fishing 1.5 miles. Riding 3 miles. Golf 4 miles.

**Open:** Easter - end September.

**Directions**

Cross the Britannia Bridge and take first slip road signed Llanfairpwll A4080, then next left signed Newborough and Brynsiencyn. Continue on A4080 for 5 miles, turning right in village at Groeslon Hotel. Continue for 1 mile to site at western end of village. O.S.GR: SH472668. GPS: 53.176217, -4.28785

**Charges 2011**

| | |
|---|---|
| Per unit incl. 2 persons and 2 children | £ 22.00 |
| extra person | £ 2.50 - £ 6.00 |
| No credit cards. | |

## Builth Wells

### Fforest Fields Caravan & Camping Park

Hundred House, Builth Wells LD1 5RT (Powys) T: 01982 570406. E: office@fforestfields.co.uk

alanrogers.com/UK6320

This secluded 'different' park is set on a family hill farm in the heart of Radnorshire. Truly rural, there are glorious views and a distinctly family atmosphere. This is simple country camping and caravanning at its best, without man-made distractions or intrusions. The facilities include 80 large pitches on level grass on a spacious and peaceful, carefully landscaped field by a stream. Electrical connections (mostly 16A) are available and there are 17 hardstanding pitches, also with electricity. Several additional areas without electricity are provided for tents. There are two new lakes, one for boating and fly fishing, the other for coarse fishing. A new reception and toilet block are planned. George and Kate, the enthusiastic owners, have opened up much of the farm for moderate or ample woodland and moorland trails which can be enjoyed with much wildlife to see. Indeed wildlife is actively encouraged with nesting boxes for owls, songbirds and bats, by leaving field margins wild to encourage small mammals and by tree planting.

**Facilities**

The toilet facilities are acceptable with baby bath, dishwashing and laundry facilities including washing machines and a dryer. Milk, eggs and orange juice are sold in reception and gas, otherwise there are few other on-site facilities. The village of Hundred House, one mile away, has a pub. Fishing. Torches are useful. Off site: Bicycle hire and golf 5 miles. Riding 10 miles.

Open: Easter - 17 November.

**Directions**

Park is 4 miles east of Builth Wells near the village of Hundred House on A481. Follow brown signs. O.S.GR: SO098535. GPS: 52.17121, -3.31621

**Charges guide**

| | |
|---|---|
| Per person | £ 3.50 |
| child | £ 2.50 |
| pitch | £ 4.50 |
| electricity | £ 2.50 |
| dog | free |

No credit cards.

# Fforest Fields
## Caravan & Camping Park

A friendly family run campsite in a quiet secluded valley with wonderful views. Many lovely walks through woodlands and up to hill tops direct from the site. Dogs are welcome by arrangement. Large level pitches and some hard standings. Lovingly maintained. Bellamy Gold for eleven years. Private fishing lake.

### See lots of photos, prices & local info on
## www.fforestfields.co.uk
### Or phone 01982 570406 for brochure

Wonderful walks lead up into the hills from Fforest Fields

Four miles from Builth Wells and the Wye Valley (On the A481)

## Caernarfon

### Plas Gwyn Caravan & Camping Park

Llanrug, Caernarfon LL55 2AQ (Gwynedd) T: 01286 672619. E: info@plasgwyn.co.uk

alanrogers.com/UK6620

In a beautiful location, this traditional, family run touring site is within the grounds of a house that was built in 1785 in the Georgian style with a colonial style veranda. The 30 touring caravan pitches are set around the perimeter of a slightly sloping grass field, and there are eight hardstandings. The separate tent field has ten pitches. There are 36 electric hook-ups (16A) of which 12 also provide water and waste water. Please note there is minimal site lighting on the caravan field and none on the tent field, a torch could be very useful. A further separate field houses five caravan holiday homes available to rent. A member of the Countryside Discovery Group.

**Facilities**

An older style building houses the toilet facilities but the fittings and tiling inside are modern and are kept neat and tidy. Controllable free hot showers, dishwashing sinks, a good laundry room (by reception), but no dedicated facilities for babies or disabled campers. Drive-over motorcaravan service point. Gas. Reception stocks basic food items, etc. Breakfast 'butties' made to order and delivered. Internet access. Off site: Llanberis and Snowdon Mountain Railway 2.5 miles. Golf 1 mile. Riding 2.5 miles. Bicycle hire 3 miles. Fishing 4 miles.

Open: 1 March - 31 October.

**Directions**

Site is on A4086, 3 miles from Caernarfon, and 2.5 miles from Llanberis. It is well signed with easy access. O.S.GR: SH522634. GPS: 53.146733, -4.212233

**Charges guide**

| | |
|---|---|
| Per unitincl. 2 persons, awning and electricity | £ 15.00 - £ 18.00 |
| extra person | £ 2.50 |
| child (0-15 yrs) | £ 1.50 - £ 2.00 |
| tent pitch | £ 4.00 - £ 11.00 |

## Caernarfon
### Bryn Gloch Caravan & Camping Park
Betws Garmon, Caernarfon LL54 7YY (Gwynedd) T: 01286 650216. E: eurig@bryngloch.co.uk
alanrogers.com/UK6600

Bryn Gloch is a well kept, family owned touring park in the impressive Snowdonia area – an unusual feature is the mountain railway which passes through the park. Neat and quiet, it takes some 160 units on five flat, wide meadows with some breathtaking views. With tarmac access roads and free areas allowed in the centre for play, of the 152 touring pitches, 80 have hardstanding, 10A electricity, water and drainage. In addition, there are 15 caravan holiday homes. Fishing is possible on the river bordering the park with a barbecue and picnic area, adventure play area and field for ball games. A range of tourist information is provided in the complex by the reception/shop and the park is very popular with walkers and cyclists. Caernarfon with its famous castle is five miles.

### Facilities
The two very clean and modern main toilet blocks include washbasins in cabins, large showers, a family bathroom (hot water £1), baby room and complete facilities for visitors with disabilities (coded access). The far field has a portacabin style unit containing all facilities, for use in peak season. Well equipped laundry and separate drying room. Motorcaravan service point and car wash. Shop (1/3-31/10). TV and games rooms with pool tables and amusement machines. Minigolf. Entrance barrier with coded access. WiFi. Off site: Pub 1 mile. ATM at garage in Ceathro 3 miles. Riding 2.5 miles, bicycle hire or golf 5 miles.

Open: All year, limited facilities 1 November - 28 February.

### Directions
From Caernarfon take A4085 signed Beddgelert. Park is just beyond Waunfawr, 5.6 miles southeast of Caernarfon. After crossing river bridge, the entrance is immediately on the right, opposite St Garmon church. O.S.GR: SH536576.
GPS: 53.095183, -4.1884

### Charges guide
| | |
|---|---|
| Per unit incl. 2 persons and electricity | £ 18.00 - £ 28.00 |
| extra person | £ 4.00 |
| child (3-16 yrs) | £ 2.00 |
| dog | £ 1.00 |

## Caernarfon
### Tafarn Snowdonia Parc Brewpub & Campsite
Waunfawr, Caernarfon LL55 4AQ (Gwynedd) T: 01286 650409. E: info@snowdonia-park.co.uk
alanrogers.com/UK6605

Set on the banks of the River Gwyrfai and amongst spectacular scenery, this no frills campsite is adjacent to the station for the Welsh Highland Railway. There are 32 grass pitches (20 with 16A electricity) of variable size. They are set in an open field and serviced by two small, basic, clean shower and toilet blocks. Enjoy riverside walks and free fishing (licence required) before calling in at the adjoining pub with its own microbrewery (listed in the CAMRA Good Beer guide) and home cooked food. Children are well catered for with a family room in the pub, two gardens (one safe for toddlers) and a playground. The campsite is located between Beddgelert and Caernarfon and four miles from the foot of Snowdon. It is an ideal location for walking, climbing, fishing, pony trekking and visiting historic castles.

### Facilities
One small toilet block in main camping field. A second block with separate showers and toilets for men and ladies, together with laundry facilities, is reached via a footbridge over the railway track. These may become stretched when site is full. Full bar, restaurant and takeaway facilities. TV. Games room. Playground. Free fishing (licence required). Off site: Riding 800 yds. Golf 3 miles. Beach and sailing 5 miles.

Open: All year.

### Directions
From Caernarfon take the A4085 for around 4 miles and campsite is on the left. The entrance is at the far end of pub/railway station car park.
O.S.GR: SH526587. GPS: 53.10611, -4.20176

### Charges 2011
| | |
|---|---|
| Per unit incl. 2 persons and electricity | £ 22.00 |
| children and dogs | free |

# Cardiff

## Cardiff Caravan Park

Pontcanna Fields, via Sophia Close, Cardiff CF11 9LB (Cardiff) T: 02920 398362

alanrogers.com/UK5925

Run by the city council, this popular site is set within acres of parkland, one mile from the city centre, ideal for visiting the many attractions of the City of Cardiff. The campsite has 73 pitches which are on a fairly open area, with 43 on a grassed grid surface with electric hook-ups (16A), the remainder are on grass. There is a public right of way through the site. Security is good with an on-site warden 24 hours a day, and security cameras constantly scanning the whole area. Remember though that you are in a city centre environment, so lock up your valuables. The Cricket Ground, Welsh Institute of Sport, the Millennium Stadium, Cardiff Castle, museums and many other attractions are within walking distance.

### Facilities

Two heated buildings each with key code entry systems, the one by reception has a laundry with washer and dryer, and facilities for disabled campers. Both have controllable hot showers. Baby facilities. Bicycle hire (the site specialises in cycles adapted for disabled visitors). Riding can be arranged. Off site: The Millennium Stadium, Glamorgan County Cricket Ground, Cardiff Bay. Local shops and services within easy walking distance. Fishing 0.25 mile, golf 4 miles.

Open: All year.

### Directions

From the A48 turn south on A4119 (Cardiff Road). Pass church on left following signs for Institute of Sport and at next traffic lights turn into Sophia Close and Gardens. Turn left at Institute of Sport and pass County Cricket Ground on right. Continue to site on left. For sat nav purposes use postcode CF11 9XR. O.S.GR: ST171772. GPS: 51.49155, -3.20313

### Charges guide

| | |
|---|---|
| Per person | £ 3.00 - £ 5.50 |
| vehicle | £ 4.00 |
| electricity | £ 3.50 |

# Colwyn Bay

## Bron-Y-Wendon Touring Caravan Park

Wern Road, Llanddulas, Colwyn Bay LL22 8HG (Conwy) T: 01492 512903. E: stay@northwales-holidays.co.uk

alanrogers.com/UK6690

Bron-Y-Wendon is right by the sea between Abergele and Colwyn Bay on the beautiful North Wales coast road. This is a quiet park which, by its own admission, is not really geared up for the family unit – there is no playground here, although there is a games room with table tennis and a TV room. The park is manicured to the highest standards and caters for a large number of seasonal caravans on pitches with gravel bases which are kept very tidy. There are a further 65 grass based, and 20 hardstanding touring pitches, all with electricity (16A) and tarmac access roads. All pitches have coastal views and the sea and beach are just a short walk away. Trailer tents are accepted, but not other tents.

### Facilities

Two toilet blocks, both with heating, provide excellent facilities including men's and women's shower rooms separate from the toilets and washbasins. Good facilities for disabled visitors. Laundry with washing machines and dryers. Mobile shop visits daily. Gas supplies. WiFi. Off site: Llanddulas village with shops and several good pubs is very near. Fishing 1 mile. Golf 4 miles. Riding 6 miles. Bicycle hire 15 miles.

Open: All year.

### Directions

From A55 Chester - Conwy road turn at Llanddulas interchange (A547), junction 23. Turn right opposite Shell garage and park is 400 yards, signed on coast side of the road. O.S.GR: SH903785. GPS: 53.29185, -3.6445

### Charges guide

| | |
|---|---|
| Per unit incl. 2 persons | £ 19.00 - £ 22.00 |
| extra person | £ 1.00 - £ 4.00 |

# Criccieth

## Llanystumdwy Camping & Caravanning Club Site

Tyddyn Sianel, Llanystumdwy, Criccieth LL52 0LS (Gwynedd) T: 01766 522855

alanrogers.com/UK6580

Overlooking mountains and sea, Llanystumdwy is one of the earliest Camping and Caravanning Club sites. Well maintained with good facilities, it is on sloping grass. However, the wardens are very helpful and know their site and can advise on the most suitable pitch and even have a supply of chocks. There are 70 pitches in total (20 ft. spacing), 45 with 10A electricity connections, spaced over two hedged fields with mainly caravans in the top field with four hardstandings for motorcaravans. Tents are located lower down. A little library with a supply of tourist information is next to the small reception. A shop and pub are in the village and a bus leaves each hour from outside the site to Pwllheli or Porthmadog.

### Facilities

A purpose-built toilet block to one side includes excellent, full facilities for disabled visitors including access ramp, one washbasin each in a cubicle for male and female and extra large sinks. Facilities for babies. Laundry (taps with fitting for disabled visitors). Gas supplies. Off site: Riding or fishing 0.5 miles. Golf 2.5 miles. Beach 3 miles.

Open: March - October.

### Directions

Follow A497 from Criccieth west and take second right to Llanystumdwy. Site is on the right. O.S.GR: SH469384. GPS: 52.920867, -4.27885

### Charges guide

| | |
|---|---|
| Per person | £ 5.53 - £ 8.17 |
| child (6-18 yrs) | £ 2.45 - £ 2.54 |
| non-member pitch fee | £ 6.46 |

For latest campsite news visit

# alanrogers.com

# Harlech
## Min-y-Don Holiday Home & Touring Park

Beach Road, Harlech LL46 2UG (Gwynedd) T: 01766 780286. E: manager@minydonholidayhomepark.co.uk
**alanrogers.com/UK6365**

Set within the Snowdonia National Park, this super park was totally rebuilt for the 2009 season to a standard that others will strive to achieve. It is a level site with first class facilities and providing 82 well drained grass touring pitches. These include 21 pitches with full services, including waste water and sewerage connections (seven with hardstanding for large motorhomes). Tents are not accepted. In a separate area there are 112 caravan holiday homes. With three miles of golden sand beaches and the Snowdon mountain range as a backdrop, Min-y-Don overlooks the famous Royal St David's Golf Course. Harlech town, dominated by its 13th-century castle, is within walking distance. A great deal of thought has made this site ideal for disabled visitors, with each pitch fronting onto smooth, level, tarmac roads which continue to the toilet and shower facilities where there are wide reserved parking bays. Key cards are required for all the facilities. Children will enjoy a secure play area, a bike track and a games field on site.

### Facilities

New toilet facilities are excellent with private cabins and underfloor heating. Large separate unit for disabled visitors. Baby room. Two private bathrooms for rent. Motorcaravan services. Laundry facilities. Play area. Football pitch. Bike track. Wildlife area. Putting green. WiFi (free). Off site: Supermarket and leisure centre 800 yds. Harlech with shops, pubs and restaurants within walking distance. Beach nearby. Coastal train. Bus service. Ffestiniog steam railway. Portmeirion. Snowdon.

Open: March - November.

### Directions

From Barmouth go north on the A496 to Harlech. Go over level crossing and turn left into Beach Road. From the north on the A496 in Harlech, right into Beach Road before level crossing. Park is on the right in 400 yards. O.S.GR: SH577314.
GPS: 52.862366, -4.11526

### Charges guide

| | |
|---|---|
| Per person | £ 5.00 - £ 6.50 |
| child (5-15 yrs) | £ 1.50 - £ 2.20 |
| pitch | £ 5.50 - £ 12.50 |
| dog (max. 2) | £ 1.00 |

---

# Harlech
## Woodlands Caravan Park

Harlech LL46 2UE (Gwynedd) T: 01766 780419. E: grace@woodlandscp.fsnet.co.uk
**alanrogers.com/UK6355**

This delightful little site is lovingly tended by its owners and has just 18 pitches for tourists, all with gravel hardstanding and electric hook-up (10A) for caravans and motorcaravans only. Tents are not accepted. There are also 22 privately owned holiday homes, and three holiday cottages. However, the location of this site certainly makes up for its diminutive size, nestling under the massive rock topped by Harlech Castle, now a designated World Heritage Site. The narrow lane running alongside the site up to the old town above, is the steepest hill in Britain. The coastal railway runs close to the site and the station is just 100 yards away. Railway noise should not be a problem (the small 'Sprinter' trains do not run at night). The 'Blue Flag' beach is only 500 yards, and the Leisure Centre with its indoor pool is 250 yards.

### Facilities

The modern stone built toilet facilities are heated, clean and tidy with controllable showers (50p), vanity style washbasins, a small laundry with a baby changing area, but with no dedicated facilities for disabled visitors. Chemical disposal point but no motorcaravan service point. Off site: Steam train pleasure trips July/August. Harlech Castle. The town also has a theatre and cinema. Nearby is Portmeirion, location of the cult TV series 'The Prisoner', 8 miles. Barmouth (market Thur, Sun) 10 miles. Golf 0.25 mile. Fishing 3 miles. Riding 3 miles.

Open: 1 March - 31 October.

### Directions

From Barmouth take A496 to Harlech and continue downhill past Royal St David's Golf Course. Fork right immediately before railway crossing, and site is 200 yards on right. DO NOT turn towards town centre which lies on B4573, it is very narrow and congested. O.S.GR: SH582314.
GPS: 52.86155, -4.107633

### Charges guide

| | |
|---|---|
| Per unit incl. 2 persons and electricity | £ 16.00 - £ 18.00 |
| extra person | £ 2.50 |
| awning | £ 2.50 |

No credit or debit cards.

For latest campsite news visit
## alanrogers.com

## Haverfordwest

### Redlands Touring Caravan & Camping Park

Hasguard Cross, Little Haven, Haverfordwest SA62 3SJ (Pembrokeshire) T: 01437 781300
E: info@redlandscamping.co.uk  alanrogers.com/UK5994

This peaceful, family run site is located in the heart of the Pembrokeshire countryside, close to many lovely sandy beaches. Redlands takes around 80 touring units in three areas divided by banks topped with pine trees, 32 hardstandings and 69 with 10A electricity. The first two areas take 60 caravans or motorcaravans and include 20 hardstandings, the third takes 19 tents on a level grassy meadow. There are fine views across rolling countryside to St Brides Bay. Reception has a small shop which is open only in peak periods. Breathable groundsheets must be used. American RVs – advance booking only. A sandy beach and the Pembrokeshire Coastal Path are 1.5 miles away.

#### Facilities

The traditional style toilet block is well kept and heated early and late season. It has all the usual requirements including two extra shower, basin and WC suites. Large utility room with washing machine, dryer and spin dryer. Ironing is free, and there are sinks for laundry and dishes. Shop. Freezers. Wet suit washing area. Dogs are welcome but must be kept on lead. Off site: Shops and ATM in Broadhaven 2 miles. Summer bus service. Fishing and boat launching 1.5 miles. Riding and sailing 5 miles. Golf 6 miles.

Open: 1 March - mid December.

#### Directions

Site 6.5 miles southwest of Haverfordwest. From Haverfordwest take the B4327 road towards Dale and site is on the right at Hasguard Cross. N.B. Do not approach via Broad Haven. O.S.GR: SM853109. GPS: 51.755567, -5.112383

#### Charges guide

| | |
|---|---|
| Per unit incl. 2 persons and electricity | £ 17.70 - £ 22.95 |
| extra person | £ 4.50 |
| dog | free - £ 1.00 |

No credit cards.

---

## Haverfordwest

### Creampots Touring Caravan & Camping Park

Broadway, Broad Haven, Haverfordwest SA62 3TU (Pembrokeshire) T: 01437 781776
alanrogers.com/UK5992

This peacefully located and beautifully manicured, garden-like park is ideal for couples and families, and is a convenient base within easy reach of beaches or for touring the local area. Creampots has 72 spacious, level pitches all with 10A electric hook-ups, including 12 with gravel hardstanding, and ten pitches for tents. There is a separate field and an overflow area taking 30 tents for the August peak holiday time. This is an ideal location for the local attractions.

#### Facilities

The single small white-washed sanitary unit is a modern building which can be heated. Two free hot showers per sex, open style washbasins. Washbasin and WC for disabled campers. These facilities were clean and tidy but may come under pressure at peak times. Tiny laundry room with just about space for one person at a time but with washing machine, dryer and sink. Gas supplies. Bread, milk, newspapers to order. Off site: Summer bus service (May-Sept) 500 m. from site entrance. Shop, post office, pub with hot food in Broad Haven 1 mile. Fishing and boat launching 1 mile. Beach 1.5 miles. Riding 4 miles. Sailing 6 miles. Golf 7 miles.

Open: March - October.

#### Directions

Site is 5 miles west of Haverfordwest. From Haverfordwest take B4341 to Broad Haven, at Broadway follow brown tourist sign on left. O.S.GR: SM882132. GPS: 51.777333, -5.072283

#### Charges guide

| | |
|---|---|
| Per unit incl. 2 persons and electricity | £ 18.90 - £ 23.70 |
| dog | free |

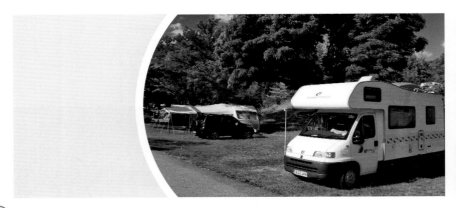

For latest campsite news visit
**alanrogers.com**

## Llandovery
### Rhandirmwyn Camping & Caravanning Club Site
Rhandirmwyn, Llandovery SA20 0NT (Carmarthenshire) T: 01550 760257
alanrogers.com/UK6070

This is a popular site with those who like a peaceful life with no on-site entertainment, just fresh air and beautiful countryside. The site is only a short drive from the magnificent Llyn Brianne reservoir and close to the Dinas RSPB nature reserve, where a two mile trail runs through oak and alder woodland alongside the River Tywi and the wildlife includes many species of birds including red kites. In a sheltered valley, there are 90 pitches on level grass, 51 electric hook-ups (16A) and 17 hardstandings. The village is within walking distance although there is a fairly steep hill to negotiate (but the return is much easier), you can take a short cut through a woodland grove.

### Facilities
The single heated sanitary block is kept very clean and tidy. Some washbasins in cubicles, dishwashing sinks and fully equipped laundry. Drive-over motorcaravan service point. Small playground with rubber base. Off site: The village has a Post Office and general store and the Royal Oak Inn serves good value meals. Farmers' market in Llandovery twice a month. Fishing 6 miles. Golf and bicycle hire 7 miles. Riding 11 miles.

Open: March - October.

### Directions
From centre of Llandovery take A483 towards Builth Wells, after a short distance turn left by the fire station, signed Rhandirmwyn, continue for about 7 miles along country lanes. O.S.GR: SN779436. GPS: 52.077017, -3.783833

### Charges guide
| | |
|---|---|
| Per person | £ 5.53 - £ 8.17 |
| child (6-18 yrs) | £ 2.45 - £ 2.54 |
| non-member pitch fee | £ 6.46 |

## Llandovery
### Erwlon Caravan & Camping Park
Brecon Road, Llandovery SA20 0RD (Carmarthenshire) T: 01550 721021. E: peter@erwlon.co.uk
alanrogers.com/UK5955

Just outside Llandovery and on the edge of the Brecon Beacons National Park, Erwlon is an attractive and welcoming campsite. Of the 110 pitches, seven are used for privately owned caravan holiday homes, 33 have seasonal caravans and 70 are for touring units. Most are on hardstanding with electricity connections and 12 have water and a drain as well. There is a flat field for tents at the bottom of the park with some electrical outlets, an open-sided, covered area for eating, food preparation and bicycle storage. The site has a relaxed atmosphere where consideration for others minimises the need for formal rules. It is ideal for young families, walkers, cyclists and fishermen.

### Facilities
New heated toilet block with washbasins in cabins, 4 family rooms (basin, shower, toilet) and a room for families and disabled visitors which includes a baby unit. Combined, well equipped laundry and dishwashing room. Motorcaravan service point. Fridge freezer. Fishing. Bicycle hire. WiFi (charge). Off site: Supermarket 500 m. Town (shops, pubs, restaurants and indoor pool) within 1 mile. Golf 1 mile. Riding 8 miles. Beaches 25 miles.

Open: All year.

### Directions
Park is about half a mile outside the town boundary of Llandovery on the A40 to Brecon. O.S.GR: SN778344. GPS: 51.99491, -3.78076

### Charges guide
| | |
|---|---|
| Per unit incl. 2 persons | £ 12.00 - £ 13.00 |
| incl. services | £ 15.00 - £ 16.00 |
| extra person | £ 1.00 |
| dog | free |
No credit cards.

## Llandrindod Wells
### Dolswydd Caravan Park
Dolswydd, Pen-y-Bont, Llandrindod Wells LD1 5UB (Powys) T: 01597 851267
E: Hughes@dolswydd.freeserve.co.uk alanrogers.com/UK6250

Dolswydd is on the edge of a pretty, traditional working farm. Peaceful and tranquil, with fine views of the Welsh hills and surrounding area, it has modern facilities and 25 good spacious pitches mainly on hardstandings, all with electrical connections (16A). The Hughes family extends a warm and friendly welcome to their little park, surrounded by hills and wandering sheep, which is ideal as a touring base or for a one night stop, but booking is recommended, especially at peak times, Bank Holidays and during the Victorian Festival (last week in August). The park is within walking distance of the local pub.

### Facilities
Modern facilities include lots of hot water, dishwashing, laundry, and a WC/washroom for disabled visitors. Fishing in the river alongside the site (free, but licence required). Off site: Within walking distance are the local pub and garage. Riding 1 mile. Golf and bicycle hire 5 miles.

Open: Easter - end October.

### Directions
Pen-y-Bont is 2 miles east of the junction of the A44 and A483 roads at Crossgates. Take A44 (Kington). Go through Pen-y-Bont and immediately after crossing cattle grid, site is on right. O.S.GR: SO117639. GPS: 52.26321, -3.28087

### Charges guide
| | |
|---|---|
| Per unit incl. 2 persons, 2 children and electricity | £ 12.00 |
| extra person | £ 1.00 |

## Llandysul

### Brynawelon Touring & Camping Park

Sarnau, Llandysul SA44 6RE (Ceredigion) T: 01239 654584. E: info@brynawlon.co.uk

alanrogers.com/UK6005

Paul and Liz Cowton have turned Brynawelon into a friendly, attractive and well appointed campsite. It is in a stunning rural location within two miles of the Ceredigion coast with its beaches, and close to the River Teifi with plenty of water based activities. All the 40 pitches have electricity hook-ups and of these 26 are serviced pitches (water and waste) on hardstanding. The remainder are on level grass. The park has ample room for children to play, an enclosed play area, an indoor games room with TV, and a sauna next to reception. Buzzards, red kites, owls and the occasional eagle can be seen from the park.

**Facilities**

New modern toilet block with toilets, showers, washbasins in cabins, two full suites in each side and a separate room for families and disabled visitors. Laundry/kitchen with washing machine, tumble dryer, ironing board and iron, fridge/freezer, microwave, kettle and toaster. Takeaway selling hot food (July/Aug). Enclosed play area. Games room. Sauna. Dog walking area. Off site: Shops and pub 1 mile. Beaches, fishing, sailing and riding 3 miles.

Open: March - 31 October.

**Directions**

Travelling north on the A487 from Cardigan turn right (southeast) at the crossroads in Sarnau village, signed Rhydlewis. Site is on the left after 650 yds. Note: the country roads from the south are not suitable for caravans and motorcaravans. O.S.GR: SN322508. GPS: 52.13001, -4.45401

**Charges guide**

| | |
|---|---|
| Per unit incl 2 persons and electricity | £ 25.00 |
| incl. 4 persons, hardstanding and services | £ 12.50 |

No credit cards.

## Llanelli

### Pembrey Country Park Caravan Club Site

Pembrey, Llanelli SA16 0EJ (Carmarthenshire) T: 01554 834369.

alanrogers.com/UK5940

This very popular Caravan Club site has a wonderful location on the edge of a 520 acre Country Park with a vast range of outdoor activities, including the use of an eight mile stretch of safe, sandy beach a mile away. This well sheltered site is set in 12 acre grounds and provides 50 large hardstanding pitches and 80 level, grass pitches for caravans and motorcaravans, all with 16A electricity. Tents are not accepted. Thoughtful landscaping has included the planting of many species of tree and a circular, one-way tarmac road provides easy access.

**Facilities**

The toilet block is of an excellent standard including washbasins in cubicles, facilities for disabled visitors and a baby room. Fully equipped laundry room. Dishwashing room and further sinks under cover. Motorcaravan service point. Gas available. Local tradesmen visit each morning selling milk, bread and newspapers. Play area. Late arrivals area (with electricity). Off site: Dogs are restricted on the beach May-Sept (follow signs).

Open: March - January.

**Directions**

Leave M4 at junction 48 onto A4138 (Llanelli). After 4 miles turn right on A484 at roundabout signed Carmarthen. Continue for 7 miles to Pembrey. The Country Park is signed off the A484 in Pembrey village; site entrance is on right 100 yds before park. O.S.GR: SN413006. GPS: 51.681817, -4.297417

**Charges guide**

| | |
|---|---|
| Per person | £ 4.70 - £ 6.20 |
| child (5-16 yrs) | £ 1.50 - £ 2.50 |
| pitch (non-member) | £ 11.90 - £ 14.80 |

## Llangadog

### Abermarlais Caravan Park

Llangadog SA19 9NG (Carmarthenshire) T: 01550 777868. E: aberma@tiscali.co.uk

alanrogers.com/UK5960

Apart from the attractions of south or mid Wales for a stay, this sheltered, family run park could also double as a useful transit stop close to the main holiday route for those travelling to Pembrokeshire. In a natural setting, up to 88 touring units are accommodated in one fairly flat, tapering five acre grass field edged by mature trees and a stream. Pitches are numbered and generously spaced around the perimeter or on either side of a central, hedged spine at the wider end, with 48 electrical hook-ups (10A) and some hardstanding. Backpackers have a small, separate area.

**Facilities**

The one small toilet block is older in style, but is clean, bright, cheerful and adequate with controllable showers. Two external, covered dishwashing sinks but no laundry facilities (nearest about 5 miles). Motorcaravan service point. Shop doubling as reception. Gas supplies. Play area with tennis and volleyball nets and play equipment. Winter caravan storage. Off site: Restaurants nearby. Pubs, shops, etc. at Llangadog. Fishing 2 miles.

Open: 14 March - 14 November.

**Directions**

Park is on the A40, between the junctions with the A4069 and A482, between Llandovery and Llandeilo. O.S.GR: SN695298. GPS: 51.951583, -3.9003

**Charges guide**

| | |
|---|---|
| Per person | £ 1.50 |
| child (5-16 yrs) | £ 1.00 |
| pitch | £ 7.00 |
| electricity | £ 2.00 |

## Llangollen

### Ty-Ucha Farm Caravan Park

Maesmawr Road, Llangollen LL20 7PP (Denbighshire) T: 01978 860677

alanrogers.com/UK6700

Only a mile from Llangollen, Ty Ucha has a rather dramatic setting, nestling under its own mountain and with views across the valley to craggy Dinas Bran castle. It is a neat, ordered park, carefully managed by the owners and providing 40 pitches (30 with 10A electrical hook-up) for caravans and motorhomes only (tents are not accepted). They are well spaced round a large, grassy field with an open centre for play. One side slopes gently and is bounded by a stream and wood in which a Nature Trail has been made. Because of overhead cables, kite flying is forbidden; no bike riding either. A path leads to various mountain walks, depending on your energy and ability. The world famous Eisteddfod is an international festival of music and dance held for six days starting on the first Tuesday of the first full week in July every year – it is a very busy time for the area.

### Facilities

The single toilet block, although of Portacabin style, is clean and well maintained and can be heated. It includes two metered showers for each sex (a little cramped). Dishwashing sink with cold water outside. No laundry facilities but there is a launderette in Llangollen. Gas supplies. Games room. Late arrivals area. Note: tents are not accepted. Off site: Hotel 0.5 miles with reasonably priced meals. Fishing 1 mile, golf 0.5 miles.

Open: Easter - October.

### Directions

Park is signed off A5 road, 1 mile east of Llangollen (250 yds). O.S.GR: SJ228411.
GPS: 52.96546, -3.14569

### Charges guide

| | |
|---|---|
| Per unit incl. 2 persons and electricity | £ 14.00 - £ 15.00 |
| extra person | £ 2.00 |

Reductions for seniors for weekly stays.
No credit cards.

## Llantwit Major

### Acorn Camping & Caravanning

Ham Lane South, Llantwit Major CF61 1RP (Vale of Glamorgan) T: 01446 794024. E: info@acorncamping.co.uk

alanrogers.com/UK5927

A peaceful, family owned, rural site, Acorn is situated on the Heritage Coast, one mile from the beach and the historic town of Llantwit Major. The 105 pitches are mostly on grass, with a few private and rental mobile homes at the far end, leaving around 90 pitches for tourers. These include 10 serviced pitches and four gravel hardstandings with 74 electric hook-ups (10A), and a separate area for tents. Reception houses a very well stocked shop which includes groceries and essentials, souvenirs, children's toys, camping gear, a delicatessen, and takeaway meals cooked to order. There is occasional aircraft noise. Site lighting is kept to a minimum to allow guests to enjoy the night sky – a torch might be useful. The Glamorgan Heritage Coastal footpath is a short walk from the site and Llantwit Major is also worth a visit, particularly St Illtud's Church for its wall paintings, medieval altar, and collection of Celtic stones.

### Facilities

A warm, modern building houses spacious shower cubicles with washbasins, ample WCs, a family/baby room, and a suite for disabled campers. Laundry facilities. Drinks machine. Shop. Gas. Snooker room. Games room (charged). Play area with free trampoline. Off site: Glamorgan Heritage Coastal footpath. Llanerch Vineyard. Cosmeston Lakes Country Park at Penarth. Sea fishing 1 mile. Riding 2 miles. Lake 4 miles. Golf, boat launching 9 miles.

Open: 1 February - 8 December.

### Directions

From east from M4 exit 33 follow signs to Cardiff airport, take B4265 for Llantwit Major. Turn left at traffic lights, through Broverton and left into Ham Lane East, finally turning left into Ham Manor Park and follow signs to campsite. From west: M4 exit 35, turn south on A473 for 3 miles, then left on A48, turning right at Pentre Meyrick towards Llantwit Major on B4268/70. Left at roundabout on B4265, over mini-roundabout, right at traffic lights into Llanmaes Road, left at mini-roundabout, continue around back of the town, left at mini-roundabout, and right into Ham Lane East and as above. O.S.GR: SS974678. GPS: 51.40409, -3.48181

### Charges guide

| | |
|---|---|
| Per unit incl. 2 persons and electricity | £ 13.80 - £ 14.95 |
| extra person | £ 4.50 |
| dog | £ 0.65 |

## Llanwrda

### Springwater Lakes

Harford, Llanwrda SA19 8DT (Carmarthenshire) T: 01558 650788. E: bookings@springwaterlakes.com

alanrogers.com/UK5880

Set in 20 acres of Welsh countryside, Springwater offers a selection of fishing lakes to keep even the keenest of anglers occupied. However, it is not just anglers who will enjoy this site – it is a lovely base to enjoy the peace and tranquillity of this part of Wales. Springwater offers 30 spacious, flat pitches either on grass or gravel hardstanding, all with 16A electricity. Future plans include fully serviced pitches. Malcolm and Shirley Bexon are very proud of their site and welcome all visitors with a smile. This is not a site for children unless they enjoy fishing (no play areas). If you want to learn about fishing Malcolm will be happy to help.

### Facilities

The modern toilet block is very clean and includes facilities for disabled visitors (there is also wheelchair access to the lakes for fishing). Fishing. Tackle/bait shop. Off site: Spar shop and garage 500 yards, other shops 5 miles. Bicycle hire and riding 2 miles. Golf 4 miles.

Open: 1 March - 31 October.

### Directions

From A40 at Llanwrda take A482 to Lampeter. After 6 miles go through village of Pumsaint and site is 2 mile further on the left, just before garage shop. O.S.GR: SN642429. GPS: 52.067417, -3.98225

### Charges guide

| | |
|---|---|
| Per unit incl. 2 persons and electricity | £ 19.00 |
| extra person (over 2 yrs) | £ 5.00 |
| dog | free - £ 2.00 |

No credit cards.

## Machynlleth

### Morben Isaf Touring & Holiday Home Park

Derwenlas, Machynlleth SY20 8SR (Powys) T: 01654 781473. E: manager@morbenisaf.co.uk

alanrogers.com/UK6245

Morben Isaf provides 13 touring pitches with multi-services, all with electricity (16A), water tap, waste water drain and a satellite TV hook-up. There is further grassy space below the touring pitches beyond the fishing lake which is normally used as a play field and football pitch but can accommodate around 30 tents who do not need any services. On a lower level, behind the site manager's bungalow, barely visible from the touring site, are 87 privately owned caravan holiday homes. Also on the site is an unfenced coarse fishing lake which campers are free to use. Machynlleth is a market town, home of Owain Glyndwr's fifteenth century Welsh Parliament building and the Celtica Centre, and is also close to the Tal-y-Llyn Steam Railway, the Centre for Alternative Technology, Corris Craft Centre and King Arthur's Labyrinth. Adjacent to the site is the Dyfi Osprey Project visitor centre – for the first time in 2007, a nest platform was erected and was occupied by a pair of ospreys. This park is in a convenient location for an overnight halt, or a short stay whilst visiting all these attractions.

### Facilities

Small but well equipped, heated modern toilet block includes spacious controllable showers, baby changing and child seats in both ladies' and men's. Facilities for disabled campers. Well equipped laundry. Powered motorcaravan service point. Internet access (free). Off site: Pub serving hot food 1.5 miles. Leisure Centre, shops and services in Machynlleth 3 miles (market on Wednesday). Dyfi Osprey Project visitor centre adjacent. Centre for Alternative Technology 6 miles.

Open: Mid March - 31 October.

### Directions

Site is 2.5 miles southwest of Machynlleth beside A487. O.S.GR: SN706986. GPS: 52.570067, -3.91145

### Charges guide

| | |
|---|---|
| Per unit incl. 2 persons and electricity | £ 16.00 - £ 18.50 |
| tent (2 persons) | £ 12.50 |

## Moelfre

### Home Farm Caravan Park

Marianglas, Anglesey LL73 8PH (Isle of Anglesey) T: 01248 410614. E: enq@homefarm-anglesey.co.uk
**alanrogers.com/UK6640**

A tarmac drive through an open field leads to this neatly laid out quality park, with caravan holiday homes to one side. Nestling below what was once a Celtic hill fort, later decimated as a quarry, the park is edged with mature trees and farmland. A circular, tarmac access road leads to the 102 well spaced and numbered touring pitches. With five types available, there are pitches for everyone; ranging from grass with no electricity, to oversized, deluxe hardstandings with electricity, water tanks/taps, waste water drain and TV hook-ups. All electricity is 16A and there are separate well maintained grass fields/areas for tents. Some areas are slightly sloping. The 'pièce de résistance' must be the children's indoor play area, large super adventure play equipment, complete with tunnels and bridges on safe rubber matting, not to mention an outside fenced play area and fields for sports, football, etc. and walking. Various beaches, sandy or rocky, are within a mile. A member of the Best of British Group.

**Facilities**

Two purpose built toilet blocks, one part of the reception building, are of similar design, can be heated and are maintained to a high standard. En-suite provision for people with disabilities (with key). Excellent small bathroom for children with baby bath and curtain for privacy. Family room (with key). Laundry room. Motorcaravan service point. Ice pack service. Reception provides basic essentials, gas and some caravan accessories. Indoor and outdoor play areas. TV and pool table. Small library. Hard tennis (extra charge) with racquet hire. Off site: Restaurants, shops and ATM at Benllech 2 miles. Beach 1 mile. Fishing and golf 2 miles. Riding 8 miles.

**Open:** April - October.

**Directions**

From the Britannia Bridge take second exit left signed Benllech and Amlwch on the A5025. Two miles after Benllech keep left at roundabout and park entrance is 300 yards on the left beyond the church. O.S.GR: SH499850. GPS: 53.34055, -4.256367

**Charges guide**

| | |
|---|---|
| Per unit incl. 2 persons and electricity | £ 17.00 - £ 25.50 |
| extra person | £ 3.50 - £ 6.00 |
| child (5-16 yrs) | £ 2.00 - £ 4.00 |
| dog (max. 2) | £ 1.00 - £ 2.00 |

## Monmouth

### Glen Trothy Caravan & Camping Park

Mitchel Troy, Monmouth NP25 4BD (Monmouthshire) T: 01600 712295. E: enquiries@glentrothy.co.uk
**alanrogers.com/UK5890**

Glen Trothy is a pretty park on the banks of the river Trothy and visitors are greeted by an array of colourful flowerbeds and tubs around the entrance and reception area. Three fields provide level touring and tent pitches. The first and largest field has a circular gravel road with seasonal pitches arranged on the outer side and touring pitches on the inner side. These have slabs for vehicle wheels and electricity hook-ups. The second field, just past the toilet block, has pitches for trailer tents and tents only (16 with electricity), whilst the camping field is for tents only (no cars allowed on this area). The owners, Horace and Merle Price, are working hard on their site bringing its facilities up-to-date, recently adding security barriers at the entrance.

**Facilities**

The sanitary block is old and a little tired (possibly stretched at peak times). Facilities for disabled visitors. Laundry and dishwashing. Tourist information in hut opposite reception. Dogs are not accepted. Only purpose built barbecues are allowed. Small play area. Off site: Golf, canoeing, shopping and supermarkets at the historic town of Monmouth 1.5 miles. The Wye Valley and the Forest of Dean are nearby for outings.

**Open:** 1 March - 31 October.

**Directions**

At Monmouth, take A40 east to Abergavenny. Exit a first junction and at T-junction, where site is signed, turn left onto B4284. Follow signs for Mitchel Troy. Site is on right just past village sign. O.S.GR: SO495105. GPS: 51.790967, -2.7341

**Charges guide**

| | |
|---|---|
| Per unit incl. 2 persons and electricity | £ 14.00 |

For latest campsite news visit
**alanrogers.com**

## Montgomery

### Daisy Bank Touring Caravan Park

Snead, Montgomery SY15 6EB (Powys) T: 01588 620471. E: enquiries@daisy-bank.co.uk

alanrogers.com/UK6330

For adults only, this pretty, tranquil park in the Camlad Valley has panoramic views, and is an ideal base for walkers. Attractively landscaped with 'old English' flower beds and many different trees and shrubs, this small park has been carefully developed. The Welsh hills to the north and the Shropshire hills to the south overlook the three fields which provide a total of 83 pitches. The field nearer to the road (perhaps a little noisy) is slightly sloping but there are hardstandings for motorcaravans, while the second field is more level. All pitches have 16A electricity, water and waste water drainage and TV hook up. With many walks in the area, including Offa's Dyke, a series of walk leaflets is available centred on Bishop's Castle three miles away. The owners will site your caravan for you and there is a late arrivals area with electricity. The code for the security gate at the entrance is obtained at registration. Although technically in Wales, the park is 500 yards from the Shropshire border, an area rich in history.

**Facilities**

The well equipped, heated toilet block now incorporates modern, en-suite units (6 with shower, WC and washbasin, 2 with WC and washbasin and facilities for disabled visitors). Dishwashing sinks at the rear of the block are covered. Laundry facilities. Shop in reception (operates an honesty policy at certain times). Gas supplies. Brick built barbecues. Small putting green (free loan of clubs and balls). Bicycle hire. Small library. WiFi (charged). Off site: Supermarket 2 miles. Many eating places near. Fishing 3 miles. Golf and riding 10 miles.

Open: All year.

**Directions**

Site is by the A489 road 2 miles east of Churchstoke in the direction of Craven Arms. O.S.GR: SO302930. GPS: 52.529917, -3.0297

**Charges guide**

| Per unit incl. 2 persons and services | £ 17.00 - £ 22.00 |
| extra person | £ 5.00 |
| tent (per person) | £ 7.00 - £ 8.00 |
| dog | £ 1.00 |

---

## Montgomery

### Bacheldre Watermill Caravan Park

Churchstoke, Montgomery SY15 6TE (Powys) T: 01588 620489. E: info@bacheldremill.co.uk

alanrogers.com/UK6310

A delightful little site, Bacheldre has just 25 pitches arranged around the perimeter of a grass meadow, with no site road. There is just one lamp on the outside of the toilet block and three small lights on the perimeter so torches are useful. However, there are 18 electric hook-ups (10A) and ten hardstandings. Ideal for tenters and small units, it is not really suitable for larger units (20 ft. plus) and American RVs. The watermill is fully operational, producing high quality organic wheat flour, which can be purchased from reception, together with eggs and bread. The mill is not normally accessible, although guided tours can be arranged. Note: there are obvious hazards for small children – a deep, partially fenced millpond, moving waterwheel and the stream.

**Facilities**

A portacabin provides the usual facilities including one controllable hot shower per sex with dishwashing sinks in a separate room. Calor gas stocked. Off site: Walking and cycling along Offa's Dyke 800 yards from site. Clun Castle ruins are worth a visit. Steam enthusiasts are well catered for with the Welshpool and Llanfair light railway. Supermarket at Churchstoke 2 miles.

Open: All year.

**Directions**

Bacheldre is just off the A489 between Newtown and Churchstoke, about 9 miles east of Newtown and 2 miles west of Churchstoke. Turn into narrow lane (signed Bacheldre Mill), over the bridge and site entrance is almost immediately on your right. O.S.GR: SO243929. GPS: 52.52749, -3.11879

**Charges guide**

| Per unit incl. 2 persons | £ 10.00 - £ 13.00 |
| extra person | £ 2.00 |
| awning | £ 2.50 |

For latest campsite news visit
alanrogers.com

# Montgomery

## Smithy Park

Abermule, Montgomery SY15 6ND (Powys) T: 01584 711280. E: info@bestparks.co.uk
alanrogers.com/UK6305

Smithy Caravan Park is set in four acres of landscaped ground bordered by the River Severn and the Shropshire Union Canal in the tranquil rolling countryside of central Wales. It does have 60 privately owned caravan holiday homes, but the touring area is separate and also has the benefit of being closest to the river with the best views and a small picnic and seating area on the bank. This area has 26 fully serviced hardstanding pitches (16A electricity, water, waste water and satellite TV hook-ups). A newly installed timber chalet is located in one corner of the touring area and provides all the sanitary facilities. This is a well run site, which is under the same ownership as Westbrook Park, with a resident manager on site here. The village has two local pubs, a shop and a bus service – all within easy walking distance. American RVs are accepted with prior notice. Kite flying or cycling on the park are not permitted.

### Facilities

The new timber clad chalet building provides two good sized showers per sex, washbasins in cubicles, a family room suitable for the less able (there is a step up to the building). Utility room housing a laundry with washing machine, dryer and dishwashing sink. Fishing in the river Severn. Fenced playground. Gas stocked. Off site: Bus stop in village opposite end of site access road. Supermarkets and all other services in Newtown 3 miles. Golf 3 miles. Riding 5 miles.

Open: 1 March - 30 October.

### Directions

Site is 3 miles north of Newtown in the village of Abermule. Turn off the A483 into village, and turn down the lane beside the Waterloo Arms, opposite the village shop and Post Office. Site is at end of lane. O.S.GR: SO161948.
GPS: 52.544217, -3.238717

### Charges guide

| Per unit incl. 2 persons and electricity | £ 14.00 - £ 20.00 |
| extra person | £ 4.00 |
| child (4-10 yrs) | £ 4.00 |
| dog | £ 1.00 |

# Newcastle Emlyn

## Cenarth Falls Holiday Park

Cenarth, Newcastle Emlyn SA38 9JS (Ceredigion) T: 01239 710345. E: enquiries@cenarth-holipark.co.uk
alanrogers.com/UK6010

The Davies family has developed an attractively landscaped, part wooded holiday home park with 86 privately owned units and three for hire. However, a neat level cared for, sheltered grassy area at the top of the park provides 30 touring pitches, accessed via a semicircular tarmac road, and all with shingle hardstanding and electricity (16A). A sunken, kidney shaped outdoor pool with landscaped surrounds and sunbeds is a focal point. The Coracles Health and Country Club provides an indoor pool, spa, sauna and steam rooms and fitness suite (reduced rates for campers). It also provides a bar, restaurant area, adult-only lounge and a large function room where live entertainment is organised during the main season. Everything is of a high quality. A footpath leads to the village and the famous Cenarth Falls. The National Coracle Centre is well worth a visit. A member of the Best of British Group.

### Facilities

The excellent, heated sanitary block has easy ramped access, even to the chemical disposal unit. Accessed by key, it uses a 'P.I.R.' system that controls heating, lighting, water and air freshener on entry – very efficient. Tiled with non-slip floors, both men and ladies have an en-suite provision for disabled visitors (doubling as a family room), spacious well equipped showers and one of the washbasins in a roomy private cabin. Laundry room with two washing machines, two dryers and ironing facilities (used by the whole park). No laundry sinks, but two dishwashing sinks are under cover. Gas supplies. Outdoor pool (mid May-mid Sept). Coracles Health and Country Club (see above). Play area. Games room with pool table and electronic games. No dogs on touring field (16/7-3/9). Off site: Shop within 0.5 miles. Fishing 0.25 miles. Riding 7 miles. Bicycle hire 8 miles. Golf 10 miles.

Open: 1 March - 16 December.

### Directions

Follow A484 Cardigan - Newcastle Emlyn road and park is signed before Cenarth village.
O.S.GR: SN265421. GPS: 52.0499, -4.531717

### Charges 2011

| Per unit incl. up to 4 people and electricity | £ 15.00 - £ 26.00 |

Wales

For latest campsite news visit
**alanrogers.com**

249

## Newport

### Tredegar House Country Park Caravan Club Site

Coedkernen, Newport NP10 8TW (Newport) T: 01633 815600

alanrogers.com/UK6060

This immaculate Caravan Club site is ideally situated for breaking a journey or for longer stays. It can accommodate 80 caravans, all with 16A electricity hook-up and 47 with gravel hardstanding. A further grass area is allocated for 20 tents, with its use limited to families and couples – no single sex groups are accepted. The site itself is set within the gardens and park of Tredegar House, a 17th century house and country park which is open to the public to discover what life was like 'above and below stairs'. The park entrance gates are locked at dusk so contact the site reception for details of latest arrival times. Some road noise may be expected at times, but otherwise this is an excellent site.

#### Facilities

The sanitary block is of an excellent standard with a digital lock system. It includes washbasins in cubicles. Facilities for disabled visitors. Baby and toddler bathroom. Laundry. Good motorcaravan service point. Calor gas available. Tredegar House visitors' centre with tea rooms, gift shop and craft workshops (Easter-Sept). Adventure play area in the park. Off site: Large supermarket 0.5 miles. Newport 3 miles. Cardiff 9 miles. Bus service 10 minutes walk.

Open: All year.

#### Directions

From M4 take exit 28 or from A48 junction with the M4 follow brown signs for Tredegar House. The caravan park is indicated to the left at the house entrance. O.S.GR: ST284852.
GPS: 51.56148, -3.03341

#### Charges guide

| | |
|---|---|
| Per person | £ 4.10 - £ 5.60 |
| child (5-16 yrs) | £ 1.30 - £ 2.15 |
| pitch incl. electricity (non-member) | £ 11.50 - £ 14.20 |

## Newport

### Cwmcarn Forest Drive Campsite

Cwmcarn, Crosskeys, Newport NP11 7FA (Newport) T: 01495 272001. E: cwmcarn-vc@caerphilly.gov.uk

alanrogers.com/UK5930

This forest site, run by Caerphilly Council, is set in a narrow, sheltered valley with magnificent wooded slopes. The park is not only central for the many attractions of this part of Wales, but there is also much of the natural environment to enjoy including a small fishing lake and the seven mile forest drive. The site has a slightly wild feel, but is well located and has 27 well spaced, flat pitches, most with 15A electricity (three with concrete hardstanding), spread over three small fields between the new Visitor Centre and the small lake. Wardens are on hand daily. The Visitor Centre and campsite reception are open 09.00-17.00 (18.00 at weekends, Oct-Easter Fridays 09.00-16.30 pm). The forest drive (open daily in season) has several car parks en-route where visitors can stop to enjoy the great views, many picnic and barbecue areas, wood carvings and a play area. The climb up to the Twmbarlwm ancient hill fort is well worth making with its magnificent views across the Severn to Somerset, Devon and Gloucestershire.

#### Facilities

The single, heated toilet block includes toilet facilities for disabled visitors, laundry facilities, small cooker and fridge. Visitor Centre has a coffee shop selling refreshments and snacks. Guided walks and the popular Twrch (9 miles) mountain bike trail. Dogs accepted by prior arrangement. Off site: Shops, leisure centre and takeaway food in village less than 1 mile. Riding 2 miles. Golf 3 miles.

Open: All year excl. 23 December - 2 January.

#### Directions

Cwmcarn Forest Drive is well signed from junction 28 on the M4. From the Midlands and the 'Heads of the Valleys' road (A465), take A467 south to Cwmcarn. O.S.GR: ST230935.
GPS: 51.63771, -3.11877

#### Charges guide

| | |
|---|---|
| Per unit incl. 2 persons and electricity | £ 14.00 - £ 18.00 |
| extra person | £ 4.00 - £ 6.00 |
| child (2-11 yrs) | £ 1.50 - £ 3.00 |
| dog | free |

For latest campsite news visit
**alanrogers.com**

## Newtown

### Cringoed Caravan Park

Cringoed, Llanbrynmair, Newtown SY19 7DR (Powys) T: 01650 521237. E: susan.mathers.@virgin.net

alanrogers.com/UK6240

Cringoed is a pleasant, peaceful, small park with a river to one side, hills on the other and trees at either end. There are 30 spacious pitches available for touring and these are in a level open field, each with hardstanding and 16A electricity. About 36 caravan holiday homes are placed at either end of the site, some amongst trees and some in a newer, more open area. There are also ten tent pitches, some with electricity. This is a relaxing base where you can sit and listen to the river and watch the wildlife, but it is also within easy reach of some of mid-Wales' best scenery and not far from the coast. Paul and Sue Mathers continue landscaping the site and will make you very welcome.

#### Facilities

The single toilet block is neat, modern and quite adequate. Laundry and dishwashing. Adventure play area. Small tourist information room. Off site: Shops 1 mile. ATM at Spar in Carno 6 miles. Bicycle hire 1 mile. Fishing 5 miles. Golf 8 miles. Riding 12 miles.

Open: 7 March - 30 November.

#### Directions

From the A470 between Newton and Machynlleth in the village of Llanbrynmair take the B4518 signed Staylittle (caravan signs). After 1 mile just before bridge turn right, go over site bridge and turn right into site. O.S.GR: SH887013.
GPS: 52.598333, -3.644383

#### Charges guide

| | |
|---|---|
| Per unit incl. 2 persons and electricity | £ 14.00 - £ 17.00 |
| extra person | £ 6.00 |
| child (3-14 yrs) | £ 3.00 |
| dog | free |

No credit cards.

## Pembroke

### Freshwater East Caravan Club Site

Trewent Hill, Freshwater East, Pembroke SA71 5LJ (Pembrokeshire) T: 01646 672341

alanrogers.com/UK5990

This Caravan Club site in the Pembrokeshire Coast National Park is open to non-members (for all units). At the bottom of a hill, it has 130 mainly level pitches bounded by trees, all with 16A electrical hook-ups and half on hardstanding. There are a further 12 pitches for tents. The beach and the Pembroke Coastal Path are about a five minute walk. This is an excellent area for walking with magnificent cliff views and bird watching. You will find St David's, the smallest cathedral city, well worth a visit. Note: TV aerial connections are available, but you will need your own extension cable.

#### Facilities

The two heated toilet blocks are modern and clean with washbasins in cubicles, and free hairdryers or sockets for your own. Facilities for disabled visitors. Fully equipped laundry rooms. Waste point for motorcaravans. Gas supplies. Reception keeps basic food items. Information kiosk. Small play area. Off site: Public transport 1 mile. Shop 0.5 miles. Beach 400 yds. Fishing 5 miles.

Open: 27 March - 26 October.

#### Directions

From the east on A477, fork left 1.25 miles past Milton onto A4075 Pembroke road. After 2 miles in Pembroke immediately (after railway bridge) turn sharp left at roundabout on A4139 Tenby road. In 1.75 miles in Lamphey turn right onto B4584 signed Freshwater East. In 1.75 miles turn right signed Stackpole and Trewent and after 400 yds. at foot of hill, right into lane at Club sign. Do not tow to the beach area. O.S.GR: SS015979.
GPS: 51.645262, -4.872512

#### Charges guide

| | |
|---|---|
| Per person | £ 4.20 - £ 5.50 |
| child (5-16 yrs) | £ 1.30 - £ 2.15 |
| pitch incl. electricity (non-member) | £ 11.70 - £ 14.20 |

## Penmaenmawr

### Tyddyn Du Touring Park

Conwy Old Road, Penmaenmawr LL34 6RE (Conwy) T: 01492 622300. E: stay@tyddyndutouringpark.co.uk
alanrogers.com/UK6695

This attractively landscaped campsite for adults only is conveniently situated close to the A55 and positioned on a hillside with panoramic views across Conwy Bay to The Great Orme at Llandudno and Puffin Island. Offering peace and quiet in a superb location between mountains and the sea and being within easy reach of Conwy, Snowdonia National Park and many historic regions of North Wales, this is an ideal base for exploring the area. Tarmac roads connect the three levels which are tiered to maximise the views for everyone. There are 92 touring pitches on either grass or hardstanding and all have 16A electricity. One modern, roomy and well equipped utility building houses separate facilities for men and women, whilst an additional, older, more traditional sanitary block is located at the top of the site. Some traffic noise from the A55 can be heard but this should not spoil the enjoyment of this pretty campsite. Units over 26 ft. in length are not accepted No arrivals before 14.00 please and visitors under the age of 18 are not allowed on site.

**Facilities**

Two well maintained sanitary blocks provide showers, open style washbasins and hairdryers. En-suite facilities for disabled visitors (Radar key). Motorcaravan service point (care needed to access). Well equipped laundry room. Small library. £5 (cash only) refundable deposit for entry card. Off site: Shops and restaurants within 1 mile. Pub at entrance to park. Sandy beach 10-15 minutes walk. Fishing and sailing 1 mile. Golf 0.5 miles. Conwy 4 miles. Llandudno 9 miles.

Open: 22 March - 31 October.

**Directions**

From the A55 take exit 16 and at roundabout signed Penmaenmawr turn immediately sharp left into Ysguborwen Road. Entrance to park is about 300 yards on the right. O.S.GR: SH728768. GPS: 53.27425, -3.90632

**Charges guide**

| | |
|---|---|
| Per unit incl. 2 adults and electricity | £ 18.00 - £ 20.00 |
| extra person (over 18 yrs) | £ 2.00 |
| awning | £ 1.00 - £ 2.00 |

## Pontarddulais

### River View Touring Park

The Dingle, Llanedi, Pontarddulais SA4 0FH (Carmarthenshire) T: 01269 844876
E: info@riverviewtouringpark.com  alanrogers.com/UK5945

Keith and Kath Brasnett with their warm welcome and helpful efficiency ensure that this park remains attractive, quiet and friendly. Nestling in the valley of the River Gwili, it is made up of three fields: one by the river which is kept mainly for adults and two on a plateau up a steep slope on the opposite side of the lane. Particular care has been taken to protect the natural environment. There are 60 level, generously sized pitches of which 45 are touring pitches, the remainder seasonal. All have electricity (16A), 20 have hardstandings and five are fully serviced. This is a popular rural retreat for young families and older couples. The park is close to the end of the M4, allowing easy access and there is plenty to do or see in the near vicinity, castles, gardens, beaches, wildfowl reserves and a water park, also there is an SSSI immediately at the back of the site. The bird life visible from the site is varied and includes buzzards and red kites, and dippers on the river. The toilet block, including an en-suite family room with baby changing facilities and one for the disabled, is modern and equipped to a very high standard, including underfloor heating and automatic lighting.

**Facilities**

The modern, heated, toilet block is spotless with spacious showers, family room and suite for disabled visitors. New laundry with sinks, washing machine, tumble dryer, iron and ironing board. Small shop for basics and local fresh produce. Large grassy recreation area on main field. Fishing. Off site: Shop, bar and restaurant 1 mile. Bicycle hire and golf 5 miles. Beach 12 miles.

Open: 1 March - 6 December.

**Directions**

From the M4 exit 49 take A483 signed Llandeilo. Take the first turn left (after layby) and park is on left after 300 yds. O.S.GR: SN578086. GPS: 51.75817, -4.06288

**Charges guide**

| | |
|---|---|
| Per unit incl. 2 persons and electricity | £ 13.00 - £ 17.00 |
| incl. services | £ 15.50 - £ 19.50 |
| extra person | £ 2.50 - £ 3.00 |
| infant (under 4 yrs) | £ 1.00 |
| dog | free - £ 1.00 |

No credit cards.

For latest campsite news visit
alanrogers.com

## Prestatyn

### Nant Mill Family Touring Caravan & Tenting Park

Gronant Road, Prestatyn LL19 9LY (Denbighshire) T: 01745 852360. E: nantmilltouring@aol.com
alanrogers.com/UK6660

This traditional style, family owned and run park of around five acres, takes some 150 units arranged over four fields. There are some distant sea views to be had from many pitches. These are carefully allocated to ensure that the largest, central, sloping field is reserved for families. A smaller more intimate field for tents only is to one side of this and two small paddocks on the other side are for couples who might prefer a quieter, more level location. There are 96 electrical connections (10/16A) but tents are not permitted on pitches with hook-ups. The best beach is the Blue Flag Prestatyn central beach which is about half a mile from the site.

#### Facilities

The main toilet block is older in style but very well kept, with showers. Baby changing. Extra showers are in a small modern 'portacabin' style unit alongside. Showers are charged (50p), with a £1 deposit for the cubicle key. A separate portacabin unit with ramp provides a full suite of services for disabled visitors. Large laundry room. Playground and play field. Off site: Beach 0.5 mile. Sea fishing 0.5 mile. Golf 0.5 miles. Bicycle hire 4 miles.

Open: Easter - mid October.

#### Directions

Site entrance is 0.5 mile east of Prestatyn on the A548 coast road. O.S.GR: SJ073832. GPS: 53.33765, -3.3932

#### Charges 2011

| | |
|---|---|
| Per unit incl. 2 persons and electricity | £ 17.00 - £ 21.50 |
| extra person (over 3 yrs) | £ 1.50 |

No credit/debit cards.

## Pwllheli

### Hafan y Môr Holiday Park

Pwllheli LL53 6HJ (Gwynedd) T: 07949 642 534
alanrogers.com/UK6575

One of Haven's flagship parks, Hafan y Mor has a substantially redeveloped leisure and activity area. The park is set on the coast with direct access to the beach. A full range of clubs is provided for toddlers to teens and there is a popular splash zone and adventure playground. This is a large park with 700 caravan holiday homes for rent or privately owned. The site is has been well designed and with hedges, trees, planting, green spaces and lakes. The 74 touring pitches are in a separate area and all have 16A electricity, with a choice of hardstanding or grass. Tents are not accepted on this site.

#### Facilities

Sanitary facilities are in new portacabin style units. Two children's units, two family shower units, three baby changing units. Facilities for disabled visitors. Washing machines and dryers. Two well stocked supermarkets with bakery, off licence. Hire shop. Bars. 'Starbucks' coffee bar. Afon Gardens restaurant, Lakeside Inn with Grill menu, Fish and Chips, 'Burger King'. Fast food takeaway. WiFi. Indoor pool with flumes and slides. Entertainment and activity programmes. WiFi (charge). Off site: Llyn peninsula beaches.

Open: March - 2 November.

#### Directions

From Caernarfon take the A499 to Pwllheli, then A497 to Pothmadog. Park is on the right, about 3 miles out of Pwllheli. From the Midlands and the South M54 to Telford, A5 past Oswestry and Llangollen. Take A494 to Bala. In Bala turn right for Porthmadog. Turn left at roundabout in Porthmadog, signed Criccieth and Pwllheli. Park is on the left, 3 miles out of Criccieth. O.S.GR: SH427367. GPS: 52.906137, -4.334579

#### Charges guide

Contact the park.

## Pwllheli

### Bolmynydd Camping Park

Llanbedrog, Pwllheli LL53 7UP (Gwynedd) T: 07882 850 820. E: info@bolmynndd.co.uk
alanrogers.com/UK6585

The drive to Bolymynydd is not for the faint hearted. The roads are extremely narrow with plenty of bends, and are not recommended for large units. However, those who do make the drive are rewarded with spectacular views and a campsite which is ideal for tents and those who wish for peace and quiet in a wonderful rural setting. One field is available for tents, and other fields offer safe play areas for young children. With 16 seasonal caravan pitches and 40 tent pitches, the owners request that you telephone ahead to discuss access and availability.

#### Facilities

One clean sanitary block, maintained to a high standard (may be under pressure in peak season). Separate modern showers, toilets and open style washbasins. Baby bath in well equipped laundry room. No motorcaravan service point. Off site: Five minute walk to small supermarket and pub. Riding, beach and sailing 400 yds. Fishing 1 mile. Golf 3 miles.

Open: Easter - 31 October.

#### Directions

From Pwllheli take the A499 toward Abersoch. After 4 miles pass through Llanbedrog and at the campsite sign turn sharp left. Site is on the left. O.S.GR: SH325530. GPS: 52.85231, -4.48844

#### Charges guide

| | |
|---|---|
| Per unit incl. 2 persons | £ 16.00 - £ 22.00 |
| extra person | £ 3.00 - £ 8.00 |

No credit cards.

For latest campsite news visit
**alanrogers.com**

## Saint Davids
### Caerfai Bay Caravan & Tent Park

Caerfai Road, Saint Davids SA62 6QT (Pembrokeshire) T: 01437 720274. E: info@caerfaibay.co.uk

alanrogers.com/UK5995

About as far west as one can get in Wales, St David's is Britain's smallest city, noted for its Cathedral and Bishops Palace. This cliff-top park in West Wales has direct access to the Pembrokeshire Coastal Path and a magnificent sandy beach is just a few minutes away, down the path from the car park by the site entrance. Altogether there are 105 touring pitches and 45 electric hook-ups (10A). Main access roads are tarmac. The camping area is spread over three open and sloping fields (chocks are often necessary). All have magnificent views over St Brides Bay. The caravan field also has a small number of holiday homes and is closest to reception. The second and third fields are for tents and motorcaravans, almost all on grass with a few hardstandings available. Caerfai Farm Shop is just across the lane (opens end of May), and other shops and services are just one mile away. Site lighting is deliberately minimal, so a torch would be useful.

#### Facilities

Three main buildings house the sanitary facilities, one by reception which is heated, contains facilities for disabled visitors and families and a room with sinks, microwave and hot drinks machine. Adjacent a small new block offers 3 unisex cubicles (WC and basin). The third in the tent field (extensively refurbished) includes 4 family rooms. Motorcaravan services. Bicycle storage. Wet suit washing facility and enclosed drying area. Gas. Barbecue stands for hire. Off site: Walk the Pembrokeshire coastal path, visit Ramsey Island Bird and Grey Seal Reserve. Sea fishing 400 yds. Indoor pool and bicycle hire 1 mile. Golf 2 miles. Riding 10 miles. Boat launching 1.5 or 3 miles.

Open: 1 March - 14 November.

#### Directions

From Haverfordwest take the A487 to St Davids. On passing the city boundary, turn left into lane immediately before the National Park Visitor Centre (site signed), and continue on for 0.75 mile to site entrance on right. O.S.GR: SM759244. GPS: 51.872983, -5.2569

#### Charges 2011

| | |
|---|---|
| Per unit incl. 2 persons and electricity | £ 17.75 - £ 21.75 |

Discounts for early payment, and for senior citizens in low season.

# CAERFAI BAY CARAVAN & TENT PARK

Quiet family-run park uniquely situated in St Davids and within Pembrokeshire Coast National Park. The perfect spot to relax on the beach and explore Pembrokeshire.
• Electric Hook-up Points • Launderette • Family Rooms
• Free Hot Showers • Disabled Toilet & Shower • Dogs restricted
Call: 01437 720274 or visit: www.caerfaibay.co.uk

## Saundersfoot
### Moreton Farm Leisure Park

Moreton, Saundersfoot SA69 9EA (Pembrokeshire) T: 01834 812016. E: moretonfarm@btconnect.com

alanrogers.com/UK5980

Moreton Farm has been developed in a secluded valley, a 10-20 minute walk from Saundersfoot and four miles from Tenby. It provides 30 caravan (all with 16A electricity, and including 17 with hardstanding) and 30 tent pitches on two sloping, neatly cut grass fields, with 12 pine holiday lodges and four cottages for letting occupying another field. The site is approached under a railway bridge (height 10 ft. 9 ins, width across the top 6 ft. 6 ins, but with alternative access over the railway line for slightly larger vehicles just possible). There are a few trains during the day, none at night. This is a quiet family site. An attractive lake at the bottom of the valley is home to ducks, geese and chickens (no fishing). Pembroke and Carew castles and a variety of visitor attractions are close.

#### Facilities

The toilet blocks (which can be heated) are light and airy, providing preset hot showers (on payment). Unit for disabled visitors with ramp (shower, toilet and washbasin). Baby bath. Laundry facilities. Fenced, outside clothes drying area. Small shop for basics and gas. Playground. Bicycle hire can be arranged. No dogs or other pets are accepted. Off site: Fishing and riding 1 mile. Golf 4 miles.

Open: 1 March - 31 October.

#### Directions

From A477 Carmarthen - Pembroke road take the A478 for Tenby at Kilgelly. Park is signed on left after 1.5 miles. Watch carefully for sign and park is 0.5 miles up poorly made-up road and under bridge. O.S.GR: SN116050. GPS: 51.711983, -4.727683

#### Charges guide

| | |
|---|---|
| Per unit incl. 2 persons incl electricity | £ 15.00 - £ 19.00 |
| extra person | £ 2.00 |

## Tenby

### Manorbier Country Park

Station Road, Manorbier, Tenby SA70 7SN (Pembrokeshire) T: 01834 871952. E: enquiries@countrypark.co.uk
alanrogers.com/UK5985

This area of southwest Wales is quite attractive, with a variety of historic buildings, sandy beaches and an extensive coastal footpath. This campsite has 103 caravan holiday homes and 28 seasonal units, which leaves only around 22 pitches for tourists. There are seven orderly rows of concrete and gravel hardstanding pitches set into a level grass field; 32 pitches have electric hook-ups (16A), cable TV and a shared water tap, four are multi-service pitches (electricity, water, waste water, sewage and TV). Additionally, ten grass pitches are on the opposite side of the car park with electric hook-ups, and four grass pitches at the front of the main field with no services. Cars park away from the caravans on a wide tarmac parking area. A small grassy recreation area is at one end of the touring site, with an adventure playground. The complex offers a bar with family entertainment each evening, a good value restaurant, wellness centre and an indoor pool. Larger units should book in advance and motorhomes over 25 feet in length are not accepted.

### Facilities

A single building at one end of the car parking area provides all toilet facilities, it can be heated, and has controllable hot showers (on payment), a multi-purpose room suitable for families, babies and disabled campers. Small laundry room and dishwashing sinks outside under cover. Shop. Bar and restaurant. Indoor heated swimming and paddling pools. Jacuzzi. Sauna and steam room, vertical solarium, gym and tennis (all charged). Adventure play area and playground. Dogs are not accepted. Off site: Bicycle hire, boat launching, sailing and beach 1.5 miles. Golf and riding 3 miles. Adjacent garden centre restaurant serves cream teas and Sunday lunches. Fish and chip bar opposite. Manorbier Castle overlooks the sandy beach. Tenby 6 miles.

Open: 1 March - 31 October.

### Directions

From Tenby take A4139 towards Pembroke, passing through Penally and Lydstep. At crossroads (Manorbier signed to left) continue straight on following signs to the station. Turn right by Baptist Chapel into Station Road, and continue to site entrance (do not go into Manorbier village). O.S.GR: SS068991. GPS: 51.657917, -4.794283

### Charges guide

| | |
|---|---|
| Per unit incl. up to 4 persons | £ 16.50 - £ 23.50 |
| extra person | £ 2.00 |
| awning | £ 2.00 |

## Tenby

### Trefalun Park

Devonshire Drive, Saint Florence, Tenby SA70 8RD (Pembrokeshire) T: 01646 651514. E: trefalun@aol.com
alanrogers.com/UK5982

Only four miles from Tenby and the beaches of Carmarthen Bay, Trefalun Park is an open, well laid out campsite with a friendly atmosphere engendered by the owners. The 100 pitches, including ten occupied by caravan holiday homes in their own enclave and 22 seasonal units, are mainly level, although the park has gentle slopes. There are 37 seasonal pitches, 55 hardstandings, of which 24 are 'super' pitches. Pitches generously sized with electric (10/16A) plus a separate paddock with nine pitches for tents not requiring hook up. This park will suit those, particularly families, looking for a quiet holiday and also the more active who favour walking, cycling or watersports. A large fenced recreational area has a variety of adventure type play equipment and a football pitch. A wildlife park is about 600 yards away opposite the turning to Trefalun Park. Pembroke and Manorbier with their respective castles are only four and five miles away and there are many other historic monuments close by.

### Facilities

Modern heated toilet block, with some washbasins in cabins. Water to showers and laundry and dishwashing sinks is metered (20p). Separate, fully equipped suite for disabled visitors and families. Separate baby room. Laundry. Play area. Gas sold. Off site: Shop, pub (with food) and outdoor pool 1.5 miles. Fishing, riding and wildlife park 600 yds. Golf 3 miles. Tenby with all town facilities, beach, boat launching and sailing 4 miles.

Open: 26 March - 30 October.

### Directions

From the A477 at Sageston (about 4 miles east of Pembroke) turn southeast just to the east of the village on B4318 signed for the Wildlife Park. Trefalun Park is signed to the left after 2.5 miles, opposite the entrance to the Wildlife Park. GPS: 51.69326, -4.75340

### Charges 2011

| | |
|---|---|
| Per pitch | £ 12.00 - £ 19.00 |
| incl. services | £ 14.00 - £ 21.50 |
| 'super' pitch | £ 16.00 - £ 24.50 |

For latest campsite news visit
## alanrogers.com

## Wrexham

### James' Caravan Park

Ruabon, Wrexham LL14 6DW (Wrexham) T: 01978 820148. E: ray@carastay.demon.co.uk

alanrogers.com/UK6680

Open all year, this park has attractive, park-like surroundings with mature trees and neat, short grass. However, edged by two main roads it is subject to some road noise. The old farm buildings and owner's collection of original farm machinery, carefully restored and maintained, add interest. The park has over 40 pitches, some level and some on a slope, with informal siting giving either a view or shade. Electricity (6/10A) is available all over, although a long lead may be useful. Tourist information and a free freezer for ice packs are in the foyer of the toilet block. This is a useful park with easy access from the Wrexham - Oswestry (A483) road.

| Facilities | Directions |
|---|---|
| The heated toilet block offers roomy showers with a useful rail to help those of advancing age with feet washing. En-suite facilities for visitors with disabilities complete with special 'clos-o-mat' toilet! Motorcaravan service point. Gas available. Off site: The village is a 10 minute walk with a Spar shop, fish and chips, a restaurant, launderette and four pubs. Golf 3 miles. | Park is at junction of A483/A539 Llangollen road and is accessible from the west-bound A539. O.S.GR: SJ302434. GPS: 52.98286, -3.04093 |

Open: All year.

**Charges guide**

| | |
|---|---|
| Per unit incl. 2 persons and electricity | £ 12.00 |
| extra person | £ 2.00 |
| awning | £ 2.00 |
| gazebo | £ 5.00 |
| dog | £ 1.00 |

No credit cards.

James Caravan Park

Idyllic Park with mature trees, well cared for grass, renovated buildings and all modern facilities

ray@carastay.demon.co.uk • Tel: 01978 820148 • Ruabon, LL14 6DW

## Wrexham

### Plassey Leisure Park

Eyton, Wrexham LL13 0SP (Wrexham) T: 01978 780277. E: enquiries@plassey.com

alanrogers.com/UK6670

The Plassey has been carefully developed over the past 45 years, the latest improvements including landscaping, car parking and low level lighting installed around the park. Originally a dairy farm, the park is set in 247 acres of the Dee Valley and offers an extensive range of activities. It has been divided into discreet areas with pitches around the edges. There are 90 touring pitches with electrical connections (16A), including 30 new fully serviced pitches with hardstanding. Five further areas accommodate 120 seasonal caravans. There is much to do and to look at in the rural setting at the Plassey. The Edwardian farm buildings have been tastefully converted to provide a restaurant, coffee shop, health, beauty and hair studio, a small garden centre and 16 different craft and retail units, open all year. Unusually there is also a small brewery on site, producing its own unique Plassey Bitter! In addition to recent landscaping to the park, the pool and the golf clubhouse have been refurbished to provide improved facilities. A member of the Best of British Group.

| Facilities | Directions |
|---|---|
| Some refurbished toilet facilities are supplemented by a new heated block with individual washbasin cubicles, a room for disabled visitors or families. Laundry. Motorcaravan services. Shop (with gas). Club room with games room for children. Heated indoor pool with sun bed, sauna and new viewing area (charged). Adventure play area. Nine hole golf course. Fishing lakes. Wildlife meadow and countryside footpaths. No bicycles, skateboards or footballs permitted. Winter caravan storage. Luxury Holiday homes for hire. Off site: Riding 2 miles. Bicycle hire 5 miles. | Follow brown and cream signs for The Plassey from the A483 Chester - Oswestry bypass onto the B5426 and park is 2.5 miles. Also signed from the A528 Marchwiel - Overton road. O.S.GR: SJ349452. GPS: 53.00257, -2.96208 |

Open: February - November.

**Charges 2011**

| | |
|---|---|
| Per unit incl. 2 persons and electricity | £ 13.50 - £ 24.50 |
| incl. services | £ 19.50 - £ 32.75 |
| extra person (over 5 yrs) | £ 4.50 |
| dog | £ 2.00 |

Includes club membership, coarse fishing, badminton and table tennis (own racquets and bats required).

For latest campsite news visit
## alanrogers.com

# Insurance Service

**High quality, low cost insurance you can trust**

Price Beater
**GUARANTEE***

Caravan
Insurance
**SAVE
UP TO
60%**

We've been entrusted with readers' campsite-based holidays since 1968, and they have asked us for good value, good quality insurance.

We have teamed up with Shield Total Insurance – one of the leading names in outdoor leisure insurances – to bring you peace of mind and huge savings. Call or visit our website for a no obligation quote – there's no reason not to – and trust us to cover your valued possessions for you.

\* Price Beater **GUARANTEE**
Motorhomes and Static Caravans
We guarantee to beat any genuine 'like for like' insurance renewal quote by at least £25. Subject to terms & conditions.

• Caravans - **Discounts up to 60%**

• Park Homes - **Fantastic low rates**

• Cars - *COMING SOON*

**Instant quote**

## Call **0844 824 6314**

**alanrogers.com/insurance**

From gentle rolling hills and rugged coastlines to dramatic peaks, punctuated with beaut lochs, Scotland is a lan steeped in history that provides superb opportunities to enjoy wild, untamed and spectacular scenery.

Probably the most striking thing about Scotland is the vast areas of uninhabited landscape. Southern Scotland boasts beautiful fertile plains, woodlands and wild sea coasts. It also has a rich heritage with ancient castles, abbeys and grand houses. Further north are the Trossachs with their heather-clad hills, home of Rob Roy, the folk hero. The Highlands and Islands, including Skye, Mull and Islay, have some of the most dramatic landscapes in Europe, dominated by breathtaking mountain ranges, such as Ben Nevis and the Grampians, plus deep glistening lochs: the largest being Loch Ness, where the monster reputedly lives. And lying at the very edge of Europe, the islands of the Inner and Outer Hebrides share a rugged natural beauty, with unspoilt beaches and an abundance of wildlife. The two largest cities, Edinburgh and Glasgow, have their own unique attractions. The capital, Edinburgh, with magnificent architecture, comprises the medieval Old Town and the Georgian New Town, with the ancient castle standing proud in the middle. A short distance to the west, Glasgow has more parks and over 20 museums and galleries, with works by Charles Rennie Mackintosh scattered around the city.

### Places of interest

*Lowlands:* Floors Castle near Kelso; Museum of Scotland and Balmoral Castle in Edinburgh; People's Palace, Burrell Collection in Pollock Park, Glasgow; Sweetheart Abbey near Dumfries; New Lanark World Heritage Site; Melrose Abbey.

*Heart of Scotland:* fishing town of Oban; Stirling Castle and Wallace Monument; Loch Lomond; Pitlochry; university town of St Andrews; Aberdeen; Dunfermline Abbey; fishing villages of Crail and Anstruther; Famous Grouse Experience in Crieff.

*Highlands and Islands:* Fort William; Eilean Donan Castle near Dornie; the Cairngorms; Highland Wildlife Part at Kingussie; Inverness; Aviemore; Urquhart Castle near Drumnadrochit; Jacobite Steam Train, operates between Fort William and Mallaig; Dunvegan Castle on the Isle of Skye.

### Did you know?

Dunfermline Abbey is the final resting place of 22 kings, queens, princes and princesses of Scotland, including Robert the Bruce.

Whales can be seen off the west coast of the Highlands, and the Moray Firth is home to bottle-nosed dolphins.

Arbroath Abbey is the site where Scotland's nobles swore independence from England in 1320.

Since 1861, every day (except on Sundays), the one o'clock gun has boomed out from Edinburgh castle.

Charles Rennie Mackintosh, famous architect and designer, was born in Glasgow in 1868.

Eas Coul Aulin near Kylesku in Sutherland is Britain's highest waterfall at 200 metres – four times the height of Niagara.

Ben Nevis is the highest mountain in the UK.

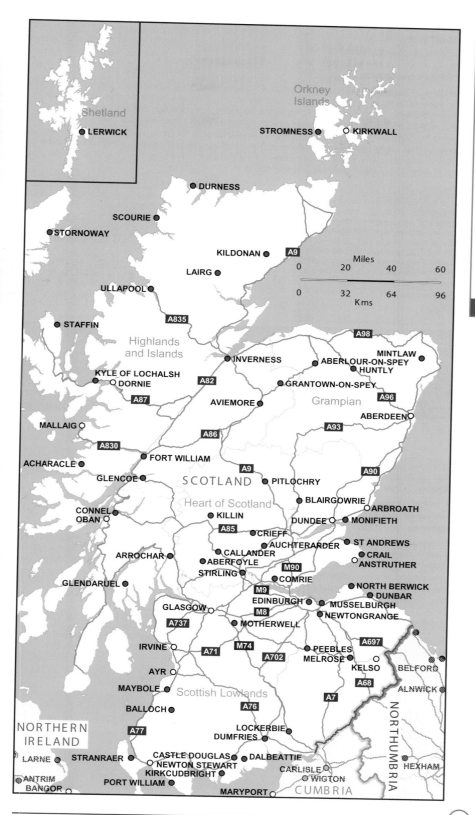

For latest campsite news visit
**alanrogers**.com

## Aberfoyle

### Trossachs Holiday Park

Aberfoyle FK8 3SA (Stirling) T: 01877 382614. E: info@trossachsholidays.co.uk

alanrogers.com/UK7230

Nestling on the side of a hill, three miles south of Aberfoyle, this is an excellent base for touring this famously beautiful area. Lochs Lomond, Ard, Venachar and others are within easy reach, as are the Queen Elizabeth Forest Park and, of course, the Trossachs. Very neat and tidy, there are 45 well laid out and marked pitches arranged on terraces with hardstanding. All have electricity and most also have water, drainage and TV connections. There is also a large area for tents. There are trees between the terraces and lovely views across the valley. The adjoining oak and bluebell woods are a haven for wildlife, with wonderful walks. You will receive a warm welcome from the friendly staff at this well run, family park. A member of the Best of British Group.

#### Facilities

A timber building houses sanitary facilities providing a satisfactory supply of toilets, showers and washbasins, the ladies' area being rather larger, with two private cabins. Laundry room. Well stocked shop (all season). Games room with TV. Play equipment (on gravel). Off site: Golf, boat launching and fishing 3 miles. Sailing 6 miles. Discount scheme arranged with a local leisure centre provides facilities for swimming, sauna, solarium, badminton, tennis, windsurfing, etc.

Open: 1 March - 31 October.

#### Directions

Park is 3 miles south of Aberfoyle on the A81 road, well signed. O.S.GR: NS544976. GPS: 56.140133, -4.3555

#### Charges guide

| Per unit incl. 2 persons | |
| --- | --- |
| and electricity | £ 14.00 - £ 20.00 |
| incl. all services | £ 16.00 - £ 22.00 |
| tent pitch incl. 2 persons | £ 14.00 - £ 18.00 |
| extra person | £ 2.00 |

TROSSACHS HOLIDAY PARK - ABERFOYLE STIRLING FK8 3SA
www.trossachsholidays.co.uk Tel: 01877 382614 (anytime)

One of the finest Environmental parks on the edge of the National Park
40 Exclusive landscaped Touring Pitches - mostly fully serviced
Holiday Caravans and Lodges For Sale and Hire
● Practical Caravan Top 100 Parks Winner 2006 - 2008 Inclusive ● Visit Scotland 5 Star Holiday Park
● 2004 Thistle Awards Customer Care ● Park of the Year ● Green Tourism Business Scheme Gold Award
● David Bellamy 10 Year Gold Award

## Aberlour-on-Spey

### Aberlour Gardens Caravan & Camping Park

Aberlour-on-Spey AB38 9LD (Moray) T: 01340 871586. E: Aberlourgardens@aol.com

alanrogers.com/UK7540

This pleasant park is within the large walled garden of the Aberlour Estate on Speyside. The owners have made many improvements to the sheltered, five-acre, family-run park which provides a very natural setting amidst spruce and Scots pine. Of the 73 level pitches, 35 are for touring units leaving the remainder for holiday homes (two for rent) and seasonal units. All pitches have 10A electrical connections and nine are 'all-weather' pitches. This is an ideal area for walking, bird watching, salmon fishing and pony trekking or for following the only Malt Whisky Trail in the world, while Aberlour has a fascinating old village shop – a time capsule. A member of the Best of British Group.

#### Facilities

The ladies' toilet block has been refurbished. The one for men is traditional in style (refurbishment planned) with four large showers. Facilities for visitors with disabilities can also be used as family or baby changing room. Laundry facilities. Motorcaravan service point. Small licensed shop stocking basics and with an information area. Play area. Caravan storage. Off site: Riding 0.5 miles. Swimming and bicycle hire 1 mile. Fishing 1 or 5 miles. Golf 4 miles.

Open: 1 March - 28 December.

#### Directions

Turn off A95 midway between Aberlour and Craigellachie onto unclassified road. Site signed in 500 yds. Vehicles over 10'6" high should use the A941 Dufftown road (site signed). O.S.GR: NJ282432. GPS: 57.47485, -3.1986

#### Charges guide

| Per unit incl. 2 persons | £ 11.65 - £ 18.40 |
| --- | --- |
| extra person (over 5 yrs) | £ 2.00 |
| dog | free |
| backpacker and tent (per person) | £ 6.70 - £ 7.80 |

For latest campsite news visit
**alanrogers.com**

## Acharacle

### Resipole Farm Caravan & Camping Park

Loch Sunart, Acharacle PH36 4HX (Highland) T: 01967 431235. E: info@resipole.co.uk
alanrogers.com/UK7800

This quiet, open park is marvellously set on the banks of Loch Sunart, eight miles from Strontian, on the Ardnamurchan peninsula. It is a must for anyone seeking peace and tranquillity and really worth the journey. With views across the water and regularly visited by wild deer, Resipole Farm offers a good base for exploring the whole of this scenic area or, more locally, for fishing, boating (launching from the site's own slipway) and walking in the unspoilt countryside. There are 48 level and well drained touring pitches here, 40 with electricity (10/16A). Tents are sited by the hedges. This is a good location for day trips to Mull via the Lochaline ferry.

**Facilities**

The central, modern sanitary block can be heated and is kept very clean. Excellent provision for visitors with disabilities. Laundry facilities. Motorcaravan service point. Caravan storage. Art gallery and studios.

Open: Easter/1 April - 31 October.

**Directions**

From A82 Fort William road, take Corran ferry located 5 miles north of Ballachulish and 8 miles south of Fort William. Leaving ferry, turn south along the A861. Park is on the north bank of Loch Sunart, 8 miles west of Strontian. Single track road for 8 miles approaching Resipole - care needed.
O.S.GR: NM676740. GPS: 56.710933, -5.720217

**Charges guide**

| | |
|---|---|
| Per unit incl. 2 persons and electricity | £ 18.50 |
| extra person | £ 3.00 |
| child (5-16 yrs) | £ 2.00 |
| backpacker tent incl. 2 persons | £ 12.00 |

## Arrochar

### Forest Holidays Ardgartan

Ardgartan, Arrochar G83 7AR (Dunbartonshire) T: 01301 702293. E: fe.holidays@forestry.gsi.gov.uk
alanrogers.com/UK7260

Forest Holidays is a partnership between the Forestry Commission and The Camping and Caravanning Club. Ardgartan is a rugged site in the Argyll Forest Park. Splendidly situated with mountains all around and lovely views of Loch Long, there are lots of sightseeing and activity opportunities. The 175 pitches are in sections which are well divided by grass giving an uncrowded air. Most with hardstanding and marked by numbered posts, they are accessed from hard surfaced roads and 54 have electricity. There are additional grass areas for tents. Midges can be a problem in this area of Scotland – go prepared. At the northern end of the Cowal Peninsula, the site is on a promontory on the shores of Loch Long, with good sea fishing and facilities for launching small boats. Walking and climbing, as well as sea and river fishing (permits obtainable locally), are all possible nearby. The site gate is locked 22.00-07.30.

**Facilities**

The main toilet block is opposite the reception and shop. Refurbished in 2009 it includes facilities for disabled visitors and babies. Launderette. Play equipment (bark surfaces). Raised barbecues are allowed. Bicycle hire. Fishing. Boat launching. Off site: Arrochar village (2 miles) has fuel, general stores and a restaurant.

Open: All year.

**Directions**

From A82 Glasgow - Crianlarich road take A83 at Tarbet signed Arrochar and Cambletown. Site is 2 miles past Arrochar, the entrance on a bend.
O.S.GR: NN275030. GPS: 56.188783, -4.781667

**Charges guide**

| | |
|---|---|
| Per unit incl. 2 persons | £ 10.00 - £ 20.50 |

Discounts for families, disabled guests and senior citizens.

## Auchterarder

### Auchterarder Caravan Park

Nether Coul, Auchterarder PH3 1ET (Perth and Kinross) T: 01764 663119. E: info@prestonpark.co.uk

alanrogers.com/UK7270

This is a charming small park, purpose designed and landscaped by the owners Stuart and Susie Robertson. In a sheltered position, it is conveniently situated for exploring central Scotland and the Highlands with many leisure activities close at hand (particularly golf) and within walking distance of the village (one mile). The 21 original pitches, all with electricity (6A) and hardstanding, 12 with drainage, are well spaced around the edge of the elongated, level grass park. Marked pitches with grass frontage back on to raised banks which are planted with trees. Further pitches have been developed to one side of the site. There is a trout fishing pond (exclusively for campers) and a woodland walk.

**Facilities**

Toilet facilities (with key system) include controllable, well equipped hot showers. A toilet for disabled visitors is provided in both the male and female units. Laundry room with sink and washing machine; an iron can be provided. Fishing. Caravan storage. Off site: Village 1 mile. Golf 1 mile. Bicycle hire and riding 4 miles. The historic cities of Perth and Stirling are less than half an hour's drive away.

Open: All year.

**Directions**

Park is between the A9 and A824 roads east of Auchterarder village, only 2 miles from the main road. It is reached by turning on to the B8062 (Dunning) road from the A824. O.S.GR: NN964138. GPS: 56.304333, -3.676167

**Charges guide**

| | |
|---|---|
| Per unit incl. up to 4 persons | £ 14.50 |
| extra person (over 5 yrs) | £ 1.00 |
| No credit cards. | |

## Aviemore

### Forest Holidays Glenmore

Aviemore PH22 1QU (Highland) T: 01479 861271. E: info@forestholidays.co.uk

alanrogers.com/UK7680

Forest Holidays is a partnership between the Forestry Commission and The Camping and Caravanning Club. This site is attractively laid out in a fairly informal style in several adjoining areas connected by narrow part gravel, part tarmac roads, with access to the lochside. One of these areas, the Pinewood Area, is very popular and has 32 hardstandings (some distance from the toilet block). Of the 260 marked pitches on fairly level, firm grass, 122 have electricity (16A). This site with something for everyone would be great for family holidays. The Glenmore Forest Park lies close to the sandy shore of Loch Morlich amidst conifer woods and surrounded on three sides by the impressive Cairngorm mountains.

**Facilities**

New toilet and shower blocks. Next to the site is a range of amenities including a well stocked shop (open all year), a café serving a variety of meals and snacks, and a Forestry Commission visitor centre and souvenir shop. Barbecues are not permitted in dry weather. Sandy beach. Off site: The Aviemore centre with a wide range of indoor and outdoor recreation activities including skiing 7 miles. Golf within 15 miles. Fishing and boat trips.

Open: All year.

**Directions**

Immediately south of Aviemore on B9152 (not the A9 bypass) take B970 then follow sign for Cairngorm and Loch Morlich. Site entrance is on right past the loch. O.S.GR: NH976097. GPS: 57.167033, -3.694717

**Charges guide**

| | |
|---|---|
| Per unit incl. 2 persons | £ 11.00 - £ 25.50 |
| extra person | £ 5.25 - £ 8.25 |
| child | £ 2.75 - £ 4.25 |

## Balloch

### Lomond Woods Holiday Park

Tullichewan, Old Luss Road, Balloch G83 8QP (West Dunbartonshire) T: 01389 755000 E: lomondwoods@holiday-parks.co.uk  alanrogers.com/UK7240

A series of improvements over the last few years has made this one of the top parks in Scotland. Almost, but not quite, on the banks of Loch Lomond, this landscaped, well planned park is suitable for both transit or longer stays. Formerly known as Tullichewan Holiday Park, it takes 110 touring units on well spaced, numbered pitches on flat or gently sloping grass. Most have hardstanding, all have electrical connections (10A) and 27 have water and waste water too. Watersport activities and boat trips are possible on Loch Lomond, with a visitor attraction, 'Lomond Shores', opened nearby.

**Facilities**

The single large heated, well kept toilet block includes some showers with WCs, baths for ladies, a shower room for disabled visitors and two baby baths. Covered dishwashing sinks. Launderette. Motorcaravan service points. Games room. Playground. Caravan storage. American motorhomes accepted with prior notice. WiFi (charged). Off site: Fishing and boat launching 400 yards. Riding 4 miles. Golf 5 miles. Balloch (5 minutes).

Open: All year.

**Directions**

Turn off A82 road 17 miles northwest of Glasgow on A811 Stirling road. Site is in Balloch at southern end of Loch Lomond and is well signed. O.S.GR: NS389816. GPS: 56.00155, -4.592233

**Charges guide**

| | |
|---|---|
| Per unit incl. up to 2 persons and electricity | £ 18.00 - £ 26.00 |
| extra person | £ 2.00 |
| dog | £ 0.50 |

For latest campsite news visit
alanrogers.com

## Blairgowrie

### Nether Craig Caravan Park

By Alyth, Blairgowrie PH11 8HN (Perth and Kinross) T: 01575 560204
E: nethercraigholidaypark@btconnect.com  **alanrogers.com/UK7280**

Nether Craig is a family run touring park, attractively designed and beautifully landscaped, with views across the Strathmore valley to the long range of the Sidlaw hills. The 40 large pitches are accessed from a circular, gravel road; 26 have hardstanding (for awnings too) and all 40 have 10A electricity. The majority are level and there are nine large tent pitches on flat grass. There is a personal welcome for all visitors at the attractive wooden chalet beside the entrance (with a slope for wheelchairs) which doubles as reception and shop providing the necessary essentials, gas and tourist information. A one mile circular woodland walk from the park has picnic benches and a leaflet guide is provided. Otherwise you can just enjoy the peace of the Angus Glens by hill walking, bird watching, fishing or pony trekking. Alyth with its Arthurian connections is only four miles away and Glamis Castle, the childhood home of the Queen Mother, is nearby, as is the beautiful Glenshee and Braemar with its castle.

**Facilities**

The central, purpose built toilet block is modern, well equipped and maintained, and can be heated. Unit for disabled visitors (entry by key). Separate sinks for dishwashing and clothes are in the laundry room (metered hot water), plus a washing machine, dryer and iron, and clothes line. Shop. Play area. Small football field. There is also fishing on siet as well as bicycle hire and caravan storage. Off site: Fishing 2 miles. Riding 4 miles. Golf within 4 miles. Boat launching 6 miles.

Open: 15 February - 13 January.

**Directions**

From A926 Blairgowrie - Kirriemuir road, at roundabout south of Alyth join B954 (Glenisla). Follow caravan signs for 4 miles and turn right onto unclassified road (Nether Craig). Park is on left after 0.5 miles. O.S.GR: NO265528. GPS: 56.6614, -3.1998

**Charges guide**

| | |
|---|---|
| Per unit incl. 2 persons and electricity | £ 15.50 - £ 17.50 |
| extra person | £ 1.00 |

---

## Callander

### The Gart Caravan Park

Stirling Road, Callander FK17 8LE (Perth and Kinross) T: 01877 330002. E: enquiries@theholidaypark.co.uk
**alanrogers.com/UK7220**

Gart Caravan Park is situated within the Loch Lomond and Trossachs National Park, just a mile from the centre of Callander. Surrounded by mature trees, this attractive, family run park is peaceful and spacious. All is kept in a pristine condition and a very warm welcome awaits on arrival with a superb information pack given to all. The 128 all grass touring pitches are reasonably level, open plan and marked, with electricity (16A), water and drain. Tents or pup tents are not accepted, groundsheets are not permitted. Privately owned caravan holiday homes are located away from the touring section near the river which runs for 200 m. along the park boundary. This is an area steeped in history with possible excursions including the Rob Roy Visitor Centre, the medieval Castle of Doune, or a sail on the steamship Sir Walter Scott on Loch Katrine. For the more active there are recommended local walks or fishing in the park's private stretch of river. There is some road noise during daytime.

**Facilities**

Modern heated central facilities are immaculate, kept spotlessly clean with toilets and showers, plus extra areas with showers, baby changing and hair washing basins. Separate facilities for disabled visitors. Fully equipped laundry. Drive-over motorcaravan service point. Gas sales. No shop on site but a breakfast car arrives at 09.00 with papers and basic provisions. Large adventure play area, part undercover. Separate field for ball games. Free fishing (not Sundays). Max. two dogs permitted. Off site: Golf and bicycle hire 1 mile. Riding 6 miles. Bus 1 mile.

Open: 1 April - 15 October.

**Directions**

From the south take M9. Near Stirling, leave at exit 10 and follow A84 through Doune. Park is on the left, 1 mile before Callander town centre. O.S.GR: NN643070. GPS: 56.2365, -4.1891

**Charges guide**

| | |
|---|---|
| Per unit incl. services | £ 19.50 |
| awning | £ 2.00 |
| Reduced rates for the over 50s. | |

## Castle Douglas
### Barlochan Caravan Park
Palnackie, Castle Douglas DG7 1PF (Dumfries and Galloway) T: 01557 870267. E: info@barlochan.co.uk
alanrogers.com/UK6945

Barlochan Caravan Park is situated on a hillside overlooking the Urr Estuary on the Solway Coast close to Dalbeattie and Castle Douglas, with the small village of Palnackie being a short walk away. Set on terraces, level, marked and numbered, most of the touring and tent pitches are on grass with a limited number of hardstandings available. There are 12 with electrical connections (16A). In addition, 55 mobile homes (five for rent) are positioned on terraces high above the touring areas and screened by mature shrubs and trees. Just to the left of the entrance there is a minigolf course and an adventure play area screened from the park with mature trees.

### Facilities
The refurbished sanitary facilities are kept spotlessly clean. Shower cubicles have recently been made larger suitable for wheelchair entry, but if required there is also a separate unit with WC and basin. Fully equipped laundry with outside drying area. Dishwashing under cover. Reception and well stocked shop. Large games/TV room. Off site: Fishing 400 yds. Bicycle hire 6 miles. Golf 7 miles. Riding 10 miles. Beach 10 miles.

Open: Easter - end October.

*See advertisement on page 275.*

### Directions
From Dumfries take A711 west to Dalbeattie. Continue through Dalbeattie for 0.5 miles and bear left at T-junction signed Auchencairn. Site is 2 miles on the right. O.S.GR: NX819571 GPS: 54.895023, -3.842564

### Charges guide
| | |
|---|---|
| Per unit incl. 2 persons and electricity | £ 15.89 - £ 20.95 |
| extra person | £ 1.25 - £ 1.85 |
| dog | £ 2.35 |

## Castle Douglas
### Loch Ken Holiday Park
Parton, Castle Douglas DG7 3NE (Dumfries and Galloway) T: 01644 470282
E: penny@lochkenholidaypark.co.uk  alanrogers.com/UK6940

Loch Ken Holiday Park sits right on the shore of the loch, adjacent to the RSPB bird reserve and the Galloway Forest Park – it is a peaceful haven in an area of outstanding beauty. This is a family owned park with 52 touring pitches and 33 caravan holiday homes, ten of which are for rent. The touring pitches, all with 10A electricity, are quite separate and are arranged in a mostly open-plan way on a large, neatly mown grass area beside the water. Some of this area is gently undulating. Mature trees border the park and provide an area for walking dogs.

### Facilities
The toilet block is old and fairly basic, but is kept clean. Showers 50p. Facilities for disabled visitors, a laundry and dishwashing are also old and in need of refurbishment (planned). Gas supplies. Well stocked shop. Small play area. Bicycles, canoes and dinghies for hire. Boat launching (permit). Fishing (permit). Off site: Bars and restaurants in Castle Douglas, 9 miles. Kirkcudbright 15 miles. Golf and riding 7 miles. Skiing 0.5 miles.

Open: 1 March - 31 October.

### Directions
From Castle Douglas take the A713 north for 7 miles. Site entrance is on left in Parton. O.S.GR: NX688701. GPS: 55.0104, -4.05568

### Charges guide
| | |
|---|---|
| Per unit incl. 2 persons, 2 children (0-10 yrs), electricity | £ 14.00 - £ 18.00 |
| tent, no electricity | £ 11.00 - £ 13.00 |
| extra person over 10 yrs | £ 2.00 |
| dog | £ 2.00 |

## Castle Douglas
### Mossyard Caravan Park
Gatehouse of Fleet, Castle Douglas DG7 2ET (Dumfries and Galloway) T: 01557 840226
E: enquiry@mossyard.co.uk  alanrogers.com/UK6890

Mossyard is a family run park set within a working farm right beside the sea in a sheltered bay. The park and farmhouse appear together suddenly over the horizon and in the distance as you approach, with some breathtaking views across the Solway where the Galloway Hills and the waters of Fleet Bay meet. There are 37 grass pitches, 12 for caravans and motorcaravans on an elevated area that slopes in parts. The remaining 25 pitches for any unit are on a level field which adjoins the beach but is a little way from the sanitary facilities. Electrical connections (16A) are available to all. This is a wonderful park for outdoor activities such as watersports and fishing where small craft can be launched from site.

### Facilities
Some of the farm buildings around the main farmhouse have been utilised for the toilet facilities, which are of traditional design. Showers are coin-operated (20p). Roomy facilities for disabled visitors can also be used as a family bathroom. Purpose built building with laundry, dishwashing area and information room with freezer and fridge for visitors' use. No shop. Off site: Gatehouse of Fleet with shops, pubs and restaurants 4 miles.

Open: 26 March - 31 October.

### Directions
Take A75 road from Dumfries towards Stranraer and park is signed to the left, 4 miles west of Gatehouse of Fleet, about 1 mile down a single track farm road. O.S.GR: NX547518. GPS: 54.840183, -4.26015

### Charges guide
| | |
|---|---|
| Per unit incl. 2 persons and electricity | £ 15.00 - £ 17.00 |

## Comrie

### Twenty Shilling Wood Caravan Park

Comrie PH6 2JY (Perth and Kinross) T: 01764 670411. E: alowe20@aol.com

alanrogers.com/UK7310

Everyone gets a warm welcome from the Lowe family when they arrive at Twenty Shilling Wood. Set amongst 10.5 acres of wooded hillside, this unusual park has a few touring pitches for caravans and motorcaravans (no tents), plus a number of owner occupied caravan holiday homes. However, with terracing and landscaping, not many of these are visible and flowering trees and shrubs help to hide them. The lowest level is the entrance where there is a late arrivals area and visitor car park. You will be escorted to your pitch. There are just ten level touring pitches on gravel with grass bays between them, all with electricity hook-ups (10A). Television reception is poor.

#### Facilities

The clean and spacious toilet blocks have some washbasins in cubicles for both men and women. Dishwashing area and laundry. No shop but rolls, milk and papers can be ordered at reception. Games room with pool table, table tennis (both free) and lounge area. Fenced adventure playground for all ages. Only two dogs per pitch are accepted. Off site: Buses pass the gate. Comrie 1 mile. Golf or fishing within 1 mile, riding or bicycle hire 6 miles. Loch Earn 11 miles.

Open: 1 April - 17 October.

#### Directions

Park is on north side of A85 Crieff - Lochearnead road, about 0.75 miles west of B827 junction, 0.5 miles west of Comrie. O.S.GR: NN762222. GPS: 56.375217, -4.0065

#### Charges guide

| | |
|---|---|
| Per unit incl. 2 persons and electricity | £ 16.00 |
| extra person (over 2 yrs) | £ 1.75 |
| dog (max. 2) | free |
| awning (rock pegs required) | £ 1.50 |

## Connel

### Oban Camping & Caravanning Club Site

Barcaldine, By Connel PA37 1SG (Argyll and Bute) T: 01631 720348

alanrogers.com/UK7810

Owned by the Camping and Caravanning Club, this site at Barcaldine, 12 miles north of Oban, is a small, intimate site taking 75 units. Arranged within the old walled garden of Barcaldine House, the walls give it some protection from the wind and make it quite a sun trap. There are 23 level, fairly small pitches with hardstanding and 52 electrical hook-ups (16A). (It can be wet underfoot in bad weather). Being a small site, it has a very cosy feel to it, due no doubt to the friendly welcome new arrivals receive. Unusually for a club site there is a lounge bar selling very reasonably priced meals most evenings. Through the garden gate, one is immediately in the Barcaldine forest with its miles of forest tracks, absolutely perfect for both walking and mountain biking.

#### Facilities

The central toilet block can be heated and is kept very clean with free hot showers, hair dryers and plenty of washbasins and WCs. Excellent unit for disabled visitors. Laundry. Motorcaravan service point. Small shop open a few hours each day for basic provisions and gas. Small play area with effective safety base. WiFi. Off site: Sea Life Centre 2 miles. Bus every hour outside gate.

Open: 2 April - 2 November.

#### Directions

Entrance is off the A828 road on south side of Loch Creran, 6 miles north of Connel Bridge. From the south, go past Barcaldine House and site is 300 yards on right. O.S.GR: NM966420. GPS: 56.5265, -5.309933

#### Charges guide

| | |
|---|---|
| Per person | £ 5.65 - £ 8.35 |
| non-member pitch fee | £ 6.60 |

## Crail

### Sauchope Links Park

Crail KY10 3XJ (Fife) T: 01333 450 460. E: info@sauchope.co.uk

alanrogers.com/UK7285

Sauchope Links Park is a member of the Largo Leisure Parks group with a good range of facilities on offer, notably a heated swimming pool, an indoor recreation room and a play area for children. The site's location is very attractive with miles of rocky shore to be explored. Pitches here are grassy and of a good size. A number of fully serviced pitches are available and also hardstandings. Alternatively, a number of mobile homes and micro lodges (small wooden chalets) are available for rent. The village of Crail, a short walk from Sauchope Links Park, is the most easterly of Fife's fishing ports.

#### Facilities

Small shop. Games room. Play areas. Tourist information. Mobile homes and other accommodation for rent. Off site: Top class golf (Crail golf club is the seventh oldest in the world and the Royal and Ancient club at St Andrews needs little introduction). Walking and cycle tracks. Fishing. Riding. Scone Palace. Craigtoun Country Park.

Open: 21 March - 31 October.

#### Directions

Approaching from St Andrews on the A918, on entering Crail at a sharp right hand corner, turn left down an unclassified road. Site is signed 400 yards on right. Follow signs to the site which is down by the sea. O.S.GR: NO620078. GPS: 56.261606, -2.612724

#### Charges guide

| | |
|---|---|
| Per unit | £ 14.00 - £ 25.00 |

## Crieff

### Braidhaugh Holiday Park

South Bridgend, Crieff PH7 4DH (Perth and Kinross) T: 01764 652951. E: info@braidhaugh.co.uk
**alanrogers.com/UK7275**

Braidhaugh is a member of the Largo Leisure Parks group and is situated on the banks of the River Earn among the scenic surroundings of Perthshire. There are 39 touring pitches, all with electricity, water and drainage. The site is well located for exploring Central Scotland, as well as being within walking distance of shops, restaurants, places of interest and many sporting facilities. The Earn is renowned for its salmon and trout fishing and permits can be purchased from the reception. The small shop stocks the essentials and a larger supermarket is close at hand. Other on-site amenities include a games room with television. For younger children, there is an outdoor play area.

**Facilities**

Small shop. Games room. Play areas. Fishing. Tourist information. Mobile homes and other accommodation for rent. Off site: Top class golf (courses at Muthill, Crieff and Comrie). Walking and cycle tracks. Fishing. Riding. Leisure centre.

Open: All year.

**Directions**

Approaching from Perth, drive through Crieff and turn left onto the A822 (Stirling). At the bottom of the hill cross a bridge over the River Earn. Turn right immediately after the bridge and take the first right to enter park. O.S.GR: NN855209.
GPS: 56.366771, -3.853455

**Charges guide**

| Per unit | £ 20.00 - £ 23.00 |
|---|---|

## Dalbeattie

### Sandyhills Bay Leisure Park

Sandyhills, Dalbeattie DG5 4NY (Dumfries and Galloway) T: 01387 780257. E: info@sandyhills-bay.co.uk
**alanrogers.com/UK6880**

Sandyhills Bay is a small, quiet park beside a sheltered, sandy beach. Reception is on the left through a car park used by visitors either walking the hills or enjoying the beach. Beyond is a large flat camping area, above which, divided by a tree lined hedge, are 60 pitches, half taken by mobile homes situated around the perimeter. The 30 touring pitches, 28 with electrical connection (16A) are in the centre of the all grassed flat area and wigwams are available to hire. This is an excellent family park, with the beach and a children's play area at the site, whilst up the hill next to the park is an 18-hole golf course where you can enjoy a bar meal in the clubhouse.

**Facilities**

The sanitary facilities are of traditional design, situated in one central block to the side of the touring area. Laundry room (tokens from reception). Shop and small takeaway. New adventure play area by the beach. Visitors can also use the facilities at Brighouse Bay, the largest park in the Gillespie Group. Barrier at entrance and beach car park (returnable deposit). Off site: Clifftop walk from Sandyhills to Rockcliffe (10 miles).

Open: Easter - 31 October.

**Directions**

From Dumfries take A710 Solway coast road (about 16 miles). Site is on left just after signs for Sandyhills. O.S.GR: NX890549. GPS: 54.879017, -3.731033

**Charges guide**

| Per unit incl. 2 persons and electricity | £ 16.40 - £ 21.70 |
|---|---|
| extra person | £ 1.95 |
| child (4-15 yrs) | £ 1.15 |

*See advertisement on page 275.*

## Dalbeattie

### Glenearly Caravan Park

Dalbeattie DG5 4NE (Dumfries and Galloway) T: 01556 611393. E: enquiries@glenearlycaravanpark.co.uk
**alanrogers.com/UK6870**

Glenearly is owned and managed by Mr. and Mrs. Jardine. Rurally located, it has been tastefully developed from farmland into a touring and mobile home, all year park. There are 39 marked, open pitches, all with 16A electrical connections (and TV), most on hardstandings. Seasonal units use some pitches. Walls and shrubs divide the touring section from the caravan holiday homes (two for rent), with mature trees around the perimeter. There are attractive views over the hills and forest of Barhill and buzzards, yellow wagtails, woodpeckers and goldfinch are some of the birds that can be seen, along with the park's own donkeys and ponies. A ten minute stroll brings you into the small town of Dalbeattie.

**Facilities**

Situated in the centre of the touring area, the toilets and showers are fitted out to a high standard. Unit for disabled visitors or families. Laundry room with washing machines and dryer and an outside drying area. Large games room. Play area. Off site: Shops, pubs, restaurants, etc. at Dalbeattie. Bicycle hire at Mabie Forest just 3 miles from Dumfries on the A710.

Open: All year.

**Directions**

From Dumfries take A711 towards Dalbeattie. 6 miles beyond Beeswing, after passing sign for Edingham Farm, park is signed with entrance on right (beside a bungalow). O.S.GR: NX834626. GPS: 54.944867, -3.822283

**Charges guide**

| Per unit incl. 2 persons and electricity | £ 16.00 - £ 18.00 |
|---|---|
| dog | free |

For latest campsite news visit
**alanrogers.com**

## Dumfries
### Southerness Holiday Village
Southerness, Dumfries DG2 8AZ (Dumfries and Galloway) T: 01387 880256
E: enquiries@parkdeanholidays.co.uk **alanrogers.com/UK6875**

Set beside a two mile stretch of sandy beach, at the foot of the beautiful Galloway Hills, is Southerness Holiday Village. Part of the Parkdean Group, it is a large park with the main emphasis on caravan holiday homes. However, there are also 100 open plan pitches for caravans, motorcaravans and tents. Set away from the static units, these are divided into two areas, some on level hardstanding with water taps, others on grass and all with 16A electrical connections. The light and airy reception office displays local information including a weekly 'What's On' programme as the main leisure complex is located a short walk from the touring area. This park is well organised with lots going on for all the family.

**Facilities**

A modern toilet block provides en-suite facilities throughout (key entry). Well maintained, it is kept very clean by on-site wardens. Excellent unit for disabled visitors. Well equipped laundry. Shop. Bar with large TV. Bistro, takeaway and coffee shop. Indoor swimming pool. Indoor soft play area. Amusement arcade. Bowling (charge). Evening entertainment programme in the Sunset Show bar. Outdoor adventure play area. Crazy golf. Nature trails. Off site: Golf course adjacent. Fishing 2 miles. Bus from outside gate.

Open: Before Easter - 31 October.

**Directions**

From Dumfries take A710 Solway Coast road for about 10 miles. Sign for Holiday Village is on the left. O.S.GR: NX974545. GPS: 54.87613, -3.60037

**Charges guide**

| | |
|---|---|
| Per unit incl. 4 persons | £ 12.50 - £ 29.00 |
| incl. services | £ 14.50 - £ 33.00 |
| dog | £ 2.00 - £ 3.00 |

## Dunbar
### Belhaven Bay Caravan & Camping Park
Belhaven Bay, West Barns, Dunbar EH42 1TU (East Lothian) T: 01368 865956
E: belhaven@meadowhead.co.uk **alanrogers.com/UK7065**

Located in the John Muir Country Park, Belhaven Bay Caravan Park is just one mile from the historic town of Dunbar, where the ancient castle ruin stands guard over the town's twin harbours. This is an excellent family park with easy access to the beach and to the clifftop trail which has spectacular views capturing the beauty of the countryside and seascapes. The park's 66 caravan holiday homes (five for rent) are located quite separately from the touring and tent areas. These are surrounded by mature trees and are arranged in large open bays. There is a new tent and touring area with electricity points, so now there are 60 reasonably level, mostly grass touring pitches, 48 with electricity (10A).

**Facilities**

Facilities are central and include a unit for disabled visitors. Laundry room. Motorcaravan service point. Reception also has a small shop and tourist information. Cyber Café and WiFi internet access. Play area and ball game area. Off site: Golf 1 mile. Riding and boat launching 2 miles. Bus stop at entrance.

Open: 13 March - 31 October.

**Directions**

From the A1 (north or south) exit at the Thistley Cross roundabout west of Dunbar. Park is about 1 mile down the A1087 towards Dunbar. O.S.GR: NT655784. GPS: 55.996767, -2.545117

**Charges guide**

| | |
|---|---|
| Per unit incl. 2 persons | £ 17.00 - £ 25.00 |

*See advertisement on page 269.*

## Durness
### Sango Sands Oasis Caravan & Camping Site
Durness via Lairg IV27 4PZ (Highland) T: 01971 511726. E: keith.durness@btinternet.com
**alanrogers.com/UK7735**

Sango Sands Oasis is a quiet, ten acre site overlooking the beautiful Sango Bay, a Blue Flag beach. The site was established by the family in 1978 and they have worked hard improving the facilities over the years. There are 82 pitches for tents and touring caravans, 48 with electricity hook-ups (16A). The land is well drained and fairly level. It is possible to see whales, porpoise, dolphins and seals from the site plus a variety of sea birds which nest nearby. An ideal area for walkers, including the less adventurous, there are numerous marked paths and there is an excellent variety of angling, from rivers to the sea.

**Facilities**

Traditional toilet and shower blocks are lit at night but a torch may be useful. Free showers with curtains. Showers and toilets are separate. With the beach so close don't be surprised to find sand in the showers. En-suite facilities for disabled visitors. Laundry. Campers' kitchen with cooking rings. Café, bar and licensed restaurant. TV. Games room with pool and darts. Off site: Two grocery stores in the village. Golf 2 km. Boat launching 3 km.

Open: All year.

**Directions**

From Thurso take the North Coast road (A836 as far as Tongue, where it continues on as the A838 to Durness). Site is on the right in the village. From Ullapool take A835 north to Ledmore Junction then left on A837. After 8 miles take A894 to Laxford Bridge. Turn left on A838. Durness is 19 miles. O.S.GR: NC420668. GPS: 58.56449, -4.74221

**Charges guide**

| | |
|---|---|
| Per person | £ 1.50 - £ 5.50 |
| electricity | £ 3.00 |

For latest campsite news visit
**alanrogers.com**

## Edinburgh
### Linwater Caravan Park
West Clifton, East Calder, Edinburgh EH53 0HT (Edinburgh) T: 01313 333326. E: linwater@supanet.com
alanrogers.com/UK7045

This delightful small family run park is set in the countryside but is still close to the city of Edinburgh. The park is level and the 60 large touring pitches are a mixture of grass and hardstanding; 49 have 16A electricity connections. Parts of the park are screened off by trees and fences. Two sides are sheltered by trees and shrubs and one side is open with views over fields. With just the occasional sound of aircraft from the airport, it is difficult to believe that you are so close to a major city. Linwater is a useful park for visiting Edinburgh and areas outside the city. The reception area has a wealth of information on places to visit. Just four miles down the road is a 'park and ride' scheme and the purchase of a Day Saver ticket is a cheap way to get into Edinburgh and to explore the area. The Falkirk Wheel, houses, castles and gardens are all within easy reach.

| Facilities | Directions |
|---|---|
| The modern and well maintained heated sanitary block has private cabins. Facilities for disabled visitors. Laundry. Gas supplies. Milk, bread and newspapers to order (by 21.00 for the next morning). Home produced free range eggs and bacon from reception (and strawberries in season). Sand pit. Three timber tents for hire. Off site: Fishing 1 mile. | From the A720 Edinburgh bypass, leave at sign for Wilkieston on the A7. In Wilkieston turn right at traffic lights (park signed). Continue to next sign indicating left and site 1 mile further on the right. O.S.GR: NT102697. GPS: 55.91104, -3.43588 |

Open: 13 March - 1 November.

Charges guide

| | |
|---|---|
| Per unit incl. 2 persons | £ 12.00 - £ 15.00 |
| tent incl. 2 persons | £ 10.00 - £ 13.00 |
| extra person | £ 3.00 |
| child (5-18 yrs) | £ 1.50 |

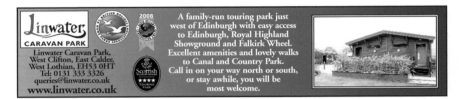

Linwater Caravan Park, West Clifton, East Calder, West Lothian, EH53 0HT Tel: 0131 333 3326 queries@linwater.co.uk www.linwater.co.uk

2008

A family-run touring park just west of Edinburgh with easy access to Edinburgh, Royal Highland Showground and Falkirk Wheel. Excellent amenities and lovely walks to Canal and Country Park. Call in on your way north or south, or stay awhile, you will be most welcome.

## Edinburgh
### Edinburgh Caravan Club Site
35-37 Marine Drive, Edinburgh EH4 5EN (Edinburgh) T: 01313 126874
alanrogers.com/UK7050

Situated as it is on the northern outskirts and within easy reach of the city of Edinburgh, this large, busy Caravan Club site (open to non-members) provides an ideal base for touring. Enter the site through rather grand gates to find the visitors' car park and reception to the left. There are 147 large flat pitches (103 hardstandings, 12 with water tap and waste water disposal) with electric hook-ups (16A) and TV aerial and provision for 50 tents in a separate field (hook-ups available) with a covered cooking shelter and bicycle stands close by.

| Facilities | Directions |
|---|---|
| Two heated, well kept toilet blocks provide washbasins in cubicles, hair and hand dryers, an en-suite room for campers with disabilities, plus a baby and toddler room with child-size facilities. Each block houses a dishwashing and vegetable preparation area, and a laundry. Drying room. No shop, but milk, bread, and newspapers can be ordered, with ice creams and gas from reception. Fenced play area. Boules. Dog walk in the only natural wood in Edinburgh (part of the site). WiFi internet access. Off site: Bicycle hire nearby. Health club (with internet access) 400 yds – ask at site for introduction card. | Turn right off A720 at Gogar roundabout at end of bypass signed City Centre, A8). Shortly turn left on to A902 (Forth Road Bridge), then right onto A90. At Blackhall junction traffic lights fork left into Telford Road (A902). At Crewe Toll roundabout turn left (B9085) and at T-junction (after bridge) turn right at traffic lights towards Leith, A901. Turn left at traffic lights (Silverknowes, Davidson's Mains). In half a mile at roundabout turn right into Marine Drive. Site is half a mile on the left. O.S.GR: NT212768. GPS: 55.97755, -3.2645 |

Open: All year.

Charges guide

| | |
|---|---|
| Per person | £ 4.70 - £ 6.20 |
| child (5-16 yrs) | £ 1.50 - £ 2.50 |
| pitch incl. electricity (non-member) | £ 11.90 - £ 14.80 |
| Tent campers apply to site. | |

# Edinburgh

## Mortonhall Caravan & Camping Park

38 Mortonhall Gate, Frogston Road East, Edinburgh EH16 6TJ (Edinburgh) T: 01316 641533
E: mortonhall@meadowhead.co.uk   alanrogers.com/UK6990

Mortonhall Park makes a good base to see the historic city of Edinburgh and buses to the City leave from the park entrance every ten minutes (parking in Edinburgh is not easy). Although only four miles from the city centre, Mortonhall is in quiet mature parkland, in the grounds of the Mortonhall estate, and easy to find with access off the bypass. There is room for 250 units mostly on numbered pitches on a slight slope with nothing to separate them, but marked by jockey wheel points. Over 180 places have electricity (10/16A), several with hardstanding, water and drainage as well, and there are many places for tents. The park is very popular but only part is reserved and tourists arriving early may find space. An attractive courtyard development houses a lounge bar and restaurant, open all year and to all, with good value meals in pleasant surroundings. There are mobile homes (20) and wooden family camping cabins (wigwams) for rent.

### Facilities

Two modern toilet blocks with outside, but covered dishwashing sinks, but the only cabins are in the third excellent facility at the top of the park, which has eight unisex units incorporating shower, washbasin and WC. The courtyard area provides further basic facilities and portacabin type units are added for the high season to serve the large number of tents. Facilities for disabled visitors. Laundry room with washing machines and dryer. Motorcaravan services. Bar/restaurant. Self-service shop (all season). Games and TV rooms. Play area. Late arrivals area with hook-ups. Torches useful in early and late season. Security lockers. Internet access at reception (£1 per half an hour). WiFi internet access (£5 per day). Off site: Bus from site gate. Golf courses and driving range 2 miles. Riding 2 miles. Bicycle hire 4 miles.

Open: 20 March - 4 January.

### Directions

Park is well signed south of the city, 5 minutes from A720 city bypass. Take the Mortonhall exit from the Straiton junction and follow camping signs. Entrance road is alongside the Klondyke Garden Centre. O.S.GR: NT262686. GPS: 55.902889, -3.181705

### Charges guide

| | |
|---|---|
| Per unit incl. 2 persons and electricity | £ 13.75 - £ 28.50 |
| tent pitch (4 persons) | £ 11.75 - £ 22.00 |
| extra person (5 yrs and over) | £ 2.50 |
| dog | £ 3.00 |

## Fort William

### Linnhe Lochside Holidays

Corpach, Fort William PH33 7NL (Highland) T: 01397 772376. E: relax@linnhe-lochside-holidays.co.uk

alanrogers.com/UK7850

This quiet well run park has a very peaceful situation overlooking Loch Eil, and it is beautifully landscaped with wonderful views. There are individual pitches with hardstanding for 65 touring units (12 seasonal) on terraces leading down to the water's edge. They include 32 with electricity connection (16A), water and drainage, plus 30 with electricity only (10A). A separate area on the lochside takes 15 small tents (no reservation). There are also 60 caravan holiday homes and 14 centrally heated pine chalets for hire. Fishing is free on Loch Eil and you are welcome to fish from the park's private beach or bring your own boat and use the slipway and dinghy park. About five miles from Fort William on 'The Road to the Isles', the park is conveniently placed for touring the Western Highlands. Easily accessible are Ben Nevis and the Nevis range (cable car to 2,000 feet), geological, Jacobite and Commando museums, distillery visits, seal island trips, the Mallaig steam railway and the Caledonian Canal.

### Facilities

Toilet facilities are excellent, heated in the cooler months and include baths (£1). Dishwashing room. First class laundry and separate outdoor clothing drying room (charged per night). Self-service, licensed shop (end May-end Sept). Gas supplies. Barbecue area. Toddlers' play room and two well equipped play areas on safe standing. Large motorhomes are accepted but it is best to book first. Caravan storage. Up to two dogs per pitch are accepted. Off site: Bicycle hire 2.5 miles. Riding, golf and skiing 5 miles.

Open: 15 December - 31 October.

### Directions

Park entrance is off A830 Fort William - Mallaig road, 1 mile west of Corpach. O.S.GR: NN072772. GPS: 56.847817, -5.16025

### Charges guide

| | |
|---|---|
| Per unit incl. 2 persons and electricity | £ 17.00 - £ 19.25 |
| extra person | £ 2.75 |
| child (3-15 yrs) | £ 1.50 |
| dog | £ 1.50 |

Seasonal rates available.

Touring, camping, chalets and caravans. Fantastic views. Wildlife and free fishing. Friendly 5 star park.

Corpach, Fort William
Scotland PH33 7NL

Tel. 01397772376 • www.linnhe-lochside-holidays.co.uk

## Fort William

### Glen Nevis Caravan & Camping Park

Glen Nevis, Fort William PH33 6SX (Highland) T: 01397 702191. E: camping@glen-nevis.co.uk
alanrogers.com/UK7830

Just outside Fort William in a most attractive and quiet situation with views of Ben Nevis, this spacious park is used by those on active pursuits as well as sightseeing tourists. It comprises eight quite spacious fields, divided between caravans, motorcaravans and tents (steel pegs required). It is licensed for 250 touring caravans but with no specific tent limits. The large touring pitches, many with hardstanding, are marked with wooden fence dividers, 174 with electricity (13A) and 100 also have water and drainage. The park becomes full in the peak months but there are vacancies each day. If reception is closed (possible in low season) you site yourself. There are regular security patrols at night in busy periods. The park's own modern restaurant and bar with good value bar meals is a short stroll from the park, open to all. A well managed park with bustling, but pleasing ambience, watched over by Ben Nevis. Around 1,000 acres of the Glen Nevis estate are open to campers to see the wildlife and explore this lovely area.

### Facilities

The four modern toilet blocks with showers (extra showers in two blocks); and units for disabled visitors. An excellent block in Nevis Park (one of the eight camping fields) has some washbasins in cubicles, showers, further facilities for disabled visitors, a second large laundry room and dishwashing sinks. Motorcaravan service point. Shop (Easter-mid Oct), barbecue area and snack bar (May-mid Sept). Play area on bark. Off site: Pony trekking, golf and fishing near.

Open: 15 March - 31 October.

### Directions

Turn off A82 to east at roundabout just north of Fort William following camp sign. O.S.GR: NN124723. GPS: 56.804517, -5.073917

### Charges guide

| | |
|---|---|
| Per person | £ 1.60 - £ 2.50 |
| child (5-15 yrs) | £ 0.80 - £ 1.30 |
| pitch incl. awning | £ 4.40 - £ 12.00 |
| serviced pitch plus | £ 2.00 - £ 3.00 |

## Glencoe

### Invercoe Caravan & Camping Park

Invercoe, Glencoe PH49 4HP (Argyll and Bute) T: 01855 811210. E: holidays@invercoe.co.uk

alanrogers.com/UK7790

On the edge of Loch Leven, surrounded by mountains and forest, Iain and Lynn Brown are continually developing this attractively located park in its magnificent historical setting. It provides 63 pitches for caravans, motorcaravans or tents on level grass (can be a bit wet in bad weather) with gravel access roads (some hardstandings). You choose your own numbered pitch, those at the loch side being very popular. The only rules imposed are necessary for safety because the owners prefer their guests to feel free and enjoy themselves. This is a park you will want to return to again and again. There is much to do for the active visitor with hill walking, climbing, boating, pony riding and sea loch or fresh water fishing in this area of outstanding natural beauty.

### Facilities

The well refurbished toilet block can be heated. Dishwashing under-cover, excellent laundry facilities with a drying room. New large under-cover eating area. Motorcaravan service point comprising multi-drainage point, fresh water, dustbins, and chemical disposal point. Shop (Easter-end Oct). Play area with swings. Fishing. New fore-shore hardstanding with slipway. WiFi. Off site: The village with pub and restaurant is within walking distance. Visitors' Centre at Glencoe 2 miles. Bicycle hire 2 miles. Golf 3 miles.

Open: All year.

### Directions

Follow A82 Crianlarich - Fort William road to Glencoe village and turn onto the B863; park is 0.5 miles along, well signed. O.S.GR: NN098594.
GPS: 56.686567, -5.105983

### Charges guide

| | |
|---|---|
| Per unit incl. 2 persons and electricity | £ 19.00 - £ 22.00 |
| extra person | £ 3.00 |
| child (3-15 yrs) | £ 1.00 |

Senior citizens less £1 per person outside July/Aug.

## Glendaruel

### Glendaruel Caravan Park

Glendaruel PA22 3AB (Argyll and Bute) T: 01369 820267. E: mail@glendaruelcaravanpark.co.uk

alanrogers.com/UK7860

Glendaruel is in South Argyll, in the area of Scotland bounded by the Kyles of Bute and Loch Fyne, yet is less than two hours by road from Glasgow and serviced by ferries from Gourock and the Isle of Bute. There is also a service between Tarbert and Portavadie. Set in the peaceful wooded gardens of the former Glendaruel House in a secluded glen surrounded by the Cowal hills, it makes an ideal centre for touring this beautiful area. The park takes 35 units on numbered hardstandings with 10A electricity, plus 15 tents, on flat oval meadows bordered by over 50 different varieties of mature trees. In a separate area are 28 privately owned holiday homes and two for rent. The converted stables of the original house provide an attractive little shop selling basics, local produce, venison, salmon, wines (some Scottish!) and tourist gifts. Glendaruel is a park for families with young children or for older couples to relax and to enjoy the beautiful views. The Craig family provides a warm welcome and will advise you where to eat and what to do – they are justifiably proud of their park and its beautiful environment.

### Facilities

The toilet block is ageing but it is kept very neat and tidy and can be heated. Washing machine and dryer. A covered area has picnic tables for use in bad weather and dishwashing sinks. Shop (hours may be limited in low season). Gas available. Games room with pool table, table tennis and video games. Behind the laundry is a children's play centre for under 12s and additional play field. Fishing. Torches advised. Off site: Sea fishing and boat slipway 5 miles, adventure centre (assault courses, abseiling and rafting) and sailing school close. Golf 12 miles.

Open: 28 March - 26 October.

### Directions

Entrance is off A886 road 13 miles south of Strachur. Alternatively there are two ferry services from Gourock to Dunoon, then on B836 which joins the A886 about 4 miles south of the park - this route not recommended for touring caravans. Do not use sat nav as this takes you along a very narrow back road and there is no entrance from here. Note: the park has discount arrangements with Western Ferries so contact the park before making arrangements (allow 7 days for postage of tickets). O.S.GR: NS001865.
GPS: 56.033967, -5.212833

### Charges guide

| | |
|---|---|
| Per person | £ 3.00 |
| child (3-15 yrs) | £ 1.50 |
| pitch incl. electricity | £ 10.00 |

# Grantown-on-Spey

## Grantown-on-Spey Caravan Park

Seafield Avenue, Grantown-on-Spey PH26 3JQ (Highland) T: 01479 872474. E: warden@caravanscotland.com
alanrogers.com/UK7670

John Fleming takes care of this excellent park. Peacefully situated on the outskirts of the town, with views of the mountains in the distance, the park consists of well-tended gravel (raked so that it is perfect for each occupant) and grass pitches. There are 100 pitches for caravans or motorcaravans, all have electricity (10A or 16A) and 57 offer fresh and waste water facilities. In addition to this there are a number of super pitches also offering 16A electric, WiFi internet connection and individual Sky TV box. A further 12 pitches are used for seasonal occupation, and there is space for 50 or more tents. WiFi internet is also available for a small charge on every pitch. Trees and flowers are a feature of this landscaped location. The wardens escort visitors to their pitch and will help to site caravans if necessary. Caravan holiday homes are located in a separate area of the park.

### Facilities

New toilet and shower block complete with laundry and drying room. A further block provides good, clean toilet facilities, with new wash cabins for ladies. Facilities for disabled visitors. Dishwashing sinks. Laundry room. Motorcaravan service point. Gas cylinders, ice creams, cold drinks and camping accessories available at reception. Games room. Touring and motorcaravan secure storage. Off site: Fishing, golf and mountain bike hire within 1 mile. Riding 3 miles.

Open: 1 March - 31 October.

### Directions

Go into the town. Turn north at Bank of Scotland. Park straight ahead half a mile. O.S.GR: NJ028283. GPS: 57.3348, -3.618617

### Charges guide

| | |
|---|---|
| Per unit incl. 2 persons and 10A electricity | £ 18.00 - £ 23.00 |
| small 2-man tent | £ 10.00 - £ 15.00 |
| extra person | £ 2.00 - £ 4.00 |

# Huntly

## Huntly Castle Caravan Park

The Meadow, Huntly AB54 4UJ (Aberdeenshire) T: 01466 794999. E: enquiries@huntlycastle.co.uk
alanrogers.com/UK7550

Huntly Caravan Park was opened in '95 and its hard-working owners, the Ballantynes, are justly proud of their neat, well landscaped 15 acre site that is managed under contract for the Caravan Club (non-members welcome). The 11 level grass and 41 hardstanding touring pitches are separated and numbered, with everyone shown to their pitch. Arranged in three bays with banks of heathers and flowering shrubs separating them, most pitches have electric hook-ups (16A) and 15 are fully serviced with water and waste water. Two bays have central play areas and all three have easy access to a toilet block, as has the camping area. Campers are provided with a covered cooking shelter (with work tops) should the weather turn inclement. The park also has 33 privately owned caravan holiday homes (three to hire). An Activity Centre near the entrance contains two indoor safe play areas (one for up to two yrs old, the other up to height 1.37 metres). There are snooker and pool tables, table tennis, badminton and short tennis. The area abounds with things to do, from forest trails to walk or cycle, a falconry centre, malt whisky distilleries and an all year Nordic ski track.

### Facilities

The three heated toilet blocks are well designed and maintained, with washbasins (in cubicles for ladies) and large showers. Each block also has a family shower room, dishwashing sinks and a room for disabled visitors. Laundry room. Milk and papers may be ordered at reception. Activity centre (charged and facilities are also open to the public; open weekends and all local school holidays). Off site: Huntly is 10 minutes walk. Fishing, golf or bicycle hire within 1 mile. Riding 5 miles.

Open: 1 April - 1 November.

### Directions

Site is well signed from A96 Keith - Aberdeen road. O.S.GR: NJ526402. GPS: 57.45205, -2.7916

### Charges 2011

| | |
|---|---|
| Per unit incl. 2 persons and electricity | £ 17.00 - £ 21.00 |
| extra person | £ 4.50 |
| child (5-16 yrs) | £ 1.80 - £ 2.50 |

For latest campsite news visit
**alanrogers.com**

## Inverness

### Torvean Caravan Park

Glenurquhart Road, Inverness IV3 6JL (Highland) T: 01463 220582

alanrogers.com/UK7690

Torvean is a small and neat, select touring park for caravans and motorhomes only. It is situated on the outskirts of Inverness beside the Caledonian Canal and is within easy reach of the town's amenities which include an ice rink, theatre and leisure sports centre. Excursions to the coast and Highlands, including Loch Ness, are possible in several directions. The pitches on level grass are clearly marked with a tarmac access road and street lighting giving a very neat appearance. There are 47 touring pitches (27 with 10A electricity, 18 fully serviced with fresh water tap, waste water disposal and electricity).

#### Facilities

Two heated toilet blocks are of good quality – ladies have two cubicles with washbasin and toilet and a hair washing cubicle. Controllable hot showers on payment. Suite for disabled visitors with toilet and shower over a bath. Launderette. Motorcaravan service point. Gas supplies. Play area. Only one dog per unit is accepted. Off site: Golf adjacent, bicycle hire or fishing 3 miles.

Open: Easter - end October.

#### Directions

Park is off the main A82 road on the southwest outskirts of the town on the west side of the Tomnahurich Canal Bridge (looks like a railway crossing rather than a bridge). O.S.GR: NH638438. GPS: 57.4654, -4.245517

#### Charges guide

| | |
|---|---|
| Per unit incl. 2 persons | £ 9.00 - £ 9.50 |
| de-luxe pitch incl. electricity | £ 12.50 - £ 13.00 |
| extra person | £ 2.00 |

No credit cards.

## Kildonan

### Seal Shore Camping & Touring Site

Kildonan, Isle of Arran KA27 8SE (North Ayrshire) T: 01770 820320. E: enquiries@campingarran.com

alanrogers.com/UK7025

A warm welcome awaits here on the Island of Arran from the resident owner, Maurice Deighton. Located on the southernmost point of the island, this is a quiet and peaceful park situated along its own private beach with wonderful sea views. The open, grassy area, sloping in parts, takes caravans, motorcaravans and tents with eight electrical connections (16A). The reception doubles as a shop selling basics with a TV room adjacent. There are communal picnic and barbecue areas. The Kildonan Hotel is next door serving restaurant and bar meals. Permits are available for loch fishing and charters available from the owner, a registered fisherman. Golfers can choose from seven golf courses.

#### Facilities

The good toilet block is clean and tidy and includes full facilities for disabled visitors that double as a baby room. No laundry but you may use the owner's washing machine, dryers and iron. Indoor dishwashing with fridge and freezer for campers' use. Shop. Camping gas. Fishing. Sailing. Covered barbecue area. Off site: Nearest golf course at Whiting 4 miles. Heritage Museum in Brodick and to the North of the Island Lochranza castle and distillery.

Open: March - October.

#### Directions

From Brodick take A841 south for 12 miles to sign for Kildonan. Site is downhill, on the seashore, next to the Kildonan Hotel. O.S.GR: NS022209. GPS: 55.44100, -5.11397

#### Charges guide

| | |
|---|---|
| Per unit incl. 2 persons and electricity | £ 16.50 |
| extra person | £ 6.00 |
| child (6-15 yrs) | £ 3.00 |
| tent pitch | £ 1.00 - £ 4.00 |

## Killin

### Loch Tay Highland Lodges

Milton Morenish Estate, by Killin, Loch Tay FK21 8TY (Perth and Kinross) T: 01567 820323

E: info@lochtay-vacations.co.uk  alanrogers.com/UK7315

Loch Tay Highland Lodges Leisure Park is situated in the central highlands on the shores of Loch Tay. Arguably one of the most beautiful areas of Scotland surrounded by mountains, rivers and lochs and still within easy driving distance of Edinburgh, Stirling or Glasgow. Loch Tay Highland Lodges are just a short drive from the scenic village of Killin and the picturesque Falls of Dochart. Highland Perthshire is renowned for its wealth of historical sites, natural beauty and wildlife. Tent pitches are grassy and of a good size. A good selection of chalets and lodges is available for rent. Motorcaravans are not accepted.

#### Facilities

Restaurant. Small shop. Games room. Play area. Equestrian centre. Marina. Sailing. Archery. Canoeing. Quad biking. Chalets, yurts, tepees and other accommodation for rent. No camp fires. Off site: Deer stalking. White water rafting. Wildlife safaris. Golf (Pitlochry, Aberfeldy and Taymouth Castle). Fishing. Whisky tours. Ben Lawers nature reserve.

Open: All year.

#### Directions

Loch Tay Highland Lodges Leisure Park is situated between Aberfeldy and Killin on the A827. O.S.GR: NN612359. GPS: 56.494024, -4.250357

#### Charges guide

| | |
|---|---|
| Per tent | £ 15.00 - £ 18.00 |

For latest campsite news visit
# alanrogers.com

# Kirkcudbright
## Brighouse Bay Holiday Park

332

Brighouse Bay, Borgue, Kirkcudbright DG6 4TS (Dumfries and Galloway) T: 01557 870267
E: info@gillespie-leisure.co.uk  alanrogers.com/UK6950

Hidden away within 1,200 exclusive acres, on a quiet, unspoilt peninsula, this spacious family park is only some 200 yards through bluebell woods from a lovely sheltered bay. It has exceptional all weather facilities, as well as golf and pony trekking. Over 90% of the 210 touring caravan pitches have electricity (10/16A), some with hardstanding and some with water, drainage and TV aerial. The three tent areas are on fairly flat, undulating ground and some pitches have electricity. There are 120 self-contained holiday caravans and lodges of which about 30 are let, the rest privately owned. On site leisure facilities include a golf and leisure club with 16.5 m. pool, water features, jacuzzi, steam room, fitness room, games room (all on payment), golf driving range, bowling green and clubhouse bar and bistro. The 18-hole golf course extends onto the headland with superb views over the Irish Sea to the Isle of Man and Cumbria. A nine-hole family golf course is a popular attraction. Like the park, these facilities are open all year. The TRSS Approved Pony Trekking Centre, also open all year, offers treks for complete beginners and a range of hacks for the more experienced. Also available are 'weenie rides' for under fives, riding lessons and stable management sessions for adults and children. This is a well run park of high standards and a member of the Best of British Group.

## Facilities

The large, well maintained main toilet block includes 10 unisex cabins with shower, basin and WC, and 12 with washbasin and WC. A second, excellent block next to the tent areas has en-suite shower rooms (one for disabled visitors) and bathroom, separate washing cubicles, showers and baby room. One section is heated in winter. Laundry facilities. Motorcaravan service point. Gas supplies. Licensed supermarket. Bar, restaurant and takeaway (all year). Golf (new practise area) and Leisure Club with indoor pool (all year). Play area (incl. new one for under 5s). Riding centre. Mountain bike hire. Quad bikes, boating pond, 10-pin bowling, playgrounds, putting. Nature trails. Coarse fishing ponds plus sea angling and an all-tide slipway for boating enthusiasts. Caravan storage. New purpose built chalet for tourist information and leisure facility bookings.

Open: All year.

## Directions

In Kirkcudbright turn onto A755 and cross river bridge. In 400 yards turn left onto B727 at international camping sign. Or follow Brighouse Bay signs off A75 just east of Gatehouse of Fleet. O.S.GR: NX630455. GPS: 54.7875, -4.1291

## Charges guide

| | |
|---|---|
| Per unit incl. 2 persons and electricity | £ 18.40 - £ 24.25 |
| extra person | £ 2.45 |
| child (4-15 yrs) | £ 1.65 |

Contact site for full charges.
Golf packages in low season.
Camping Cheques accepted.

## Kirkcudbright

### Seaward Caravan Park

Dhoon Bay, Kirkcudbright DG6 4TJ (Dumfries and Galloway) T: 01557 870267. E: info@seaward-park.co.uk

alanrogers.com/UK6900

Seaward Caravan Park is little sister to the much larger Brighouse Bay Holiday Park, 3.5 miles away. Set in an idyllic location overlooking the bay, this park is suitable for all units. The terrain is slightly undulating, but most of the numbered pitches are flat and of a good size. There are 35 pitches (21 hardstandings) designated for caravans and motorcaravans, a further 14 for tents, plus 43 caravan holiday homes (six for hire). Electricity hook-ups (16A) are on 32 of the touring pitches and 12 are also serviced with water and drain. This is a quiet park with excellent views ideally suited for that relaxing holiday or for touring the region.

### Facilities

The principal, fully equipped toilet block is to the rear of the park. Four rooms with en-suite facilities are also suitable for disabled campers. Well equipped baby room. Laundry facilities. No motorcaravan service point but the manager can lift a manhole cover to empty waste water tanks. The reception/shop stocks basic provisions, books, gifts, gas, and tourist information. Unsupervised heated outdoor swimming pool with sunbathing area (15/5-15/9). Central play area with bark surface, rocking horse, table tennis and picnic tables. Excellent games room. Pitch and putt. Off site: Beach and sea angling nearby. Riding or bicycle hire 3.5 miles. Kirkcudbright 2.5 miles.

Open: 1 March - 31 October.

### Directions

In Kirkcudbright turn onto A755 signed Borgue. Go over river bridge and after 400 yards turn left onto B727 at international camping sign. Proceed with caution when turning right into site entrance as the turn is tight. O.S.GR: NX680510. GPS: 54.819767, -4.082117

### Charges guide

| | |
|---|---|
| Per unit incl. 2 persons and electricity | £ 16.40 - £ 21.70 |
| extra person | £ 1.95 |
| child (4-15 yrs) | £ 1.50 |

*See advertisement on page 275.*

---

## Kyle of Lochalsh

### Reraig Caravan Site

Balmacara, Kyle of Lochalsh IV40 8DH (Highland) T: 01599 566215. E: warden@reraig.com

alanrogers.com/UK7760

This is a small, level park close to Loch Alsh with a wooded hillside behind (criss-crossed with woodland walks). Set mainly on well cut grass, it is sheltered from the prevailing winds by the hill and provides just 45 numbered pitches. There are electrical connections (10A) and 35 hardstandings (two without electricity). Large tents and trailer tents are not accepted at all. Small tents are permitted at the discretion of the owner, so it would be advisable to telephone first if this affects you. Reservations are not taken so it may be best to arrive before late afternoon in July and August. Awnings are not permitted during July and August in order to protect the grass. The ground can be stony so there could be problems with tent pegs. Reraig makes a good base from which to explore the area, the Isle of Skye and the pretty village of Plockton with its palm trees (remember Hamish Macbeth on TV?).

### Facilities

The single sanitary block has been extensively refurbished and is kept immaculately clean. Children have their own low basins. Controllable hot showers are on payment (10p for 2 minutes). Sinks for laundry and dishwashing. A slope replaces the small step into the ladies and sink rooms. Motorcaravan drainage point. Off site: Adjacent to the park is the Balmacara Hotel (with bar), shop (selling gas), sub-post office and off licence.

Open: 1 May - 30 September.

### Directions

On A87, park is 2 miles west of the junction with the A890, beside the Balmacara hotel. O.S.GR: NG815272. GPS: 57.283133, -5.626517

### Charges guide

| | |
|---|---|
| Per unit incl. 2 persons and electricity | £ 13.80 - £ 14.30 |
| extra person (13 yrs or over) | £ 3.00 |
| awning (May, June , Sept only) | £ 3.00 |

For latest campsite news visit

## alanrogers.com

## Lairg
### Woodend Camping & Caravan Park
Achnairn, Lairg IV27 4DN (Highland) T: 01549 402248
alanrogers.com/UK7720

Woodend is a delightful, small park overlooking Loch Shin and perfect for hill walkers and backpackers. Peaceful and simple, it is owned and run by Mrs Cathie Ross, who provides a wonderfully warm Scottish welcome to visitors. On a hill with open, panoramic views across the Loch to the hills beyond and all around, the large camping field is undulating and gently sloping with some reasonably flat areas. The park is licensed to take 55 units and most of the 30 electrical hook-ups (16A) are in a line near the top of the field, close to the large, fenced play area which has several items of equipment on grass. There are opportunities for fishing and hill walking. The famous Falls of Shin with a Visitor Centre is an ideal place to see the salmon leap (about 10 miles).

### Facilities
The sanitary facilities are of old design but kept very clean and are quite satisfactory. Laundry with two machines and a dryer. Kitchen with dishwashing sinks and eating room for tent campers. Reception is at the house, Sunday papers, daily milk and bread may be ordered. Fishing licences for the Loch (your catch will be frozen for you). Off site: Mountain bikes can be hired in Lairg, 5 miles. Several scenic golf courses within 20-30 miles.

Open: 1 April - 30 September.

### Directions
Achnairn is near the southern end of Loch Shin. Turn off the A838 single track road at signs for Woodend. From the A9 coming north take the A836 at Bonar Bridge, 11 miles northwest of Tain. O.S.GR: NC558127. GPS: 58.080267, -4.44705

### Charges guide
| | |
|---|---|
| Per unit incl. electricity | £ 10.00 |
| tent | £ 8.00 |
| No credit cards. | |

## Lerwick
### Clickimin Caravan & Camp Site
Clickimin Leisure Complex, Lochside, Lerwick ZE1 0PJ (Shetlands) T: 01595 741000
E: clickimin.centre@srt.org.uk  alanrogers.com/UK7980

The caravan and camping site is in the grounds of the Clickimin leisure complex, but it is not dominated by the building with its swimming pool and restaurant, etc. The site is arranged in two tiers which are well laid out with a tarmac road in the centre of each tier. The lower grass tier is separated into areas by shrubs and provides a camping area for 30 tents. The upper tier has 50 touring pitches, each with a large gravel area and divided from its neighbour by a wide impressed concrete section for sitting out. A small lamp post with electricity, water and waste disposal points is provided at each pitch. From the pitches there is a view across a lake with its ruined 'broche' that is floodlit at night. The site is on the edge of Lerwick (ferry terminal), but with easy access to the town and its facilities. Lerwick is ideal as a base to explore Shetland. Travel between the islands is exceptionally easy with drive on and off ferries running regularly between the islands and booking not essential. Daily ferries go to Shetland from Orkney and Aberdeen.

### Facilities
The modern toilet block is clean and includes a toilet and shower cubicle for disabled visitors. Large, warm and well equipped laundry and drying room with an area for food preparation. Bar (evenings). Café and takeaway. Heated indoor and outdoor swimming pools. Off site: Shop and bicycle hire within 1 mile. Golf 3 miles. Riding 12 miles.

Open: May - September.

### Directions
Site is on the west side of Lerwick and is signed as you start to leave Lerwick. Take the A969 north or south. Just before leaving the town is the road North Lochside (turn south) or South Lochside (turn north). Clickimin Leisure Centre is on this road. O.S.GR: HU464413. GPS: 60.15348, -1.15934

### Charges guide
| | |
|---|---|
| Per unit incl. electricity | £ 11.10 |
| tent | £ 5.30 - £ 9.90 |

For latest campsite news visit
## alanrogers.com

## Lockerbie

### Hoddom Castle Caravan Park

Hoddom, Lockerbie DG11 1AS (Dumfries and Galloway) T: 01576 300251. E: hoddomcastle@aol.com

alanrogers.com/UK6910

The park around Hoddom Castle is landscaped, spacious and well laid out on mainly sloping ground with many mature and beautiful trees, originally part of an arboretum. The drive to the site is just under a mile long with a one way system. Many of the 120 numbered pitches have good views of the castle and have gravel hardstanding with grass for awnings. Most have electrical connections (16A). In front of the castle are flat fields used for tents and caravans with a limited number of electricity hook-ups. The oldest part of Hoddom Castle itself is a 16th century Borders Pele Tower, or fortified Keep. This was extended to form a residence for a Lancashire cotton magnate, became a youth hostel and was then taken over by the army during WW2. Since then parts have been demolished but the original 'Border Keep' still survives, unfortunately in a semi-derelict state. The site's bar and restaurant have been developed in the courtyard area from the coach houses, and the main ladies' toilet block was the stables. Amenities include a comfortable bar lounge with a TV. The park's nine-hole golf course is in an attractive setting alongside the Annan river, where fishing is possible for salmon and trout (tickets available). Coarse fishing is also possible elsewhere on the estate. This is a peaceful base from which to explore historic southwest Scotland.

### Facilities

The main toilet block can be heated and very well appointed. Washbasins in cubicles, 3 en-suite cubicles with WC and basin (one with baby facilities) and an en-suite shower unit for disabled visitors. Two further tiled blocks, kept very clean, provide washbasins and WCs only. Well equipped laundry room at the castle. Motorcaravan service point. Licensed shop at reception (gas available). Bar, restaurant and takeaway (restricted opening outside high season). Games room. Large, grass play area. Crazy golf. Mountain bike trail. Fishing. Golf. Guided walks (high season). Caravan storage. Off site: Tennis nearby.

Open: 1 April - 30 October.

### Directions

Leave A74M at junction 19 (Ecclefechan) and follow signs to park. Leave A75 at Annan junction (west end of Annan by-pass) and follow signs. O.S.GR: NY155725. GPS: 55.041367, -3.311

### Charges guide

| | |
|---|---|
| Per unit incl. 2 persons | £ 9.00 - £ 16.00 |
| incl. electricity | £ 12.00 - £ 19.00 |
| extra person | £ 3.00 |
| child (7-16 yrs) | £ 1.00 |

- Fishing
- Walking
- Golf
- Cycle Hire

ENQUIRIES: The Warden, Hoddom Castle, Hoddom, Lockerbie DG11 1AS
Tel: 01576 300251 • www.hoddomcastle.co.uk • Email: hoddomcastle@aol.com

## Maybole

### Culzean Castle Camping & Caravanning Club Site

Maybole KA19 8JJ (South Ayrshire) T: 01655 760627

alanrogers.com/UK7010

With wonderful views of the Firth of Clyde and over to the Isle of Arran, this quiet Camping and Caravanning Club site is next door to Culzean Castle (pronounced Kullayne). Visitors are given a pass to walk in the grounds (when open) with their 17 miles of footpaths as many times as they wish. The campsite has 90 pitches, some level others slightly sloping, and 60 have electrical hook-ups (10A). A few level pitches are suitable for motorcaravans and 20 pitches have hardstanding. American style motorhomes (more than 25 ft.) must contact the site prior to arrival as large pitches are limited.

### Facilities

The toilet blocks, kept very clean, can be heated and include some washbasins in cubicles. Unit for disabled visitors has a WC, washbasin and shower – an excellent facility. Dishwashing sinks. Well equipped laundry. Small shop for basics opens for short periods morning and evening. Adventure playground. Off site: Golf or bicycle hire 4 miles. Fishing 8 miles. Buses pass the gate.

Open: 30 March - 30 October.

### Directions

From Maybole follow signs for Culzean Castle and Country Park, turning in the town on B7023 which runs into the A719. Country Park entrance is clearly signed on right after 3.75 miles; entrance to caravan park is on the right in Country Park drive. O.S.GR: NS247103. GPS: 55.35345, -4.76945

### Charges guide

| | |
|---|---|
| Per person | £ 4.90 - £ 7.25 |
| child (6-18 yrs) | £ 2.15 - £ 2.25 |
| non-member pitch fee | £ 5.65 |

For latest campsite news visit
**alanrogers.com**

## Maybole

### The Ranch Holiday Park

Culzean Road, Maybole KA19 8DU (South Ayrshire) T: 01655 882446

alanrogers.com/UK7015

This holiday park is situated in the Ayrshire countryside, four miles from the small town of Maybole. The Ranch, a Caravan Club affiliated site, is managed by the McAuley family. Barrier controlled, the park is beautifully set out with 60 spacious touring pitches, all with 16A electricity connections and including eight super pitches. Most are on level hardstanding with a few level, all grass pitches arranged open plan facing a huge playing field. There are also 65 caravan holiday homes, one for rent. There are plans to extend the number of touring pitches and holiday homes. The superb facilities include a private Leisure Centre with an indoor heated pool, sauna, solarium and well equipped gym. This is complete with changing room, toilets, shower and free hair dryers. To the rear is a small unfenced play park adjacent to the small camping area which has undercover seating for those rainy days. A 'Wee Honesty Shop' offers exchange books and magazines and a kiddies corner for children under the age of five. This is an excellent park for relaxing and enjoying the amenities or for touring the area with nearby sandy beaches at Maybole Shore and Croy Bay plus the wonderful freak of nature, where the laws of gravity are turned upside down at the Electric Brae, where you can see water run uphill.

### Facilities

The sanitary facilities are away from the touring area and older ones in style, but kept spotlessly clean, (there are plans for a new block). Washbasins in vanity units, four in cubicles with WCs for ladies. Large preset showers. Individual unit with WC and basin for disabled visitors. Purpose built wooden building housing well equipped laundry with dishwashing area on the end. No shop but reception has a good information area. Off site: Golf courses at Turnberry and fishing at Mochram Loch.

Open: March - October (and weekends).

### Directions

From Maybole turn onto B7023 (signed Culzean Maidens) for 1 mile and site is signed on left. O.S.GR: NS286102 GPS: 55.3559, -4.7061

### Charges guide

| | |
|---|---|
| Per unit incl. 2 persons | £ 10.60 - £ 16.60 |
| extra person | £ 3.30 - £ 4.80 |
| child | £ 1.10 - £ 1.60 |

---

## Melrose

### Gibson Park Caravan Club Site

High Street, Melrose TD6 9RY (Borders) T: 01896 822969

alanrogers.com/UK7030

This is an ideal transit park, being so close to the A68, but is also a perfect base for exploring this Southern Scotland area or indeed a trip to Edinburgh, as this is only 35 miles away by car or one of the regular buses which run from the park entrance. This small, three acre park has only 60 touring pitches plus, unusually, an extra 12 tent pitches (summer only) next to the adjacent rugby pitch. All touring pitches have electricity (16A) and TV connections (otherwise it is a bad signal here), 57 have hardstanding and ten are serviced with water and drainage. A one-way system on the tarmac roads is in operation. This is Sir Walter Scott country – visit Abbotsford House, his romantic mansion on the banks of the River Tweed. Melrose's Abbey ruins are believed to be the final resting place of Robert the Bruce and the starting place of St Cuthbert's Way.

### Facilities

First rate toilet facilities are in a new building with spacious showers, washbasins in cabins, centrally heated and all fitted out with purpose made faced boarding giving a very pleasing finish. Laundry facilities. Separate room with shower and WC for disabled visitors. Motorcaravan service point. Gas is available. Security barrier (operated by card). Off site: Situated on the edge of the little town of Melrose, a five minute walk, shops, pubs and restaurants are all in easy reach. Play area next to site.

Open: All year.

### Directions

Turn left off A68 Jedburgh - Lauder road at roundabout about 2.5 miles past Newton St Boswell onto A6091 Galashiels road. In about 3.25 miles at roundabout turn right onto B6374 to Melrose (not at first turning into town). Site is on right at filling station opposite Melrose Rugby Club, just before entering town centre. O.S.GR: NT545340. GPS: 55.598017, -2.72413

### Charges guide

| | |
|---|---|
| Per person | £ 4.80 - £ 6.20 |
| child (5-16 yrs) | £ 1.50 - £ 2.50 |
| pitch incl. electricity (non-members) | £ 12.00 - £ 14.80 |

For tent pitches apply to site.

---

For latest campsite news visit

**alanrogers.com**

## Mintlaw

### Aden Country Park Caravan Park

Station Road, Mintlaw AB42 8FQ (Aberdeenshire) T: 01771 623460

alanrogers.com/UK7530

Aden Country Park is owned by the local authority and is open to the public. The caravan and camping site is on one side of the park. Beautifully landscaped and well laid out with trees, bushes and hedges, it is kept very neat and tidy. It provides 48 numbered pitches for touring units, with varying degrees of slope (some level) and all with electrical hook-ups (16A), plus an area for tents. There are also 12 caravan holiday homes. The park is in a most attractive area and one could spend plenty of time enjoying all it has to offer. Attractions for visitors include an Agricultural Heritage Centre, Wildlife Centre, Nature Trail and restaurant, as well as open and woodland areas with a lake, for walking and recreation.

### Facilities

The modern toilet block is clean, with good facilities for disabled visitors. It can be heated and provides free, preset hot showers, hairdryer for ladies, and a baby bath, but no private cabins. Dishwashing and laundry facilities (metered). Motorcaravan service point. Gas supplies. Small shop in reception area. Restaurant in the Heritage Centre. Games areas. Play equipment (safety surfaces). Dog exercise area. Off site: Shops in Mintlaw 0.5 miles. Fishing 1 mile. Riding 2 miles.

Open: Easter - 25 October.

### Directions

Approaching Mintlaw from west on A950 road, park is shortly after sign for Mintlaw station. From east, go to the western outskirts of village and entrance is on left – Aden Country Park and Farm Heritage Centre. O.S.GR: NJ985484. GPS: 57.52475, -2.026117

### Charges guide

| | |
|---|---|
| Per unit incl. electricity | £ 13.40 - £ 15.00 |
| tent (2 persons) | £ 6.40 - £ 7.10 |
| awning | £ 2.00 |

## Monifieth

### Riverview Holiday Park

Marine Drive, Monifieth DD5 4NN (Angus) T: 01382 535471. E: info@riverview.co.uk

alanrogers.com/UK7410

A quiet, family park, Riverview overlooks a long sandy beach and has magnificent views over the River Tay towards the Kingdom of Fife and yet is within walking distance of Monifieth town. The park is neatly set out with flowering shrubs and bushes dividing 40 numbered touring pitches. Some enjoying river views, they are grassy and level, each with 16A electricity and two also with water and drainage. Bordering the park are 46 privately owned caravan holiday homes and four to rent. At the entrance to the park is a small reception office and separate tourist information room and a leisure suite with sauna, steam baths and gym (charge). There is an indoor games room with a pool table and a play area for small children. A small outdoor adventure play area is provided for children under 12 years of age with seats alongside for supervision. A member of the Best of British Group.

### Facilities

The spotlessly clean amenity block (key entry) has open washbasins, one in a cabin with WC, and preset showers. Baby bath. Full facility for disabled visitors. Well equipped laundry. Leisure suite. Games room and play area. Adventure play area. Off site: Picnic areas and small boat slipway adjacent. Opposite the Riverview recreation park offers football pitches, putting, crazy golf, tennis, bowling as well as a well equipped adventure play park. Golf 800 yds. Fishing 2 miles. Riding 3 miles. Dundee city 5 miles. Bus service nearby.

Open: 1 April - 31 October.

### Directions

From Dundee follow signs for Monifieth on the A930, after passing Tesco. Turn right at sign for golf course and right again under railway bridge. Park is signed on the left. O.S.GR: NO501322. GPS: 56.47995, -2.811533

### Charges guide

| | |
|---|---|
| Per unit incl. 2 adults | |
| and 2 children | £ 13.00 - £ 15.00 |
| extra person | £ 2.00 |
| awning | £ 2.00 |

For latest campsite news visit

## alanrogers.com

## Motherwell

### Strathclyde Country Park Caravan Site

Strathclyde Country Park, 366 Hamilton Road, Motherwell ML1 3ED (North Lanarkshire) T: 01698 402060
E: strathclydepark@northlan.gov.uk **alanrogers.com/UK7000**

The 1,200 acre Country Park is a large green area less than 15 miles from the centre of Glasgow. Well kept and open to all, it provides many amenities and sports facilities. The touring site, part of the park, is suitable for both overnight or longer stays (max. 14 days) and has 80 numbered pitches for caravans or tents, 70 with electrical connections (10A). Arranged in semicircular groups on flat grass they are served by made-up access roads and the site is well lit. As it is close to the motorway, there may be some traffic noise. The Country Park provides nature trails, a children's adventure play area, sandy beaches and coarse fishing, with an 18-hole golf course two miles away. In addition there is a large watersports centre offering sailing, water skiing, windsurfing, canoeing, rowing (all with craft for hire), a water bus, a selection of family 'fun boats' and bicycle hire, plus Scotland's own theme park nearby.

#### Facilities

Four solidly built toilet blocks make a good provision. Enclosed sinks for dishwashing or food preparation. Laundry in two blocks (irons from reception). Block 4 has facilities for visitors with disabilities, block 3 has a baby room. Motorcaravan services. Shop within reception sells basic provisions. Play equipment. Bicycle hire. American motorhomes accepted up to 22 ft. Barrier card and toilet block key £10 deposit. Off site: Bar and restaurant facilities (100 yds) in the Country Park. Fishing 400 yards. Bus 1 mile.

Open: Easter - 18 October.

#### Directions

Take exit 5 from the M74 and follow sign for Strathclyde Country Park. Turn first left for site. O.S.GR: NS720584. GPS: 55.803917, -4.046733

#### Charges guide

| | |
|---|---|
| Per caravan pitch incl. 2 persons and electricity | £ 13.65 |
| tent pitch (4 persons) | £ 9.05 |
| extra person | £ 1.30 |
| child | £ 1.15 |

No credit cards.

---

## Musselburgh

### Drum Mohr Caravan Park

Levenhall, Musselburgh EH21 8JS (East Lothian) T: 01316 656867. E: bookings@drummohr.org
alanrogers.com/UK6980

This family owned, attractively laid out touring park is on the east side of Edinburgh. It is a secluded, well kept modern park, conveniently situated for visits to Edinburgh, the Lothian and Borders regions. It has been carefully landscaped and there are many attractive plants, flowers and hedging. There are 120 individual pitches, 40 with hardstanding, for touring units of any type, well spaced out on gently sloping grass in groups of 12 or more, marked with white posts. All have electric hook-ups and 13 are fully serviced with water and a drain. Free space is left for play and recreation. Twelve chalets are available to rent. Musselburgh centre is 1.5 miles, Edinburgh 7, with a frequent bus service to the latter.

#### Facilities

The two toilet blocks are clean, attractive, of ample size and can be heated. Free hot water to washbasins (one cabin for men, two for ladies in each block) and to four external dishwashing sinks, showers and laundry sinks. Baby changing facilities. Laundry facilities in each block. Motorcaravan service point. Well stocked, shop (gas available, bread and papers to order). Playground on sand. Excellent dog walk. Caravan storage. Security barrier with code access. No late night arrivals area. WiFi (on payment). 'Bothy' for hire. Off site: Golf course adjacent.

Open: All year.

#### Directions

From Edinburgh follow A1 signs for Berwick on Tweed for 6-7 miles. Turn off for Wallyford and follow camp and Mining Museum signs. From south follow A1 taking junction after Tranent village (A199 Musselburgh) and follow signs. O.S.GR: NT371732. GPS: 55.950033, -3.011667

#### Charges 2011

| | |
|---|---|
| Per unit incl. 2 persons and electricity | £ 18.00 - £ 21.00 |

For latest campsite news visit
**alanrogers.com**

## Newtongrange

### Lothianbridge Caravan Park

Craigesk, Newtongrange EH22 4TP (Mid Lothian) T: 01316 636120. E: lothianbridge@tiscali.co.uk

alanrogers.com/UK7035

You will receive a warm welcome at this small, family run park. It is situated beside the A7, a major road into Edinburgh, and the entrance is through a disused but very grand railway viaduct which crosses one side. The park is level with hardstanding and grass pitches, 45 of which are for touring. The central area is grassed with some electrical points (long leads useful for some) and newly planted trees. A key controls access to the park and the sanitary facilities. There are several picnic tables for visitors to use and tall trees and shrubs provide a green perimeter. The family live on site so they are able to see and let in late arrivals. It is very easy to get into Edinburgh from here and to visit other places of interest. There is public transport 450 yards from the entrance.

| Facilities | Directions |
|---|---|
| A modern toilet block also housing a well equipped en-suite for disabled visitors. Laundry facilities, iron (from reception) and microwave. No shop but a few items are available in peak season. Motorcaravan service point. Play area. Free WiFi internet access. Two bungalows available to rent. Off site: Supermarket (24 hour) 2 miles with ATM. Golf, riding and fishing all within 5 miles. Beach 8 miles.<br><br>Open: 1 April - 6 January. | Travelling on the A7, just southeast of Edinburgh and due west of Newtongrange, the site is clearly marked by brown camping signs. A large viaduct marks the entrance. O.S.GR: NT326648.<br>GPS: 55.87131, -3.07633 |

**Charges guide**

| Per unit incl. 2 persons | |
|---|---|
| and children under 5 yrs | £ 14.00 - £ 16.00 |
| electricity | £ 2.00 |
| extra person | £ 2.00 |
| child (5-17 yrs) | £ 1.00 |

## North Berwick

### Tantallon Caravan & Camping Park

Tantallon Road, North Berwick EH39 5NJ (East Lothian) T: 01620 893348. E: tantallon@meadowhead.co.uk

alanrogers.com/UK7060

Tantallon is a large park with views over the Firth of Forth and the Bass Rock. The park has 147 quite large, grass touring pitches in two lower, more sheltered areas (Law Park), with the rest having good views at the top (Bass Park). Many have some degree of slope. There are 75 electrical connections (10A) and ten pitches also with water and waste water. Each area has its own sanitary facilities, the top block a little way from the end pitches. About 55 caravan holiday homes for sale or hire are in their own areas. Wooden wigwams are also available. This a mature, well managed park with good facilities. This area is a popular venue for bird-watchers with its world famous gannet colony. Tantallon and Dirleton Castles are also nearby. Access to the beach is through the golf course and then down the road or via cliff paths.

| Facilities | Directions |
|---|---|
| Bass Park has 8 unisex units with shower, washbasin and toilet. The other areas have open washbasins. Two heated units for disabled visitors. Good launderette with spin dryer and free iron. Motorcaravan service point. Reception sells a few ices, chocolate bars, cold drink and newspapers at weekends. Games room with pool table and TV. Internet access in reception and WiFi. Good playground and better than average putting green. Dogs are only accepted by prior arrangement. Off site: Tesco supermarket within walking distance. Golf next door, sea fishing, safe sandy beaches in walking distance. Town (with footpath) 1 mile. Riding 5 miles. Bicycle hire 1 mile.<br><br>Open: 13 March - 31 October. | Park is beside the A198 just to the east of North Berwick, which lies between Edinburgh and Dunbar. It is easily accessible from the A1.<br>O.S.GR: NT567850. GPS: 56.05575, -2.690833 |

**Charges guide**

| Per unit incl. 2 persons | £ 13.50 - £ 26.00 |
|---|---|
| extra person (over 5 yrs) | £ 2.50 |
| dog | £ 3.00 |

*See advertisement on page 269.*

For latest campsite news visit

# alanrogers.com

## Peebles

### Crossburn Caravan Park

Edinburgh Road, Peebles EH45 8ED (Borders) T: 01721 720501. E: enquiries@crossburncaravans.co.uk
alanrogers.com/UK6960

A peaceful, friendly small park, suitable as a night stop, Crossburn is on the south side of the A703 road, half a mile north of the town centre. The entrance has a fairly steep slope down to reception and the shop which also sells a very large selection of caravan and camping accessories. Passing the caravans for sale and the holiday homes you might think that this is not the site for you, but persevere as the touring area is very pleasant, with attractive trees and bushes. Of the 40 pitches, all have electricity (16A), 20 have hardstanding and eight are fully serviced. There is also a sheltered area for tents. If you decide to stay longer, the area has many places to visit and things to do. From historic homes, abbeys, woodland walks, fishing, horse riding, golf and canoeing – it's all there. Edinburgh is only 40 minutes drive. Perhaps the night halt may turn into a longer visit.

#### Facilities

There are two toilet blocks, the smaller one (which can be heated) with fairly basic facilities, the other more modern with washbasins in cubicles, free hairdryers and spacious, controllable free showers. Campers' kitchen (key at reception) with free use of an electric hot plate, kettle and fridge. Shop. Adjacent is a large games room with snooker table and games machines. Good play area on bark chippings. Riverside dog walk. Card operated barrier (£10 deposit). Off site: Buses from site gate or in Peebles (a short walk).

Open: Easter/1 April - end October.

#### Directions

Park is by the A703 road, about 0.5 miles north of Peebles. O.S.GR: NT248417.
GPS: 55.662167, -3.193333

#### Charges guide

| | |
|---|---|
| Per unit incl. 2 persons and awning | £ 16.00 - £ 18.00 |
| incl. services | £ 20.00 |

## Pitlochry

### Tummel Valley Holiday Park

Tummel Bridge, Pitlochry PH16 5SA (Perth and Kinross) T: 01882 634221
E: enquiries@parkdeanholidays.co.uk  alanrogers.com/UK7305

Set in the Tay Forest Park on the banks of the River Tummel, this large family holiday park is part of the Parkdean Group. Divided into two areas by the roadway, the main emphasis is on chalets to let on the side that overlooks the river. Privately owned caravan holiday homes and touring pitches are on the other, quieter side. The 26 touring pitches, open plan with hardstanding, electricity hook-up and a shared water point, overlook a small fishing lake which is an added attraction for all the family. On arrival, you should turn right and park, then cross back to book in. The leisure complex with indoor and outdoor activities is on the river side, as is the reception office.

#### Facilities

The very clean toilet block has vanity style washbasins, preset showers and a bathroom in each section. Good facilities for disabled visitors. Well equipped laundry. Chemical disposal but no motorcaravan service point. Shop. Riverside entertainment complex with bar with terrace, restaurant and takeaway. Indoor heated pool and toddlers' splash pool. Solarium and sauna. Amusements. Separate area with pool tables. All weather sports court. Adventure play area. Crazy golf. Nature trails. Bicycle hire. Fishing. Max. 2 dogs per unit. Off site: Golf and riding 10 miles. Buses leave near park entrance.

Open: 24 March - 1 November.

#### Directions

Travel through Pitlochry. After 2 miles turn left on B8019 to Tummel Bridge (10 miles). Park is on both the left and right. Tourers should turn right and park, then return to reception on the left.
O.S.GR: NN764590. GPS: 56.70742, -4.02002

#### Charges guide

| | |
|---|---|
| Per unit incl. 4 persons and electricity | £ 13.00 - £ 32.00 |
| dog | £ 2.00 - £ 3.00 |

For latest campsite news visit
**alanrogers.com**

## Pitlochry
### Blair Castle Caravan Park

Blair Atholl, Pitlochry PH18 5SR (Perth and Kinross) T: 01796 481263. E: mail@blaircastlecaravanpark.co.uk
alanrogers.com/UK7300

This attractive, well kept park is set in the grounds of Blair Castle, the traditional home of the Dukes of Atholl. It has a wonderful feeling of spaciousness with a large central area left free for children's play or for general use. There is space for 277 touring units with 190 electricity connections (10/16A), 144 hardstandings and 44 fully serviced pitches with water and waste water facilities also. Caravan holiday homes, 83 privately owned and 27 for hire, are in separate areas. A quality park, quiet at night and well managed. The castle is open to the public, its 30 fully furnished rooms showing a picture of Scottish life from the 12th century to the present day, while the beautiful grounds and gardens are free to those staying on site. The castle grounds provide many walking trails and the village is within walking distance with hotels, shops, a water mill craft centre and folk museum.

### Facilities

The five toilet blocks can be heated and are of excellent quality and very clean. Large hot showers, some incorporating WC and washbasin, and further cubicles with WC and washbasin. Facilities for disabled visitors with bath or shower, WCs and washbasins. Baby changing mats. Motorcaravan service point. Reception (WiFi), shop, games room (Wii games consoles for hire), laundry and internet gallery. Gas supplies. American motorhomes are accepted (max. 30 ft or 5 tons). Off site: Mountain bike hire, riding, golf and fishing within 1 mile.

Open: 28 February - 28 November.

### Directions

From A9 just north of Pitlochry take B8079 into Blair Atholl. Park is in grounds of Blair Castle, well signed. O.S.GR: NN868659. GPS: 56.767039, -3.845791

### Charges 2011

| Per unit incl. 2 persons | |
|---|---|
| and electricity | £ 20.00 - £ 23.00 |
| extra person | £ 2.00 |
| child (5-14 yrs) | £ 1.50 |
| dog (max. 2) | £ 1.00 |

## Pitlochry
### The River Tilt Park

Golf Course Road, Blair Atholl, Pitlochry PH18 5TB (Perth and Kinross) T: 01796 481467
E: stuart@rivertilt.co.uk  alanrogers.com/UK7295

This good quality, family owned park is set on the banks of the River Tilt, a short walk from the village of Blair Atholl, where the 16th century Blair Castle stands proud. There are 51 caravan holiday homes including three for rent. Two central areas have been set aside for touring caravans, motorcaravans and tents, with 31 pitches mostly with hardstanding. Divided by mature shrubs and hedges, all have 10A electricity connections, 18 have water and a drain. One of the areas is reserved for dog owners and their pets. The Steadings Spa provides an indoor pool, solarium, steam room, spa pool and multigym, plus Waves hair salon. Also open to the public, there are charges for these facilities. The park also has an award winning restaurant. Adjacent are a riverside walk and a golf course. There may be some noise from the railway line that runs alongside the park.

### Facilities

The purpose built toilet block is centrally situated (with key entry) and provides en-suite toilet and washbasin cabins and individual large preset showers, one suitable for disabled visitors. Baby facilities. Well equipped laundry. Motorcaravan service point. Bar and restaurant. Leisure spa complex with indoor pool, etc. Hair salon. Tennis. Max. 2 dogs per pitch. No ball games. Off site: Private fishing and golf adjacent. Bicycle hire and riding 1 mile. Pitlochry with its famous salmon leap 6 miles. Bus or train from Blair Atholl.

Open: 17 March - 13 November.

### Directions

From the A9 just north of Pitlochry, take B8079 into Blair Atholl and follow signs for River Tilt. O.S.GR: NN874655. GPS: 56.76538, -3.83962

### Charges guide

| Per unit incl. 2 persons | £ 10.00 - £ 16.00 |
|---|---|
| incl. electricity | £ 12.00 - £ 18.00 |
| extra person | £ 1.00 |
| dog | £ 2.00 |

## Port William

### Kings Green Caravan Park

South Street, Port William DG8 9SG (Dumfries and Galloway) T: 01988 700489. E: enquiries@portwilliam.com

alanrogers.com/UK6885

Kings Green Caravan Park is now owned and run by the Port William Community Association. Kept very natural and situated beside the sea overlooking Luce Bay and the Mull of Galloway, it is within walking distance of Port William, well known for its harbour and fishing community. The all grass, open site provides 30 marked and numbered pitches for caravans, motorcaravans and tents (21 with 10A electricity). On arrival visitors are given a welcome pack which includes a guide on the history of the area and local information. Second Sands at the northern end of the village is perfect for the launching and recovery of boats at any stage of the tide and provides wheelchair and pushchair access to the beach. When we inspected the park, volunteers were in charge. Reception may not therefore always be open. You are invited to park and details of reserved pitches are placed on the notice board.

### Facilities

The small toilet block (key entry) is kept very clean and has vanity style washbasins, free electric showers and hair dryers. Facilities for disabled visitors include WC and washbasin (Radar key). Small basic outdoor dishwashing. New Laundry with washing machine and drier. Large play and ball game area adjacent. Off site: Shops, restaurants and bars in Port William. Local walks and cycle routes. Fishing 50 yds. Golf 2 miles. Sailing and boat launching 600 yds. Riding 3 miles. Bladnoch distillery and the Isle of Whithorn just a short drive away or further to Stranraer with boats to Ireland.

Open: 30 March - 31 October.

### Directions

From Dumfries, take A75 to Newton Stewart. Follow A714 to Wigtown, then B7085 to Port William. O.S.GR: NX337433. GPS: 54.755967, -4.581533

### Charges guide

Per unit incl. 2 persons and electricity £ 11.00 - £ 13.00

## Saint Andrews

### Craigtoun Meadows Holiday Park

Mount Melville, Saint Andrews KY16 8PQ (Fife) T: 01334 475959. E: craigtoun@aol.com

alanrogers.com/UK7290

This attractively laid out, good quality park has individual pitches and good facilities and, although outnumbered by caravan holiday homes, the touring section is an important subsidiary. Its facilities are both well designed and comprehensive. With 67 units taken on gently sloping land, caravans go on individual hardstandings with grass alongside for awnings on most pitches. All caravan pitches are large (130 sq.m) and are equipped with electricity (16A), water and drainage. There are 15 larger 'patio pitches' with summer house, barbecue patio, picnic table and chairs, partially screened. Tents are taken on a grassy meadow at one end, also with electricity available. The 157 caravan holiday homes stand round the outer parts of the site; 27 are owned and let by the park. Buses pass the entrance and Craigtoun park with boating pond and miniature railway, etc. is within walking distance. This is a well run park, two miles from St Andrews with its golf courses and long, sandy beaches, from where there is a picturesque view of St Andrews and its ruined Abbey and Castle.

### Facilities

An excellent, de-luxe, centrally heated sanitary building serves the touring area. All washbasins are in cabins and each toilet has its own basin. Showers are unisex, as are two bathrooms, with hand and hair dryers. Facilities for disabled visitors and babies. Dishwashing room. Launderette. Shop and licensed restaurant (both restricted hours in low seasons), also providing takeaway. Games room. Well equipped playground, play field and 8 acres of woodland. Barbecue area. Tennis. Information room. Dogs and other pets are not accepted. Off site: Golf or bicycle hire 1.5 miles. Fishing 5 miles. Riding 6 miles.

Open: 15 March - 15 November.

### Directions

From M90 junction 8 take A91 to St Andrews. Just after sign for Guardbridge (to left, A919), turn right at site sign and sign for Strathkinness. Go through village, over crossroads at end of village, left at next crossroads, then 0.75 miles to park. O.S.GR: NO482151. GPS: 56.324617, -2.83745

### Charges guide

Per unit £ 18.00 - £ 24.50
tent £ 18.00

Only 'breathable' type groundsheets may be used in awnings.

## Scourie

### Scourie Caravan & Camping Park

Harbour Road, Scourie IV27 4TG (Highland) T: 01971 502060

alanrogers.com/UK7730

Mr Mackenzie has carefully nurtured this park over many years, developing a number of firm terraces with 60 pitches which gives it an attractive layout – there is nothing regimented here. Perched on the edge of the bay in an elevated position, practically everyone has a view of the sea and a short walk along the shore footpath leads to a small sandy beach. The park has tarmac and gravel access roads, with well drained grass and hardstanding pitches, some with 10A electric hook-ups. A few are on an area which is unfenced from the rocks (young children would need to be supervised here). Reception, alongside the modern toilet block, contains a wealth of tourist information and maps. There are very good facilities for disabled visitors on the park and at the restaurant, although the ramps leading to them are a little steep. Mr Mackenzie claims that this is the only caravan park in the world from where, depending on the season, you can see palm trees, Highland cattle and Great Northern divers from your pitch. Red throated divers have also been seen. Trips to Handa Island (a special protection area for seabird colonies) are available from here and Tarbet. The clear water makes this area ideal for diving.

**Facilities**

The toilet facilities can be heated. Showers have no divider or seat. Laundry. Motorcaravan service point. The 'Anchorage' restaurant at the entrance to the park (used as reception at quiet times) serves meals at reasonable prices, cooked to order (I/4-30/9). Boat launching. Fishing permits can be arranged. Off site: Village with shop and post office, gas is available from the petrol station and mobile banks visit regularly.

Open: Easter/1 April - 30 September, but phone first to check.

**Directions**

Park is by Scourie village on A894 road in northwest Sutherland. O.S.GR: NC153446.
GPS: 58.351417, -5.156767

**Charges guide**

| | |
|---|---|
| Per unit incl. 2 persons | £ 12.00 - £ 16.00 |
| electricity | £ 2.00 |
| extra person | £ 2.50 |
| child (3-16 yrs) | £ 1.50 |

No credit cards.

## Staffin

### Staffin Caravan & Camping Site

Staffin IV51 9JX (Isle of Skye) T: 01470 562213. E: staffincampsite@btinternet.com

alanrogers.com/UK7750

This small camping site is just outside Staffin, where the broad sweep of the bay is dotted with working crofts running down to the sea. With 50 pitches, 26 with electricity (16A), some slope but many are reasonably level, with improved hardstanding for caravans and motorcaravans. The entrance to the site from the main road is by a single track road. A marked walk from the site leads to the seashore and slipway (good for walking dogs). Skye has many activities to offer and for the truly dedicated walker the Cuillins are the big attraction and the hills above Staffin are demanding in places!

**Facilities**

The modern sanitary block includes large, controllable showers. There are some hot water dishwashing sinks and a laundry. Large hardstanding area and motorcaravan service point. Gas available. Bicycle hire. Off site: Fishing or boat launching 1 mile. Riding 9 miles. Staffin village is 400 yards and has a large shop (open six days a week), and a restaurant. The Columbia centre in the village provides internet access.

Open: 1 April - 30 September.

**Directions**

Site is 15 miles north of Portree on A855 (2 miles of single track at the start), just before 40 mph signs on the right. O.S.GR: NG496668.
GPS: 57.622017, -6.196

**Charges guide**

| | |
|---|---|
| Per unit incl. 2 persons and electricity | £ 11.50 - £ 13.50 |
| extra person | £ 1.50 |

No credit cards.

For latest campsite news visit
**alanrogers.com**

## Stirling

### Witches Craig Caravan Park

Blairlogie, Stirling FK9 5PX (Stirling) T: 01786 474947. E: info@witchescraig.co.uk
alanrogers.com/UK7320

Witches Craig is a neat and tidy park, nestling under the Ochil Hills. All 60 pitches have 10A electricity and hardstanding, seven of these being large (taking American style motorhomes easily). Reasonably level, the park covers five well maintained acres with the grass beautifully manicured. Being by the A91, there is some daytime road noise. Trees have been planted to try to minimise this but the further back onto the park you go, the less the traffic is heard. The area has a wealth of historic attractions, starting with the Wallace Monument which practically overlooks the park. Its 220 ft. tower dominates the surrounding area and the climb up its 246 steps gives spectacular views. Stirling is known as the 'Gateway to the Highlands' and its magnificent castle is world renowned. Seven residential park homes are well kept and surrounded by flowering shrubs.

#### Facilities

The modern, heated toilet block is well maintained, and includes one cubicle with washbasin and WC each for ladies and men. Free controllable showers. Baby bath and mat. Good unit for disabled campers. Dishwashing sinks. Laundry, with free fridge/freezer facilities. Bread, milk, drinks and papers are available daily (supermarket 2.5 miles). Large fenced play area. Field for team games. Off site: Riding or bicycle hire 2 miles, fishing 3 miles, golf 1 mile. Buses stop at the park entrance. Within 10 miles there are castles, museums, cathedrals and parks. There are many walks from the site into the Ochil Hills.

Open: 1 April - 31 October.

#### Directions

Park is on the A91, 3 miles northeast of Stirling.
O.S.GR: NS822968. GPS: 56.148033, -3.898667

#### Charges guide

| | |
|---|---|
| Per unit incl. 2 persons and electricity | £ 17.00 - £ 20.00 |
| extra person | £ 2.00 |
| child (2-13 yrs) | £ 1.00 |
| awning (no groundsheet) | £ 2.00 |

£5 deposit for key to facilities.

## Stornoway

### Laxdale Holiday Park

6 Laxdale Lane, Stornoway HS2 0DR (Isle of Lewis) T: 01851 706966. E: info@laxdaleholidaypark.com
alanrogers.com/UK7920

Whilst not in the most scenic of locations, this good park is well placed for touring. Surrounded by trees, it is on the edge of Stornaway (ferry port) and is well laid out with a tarmac road running through the centre. A level hardstanding area for touring caravans has 14 electricity hook-ups plus two for tents and a grassy area for the tents gently slopes away to the trees and boundary. There are five holiday caravans and a self catering holiday bungalow available for rent on the site, plus a bunkhouse. The site is centrally situated in an ideal spot for touring the Isle of Lewis with easy access to all parts of the island. The Butt of Lewis, the Callanish standing stones and the Black House Village are all within easy reach as well as many other attractions. Some parts have rocky coastal scenery but there are some lovely beaches around the island. The main road south leads to Harris passing through the mountainous area to the south of the Isle of Lewis. Ferries come into Stornoway from Ullapool and also Uig (Skye) to Tarbert (north Harris). Ferries to Berneray/North Uist go from Leverburgh in the south of Harris.

#### Facilities

The well maintained and modern toilet block is heated and raised above the hardstanding area. Access is via steps or a gravel path to the ramp. Good (but narrow) showers with dividing curtain (50p). Well equipped laundry with washing machine, dryer, iron and board, sink and clothes line. Telephone. WiFi in reception. Off site: Bus stop 200 m. The busy fishing port of Stornoway has a comprehensive range of shops and restaurants. New sports centre with swimming pool. Library with free internet access.

Open: 1 April - 31 October.

#### Directions

From Stornoway take the A857 for 1 mile then take the second turning on the left past the hospital.
O.S.GR: NB420348. GPS: 58.22738, -6.39254

#### Charges guide

| | |
|---|---|
| Per person | £ 2.00 - £ 3.00 |
| child (5-15 yrs) | £ 2.00 |
| pitch | £ 5.00 - £ 8.00 |
| electricity | £ 2.00 |

Credit cards accepted (over £50).

For latest campsite news visit
**alanrogers.com**

## Stranraer

### Aird Donald Caravan Park

London Road, Stranraer DG9 8RN (Dumfries and Galloway) T: 01776 702025. E: enquiries@aird-donald.co.uk

alanrogers.com/UK7020

Aird Donald is a good stopping off place when travelling to and from the Irish ferries, but it is also useful for seeing the sights around Stranraer. This tidy park comprises 12 acres surrounded by conifers, flowering trees and shrubs and the 300 yard drive is lit and lined with well trimmed conifers. There are grass areas for caravans or tents and hardstandings with electricity hook-up (these are very handy for hardy winter tourers). A small play area caters for young children, but the local leisure centre is only a walk away and provides swimming, table tennis, gym, etc, and a theatre that hosts everything from country and western to opera.

**Facilities**

Two toilet blocks, the new block modern and heated. Kept very clean with excellent, tiled facilities, this one is kept locked with a key deposit of £5. There are two types of shower, an electric one which is metered (20p) and two others which are free (strange, because they are all excellent). Unit for visitors with disabilities has a washbasin and WC. Small laundry. Motorcaravan services. Play area.

Open: All year.

**Directions**

Enter Stranraer on A75 road. Watch for narrow site entrance on left entering town, opposite school. O.S.GR: NX075605. GPS: 54.90185, -5.006217

**Charges 2011**

| | |
|---|---|
| Per unit incl. 2 persons and electricity | £ 16.00 - £ 18.00 |

No credit cards.

## Stromness

### Point of Ness Caravan & Camping Site

Well Park, Ness Road, Stromness KW16 3DN (Orkney) T: 01856 873535. E: recreation@orkney.gov.uk

alanrogers.com/UK7950

This quiet site is in an idyllic position bounded by the sea one side (an entrance to the harbour). It is sheltered by the land from the open sea and has views to the mountains and the island of Hoy. There is a rocky beach close by and walks from the site. It is a level, firm grassy site, protected from the small drop to the sea by a low fence. Access to the steps to the sea is gained by a gate in the fence. Whilst being located at one end of Orkney, it is still easy to visit the Churchill Barriers and the Italian Chapel as well as the closer Maes Howe and Skara Brae sites. Regular ferries come into Stromness from Thurso. Don't be surprised if the seals come to watch you. Ferries to other islands go from various ports and it is sometimes necessary to book in advance.

**Facilities**

The well maintained traditional style toilet block has good-sized showers (20p) with curtains separating the changing area. Well equipped laundry. Telephone and tourist information. Lounge for campers is at one end of the block. Off site: Fishing, golf and bicycle hire all nearby.

Open: 28 April - 30 September.

**Directions**

Site is just west of Stromness and is signed from the town. Campers can walk along the narrow high street to the site on the edge of the town. Caravans and motorcaravans are advised to take the road at the back of the town (about 2 miles) that is clearly marked. O.S.GR: HY256079. GPS: 58.95443, -3.30041

**Charges guide**

| | |
|---|---|
| Per pitch | £ 4.40 - £ 8.30 |

No credit cards.

## Ullapool

### Ardmair Point Caravan Park

Ardmair Point, Ullapool IV26 2TN (Highland) T: 01854 612054. E: sales@ardmair.com

alanrogers.com/UK7710

This spectacularly situated park, overlooking the little Loch Kanaird, just round the corner from Loch Broom, has splendid views all round. The 68 touring pitches are arranged mainly on grass around the edge of the bay, in front of the shingle beach. Electrical hook-ups (10A) are available and some gravel hardstandings are on the other side of the access road, just past the second toilet block. Tent pitches, together with cheaper pitches for some tourers are in a large field behind the other sanitary facilities. Scuba diving is popular at Loch Kanaird because the water is so clear.

**Facilities**

Two toilet blocks, both with good facilities. One block has wonderful views from the large windows in the launderette and dishwashing rooms. Large en-suite rooms for disabled visitors. Motorcaravan service point. Shop. Play area. Fishing. Sailing and boating (with your own boat). Off site: Ullapool 3 miles. Golf and bicycle hire 3 miles.

Open: 1 April - late September, depending on the weather.

**Directions**

Park is off the A835 road, 3 miles north of Ullapool. O.S.GR: NH109983. GPS: 57.933967, -5.197017

**Charges guide**

| | |
|---|---|
| Per unit incl. 2 persons and electricity | £ 15.00 - £ 20.00 |

288

For latest campsite news visit

alanrogers.com

With a diversity of unspoilt landscapes, ranging from wild coastlines to green valleys, rugged mountains and shimmering lakes, to the natural phenomenon of the Giant's Causeway, Northern Ireland, though small, is crammed full of sights offering something for everyone.

## NORTHERN IRELAND COMPRISES THE FOLLOWING COUNTIES: ANTRIM, ARMAGH, DOWN, FERMANAGH, LONDONDERRY AND TYRONE

The rugged coastline of the Causeway Coast and the nine Glens of Antrim, in the north, is an Area of Outstanding Natural Beauty, with white sandy shores and little bays, tranquil forests and romantic ruins and castles, full of tales of the ancient Irish Giants and other myths and legends. At over 60 million years old, with a mass of 4,000 tightly packed basalt columns, each a polygon shape, the Giant's Causeway is a popular attraction. One of the most beautiful regions is in the west around Londonderry, a delightful walled city set on a hill on the banks of the Foyle estuary. Further south is the beautiful region of Fermanagh, with glistening lakes and little islands all surrounded by lush green fields, hillsides and forests. The large lake of Lough Erne is to be found here: made up of two channels, the lower and upper Loughs, the meeting point of these channels is Enniskillen, a town steeped in history, boasting numerous preserved buildings including a castle. Across to the eastern shores lies the ancient Kingdom of Down, with its endless miles of spectacular coastline, little fishing villages, country parks and the Mountains of Mourne. And, ringed by hills, sea lough and river valley is Belfast, a bustling city full of theatres, concert halls, art galleries and restaurants.

### Places of interest

*Antrim:* Antrim Lough Shore Park; Rathlin Island; Giant's Causeway; Dunluce Castle near Portrush.

*Belfast & environs:* Belfast zoo and castle; Irish Linen Centre in Lisburn; Carrickfergus Castle.

*Armagh:* Gosford Forest Park near Markethill; Lough Neagh Discovery Centre on Oxford Island.

*Down:* County Museum and Downpatrick Cathedral; Mourne Mountains; Castlewellan forest park; Ballycopeland Windmill near Millisle.

*Fermanagh:* Enniskillen Castle and Castle Coole; village of Belleek; Marble Arch Caves, near Lough Macnean; Devenish Island on Lough Erne.

*Londonderry:* St Columb's Cathedral, Harbour Museum, Foyle Valley Railway Centre in Derry.

*Tyrone:* Omagh; Beaghmore stone circles near Cookstown; Dungannon; Sperrin Mountains.

### Did you know?

Northern Ireland measures 85 miles from north to south and is about 110 miles wide.

The world's most famous ship, the Titanic, was built in Belfast.

Legend has it that the rugged Giant's Causeway was built by Finn McCool, the legendary Irish Giant, when he travelled to Scotland to bring back his sweetheart.

At 2,240 yards an Irish mile is 480 yards longer than a standard English mile.

Mountsandel near Coleraine is where Ireland's first known house was built 9,000 years ago.

For latest campsite news visit
**alanrogers.com**

## Antrim

### Six Mile Water Caravan & Camping Park

Lough Road, Antrim BT41 4DG (Co. Antrim) T: 028 9446 4963. E: sixmilewater@antrim.gov.uk

alanrogers.com/UK8330

Six Mile Water is located at the Lough Shore Park and is adjacent to the Antrim Forum leisure complex, a major amenity area that includes swimming pools, a bowling green, an adventure playground for children, fitness and health gyms and sports fields. Managed by Antrim Borough Council, the park is easily accessible when travelling to and from the ports of Belfast and Larne, making it perfect for stopovers. There are now 37 pitches with 13A electricity, arranged in a herringbone layout of hardstandings with grass for awnings, and a grass area for 30 tents to one side, plus picnic and barbecue areas. Advance booking is advisable. Six Mile Water is central for sightseeing in the area including the Antrim Castle Gardens and Clotworthy Arts Centre and for shopping in Antrim town. The Lough Shore Park offers visitors boating and water activities and boat launching on the beautiful Lough Neagh, as well as walking and cycling the Lough Shore Trail which takes in 25 places of interest along its 128 mile cycle route. The nearby golf club also offers a 20 bay driving range.

**Facilities**

The small, modern toilet block provides toilets, washbasins and showers and facilities for disabled campers. Baby changing unit. Laundry room. TV lounge and games room. Fishing and boat launching. Off site: The facilities of Lough Shore Park, including a café, open all year round. Antrim Forum leisure centre. Bus service 1 mile. Shops, pubs and restaurants within 1.5 miles. Golf 1.5 miles. Riding 6 miles.

Open: March - October and weekends in Feb. and Nov.

**Directions**

Site is 1 mile south of the city centre. Follow signs for Antrim Forum and Lough Shore Park. On the Dublin road, turn off into Lough Road. Pass Antrim Forum and park is at the end of the road (with speed bumps). GPS: 54.71533, -6.23375

**Charges guide**

| | |
|---|---|
| Per unit incl. electricity | £ 18.00 - £ 20.00 |
| tent | £ 18.00 |

## Six Mile Water Caravan and Camping Park

**Lough Road, Antrim, Northern Ireland, BT41 4DG**

Situated on the shores of Lough Neagh, an ideal base for Northern Ireland. On-site facilites include: TV lounge, games room, modern toilet and shower block, WiFi internet access, fully equipped laundry room, electric hook-up for 37 pitches and 30 camping sites. Maximum stay 14 nights. Open March - October and weekends only during February and November.

**Tel: 028 9446 4963   Email: sixmilewater@antrim.gov.uk**
**www.antrim.gov.uk/caravanpark**

## Ballymoney

### Drumaheglis Caravan Park

36 Glenstall Road, Ballymoney BT53 7QN (Co. Antrim) T: 028 2766 0280. E: drumaheglis@ballymoney.gov.uk

alanrogers.com/UK8340

A caravan park which continually maintains high standards, Drumaheglis is popular throughout the season. Situated on the bank of the lower River Bann, approximately four miles from the town of Ballymoney, it appeals to watersports enthusiasts or makes a very good base for exploring this scenic corner of Northern Ireland. This attractive site is well laid out with trees, shrubs, flower beds and tarmac roads. There are 35 serviced pitches for touring units with hardstanding, electricity (5/16A), water points and drainage. The marina offers facilities for boat launching, waterskiing, cruising, canoeing and fishing. Getting out and about can take you to the Giant's Causeway, seaside resorts such as Portrush or Portstewart, the sands of Whitepark Bay, the Glens of Antrim or the picturesque villages of the Antrim coast road. Ballymoney is popular for shopping and the Joey Dunlop leisure centre provides a high-tech fitness studio, sports hall, etc. There is much to see and do within this Borough and of interest is the Ballymoney museum in Townhead Street.

**Facilities**

Modern toilet blocks are very clean and well maintained. Facilities for disabled visitors. Baby changing facilities and four en-suite shower rooms. Washing machine and dryer. Basic shop. Play area. Barbecue and picnic areas. Barrier with key system. Fishing. Boat launching. Off site: Marina. Bus service from park entrance. Bicycle hire and golf 4 miles. Riding 6 miles. Beach 10 miles.

Open: 17 March - end October.

**Directions**

From A26/B62 Portrush - Ballymoney roundabout continue for about 2 miles on the A26 towards Coleraine. Site is clearly signed - follow International camping signs. GPS: 55.07212, -6.59082

**Charges guide**

| | |
|---|---|
| Per unit incl. electricity | £ 19.00 - £ 20.00 |
| tent pitch | £ 14.00 |

For latest campsite news visit
**alanrogers.com**

## Belcoo

### Rushin House Caravan Park

Holywell, Belcoo, Enniskillen BT93 5DU (Co. Fermanagh) T: 028 6638 6519

E: enquiries@rushinhousecaravanpark.com **alanrogers.com/UK8515**

Although situated in Northern Ireland, this park, opened in 2007, is almost on the border with the Republic of Ireland. It has been carefully landscaped from farmland that sloped down to the tranquil Lough MacNean. There are 24 fully serviced pitches on hardstanding which form a friendly circle surrounding a fairy thorn tree. There is also a small camping area. The toilet block, boat jetty, picnic tables and play areas are only a short walk away from the pitches. The helpful owners live on site and are on call most of the time. This park provides a peaceful haven to relax after returning from days out in lovely Fermanagh. At the farm entrance are the stark ruins of Templerushin Church and nearby is St Patrick's Holy Well.

| Facilities | Directions |
| --- | --- |
| Heated toilet block, beautifully appointed, with laundry and adjoining kitchen area. Separate facilities for disabled campers. Payphone. Boat jetty. Play area. All-weather sports facility. Picnic area. Tourist Information. Off site: Golf course nearby. Twin border towns of Belcoo and Blacklion are charming and well provided with shops and restaurants. Within 25 miles are historic Enniskillen, Marble Arch caves, Belleek Pottery, two National Trust properties. | From Enniskillen follow the A4 for 13 miles to Belcoo. Turn right on to the B52 towards Garrison and in about 1 mile you will see the signs for Rushin House. GPS: 54.306584, -7.89505 |

**Charges guide**

| | |
| --- | --- |
| Per unit incl. services | £ 22.00 |
| awning | £ 2.00 |

Open: 11 March - 31 October.

## Bushmills

### Ballyness Caravan Park

40 Castlecatt Road, Bushmills BT57 8TN (Co. Antrim) T: 028 2073 2393. E: info@ballynesscaravanpark.com
**alanrogers.com/UK8360**

Ballyness is immaculately cared for and is designed with conservation in mind. In keeping with the surrounding countryside, it is extensively planted with native trees and shrubs. A pathway encircles several ponds which attract local wildlife and birds. The overall appearance of this park, with its white stone pillared entrance gate and broad tarmac drive is attractive. There are 48 hardstanding pitches all with electricity, water and drainage. Privately owned caravan holiday homes are placed away from the touring pitches. The village of Bushmills, with its famous Whisky Distillery, is within walking distance. The Giant's Causeway and the majestic Antrim coast are only a short drive.

| Facilities | Directions |
| --- | --- |
| One spotlessly clean and well decorated, cottage style heated sanitary block (key coded). Facilities for disabled visitors (toilet and shower). Shop for basic food supplies, gas and campers' essentials. Family room with bath. Laundry room. Play area and play park. WiFi and internet. Off site: Bus service 0.5 miles. Bicycle hire 1 mile. Beach and fishing 1 mile. Boat launching and championship golf courses 1.5 miles. Riding 5 miles. | From M2 follow A26. At Ballymoney turn right on B66 towards Dervock and turn left. Stay on B66 and site is 5.5 miles on right. GPS: 55.20121, -6.52096 |

**Charges guide**

| | |
| --- | --- |
| Per unit incl. 2 persons, electricity, water and drainage | £ 20.00 |
| extra person (over 6 yrs) | £ 1.00 |
| awning or pup tent | £ 2.00 |

Open: 17 March - 31 October.

For latest campsite news visit

# alanrogers.com

## Bushmills
### Bush Caravan Park

97 Priestland Road, Bushmills BT57 8UJ (Co. Antrim) T: 028 2073 1678. E: bushcaravanpark@tiscali.co.uk
alanrogers.com/UK8350

A good base for touring the North Antrim Coast, this family run park is only minutes away from two renowned attractions, the Giant's Causeway and the Old Bushmills Distillery. Located just off the main Ballymoney - Portrush Road (B62), it is approached by a short drive. The park is partly surrounded by mature trees and hedging, but views across the countryside can still be appreciated. Tarmac roads lead to 47 well laid out and spacious pitches with hardstanding and 16A electricity or to a grass area for pup tents. Unique features on site are murals depicting the famed scenery, sights and legends of the Causeway coast. The enthusiastic owners may organise tours to the distillery and coastal trips.

**Facilities**

The toilet block (opened by keypad) is modern, clean and equipped to a high standard. Facilities include controllable showers with excellent provision for visitors with disabilities (can also be used by families). Washing machine and dryer. Central play area. Recreation room for all ages. Off site: Riding 2 miles. Golf and fishing 3 miles. Bicycle hire and boat launching 4 miles. Beach 3 miles.

Open: Easter - 31 October.

**Directions**

From the A26 turn onto the B62 for 7 miles. Turn onto the B17 Priestlands Road and site is immediately on the left. GPS: 55.17103, -6.57114

**Charges guide**

| | |
|---|---|
| Per unit incl. 2 persons and electricity | £ 20.00 |
| awning | £ 2.00 |

## Coleraine
### Tullans Farm Holiday Park

46 Newmills Road, Coleraine BT52 2JB (Co. Londonderry) T: 028 7034 2309. E: tullansfarm@hotmail.com
alanrogers.com/UK8590

A well run family park convenient for the Causeway coast, Tullans Farm has a quiet, heart of the country feel, yet the University town of Coleraine is within a mile, the seaside resorts of Portrush and Portstewart five miles and a shopping centre a five minute drive. The toilet block is clean and attractive flower displays add to the park's well cared for appearance. Around the park roads are gravel and the 36 pitches are on hardstanding; all with electric hook-ups (10A), water and drainage. In season the owners organise barbecues, barn dances and line dancing (raising funds for charity). A central building houses the reception, toilet block and TV room. Plans have been passed for an extension to provide caravan holiday home accommodation.

**Facilities**

The toilet and shower rooms, including a family shower unit, are spacious, modern and include facilities for visitors with disabilities. Laundry and washing up room with sinks, washing machine, dryers and fridge. Play areas. TV lounge. Games room. Caravan storage. Off site: Public transport in Coleraine 1 mile. Fishing and riding 1.5 miles. Golf and bicycle hire 5 miles. Beach 5 miles.

Open: March - 30 September.

**Directions**

From the Lodge Road roundabout (south end of Coleraine) turn east onto A29 Portrush ring road and proceed for 0.5 miles. Turn right at sign for park and Windy Hall. Park is clearly signed on left. GPS: 55.12557, -6.63923

**Charges guide**

| | |
|---|---|
| Per unit incl. all persons | £ 20.00 |
| tent | £ 10.00 - £ 18.00 |

## Dungannon
### Dungannon Park

Moy Road, Dungannon BT71 6DY (Co. Tyrone) T: 028 8772 8690. E: dpreception@dungannon.gov.uk
alanrogers.com/UK8550

This small touring park nestles in the midst of a 70 acre park with a multitude of tree varieties, brightly coloured flower beds and a charming 12 acre fishing lake. The 12 pitches, some with lake views, are on hardstanding each with dedicated water, waste and 16A electricity connections. Hedging provides some separation. There is also an unmarked grass area for tents. Run by Dungannon Council the park, which also incorporates tennis courts, football and cricket pitches, lies about one mile south of Dungannon town. A modern Visitor Amenity Centre houses reception, sanitary facilities, a TV/lounge area and vending machines. Walkers can enjoy three miles of parkland paths which, from the higher ground, command views of the surrounding countryside and Lough Neagh.

**Facilities**

Sanitary facilities are to the rear of the Amenity Centre and include showers (by token), washbasins, baby changing mat and spacious unit for disabled visitors. Laundry room with washing machine and dryer. Excellent play area. TV lounge. Tennis. Fishing. Walking. Orienteering. Off site: Bus stop and shop at main entrance to park. Restaurants, shops, leisure facilities in Dungannon. Interesting walking and cycling in Clogher Valley. Local markets.

Open: 1 March - 31 October.

**Directions**

Leave M1 motorway at junction 15 to join the A29 towards Dungannon. Turn left at second traffic lights signed Dungannon Park. GPS: 54.390217, -6.757967

**Charges guide**

| | |
|---|---|
| Per unit incl. services | £ 15.00 |
| tent | £ 10.00 |

For latest campsite news visit
**alanrogers.com**

## Kilkeel

### Cranfield Caravan Park

123 Cranfield Road, Cranfield West, Kilkeel BT34 4LJ (Co. Down) T: 028 4176 2572
E: jimchestnut@btconnect.com  alanrogers.com/UK8405

On the shores of Carlingford Lough with direct access to a Blue Flag beach, this friendly, family-run park immediately impresses with its well cared for flower beds, neat hedging, cordyline palms and the elegant building which incorporates the family home and reception. Despite the many privately owned caravan holiday homes on site, touring pitches are kept separate and situated towards the park entrance. Most pitches have a sea view, hardstanding and all have tower units providing an electricity hook-up (10A), water, waste water point and TV outlet. Tents are not accepted. Situated at Northern Ireland's most southerly point, the surrounding scenery of the Mourne Mountains, the Lough and distant vistas is stunning. A focal point is the Haulbowline lighthouse, off Cranfield Point, built in the 1800s.

| Facilities | Directions |
|---|---|
| A modern, heated toilet block (entrance by key) is well maintained with tiled walls/floors, preset showers (token) and open style washbasins. Excellent suite for disabled visitors doubles as a family room, also a night WC (by key). Dishwashing sinks and well equipped laundry in a separate building. Play area (outside park). Sea fishing, boat launching and beach (with lifeguard). Off site: Kilkeel town (3.5 miles). Golf, hill walking in the Mournes. | Travelling southeast on A2 Newry - Kilkeel Road turn right about 5.5 miles after passing through Rostrevor onto local road, signed Cranfield/Greencastle. If approaching from Kilkeel follow signs for Cranfield West. Site signed at end of road. GPS: 54.029933, -6.0683 |

Open: 17 March - 31 October.

Charges guide

| | |
|---|---|
| Per unit incl. all persons and electricity | £ 19.00 |
| awning | £ 1.50 |

## Kilkeel

### Sandilands Caravan Park

30 Cranfield Road, Cranfield East, Kilkeel BT34 4LJ (Co. Down) T: 028 4176 3634
E: info@chestnuttholidayparks.com  alanrogers.com/UK8407

In the very popular area of Cranfield, Sandilands is set slightly apart from its neighbours, looking south east over the Irish Sea rather than Carlingford Lough. The park largely comprises privately owned caravan holiday homes, but has an attractive and enclosed area for 30 touring units, although roughly half of these pitches can be seasonally held. It makes the most of its coastal plain situation to the immediate south of the Mourne Mountains. Kilkeel and the mountain foothills can be reached in a few minutes by car. Sandilands is pleasantly laid out with an inviting entrance and may be just the answer for those seeking a quieter location whilst visiting the area.

| Facilities | Directions |
|---|---|
| Laundry and toilet block (entrance to all facilities by key) is well maintained. It has preset showers (token) and open style washbasins and a night WC. There are no dedicated facilities for disabled visitors. Play area and small football pitch. Off site: Sea fishing and boat launching nearby. Pretty village of Rostrevor, well known for its ceilidhs and Irish music 7 miles. | From the north leave the A2 in the middle of Kilkeel and follow signs for Cranfield East until the sign for Sandilands appears on the left. From Newry pass through Rostrevor and after about 6 miles look for signs to Cranfield East. GPS: 54.029932, -6.058391 |

Open: 17 March - 31 October.

Charges guide

| | |
|---|---|
| Per unit incl. services | £ 19.00 |
| awning | £ 1.00 |

## Kilkeel

### Chestnutt Caravan Park

3 Grange Road, Kilkeel, Newry BT34 4LW (Co. Down) T: 028 4176 2653. E: info@chestnuttholidayparks.com
alanrogers.com/UK8410

Chestnutt Caravan Park is one of the best in the southernmost corner of Northern Ireland. There are two areas designated for touring units, one on each side of the entrance road and all pitches have electricity, light, water and waste. The park is surrounded by dramatic scenery and unspoilt countryside and is an attractive choice for a beach-based holiday. The adjacent beach, with lifeguard, tennis court, small football pitch and playpark will keep youngsters happy all day. The backdrop of the Mourne Mountains to the north give the area shelter.

| Facilities | Directions |
|---|---|
| Each touring section has its own toilet block with token operated showers. The large well equipped laundry (also token operated), toilets and full facilities for disabled campers have been completely refurbished. Shop, restaurant and takeaway (all open Easter weekend, July/Aug). Tennis. Play area. WiFi is available throughout the park (small charge). Off site: Sea canoeing and other water sports, sea fishing and golf are all available nearby. | From the north follow the A2 from Newcastle and at Kilkeel follow signs for Cranfield West and then Chestnutt Holiday Park. From Newry, pass through Rostrevor and about 6 miles further you will see signs for Cranfield West. GPS: 54.030864, -6.068868 |

Open: 17 March - 31 October.

Charges guide

| | |
|---|---|
| Per unit incl. services | £ 18.00 |
| awning | £ 1.00 |

For latest campsite news visit
**alanrogers.com**

## Killyleagh

### Delamont Country Park Camping & Caravanning Club Site

Delamont Country Park, Downpatrick Road, Killyleagh BT30 9TZ (Co. Down) T: 028 4482 1833
E: delamont.site@thefriendlyclub.co.uk   alanrogers.com/UK8460

This is Northern Ireland's first Camping and Caravanning Club site and is now one of the country's more popular sites. Facilities on the campsite itself are excellent and it has an orderly, neat and tidy appearance. Reception stands beside the entrance to the site and the sanitary block towards the rear. The 65 all weather pitches on level terrain all have electricity, plus water and waste hook-ups. The site is surrounded by trees and the rich vegetation of the country park, and the young shrubs and trees around the pitches are slowly maturing. Within the boundaries of Delamont Country Park, it is an idyllic location for those seeking an 'away from it all' feel, yet wanting to be within easy reach of the major attractions. The country park is a designated Area of Outstanding Natural Beauty and commands from its highest point, breathtaking vistas of Strangford Lough and surrounding countryside.

**Facilities**

The single modern toilet block, with heating, has wash cubicles and a baby bath. En-suite facilities for disabled visitors. Laundry sinks, washing machine and dryer; dishwashing inside. Small shop area selling basics. Adventure playground and miniature railway in country park. Free admittance to country park for campers. WiFi (charged). Off site: Tyrella beach 7 miles. Fishing and riding 1 mile. Golf 4 miles.

Open: 8 March - 6 November.

**Directions**

From Belfast follow A22 southeast to village of Killyleagh. Pass through village and site entrance is on left after 1 mile. GPS: 54.38656, -5.67657

**Charges guide**

| | |
|---|---|
| Per unit incl. 2 persons | £ 15.10 - £ 21.30 |
| non-member pitch fee | £ 22.10 - £ 28.30 |

## Larne

### Curran Caravan Park

131 Curran Road, Larne BT40 1DD (Co. Antrim) T: 028 2827 3797. E: robinsonsservicestation@hotmail.co.uk
alanrogers.com/UK8320

Attractive garden areas add to the charm of this small, neat park which has recently been purchased by the owner of the garage/shop opposite. It is very conveniently situated for the ferry terminal and only a few minutes walk from the sea. The new owner has been making some upgrades and now provides four hardstanding pitches for motorcaravans. The 34 pitches, all with electricity connections (14A), give reasonable space off the tarmac road and there is a separate tent area of 1.5 acres. Larne market is on Wednesdays. You may consider using this site as a short term base for discovering the area as well as an ideal overnight stop, especially for early or late ferry crossings. The warden can usually find room for tourists so reservations are not normally necessary.

**Facilities**

The toilet block is clean and adequate without being luxurious but there are no facilities for disabled visitors. Laundry room with dishwashing facilities. Bowls and putting adjacent and also play areas with good equipment and safety surfaces. Late arrivals can call at the garage if open. Off site: Train station and bus stop within a few minutes walk. Bicycle hire 0.5 miles. Golf 2 miles. Boat launching 500 yds. Many other amenities are very close including a shop (100 yds), restaurants, tennis and a leisure centre with swimming pool (300 yds).

Open: Easter - 31 October.

**Directions**

Immediately after leaving the ferry terminal, turn right and follow camp signs. Site is 400 yards on the left. GPS: 54.84995, -5.80818

**Charges guide**

| | |
|---|---|
| Per caravan, motorcaravan or large tent incl. electricity and awning | £ 15.00 |
| tent | £ 10.00 |

## Larne

### Carnfunnock Country Park Caravan Park & Campsite

Coast Road, Drain's Bay, Larne BT40 2QG (Co. Antrim) T: 028 2827 0541. E: carnfunnock@larne.gov.uk

alanrogers.com/UK8310

In a magnificent parkland setting overlooking the Irish Sea and Scotland, what makes this touring site popular is its scenic surroundings and convenient location. It is 3.5 miles north of the market town of Larne on the famed Antrim Coast Road and offers 28 level 'super' pitches and three extra long pitches, all with hardstanding, water, electricity (15A), drainage, individual pitch lighting and ample space for an awning. The site has a neat appearance with a tarmac road following through to the rear where a number of pitches are placed in a circular position with allocated space for tents. Run by the Borough Council and supervised by a manager, the surrounding Country Park is immaculately kept. The Visitor Centre includes a gift shop and information about local attractions and the restaurant/coffee shop is pleasant and looks towards the sea. Spending time around the parkland, you find a walled time garden with historic sundials, a maze, forest walk, children's adventure playground, putting green, nine-hole golf course, wildlife garden and miniature railway. There is also a summer events programme.

### Facilities

A small building beside the entrance gates houses the toilet facilities (entry by key) which have had a major refurbishment and are kept very clean. There are shower units, a family bathroom and facilities for disabled visitors. Baby changing room. Off site: Facilities of the adjacent Country Park include: gift shop, restaurant and coffe shop. Adventure playground. Maze. Putting green. 9-hole golf course. Forest walk. Larne with buses 3.5 miles. Fishing and boat launching 400 yds. Riding 7 miles.

Open: Easter - 31 October.

### Directions

From ferry terminal in Larne, follow signs for Coast Road and Carnfunnock Country Park; well signed 3.5 miles on A2 coast road.
GPS: 54.888193, -5.845231

### Charges guide

| | |
|---|---|
| Per caravan or motorcaravan incl. electricity and awning | £ 18.00 - £ 20.00 |
| tent incl. 2 persons | £ 11.00 - £ 12.00 |
| tent (per extra person) | £ 2.00 |

## Newcastle

### Tollymore Forest Caravan Park

178 Tullybrannigan Road, Newcastle BT33 OPW (Co. Down) T: 028 4372 2428

alanrogers.com/UK8420

This popular park, for touring units only, is located within the parkland of Tollymore Forest which is noted for its scenic surroundings. The forest park is approached by a majestic avenue of Himalayan cedars and covers an area of almost 500 hectares. Situated two miles from the beaches and resort of Newcastle, it is backed impressively by the Mourne mountains. The open grassy site is attractively laid out with hardstanding pitches, 72 of which have electricity (6A). The Forestry Service Rangers are very helpful and ensure that the caravan site is efficiently run and quiet, even when full. Exploring the park is part of the pleasure of staying here. The stone bridges and entrance gates are of particular interest. The picturesque Shimna and Spinkwee rivers rise in the Mournes and flow through the park. Tree lovers appreciate the arboretum with its many rare species.

### Facilities

The timbered toilet blocks have wash cubicles, showers, dishwashing and laundry area. Fishing (permit required). Off site: Confectionery shop and tea room nearby in high season. Small grocery shop a few yards from the exit gate of the park with gas available.

Open: All year.

### Directions

Approach Newcastle on the A24. Before entering the town, at roundabout, turn right on to A50 signed Castlewellan and follow signs for Tollymore Forest Park. GPS: 54.22630, -5.93449

### Charges guide

| | |
|---|---|
| Per unit incl. car and occupants | £ 10.00 - £ 14.00 |
| electricity | £ 1.50 |

For latest campsite news visit
**alanrogers.com**

Famed for its folklore, traditional music, and friendly, hospitable people, the Republic of Ireland offers spectacular scenery contained within a relatively compact area. With plenty of beautiful areas to discover, and a decidedly relaxed pace of life, it is an idea place to unwind.

**IRELAND IS MADE UP OF FOUR PROVINCES: CONNAUGHT, LEINSTER, MUNSTER AND ULSTER, COMPRISING 32 COUNTIES, 26 OF WHICH FALL IN THE REPUBLIC OF IRELAND**

Ireland is the perfect place to indulge in a variety of outdoor pursuits while taking in the glorious scenery. There are plenty of way-marked footpaths, which lead through woodlands, across cliffs, past historical monuments and over rolling hills. The dramatic coastline, with its headlands, secluded coves and sandy beaches, is fantastic for watersports: from sailing to windsurfing, scuba diving and swimming; or for just simply relaxing and watching the variety of seabirds that nest on the shores. The Cliffs of Moher, in particular, is a prime location for birdwatching and Goat Island, just offshore, is where puffins make their nesting burrows. Fishing is another popular activity; the country is full of pretty streams, rivers, hidden lakes and canals, which can all be explored by hiring a boat. In the south the beautiful Ring of Kerry is one of the most visited regions. This 110-mile route encircles the Inveragh Peninsula, and is surrounded by mountains and lakes. Other sights include: the Aran Islands, home to some of the most ancient Christian and pre-Christian remains in Ireland, and the Rock of Cashel, with its spectacular group of medieval buildings; not to mention the bustling cities of Dublin, Galway and Cork.

### Places of interest

*Connaught:* Boyle Abbey; Connemara National Park; Céide Fields at Ballycastle; Kylemore Abbey; Aran Islands; Galway city; Westport; Sligo Abbey; megalithic tombs of Carrowmore.

*Leinster:* Wicklow Mountains National Park; Rock of Cashel; Killkenny Castle; Guinness brewery, Trinity College and National Museum in Dublin; Dunmore Cave at Ballyfoyle; Wexford Wildfowl Reserve.

*Munster:* harbour towns of Kinsale and Clonakilty; Blarney Castle in Cork; historical city of Limerick with 13th century castle fortress and old town; Ring of Kerry; Bunratty Castle; Cliffs of Moher; Killarney National Park.

*Ulster:* Glenveagh National Park; Slieve League, the highest sea cliffs in Europe; Donegal Castle; Newmills Corn and Flax Mills in Letterkenny.

### Did you know?

The official currency of the Republic of Ireland is the Euro.

The international dialling code for the Republic of Ireland is 00 353 (then drop the first '0' of the number).

The Blarney Stone, reputedly cast with a spell by a witch to reward a king who saved her from drowning, is said to bestow the gift of eloquence on all those who kiss it.

The harp is a symbol of the Irish people's love of music: since Medieval times it has been the official emblem for Ireland.

Hurling is the oldest native sport.

On display in Trinity College, the Book of Kells is one of the oldest books in the world, written around the year 800 AD.

For latest campsite news visit

alanrogers.com

# Athlone

## Lough Ree (East) Caravan & Camping Park

Ballykeeran, Athlone (Co. Westmeath) T: 090 647 8561. E: athlonecamping@eircom.net

alanrogers.com/IR8960

This touring park is alongside the river, screened by trees but reaching the water's edge. Drive into the small village of Ballykeeran and the park is discreetly located behind the main street. The top half of the site is in a woodland situation and after the reception and sanitary block, Lough Ree comes into view and the remaining pitches run down to the shoreline. There are 60 pitches, 20 with hardstanding and 52 with electricity (6A). With fishing right on the doorstep there are boats for hire locally and the site has its own private mooring buoys, plus a dinghy slip and harbour. A restaurant and 'singing' pub are close.

### Facilities

The toilet block is clean without being luxurious. Hot showers (€ 1). Dishwashing sinks outside. Laundry room (wash and dry € 8). A wooden chalet houses a pool room with open fire and campers' kitchen (no cooking facilities). Off site: Riding 4 km. Golf 8 km.

Open: 1 April - 30 September.

### Directions

From Athlone take N55 towards Longford for 4.8 km. Park is in the village of Ballykeeran, clearly signed. GPS: 53.44815, -7.88992

### Charges guide

| | |
|---|---|
| Per unit incl. 2 persons and electricity | € 23,00 |

No credit cards.

# Athy

## Forest Farm Caravan & Camping Park

Dublin Road, Athy (Co. Kildare) T: 059 863 1231. E: forestfarm@eircom.net

alanrogers.com/IR9080

This site makes an excellent stopover if travelling from Dublin to the southeast counties. It is also ideally placed to visit local places of interest including the Shackleton exhibition, the Japanese Gardens and the Irish National Stud. Part of a working farm, the campsite spreads to the right of the modern farmhouse, which also provides B&B and holiday apartments. The owners have cleverly utilised their land to create a site which offers 64 unmarked touring pitches on level ground. Of these, 32 are for caravans, all with electricity and ten with hardstanding, and 32 places are available for tents. Full Irish breakfasts are served at the farmhouse and farm tours are arranged on request. The park is signed on the N78 and approached by a 500 m. avenue of tall pines.

### Facilities

The centrally located, red brick toilet block is heated and double glazed, providing quality amenities. Spacious shower unit for disabled visitors. Family room with shower and WC. Laundry room. Campers' kitchen with fridge and freezer, cooker, table and chairs. Comfortable, large lounge/games room (a TV can be provided). Sand pit and picnic tables. Off site: Shop, bar and restaurant 3 km. Golf courses nearby. Course and game fishing 4 km.

Open: All year.

### Directions

Site is 4.8 km. northeast of Athy town off the main N78 Athy - Kilcullen road. GPS: 53.0139, -6.9256

### Charges guide

| | |
|---|---|
| Per person | € 4,00 |
| child | € 2,00 |
| pitch incl. electricity | € 2,00 |
| hiker, cyclist or motorcyclist incl. tent | € 6,00 |

# Ballaghaderreen

## Willowbrook Camping & Caravan Park

Kiltybranks, Ballaghaderreen (Co. Roscommon) T: 094 986 1307. E: info@willowbrookpark.com

alanrogers.com/IR8815

This is a campsite with a difference. Willowbrook is a small family run caravan and camping park, which offers a unique holiday in an unspoiled part of Ireland. It has eight hardstanding pitches with electricity and a central level grass area without power, all with ample water points. An additional tenting area is available in the adjoining field. The main difference is that meditation, Tai Chi and other relaxation techniques, all adding to the tranquillity of the setting, are organised by Dave and Lin Whitefield whose aim is to ensure their guests relax and unwind in this idyllic hideaway. Archery, guided walks on the Suck Valley Way and in the Ox and Curlieu mountains, and coarse fishing for more active relaxation are also provided. This is a clean and well cared for park.

### Facilities

The toilet block is immaculate and lit at night, with separate shower cubicles and facilities for disabled campers. Laundry room. Campers' kitchen with microwave, kettle and toaster. Bunkhouse (sleeps 12). Library and reading room with TV. Fishing. Torches useful. Off site: Local sporting activities available include tennis, golf and fishing.

Open: All year.

### Directions

Park is 6 km. from Ballaghaderreen. Take the R293 from Ballaghaderreen towards Castlerea and Ballyhaunis, then the R325 over the bridge. Bear left, still towards Castlerea and Ballyhaunis for 1.5 km. Turn right at sign to site in 500 m. GPS: 53.86672, -8.60214

### Charges guide

| | |
|---|---|
| Per unit incl. 2 persons and electricity | € 23,00 |
| family tent incl. 2 adults and 2 children | € 24,00 |

No credit cards.

For latest campsite news visit
**alanrogers.com**

## Bantry

Eagle Point Caravan & Camping Park

Ballylickey, Bantry (Co. Cork) T: 027 506 30. E: eaglepointcamping@eircom.net

alanrogers.com/IR9510

Midway between the towns of Bantry and Glengarriff, the spectacular peninsula of Eagle Point juts into Bantry Bay. The first impression is of a spacious country park rather than a campsite. As far as the eye can see this 20 acre, landscaped, part-terraced park, with its vast manicured grass areas separated by mature trees, shrubs and hedges, runs parallel with the shoreline providing lovely views. Suitable for all ages, this is a well run park mainly for touring units, with campers pitched mostly towards the shore. It provides 125 pitches with electricity (6A), although many are seasonally occupied. For wet weather, a timbered building towards the water's edge houses three lounges, two for children and all with TV. The brightly decorated interior is guaranteed to brighten the dullest of days. Eagle Point makes an excellent base for sightseeing throughout West Cork and Kerry and its sheltered location makes it ideal for watersports enthusiasts. Swimming is safe and there is a slipway for small craft.

### Facilities

Three well maintained, well designed toilet blocks are of a high standard. Laundry. Motorcaravan services. Play area. Tennis. Football field, well away from the pitches. Fishing. Boat launching. Supermarket at park entrance. Dogs are not accepted. Off site: Bicycle hire 6 km. Riding 10 km. Golf 2 km.

Open: 22 April - 25 September.

### Directions

Take N71 to Bandon, then R586 Bandon to Bantry. From Bantry take N71 to Glengarriff. 6.4 km. from Bantry; park entrance is opposite EMO petrol station. GPS: 51.718333, -9.455278

### Charges guide

| | |
|---|---|
| Per unit incl. 2 persons and electricity | € 30,00 - € 32,00 |
| extra person | € 10,00 |
| child | € 3,00 |
| motorcyclist, hiker or cyclist (per person) | € 12,00 |

## Belleek

Belleek Caravan & Camping Park

Belleek, Ballina (Co. Mayo) T: 096 715 33. E: lenahan@belleekpark.com

alanrogers.com/IR8750

Belleek has a quiet woodland setting, only minutes from Ballina, a famed salmon fishing centre. With excellent pitches and toilet block, the family owners are committed to ensuring that it is immaculate at all times. From the entrance gate, the park is approached by a drive that passes reception and leads to 58 well spaced pitches. With a very neat overall appearance, 32 pitches have hardstanding, 45 have electricity hook-ups, and you may choose your pitch. Sports facilities within a short distance of the park include a swimming pool, tennis and bicycle hire. There is a Blue Flag beach at Ross. Other local attractions are Ceide Fields (Neolithic farm), Down Patrick Head, Mayo North Heritage Centre or a seaweed bath at Kilcullen's Bath House, Enniscrone.

### Facilities

Spotlessly clean, tastefully decorated toilet block providing showers (€ 1.00 token). Baby bath. Facilities for disabled visitors. Laundry facilities. Reception includes a shop (June-Sept) and a tea room also serving breakfast. Campers' kitchen and emergency accommodation with beds provided. TV room. Games room. Play area. Ball game area. Tennis. Barbecue area. Off site: Fishing 1 km. Bicycle hire 2 km. Golf 3.5 km. Beach 10 km.

Open: 15 March - 1 November, by arrangement all year.

### Directions

Take R314 Ballina - Killala road. Park is signed on right after about 3 km. GPS: 54.1345, -9.1585

### Charges guide

| | |
|---|---|
| Per unit incl. 2 persons | € 19,00 |
| extra person | € 5,00 |
| child | € 2,50 |
| electricity (10A) | € 4,00 |
| hiker/cyclist and tent | € 9,00 |

Low season discounts for stays of 3 or more nights when pre-paid.

For latest campsite news visit
**alanrogers.com**

## Bennettsbridge

### Nore Valley Park

Annamult, Bennettsbridge (Co. Kilkenny) T: 056 772 7229. E: norevalleypark@eircom.net

alanrogers.com/IR9230

This lovely site is set on a grassy hill overlooking the valley of the River Nore, with a woodland setting behind. Situated on a working farm, it offers 70 touring pitches, 50 of which have 6A electricity. There is an additional area for tents and four mobile homes for rent. The owners, Samuel and Isobel, are proud of their park and her baking and jams must be sampled. An attractive courtyard houses several unusual facilities including a sand pit and a straw loft play area for wet weather. Animal park, outdoor chess, tractor rides and go-karts in the fields.

**Facilities**

The modern toilet block is kept clean and can be heated. Two units suitable for disabled visitors. Laundry room with washing machine and dryer. Motorcaravan services. The original block in the courtyard is used mainly in the low season. Shop (basic items such as milk, bread and camping gaz) and café (June-Aug). Comfortable lounge. Games room. Play area. Minigolf. Off site: Bennettsbridge 3 km. Outdoor pursuits nearby such as canoeing, walking and fishing 4 km. Riding 6 km. Golf 10 km.

Open: 1 March - 31 October.

**Directions**

From Kilkenny take R700 to Bennettsbridge. Just before the bridge turn right at sign for Stoneyford and after about 3 km. site is signed Nore Valley Park. GPS: 52.56307, -7.19506

**Charges guide**

| | |
|---|---|
| Per unit incl. 2 persons and electricity | € 21,00 - € 23,00 |
| extra person | € 4,00 |

## Blarney

### Blarney Caravan & Camping Park

Stone View, Blarney (Co. Cork) T: 021 451 6519. E: con.quill@camping-ireland.ie

alanrogers.com/IR9480

There is a heart of the country feel about this 'on the farm' site, yet the city of Cork is only an 8 km. drive. What makes this friendly, family run park so appealing is its secluded location and neatly laid out, open appearance. The terrain on the three acre park is elevated and gently sloping, commanding views towards Blarney Castle and the surrounding mountainous countryside. The 80 pitches, 39 of which have hardstanding and 10A electrical connections, are with caravans near the entrance and tents pitched slightly further away. There are gravel roads, well tended young shrubs and a screen of mature trees. Tidy hedging marks the park's perimeter.

**Facilities**

Excellent toilet facilities are housed in converted farm buildings. Reception and small shop are now at entrance. Good facilities for disabled visitors. Laundry room. Campers' kitchen. Motorcaravan service point. Shop (1/6-31/8). TV lounge. Internet and WiFi (charged). Delightful 18-hole golf and pitch and putt course. Off site: Bar and restaurant 100 m. serving food all day. Within easy reach of the ports of Cork and Rosslare.

Open: 1 April - 25 October.

**Directions**

Site is 8 km. northwest of Cork, just off the N20. Take N20 from Cork for about 6 km. and then left on R617 to Blarney. Site clearly signed at Top Filling station in village, in 2 km. GPS: 51.94787, -8.54622

**Charges guide**

| | |
|---|---|
| Per unit incl. 2 persons and electricity | € 24,00 - € 27,00 |
| extra person | € 6,50 |
| child | € 3,00 |

## Boyle

### Lough Key Caravan & Camping Park

Lough Key Forest Park, Boyle (Co. Roscommon) T: 071 966 2212. E: info@loughkey.ie

alanrogers.com/IR8825

This caravan and camping park is set deep in the 320 hectares of the Lough Key Forest Park. Comprising mixed woodland including giant red cedar, beech, ash and oak trees, the forest is bounded by Lough Key and incorporates several of its islands. The rustic design of the main building on the park (which houses reception, a campers' kitchen, a TV room, and the sanitary and laundry facilities) blends well with the wooded environment. The well landscaped, five hectare site provides space for 52 touring units with electricity connections and ample water points. There is a separate area for tents. The history of the parkland goes back to 1184.

**Facilities**

The main toilet block includes metered hot showers (€ 2). Facilities for disabled campers (key required). Campers' kitchen and sheltered eating area. Laundry. TV room. Play area in the centre of the park with adventure type play equipment in a hedged areas. Forest walks and trails. Boat tours and hire. Off site: Restaurant at Rockingham harbour. Nearby town of Boyle for bars, restaurants and entertainment 3 km. Bicycle hire and golf 5 km.

Open: Easter - mid September.

**Directions**

Park is 4 km. east of Boyle on the N4 Dublin - Sligo Road. GPS: 53.98125, -8.235167

**Charges guide**

| | |
|---|---|
| Per pitch | € 10,00 - € 20,00 |
| electricity | € 2,00 |
| No credit cards. | |

## Caherdaniel

### Wave Crest Caravan & Camping Park

Caherdaniel (Co. Kerry) T: 066 947 5188. E: wavecrest@eircom.net

alanrogers.com/IR9560

It would be difficult to imagine a more dramatic location than Wave Crest's on the Ring of Kerry coast. Huge boulders and rocky outcrops tumble from the park entrance on the N70 down to the seashore which forms the most southern promontory on the Ring of Kerry. There are spectacular southward views from the park across Kenmare Bay to the Beara peninsula. Sheltering on grass patches in small coves that nestle between the rocks and shrubbery, are 65 hardstanding pitches and 20 on grass offering seclusion. Electricity connections are available (13A). This park would suit older people looking for a quiet, relaxed atmosphere. A unique feature is the TV room, an old stone farm building with a thatched roof. Its comfortable interior includes a stone fireplace heated by a converted cast iron marker buoy. Caherdaniel is known for its cheerful little pubs and distinguished restaurant. The Derrynane National Park Nature Reserve is only a few kilometres away, as is Derrynane Cove and Bay.

| Facilities | Directions |
|---|---|
| Two blocks house the sanitary and laundry facilities and include hot showers on payment (€ 1). Small shop and takeaway service (June-Sept). Small play area. Fishing and boat launching. Off site: Riding 1 km. Bicycle hire and golf 10 km. Small beach near and Derrynane Hotel with bar and restaurant. | On the N70 (Ring of Kerry), 1.5 km. east of Caherdaniel. GPS: 51.75881, 10.09112 |

Open: All year.

Charges guide

| | |
|---|---|
| Per unit incl. 2 persons and electricity | € 27,00 |
| extra person | € 6,00 |
| child | € 2,00 |

## Cahir

### The Apple Camping & Caravan Park

Moorstown, Cahir (Co. Tipperary) T: 052 74 414 59. E: con@theapplefarm.com

alanrogers.com/IR9410

This fruit farm and campsite combination offers an idyllic country holiday venue in one of the most delightful situations imaginable. For tourers only, it is located off the N24, midway between Clonmel and Cahir. The park has 32 pitches in a secluded situation behind the barns and are mostly grass with a few hardstandings, with electricity to 25. Entrance is by way of a 300 m. drive flanked by the orchard fields and various non-fruit tree species, which are named and of interest to guests who are free to spend time walking the paths around the farm. When we visited, strawberries were being gathered – the best we had tasted all season – and award winning apple juice, cordials, jams, etc. are also sold by Con and Noreen in the farm shop. Reception is housed with the other site facilities in a large farmyard barn. Although a rather unusual arrangement, it is central and effective. The towns of Cahir and Clonmel are of historic interest and the countryside around boasts rivers, mountains, Celtic culture and scenic drives.

| Facilities | Directions |
|---|---|
| Toilet facilities, kept very clean, quite modern in design and with heating, comprise showers, washbasins with mirrors, electric points, etc. in functional units occupying two corners of the large floor space. Facilities for disabled visitors. Also in the barn are dishwashing sinks, washing machine and a fridge/freezer for campers to use. Good motorcaravan service point. Good tennis court (free). Play area. Dogs only accepted by prior arrangement. Off site: Fishing, golf, bicycle hire and riding within 6 km. | Park is 300 m. off main N24, 9.6 km. west of Clonmel, 6.4 km. east of Cahir. GPS: 52.37663, -7.84262 |

Open: 1 May - 30 September.

Charges guide

| | |
|---|---|
| Per unit incl. 2 persons and electricity | € 15,50 |
| extra person | € 6,50 |
| child | € 4,50 |

Less 20% for groups of 4 or more.

## Cahirciveen

### Mannix Point Camping & Caravan Park

Cahirciveen (Co. Kerry) T: 066 947 2806. E: mortimer@campinginkerry.com

alanrogers.com/IR9610

A tranquil, beautifully located seashore park, it is no exaggeration to describe Mannix Point as a nature lovers' paradise. Situated in one of the most spectacular parts of the Ring of Kerry, overlooking the bay and Valentia Island, the rustic seven-acre park commands splendid views in all directions. The park road meanders through the level site and offers 42 pitches of various sizes and shape, many with shelter and seclusion. There are 42 electrical connections (10A) available. A charming, old flower bedecked fisherman's cottage has been converted to provide facilities including reception, excellent campers' kitchen and a cosy sitting room with turf fire. There is no television, but compensation comes in the form of a knowledgeable, hospitable owner who is a Bord Fáilte registered local tour guide. A keen gardener, Mortimer Moriarty laid out the site over 20 years ago and his intention to cause as little disruption to nature as possible has succeeded. The site opens directly onto marshland which teems with wildlife (a two acre nature reserve) with direct access to the beach and seashore. This park retains a wonderful air of Irish charm aided by occasional impromptu musical evenings. A viewing platform allows observation of seals and birdlife and to consider the secrets of the park sculpture, 'the pinicle'. This is also an ideal resting place for people walking the Kerry Way.

### Facilities

Toilet and shower facilities were clean when we visited. Modern and well equipped campers' kitchen and dining area. Comfortable campers' sitting room. Laundry facilities with washing machines and dryer. Motorcaravan service point. Picnic and barbecue facilities. Fishing and boat launching from site. Off site: Bicycle hire 800 m. Riding 3 km. Golf 14 km. Pubs, restaurants and shops 15 minutes walk. Watersports, bird watching, walking and photography. Local cruises to Skelligs Rock with free transport to and from the port for walkers and cyclists.

Open: 15 March - 15 October.

### Directions

Park is 300 m. off the N70 Ring of Kerry road, 800 m. southwest of Cahirciveen (or Cahersiveen) on the road towards Waterville.
GPS: 51.941517, -10.24465

### Charges guide

| | |
|---|---|
| Per unit incl. 2 persons and electricity | € 27,00 |
| extra person | € 6,00 |

Reductions for activity groups and rallies if pre-paid.
No credit cards.

## Castlebar

### Lough Lannagh Caravan Park

Old Westport Road, Castlebar (Co. Mayo) T: 094 902 7111. E: info@loughlannagh.ie

alanrogers.com/IR8810

Lough Lannagh is an attractive holiday village on the lake shore which comprises good quality accommodation, self catering cottages and a caravan park. It is within walking distance of Castlebar with its many restaurants, pubs, theatres and shops. County Mayo's main attractions are also within a short drive. The caravan park has 20 touring pitches, well laid out in a separate dedicated corner of the village, all on hardstanding with electric connections. There is a separate grass area for tents. One reception area serves all and is situated to the right of the security barrier; check in prior to 18:00. When not out and about, there are many on site activities for all the family. The main attraction is the fitness suite, sauna and steam room, plus reflexology and other therapies available. Popular with the young are the organised activities in July/August. Anglers need only travel 500 metres.

### Facilities

One modern heated sanitary block provides washbasins and well equipped, preset showers. En-suite unit for disabled visitors. Laundry room with sink, washing machines and dryers. Café (serving breakfast). Fitness suite (free entry and over 18s only admitted). Table tennis. Boules. Badminton. Tennis. Dogs are not accepted in July/Aug.

Open: 22 April - 30 September.

### Directions

To get to Castlebar take the N5, N60 or N84. At Castlebar ring road follow directions for Westport. Site is signed on all approach roads to the Westport roundabout. GPS: 53.8491, -9.3119

### Charges 2011

| | |
|---|---|
| Per unit incl. 2 persons, electricity and hardstanding | € 21,00 - € 28,00 |
| tent incl. 2 persons (no car) | € 15,00 - € 18,00 |
| child | € 1,50 |

For latest campsite news visit
**alanrogers.com**

## Castlebar
### Carra Caravan & Camping Park
Belcarra, Castlebar (Co. Mayo) T: 094 903 2054. E: post@mayoholidays.com
alanrogers.com/IR8790

This is an ideal location for those seeking a real Irish village experience in a 'value for money' park. Small, unpretentious and family run, it is located in Belcarra, a regular winner of the 'Tidiest Mayo Village' award. Nestling at the foot of a wooded drumlin, it is surrounded by rolling hills and quiet roads which offer an away from it all feeling, yet Castlebar the county's largest town is only an 8 km. drive. On the pleasant 1.5 acre park, the 20 unmarked touring pitches, seven with electric hook-up (13A), are on flat ground enclosed by ranch fencing and shaded in parts by trees. An additional novel idea at Carra are eight horse-drawn caravans for hire. Also of interest are the talks that the owner Sean and daughter Deirdre give on the area. There are recommended walks and maps provided. New to the area is the National Museum of Country Life at Turlough (8 km) which is now a super attraction.

**Facilities**

The basic toilet block has adequate, well equipped showers (€ 1). Combined kitchen with dishwashing, laundry area with fridge/freezer, sink, table, chairs, washing machine and dryer. Comfortable lounge with TV, books and magazines located at reception. Off site: Village shops, a post office and 'Flukies' cosy bar which serves Irish breakfast and where Irish stew is a speciality. Leisure centre and tennis courts. Free fishing area and special walkway to the river. Golf 8 km.

Open: 23 April - 1 October.

**Directions**

From Castlebar follow the N84 towards Ballinrobe. On the outskirts of Castlebar, 100 m. after the railway bridge turn left for Belcarra (Ballycarra) 8 km. GPS: 53.80205, -9.21622

**Charges guide**

| | |
|---|---|
| Per unit incl. all persons and electricity | € 16,00 |

No credit cards.

## Castlegregory
### Anchor Caravan Park
Castlegregory (Co. Kerry) T: 066 713 9157. E: anchorcaravanpark@eircom.net
alanrogers.com/IR9550

Of County Kerry's three long, finger like peninsulas which jut into the sea, Dingle is the most northerly. Anchor Caravan Park is 20 km. west of Tralee, the main town, and under 4 km. south of Castlegregory on Tralee Bay. Its situation, just 150 m. from a fine sandy beach, provides ideal opportunities for safe bathing, boating and shore fishing. A secluded and mature, five acre park, it is enclosed by shrubs and trees that give excellent shelter. There are 30 pitches, all with electric hook-ups and some also with drainage and water points. Although there are holiday homes for hire, these are well apart from the touring pitches. The approach roads to the park are narrow and may be difficult for larger units. In this area of great beauty, miles of sand abound and taking in the panorama of mountain scenery from the top of the Connor Pass is a wonderful experience. Dingle and the beautiful Slea Head Drive are within easy reach by car. A boat trip to the Blasket Islands from Dunquin would be a worthwhile excursion.

**Facilities**

Toilet facilities (entry by key) are kept very clean and provide showers on payment (€ 0,50), two private cabins, some low level basins and a toilet with handrail. No facilities for disabled campers. Laundry facilities (incl. drying room, clothes lines and ironing). Campers' kitchen with fridges, freezers and seating. Motorcaravan services. Two play areas. Games and TV rooms. Off site: Beautiful sandy beach 2 minutes. Fishing 2 km. Riding and bicycle hire 3 km. Golf 4 km.

Open: Easter - 30 September.

**Directions**

From Tralee follow the N86 Dingle coast road for 19 km. At Camp take the R560 towards Castlegrogory. The park is signed from Camp junction. GPS: 52.24393, -9.98579

**Charges guide**

| | |
|---|---|
| Per unit incl. 2 persons and electricity | € 20,00 - € 22,00 |
| extra person | € 5,00 |
| child | € 2,00 |

No credit cards.

For latest campsite news visit
## alanrogers.com

## Clondalkin

### Camac Valley Tourist Caravan & Camping Park

Green Isle Road, Clondalkin Dublin 22 (Co. Dublin) T: 014 640 644. E: reservations@camacvalley.com

alanrogers.com/IR9100

Opened in 1996, this campsite is not only well placed for Dublin, but also offers a welcome stopover if travelling to the more southern counties from the north of the country, or vice versa. Despite its close proximity to the city, being located in the 300-acre Corkagh Park gives it a 'heart of the country' atmosphere. There are 163 pitches, 48 for tents placed to the fore and hardstandings for caravans laid out in bays and avenues with electrical connections, drainage and water points. Maturing trees and shrubs separate pitches and roads are of tarmac. Beyond the entrance gate and forecourt stands an attractive timber fronted building housing the site amenities.

**Facilities**

Heated sanitary facilities include good sized showers (token). Facilities for disabled visitors. Baby room. Laundry. Shop and coffee bar. Playground with wooden play frames and safety base. Fishing. Electronic gate controlled from reception and 24 hour security. Off site: Bicycle hire 1.5 km. Golf 6 km. Riding 9 km.

Open: All year.

**Directions**

From north follow signs for West Link and M50 motorway. Exit M50 at junction 9 onto N7 Cork road. Site is on right of dual-carriageway (beside Green Isle Hotel) after 2 km. and is clearly signed. At City West business park, cross over bridge and return on dual-carriageway following site signs - site is on left after 800 m. GPS: 53.30445, -6.41533

**Charges guide**

| Per unit incl. 2 persons | € 19,00 - € 24,00 |
| incl. up to 4 children | € 26,00 |
| electricity (10A) | € 5,00 |

## Cong

### Cong Caravan & Camping Park

Lisloughrey, Quay Road, Cong (Co. Mayo) T: 094 954 6089. E: info@quietman-cong.com

alanrogers.com/IR8740

It would be difficult to find a more idyllic and famous spot for a caravan park than Cong. Situated close to the shores of Lough Corrib, Cong's scenic beauty was immortalised in the film 'The Quiet Man'. This well kept park is 1.6 km. from the village of Cong, near the grounds of the magnificent and renowned Ashford Castle. The owner's house that incorporates reception, shop and the hostel, stands to the fore of the site. Toilet facilities and the holiday hostel accommodation are entered from the courtyard area. The 40 grass pitches, 36 with electricity, are placed at a higher level to the rear, with the sheltered tent areas below and to the side. The park can be crowded and busy in high season.

**Facilities**

Toilet facilities are tastefully decorated, kept clean and are heated when necessary. Hot showers with curtains (€ 1 charge). Campers' kitchen. Launderette service. Shop. Full Irish and continental breakfast, dinner and packed lunch orders, and home baked bread and scones purchased in the shop. Barbecue, games room and play area. TV lounge. Bicycle hire. Off site: Riding and golf within 2 km. Fishing and boat slipway 500 m.

Open: All year.

**Directions**

Leave N84 road at Ballinrobe to join R334/345 signed Cong. Turn left at end of the R345 (opposite entrance to Ashford Castle), slow down take next road on right (about 300 m) and the park is on right (200 m). GPS: 53.53945, -9.27263

**Charges guide**

| Per unit incl. 2 persons and electricity | € 26,00 - € 30,00 |

## Corofin

### Corofin Village Camping & Caravan Park

Main Street, Corofin (Co. Clare) T: 065 683 7683. E: info@corofin.camping.com

alanrogers.com/IR9460

This compact green oasis in the centre of the village of Corofin occupies one acre and adjoins the family's hostel. The owners, Jude and Marie Neylon, live on the site and have a policy of always having a family member on hand at all times. They are very environmentally aware and have excellent recycling facilities. The 16 touring pitches all have electricity and there are ample water points. The site now includes a small separate tent area which is quite private and well sheltered. This little site is neat and well maintained and makes an ideal base for sightseeing throughout Clare.

**Facilities**

The sanitary block is bright and clean with free hot showers. Separate facilities for disabled campers. Laundry room with washing machine and dryer. Campers' kitchen. TV and games room. CCTV security. Free WiFi. Torches useful. Site is not suitable for large units. Off site: Fishing and boat launching 2 km. Riding 8 km. Bicycle hire 10 km. Golf 20 km. Beach 20 km.

Open: 1 April - 30 September.

**Directions**

Corofin village is 12 km. from Ennis, from where you take the N85 towards Ennistymon and after 2 km. (well signed) turn right onto R476. Site is in the centre of the village. GPS: 52.9407, -9.058933

**Charges guide**

| Per unit incl. 2 persons and electricity | € 25,00 |
| extra person | € 5,00 |
| No credit cards. | |

For latest campsite news visit

**alanrogers.com**

## Donard

### Moat Farm Caravan & Camping Park

Donard (Co. Wicklow) T: 045 404 727. E: moatfarm@ireland.com

alanrogers.com/IR9160

Providing a true feel of the countryside, this park is part of a working sheep farm. It offers incredible vistas across a scenic landscape, yet is within driving distance of Dublin and Rosslare. Driving into the village of Donard you little suspect that alongside the main street lies a pleasant, well cared for and tranquil five acre campsite. The entrance is approached by way of a short road where the ruins of a Medieval church sit high overlooking the forecourt and reception. There are 40 pitches for caravans and tents. Spacious pitches with hardstanding line both sides of a broad avenue, incorporating ample space for awnings and all with electricity and drainage. A large field takes tents and further caravans. The site makes a good base for touring or walking, for this area is a walker's paradise with a 30 minute circular walk around the perimeter of the site. Those with larger units should phone to check accessibility.

**Facilities**

The toilet block is kept very clean and includes spacious showers. Facilities for visitors with disabilities. Well equipped laundry room. Good quality campers' kitchen. Large recreation/entertainment room with open fire. Three large barbecues and patio area. Caravan storage. Off site: Mountain climbing or sites of archaeological interest nearby. Fishing 3 km. Golf and riding 13 km. Bicycle hire 15 km.

Open: 15 March - 30 September.

**Directions**

Park is 16.5 km. south of Blessington. Leave the M50 Dublin ring motorway at exit 10 to join N81 southwest for 19 km. to Blessington. Continue on N81 for a further 16.5 km. and turn left at Old Toll House pub onto local road and follow signs to park in Donard village (3.5 km). GPS: 53.0212, -6.61562

**Charges guide**

| | |
|---|---|
| Per unit incl. 2 persons and electricity | € 23,00 |
| extra person | € 5,00 |
| child | € 3,00 |
| motorcyclist, cyclist or hiker incl. tent | € 10,00 |

No credit cards.

## Doolin

### Nagle's Doolin Camping & Caravan Park

Doolin (Co. Clare) T: 065 7074458. E: ken@doolincamping.com

alanrogers.com/IR9465

This neat and tidy seaside site is located just one kilometre from the cliffs of Moher, and a short ferry ride from the sparsely populated Aran Islands. The nearby village of Doolin, famed for its traditional music, has a good range of shops, restaurants and pubs. The four-hectare site, which enjoys spectacular views over the bay to Conemara, has 99 level, grassy pitches, 55 for touring (with 10A electricity, water and drainage). They are not separated by hedges, but the site is divided into bays by limestone walls. There is excellent WiFi coverage over the whole site. Walkers and nature lovers will be in their element among the rare species of flowers and insects found in this limestone region known as the Burren. Doolin itself is home to a number of traditional pubs with lively, impromptu music sessions featuring musicians from Ireland and overseas. A complete contrast is offered by the many signposted coastal walks along the eight-kilometre headland, with its panoramic views towards the Aran Islands, just 20 minutes away by high-speed ferry.

**Facilities**

One modern, well equipped toilet block is unheated but has good facilities including en-suite unit for disabled visitors. Laundry with 3 washers and 3 dryers (charged). Kitchen with cooking rings (charged), fridge/freezer and dishwashing sinks with hot water. Shop (June-Aug). Motorcaravan service point. Gas. WiFi throughout. Off site: Pitch and putt, boat launching and ferry to Aran Islands all 300 m. Fishing, riding, bicycle hire, shops, hot food and bars within 1-2 km. Golf 10 km.

Open: Open St Patrick's weekend to mid/end October (check with site).

**Directions**

From Limerick take N85 round Ennis to Ennistimon, then N67 towards Lisdoonvarna. After 11 km. turn left for Doolin and then Doolin Pier. Site signed. From Galway take N18 and then in 20 km. N67 to Lisdoonvarna and follow signs as above. GPS: 53.01677, -9.402

**Charges guide**

| | |
|---|---|
| Per unit incl. 2 persons and electricity | € 21,00 - € 23,00 |
| extra person | € 7,00 |
| child | € 3,00 |

## Dungarvan

### Casey's Caravan & Camping Park

Clonea, Dungarvan (Co. Waterford) T: 058 419 19

alanrogers.com/IR9330

This is a very large park by Irish standards. Set on 20 acres of flat grass, edged by mature trees, this family run park is well managed and offers 284 pitches which include 110 touring pitches all with electrical hook-ups and 39 with hardstanding. There is even a large, open and flat field without services for high-season overspill arrivals. The remainder are occupied by caravan holiday homes. There is direct access from the park to a sandy, 'Blue Flag' beach with a resident lifeguard during July and August. A highly recommended leisure centre is adjacent should the weather be inclement. The park is 5.5 km. from Dungarvan, a popular town for deep sea angling, from where charter boats can be hired and three, 18-hole golf courses are within easy driving distance. Suggested drives include the scenic Vee, the Comeragh Mountain Drive and the coast road to Tramore – the last having a series of magical coves and the remains of old copper mines. The pretty 'English' village of Lismore and the picturesque and historic town of Youghal, once home to Sir Walter Raleigh, are each about 30 km. drive away.

#### Facilities

The central toilet block (key system), has good facilities kept spotlessly clean. Showers on payment (€ 1). Small laundry with washing machine and dryer. A further modern block provides an excellent campers' kitchen, laundry room and toilet for disabled visitors. Large adventure play area. Large, well equipped games room. TV lounge. Minigolf. Gas supplies. Full time security staff in high season. Tiny tots play area for those under 4 yrs. Off site: Two village stores near the beach. Hotel for food and drink. Golf 5 km. Fishing 4 km. Riding 20 km.

Open: 21 April - 11 September.

#### Directions

From Dungarvan centre follow R675 east for 3.5 km. Look for signs on the right to Clonea Bay and site. Site is about 1.5 km. GPS: 52.094767, -7.546167

#### Charges guide

| Per unit incl. 2 persons | |
|---|---|
| and electricity | € 27,00 - € 31,00 |
| extra person | € 7,00 - € 8,00 |
| child | € 3,00 |
| hiker, biker, cyclist | € 10,00 - € 10,50 |

No credit cards.

CASEY'S CARAVAN & CAMPING PARK

Grade Category 4★ • Bord Failte Registered • Bord Failte / ICC Park Awards
Best 4★ 2004 • 2000 & 2002 Overall Winner Best Park
2001 & 2002 Personal Choice Awards • Merit Award 4★ 2003

Top class facilities including; playground, electric sites for tents & tourers (10A), crazy golf, games & TV rooms and also laundry & kitchen facilities. The park is situated next to EU Blue Flag beach. 2 shops with takeaway are also nearby.

Dungarvan town is 5.5km away and there's a choice of scenic views to visit. Adjacent hotel with 19 metre pool and leisure centre with bowling alley. Other activities can include deep sea and river angling and an 18 hole golf course which are all within easy reach.

Best Coastal park 2008
Best Seaside Park Award 2007
Ambience Award 2006

Clonea, Dungarvan, Co Waterford    Tel: +353 (0)58 41919

## Fermoy

### Blackwater Valley Caravan & Camping Park

Mallow-Killarney Road, Fermoy (Co. Cork) T: 025 321 47. E: blackwatervalleycaravanpark@gmail.com

alanrogers.com/IR9470

The location of this park provides the best of both worlds, as it backs onto green fields adjacent to the Blackwater river, yet is within 200 metres of Fermoy town. Pat and Nora Ryan live overlooking the park which ensures supervision and prompt attention. Well situated for touring, there are 25 pitches, all with hardstanding and electricity connections (13A). Water taps are convenient to all pitches. Considerable additional space for tents is available towards the rear of the park. There are five caravan holiday homes to rent. Fermoy provides local amenities, such as a cinema, restaurants and pubs, many of these providing traditional music. The park owners also own the stretch of the Blackwater that is alongside – a huge plus for all campers who fancy trying their hand at fishing.

#### Facilities

Modern, tiled toilet block provides the usual facilities including an en-suite shower room for disabled visitors. Laundry room with ironing facilities. Campers' kitchen with cooking facilities and dining area. TV and games room. Motorcaravan service point. Off site: Fishing adjacent. Internet access 100 m. Bicycle hire 1 km. Golf 3.5 km. Beach 35 km. Petrol station with gas across the road.

Open: 15 March - 31 October.

#### Directions

In Fermoy town take the N72 for Mallow. Park is 200 m. from junction. GPS: 52.141498, -8.281873

#### Charges guide

| Per unit incl. 2 persons and electricity | € 24,00 |
|---|---|
| extra person | € 6,00 |
| child | € 3,00 |

No credit cards.

For latest campsite news visit

# alanrogers.com

## Glandore
### The Meadow Camping Park
Glandore (Co. Cork) T: 028 332 80. E: meadowcamping@eircom.net
alanrogers.com/IR9500

The stretch of coast from Cork to Skibbereen reminds British visitors of Devon before the era of mass tourism. This is rich dairy country, the green of the meadows matching the emerald colours of the travel posters. Thanks to the warm, wet Gulf Stream climate, it is also a county of gardens and keen gardeners. The Meadow is best described not as a site but as a one-acre garden surrounded, appropriately, by lush meadows. The owners, who live on the park, have cunningly arranged accommodation for 19 pitches, 14 with 6A electric hook-ups, among the flower beds and shrubberies of their extended garden. There are 12 hardstandings. Among the homely features are a campers' kitchen and dining area.

**Facilities**

Facilities are limited but well designed and maintained with brand new solar panels. Showers on payment. Washing machine and dryer. Larger units may be accepted depending on length and available space; contact park before arrival. Football and cycling are not permitted on the park. Off site: Riding 5 km. Fishing, swimming, boat launching and sailing at Glandore 2 km. Bicycle hire 10 km. Golf 19 km.

Open: Easter - 15 September.

**Directions**

Park is 1.5 km. east of Glandore, off N71 road, on R597 midway between Leap and Rosscarbery (coast road). Approach roads are very narrow. GPS: 51.56693, -9.09702

**Charges guide**

| | |
|---|---|
| Per unit incl. 2 persons and electricity | € 23,00 |
| extra person | € 6,00 |
| child (under 16 yrs) | € 3,00 |

No credit cards.

## Glenbeigh
### Glenross Caravan & Camping Park
Glenbeigh (Co. Kerry) T: 066 976 8451. E: info@killarneycamping.com
alanrogers.com/IR9600

Its situation on the spectacular Ring of Kerry and the Kerry Way footpath gives Glenross an immediate advantage, and scenic grandeur around every bend of the road is guaranteed as Glenbeigh is approached. Quietly located before entering the village, the park commands stunning views of Rossbeigh Strand, (within walking distance) and the Dingle Peninsula. On arrival, a good impression is created with the park well screened from the road and with new stone entrance and gates. With 30 touring pitches, all with hardstanding and 10A electricity, and six caravan holiday homes, the park is attractively laid out with a dedicated small tent area.

**Facilities**

Well maintained modern toilet block includes facilities for laundry and dishwashing. Motorcaravan service point. Games room. Bicycle hire. Shelter for campers and new dining area. Off site: Playground at Blue Flag Rossbeigh beach (5 minutes). Watersports and tennis nearby. Riding and fishing 200 m.

Open: 29 April - 26 September.

**Directions**

Park is on the N70 Killorglin - Glenbeigh road, on the right just before entering the village. GPS: 52.05887, -9.93198

**Charges guide**

| | |
|---|---|
| Per unit incl. 2 persons | € 29,00 - € 30,00 |
| extra person | € 3,00 - € 8,00 |

No credit cards.

## Keel
### Keel Sandybanks Caravan & Camping Park
Keel, Achill Island (Co. Mayo) T: 098 432 11. E: info@achillcamping.com
alanrogers.com/IR8730

This is a park offering a taste of island life and the opportunity to relax in dramatic, scenic surroundings. Achill, Ireland's largest island, is 24 km. long and 19 km. wide and is connected to the mainland by a bridge. The site is situated beside Keel village and approached by the R319 from the swivel bridge at Achill Sound. Although there are static holiday mobile homes on this site, the 42 pitches for caravans and 42 for tents are kept separate. Some with hardstanding are located at the perimeter fence overlooking the beach. Although sand based, the ground is firm and level. Roads are tarmac and there is direct access to the beach which is supervised by lifeguards.

**Facilities**

Two modern toilet blocks serve the site, one at the entrance gate beside reception and the other in a central position. Heated facilities include WCs (one for disabled visitors), washbasins and hot showers (on payment). Hair and hand dryers. Play area. TV room. Watersports enthusiasts can enjoy surfing, canoeing and board sailing on Keel Strand and Lough. Fishing trips. Off site: Bicycle hire and golf 200 m. Riding 6 km. In the village there is a food shop, restaurants and music at night in the pubs.

Open: 22 April - 12 September.

**Directions**

From Achill Sound follow the R319 for 16 km. Site is on the left before Keel village. GPS: 53.97535, -10.0779

**Charges guide**

| | |
|---|---|
| Per unit incl. 2 persons and electricity | € 19,00 - € 22,00 |
| child | € 2,00 |
| extra person | € 3,00 |

For latest campsite news visit
**alanrogers.com**

## Killarney

### Killarney Flesk Caravan & Camping Park

Muckross Road, Killarney (Co. Kerry) T: 06466 317 04. E: killarneylakes@eircom.net

alanrogers.com/IR9640

At the gateway to the National Park and Lakes, near Killarney town, this family run, seven-acre park has undergone extensive development and offers high quality standards. Pitches vary in size and spacing and have electricity (10A). Many pitches have a good grass area for awnings, and 11 also have dedicated electricity, water and drainage. The grounds are neat and tidy with a feeling of space. The toilet block is central to most pitches and camp security appears to be tight. This site would appeal to young people wanting to be close to the action in Killarney. The Flesk park is under the same management as the adjacent Victoria House Hotel and, being the nearest camping park to Killarney's town centre is within easy walking distance from the shops and restaurants. Leisure facilities are available at the nearby Gleneagle Hotel. Convenient for a stroll to Ross Castle and its pier for lake cruises. The town's world famous jaunting cars pass by the entrance to the park. Nearby is the newly-restored Muckross Abbey, burned down by Oliver Cromwell in 1652, two centuries after its founding.

**Facilities**

Modern, clean toilet blocks are well designed and equipped. Baby room. En-suite facility for disabled campers (key operated). Laundry room. Campers' kitchen. Games room. Night time security checks. Winter caravan storage. Off site: Adjacent hotel (same ownership) with bar and restaurant. Fishing 300 m. Boat launching 2 km.

Open: 17 April - 30 September.

**Directions**

From Killarney follow the N71 and signs for Killarney National Park. Site is 1.5 km. on the left beside the Victoria House Hotel. GPS: 52.04304, -9.49954

**Charges guide**

| | |
|---|---|
| Per unit incl. 2 persons and electricity | € 30,00 - € 31,00 |
| extra person | € 8,50 |
| child (under 14 yrs) | € 3,00 |

## Killarney

### Donoghues White Villa Farm Caravan & Camping Park

Lissivigeen, Killarney - Cork Road N22, Killarney (Co. Kerry) T: 064 662 0671. E: killarneycamping@eircom.net

alanrogers.com/IR9630

This is a very pleasing small touring park in scenic surroundings off the N22 Cork-Killarney road. Set in the countryside surrounded by green fields, yet is only five minutes away from Killarney town. There are many trees and shrubs around the park but dominant is a magnificent view of the MacGillicuddy's Reeks. There are 30 pitches for caravans and tents, 20 with hardstanding and a grass area for awnings, electricity (10A), water points and night lighting. One pitch is designated for disabled campers and there is a key-operated en-suite facility for their use. An unusual novelty is that old school desks are placed in pairs around the site as picnic tables, plus an antique green telephone box. One can also enjoy walking through the oak wood, fishing on the Flesk or visiting the site's own National Farm Museum. There is a pleasant old-fashioned charm about the White Villa park. Some visitors might fondly describe it as 'camping as it used to be' while others might argue that 'camping as it should be' would better suit, since most of White Villa's facilities compare well with any competitor in the area.

**Facilities**

The toilet block, a sandstone coloured building, is kept spotlessly clean and houses showers on payment (€ 1), a good toilet/shower room for disabled visitors, laundry room and dishwashing sinks. Motorcaravan service area. Campers' kitchen with TV. Play area. Max. 2 dogs (not certain breeds). Daily coach tours from park. Off site: Riding, golf and bicycle hire 3 km. Pub/restaurant 1 km. Killarney town 5 minutes, the National Park is 10 minutes away.

Open: Easter - 2 October.

**Directions**

Park is 3 km. east from Killarney town on N22 Cork road. Park entrance is 300 m. east of N22/N72 roundabout. From Killarney follow N22 Cork road signs and White Villa Farm finger signs from Park Road roundabout. From Kenmare take R569 via Kilgarvan to the N22, or N71 to Killarney, then the N22 Cork road. GPS: 52.04724, -9.45358

**Charges guide**

| | |
|---|---|
| Per unit incl. 2 persons and electricity | € 22,00 - € 23,00 |
| extra person | € 6,00 |
| child | € 3,00 |

No credit cards.
Seven nights for the price of six (if pre-paid).

## Killarney

### Fleming's White Bridge

Ballycasheen Road, Killarney (Co. Kerry) T: 064 663 1590. E: info@killarneycamping.com

alanrogers.com/IR9620

The main road from Cork to Killarney (N22) runs through the gentle valley of the Flesk river. Between the two sits Fleming's White Bridge Camping Park. Its ten-hectare site is within comfortable walking distance of Killarney centre. Surrounded by mature broad-leafed trees, the park is flat, landscaped and generously adorned with flowers and shrubs. It comprises 92 pitches, the majority for touring caravans on well-kept grass pitches with electricity hook-ups, although some have concrete handstanding and some pitches are reserved for tents. Well distributed around the park are three well appointed toilet blocks. This is obviously a site of which the owners are very proud. Hillary and Moira Fleming personally supervise the reception and grounds, maintaining high standards of hygiene, cleanliness and tidiness. In high season they even find time to organise on-site activities that keep children happy and parents relaxed. The park's location so close to Ireland's premier tourism centre makes this park an ideal base to explore Killarney and the southwest.

### Facilities

Three toilet blocks are of a high standard. Motorcaravan service point. Campers' drying room and two laundries. Small shop (1/6-1/9). Two TV rooms and a games room. Fishing (advice and permits provided). Canoeing (own canoes). Bicycle hire. Woodland walks. Off site: Riding 3 km. Golf 2 km.

Open: 15 March - 31 October.

### Directions

From Cork and Mallow: at N72/N22 junction continue towards Killarney and take first turn left (signed Ballycasheen Road). Proceed for 300 m. to archway entrance on left. From Limerick: follow the N22 Cork road. Pass Super Valu and The Heights Hotel take first right (signed Ballycasheen Road) and continue as above. From Kenmare: On N71, pass Gleneagles Hotel and Flesk Bridge. Turn right at traffic lights into Woodlawn Road and Ballycasheen Road and continue 2 km. to archway.
GPS: 52.05595, -9.47458

### Charges guide

| Per unit incl. 2 persons | |
|---|---|
| and electricity | € 30,00 - € 31,00 |
| extra person | € 8,00 |
| child | € 3,00 - € 11,00 |
| No credit cards. | |

## Killarney

### Fossa Caravan & Camping Park

Fossa, Killarney (Co. Kerry) T: 064 663 1497. E: fossaholidays@eircom.net

alanrogers.com/IR9590

This park is in the village of Fossa, ten minutes by car or bus (six per day) from Killarney town centre. Fossa Caravan Park has a distinctive reception building and hostel accommodation, a stimulating play area and shop. The park is divided in two – the touring caravan area lies to the right, tucked behind the main building and to the left is an open grass area mainly for campers. Touring pitches, with electricity (10/15A) and drainage, have hardstanding and are angled between shrubs and trees in a garden setting. To the rear at a higher level and discreetly placed are 30 caravan holiday homes, sheltered by the thick foliage of the wooded slopes which climb high behind the park. Not only is Fossa convenient for Killarney (5.5 km), it is also en-route for the famed Ring of Kerry, and makes an ideal base for walkers and golfers. Less than 8 km. away are the famous walk up the Gap of Dunloe, and Carrantuohill, the highest mountain in Ireland.

### Facilities

Modern toilet facilities include showers on payment. En-suite unit for campers with disabilities. Laundry room. Campers' kitchen. Shop. Takeaway (8/7-25/8). TV lounge. Tennis. Play area. Picnic area. Games room. Security patrol. Off site: Fishing and golf 2 km. Riding 3 km. Bicycle hire 5 km. Woodland walk into Killarney. A visit to Killarney National Park is highly recommended.

Open: 1 April - 30 September.

### Directions

Approaching Killarney from all directions, follow signs for N72 Ring of Kerry/Killorglin. At last roundabout join R562/N72. Continue for 5.5 km. and Fossa is the second park to the right.
GPS: 52.07071, -9.58573

### Charges guide

| Per unit incl. 2 persons | |
|---|---|
| and electricity | € 24,00 - € 26,00 |
| extra person | € 6,00 |
| child (under 14 yrs) | € 2,50 |
| hiker/cyclist incl. tent | € 8,00 - € 9,00 |

## Kilmacanogue

### Valley Stopover & Caravan Park

Killough, Kilmacanogue (Co. Wicklow) T: 012 829 565. E: rowanbb@eircom.net

alanrogers.com/IR9140

In a quiet, idyllic setting in the picturesque Rocky Valley, this small, neat, family run park is convenient for the Dublin ferries. Situated in the grounds of the family home, covering under an acre, it can be used either as a transit site or for a longer stay. It will appeal to those who prefer the more basic 'CL' type site. There are four grassy pitches with electric hook-ups, nine hardstandings, a separate area for three tents, two water points, night lighting and a security gate. Staying put here you are only minutes from Enniskerry which lies in the glen of the Glencullen river. Here you can enjoy a delight of forest walks, or visit Powerscourt, one of the loveliest gardens in Ireland. To be at the sea, travel 6 km. to Bray and you are in one of the oldest seaside resorts in the country.

#### Facilities

Toilet facilities, clean when we visited, are housed in one unit and consist of two WCs with washbasins, mirrors, etc. and a shower. Laundry sink, spin dryer. Campers' kitchen. Full cooked Irish breakfast in the family guest house. Off site: Riding 3 km. Golf 7 km. Fishing 16 km.

Open: Easter - 31 October.

#### Directions

Turn off N11 Dublin - Wexford road at Kilmacanogue, following signs for Glendalough. Continue for 1.6 km. and take right fork signed 'Waterfall'. Park is second opening on the left in about 200 m. GPS: 53.1671, -6.1634

#### Charges guide

| | |
|---|---|
| Per unit incl. 2 persons and electricity | € 20,00 |
| extra person | € 1,25 |

## Knock

### Knock Caravan & Camping Park

Claremorris Road, Knock (Co. Mayo) T: 094 938 8100. E: caravanpark@knock-shrine.ie

alanrogers.com/IR8780

This park is immediately south of the world famous shrine that receives many visitors. Comfortable and clean, the square shaped campsite is kept very neat with tarmac roads and surrounded by clipped trees. The pitches are of a decent size accommodating 50 caravans or motorcaravans, 20 tents and 18 caravan holiday homes (for rent). All pitches have hardstanding (five doubles) and there are 52 electrical connections (13A), with an adequate number of water points. There is also an overflow field. Because of the religious connections of the area, the site is very busy in August and indeed there are unlikely to be any vacancies at all for 14-16 August. Besides visiting the shrine and Knock Museum, it is also a good centre for exploring scenic Co. Mayo.

#### Facilities

Two heated toilet blocks have good facilities for disabled visitors and a nice sized rest room attached, hot showers (on payment) and adequate washing and toilet facilities. Laundry room. Gas supplies. Playground. Off site: Fishing 4.5 km. Golf and riding 11 km.

Open: 1 March - 31 October.

#### Directions

Exit from the N17 at the Knock bypass and from the roundabout follow signs to the site which is just south of the village. GPS: 53.7877, -8.9194

#### Charges guide

| | |
|---|---|
| Per unit incl. 2 persons and electricity | € 23,50 - €25,50 |
| extra person | €2,00 - € 2,50 |
| child | € 1,00 |
| No credit cards. | |

## Lauragh
### Creveen Lodge Caravan & Camping Park
Healy Pass, Lauragh (Co. Kerry) T: 06466 831 31. E: info@creveenlodge.com
alanrogers.com/IR9570

The Healy Pass is the well known scenic summit of the R574 road that crosses the Beara Peninsula, shortening the original journey from Kenmare Bay in the north to Bantry Bay in the south by nearly 70 km. As this narrow coast road starts to climb steeply, on the mountain foothills you will arrive at Creveen Lodge, a working hill farm with a quiet, homely atmosphere. The park provides 20 attractive pitches, 16 with 10A electricity and an area of hardstanding for motorcaravans. To allow easy access, the steep farm track is divided into a simple one-way system. Creveen Lodge, commanding views across Kenmare Bay, is divided among three gently sloping fields separated by trees. The park is carefully tended with neat rubbish bins and rustic picnic tables informally placed. Although not so famed as the Iveragh Peninsula, around which runs the Ring of Kerry, the northern Beara is a scenically striking area of County Kerry. This is walking and climbing countryside or, of interest nearby, is Derreen Gardens.

| Facilities | Directions |
|---|---|
| Well appointed and maintained, the small toilet block provides token operated showers (€ 1). Communal room with cooking facilities, a fridge, freezer, TV, ironing board, fireplace, tables and chairs. Reception is in the farmhouse. Play area. Off site: Water sports, riding, 'Seafare' cruises, shops and a restaurant nearby. Fishing 2 km. Bicycle hire and boat launching 9 km. | Park is on the Healy Pass road (R574) 1.5 km. southeast of Lauragh. GPS: 51.75562, -9.76193 |

Open: Easter - 31 October.

**Charges guide**

| | |
|---|---|
| Per unit incl. 2 persons and electricity | € 22,00 |
| extra person | € 3,00 |
| child | € 1,00 |

No credit cards.

## Mullingar

### Lough Ennell Camping & Caravan Park

Tudenham Shore, Mullingar (Co. Westmeath) T: 044 934 8101. E: eamon@caravanparksireland.com
alanrogers.com/IR8965

Nature and rustic charm is the visitor's first reaction on arrival at Lough Ennell Caravan Park. Set in 18 acres of mature woodland beside a Blue Flag lake, Eamon and Geraldine O'Malley run this sheltered and tranquil park with their family who live on the site. They receive a blend of visitors – seasonal residents in camping holiday homes (private and to rent), caravanners and motorcaravanners and there are ample areas for tents. Pitches are varied, sheltered with trees and natural shrubbery, and spacious with gravel or gravel and grass combinations. Electricity is available on 44 hardstanding and grass pitches and there are water points on or near all the pitches. Just an hour from Dublin, it provides a good holiday base or a useful stopover en-route to the West of Ireland. The watersports permitted on the lake include canoeing, sailing, windsurfing, boating, fishing and safe swimming. The woodlands offer ample opportunities for walking and cycling. Numerous other lakes in the area provide fishing for all varieties especially wild trout. Other activities might include tennis, horse riding, golf, dog racing and of course forest walks. Belvedere House and Tullynally Castle are nearby and the large town of Mullingar is just 6 km.

### Facilities

The toilet block provides toilets, washbasins and hot showers (€1 coin). Additional dishwashing areas are around the park. Laundry. Small shop. Café and coffee shop with takeaway. TV and games room. Play areas and area for ball games. Small lakeside beach. Fishing. Late arrivals area outside. Security including CCTV. Some breeds of dog are not accepted. Off site: Bus service 8 km. Golf 1.5 km. Riding 4 km. Bicycle hire 6 km.

Open: Easter/1 April - 30 September.

### Directions

From N4 take the N52. Follow signs for Belvedere House and take turn 300 m. south of Belvedere House (signed for site). Continue to the shores of Lough Ennell and turn left. GPS: 53.4857, -7.36299

### Charges guide

| | |
|---|---|
| Per unit incl. 2 persons and electricity | € 23,00 - € 25,00 |
| extra person | € 3,00 - € 5,00 |

No credit cards.

## Rathdrum

### Hidden Valley Caravan and Camping Park

Rathdrum (Co. Wicklow) T: 086 7272 872. E: info@irelandholidaypark.com
alanrogers.com/IR9155

This pleasant, level park occupies over seven hectares on both banks of the pretty Avonmore River near the small town of Rathdrum. It has 100 pitches arranged around a boating pond. The pitches are mostly concrete hardstandings with a few on grass. All have safe 16A electricity hook-ups and close access to a water tap and waste drainage. Across a fine footbridge is a large, flat area for tents – most of them used by families at holiday time. Spring 2010 saw major landscaping work on what must now be regarded as one of the best camping park play areas in Ireland.

### Facilities

Well equipped and very modern toilet block finished in local slate. Facilities for campers with disabilities. Motorcaravan service point. Laundry. Dishwashing and hobs for cooking. Small shop. Takeaway. Fishing in the river may be arranged. Impressive play park. Canoes and boats for hire on lake. Bicycle hire. Log cabins for rent. Off site: Golf and riding within 5 miles. Beach within 15 miles. Thomas Moore's Meeting of the Waters, the pretty town of Avoca (now better known as Ballykissangel) and Powerscourt House are within easy reach.

Open: 1 April – 30 September.

### Directions

Leave M11 at junction signed Rathnew. From this village follow signs for Rathdrum (c.15 mins). Over the bridge approaching Rathdrum turn right immediately at large new apartment building. Take care over speed humps for 100 m. Park gate is on the right. GPS: 52.938693, -6.22898

### Charges guide

| | |
|---|---|
| Per unit incl. 2 persons and electricity | € 25,00 - € 27,00 |
| extra person | € 6,00 |
| child/young person (2-25 yrs) | € 4,00 |

## Redcross Village
River Valley Caravan & Camping Park
Redcross Village (Co. Wicklow) T: 040 441 647. E: info@rivervalleypark.com
alanrogers.com/IR9150

In the small country village of Redcross, in the heart of County Wicklow, you will find this popular, family run park. Based here you are within easy reach of beauty spots such as the Vale of Avoca (Ballykissangel), Glendalough and Powerscourt, plus the safe beach of Brittas Bay. The 145 touring pitches at River Valley are mostly together in a dedicated area, all have electricity connections (6A) and offer a choice of hardstanding or grass – you select your pitch. There is a new, hardstanding area for adults only, with its own amenity block and where dogs are allowed. A late arrivals area has electricity hook-ups, water and night lighting.

### Facilities
A luxurious new sanitary block is modern and well designed. Excellent facilities for disabled visitors. Showers are on payment (€ 1). Laundry area. Campers' kitchen. Motorcaravan service points. Gas supplies. Wine/coffee bar and restaurant (1/6-31/8). TV and games room. Three tennis courts. Par 3 golf course. Beer garden with children's entertainment (July/Aug). Sports complex. Playgrounds. Caravan storage. Dogs are not accepted in July/Aug. in the family area. Off site: Riding 2 km.

Open: 12 March - 1 November.

### Directions
From Dublin follow N11 Wexford road south, bypassing Ashford and Rathnew. After passing The Beehive pub look out for Doyle's pub on the right. Turn right at the pub, then 5 km. to the park at the top of Redcross village. GPS: 52.8884, -6.14528

### Charges guide
| Per unit incl. 2 persons | |
|---|---|
| and electricity | € 25,00 - € 27,00 |
| extra person | € 6,00 |
| child (2-15 yrs) | € 4,00 |

## Roscrea
Streamstown Caravan & Camping Park
Streamstown, Roscrea (Co. Tipperary) T: 050 521 519. E: streamstowncaravanpark@eircom.net
alanrogers.com/IR9420

This family run site, set on a dairy farm in the centre of Ireland, has been open for over 30 years. It is conveniently situated off the M7 Dublin - Limerick road and makes a good overnight halt or for a longer stay if you are seeking a quiet, restful location with little to disturb the peace. There are 27 touring pitches, ten with hardstanding and separated by low hedges. The remainder are on grass and more suitable for units with awnings. This is a working farm and the owners, who are friendly and welcoming, have made some attractive improvements. What impresses most here, as well as the tidy overall appearance with neatly trimmed hedging, is the simplicity - no 'bells or whistles'.

### Facilities
The sanitary facilities, very clean when we visited, are housed in a modern block. Showers (free), toilets and washbasins (two washbasins are in cubicles). Facilities for disabled visitors in family shower room. Good laundry room. Good campers' kitchen. Small play area. TV, pool table and games room. Caravan storage. Accommodation to rent. A torch would be useful. Off site: Fishing 1.5 km. Golf 5 km. Riding 8 km.

Open: Easter - 1 October.

### Directions
Leave M7 by Roscrea exit. From Roscrea follow signs for R491 Shinrone. Continue towards Shinrone following site signs for about 2.5 km. and site entrance is on left. GPS: 52.95720, -7.83937

### Charges guide
| Per unit incl. 2 persons and electricity | € 24,00 |
|---|---|
| extra person | € 4,50 |
| child (under 14 yrs) | € 2,00 |

## Rosses Point
Greenlands Caravan & Camping Park
Rosses Point (Co. Sligo) T: 071 917 7113. E: noelineha@eircom.net
alanrogers.com/IR8690

Just off the N15 road and 8 km. from Sligo town, this is a well run park at Rosses Point, in the sand hills adjoining a championship golf course. It is thoughtfully laid out with small tents placed to the front of reception and the hardstanding touring pitches separated from the trailer tent pitches which occupy the rear. The ground is undulating and adds interest to the overall appearance. Your view depends on where you are pitched – look towards Coney Island and the Blackrock lighthouse which guards the bay, take in the sight of Benbulben Mountain or appreciate the seascape and the resort's two beaches.

### Facilities
Modern toilet facilities, recently extended and refitted, are kept exceptionally clean, with hot showers (€ 1 token). Washing machine, dryer and iron. Motorcaravan service point. Campers' kitchen. TV room beside reception. Play area and sand pit for children. Outdoor chess and draughts sets. Off site: Shop, restaurant and evening entertainment in the village. Fishing and boat launching 100 m. Golf 50 m. Bicycle hire 8 km. Riding 14 km.

Open: 30 April - 14 September.

### Directions
From Sligo city travel about 800 m. north on the N15 road, turn left onto R291 signed Rosses Point. Continue for 6.5 km. and park is on right after village. GPS: 54.30628, -8.56889

### Charges guide
| Per unit incl. 2 persons | € 19,00 - € 21,00 |
|---|---|
| extra person | € 5,00 |
| child | € 3,00 |
| electricity (10A) | € 4,00 |

## Rosslare

### Saint Margaret's Beach Caravan & Camping Park

Lady's Island, Rosslare Harbour (Co. Wexford) T: 053 913 1169. E: info@campingstmargarets.ie

alanrogers.com/IR9170

'This park is loved', was how a Swedish visitor described this family-run, environmentally-friendly caravan and camping park, the first the visitor meets near the Rosslare ferry port. Landscaping with flowering containers and maze-like sheltered camping areas and a pretty sanitary block all demonstrate the Traynor family's attention to detail. Most pitches give shelter from the fresh sea breeze and ferries can be seen crossing the Irish sea. Just metres away, the safe, sandy beach (part of the Wexford coastal path) curves around in a horseshoe shape ending in a small pier and slipway. Tourist information on the area is provided in the well stocked shop. The immediate area boasts of thatched roof cottages and cottage gardens. The park is an ideal base from which to explore the sunny southeast or as an overnight stop to prepare for touring Ireland or for departure. Local lakes and the Saltee Islands, various locations of ornithological interest, deep sea and shore fishing, and award-winning pubs and restaurants provide something for everyone.

### Facilities

The toilet block is spotless. Laundry room. Campers' kitchen including toaster, microwave and TV. Shop (June-Aug). Fresh milk and bread daily. Mobile homes for rent. Sun/TV room. Off site: Walking, beach and fishing. Boat slipway 2.5 km. Pitch and putt 2 km. Riding 6 km. Pubs and restaurants. The JFK Arboretum, Johnstown Castle and Gardens, the Irish National Heritage Park, Kilmore Quay and Marina, and Curracloe beach (featured in the film 'Saving Private Ryan').

Open: Mid March - 31 October.

### Directions

From the N25 south of Wexford town, outside village of Tagoat, follow signs for Lady's Island and Carne. After 3 km. pass Butlers Bar and take next left and continue for 2.5 km. Site is well signed.
GPS: 52.206433, -6.356417

### Charges 2011

| | |
|---|---|
| Per unit incl. 2 persons and electricity | € 20,00 - € 22,00 |
| extra person | € 2,50 |
| child (2-16 yrs) | € 1,50 |

## Roundwood

### Roundwood Caravan & Camping Park

Roundwood (Co. Wicklow) T: 012 818 163. E: info@dublinwicklowcamping.com

alanrogers.com/IR9130

In the heart of the Wicklow mountains, the hospitable owner of this park maintains high standards. It is neatly laid out with rows of trees dividing the different areas and giving an attractive appearance. There are 46 hardstanding pitches for caravans and motorcaravans, all with electricity (6A), plus 33 pitches for tents, arranged off tarmac access roads. There are excellent walks around the Varty Lakes and a daily bus service to Dublin city. Close by are the Wicklow Mountains and the Sally Gap, Glendalough, Powerscourt Gardens, plus many other places of natural beauty. Apart from its scenic location, this site is well placed for the ferry ports.

### Facilities

The renovated sanitary block is kept clean, with adequate washing and toilet facilities, plus spacious showers on payment (€ 1). Good laundry facilities, but ask at reception as machines are not self-service. Motorcaravan service point. Campers' kitchen and dining room. TV room. Adventure playground. WiFi. Off site: Roundwood village has shops, pubs, restaurants, takeaway food, and a Sunday market. Fishing within 1 km. Riding, golf 3 km. Bicycle hire 3 km.

Open: 29 April - 31 August.

### Directions

Turn off N11 Dublin - Wexford road at Kilmacanogue towards Glendalough and then 15 km. to Roundwood. Park is on the north side of the village.
GPS: 53.06924, -6.22269

### Charges 2011

| | |
|---|---|
| Per unit incl. 2 persons and electricity | € 28,00 - € 30,00 |
| extra person | € 8,00 - € 9,00 |
| child (under 14 yrs) | € 4,00 |
| dog | free |

No credit cards.

For latest campsite news visit
**alanrogers.com**

## Skibbereen

### The Hideaway Camping & Caravan Park

Skibbereen (Co. Cork) T: 028 222 54. E: skibbereencamping@eircom.net

alanrogers.com/IR9505

A sister park to The Meadow at Glandore, the Hideaway is ideally situated as a touring base for the West Cork region. It is a well run site under the constant supervision of the owners and although it enjoys tranquil surroundings, including preserved marshland, it is only ten minutes walk from the busy market town of Skibbereen. The Hideaway is a two-hectare, touring only park with 60 pitches, including 50 with hardstanding and 6A electric hook-up. The remainder are for tents. Shrubs and low hedges divide the park giving an open feel overall and commanding views across the fields and hills. One long building houses reception, the toilet facilities and a games room.

**Facilities**

The modern toilet block has non slip floors, well equipped showers (on payment). Baby room with bath. En-suite unit for disabled visitors. Laundry. Campers' dining room. Motorcaravan service point. Adventure play area. WiFi (charged). Off site: Fishing 1.6 km. Golf 2 km. Riding 4 km. Bicycle hire 1 km. Interesting towns of Skibbereen, Rosscarbery and Clonakilty.

Open: Easter - 15 September.

**Directions**

From Skibbereen town centre take R596 (signed Casteltownsend). Site is on the left after 1 km. GPS: 51.54167, -9.26008

**Charges guide**

| | |
|---|---|
| Per unit incl. 2 persons and electricity | € 23,00 |
| extra person | € 6,00 |
| child (under 16 yrs) | € 3,00 |

No credit cards.

## Strandhill

### Strandhill Caravan & Camping Park

Strandhill (Co. Sligo) T: 071 916 8111. E: strandhillcvp@eircom.net

alanrogers.com/IR8695

This seaside park is located on 20 acres of undulating grass with a sandy base with natural protection from the onshore breezes of the famous Strandhill beach. There are 55 hardstanding pitches for caravans and motorcaravans, with electricity and ample water points, and two camping areas for tents, one with views of the sea and the second more sheltered. Throughout the site many hollows provide ideal pitches for tents. Strandhill, world recognised as a surfing Mecca, also provides activities for all the family. There are miles of sandy beach and the Knocknarea Mountain provides walkers with choice.

**Facilities**

The toilet block (keys provided on deposit) is clean and fresh with hot showers (token €1.50), electric hand dryers and hairdryer. New reception building, including tv room, games room, campers kitchen, laundry and full disabled facility. Automatic gate and door control. Off site: Public transport from village. Shops, restaurants, takeaway, pubs and ATM are just beyond the park's boundary in the village. Strandhill golf course 500 m. Riding 2 km. Swimming pool and sports centre in Sligo 8 km.

Open: 14 April - 28 September.

**Directions**

Strandhill is 8 km. west of Sligo city on the R292. Site is on the airport road. GPS: 54.27242, -8.60448

**Charges guide**

| | |
|---|---|
| Per unit incl. 2 persons | € 20,00 |
| plus 2 children | € 22,00 |
| electricity (10A) | € 4,00 |
| extra person | € 3,00 - € 5,00 |

## Timoleague

### Sextons Caravan and Camping Park

R600 Timoleague/Clonakility Road, Bandon (Co. Cork) T: 023 8846347. E: info.sextons@gmail.com

alanrogers.com/IR9490

Sexton's is an unpretentious 2-star site that has been in existence for over forty years. At the time of writing the owners were proud of their recently-completed reception, allowing the old shop area to be converted into a comfortable lounge area for campers. They are also very confident that their plans to convert a part of the laundry into an en-suite facility for use by campers with disabilities will ensure their upgrading to 3-star status. The 2.5-hectare park contains 50 pitches for touring vans and tents, 30 of these on gravel hardstanding and the remainder on well kept lawn grass. Although conveniently situated for the Cork Ferry Terminal, Sexton's is situated on a quiet road between Clonakilty and Timoleague.

**Facilities**

Two small toilet blocks with free showers are in old farm buildings. Small shop (1/5-30/9). Gas. Small but comfortable camp kitchen with local TV. Sitting Room for campers. Laundry. Internet and WiFi (charged). Small playground, football field and games room. Bicycle hire can be arranged. Off site: Beaches, riding, boat launching, fishing and golf, all within 6 km.

Open: 15 March - 30 September.

**Directions**

N71 into Clonakilty, then follow R600 towards Timoleague for approx. 5 km. – site on right. Look for John Wayne statue guarding the entrance. GPS: 51.635006, -8.800821

**Charges year**

| | |
|---|---|
| Per unit incl. 2 persons and electricity | € 25,00 |
| extra person | € 3,00 - € 5,00 |

No credit cards.

For latest campsite news visit

# alanrogers.com

# Tipperary

## The Glen of Aherlow Caravan & Camping Park

Newtown, Glen of Aherlow (Co. Tipperary) T: 062 565 55. E: rdrew@eircom.net
alanrogers.com/IR9400

The owners of one of Ireland's newest parks, George and Rosaline Drew, are campers themselves and have set about creating an idyllic park in an idyllic location. This three-hectare park is set in one of Ireland's most picturesque valleys and is open all year. There are beautiful views of the wooded and hilly areas of Slievenamuck and the Galtee Mountains. There are 42 large and level touring pitches, with both hardstanding and grass places, each pair sharing a double hook-up 10A post and water point. The Drew family is happy to welcome large groups and rallies, and large units can be accommodated. The new stone-built reception, shop and coffee bar beside the gate should now be complete. The excellent facilities are located in a purpose-built toilet block. This area is an outdoor paradise with a nearby nature park and forest trails, with a 6 km. walk starting at the park entrance, and a popular retreat for adults looking for a relaxing haven. With a local pub and a restaurant just 300 m. away, this is an excellent base from which to tour attractions such as the Rock of Cashel, Cahir Castle, Holycross Abbey and many more.

### Facilities

The modern toilet block includes free showers and facilities for disabled visitors. Motorcaravan service point. Laundry room with ironing. Campers' kitchen. Recreation and TV rooms. Shop, bicycle hire and Internet café planned for 2011. Off site: Holiday homes to rent 300 m. Restaurant nearby. Outdoor activities. Fishing in Aherlow River. Golf and riding 7 km.

Open: All year.

### Directions

From Tipperary town take N24 to Bansha, then R663 to Newtown. Continue through village and pass Coach Road Inn to park in 300 m. GPS: 52.4161, -8.2105

### Charges guide

| | |
|---|---|
| Per unit incl. 2 persons and electricity | € 26,00 |
| extra person | € 6,00 |
| child (2-14 yrs) | € 5,00 |

# Tipperary

## Ballinacourty House Caravan & Camping Park

Glen of Aherlow, Tipperary (Co. Tipperary) T: 062 565 59. E: info@camping.ie
alanrogers.com/IR9370

Ballinacourty House and its cobble-stoned courtyard form the centrepiece of this south-facing park with views of the Galtee Mountains. Accessed by a tree-lined lane, the reception area is in part of the renovated 18th-century building, as is the adjoining restaurant. The park is level with 26 touring pitches with 6A electricity and 19 grassy pitches for tents. Some areas are shaded and there are open spaces to accommodate rallies and larger groups. Self-catering cottages and B&B are also available. This tranquil site is very appealing to families with young children. It is an excellent base from which to tour the Rock of Cashel, the Mitchelstown Caves, Swiss Cottage and the towns of Tipperary, Cahir and Cashel. The management has recently begun to keep farm animals in an enclosed part of the park and intends to enhance the estate's entire old walled garden. Activities in the area include horse riding and trekking, fishing for perch and brown trout, cycling, forest walks, three 18-hole golf courses, leisure centre with swimming pool, cinema theatre and pottery shop.

### Facilities

Sanitary facilities provide free hot water and showers. Baby room. Laundry with ironing facilities. Campers' kitchen. Ice pack freezing. Licensed restaurant (early booking advised). Motorcaravan services. Gas supplies. Frisbee golf. TV and games rooms. Picnic benches. Tennis. Play area. Off site: Riding, fishing, golf within 8 km.

Open: Easter - last Sunday in September.

### Directions

Follow the N24 from Tipperary or Cahir to Bansha. Turn on to R663 for about 7 miles, passing Glen Hotel after 6 miles. Follow signs for Ballinacourty House. GPS: 52.41614, -8.21047

### Charges guide

| | |
|---|---|
| Per unit incl. 2 persons and electricity | € 22,00 - € 24,00 |
| extra person | € 5,00 |
| child | € 4,00 |

## Tralee

### Woodlands Park Touring Caravan & Camping Park

Dan Spring Road, Tralee (Co. Kerry) T: 066 712 1235. E: wdlands@eircom.net

alanrogers.com/IR9650

This family-run park is located in the heart of Kerry, on the gateway to the Dingle peninsula and just north of the Ring of Kerry and Killarney. Woodlands is an ideal base, only ten minutes' walk from Tralee town centre via the town park and famous rose garden. Located on a 16-acre elevated site approached by a short road and a bridge that straddles the River Lee; once on site the town seems far removed with a countryside environment taking over. Hedging, trees, grazing fields and the distant Slieve Mish Mountain create the setting. There are 135 pitches including 85 'super' pitches with hardstanding, electricity, water and drainage and a grass area. The park has a landscaped entrance, tropical shrubs, cordyline palms and flower beds have been planted around the park. The owners of Woodlands have designed and equipped their park to a high standard including a clubhouse. The town park is home to the Kerry County Museum and the National folk theatre of Ireland with nightly performances. In addition to the river, there is a canal bank walk to Blennerville village and its famous windmill.

#### Facilities

Excellent, heated sanitary facilities include sizeable showers (€ 1 token) and provision for disabled guests. Campers' kitchen. Laundry room with washing machines and dryer. Gas for sale. Motorcaravan service point. Club house with café/snack bar. Shop. Games room. TV and adult only room. Internet and WiFi access. Fenced adventure play area. Public telephone on site. Off site: The nearby Aqua Dome offers half price admission after 18.00. Golf 6 km. Riding 2 km. Blue Flag beaches on the Dingle Peninsula. Sailing 10 km.

Open: Easter - 30 September.

#### Directions

Site is 1 km. southwest of Tralee town centre. From N21/N69/N86 junction south of Tralee follow site signs for 2.4 km. to park, 200 m. off the N86 Tralee - Dingle road. Site is 300 m. east of the Aqua Dome GPS: 52.26157, -9.70338

#### Charges guide

| | |
|---|---|
| Per unit incl. 2 persons and electricity | € 21,00 - € 24,00 |
| extra person | € 6,00 |
| child (under 16 yrs) | € 3,00 |

## Tramore

### Newtown Cove Camping & Caravan Park

Newtown Road, Tramore (Co. Waterford) T: 051 381 979. E: info@newtowncove.com

alanrogers.com/IR9340

Well run and friendly, this very attractive small park is only five minutes walk from the beautiful Newton Cove. It offers views of the famous and historic Metal Man and is 2.5 km. from Tramore beach and 11 km. from Waterford. Neatly set out on gently sloping grass are 40 pitches, with an abundance of shrubs and bushes reflecting the efforts of the owners. All pitches have 10A electrical connections, some with hardstanding also, and access is by well lit, tarmac roads. There are around 50 privately owned caravan holiday homes. A modern building at the entrance houses reception, the amenities and additional sanitary facilities. The busy holiday resort of Tramore, with a wide range of shops and eating houses, is close and there is a choice of many delightful cliff walks in the immediate vicinity. The historic town of Waterford has many interesting attractions including a very new Waterford Crystal Centre. The Copper Coast towards Dungarvan is very reminiscent of Cornwall, although the ore being mined was copper rather than tin.

#### Facilities

The main sanitary block at the bottom end of the site provides good, clean facilities including a bathroom. Showers on payment (token from reception). Excellent motorcaravan services. Campers' kitchen with cooking facilities, sheltered eating area, lounge and small laundry. Small shop (1/7-30/8). TV room. Games room. Small play area. Off site: Beach 400 m. Fishing 400 m. Golf 800 m. Riding 3 km.

Open: Easter - 25 September.

#### Directions

From Tramore on R675 coast road to Dungarvan. Turn left 2 km. from town centre, following signs. GPS: 52.14763, -7.17274

#### Charges guide

| | |
|---|---|
| Per unit incl. 2 persons and electricity | € 24,00 - € 29,00 |
| extra person | € 6,00 |
| child (3-15 yrs) | € 3,00 |
| hiker, cyclist or motorcyclist | € 8,00 - € 11,00 |

No single sex groups.

For latest campsite news visit
**alanrogers.com**

## Tuosist

### Beara Camping The Peacock

Coornagillagh, Tuosist, Post Killarney (Co. Kerry) T: 064 66842 87. E: bearacamping@eircom.net

alanrogers.com/IR9580

Five minutes from Kenmare Bay, The Peacock is a unique location for campers who appreciate the natural world, where disturbance to nature is kept to a minimum. This five-acre site offers simple, clean and imaginative camping facilities. Located on the Ring of Beara, bordering the counties of Cork and Kerry, visitors will be treated with hospitality by a Dutch couple, Bert and Klaske van Bavel, almost more Irish than the Irish, who have made Ireland their home and run the site with their family. The variety of accommodation at Beara Camping includes a hostel, caravan holiday homes, secluded hardstanding pitches with electricity and level grass areas for tenting. In addition, there are cabins sleeping two or four people and hiker huts sleeping two, ideal to avoid a damp night or to dry out. Bert and Klaske love to share with visitors the unspoiled natural terrain, its wildlife, the sheltered community campfire and advice on the walking and hiking routes in the area. The homely restaurant, displaying Bert's own acrylic paintings, boasts appetising and homemade food including breakfast with fresh bread each morning. Nearby are the Ring of Beara, stone circles, the Healy Pass, Ardea Castle, Derreen Gardens and the fishing town of Castletownbere.

#### Facilities

Three small blocks, plus facilities at the restaurant provide toilets, washbasins and free hot showers. Laundry service for a small fee. Campers' kitchens and sheltered eating area. Restaurant and takeaway (May-Oct). Pets are not permitted in rental accommodation or tents. Off site: Public transport from the gate in summer months. Pub and shop 900 m. Riding 6 km. Golf 12 km. Boating, fishing and sea angling 200 m. Beach (pebble) 500 m.

Open: 1 April - 31 December.

#### Directions

From the A22, 17 km. east of Killarney, take the R569 south to Kenmare. In Kenmare take the R571, Castletownbere road and site is 12 km. GPS: 51.8279, -9.7356

#### Charges guide

| | |
|---|---|
| Per unit incl. 2 persons and electricity | € 23,00 |
| extra person | € 3,50 |
| child (0-10 yrs) | € 2,00 |

---

## Westport

### Westport House Caravan and Camping Park

Westport House Country Park, Westport (Co. Mayo) T: 098 277 66. E: camping@westporthouse.ie

alanrogers.com/IR8770

Located in the grounds of an elegant country estate, this is a popular park. From Westport Quay, you enter the grounds of the estate by way of a tree lined road that crosses the river and leads to the site. In an attractive, sheltered area of the parkland, set in the trees, are 155 pitches. There are 65 with hardstanding and 76 electric hook-ups. Early in the season the site may not be fully prepared, and only minimal facilities may be available. There is the choice of a 'pitch only' booking, or a 'special deal' (min. stay three nights). This includes free admission to Westport House and many of the activities of the adjoining leisure park. There is a children's animal and bird park, boating and fishing on the lake and river, pitch and putt, 'slippery dip', ball pond and 'supabounce', a play adventure world, hillside train rides and a flume ride. Stay one week or more and all the above are free, plus tennis, a par 3 golf course and 20% discount on bar food in the Horse and Wagon bar on the site. Westport is an attractive town with splendid Georgian houses and traditional shop fronts. There are many good restaurants and pubs.

#### Facilities

Toilet facilities are provided at various points on the site, plus a 'super-loo' located in the farmyard buildings. Facilities for disabled visitors. Laundry facilities. Fifties style function room and bar with food and musical entertainment (all 1/6-31/8). Fishing. Tennis. Westport House and Country Park. Off site: Within 5 km. of the estate are an 18-hole golf course and deep sea angling on Clew Bay.

Open: 26 March - 15 September.

#### Directions

Take R335 Westport - Louisburgh road and follow signs for Westport Quay, then turn in through gates of Westport House and continue through estate following signs for camping. GPS: 53.8053, -9.5395

#### Charges guide

| | |
|---|---|
| Per unit incl. 2 persons and electricity | € 28,00 - € 33,00 |
| hiker or cyclist | € 25,00 - € 27,50 |
| Family weekend rates in June. | |

A visit to the Channel Islands offers a holida in part of the British Isles, yet in an area w. has a definite continent flavour. All the islands ha beautiful beaches and coves, pretty scenery and fascinating histories.

**THE CHANNEL ISLANDS ARE MADE UP OF THE ISLANDS OF: JERSEY, GUERNSEY, SARK, HERM AND ALDERNEY**

The largest of the Channel Islands is Jersey, which is also the most commercial with more entertainment on offer. It has long stretches of safe beaches for swimming and water-based activities such as windsurfing and banana rides. Caravans and motorcaravans are allowed on Jersey, but with a number of limitations (for example, length of stay, width and length of the unit). A permit is required which is obtained as part of the booking procedure with the campsite of your choice. You must book in advance but the campsite owner will advise you on all aspects of your visit.

Guernsey will suit those who prefer a quieter, more peaceful holiday. Caravans and motorcaravans are not allowed here. Guernsey too has wide, sandy beaches plus sheltered coves. The historic, harbour town of St Peter Port has steep and winding cobbled streets, with plenty of shops, cafes and restaurants.

For those who want total relaxation, one of the smaller islands – Sark or Herm, would be ideal. No cars are permitted on either of these islands. Explore on foot, by cycle or horse-drawn carriage.

Shopping on all the islands has the advantage of no VAT – particularly useful when buying cameras, watches or alcohol.

**Places of interest**

*Jersey:* St Helier; Jersey Zoo; Jersey War tunnels; Elizabeth Castle; German Underground Hospital in St Lawrence; Samarès Manor in St Clement; Shell Garden at St Aubin; Battle of Flowers Museum in St Ouen.

*Guernsey:* Castle Cornet at St Peter Port Harbour; Victor Hugo's House; Guernsey Folk Museum; German Occupation Museum; Fort Grey Shipwreck Museum; Saumarez Park.

*Sark:* La Coupée; La Seigneurie, with old dovecote and gardens; Gouliet and Boutique Caves; Le Pot on Little Sark; Venus Pool; Little Sark Village.

*Herm:* This tiny island has beautiful, quiet, golden beaches and a little harbour village and hotel. Arrive by ferry from Guernsey for a wonderful day out.

**Did you know?**

Jersey has been associated with knitting for nearly 400 years.

The Channel Islands were the only part of the British Isles to be occupied by the Germans during the Second World War.

Herm island is just one and a half miles long and only half a mile wide.

Le Jerriais is the native language of Jersey, a blend of Norse and Norman French.

**Note:** The reciprocal health services agreement between the British Government and the Channel Islands ended in April 2009. The EHIC card does not cover emergency health care as the Channel Islands are not part of the EU. Travel insurance is now essential.

## Castel

### Fauxquets Valley Campsite

Candie Road, Castel, Guernsey GY5 7QL T: 01481 255460. E: info@fauxquets.co.uk

alanrogers.com/UK9780

Situated in the rural centre of the island, Fauxquets is in a pretty sheltered valley, hidden down narrow lanes away from busy roads and is run by the Guille family. It was once a dairy farm, but the valley side has now been developed into an attractive campsite, with the old farm buildings as its centre. Plenty of trees, bushes and flowers have been planted to separate pitches and to provide shelter around the various fields which are well terraced. The 86 touring pitches are of a good size, most marked, numbered and with electricity, and there is lots of open space. There are also 15 smaller places for backpackers. The site has 23 fully equipped tents for hire, but there are no tour operators. The Haybarn licensed restaurant and bar provides breakfast, morning coffee and cake and evening meals. There is plenty of room to sit around the heated swimming pool, including a large grassy terrace with sun beds provided. A car would be useful here to reach the beaches, St Peter Port and other attractions, although there is a bus service each day (20 minutes walk).

### Facilities

Good toilet facilities have controllable showers, some washbasins in private cabins with a shower, baby bath and changing unit. Dishwashing facilities under cover and a tap for free hot water. Laundry room with free irons, boards and hairdryers. Heated swimming pool (20x45 ft.) with paddling pool. Restaurant and bar (25/6-7/9). Small shop with ice-pack hire and gas. TV room. Table football and table tennis. Small play area and play field. Bicycle hire. Torches useful. Off site: Riding and golf 2 miles. Fishing, sailing and boat launching 3 miles.

Open: April - 15 September.

### Directions

From harbour take second exit from roundabout. At top of hill, turn left at 'filter in turn' into Queens Road, then right at next filter. Follow straight through traffic lights and down hill past hospital, through pedestrian lights and straight on at next lights at top of hill. Continue for 0.75 miles, then turn right opposite sign for German Hospital. Fourth left is pedestrian entrance, cars carry on for 400 yds to gravel entrance on left. GPS: 49.46812, -2.58843

### Charges guide

| | |
|---|---|
| Per person | £ 7.00 - £ 9.00 |
| child (at school) | £ 3.50 - £ 4.70 |
| electricity (6A) | £ 3.00 |

Fully equipped tents with fridge for hire.

## Herm Island

### Seagull Campsite

The Administration Office, Herm Island GY1 3HR T: 01481 722377. E: camping@herm-island.com

alanrogers.com/UK9830

This tiny site, and indeed the island of Herm, will appeal to those who are looking for complete tranquillity and calm. Reached by boat (20 minutes and about £8.50 return fare for adults, £4.25 for children) from Guernsey, the 300 acre island allows no cars only tractors on its narrow roads and paths (no bicycles either). The campsite is a 20 minute uphill walk from the harbour, but your luggage will be transported for you by tractor. It consists of several terraced areas offering a total of 90 pitches, and 26 fully equipped tents for hire on flat grass areas. There are no electricity hook-ups. One may bring one's own tent and equipment or hire both (but not bedding, crockery and lighting) from the site. One is free to stroll around the many paths, through farmland, heath and around the coast, where there are beautiful beaches. Herm is definitely not for those who like entertainment and plenty of facilities, but for total relaxation, with the absence of any bustle and noise it takes some beating! Due to the stony footpaths on Herm, sensible walking shoes are advised.

### Facilities

Small, modern, but open, toilet block. Hot showers (£1 payment – there is a shortage of water on Herm). Laundry facility and small kitchen. Freezer for ice-packs. No dogs or pets are allowed. Torches useful. Off site: The harbour village is about ten minutes walk for small shop, gas, a post office, pub, restaurants and café. Fishing on the island.

Open: May - first w/end in September.

### Directions

Reached by boat from St Peter Port - report to Administration Office on arrival. Do not take your car as it is unlikely you will be able to park long term in St Peter Port. GPS: 49.47665, -2.45665

### Charges guide

| | |
|---|---|
| Per person | £ 6.30 |
| child (under 14 yrs) | £ 3.15 |
| transportation of luggage | £ 7.50 |

Equipped tents for hire.
Groups of single people not accepted.

## Saint Martin

### Beuvelande Camp Site

Beuvelande, Saint Martin, Jersey JE3 6EZ T: 01534 853575. E: info@campingjersey.com

alanrogers.com/UK9720

What a pleasant surprise we had when we called here – the outstanding sanitary building gives campers facilities often associated with top class hotels. A licensed restaurant with covered terrace area is also situated in this building, open morning and evening all season, but perhaps a few less hours at quiet times. There are 150 pitches, 60 with fully equipped tents for hire, but with plenty of space for those with their own. Cars may be parked next to your tent. 100 pitches have electric hook ups (5/10A). Torches would be useful. Car and bicycle hire can be arranged. This family run park prides itself on quality, cleanliness and hospitality.

### Facilities

The toilet block is tiled top to bottom and spotlessly clean, with controllable showers, two fully equipped bathrooms for disabled visitors, and a baby room. Laundry. Games room with arcade games and pool. TV room. Well stocked shop open 08.00-19.00 during peak times and stocks gas. Licensed restaurant. Ice pack and battery charging services for a small charge. Outdoor heated swimming pool (41x17 ft) with small waterslide. Play area and large playing field. Evening entertainment. Off site: Beach and sailing 1.5 miles. Fishing, golf and riding within 2 miles.

Open: 1 April - 30 September.

### Directions

On leaving the harbour by Route du Port Elizabeth, take A1 east through the tunnel and the A17. At the fourth set of traffic lights turn left on A6. Continue to Five Oaks and on to St Martin's RC church, then right into La Longue Rue, right again Rue de L'Orme then left to site. GPS: 49.21294, -2.05615

### Charges guide

| | |
|---|---|
| Per person | £ 6.00 - £ 9.00 |
| child (2-14 yrs) | £ 6.00 |

Single sex groups not accepted.

## Sark

### Pomme de Chien Campsite

Sark GY9 OSB T: 01481 832316. E: rangjill@hotmail.com

alanrogers.com/UK9870

The island where 'time stands still' is an apt description of Sark, one of the smallest inhabited Channel Islands, some 45 minutes from Guernsey by boat. Situated five minutes from the shops and ten from the beach, the Pomme de Chien campsite is small with only 50 pitches, of which eight are occupied by fully equipped tents for rent. The remainder are for campers with their own tents (no caravans, motorhomes or trailer tents of course). The pitches are large, on fairly level ground, but none have electricity. There is a warm welcome from the owners Chris and Jill Rang with the famous charm of Sark. Although you cannot take your car to the island, the Condor service via Guernsey means you can get there in a little over three hours either with your own small tent or of course you could hire some of the site's own (equipment includes everything you're likely to need except bedding and a torch). There is no airport, no cars or motorcycles and (apart from a tractor-drawn land-train up Harbour Hill) the only transport is by bicycle (which must be hired on the island) or horse-drawn carriage. However, all you are likely to need for a tranquil holiday is provided with several small shops, pubs, hotels, restaurants, a Tourist Office and even two banks!

### Facilities

Modern sanitary block with free hot showers (large, with bench and hook), toilets and washbasins. Dishwashing sinks are outside. Outside washing line. Dogs are not accepted. Torches are necessary. Baggage can be transferred from the harbour to the site by tractor trailer, at a cost of £1 per item. Off site: Bicycle hire 5 minutes. Beach and fishing 10 minutes walk.

Open: All year.

### Directions

Take the tractor drawn 'train' up Harbour Hill (you can walk but it is a ten minute hike). Once at the top take road leading off left, then second right, and follow the lane to the site entrance. Reception is at house with white gates. GPS: 49.43665, -2.36331

### Charges guide

| | |
|---|---|
| Per person | £ 7.50 |
| child | £ 5.00 |

No credit cards.

For latest campsite news visit
**alanrogers.com**

## Saint Martin

### Rozel Camping Park

Rozel, Saint Martin, Jersey JE3 6AX T: 01534 855200. E: rozelcampingpark@jerseymail.co.uk
alanrogers.com/UK9710

This family owned park is within walking distance of the famous Jersey Zoo and the pretty harbour and fishing village of Rozel, where the north coast cliff path commences. There are two main camping areas providing 130 pitches of which 120 have electric hook ups (10/16A) and 16 are used for fully equipped tents to hire. Some pitches, mainly for smaller tents are arranged on terraced areas. The remainder are on a higher, flat field where pitches are arranged in bays with hedges growing to separate them into groups. The site has provided easy access for caravans and motorcaravans, plus chemical and grey waste disposal facilities. In addition to package deals for tent hire and travel, the site offers a good range of camping equipment for hire on a daily basis. Boats are accepted by prior arrangement. The surrounding countryside is quieter than many areas of the island. A car is probably necessary to reach the main island beaches, although a bus service does run to St Helier from close by. The park itself is quietly situated at the top of a valley (the French coast can be seen on a clear day) and is surrounded by trees providing shelter.

### Facilities

Two first rate, heated sanitary buildings include a bathroom for disabled visitors with a shower, toilet and washbasin. Family shower room with small heater for cooler weather. Fully equipped laundry. Shop. Takeaway (peak season). Swimming pool (June-Sept) with children's pool and sunbathing areas. Play area. Crazy golf. Games room, reading and TV room. Torches useful. Bicycles for hire can be delivered to the site. Off site: Fishing 1 mile. Beach 2 miles. Riding 3 miles. Golf 4 miles.

Open: 21 May - 9 September.

### Directions

Leave harbour by Route du Port Elizabeth, take the A1 east through the tunnel and the A17. At fourth set of lights turn left on A6. Keep in the middle lane. Continue to Five Oaks and on to St Martin's church. Turn right, then immediately left at the Royal pub on B38 to Rozel, continue to end of road, turn right and park is on the right. GPS: 49.23841, -2.05058

### Charges guide

| | |
|---|---|
| Per person | £ 7.60 - £ 9.00 |
| child (4-11 yrs) | £ 3.80 - £ 4.50 |
| electricity | £ 1.80 |

Tent hire and travel packages.

## Saint Sampson's

### Vaugrat Camping

Route de Vaugrat, Saint Sampson's, Guernsey GY2 4TA T: 01481 257468. E: enquiries@vaugratcampsite.com
alanrogers.com/UK9770

Vaugrat Camping is a neat, well tended site, close to the beach in the northwest of the island. Owned and well run by the Laine family, it is centred around attractive and interesting old granite farm buildings dating back to the 15th century, with a gravel courtyard and attractive flower beds. It provides 150 pitches (six with electricity) on flat grassy meadows, that are mostly surrounded by trees, banks and hedges to provide shelter. Tents are arranged around the edges of the fields, giving open space in the centre, and while pitches are not marked, there is sufficient room and cars may be parked next to tents. Only couples and families are accepted. It also offers 30 fully equipped tents for hire. Housed in the old farmhouse, now a listed building, are the reception area, and shop where fresh croissants are baked every morning. Upstairs is the Coffee Barn with views to the sea, where breakfast is served; one can also sit here in the evenings. There are plans to include caravans and motorhomes subject to permission.

### Facilities

Well kept sanitary facilities are in two buildings. The first block is in the courtyard, with hot showers on payment. Unit for disabled visitors with shower, basin and toilet (although there is a 6 inch step into the building). Laundry facilities. Second block near the camping fields provides toilets, washbasins and dishwashing facilities. Shop with ice pack hire and gas (open at certain times by arrangement). Café serving breakfast only. Dogs are not accepted. Torches may be useful. Off site: Bus service within easy reach. Car or bicycle hire can be arranged. Fishing, riding and golf within 1.5 miles. Hotel and bar nearby.

Open: May - September.

### Directions

On leaving St Peter Port, turn right onto coast road for 1.5 miles. At filter turn left into Vale Road. Straight over at two sets of lights then first left turn by church. Follow to crossroads (garage opposite) turn right. Carry on past Peninsula Hotel, then second left, signed for site. Site on left after high stone wall (400 yds) with concealed entrance. GPS: 49.49584, -2.55433

### Charges guide

| | |
|---|---|
| Per person | £ 8.25 |
| child (under 14 yrs) | £ 6.50 |
| car | £ 1.50 |
| electricity | £ 5.00 |

Families and couples only.
Fully equipped tents to hire (details from site).

# Holiday Caravans and Chalets

Over recent years many of the campsites featured in this guide have added large numbers of high quality caravan holiday homes, chalets and lodges. Many park owners believe that some former caravanners and motorcaravanners have been enticed by the extra comfort this type of accommodation can now provide, and that maybe this is the ideal solution to combine the freedom of camping with all the comforts of home.

Quality is consistently high and, although the exact size and inventory will vary from park to park, if you choose any of the parks detailed here, you can be sure that you're staying in some of the best quality and best value caravan holiday homes or chalets available.

Home comforts are provided and typically these include a fridge with freezer compartment, gas hob, proper shower – often a microwave and CD player too, but do check for details. All caravan holiday homes and chalets come fully equipped with a good range of kitchen utensils, pots and pans, crockery, cutlery and outdoor furniture. Many even have an attractive wooden sundeck or paved terrace – a perfect spot for outdoors eating or relaxing with a book and watching the world go by. An efficient heating system is invariably included and some models may also incorporate air conditioning.

Regardless of model, colourful soft furnishings are the norm and a generally breezy décor helps to provide a real holiday feel.

Although some parks may have a large number of different accommodation types, we have restricted our choice to one or two of the most popular accommodation units (either caravan holiday homes or chalets) for each of the parks listed.

The caravan holiday homes here will be of modern design, and recent innovations such as pitched roofs undeniably improve their appearance.

Design will invariably include clever use of space and fittings/furniture to provide for comfortable holidays – usually light and airy, with big windows and patio-style doors, fully equipped kitchen areas, a shower room with shower, washbasin and WC, cleverly designed bedrooms and a comfortable lounge/dining area (often incorporating a sofa bed).

In general, modern campsite chalets incorporate all the best features of caravan holiday homes in a more traditional, wood-clad structure, sometimes with the advantage of an upper mezzanine floor for an additional bedroom.

Our selected parks offer a massive range of different types of caravan holiday home and chalet, and it would be impractical to inspect every single accommodation unit. Our selection criteria, therefore, primarily takes account of the quality standards of the campsite itself.

However, there are a couple of important ground rules:

- Featured caravan holiday homes must be no more than 5 years old.

- Chalets no more than 10 years old.

- All listed accommodation must, of course, fully conform with all applicable local, national and European safety legislation.

For each park we given details of the type, or types, of accommodation available to rent, but these details are necessarily quite brief. Sometimes internal layouts can differ quite substantially, particularly with regard to sleeping arrangements, where these include the flexible provision for 'extra persons' on sofa beds located in the living area.

These arrangements may vary from accommodation to accommodation, and if you're planning a holiday which includes more people than are catered for by the main bedrooms you should check exactly how the extra sleeping arrangements are to be provided!

## Charges

An indication of the tariff for each type of accommodation featured is also included, indicating the variance between the low and high season tariffs. However, given that many parks have a large and often complex range of pricing options, incorporating special deals and various discounts, the charges we mention should be taken to be just an indication. We strongly recommend therefore that you confirm the actual cost when making a booking.

We also strongly recommend that you check with the park, when booking, what (if anything) will be provided by way of bed linen, blankets, pillows etc. Again, in our experience, this can vary widely from park to park.

On every park a fully refundable deposit (usually between £100 and £250) is payable on arrival. There may also be an optional cleaning service for which a further charge is made. Other options may include sheet hire (typically £20 per unit) or baby pack hire (cot and high chair).

## UK0380 Wooda Farm Holiday Park

see report page 15

Poughill, Bude EX23 9HJ

| AR1 – CEDAR – Mobile Home | AR2 – BRAMBLES – Bungalow |
|---|---|
| **Sleeping:** 3 bedrooms, sleeps 6: 1 double, 4 singles, pillows and blankets provided | **Sleeping:** 4 bedrooms, sleeps 7: 2 doubles, 3 singles, pillows and blankets provided |
| **Living:** living/kitchen area, heating, TV, shower, seperate WC | **Living:** living/kitchen area, heating, TV, shower, seperate WC |
| **Eating:** fitted kitchen with hobs, oven, microwave, grill, fridge, freezer | **Eating:** fitted kitchen with hobs, oven, microwave, grill, dishwasher, fridge, freezer |
| **Outside:** table & chairs | **Outside:** table & chairs |
| **Pets:** not accepted | **Pets:** not accepted |

**Other** (AR1 and AR2): cot, highchair to hire

**Open:** 29 March - 31 October

| Weekly Charge | AR1 | AR2 |
|---|---|---|
| **Low Season** *(from)* | £ 300 | £ 350 |
| **High Season** *(from)* | £ 790 | £ 1100 |

## UK0970 Cofton Country Holidays

see report page 57

Starcross, Dawlish EX6 8RP

| AR1 – COACHING HOUSE – Bungalow | AR2 – TEIGN – Mobile Home |
|---|---|
| **Sleeping:** 3 bedrooms, sleeps 6: 1 double, 4 singles, pillows and blankets provided | **Sleeping:** 3 bedrooms, sleeps 8: 1 double, 4 singles, pillows and blankets provided |
| **Living:** living/kitchen area, heating, TV, shower, WC | **Living:** living/kitchen area, heating, TV, shower, WC |
| **Eating:** fitted kitchen with hobs, oven, microwave, grill, dishwasher, fridge, freezer | **Eating:** fitted kitchen with hobs, oven, microwave, grill, fridge |
| **Outside:** table & chairs | **Pets:** not accepted |
| **Pets:** not accepted | |

**Other** (AR1 and AR2): bed linen, cot, highchair to hire

**Open:** All year

| Weekly Charge | AR1 | AR2 |
|---|---|---|
| **Low Season** *(from)* | £ 330 | £ 280 |
| **High Season** *(from)* | £ 840 | £ 740 |

## UK1085 Golden Sands Holiday Park
Week Lane, Dawlish Warren EX7 0LZ

▶ see report page 58

| AR1 – BRONZE 2 BEDROOM – Mobile Home | AR2 – GOLD 3 BEDROOM – Mobile Home |
|---|---|
| Sleeping: 2 bedrooms, sleeps 6: 1 double, 2 singles, sofa bed | Sleeping: 3 bedrooms, sleeps 8: 1 double, 4 singles, sofa bed |
| Living: living/kitchen area, heating, TV, shower, WC | Living: living/kitchen area, heating, TV, shower, WC |
| Eating: fitted kitchen with hobs, oven, microwave, grill, fridge | Eating: fitted kitchen with hobs, oven, microwave, grill, fridge |
| Pets: not accepted | Pets: not accepted |

Other (AR1 and AR2): bed linen, cot, highchair to hire

Images for guideline purposes only, accommodation may vary by park

**Open:** 1 March - 31 October

| Weekly Charge | AR1 | AR2 |
|---|---|---|
| Low Season *(from)* | £ 194 | £ 305 |
| High Season *(from)* | £ 604 | £ 915 |

## UK1780 Freshwater Beach Holiday Park
Burton Bradstock, Bridport DT6 4PT

▶ see report page 85

| AR1 – BUDGET – Mobile Home | AR2 – SUPER DELUXE – Mobile Home |
|---|---|
| Sleeping: 3 bedrooms, sleeps 6: 1 double, 4 singles, pillows and blankets provided | Sleeping: 3 bedrooms, sleeps 6: 1 double, 4 singles, pillows and blankets provided |
| Living: living/kitchen area, heating, TV, shower, seperate WC | Living: living/kitchen area, heating, TV, shower, seperate WC |
| Eating: fitted kitchen with hobs, oven, grill, fridge, freezer | Eating: fitted kitchen with hobs, oven, microwave, grill, fridge, freezer |
| Outside: table & chairs | Outside: table & chairs |
| Pets: not accepted | Pets: not accepted |

**Open:** 18 March - 13 November

| Weekly Charge | AR1 | AR2 |
|---|---|---|
| Low Season *(from)* | £ 200 | £ 330 |
| High Season *(from)* | £ 650 | £ 920 |

## UK1575 Holiday Resort Unity

⊙ see report page 86

Coast Road, Brean Sands, Burnham-on-Sea TA8 2RB

| AR1 – VILLA DELUXE – Mobile Home | AR2 – LUXURY LODGE – Mobile Home |
|---|---|
| **Sleeping:** 3 bedrooms, sleeps 6: 1 double, 4 singles, pillows and blankets provided | **Sleeping:** 3 bedrooms, sleeps 6: 1 double, 4 singles, pillows and blankets provided |
| **Living:** living/kitchen area, heating, TV, shower, seperate WC | **Living:** living/kitchen area, heating, TV, shower, seperate WC |
| **Eating:** fitted kitchen with hobs, oven, microwave, grill, fridge, freezer | **Eating:** fitted kitchen with hobs, oven, microwave, grill, dishwasher, fridge, freezer |
| **Pets:** not accepted | **Outside:** table & chairs |
| | **Pets:** not accepted |

**Other** (AR1 and AR2): bed linen, cot, highchair to hire

**Open:** 1 February - 1 November

| Weekly Charge | AR1 | AR2 |
|---|---|---|
| Low Season *(from)* | £ 350 | £ 525 |
| High Season *(from)* | £ 756 | £ 1100 |

## UK2290 Sandy Balls Holiday Centre

⊙ see report page 110

Godshill, Fordingbridge SP6 2JZ

| AR1 – PINE LODGE ENSUITE – Chalet | AR2 – READY TENT – Tent |
|---|---|
| **Sleeping:** 3 bedrooms, sleeps 6: 1 double, 4 singles, pillows and blankets provided | **Sleeping:** 2 bedrooms, sleeps 6: 6 singles, pillows and blankets provided |
| **Living:** living/kitchen area, heating, TV, shower, WC | **Living:** living/kitchen area |
| | **Eating:** fitted kitchen with hobs, fridge |
| **Eating:** fitted kitchen with hobs, oven, microwave, grill, fridge, freezer | **Outside:** table & chairs |
| **Outside:** barbecue | **Pets:** not accepted |
| **Pets:** not accepted | |

**Other** (AR1 and AR2): bed linen, cot, highchair to hire

**Open:** All year

| Weekly Charge | AR1 | AR2 |
|---|---|---|
| Low Season *(from)* | £ 250 | £ 240 |
| High Season *(from)* | £ 1300 | £ 550 |

# UK2875 Chichester Lakeside Park

▶ see report page 133

Vinnetrow Road, Chichester PO20 1QH

| AR1 – GOLD – Mobile Home | AR2 – SILVER – Mobile Home |
|---|---|
| **Sleeping:** 3 bedrooms, sleeps 8: 1 double, 4 singles, sofa bed, pillows and blankets provided | **Sleeping:** 2 bedrooms, sleeps 6: 1 double, 2 singles, sofa bed, pillows and blankets provided |
| **Living:** living/kitchen area, heating, TV, shower, seperate WC | **Living:** living/kitchen area, heating, TV, shower, WC |
| **Eating:** fitted kitchen with hobs, oven, microwave, grill, fridge, freezer | **Eating:** fitted kitchen with hobs, oven, microwave, grill, fridge, freezer |
| **Pets:** not accepted | **Pets:** not accepted |

**Other** (AR1 and AR2): bed linen, cot, highchair to hire

**Open:** March - November

| Weekly Charge | AR1 | AR2 |
|---|---|---|
| Low Season (from) | £ 225 | £ 183 |
| High Season (from) | £ 666 | £ 565 |

# UK2920 Bay View Park

▶ see report page 134

Old Martello Road, Pevensey Bay BN24 6DX

| AR1 – FESTIVAL SUPER – Mobile Home | AR2 – RICHMOND DELUXE – Mobile Home |
|---|---|
| **Sleeping:** 2 bedrooms, sleeps 6: 1 double, 2 singles, sofa bed, pillows and blankets provided | **Sleeping:** 2 bedrooms, sleeps 6: 1 double, 2 singles, sofa bed, pillows and blankets provided |
| **Living:** living/kitchen area, heating, TV, shower, seperate WC | **Living:** living/kitchen area, heating, TV, shower, WC |
| **Eating:** fitted kitchen with grill, fridge | **Eating:** fitted kitchen with grill, fridge |
| **Outside:** table & chairs | **Outside:** table & chairs |
| **Pets:** not accepted | **Pets:** not accepted |

**Other** (AR1 and AR2): bed linen, cot, highchair to hire

**Open:** 1 March - 31 October

| Weekly Charge | AR1 | AR2 |
|---|---|---|
| Low Season (from) | £ 226 | £ 265 |
| High Season (from) | £ 546 | £ 619 |

## UK3085 New Beach Holiday Park

▶ see report page 135

Hythe Road, Dymchurch TN29 0JX

| AR1 – BRONZE – Chalet | AR2 – SILVER PLUS – Mobile Home |
|---|---|
| **Sleeping:** 2 bedrooms, sleeps 6: 1 double, 2 singles, sofa bed, pillows and blankets provided | **Sleeping:** 3 bedrooms, sleeps 8: 1 double, 4 singles, sofa bed, pillows and blankets provided |
| **Living:** living/kitchen area, heating, TV, shower, WC | **Living:** living/kitchen area, heating, TV, shower, WC |
| **Eating:** fitted kitchen with hobs, oven, microwave, grill, fridge | **Eating:** fitted kitchen with hobs, oven, microwave, grill, fridge |
| **Pets:** not accepted | **Pets:** not accepted |

**Other** (AR1 and AR2): bed linen, cot, highchair to hire

**Open:** 1 March - 15 January

| Weekly Charge | AR1 | AR2 |
|---|---|---|
| Low Season *(from)* | £ 134 | £ 166 |
| High Season *(from)* | £ 445 | £ 578 |

*Images for guideline purposes only, accommodation may vary by park*

## UK3850 Rivendale Caravan & Leisure Park

▶ see report page 164

Buxton Road, Alsop-en-le-Dale, Ashbourne DE6 1QU

| AR1 – SENATOR – Mobile Home | AR2 – FAMILY POD – Pod |
|---|---|
| **Sleeping:** 2 bedrooms, sleeps 6: 2 doubles, 1 single, pillows and blankets provided | **Sleeping:** sleeps 4 |
| **Living:** living/kitchen area, heating, TV, shower, WC | **Living:** heating |
| **Eating:** fitted kitchen with hobs, oven, microwave, grill, fridge, freezer | **Pets:** accepted |
| **Outside:** table & chairs, barbecue | |
| **Pets:** accepted | |

**Open:** 29 January - 31 December

| Weekly Charge | AR1 | AR2 |
|---|---|---|
| Low Season *(from)* | £ 340 | £ 280 |
| High Season *(from)* | £ 540 | £ 395 |

## UK4532 Middlewood Farm Holiday Park

▶ see report page 201

Middlewood Lane, Fylingthorpe, Robin Hood's Bay YO22 4UF

| AR1 – HOLIDAY CARAVAN 4 BERTH – Mobile Home | AR2 – HOLIDAY CARAVAN 6 BERTH – Mobile Home |
|---|---|
| Sleeping: 2 bedrooms, sleeps 4: 1 double, 2 singles, pillows and blankets provided | Sleeping: 3 bedrooms, sleeps 6: 1 double, 4 singles, pillows and blankets provided |
| Living: living/kitchen area, heating, TV, shower, WC | Living: living/kitchen area, heating, TV, shower, WC |
| Eating: fitted kitchen with hobs, oven, microwave, grill, fridge | Eating: fitted kitchen with hobs, oven, microwave, grill, fridge |
| Pets: accepted (with supplement) | Pets: accepted (with supplement) |

Other (AR1 and AR2): cot, highchair to hire

**Open:** All year

| Weekly Charge | AR1 | AR2 |
|---|---|---|
| Low Season (from) | £ 165 | £ 185 |
| High Season (from) | £ 460 | £ 555 |

## UK5300 Kneps Farm Holiday Park

▶ see report page 211

River Road, Stanah, Thornton-Cleveleys FY5 5LR

| AR1 – SUPER DELUXE – Mobile Home | AR2 – DE LUXE – Mobile Home |
|---|---|
| Sleeping: 2 bedrooms, sleeps 6: 1 double, 2 singles, sofa bed, pillows and blankets provided | Sleeping: 2 bedrooms, sleeps 6: 1 double, 3 singles, sofa bed, pillows and blankets provided |
| Living: living/kitchen area, heating, TV, shower, WC | Living: living/kitchen area, heating, TV, shower, WC |
| Eating: fitted kitchen with hobs, oven, microwave, grill, fridge | Eating: fitted kitchen with hobs, oven, microwave, grill, fridge |
| Pets: not accepted | Pets: not accepted |

Other (AR1 and AR2): cot, highchair to hire

**Open:** 1 March - 15 November

| Weekly Charge | AR1 | AR2 |
|---|---|---|
| Low Season (from) | £ 305 | £ 280 |
| High Season (from) | £ 450 | £ 425 |

**UK6950** Brighouse Bay Holiday Park

Brighouse Bay, Borgue, Kirkcudbright DG6 4TS

▶ see report page 275

| AR1 – LODGE – Chalet | AR2 – THISTLE CARAVAN – Mobile Home |
|---|---|
| Sleeping: 4 bedrooms, sleeps 8: 2 doubles, 6 singles, pillows and blankets provided | Sleeping: 2 bedrooms, sleeps 4: 1 double, 4 singles, pillows and blankets provided |
| Living: living/kitchen area, heating, TV, shower, WC | Living: living/kitchen area, heating, TV, shower, WC |
| Eating: fitted kitchen with hobs, oven, microwave, grill, fridge, freezer | Eating: fitted kitchen with hobs, oven, microwave, grill, fridge, freezer |
| Outside: table & chairs | Outside: table & chairs |
| Pets: accepted (with supplement) | Pets: accepted (with supplement) |

Other (AR1 and AR2): bed linen, cot, highchair to hire

| Open: All year | | |
|---|---|---|
| Weekly Charge | AR1 | AR2 |
| Low Season *(from)* | £ 640 | £ 345 |
| High Season *(from)* | £ 990 | £ 645 |

# Low Cost Flights

## An Inexpensive Way To Arrive At Your Campsite

Many campsites are conveniently served by a wide choice of low cost airlines. Cheap flights can be very easy to find and travellers increasingly find the regional airports often used to be smaller, quieter and generally a calmer, more pleasurable experience.

Low cost flights can make campsites in more distant regions a much more attractive option: quicker to reach, inexpensive flights, and simply more convenient.

Campsites are seeing increased numbers of visitors using the low cost flights and are adapting their services to suit this clientele. An airport shuttle service is not uncommon, meaning you can take advantage of that cheap flight knowing you will be met at the other end and whisked to your campsite. No taxi queues or multiple drop-offs.

Obviously, these low cost flights are impractical when taking all your own camping gear but they do make a holiday in campsite owned accommodation much more straightforward. The low cost airline option makes caravan holiday home holidays especially attractive: pack a suitcase and use bed linen and towels provided (which you will generally need to pre-book).

## Open All Year

The following parks are understood to accept caravanners and campers all year round. It is always wise to phone the park to check as the facilities available, for example, may be reduced.

## England

### South West England
#### Cornwall

| | | |
|---|---|---|
| Bodmin | UK0270 | Mena |
| Bodmin | UK0306 | Ruthern Valley |
| Liskeard | UK0300 | Colliford Tavern |
| Newquay | UK0165 | Monkey Tree |
| Newquay | UK0310 | Trekenning |
| Padstow | UK0430 | Padstow |
| Penzance | UK0018 | Bone Valley |
| Redruth | UK0114 | Globe Vale HP |
| Saint Ives | UK0030 | Ayr |
| Saint Martins-Looe | UK0320 | Polborder House |
| Saltash | UK0440 | Dolbeare |
| Truro | UK0180 | Carnon Downs |
| Truro | UK0185 | Cosawes |

### South West England
#### Devon

| | | |
|---|---|---|
| Braunton | UK0710 | Hidden Valley |
| Dawlish | UK0970 | Cofton |
| Dawlish | UK1010 | Lady's Mile |
| Drewsteignton | UK1250 | Woodland Springs |
| Ilfracombe | UK0690 | Stowford Farm |
| Modbury | UK0820 | Moor View |
| Newton Abbot | UK0980 | Lemonford |
| Paignton | UK0870 | Beverley |
| Plymouth | UK0810 | Riverside (Plymouth) |
| South Molton | UK0745 | Riverside (S. Molton) |
| Tavistock | UK0790 | Harford Bridge |
| Tavistock | UK0795 | The Old Rectory |

### South West England
#### Somerset, Wiltshire, West Dorset

| | | |
|---|---|---|
| Bath | UK1460 | Newton Mill |
| Bishop Sutton | UK1510 | Chew Valley |
| Bridgwater | UK1306 | Mill Farm |
| Bristol | UK1440 | Baltic Wharf |
| Glastonbury | UK1390 | Old Oaks |
| Martock | UK1420 | Southfork |
| Minehead | UK1301 | Westermill Farm |
| Salisbury | UK1640 | Greenhill Farm |
| Salisbury | UK1655 | Church Farm |
| Sparkford | UK1500 | Long Hazel |
| Taunton | UK1340 | Cornish Farm |
| Taunton | UK1350 | Quantock Orchard |
| Taunton | UK1520 | Waterrow |
| Westbury | UK1630 | Brokerswood |
| Weymouth | UK1820 | Bagwell Farm |

### Southern England

| | | |
|---|---|---|
| Banbury | UK2600 | Barnstones |
| Bere Regis | UK2050 | Rowlands Wait |
| Bletchingdon | UK2590 | Greenhill Farm |
| Cowes | UK2530 | Waverley |
| Fordingbridge | UK2290 | Sandy Balls |
| Wareham | UK2030 | Wareham Forest |

### South East England

| | | |
|---|---|---|
| Ashford | UK3040 | Broadhembury |
| Bexhill | UK2955 | Kloofs |
| Brighton | UK2930 | Sheepcote |
| Canterbury | UK3070 | Canterbury |
| Chertsey | UK2810 | Chertsey |
| Folkestone | UK3090 | Black Horse |
| Horsham | UK2940 | Honeybridge |
| Marden | UK3030 | Tanner Farm |
| Redhill | UK2800 | Alderstead Heath |
| Washington | UK2950 | Washington |

### London

| | | |
|---|---|---|
| Abbey Wood | UK3260 | Abbey Wood |
| Crystal Palace | UK3270 | Crystal Palace |

### East of England

| | | |
|---|---|---|
| Bury Saint Edmunds | UK3345 | The Dell |
| Great Yarmouth | UK3382 | Rose Farm |
| Hunstanton | UK3520 | Searles |
| Ipswich | UK3310 | Low House |
| Norwich | UK3455 | Deer's Glade |
| Peterborough | UK3580 | Ferry Meadows |
| Pidley | UK3575 | Stroud Hill |
| Swaffham | UK3470 | Breckland |
| Woodbridge | UK3322 | Run Cottage |

### Heart of England

| | | |
|---|---|---|
| Bridgnorth | UK4400 | Stanmore Hall |
| Buxton | UK3845 | Clover Fields |
| Coleford | UK4160 | Christchurch |
| Coventry | UK4075 | Hollyfast |
| Grantham | UK3765 | Woodland Waters |
| Grantham | UK3775 | Wagtail C.P. |
| Lutterworth | UK3890 | Stanford Hall |
| Matlock | UK3815 | Lickpenny |
| Meriden | UK4070 | Somers Wood |
| Moreton-in-Marsh | UK4130 | Moreton-in-Marsh |

## Open All Year continued

| | | |
|---|---|---|
| Newark | UK3940 | Smeaton's Lakes |
| Newark | UK3945 | Milestone |
| Peterchurch | UK4300 | Poston Mill |
| Ripley | UK3865 | Golden Valley |
| Shrewsbury | UK4410 | Beaconsfield |
| Shrewsbury | UK4430 | Oxon Hall |
| Skegness | UK3730 | Skegness Sands |
| Slimbridge | UK4170 | Tudor |
| Stamford | UK3760 | Tallington Lakes |
| Stourport-on-Severn | UK4210 | Lickhill Manor |
| Woodhall Spa | UK3690 | Bainland |
| Worksop | UK3920 | Riverside *(Worksop)* |

### Yorkshire

| | | |
|---|---|---|
| Pickering | UK4570 | Spiers House |

### North West England

| | | |
|---|---|---|
| Ormskirk | UK5280 | Abbey Farm |
| Preston | UK5290 | Royal Umpire |

### Cumbria

| | | |
|---|---|---|
| Appleby-in-Westmorland | UK5570 | Wild Rose |
| Penrith | UK5560 | Sykeside |
| Wigton | UK5505 | Stanwix Park |

### Northumbria

| | | |
|---|---|---|
| Belford | UK5755 | South Meadows |
| Berwick-upon-Tweed | UK5800 | Ord House |
| Durham | UK5705 | The Grange |
| Stockton-on-Tees | UK5740 | White Water |

### Wales

| | | |
|---|---|---|
| Beddgelert | UK6590 | Beddgelert |
| Caernarfon | UK6600 | Bryn Gloch |
| Caernarfon | UK6605 | Tafarn Snowdonia |
| Cardiff | UK5925 | Cardiff |
| Colwyn Bay | UK6690 | Bron-Y-Wendon |
| Llandovery | UK5955 | Erwlon |

| | | |
|---|---|---|
| Montgomery | UK6310 | Bacheldre |
| Montgomery | UK6330 | Daisy Bank |
| Newport | UK6060 | Tredegar House |
| Wrexham | UK6680 | James' |

### Scotland

| | | |
|---|---|---|
| Arrochar | UK7260 | Ardgartan |
| Auchterarder | UK7270 | Auchterarder |
| Aviemore | UK7680 | Glenmore |
| Balloch | UK7240 | Lomond Woods |
| Crieff | UK7275 | Braidhaugh |
| Dalbeattie | UK6870 | Glenearly |
| Durness | UK7735 | Sango Sands |
| Edinburgh | UK7050 | Edinburgh |
| Glencoe | UK7790 | Invercoe |
| Killin | UK7315 | Loch Tay Highland Lodges |
| Kirkcudbright | UK6950 | Brighouse Bay |
| Melrose | UK7030 | Gibson Park |
| Musselburgh | UK6980 | Drum Mohr |
| Stranraer | UK7020 | Aird Donald |

### Northern Ireland

| | | |
|---|---|---|
| Newcastle | UK8420 | Tollymore |

### Republic of Ireland

| | | |
|---|---|---|
| Athy | IR9080 | Forest Farm |
| Ballaghaderreen | IR8815 | Willowbrook |
| Caherdaniel | IR9560 | Wave Crest |
| Clondalkin | IR9100 | Camac Valley |
| Cong | IR8740 | Cong |
| Tipperary | IR9400 | Glen of Aherlow |

### Channel Islands

| | | |
|---|---|---|
| Sark | UK9870 | Pomme de Chien |

# Dogs

For the benefit of those who want to take their dogs with them or for people who do not like dogs at the parks they visit, we list here the parks that have indicated to us that they do not accept dogs. If you are planning to take your dog we do advise you to phone the park first to check – there may be limits on numbers, breeds, etc. or times of the year when they are excluded.

## Never – these parks do not accept dogs at any time:

| | | | | | |
|---|---|---|---|---|---|
| UK0065 | Wayfarers | 32 | UK3060 | Yew Tree | 131 |
| UK0115 | Tehidy | 34 | UK3120 | Gate House Wood | 138 |
| UK0250 | Pentewan Sands | 31 | UK4498 | South Cliff | 187 |
| UK0302 | South Penquite | 14 | UK5890 | Glen Trothy | 247 |
| UK0785 | South Breazle | 69 | UK5980 | Moreton Farm | 254 |
| UK0860 | Whitehill | 71 | UK6040 | Pencelli Castle | 237 |
| UK0870 | Beverley | 70 | UK7290 | Craigtoun Meadows | 285 |
| UK0940 | Holmans Wood | 52 | IR9410 | The Apple | 302 |
| UK1075 | Golden Coast | 77 | IR9510 | Eagle Point | 300 |
| UK1150 | Ruda | 53 | UK9770 | Vaugrat | 322 |
| UK1490 | Greenacres | 97 | UK9830 | Seagull | 320 |
| UK2130 | Grove Farm | 108 | UK9870 | Pomme de Chien | 321 |
| UK2300 | Ashurst | 104 | | | |

## Sometimes – these parks do not accept dogs at certain times of the year or have other restrictions, contact park:

| | | | | | |
|---|---|---|---|---|---|
| UK0010 | Chacewater | 45 | UK4760 | Riverside Meadows | 194 |
| UK0030 | Ayr | 39 | UK5350 | Holgates | 207 |
| UK0215 | Sun Haven Valley | 23 | UK5710 | Doe Park | 226 |
| UK0306 | Ruthern Valley | 13 | UK5750 | Waren | 225 |
| UK0735 | Woolacombe Sands | 80 | UK5930 | Cwmcarn Forest | 250 |
| UK0850 | Galmpton | 51 | UK5995 | Caerfai Bay | 254 |
| UK1540 | Batcombe Vale | 96 | UK6010 | Cenarth Falls | 249 |
| UK2500 | Heathfield Farm | 111 | UK6280 | Aeron Coast | 232 |
| UK2510 | Whitecliff Bay | 105 | UK6290 | Glan-y-Mor | 234 |
| UK2590 | Greenhill Farm | 107 | UK6660 | Nant Mill | 253 |
| UK3095 | Little Satmar | 135 | UK6990 | Mortonhall | 269 |
| UK3485 | Clippesby | 151 | UK7060 | Tantallon | 282 |
| UK3520 | Searles | 152 | UK7690 | Torvean | 274 |
| UK3983 | The Star | 180 | IR8810 | Lough Lanagh | 303 |
| UK4180 | Ranch | 168 | IR9150 | River Valley | 314 |
| UK4496 | Skipsea Sands | 199 | UK9710 | Rozel | 322 |
| UK4520 | Flower of May | 196 | | | |

# Fishing

We are pleased to include details of parks which provide facilities for fishing on site. Many other parks, particularly in Scotland and Ireland, are in popular fishing areas and have facilities within easy reach. Where we have been given details, we have included this information in the reports. It is always best to contact parks to check that they provide for your individual requirements.

## England

| | | |
|---|---|---|
| UK0165 | Monkey Tree | 30 |
| UK0170 | Trevella | 29 |
| UK0185 | Cosawes | 41 |
| UK0220 | Trevornick | 28 |
| UK0235 | Porth Beach | 31 |
| UK0250 | Pentewan Sands | 31 |
| UK0270 | Mena | 15 |
| UK0302 | South Penquite | 14 |
| UK0380 | Wooda Farm | 15 |
| UK0415 | Meadow Lakes | 37 |
| UK0530 | Trethiggey | 24 |
| UK0685 | Newberry Valley | 52 |
| UK0695 | Sandaway | 62 |
| UK0725 | Warcombe Farm | 66 |
| UK0745 | Riverside (S. Molton) | 73 |
| UK0750 | Minnows | 77 |
| UK0790 | Harford Bridge | 75 |
| UK0810 | Riverside (Plymouth) | 72 |
| UK0950 | River Dart | 47 |
| UK0970 | Cofton | 57 |
| UK1060 | Yeatheridge | 53 |
| UK1075 | Golden Coast | 77 |
| UK1090 | Peppermint Park | 58 |
| UK1150 | Ruda | 53 |
| UK1257 | Watermouth Cove | 60 |
| UK1390 | Old Oaks | 93 |
| UK1460 | Newton Mill | 82 |
| UK1480 | Home Farm | 88 |
| UK1520 | Waterrow | 98 |
| UK1540 | Batcombe Vale | 96 |
| UK1545 | Cheddar Bridge | 90 |
| UK1570 | Northam Farm | 87 |
| UK1575 | Unity | 86 |
| UK1580 | Warren Farm | 87 |
| UK1590 | Exe Valley | 92 |
| UK1630 | Brokerswood | 100 |
| UK1640 | Greenhill Farm | 96 |
| UK1665 | Burton Hill | 93 |
| UK1740 | Golden Cap | 84 |
| UK1760 | Wood Farm | 89 |
| UK1780 | Freshwater Beach | 85 |
| UK2130 | Grove Farm | 108 |
| UK2150 | Woolsbridge | 124 |
| UK2290 | Sandy Balls | 110 |
| UK2360 | Hill Cottage | 111 |
| UK2450 | The Orchards | 114 |
| UK2510 | Whitecliff Bay | 105 |
| UK2590 | Greenhill Farm | 107 |
| UK2610 | Bo Peep | 104 |
| UK2700 | Hurley | 113 |
| UK2810 | Chertsey | 131 |
| UK2820 | Horsley | 136 |
| UK2900 | Horam Manor | 136 |
| UK2915 | Fairfields Farm | 134 |
| UK3030 | Tanner Farm | 137 |
| UK3290 | Fen Farm | 148 |
| UK3300 | Homestead Lake | 148 |
| UK3400 | Old Brick Kilns | 150 |
| UK3430 | Kelling Heath | 158 |
| UK3455 | Deer's Glade | 156 |
| UK3480 | Little Lakeland | 152 |
| UK3520 | Searles | 152 |
| UK3555 | Wyton Lakes | 152 |
| UK3575 | Stroud Hill | 157 |
| UK3655 | Thorpe Park | 167 |
| UK3675 | Willow Holt | 182 |
| UK3680 | Ashby Park | 170 |
| UK3685 | Tattershall Lakes CP | 182 |
| UK3750 | Foreman's Bridge | 179 |
| UK3760 | Tallington Lakes | 179 |
| UK3765 | Woodland Waters | 168 |
| UK3775 | Wagtail C.P. | 169 |
| UK3855 | Callow Top | 164 |
| UK3865 | Golden Valley | 176 |
| UK3940 | Smeaton's Lakes | 175 |
| UK3945 | Milestone | 174 |
| UK3970 | Glencote | 170 |
| UK4080 | Riverside Stratford | 181 |
| UK4090 | Island Meadow | 169 |
| UK4100 | Hoburne Cotswold | 166 |
| UK4140 | Winchcombe | 183 |
| UK4150 | Croft Farm | 183 |
| UK4170 | Tudor | 178 |
| UK4190 | Kingsgreen | 172 |
| UK4210 | Lickhill Manor | 180 |
| UK4300 | Poston Mill | 175 |
| UK4310 | Luck's All | 170 |
| UK4320 | Broadmeadow | 176 |
| UK4345 | Townsend | 171 |
| UK4380 | Fernwood | 168 |
| UK4390 | Westbrook | 171 |
| UK4410 | Beaconsfield | 177 |
| UK4500 | Burton Constable | 190 |
| UK4510 | Thorpe Hall | 188 |
| UK4610 | Moorside | 203 |
| UK4640 | Goose Wood | 202 |
| UK4660 | Woodhouse Farm | 194 |
| UK4715 | Riverside Lancaster | 189 |
| UK4720 | Knight Stainforth | 199 |
| UK5272 | Moss Wood | 207 |
| UK5280 | Abbey Farm | 209 |

## Bicycle Hire

We understand that the following parks have bicycles to hire on site or can arrange for bicycles to be delivered. However, we would recommend that you contact the park to check as the situation can change.

### England

| | | |
|---|---|---|
| UK0014 | Porthtowan | 42 |
| UK0025 | Roselands | 39 |
| UK0306 | Ruthern Valley | 13 |
| UK0475 | Lower Polladras | 21 |
| UK0695 | Sandaway | 62 |
| UK0750 | Minnows | 77 |
| UK0950 | River Dart | 47 |
| UK1250 | Woodland Springs | 59 |
| UK1252 | Andrewshayes | 48 |
| UK1350 | Quantock Orchard | 97 |
| UK1390 | Old Oaks | 93 |
| UK1415 | Alpine Grove | 88 |
| UK1490 | Greenacres | 97 |
| UK1575 | Unity | 86 |
| UK1580 | Warren Farm | 87 |
| UK1590 | Exe Valley | 92 |
| UK1640 | Greenhill Farm | 96 |
| UK1725 | Hawkchurch CP | 48 |
| UK2050 | Rowlands Wait | 106 |
| UK2120 | South Lytchett Manor | 116 |
| UK2290 | Sandy Balls | 110 |
| UK2315 | Riverside (Hamble) | 112 |
| UK2450 | The Orchards | 114 |
| UK3325 | The Oaks | 153 |
| UK3330 | Moat Barn | 159 |
| UK3370 | Kessingland | 155 |
| UK3390 | Dower House | 149 |
| UK3430 | Kelling Heath | 158 |
| UK3485 | Clippesby | 151 |
| UK3520 | Searles | 152 |
| UK3655 | Thorpe Park | 167 |
| UK3660 | Walesby Woodlands | 173 |
| UK3685 | Tattershall Lakes CP | 182 |
| UK3750 | Foreman's Bridge | 179 |
| UK3855 | Callow Top | 164 |
| UK3904 | Greendale Farm | 175 |
| UK4540 | Saint Helens | 195 |
| UK4560 | Golden Square | 203 |
| UK4620 | Upper Carr | 193 |
| UK5505 | Stanwix Park | 221 |
| UK5605 | Woodclose | 217 |

### Wales

| | | |
|---|---|---|
| UK5925 | Cardiff | 240 |
| UK6040 | Pencelli Castle | 237 |
| UK6330 | Daisy Bank | 248 |
| UK6340 | Pen-y-Bont | 235 |
| UK6345 | Glanlynn | 235 |

### Scotland

| | | |
|---|---|---|
| UK6940 | Loch Ken | 264 |
| UK6950 | Brighouse Bay | 275 |
| UK7000 | Strathclyde | 281 |
| UK7230 | Trossachs | 260 |
| UK7260 | Ardgartan | 261 |
| UK7315 | Loch Tay Highland Lodges | 274 |

### Republic of Ireland

| | | |
|---|---|---|
| IR8740 | Cong | 305 |
| IR8790 | Carra | 304 |
| IR9155 | Hidden Valley HP | 313 |
| IR9400 | Glen of Aherlow | 317 |
| IR9490 | Sextons | 316 |
| IR9600 | Glenross | 308 |
| IR9620 | Flemings | 310 |
| IR9640 | Killarney Flesk | 309 |

### Channel Islands

| | | |
|---|---|---|
| UK9780 | Fauxquets | 320 |

# Golf

We understand that the following parks have facilities for playing golf on site. Where facilities are within easy reach and we have been given details, we have included this information in the individual reports. However, we recommend that you contact the park to check that they meet your requirements.

## Horse Riding

We understand that the following parks have horse riding stables on site. Where facilities are within easy reach and we have been given details, we have included this information in the individual reports. However, we recommend that you contact the park to check that they meet your requirements.

| | | | | | | |
|---|---|---|---|---|---|---|
| UK0360 | Lakefield | 17 | UK1575 | Unity | 86 |
| UK0690 | Stowford Farm | 62 | UK1780 | Freshwater Beach | 85 |
| UK0735 | Woolacombe Sands | 80 | UK2290 | Sandy Balls | 110 |
| UK1060 | Yeatheridge | 53 | UK2900 | Horam Manor | 136 |
| UK1370 | Burrowhayes | 94 | UK6950 | Brighouse Bay | 275 |

## Boat Launching

We understand that the following parks have boat slipways on site. Where facilities are within easy reach and we have been given details, we have included this information in the individual reports. However, we recommend that you contact the park to check that they meet your requirements.

| | | | | | | |
|---|---|---|---|---|---|---|
| UK0250 | Pentewan Sands | 31 | UK6950 | Brighouse Bay | 275 |
| UK0750 | Minnows | 77 | UK7025 | Seal Shore | 274 |
| UK1540 | Batcombe Vale | 96 | UK7260 | Ardgartan | 261 |
| UK2510 | Whitecliff Bay | 105 | UK7315 | Loch Tay Highland Lodges | 274 |
| UK2520 | Thorness Bay | 109 | UK7410 | Riverview | 280 |
| UK2700 | Hurley | 113 | UK7710 | Ardmair Point | 288 |
| UK3290 | Fen Farm | 148 | UK7800 | Resipole | 261 |
| UK3685 | Tattershall Lakes CP | 182 | UK7850 | Linnhe Lochside | 270 |
| UK3760 | Tallington Lakes | 179 | UK8330 | Sixmilewater | 291 |
| UK4080 | Riverside Stratford | 181 | UK8340 | Drumaheglis | 291 |
| UK4150 | Croft Farm | 183 | UK8405 | Cranfield | 294 |
| UK4210 | Lickhill Manor | 180 | UK8515 | Rushin House | 292 |
| UK4310 | Luck's All | 170 | IR8960 | Lough Ree | 299 |
| UK4500 | Burton Constable | 190 | IR8965 | Lough Ennell | 313 |
| UK5615 | Hill of Oaks | 222 | IR9510 | Eagle Point | 300 |
| UK6345 | Glanlynn | 235 | IR9560 | Wave Crest | 302 |
| UK6890 | Mossyard | 264 | IR9610 | Mannix Point | 303 |
| UK6940 | Loch Ken | 264 | | | |

## Adults Only

We list here the parks that have indicated to us that they do not accept children at any time during the year, at certain times, or in certain areas of their park.

| | | | | |
|---|---|---|---|---|
| UK0012 | Killiwerris | | UK3420 | Two Mills |
| UK0010 | Chacewater | | UK3450 | Little Haven |
| UK1510 | Chew Valley | | UK3470 | Breckland |
| UK1545 | Cheddar Bridge | | UK3325 | The Oaks |
| UK1390 | Old Oaks | | UK3904 | Greendale Farm |
| UK1500 | Long Hazel | | UK4534 | Overbrook |
| UK1355 | Lowtrow Cross | | UK4610 | Moorside |
| UK1520 | Waterrow | | UK5510 | The Larches |
| UK1640 | Greenhill Farm | | UK6330 | Daisy Bank |
| UK3410 | Sandy Gulls | | | |

# What are you looking for?

Best of British, a group of high quality, privately owned touring and holiday parks, provides you with a choice of 54 prestigious parks throughout the UK offering a variety of accommodation. You can take your tent, touring caravan or motorhome or, if you prefer, you can book a caravan holiday home, chalet or lodge for your holiday – the choice is yours! Contact the parks direct for details of their prices and their facilities.

**A warm welcome wherever you go**

Whichever Best of British park you choose, you can be sure that you will receive the warmest of welcomes and a very high standard of customer service.

**Visit the Best of British website**

Go to **www.bob.org.uk** to register for a **FREE** Best of British loyalty card and see details of the special offers available on the parks, sign up for the e-newsletter, request a full colour brochure or to email the park of your choice direct from their own pages on the website.

A brochure and/or loyalty card can also be obtained by writing to

**PO Box 28249, Edinburgh, EH9 2YZ**

(342) **Visit www.bob.org.uk**

4   Bath Chew Valley Caravan Park
    01275 332127

5   Beverley Park
    01803 661976

6   Dolbeare
    01752 851332

7   Dornafield
    01803 812732

8   Hendra Holiday Park
    01637 875778

9   Highlands End
    01308 422139

10  Merley Court Touring Park
    01590 648331

11  Oakdown
    01297 680387

12  The Old Oaks
    01458 831437

13  Polmanter
    01736 795640

14  Ross Park
    01803 812983

15  Sandy Balls Holiday Park
    0845 2702248

16  Seaview International
    01726 843425

17  Sun Valley Holiday Park
    01726 843266

18  Trethem Mill Touring Park
    01872 580504

19  Wareham Forest Tourist Park
    01929 551393

20  Waterrow Touring Park
    01984 623464

21  Webbers Park
    01395 232276

22  Wood Farm
    01297 560697

23  Wooda Farm Holiday Park
    01288 352069

24  Woodlands Grove
    01803 712598

25  Woodovis Park
    01822 832968

27  Broadhembury
    01233 620859

28  The Orchards
    01983 531331

29  Quex Park
    01843 841273

30  Tanner Farm Park
    01622 832399

32  Cenarth Falls Holiday Park
    01239 710345

33  Erwlon Caravan & Camping Park
    01550 721021/720332

34  Home Farm
    01248 410614

35  Plassey
    01978 780277

36  Trawsdir Caravan & Camping Park
    01341 280999

38  Beaconsfield
    01939 210370

39  Lincoln Farm Park
    01865 300239

40  Oxon Hall Touring Park
    01743 340868

41  Poston Mill Park
    01981 550225

42  Somers Wood Caravan Park
    01676 522978

43  Townsend
    01544 388527

45  Bainland Country Park
    01526 352903

46  Brookside Caravan Park
    01724 721369

47  Cherry Tree Caravan Site
    01507 441626

48  Highfield Farm Touring Park
    01223 262308

49  Stroudhill Park
    01487 741333

50  The Old Brick Kilns
    01328 878305

51  Two Mills Touring Park
    01692 405829

53  Newbus Grange Country Park
    01325 720973

54  Ord House Country Park
    01289 305288

55  Park Cliffe Camping & Caravan Estate
    015395 31344

56  Riverside
    015242 61272

57  Wild Rose Park
    017683 51077

59  Aberlour Gardens
    01340 871586

60  Brighouse Bay Holiday Park
    01557 870267

61  Kippford Holiday Park
    01556 620636

62  Riverview
    01382 535471

63  Trossachs Holiday Park
    01877 382614

# Been to any good campsites lately?
## We have

You'll find them here...

The UK's market leading independent guides to the best campsites

...and, new for 2011, here...

101 great campsites, ideal for your specific hobby, pastime or passion

# Want independent campsite reviews at your fingertips?

You'll find them here...

...and even here...

An exciting free app from iTunes and the Apple app store*

*available January 2011

# THE
# CARAVAN &
# MOTORHOME
## SHOWS

## The best start to your next adventure...

### MANCHESTER CENTRAL
# CARAVAN &
# MOTORHOME
## SHOW 2011   MANCHESTER 20-23 JANUARY

Come and see the widest choice of caravans and a great selection of motorhomes from leading UK and overseas manufacturers. If it's a bargain you are looking for, many exhibitors are offering amazing dea that you won't find anywhere else!

### INTERNATIONAL
# CARAVAN &
# MOTORHOME
## 2011   NEC BIRMINGHAM 11-16 OCTOBER

The UK's biggest selection of caravans, motorhomes, holiday homes, awnings, folding campers and of course accessories! The NEC is the first place to see all the latest products, have a great day out and find exactly what you want for your next holiday.

For more information visit:
www.caravanshows.com or e
info@caravanshows.co

# ηjoy your UK holidays more with The Caravan Club

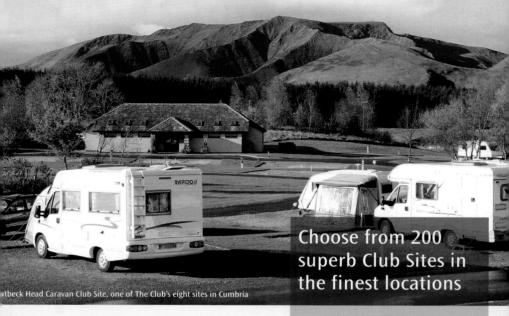

itbeck Head Caravan Club Site, one of The Club's eight sites in Cumbria

## Choose from 200 superb Club Sites in the finest locations

h the UK's increasing popularity as a holiday destination, there's
better way to discover Britain & Ireland's beauty and heritage than
staying at one of The Caravan Club's 200 quality Club Sites.

avan Club Sites are renowned for their excellence.
h most of those graded achieving 4 or 5 stars from
tBritain, you can be sure of consistently high standards.

l with over 40 Club Sites open all year, you can enjoy superb
ring all year round.

l can be assured of excellent facilities and a friendly welcome from
Resident Wardens. Why not discover the best of Britain this year?

## Why choose a Caravan Club Site?

- Choice of superb locations throughout Britain & Ireland

- Sites are immaculately maintained

- Most Club Sites are in peaceful settings, ideal for a relaxing holiday

- Care for the local environment and wildlife is paramount

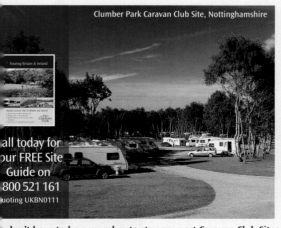

Clumber Park Caravan Club Site, Nottinghamshire

all today for
ur FREE Site
Guide on
800 521 161
uoting UKBN0111

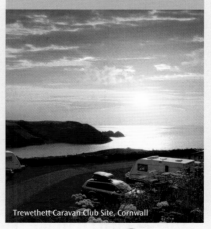

Trewethett Caravan Club Site, Cornwall

l don't have to be a member to stay on most Caravan Club Sites
: members save £8 per night on pitch fees!

## r Caravan Club Site details and
cations visit www.caravanclub.co.uk

THE
CARAVAN
CLUB

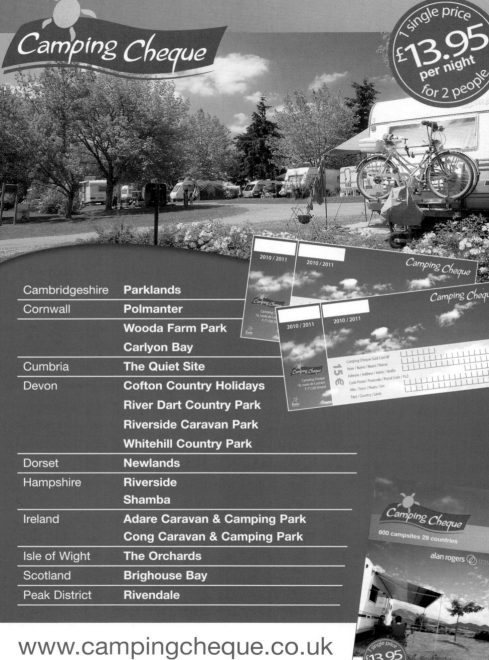

# Touring & Camping Breaks with Haven

A holiday with Haven offers great coastal locations, fabulous holiday facilities, amazing water fun, superb Touring areas and top rate entertainment for all.

## 23
**UK Coastal Holiday Parks**

## Save up to 50%* Off
2011 Holidays

## Haven highlights

* We welcome Tourers, Motorhomes, Tents & Trailer Tents
* Dedicated Touring areas with WC's, Showers & 24hr Security
* 5 pitch types from Basic grass to full facility Premier & Euro pitches
* Touring Wardens on many Parks
* Direct beach access on many Parks
* £millions recently invested on both our Touring areas and Holiday Park facilities
* Heated Pools, Kids' Clubs, Sports Facilities & daily Entertainment are all included in the pitch price

**Call or go online for a brochure & our latest offers!**

**Save more with FreedomTrail** Haven's Loyalty Club
Please call or go online

## Haven caravan + camping

**Call: 0871 230 1933** Quote: TO_ART
Open 7 days a week, 9am - 9pm

**Click: caravancamping.co.uk/art**

WINNER THE BRITISH TRAVEL AWARDS 2009 BEST CAMPING AND MOBILE TOUR OPERATOR

# Insurance Service

**High quality, low cost insurance you can trust**

Price Beater
**GUARANTEE***

Caravan Insurance
**SAVE UP TO 60%**

We've been entrusted with readers' campsite-based holidays since 1968, and they have asked us for good value, good quality insurance.

We have teamed up with Shield Total Insurance – one of the leading names in outdoor leisure insurances – to bring you peace of mind and huge savings. Call or visit our website for a no obligation quote – there's no reason not to – and trust us to cover your valued possessions for you.

* Price Beater **GUARANTEE**
Motorhomes and Static Caravans
We guarantee to beat any genuine 'like for like' insurance renewal quote by at least £25. Subject to terms & conditions.

• Caravans - **Discounts up to 60%**

• Park Homes - **Fantastic low rates**

• Cars - *COMING SOON*

**Instant quote**

## Call **0844 824 6314**

**alanrogers.com/insurance**

Scotland
*page 258*

Northern
Ireland
*page 289*

Northumbria
*page 223*

Cumbria
*page 212*

Yorkshire
*page 186*

North West
England
*page 204*

Republic of Ireland
*page 297*

Heart of England
*page 161*

East of England
*page 144*

Wales
*page 230*

Southern
England
*page 102*

South West England
*page 12*

South East
England
*page 127*

London
*page 140*

Channel Islands
*page 320*

# Town & Village Index

# Town & Village Index continued

## Town & Village Index continued

# Index by Campsite Number

## England

## Wales

# Index by Campsite Number continued

# Index by Campsite Region, County & Name

Index - Campsite Region, County & Name

# Index by Campsite Region, County & Name continued